ACCA

Advanced Financial Management

Exam Practice Kit

For exams in September 2024, December 2024, March 2025 and June 2025

First edition 2007

Seventeenth edition 2024

ISBN 9781 0355 1393 2

(previous ISBN 9781 0355 0125 0)

e-ISBN: 9781 0355 1432 8

British Library Cataloguing-in-Publication Data

A catalogue record for this book is available from the British Library

Published by

BPP Learning Media Ltd

BPP House, Aldine Place

142–144 Uxbridge Road

London W12 8AA

learningmedia.bpp.com

Printed in United Kingdom

Your learning materials, published by BPP Learning Media Ltd, are printed on paper obtained from traceable, sustainable sources.

We are grateful to the Association of Chartered Certified Accountants for permission to reproduce past examination questions. The suggested solutions in the Exam Practice Kit have been prepared by BPP Learning Media Ltd, except where otherwise stated.

A note about copyright

Dear Customer

What does the little © mean and why does it matter?

Your market-leading BPP books, course materials and e-learning materials do not write and update themselves. People write them on their own behalf or as employees of an organisation that invests in this activity. Copyright law protects their livelihoods. It does so by creating rights over the use of the content.

Breach of copyright is a form of theft – as well as being a criminal offence in some jurisdictions, it is potentially a serious breach of professional ethics.

With current technology, things might seem a bit hazy but, basically, without the express permission of BPP Learning Media:

- Photocopying our materials is a breach of copyright

- Printing our digital materials in order to share them with or forward them to a third party or use them in any way other than in connection with your BPP studies is a breach of copyright.

You can, of course, sell your books, in the form in which you have bought them – once you have finished with them. (Is this fair to your fellow students? We update for a reason.) Please note the e-products are sold on a single user licence basis: we do not supply 'unlock' codes to people who have bought them secondhand.

And what about outside the UK? BPP Learning Media strives to make our materials available at prices students can afford by local printing arrangements, pricing policies and partnerships which are clearly listed on our website. A tiny minority ignore this and indulge in criminal activity by illegally photocopying our material or supporting organisations that do. If they act illegally and unethically in one area, can you really trust them?

Contents

Question index

The headings in this checklist/index indicate the main topics of questions, but questions often cover several different topics. Since September 2015 there have been four exam sittings per year, but ACCA normally only publish a sample of the questions from the March and June papers, and from the September and December papers; these questions are denoted as 'Mar/Jun' and 'Sept/Dec' in the index below.

Topic index

Listed below are the key AFM syllabus topics and the numbers of the questions in this Kit covering those topics. We have also included a reference to the relevant Chapter of the BPP AFM Course Book, the companion to the BPP AFM Exam Practice Kit, in case you wish to revise the information on the topic you have covered.

If you need to concentrate your Exam Practice on certain topics or if you want to attempt all available questions that refer to a particular subject, you will find this index useful.

Syllabus topic	Question numbers	Course Book chapter
A1: Role of senior financial advisor	2, 6, 11, 52	1
A2: Financial strategy formulation	3, 4, 5, 6, 7, 8, 19, 27, 46, 47, 52, ME4 Q2	2
A3: Corporate environmental, social, governance and ethical issues	1, 6, 16, 27, 51, 56, 57, ME2 Q1	1
A4: Management of international trade and finance	3, 32, 55, 56	16
A5: Strategic business and financial planning	4, ME2 Q2, ME3 Q1	16
A6: Dividend policy and transfer pricing	1, 2, 3, 7, 45	16
B1: Discounted cash flow techniques	9, 10, 14, 18, 30, 51, 52, 53, 56, 57	3
B2: Option pricing theory	12, 13, 18, 51, 57	4
B3: Impact of financing and APV	15, 16, 17, 28, 42, 47, 52, 54, 55, ME1 Q3	6 and 7
B4: Valuation and free cash flows	7, 18, 22, 30, 45, 48	8
B5: International investment and financing	46, 49, 56, ME2 Q2, ME3 Q3, ME4 Q1	5
C1: Acquisitions and other growth strategies	19, 20, 21, 22, 24, 25, 48, 49, ME3 Q1, ME3 Q2	9
C2: Valuation for acquisition and mergers	2, 19, 20, 21, 22, 23, 24, 25, 28, 45, 48, 50, ME1 Q1, ME3 Q1, ME3 Q2	8
C3: Regulatory issues	48, 54, ME1 Q1, ME2 Q1	9
C4: Financing acquisitions and mergers	20, 21, 22, 23, 54	10
D1: Financial reconstruction	26, 28, 29, 47, 54, ME2 Q1	14
D2: Business reorganisation	27, 28, 29, 30, 46, 50, 56, ME1 Q3	15
E1: Treasury function	32, 33, 36, 38, 39, 42, 44	11 and 12

Syllabus topic	Question numbers	Course Book chapter
E2: Foreign exchange hedging	32, 33, 34, 35, 36, 37, 45, 49 58, ME1 Q2, ME2 Q3	12 and 13
E3: Interest rate hedging	38, 39, 40, 41, 42, 43, 44, 58	13

ME1 is Mock Exam 1, ME2 is Mock Exam 2 etc.

The exam

 Videos can be viewed by accessing your ebook version on VitalSource.

Computer-based exams

Strategic Professional exams are all computer-based exams (CBE).

Approach to examining the syllabus

The Advanced Financial Management syllabus is assessed by a 3 hour 15 minute exam. The pass mark is **50%.** All questions in the exam are **compulsory**.

Examining team's general comments

If you are preparing to sit AFM you should pay particular attention to the following in order to maximise your chances of success.

(a) Know your stuff

- Develop a sound knowledge of the entire AFM syllabus. Augment studying the manuals with wider reading of the financial press, finance textbooks, articles in Student Accountant and financial journals.

- You should expect and be prepared for questions from a range of syllabus areas and more than one area may be tested in a single question. Be prepared for questions that require you to consider a number of areas of the syllabus within one question.

(b) Question practice

- Work through the past exam questions under exam conditions and to time. Doing past questions will help you build your speed and efficiency in answering questions and help you build knowledge of how to make your answer relevant to the scenario in the question.

(c) Address the requirement and scenario

- Your answer must relate to the scenario in question. Context is very important for higher-level exams. General answers will gain fewer or even no marks.

- In your exams, good time management techniques and habits are essential in ensuring success. Make sure that you are able to answer all parts of each question and manage your time effectively so that you make a reasonable attempt at each part of each question. Good time management skills are essential.

- Often parts of a requirement may ask for more than one aspect. Make sure that you can answer, and do answer, everything each part of each requirement is asking for.

- Make sure you answer the requirements correctly. For example, if the question asks you to explain, it is not enough just to list. If the question asks you to assess, it is not enough just to explain.

(d) Communicate concisely

- For the written parts of any question, remember it is generally a mark for each relevant point. Repeating a point does not get you any extra marks and it wastes time. Avoid repetition.

- Don't use incomplete sentences when making a point. Marks are awarded for complete points made in full sentences. However, you can use bullet points and numbered paragraphs, and headings when appropriate, to structure an answer to a question. But points made should be in complete sentences.

(e) Think before you start and manage your time

- Pay attention to the number of marks available – this provides you with a clear indication of the amount of time you should spend on each question part.

- Use your exam time effectively. The questions may contain a substantial amount of information that you will need to sort out and apply properly and you should plan your answer before beginning to write it.

Format of the exam

100 marks, two sections, each section 50 marks.

		Marks
Section A	One compulsory question. Longer questions will cover topics from across the syllabus but will tend to be based on one major area – for example a cross-border merger question (major topic) might bring in ethical issues (smaller topic). **Ten professional skills marks are available.** This is new from September 2022 onwards and explained later in this section.	50
Section B	Two compulsory 25-mark questions. All topics and syllabus sections will be examinable in either Section A or Section B of the exam, but every exam will have questions which have a focus on syllabus Sections B (advanced investment appraisal) and E (advanced risk management). **Ten professional skills marks are available (5 marks in each section B question).** This is new from September 2022 onwards and explained later in this section.	50

Remote invigilated exams

In certain geographical areas it may be possible for you to take your exam remotely. This option, which is subject to strict conditions, can offer increased flexibility and convenience under certain circumstances. Further guidance, including the detailed requirements and conditions for taking the exam by this method, is contained on ACCA's website at https://www.accaglobal.com/an/en/student/exam-entry-and-administration/about-our-exams/remote-exams/remote-session-exams.html.

Analysis of past exams

The table below provides details of when each element of the syllabus has been examined in the ten most recent sittings and the question number and section in which each element was examined. We have also included a reference to the relevant Chapter of the BPP AFM Course Book, the companion to the BPP AFM Exam Practice Kit, in case you wish to revise the information on the topic covered.

Course Book chapter		Sep/Dec 2023	Mar/Jun 2023	Sep 2022	Mar/Jun 2022	Sep/Dec 2021	Mar/Jun 2021	Sep/Dec 2020	Mar 2020	Sep/Dec 2019	Mar/Jun 2019
	ROLE OF SENIOR FINANCIAL ADVISER										
1	Financial strategy formulation		A	A	A		B	A		B	A
2	Financial strategy evaluation	B	B					A		B	
16	Planning and trading issues for multinationals				A	A		B			
	ADVANCED INVESTMENT APPRAISAL										
3	Discounted cash flow techniques		B	A	A		B		B	A	A
4	Application of option pricing theory to investment decisions			A		A				B	
5	International investment	A	B		A		A			B	
6	Cost of capital and changing risk					A					B
7	Financial and credit risk							A			
	ACQUISITIONS AND MERGERS										
8	Valuation techniques		A,B			B	A		A	B	
9	Strategic and regulatory issues		A				A	A	A	B	

Course Book chapter		Sep/Dec 2023	Mar/Jun 2023	Sep 2022	Mar/Jun 2022	Sep/Dec 2021	Mar/Jun 2021	Sep/Dec 2020	Mar 2020	Sep/Dec 2019	Mar/Jun 2019
10	Financing acquisitions						A		A	B	
	CORPORATE RECONSTRUCTION AND REORGANISATION										
14	Financial reconstruction					B					
15	Business reorganisation			B	B	B	A				B
	TREASURY AND ADVANCED RISK MANAGEMENT TECHNIQUES										
11	Role of the treasury function			B		B	B		B		B
12	Managing foreign currency risk			B	B		B		B	A	
13	Managing interest rate risk	B				B		B			B

IMPORTANT! The table above gives a broad idea of how frequently major topics in the syllabus are examined. It should **not** be used to question spot and predict, for example, that Topic X will not be examined because it came up two sittings ago. The examining team's reports indicate that they are well aware that some students try to question spot. They avoid predictable patterns and may, for example, examine the same topic two sittings in a row, particularly if there has been a recent change in legislation.

 Videos can be viewed by accessing your ebook version on VitalSource.

Syllabus and Study Guide

The complete AFM syllabus and study guide can be found by visiting the exam resource finder on the ACCA website.

Syllabus changes

Helping you with your revision

BPP Learning Media – ACCA Content Partner

As an ACCA Content Partner, BPP Learning Media gives you the opportunity to use the revision materials created by BPPs expert team of Subject Matter Experts who have years of experience authoring Professional Qualification Content. The Subject Matter Experts ensure the content covers the depth and breadth of the syllabus and provides excellent support for your revision.

BPP Learning Media do everything possible to ensure the material is accurate and up-to-date when sending to print. In the event that any errors are found after the print date, they are uploaded to the following website: www.bpp.com/learningmedia/Errata.

The structure of this Exam Practice Kit

This Exam Practice Kit is divided into two sections. The questions in Section A are 25 mark questions which are mainly focused on specific syllabus areas. Section B contains a number of 50 mark questions which generally cover at least two different syllabus areas. There are also four mock exams which provide sufficient opportunity to refine your knowledge and skills as part of your final exam preparations.

Question practice

This is the most important thing to do if you want to get through. Many of the most up-to-date exam questions are in this Kit. Practice doing them under timed conditions, then go through the answers and go back to the Course Book for any topic you are really having trouble with. Come back to a question a week later and try it again – you will be surprised at how much better you are getting. Be very ruthless with yourself at this stage – you have to do the question in the time, without looking at the answer. This will really sharpen your wits and make the exam experience less worrying. Just keep doing this and you will get better at doing questions and you will really find out what you know and what you don't know.

 Videos can be viewed by accessing your ebook version on VitalSource.

Selecting questions

To help you plan your revision, we have provided a full topic index which maps the questions to topics in the syllabus (see page vii).

Making the most of question practice

At BPP Learning Media we realise that you need more than just questions and model answers to get the most from your question practice.

- Our Top tips included for certain questions provide essential advice on tackling questions, presenting answers and the key points that answers need to include.
- We show you how you can pick up Easy marks on some questions, as we know that picking up all readily available marks often can make the difference between passing and failing.
- We include marking guides to show you what the examining team rewards

Attempting mock exams

https://www.accaglobal.com/gb/en/student/exam-support-resources/professional-exams-study-resources/p4/examiners-reports1.html

This Kit has four mock exams, including the ACCA Specimen Exam, which provide practice at coping with the pressures of the exam day. We strongly recommend that you attempt them under exam conditions. All the mock exams reflect the question styles and syllabus coverage of the exam.

Topics to revise

Any part of the syllabus could be tested in the compulsory Section A question, therefore it is essential that you learn the entire syllabus to maximise your chances of passing. There are no short cuts – trying to spot topics is dangerous and will significantly reduce the likelihood of success.

As this is an advanced level exam, it assumes knowledge of the topics covered in Financial Management (FM), including business valuation techniques, investment appraisal techniques, cost of capital and risk management. You should revise these topics if necessary as they impact on your understanding of the more advanced techniques.

From September 2018 every exam will contain a question which has a clear focus on syllabus Section B (advanced investment appraisal) and on Section E (treasury and advanced risk management) so these syllabus sections are especially important.

It's also useful to keep reading the business pages during your revision period and not just narrowly focus on the syllabus. Remember that the examining team has stressed that this exam is about how organisations respond to real-world issues, so the more you read, the more practical examples you will have of how organisations have tackled real-life situations.

Essential skills areas to be successful in Advanced Financial Management

We think there are three areas you should develop in order to achieve exam success in AFM:

(a) **Knowledge application:** technical knowledge accounts for a high percentage of the marks in the AFM exam and it is essential to have a good knowledge of all syllabus areas.

(b) **AFM Professional skills:** these are worth 20% of the marks in the AFM exam (from September 2022 onwards) and are explained in detail in this section.

(c) **Exam success skills:** these are general skills required in the application of good exam technique and apply to any exam.

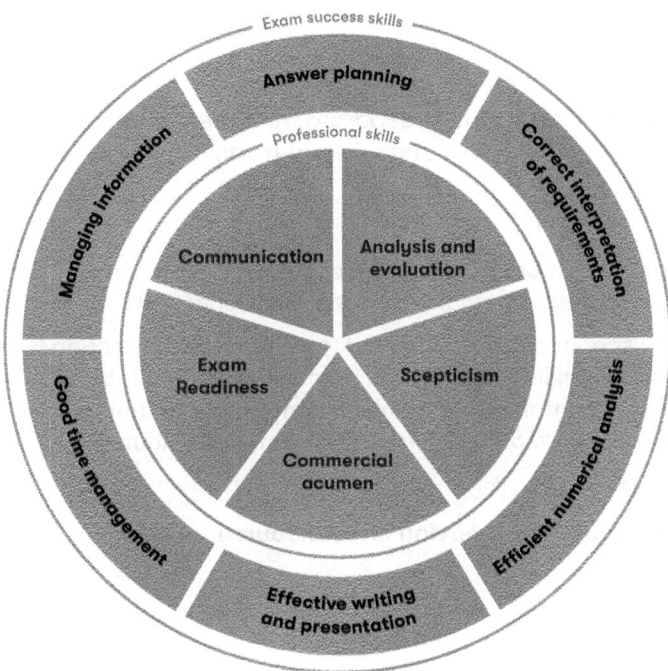

AFM professional skills

From the September 2022 exam onwards, 20 marks will be available for demonstrating the 'professional skills' that would be expected from a proficient senior financial professional.

There are four professional skills – these skills are important and are worth 20 marks in the exam, a brief summary of each skill is given below.

ACCA professional skill: Definition	Three aspects of each professional skill
Communication To express yourself clearly and convincingly through an appropriate medium, while being sensitive to the needs of the intended audience	Inform target audience using clear format Persuade with logical argument Appropriate use of technology
Commercial acumen To show awareness of the wider business and external factors affecting business, and use commercially sound judgement and insight to resolve issues and exploit opportunities.	Practical considerations Recognise constraints Awareness of alternative opportunities to those suggested

ACCA professional skill: Definition	Three aspects of each professional skill
Analysis and evaluation To appraise information objectively and to draw logical conclusions, recognising the impact on relevant stakeholders.	Consider the meaning of data Assess impact on stakeholders Apply analysis to the company in the question
Scepticism To probe, question and challenge information and views presented to you, to fully understand business issues and to establish facts objectively, based on ethical and professional values.	Question the validity of approaches Challenge opinions Identify new information needed

Professional skills marks should not be thought of as being separate from the technical content of an answer; they are earned by providing comprehensive and relevant responses to the technical requirements of a question.

These skills are covered in more detail in the AFM Course Book.

All of the professional skills will be examined in Section A of the exam, which is a single 50-mark case study. 10 of the 50 marks will be allocated to demonstrating professional skills.

Section B will consist of two compulsory scenario-based 25-mark questions. Each section B question will allocate 5 marks to professional skills, so 10 marks in total will be available for professional skills marks in Section B. **Each section B question will contain a minimum of two professional skills from Analysis and Evaluation, Scepticism and Commercial Acumen.**

 Videos can be viewed by accessing your ebook version on VitalSource.

Exam success skills

Passing the AFM exam also requires the development of excellent exam technique through question practice.

We consider the following six skills to be vital for exam success.

Exam success skill 1

The CBE functionality demonstrated below can help you to manage this information on the screen.

In a computer-based exam (CBE) the **highlighter tool** provided in the toolbar at the top of the screen offers a range of colours:

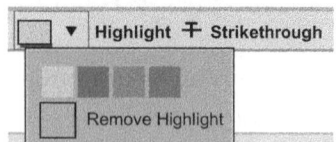

This allows you to choose **different colours to answer different aspects to a question**. For example, if a question asked you to discuss the pros and cons of an issue then you could choose a different colour for highlighting pros and cons within the relevant section of a question.

The **strikethrough function** allows you to delete areas of a question that you have dealt

with – this can be useful in managing information if you are dealing with numerical questions because it can allow you to ensure that all numerical areas have been accounted for in your answer.

The CBE also allows you **to resize windows** by clicking on the bottom right-hand corner of the window as highlighted in the following section:

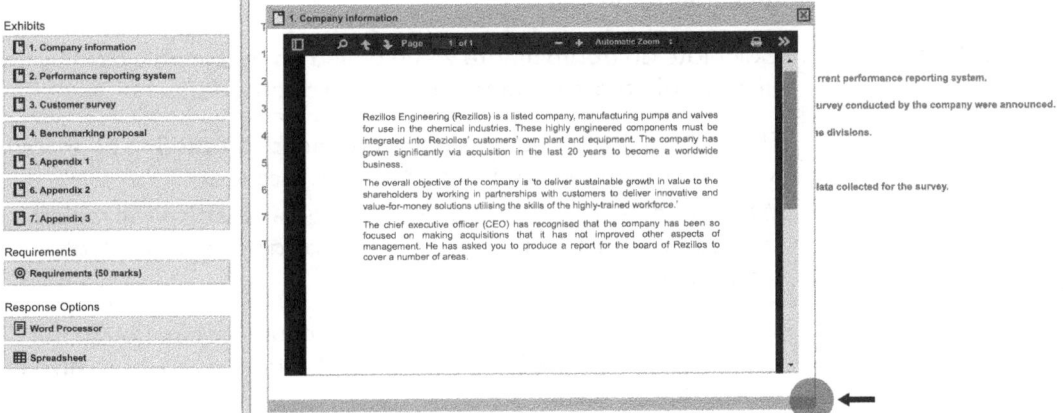

This functionality allows you to **display a number of windows at the same time**, so this could allow you review:

- The question requirements and the exhibit relating to that requirement at the same time; or
- The window containing your answer (whether a word processing or spreadsheet document) and the exhibit relating to that requirement, at the same time.

Exam success skill 2

The active verb used often dictates the approach that written answers should take (eg 'explain', 'discuss', 'evaluate'). It is important you identify and use the verb to define your approach. The **correct interpretation of the requirements** skill means correctly producing only what is being asked for by a requirement. Anything not required will not earn marks.

Advice on developing this skill

This skill can be developed by analysing question requirements and applying this process:

Step 1   Read the requirement

Firstly, read the requirement a couple of times slowly and carefully and **highlight the active verbs**. Use the active verbs to define what you plan to do. Make sure you identify any sub-requirements within a requirement; this **often signalled by the use of the word 'and'** within a requirement.

Important active verbs for AFM include the following:

Verb	Meaning
Advise	This requires you to provide someone with useful information, or to **tell them what you think they should do** based on a consideration of the issues presented in a scenario.
Analyse	This requires you **break an issue into separate parts** and discuss, examine, or interpret each part. This may require you to **give reasons for** the current situation or what has happened.
Apply	This requires you to put a concept into action by applying it **to the scenario** in a relevant way.

Verb	Meaning
Assess	This requires you to **judge the importance** or estimate the nature, quality or significance of an issue.
Discuss	This will require you to consider and debate/argue about the **pros and cons** of an issue.
Estimate	Calculate an **approximate value** based on reasonable assumptions, and explain those assumptions, where appropriate.
Evaluate	This will require you to present a **'balanced' discussion** of an issue looking at both the positive and negative issues. Where numbers feature in a question, an evaluation will require you to use the numbers provided to create a value from which **a judgement** can be made.
Explain	This involves making an idea clear and could require you to, for example, show logically how a concept is developed, or to **give the reason for** an event.
Recommend	If you are asked to **'recommend'** then you are expected to **use details presented in the scenario** to create a logical and **justified** course of action.

Step 2 Read the rest of the question

By reading the requirement first, you will have an idea of what you are looking out for as you read through the case overview and exhibits. This is a great time saver and means you don't end up having to read the whole question in full twice. You should do this in an active way – see Exam success skill 1: Managing Information.

Step 3 Read the requirement again

Read the requirement again to remind yourself of the exact wording before starting your written answer. This will capture any misinterpretation of the requirements or any missed requirements entirely. This should become a habit in your approach and, with repeated practice, you will find the focus, relevance and depth of your answer plan will improve.

Exam success skill 3

Answer planning: Priorities, structure and logic

This skill requires the planning of the key aspects of an answer which accurately and completely responds to the requirement.

Advice on developing this skill

Everyone will have a preferred style for an answer plan. For example, it may be a mind map, bullet-pointed lists or simply annotating the question paper. Choose the approach that you feel most comfortable with, or, if you are not sure, try out different approaches for different questions until you have found your preferred style.

In a **computer-based exam** you can use the copy and paste functions to **copy the question requirements to the beginning of your answer**. This will allow you to ensure that your answer plan addresses all parts of the question requirements.

You can also **copy the question requirements to the main body your answer.** This will allow you to create sub-headings for your answer, again ensuring that your answer addresses all parts of the question requirements.

Copying and pasting simply involves highlighting the relevant information and either right clicking to access the copy and paste functions, or alternatively using Ctrl C to copy and Ctrl V to paste.

Exam success skill 4

Efficient numerical analysis

This skill aims to maximise the marks awarded by making clear to the marker the process of arriving at your answer. This is achieved by laying out an answer such that, even if you make a few errors, you can still score subsequent marks for follow-on calculations. It is vital that you do not lose marks purely because the marker cannot follow what you have done.

It is important to use the spreadsheet provided to produce a clear and efficient numerical analysis.

It is **not a sensible idea** to perform calculations on a calculator and then manually transfer them to the spreadsheet because this will not show the marker where numbers have come from.

It is important to remember that, in an exam situation, it is difficult to get every number 100% correct. It is important that you do not spend too long on any single calculation. If you are struggling with a solution then **make a sensible assumption, state it and move on**.

Using a spreadsheet allows you to **show the marker how numerical values have been calculated**, because the basis for a calculation is displayed if the marker clicks onto a cell.

Clear labelling should also help to show the marker what the numbers are intended to mean.

For example, in the following spreadsheet the marker can see that the highlighted calculation in cell F16 is calculated as 25% of the change in revenue given in cell C7 because this is what is recorded in the spreadsheet cell (as shown in the first row). The marker can also see from the **heading** in cell C4 that the value in cell C7 is a measure of the increase in sales revenue.

F16	▾ : × ✓ fx	=-0.25*F7								
◢	A	B	C	D	E	F	G	H	I	J
2		part a	Workings							
3										
4			increase in revenue			$m		Notes		
5			20X6 revenue			133900		2% margin		
6			20X5 revenue			130000		3% growth		
7			change			3900				
8										
9			Divided capacity			$m				
10										
11				Pre-tax operating profit		2678				
12				interest		**-820**				
13						1858				
14				tax 30%		-557.4				
15										
16				spending on new capacity		**-975**				
17										
18				**dividend capacity**		**325.6**				

Workings

If the workings are visible in the cell and reflect straightforward calculations, then there is **less need to show detailed workings**. For example, in cell F16 in the previous spreadsheet extract workings are helpful, but in cell F14 there is no real need for workings as the marker will be able to follow the logic by looking at the basis for the calculation in F14, which will be something like =-F13*0.3.

However, **a workings section** (as shown in the previous spreadsheet) will sometimes be a useful feature of a spreadsheet answer if more detailed calculations are involved. A workings section reduces the likelihood of errors being made (if calculations are complex).

Keep your workings as clear and simple as possible and ensure they are cross-referenced to the main part of your answer. Where it helps, provide brief narrative explanations to help the marker understand the steps in the calculation. This means that if a mistake is made you should not lose any subsequent marks for follow-on calculations.

Spreadsheet short-cuts

You can also use useful spreadsheet short-cuts to improve the efficiency of numerical analysis. For AFM, useful short-cuts include the ability to calculate totals and averages, to insert different currency symbols and also to calculate NPV, IRR and MIRR.

Further details are given in the following table:

Function	Guidance & examples
Sum	=SUM(A1:A10) adds all the numbers in spreadsheet cells A1 to A10.
Average	=AVERAGE(A1:A10) averages the numbers in spreadsheet cells A1 to A10.
NPV	Net present value is based on future cash flows, assuming that the first cash flow is in one year's time.
	For example, if the future cash flows from a project arise over five years and need to be discounted at 10% then the formula could be as follows:
	=NPV(0.1, B10:F10)
	This would give the present value of cash flows from time period 1-5, the cash outflow in time 0 would then need to be deducted to calculate the net present value.
IRR	Internal rate of return is based on future cash flows (looking at cash outflows and inflows) in each year of a project, from time 0 onwards.
	For example, to identify the internal rate of return of a project arising over five years (involving time periods 0-5), the formula could be as follows:
	=IRR(A10:F10)
MIRR	Modified internal rate of return is based on future cash flows (looking at cash outflows and inflows) in each year of a project, from time 0 onwards.
	The formula is =MIRR (values, finance rate, reinvestment rate). The finance rate and reinvestment rate will normally be the same.
	For example, to identify the MIRR of the future cash flows from a project arising over five years (involving time periods 0-5) where the cost of capital to be applied to cash outflows (the finance rate) and cash inflows (reinvestment rate) is 10%, then the formula could be as follows:
	=MIRR(A10:F10, 0.1, 0.1)

Where numerical calculations require commentary then this can be provided in a word processing document with a **reference to calculations provided within the spreadsheet**.

Exam success skill 5

Effective writing and presentation

Written answers should be presented so that the marker can clearly see the points you are making, presented in the format specified in the question. The skill is to provide efficient written answers with sufficient breadth of points that answer the question, in the right depth, in the time available.

Advice on developing this skill

Step 1   **Use headings**

Using the headings and sub-headings from your answer plan will give your answer structure, order and logic. This will ensure your answer links back to the requirement and is clearly signposted, making it easier for the marker to understand the different points you are making. Underlining your headings will also help the marker.

Step 2   **Write your answer in short, but full, sentences**

Use short, clear sentences with the aim that every sentence should say something different and generate marks. Write in full sentences, ensuring your style is professional.

Exam success skill 6

Good time management

This skill means planning your time across all the requirements so that all tasks have been attempted at the end of the 3 hours 15 minutes available and actively checking on time during your exam. This is so that you can flex your approach and prioritise requirements which, in your judgement, will generate the maximum marks in the available time remaining.

Planning time

In AFM it is **crucial to spend time on planning before starting to write your answer**. This allows time for a candidate to immerse themselves in the question scenarios. Approximately 20% of your time should be allocated to planning to ensure that you are able to assimilate the key features of the scenario before starting to write.

For a 50-mark question, planning time should be 50 marks × 1.95 × 0.2 = **20 minutes**.

For a 25-mark question, planning time would be 25 marks × 1.95 × 0.2 = **10 minutes** per question.

Writing time

For time management purposes, candidates should allocate time based on the technical marks available. Professional skills marks should not be thought of as separate requirements as they are earned by providing comprehensive and relevant responses to the technical requirements.

Writing time can be calculated by **multiplying the technical mark allocation for each requirement by 1.95 minutes** (as the 20% of time spent planning is exactly offset by the extra 20% of marks available for professional skills marks).

So, time planning for a 25-mark question with, for example, a 12-mark part a and a 10 mark part b (and 5 professional skills marks) should be as follows:

Total time: 25 marks × 1.95 minutes per mark = 49 minutes

Planning time: 49 minutes × 0.2 = 10 minutes

Writing time: part a = 12 × 1.95 minutes per mark = 23 minutes

Writing time: part b = 8 × 1.95 minutes per mark = 16 minutes

At the beginning of a question, work out the amount of time you should be spending on each requirement and make a note of this on your plan.

Keep an eye on the clock

Aim to attempt all requirements, but be ready to be ruthless and move on if your answer is not going as planned. The challenge for many is sticking to planned timings. Be aware this is difficult to achieve in the early stages of your studies and be ready to let this skill develop over time.

Avoid discussing issues at great length, remember that the Strategic Professional Options examinations are normally marked on the basis **of one mark per point, possibly with an extra mark for more fully developing the same point**.

If you find yourself running short on time and know that a full answer is not possible in the time you have, consider recreating your plan in overview form and then add key terms and details as time allows. Remember, some marks may be available, for example, simply stating a conclusion which you don't have time to justify in full.

Question practice

Question practice is a core part of learning new topic areas. When you practise questions, you should focus on improving the Exam success skills – personal to your needs – by obtaining feedback or through a process of self-assessment.

If sitting this exam as a computer-based exam, practising as many exam-style questions as possible in the ACCA CBE practice platform will be the key to passing this exam. You should attempt questions under timed conditions and ensure you produce full answers to the discussion parts as well as doing the calculations. Also ensure that you attempt all mock exams under exam conditions.

ACCA have launched a free on-demand resource designed to mirror the live exam experience helping you to become more familiar with the exam format. You can access the platform via the Study Support Resources section of the ACCA website navigating to the CBE question practice section and logging in with your myACCA credentials.

Questions

ROLE OF THE SENIOR FINANCIAL ADVISER IN THE MULTINATIONAL ORGANISATION

The questions in this part of the Exam Practice Kit mainly cover Section A of the AFM syllabus which is the subject of Chapters 1, 2, and 16 of the BPP Course Book.

---

1 Cadnam (Sep/Dec 2019, amended) (49 mins)

(a) Calculate the forecast dividend capacity of Cadnam Co for 20X6. **(5 marks)**

(b) Discuss the viability and financial impacts of Cadnam Co seeking to maintain its current dividend policy, supporting your answers with relevant calculations.

Note. 4 marks are available for calculations in part (b). **(8 marks)**

(c) Discuss the governance and ethical issues associated with Cadnam Co's dividend and directors' remuneration policies. **(7 marks)**

Professional marks will be awarded for the demonstration of skill in analysis and evaluation, scepticism and commercial acumen in your answer. **(5 marks)**

(Total = 25 marks)

Exhibit 1: Cadnam Co

Cadnam Co is a large company in the support services sector.

Cadnam Co's most recent annual report, for the year ended 31 December 20X5, acknowledged challenges for the company, including financing the major investment programme required to meet its clients' increasing expectations. Cadnam Co also faced upward pressure on employment costs, fuelled by a 'fair wage' campaign which adversely compared wage rises in the support services sector with increases in dividends and directors' remuneration, and a consequent government enquiry into low pay in the sector.

Cadnam Co's board, however, was confident that the company would be able to renew a number of large contracts that were coming up for review. The report stressed the strength of Cadnam Co's senior management team as a vital success factor. Directors' remuneration packages thus reflected the need to, in a competitive labour market, retain its directors at senior level.

In the stakeholder engagement section of its annual report, Cadnam Co highlighted that it had fulfilled its aim of guaranteeing investors a consistent rise in dividends, and its board was confident that Cadnam Co would be able to maintain the recent rate of dividend increase. The report also stated that Cadnam Co was looking to publish a full integrated report over the next couple of years.

Dividend policy

At Cadnam Co's last annual general meeting, there were no questions about the level of profits, dividends or directors' remuneration. However, a recent investment analysts' report on the support services sector highlighted Cadnam Co as a company which might have problems in the next few years. The report suggested that Cadnam Co's investment and dividend policies could not both be maintained. It highlighted one of Cadnam Co's principal competitors, Holmsley Co, as a company whose policies it believed would sustain long-term growth. It highlighted directors' remuneration as an area where Holmsley Co's policies were more likely to encourage long-term value creation and share price increases than Cadnam Co's policies.

Cadnam Co's board is currently considering the comments made by the investment analysts, and also assessing what the dividend for 20X6 should be.

 **BPP**

Exhibit 2: Recent financial data and directors' remuneration

Cadnam Co

	20X2	20X3	20X4	20X5
	$m	$m	$m	$m
Profit after tax	1,380	1,490	1,550	1,580
Dividends	765	840	925	1,020
Investment in additional assets	282	312	584	864
Share price ($)	$4.88	$5.35	$5.61	$5.75

Holmsley Co

	20X2	20X3	20X4	20X5
	$m	$m	$m	$m
Profit after tax	1,485	1,590	1,700	1,830
Dividends	560	590	621	654
Investment in additional assets	595	625	660	690
Share price	$5.04	$5.23	$5.55	$5.93

There have been no changes in the issued share capital of Cadnam Co and Holmsley Co since 20X1.

Directors' remuneration:

	Cadnam Co	Holmsley Co
Average salary executive director	$550,000	$550,000
Performance bonus	Maximum 25% of salary	Maximum 30% of salary
Loyalty bonus	Maximum 10% of salary	None
Share options	None	Options to be exercised on 31 December 20X8 at an exercise price of $7.00

Exhibit 3: Cadnam Co 20X6 forecast

Forecasts prepared by Cadnam Co's finance director for 20X6 predict that:

- Cadnam Co's pre-tax operating profit for 20X6 will be $2,678 million, an increase of 3% compared with 20X5. The operating profit margin will be 2%, the same as for 20X5.
- The tax rate will be 30%.
- Average debt in 20X6 will be $10,250 million and predicted year-end gearing will be 41.3%. The average pre-tax interest rate on the debt will be 8%.
- The investment required to keep the non-current asset base at its present productive capacity in 20X6 will be $2,430 million, which has been included in the calculation of operating profit as depreciation.
- Investment required in additional assets in 20X6 will be $0.25 for every $1 increase in revenue.

2 Chithurst (Sep/Dec 2016, amended)   (49 mins)

(a) Discuss the benefits and drawbacks of the dividend policies which the three companies appear to have adopted. Provide relevant calculations to support your discussion.

Note. Up to 5 marks are available for the calculations.   **(14 marks)**

(b) Discuss how the market capitalisation of the three companies compares with your valuations calculated using the dividend valuation model. Use the data provided to calculate valuations based on growth rates for the last three years.

Note. Up to 3 marks are available for the calculations.   **(6 marks)**

Professional marks will be awarded for the demonstration of skill in analysis and evaluation, scepticism and commercial acumen in your answer.   **(5 marks)**

     (Total = 25 marks)

Exhibit 1: Financing the bid for Chithurst Co

Chithurst Co gained a stock exchange listing five years ago. At the time of the listing, members of the family who founded the company owned 75% of the shares, but now they only hold just over 50%. The number of shares in issue has remained unchanged since Chithurst Co was listed. Chithurst Co's directors have continued the policy of paying a constant dividend per share each year which the company had before it was listed. However, investors who are not family members have become increasingly critical of this policy, saying that there is no clear rationale for it. They would prefer to see steady dividend growth, reflecting the increase in profitability of Chithurst Co since its listing.

Exhibit 2: Financial information for Chithurst and two other companies in its sector

The finance director of Chithurst Co has provided its board with details of Chithurst Co's dividends and investment expenditure, compared with two other similar-sized companies in the same sector, Eartham Co and Iping Co. Each company has a 31 December year end.

	Chithurst Co			Eartham Co			Iping Co		
	Profit for year after interest and tax	Dividend paid	New investment expenditure	Profit for year after interest and tax	Dividend paid	New investment expenditure	Profit for year after interest and tax	Dividend paid	New investment expenditure
	$m	$m	$m	$m	$m	$m	$m	$m	$m
20X2	77	33	18	95	38	30	75	35	37
20X3	80	33	29	(10)	15	15	88	17	64
20X4	94	33	23	110	44	42	118	39	75
20X5	97	33	21	120	48	29	132	42	84

 **BPP**

Exhibit 3: Other financial information

Other financial information relating to the three companies is as follows:

	Chithurst Co	Eartham Co	Iping Co
Cost of equity	11%	14%	12%
Market capitalisation $m	608	1,042	1,164
Increase in share price in last 12 months	1%	5%	10%

Chithurst Co's finance director has estimated the costs of equity for all three companies.

None of the three companies has taken out significant new debt finance since 20X1.

3 Chawan (June 2015, amended)   (49 mins)

(a) Explain what a dark pool network is and why Chawan Co may want to dispose of its equity stake in Oden Co through one, instead of through the stock exchange where Oden Co's shares are listed.   **(4 marks)**

(b) Discuss whether or not Chawan Co should dispose of its equity stake in Oden Co.

Provide relevant calculations to support the discussion.

Note. Up to 8 marks are available for the calculations.   **(16 marks)**

Professional marks will be awarded for the demonstration of skill in analysis and evaluation, scepticism and commercial acumen in your answer.   **(5 marks)**

(Total = 25 marks)

Exhibit 1: Chawan Co & Oden Co

Chawan Co

The treasury department of Chawan Co, a listed company, aims to maintain a portfolio of around $360 million consisting of equity shares, corporate bonds and government bonds, which it can turn into cash quickly for investment projects. Chawan Co is considering disposing of 27 million shares, valued at $2.15 each, which it has invested in Oden Co.

The head of Chawan Co's treasury department is of the opinion that, should the decision be made to dispose of its equity stake in Oden Co, this should be sold through a dark pool network and not sold on the stock exchange where Oden Co's shares are listed. In the last few weeks, there have also been rumours that Oden Co may become subject to a takeover bid.

Oden Co

Oden Co operates in the travel and leisure (T&L) sector, and the poor weather conditions in recent years, coupled with a continuing recession, have meant that the T&L sector is underperforming. Over the past three years, sales revenue fell by an average of 8% per year in the T&L sector. However, there are signs that the economy is starting to recover, but this is by no means certain.

Exhibit 2: Recent financial statement (extracts) for Oden Co

Given below are extracts from the recent financial statements and other financial information for Oden Co and the T&L sector.

ODEN CO

YEAR ENDING 31 MAY

	20X3	20X4	20X5
	$m	$m	$m
Total assets	1,100	1,132	1,106
Equity			
Ordinary shares ($0.50)	300	300	300
Reserves	305	329	311
Total equity	605	629	611
Total non-current liabilities	365	368	360
Total current liabilities	130	135	135
Total equity and liabilities	1,100	1,132	1,106

ODEN CO

YEAR ENDING 31 MAY

	20X3	20X4	20X5
	$m	$m	$m
Sales revenue	1,342	1,335	1,185
Operating profit	218	203	123
Finance costs	(23)	(27)	(35)
Profit before tax	195	176	88
Taxation	(35)	(32)	(16)
Profit for the year	160	144	72

Exhibit 3: Other financial information for Oden Co and the T&L sector

OTHER FINANCIAL INFORMATION (BASED ON ANNUAL FIGURES TILL 31 MAY OF EACH YEAR)

	20X2	20X3	20X4	20X5
Oden Co average share price ($)	2.10	2.50	2.40	2.20
Oden Co dividend per share ($)	0.15	0.18	0.20	0.15
T&L sector average share price ($)	3.80	4.40	4.30	4.82
T&L sector average earnings per share ($)	0.32	0.36	0.33	0.35
T&L sector average dividend per share ($)	0.25	0.29	0.29	0.31
Oden Co's equity beta	1.5	1.5	1.6	2.0
T&L sector average equity beta	1.5	1.4	1.5	1.6

The risk-free rate and the market return have remained fairly constant over the last ten years at 4% and 10% respectively.

 BPP

4 High K (Sep/Dec 2017, amended)   (49 mins)

(a) Evaluate High K Co's financial performance. You should indicate in your discussion areas where further information about High K Co would be helpful.

Provide relevant calculations for ratios and trends to support your evaluation.

Note. Up to 8 marks are available for calculations.   (16 marks)

(b) Discuss how High K Co may seek to finance an investment programme.   (4 marks)

Professional marks will be awarded for the demonstration of skill in analysis and evaluation, scepticism and commercial acumen in your answer.   (5 marks)

(Total = 25 marks)

Exhibit 1: High K Co

High K Co is one of the three largest supermarket chains in the country of Townia. Its two principal competitors, Dely Co and Leminster Co, are of similar size to High K Co. In common with its competitors (but see below), High K Co operates three main types of store:

- Town centre stores – these sell food and drink and a range of small household items. High K Co's initial growth was based on its town centre stores, but it has been shutting them over the last decade, although the rate of closure has slowed in the last couple of years.

- Convenience stores – these are smaller and sell food and drink and very few other items. Between 20X3 and 20Y3, High K Co greatly expanded the number of convenience stores it operated. Their performance has varied, however, and since 20Y3, High K Co has not opened any new stores and closed a number of the worst-performing stores.

- Out-of-town stores – these sell food and drink and a full range of household items, including large electrical goods and furniture. The number of out-of-town stores which High K Co operated increased significantly until 20Y0, but has only increased slightly since.

The majority of town centre and out-of-town stores premises are owned by High K Co, but 85% of convenience stores premises are currently leased.

High K Co also sells most of its range of products online, either offering customers home delivery or 'click and collect' (where the customer orders the goods online and picks them up from a collection point in one of the stores).

20Y6 results

High K Co's year end is 31 December. When its 20Y6 results were published in April 20Y7, High K Co's chief executive emphasised that the group was focusing on:

- Increasing total shareholder return by improvements in operating efficiency and enhancement of responsiveness to customer needs

- Ensuring competitive position by maintaining flexibility to respond to new strategic challenges

- Maintaining financial strength by using diverse sources of funding, including making use in future of revolving credit facilities

Exhibit 2: Changes in High K's environment

Since April 20Y7, Dely Co and Leminster Co have both announced that they will be making significant investments to boost online sales. Dely Co intends to fund its investments by closing all its town centre and convenience stores, although it also intends to open more out-of-town stores in popular locations.

The government of Townia was re-elected in May 20Y7. In the 18 months prior to the election, it eased fiscal policy and consumer spending significantly increased. However, it has tightened fiscal policy since the election to avoid the economy overheating. It has also announced an investigation into whether the country's large retail chains treat their suppliers unfairly.

 BPP

Exhibit 3: Financial information

Extracts from High K Co's 20Y6 financial statements and other information about it are given below:

HIGH K CO

STATEMENT OF PROFIT OR LOSS EXTRACTS YEAR ENDING 31 DECEMBER (ALL AMOUNTS IN $m)

	20Y4	20Y5	20Y6
Sales revenue	23,508	23,905	24,463
Gross profit	1,018	1,211	1,514
Operating profit	204	407	712
Finance costs	(125)	(115)	(100)
Profit after tax	52	220	468
Dividends	150	170	274

HIGH K CO STATEMENT OF FINANCIAL POSITION EXTRACTS YEAR ENDING 31 DECEMBER (ALL AMOUNTS IN $m)

	20Y4	20Y5	20Y6
Non-current assets	10,056	9,577	8,869
Cash and cash equivalents	24	709	1,215
Other current assets	497	618	747
Total non-current and current assets	10,577	10,904	10,831
Equity			
Ordinary shares ($1)	800	800	800
Reserves	7,448	7,519	7,627
Total equity	8,248	8,319	8,427
Non-current liabilities	1,706	1,556	1,246
Current liabilities	623	1,029	1,158

Other financial information

Market price per share			
(in $, $3.89 at end of 20Y3, $3.17 currently)	3.54	3.34	3.23
Dividend yield (%)	5.30	6.36	10.60
Segment information			
Revenue ($m)			
Town centre stores	5,265	5,189	5,192
Convenience stores	3,786	3,792	3,833
Out-of-town stores	10,220	10,340	10,547
Store revenue	19,271	19,321	19,572
Online sales	4,237	4,584	4,891
Number of stores			
Town centre stores	165	157	153
Convenience stores	700	670	640
Out-of-town stores	220	224	227

5 Tillinton (Sep 2018, amended)   (49 mins)

(a) Evaluate Tillinton Co's performance and business prospects in the light of the chief executive's comments and Steph Slindon's concerns. Provide relevant calculations for ratios and trends to support your evaluation.

   Note. 8 marks are available for the calculations.   **(16 marks)**

(b) Discuss how behavioural factors may have resulted in Tillinton Co's share price being higher than is warranted by a rational analysis of its position.   **(4 marks)**

Professional marks will be awarded for the demonstration of skill in analysis and evaluation, scepticism and commercial acumen in your answer.   **(5 marks)**

(Total = 25 marks)

Exhibit 1: Tillinton Co

Tillinton Co is a listed company which has traditionally manufactured children's clothing and toys with long lives. Five years ago, it began manufacturing electronic toys and has since made significant investment in development and production facilities. The first electronic toys which Tillinton Co introduced into the market were received very well, partly as it was seen to be ahead of its competitors in making the most of the technology available.

The country where Tillinton Co is listed has seen a significant general increase in share prices over the last three years, with companies in the electronic goods sector showing particularly rapid increases.

Statement by Tillinton Co's chief executive

Assume it is now September 20X3. Tillinton Co's annual report for the year ended 31 March 20X3 has just been published. Its chief executive commented when announcing the company's results:

> I am very pleased to report that revenue and gross profits have shown bigger increases than in 20X2, resulting in higher post-tax earnings and our company being able to maintain increases in dividends. The sustained increase in our share price clearly demonstrates how happy investors are with us. Our cutting-edge electronic toys continue to perform well and justify our sustained investment in them. Our results have also

benefited from improvements in operational efficiencies for our older ranges and better working capital management. We are considering the development of further ranges of electronic toys for children, or developing other electronic products for adults. If necessary, we may consider scaling down or selling off our operations for some of our older products.

Steph Slindon represents an institutional investor who holds shares in Tillinton Co. Steph is doubtful whether its share price will continue to increase, because she thinks that Tillinton Co's situation may not be as good as its chief executive suggests and because she believes that current share price levels generally may not be sustainable.

Exhibit 2: Information from Tillinton's financial statements

Extracts from Tillinton Co's financial statements for the last three years and other information about it are given below.

TILLINTON CO STATEMENT OF PROFIT OR LOSS IN YEARS ENDING 31 MARCH (ALL AMOUNTS IN $m)

	20X1	20X2	20X3
Sales revenue	1,385	1,636	1,914
Gross profit	381	451	528
Operating profit	205	252	300
Finance costs	(46)	(50)	(66)
Profit before tax	159	202	234
Taxation	(40)	(51)	(65)
Profit after tax	119	151	169
Dividends	(60)	(72)	(84)

TILLINTON CO STATEMENT OF FINANCIAL POSITION IN YEARS ENDING 31 MARCH (ALL AMOUNTS IN $m)

	20X1	20X2	20X3
Non-current assets	2,070	2,235	2,449
Cash and cash equivalents	10	15	15
Other current assets	150	130	125
Total non-current and current assets	2,230	2,380	2,589
Equity			
Ordinary shares ($0.50)	400	400	400
Reserves	805	884	969
Total equity	1,205	1,284	1,369
Non-current liabilities	920	970	1,000
Current liabilities	105	126	220
Total equity and liabilities	2,230	2,380	2,589

Exhibit 3: Other financial information

	20X1	20X2	20X3
Market price per $0.50 share ($2.50 at 31 March 20X0, $5.06 in Sept 20X3)	$2.76	$3.49	$4.44
Earnings per share ($)	0.15	0.19	0.21
Dividend per share ($)	0.075	0.09	0.105

Analysis of revenue

	20X1	20X2	20X3
Electronic toys		319	390
(% change from previous year in brackets)	249	(+28%)	(+22%)
Non-electronic toys		350	404
(% change from previous year in brackets)	302	(+16%)	(+15%)
Clothing		967	1,120
(% change from previous year in brackets)	834	(+16%)	(+16%)

Analysis of gross profit

	20X1	20X2	20X3
Electronic toys		112	113
(% change from previous year in brackets)	100	(+12%)	(+1%)
Non-electronic toys		88	105
(% change from previous year in brackets)	72	(+22%)	(+19%)
Clothing		251	310
(% change from previous year in brackets)	209	(+20%)	(+24%)

Gross profit margin %

	20X1	20X2	20X3
Electronic toys	40.2%	35.1%	29.0%
Non-electronic toys	23.8%	25.1%	26.0%
Clothing	25.1%	26.0%	27.7%

Note. None of Tillinton Co's loan finance in 20X3 is repayable within one year.

6 Arthuro (Mar/Jun 2018, amended)   (49 mins)

(a) Estimate whether Arthuro Co's forecast dividend capacity for a 'normal' year is sufficient for it to maintain its dividend level of $0.74 per equity share.   **(10 marks)**

(b)

   (i)   From Arthuro Co's viewpoint, discuss the financial benefits of, and problems with the decision to increase its level of dividend from Bowerscots Co.   **(5 marks)**

   (ii) Discuss the agency problems, and how they might be resolved, with this decision.   **(5 marks)**

Professional marks will be awarded for the demonstration of skill in analysis and evaluation, scepticism and commercial acumen in your answer.   **(5 marks)**

(Total = 25 marks)

Exhibit 1: Arthuro Co

Arthuro Co is based in Hittyland and is listed on Hittyland's stock exchange. Arthuro Co has one wholly owned subsidiary, Bowerscots Co, based in the neighbouring country of Owlia. Hittyland and Owlia are in a currency union and the currency of both countries is the $.

Arthuro Co purchased 100% of Bowerscots Co's share capital three years ago. Arthuro Co has the power under the acquisition to determine the level of dividend paid by Bowerscots Co. However, Arthuro Co's board decided to let Bowerscots Co's management team have some discretion when making investment decisions. Arthuro Co's board decided that it should receive dividends of 60% of Bowerscots Co's post-tax profits and has, until now, allowed Bowerscots Co to use its remaining retained earnings to fund investments chosen by its management. A bonus linked to Bowerscots Co's after-tax profits is a significant element of Bowerscots Co's managers' remuneration.

Bowerscots Co operates in a very competitive environment. Recently, a senior member of its management team has left to join a competitor.

Exhibit 2: Arthuro Co's dividend policy

Until three months ago, Arthuro Co had 90 million $2 equity shares in issue and $135 million 8% bonds. Three months ago it made a 1 for 3 rights issue. A number of shareholders did not take up their rights, but sold them on, so there have been changes in its shareholder base. Some shareholders expressed concern about dilution of their dividend income as a result of the rights issue. Therefore, Arthuro Co's board felt it had to promise, for the foreseeable future, at least to maintain the dividend of $0.74 per equity share, which it paid for the two years before the rights issue.

Arthuro Co's board is nevertheless concerned about whether it will have sufficient funds available to fulfil its promise about the dividend. It has asked the finance director to forecast its dividend capacity based on assumptions about what will happen in a 'normal' year. The finance director has made the following assumptions in the forecast:

(1) Sales revenue can be assumed to be 4% greater than the most recent year's of $520 million.

(2) The operating profit margin can be assumed to be 20%.

(3) Operating profit can be assumed to be reported after charging depreciation of $30 million and profit on disposal of non-current assets of $5.9 million. The cost of the non-current assets sold can be assumed to be $35 million and its accumulated depreciation to be $24.6 million. Depreciation is allowable for tax and the profit on disposal is fully chargeable to tax.

(4) The net book value of non-current assets at the year end in the most recent accounts was $110 million. To maintain productive capacity, sufficient investment to increase this net book value figure 12 months later by 4% should be assumed, in line with the increase in sales. The calculation of investment required for the year should take into account the depreciation charged of $30 million, and net book value of the non-current assets disposed of during the year.

(5) A $0.15 investment in working capital can be assumed for every $1 increase in sales revenue.

(6) Bowerscots Co's pre-tax profits can be assumed to be $45 million.

Arthuro Co's directors have decided that, to ensure that there is a sufficient dividend capacity to maintain the current dividend level, 100% of the post-tax profits of Bowerscots Co should now be paid as a dividend.

Exhibit 3: Taxation

Arthuro Co pays corporation tax at 30% and Bowerscots Co pays corporation tax at 20%. A withholding tax of 5% is deducted from any dividends remitted by Bowerscots Co. There is a bilateral tax treaty between Hittyland and Owlia. Corporation tax is payable by Arthuro Co on profits declared by Bowerscots Co, but Hittyland gives full credit for corporation tax already paid in Owlia. Hittyland gives no credit for withholding tax paid on dividends in Owlia.

 **BPP**

7 Lamri (December 2010, amended)   (49 mins)

(a) Calculate Lamri's dividend capacity for the coming year prior to implementing TE's proposal and after implementing the proposal.   (14 marks)

(b) Comment on the impact of implementing TE's proposal and suggest possible actions Lamri may take as a result.   (6 marks)

Professional marks will be awarded for the demonstration of skill in analysis and evaluation, scepticism and commercial acumen in your answer.   (5 marks)

(Total = 25 marks)

Exhibit 1: Lamri Co

Lamri Co (Lamri), a listed company, is expecting sales revenue to grow to $80 million next year, which is an increase of 20% from the current year. The operating profit margin for next year is forecast to be the same as this year at 30% of sales revenue. In addition to these profits, Lamri receives 75% of the after-tax profits from one of its wholly owned foreign subsidiaries, Magnolia Co (Magnolia), as dividends. However, its second wholly owned foreign subsidiary, Strymon Co (Strymon), does not pay dividends.

Lamri is due to pay dividends of $7.5 million shortly and has maintained a steady 8% annual growth rate in dividends over the past few years. The company has grown rapidly in the last few years as a result of investment in key projects and this is likely to continue.

For the coming year it is expected that Lamri will require the following capital investment.

- An investment equivalent to the amount of depreciation to keep its non-current asset base at the present productive capacity. Lamri charges depreciation of 25% on a straight-line basis on its non-current assets of $15 million. This charge has been included when calculating the operating profit amount.

- A 25% investment in additional non-current assets for every $1 increase in sales revenue.

- $4.5 million additional investment in non-current assets for a new project.

Lamri also requires a 15% investment in working capital for every $1 increase in sales revenue.

Strymon produces specialist components solely for Magnolia to assemble into finished goods. Strymon will produce 300,000 specialist components at $12 variable cost per unit and will incur fixed costs of $2.1 million for the coming year. It will then transfer the components to Magnolia at full cost price, where they will be assembled at a cost of $8 per unit and sold for $50 per unit. Magnolia will incur additional fixed costs of $1.5 million in the assembly process.

Exhibit 2: Transfer pricing concerns

Tax-Ethic (TE) is a charitable organisation devoted to reducing tax avoidance schemes by companies operating in poor countries around the world. TE has petitioned Lamri's board of directors to reconsider Strymon's policy of transferring goods at full cost. TE suggests that the policy could be changed to cost plus 40% mark-up. If Lamri changes Strymon's policy, it is expected that Strymon would be asked to remit 75% of its after-tax profits as dividends to Lamri.

Exhibit 3: Other information

(1) Lamri's outstanding non-current liabilities of $35 million, on which it pays interest of 8% per year, and its 30 million $1 issued equity capital will not change for the coming year.

(2) Lamri's, Magnolia's and Strymon's profits are taxed at 28%, 22% and 42% respectively. A withholding tax of 10% is deducted from any dividends remitted from Strymon.

(3) The tax authorities where Lamri is based charge tax on profits made by subsidiary companies but give full credit for tax already paid by overseas subsidiaries.

(4) All costs and revenues are in $ equivalent amounts and exchange rate fluctuations can be ignored.

8 Moonstar (Sep/Dec 2015, amended)   (49 mins)

(a) Calculate the amounts in $ which each of the tranches can expect to receive from the securitisation arrangement proposed by the non-executive director and discuss how the variability in rental income affects the returns from the securitisation.   **(11 marks)**

(b) Discuss the benefits and risks for Moonstar Co associated with the securitisation arrangement that the non-executive director has proposed.   **(5 marks)**

(c) Discuss whether a Mudaraba contract would be an appropriate method of financing the investment and discuss why the bank may have concerns about providing finance by this method.   **(4 marks)**

Professional marks will be awarded for the demonstration of skill in analysis and evaluation, scepticism and commercial acumen in your answer.   **(5 marks)**

(Total = 25 marks)

Exhibit 1: Moonstar Co

Moonstar Co is a property development company which is planning to undertake a $200 million commercial property development. Moonstar Co has had some difficulties over the last few years, with some developments not generating the expected returns and the company has at times struggled to pay its finance costs. As a result, Moonstar Co's credit rating has been lowered, affecting the terms it can obtain for bank finance. Although Moonstar Co is listed on its local stock exchange, 75% of the share capital is held by members of the family who founded the company. The family members who are shareholders do not wish to subscribe for a rights issue and are unwilling to dilute their control over the company by authorising a new issue of equity shares. Moonstar Co's board is therefore considering other methods of financing the development, which the directors believe will generate higher returns than other recent investments, as the country where Moonstar Co is based appears to be emerging from recession.

Exhibit 2: Securitisation proposals

One of the non-executive directors of Moonstar Co has proposed that it should raise funds by means of a securitisation process, transferring the rights to the rental income from the commercial property development to a special purpose vehicle. Her proposals assume that the leases will generate an income of 11% per year to Moonstar Co over a ten-year period. She proposes that Moonstar Co should use 90% of the value of the investment for a collateralised loan obligation which should be structured as follows:

- 60% of the collateral value to support a tranche of A-rated floating rate loan notes offering investors central bank base rate plus 150 basis points

- 15% of the collateral value to support a tranche of B-rated fixed rate loan notes offering investors 12%

- 15% of the collateral value to support a tranche of C-rated fixed rate loan notes offering investors 13%

- 10% of the collateral value to support a tranche as subordinated certificates, with the return being the excess of receipts over payments from the securitisation process

The non-executive director believes that there will be sufficient demand for all tranches of the loan notes from investors. Investors will expect the income stream from the development to be low risk, as they will expect the property market to improve with the recession coming to an end and enough potential lessees to be attracted by the new development.

The non-executive director predicts that there would be annual costs of $200,000 in administering the loan. She acknowledges that there would be interest rate risks associated with the proposal, and proposes a fixed for variable interest rate swap on the A-rated floating rate notes, exchanging central bank base rate for 9.5%.

However, the finance director believes that the prediction of the income from the development that the non-executive director has made is over-optimistic. He believes that it is most likely that

 BPP

the total value of the rental income will be 5% lower than the non-executive director has forecast. He believes that there is some risk that the returns could be so low as to jeopardise the income for the C-rated fixed rate loan note holders.

Exhibit 3: Islamic finance

Moonstar Co's chairman has pointed out that a major bank in the country where Moonstar Co is located has begun to offer a range of Islamic financial products. The chairman has suggested that a Mudaraba contract would be the most appropriate method of providing the funds required for the investment.

ADVANCED INVESTMENT APPRAISAL

Questions in this part of the Exam Practice kit mainly cover Section B of the AFM syllabus, the subject of Chapters 3–7 of the BPP Course Book.

9 Fernhurst (Sep/Dec 2016, amended)   (49 mins)

(a) Evaluate the financial acceptability of the investment in the Milland and calculate and comment on the investment's duration.   (12 marks)

(b) Calculate the percentage change in the selling price required for the investment to have a zero net present value, and discuss the significance of your results.   (4 marks)

(c) Discuss the non-executive director's comments on net present value.   (4 marks)

Professional marks will be awarded for the demonstration of skill in analysis and evaluation and scepticism in your answer.   (5 marks)

(Total = 25 marks)

Exhibit 1: Fernhurst Co

Fernhurst Co is a manufacturer of mobile communications technology. It is about to launch a new communications device, the Milland, which its directors believe is both more technologically advanced and easier to use than devices currently offered by its rivals.

Exhibit 2: Investment in the Milland

The Milland will require a major investment in facilities. Fernhurst Co's directors believe that this can take place very quickly and production be started almost immediately.

Fernhurst Co expects to sell 132,500 units of the Milland in its first year. Sales volume is expected to increase by 20% in Year 2 and 30% in Year 3, and then be the same in Year 4 as Year 3, as the product reaches the end of its useful life. The initial selling price in Year 1 is expected to be $100 per unit, before increasing with the rate of inflation annually.

The variable cost of each unit is expected to be $43.68 in Year 1, rising by the rate of inflation in subsequent years annually. Fixed costs are expected to be $900,000 in Year 1, rising by the rate of inflation in subsequent years annually.

The initial investment in non-current assets is expected to be $16,000,000. Fernhurst Co will also need to make an immediate investment of $1,025,000 in working capital. The working capital will be increased annually at the start of each of Years 2 to 4 by the inflation rate and is fully recoverable at the end of the project's life. Fernhurst Co will also incur one-off marketing expenditure of $1,500,000 post-inflation after the launch of the Milland. The marketing expenditure can be assumed to be made at the end of Year 1 and be a tax-allowable expense.

Fernhurst Co pays company tax on profits at an annual rate of 25%. Tax is payable in the year that the tax liability arises. Tax-allowable depreciation is available at 20% on the investment in non-current assets on a reducing balance basis. A balancing adjustment will be available in Year 4. The realisable value of the investment at the end of Year 4 is expected to be zero.

The expected annual rate of inflation in the country in which Fernhurst Co is located is 4% in Year 1 and 5% in Years 2 to 4.

The applicable cost of capital for this investment appraisal is 11%.

Other calculations

Fernhurst Co's finance director has indicated that besides needing a net present value calculation based on this data for the next board meeting, he also needs to know the figure for the project's duration, to indicate to the board how returns from the project will be spread over time.

 BPP

Failure of launch of the Milland

The finance director would also like some simple analysis based on the possibility that the marketing expenditure is not effective and the launch fails, as he feels that the product's price may be too high. He has suggested that there is a 15% chance that the Milland will have negative net cash flows for Year 1 of $1,000,000 or more. He would like to know by what percentage the selling price could be reduced or increased to result in the investment having a zero net present value, assuming demand remained the same.

Exhibit 3: Assessment of new products

Fernhurst Co's last board meeting discussed another possible new product, the Racton, and the finance director presented a range of financial data relating to this product, including the results of net present value and payback evaluations. One of the non-executive directors, who is not a qualified accountant, stated that they found it difficult to see the significance of the different items of financial data. Their understanding was that Fernhurst Co merely had to ensure that the investment had a positive net present value and shareholders were bound to be satisfied with it, as it would maximise their wealth in the long term.

10 Riviere (December 2014, amended)   (49 mins)

(a) Discuss the aims of a free trade area, such as the EU, and the possible benefits to Riviere Co of operating within the EU.   (4 marks)

(b) Calculate the figures which have not been provided for project Drugi and recommend which project should be accepted. Provide a justification for the recommendation and explain what the value at risk measures.   (10 marks)

(c) Discuss the possible legal risks of investing in project Drugi which Riviere Co may be concerned about and how these may be mitigated.   (6 marks)

Professional marks will be awarded for the demonstration of skill in analysis and evaluation, scepticism and commercial acumen in your answer.   (5 marks)

(Total = 25 marks)

Exhibit 1: Riviere Co

Riviere Co is a small company based in the European Union (EU). It produces high quality frozen food which it exports to a small number of supermarket chains located within the EU as well. The EU is a free trade area for trade between its member countries.

Riviere Co finds it difficult to obtain bank finance and relies on a long-term strategy of using internally generated funds for new investment projects. This constraint means that it cannot accept every profitable project and often has to choose between them.

Exhibit 2: New projects

Riviere Co is currently considering investment in one of two mutually exclusive food production projects: Privi and Drugi. Privi will produce and sell a new range of frozen desserts exclusively within the EU. Drugi will produce and sell a new range of frozen desserts and savoury foods to supermarket chains based in countries outside the EU. Each project will last for five years and the following financial information refers to both projects.

PROJECT DRUGI ANNUAL AFTER-TAX CASH FLOWS EXPECTED AT THE END OF EACH YEAR

Year	Current	1	2	3	4	5
Cash flows (€'000)	(11,840)	1,230	1,680	4,350	10,240	2,200

	Privi	Drugi
Net present value	€2,054,000	€2,293,000
Internal rate of return	17.6%	Not provided
Modified internal rate of return	13.4%	Not provided
Value at risk (over the project's life)		
95% confidence level	€1,103,500	Not provided
90% confidence level	€860,000	Not provided

Both projects' net present value has been calculated based on Riviere Co's nominal cost of capital of 10%. It can be assumed that both projects' cash flow returns are normally distributed and the annual standard deviation of project Drugi's present value of after-tax cash flows is estimated to be €400,000. It can also be assumed that all sales are made in € (Euro) and therefore the company is not exposed to any foreign exchange exposure.

The standardised value for a 90% confidence level is 1.282 standard deviations, and for a 95% confidence level the standardised value is 1.645 standard deviations.

Exhibit 3: Legal risks

Notwithstanding how profitable project Drugi may appear to be, Riviere Co's board of directors is concerned about the possible legal risks if it invests in the project because they have never dealt with companies outside the EU before.

11 Hathaway (March 2020, amended) (49 mins)

(a)

(i) Evaluate the financial acceptability of the project chi investment proposal based on the chief engineer's forecasts, assuming regulatory approval is granted in one year's time. **(6 marks)**

(ii) Calculate the expected net present value of the proposal based on the finance director's assumptions about the likelihood of a recession and the potential impact on project chi's cash flows. **(2 marks)**

(iii) Calculate the net present value of the finance director's alternative option for the technology and advise the board whether this is worth pursuing. **(3 marks)**

(iv) Recommend whether the board should proceed with the application for regulatory approval after taking into consideration Hathaway Co's 70% approval rate with its regulatory applications or to sell the concept now to Gepe Co. Include in your analysis any comments on your findings. **(5 marks)**

(b) Explain the rationale for implementing post-completion audits. Suggest ways in which Hathaway Co may have benefited if this had been applied to projects lambda and kappa. **(4 marks)**

Professional marks will be awarded for the demonstration of skill in analysis and evaluation, scepticism and commercial acumen in your answer. **(5 marks)**

(Total = 25 marks)

Exhibit 1: Hathaway Co

Hathaway Co operates in the aviation industry, manufacturing safety equipment for commercial aircraft. The company has a policy of carefully appraising new investment opportunities, including the detailed analysis of all cost and revenue assumptions prior to their approval.

Project chi

Hathaway Co's board is reviewing a potential investment, project chi. The company's engineers have developed a new technology which can detect the potential for mechanical failure with a greater degree of accuracy than has previously been the case. Early test results have been extremely encouraging.

If the board accepts the engineers' proposal, Hathaway Co would need to submit an application to the relevant regulatory authority. It is expected regulatory approval would be granted in one year's time. Manufacturing and sales would commence immediately after being granted regulatory approval. Hathaway Co's chief engineer presented an investment case for project chi to the board, including a summary of the following cost and revenue forecasts and assumptions.

Hathaway Co is expected to sell 3,000 units in the first year of production with demand increasing by 5% in each subsequent year of its four-year life. These sales forecasts are based on a contribution of $5,000 per unit in the first year of production and increasing at 2% per year in subsequent years. Annual fixed costs of $8.7m are expected in the first year of production, increasing at 3% per year throughout the life of the project.

An investment in plant and machinery of $12m will be required as soon as regulatory approval has been granted. Tax allowable depreciation is available on the plant and machinery at an annual rate of 20% on a straight-line basis. A balancing adjustment is expected at the end of the project when the plant and machinery will be scrapped.

Tax is payable at 20% in the year in which profits are made. The relevant cost of capital to be used in the appraisal is 12%.

Exhibit 2: Project chi extra information

The finance director, however, raised the following objections and consequences to the chief engineer's presentation.

The chief engineer's cost and revenue assumptions ignore the possibility of a recession, which has a 20% probability of occurring. In a recession, the total present values for the four years of production are likely to be 40% lower. The finance director also believes there is an alternative, mutually exclusive, development opportunity based on the new technology although this would still depend on it being granted regulatory approval. This alternative option would incur an identical investment cost of $12m but generate annual, inflation adjusted, post-tax cash flows of $3.43m over its seven-year life from year two onwards.

The investment case assumes regulatory approval is certain whereas historically only 70% of Hathaway Co's applications have been approved. In one year's time, if the regulatory application is not approved, it is assumed that the concept can be sold to Gepe Co for $1.0m at that time. If the board rejects the proposal now, assume the concept can be sold for $4.3m immediately.

Exhibit 3: Projects lambda and kappa

A recent board meeting discussed two recent investments, projects lambda and kappa, both involving the construction of new manufacturing plants for safety equipment. Both projects are now operational although project lambda experienced significant time delays and cost overruns while project kappa was under budget and within schedule.

On closer examination, the directors noticed that project lambda's revenue far exceeded initial expectations, whereas project kappa's revenue was much less than originally expected. On balance, Hathaway Co's chief executive officer suggested that each project's successes compensated for their respective failings and that this was to be expected when making predictions about the future in an investment plan. However, one of the directors suggested the company could benefit from the introduction of post-completion audits. The directors agreed to discuss this in greater depth at the next board meeting.

12 MMC (June 2011, amended) (49 mins)

(a) Estimate the financial impact of the directors' decision to delay the production and marketing of the game. The Black–Scholes option pricing (BSOP) model may be used, where appropriate. A BSOP spreadsheet is available on the ACCA practice platform to complete the relevant calculations. **(9 marks)**

(b) Briefly discuss the implications of the answer obtained in part (a) above. **(6 marks)**

(c) Discuss how a decrease in the value of each of the determinants of the option price in the Black–Scholes option pricing model for European options is likely to change the price of a call option. **(5 marks)**

Professional marks will be awarded for the demonstration of skill in analysis and evaluation, scepticism and commercial acumen in your answer. **(5 marks)**

(Total = 25 marks)

Exhibit 1: MMC

MesmerMagic Co (MMC) is considering whether to undertake the development of a new computer game based on an adventure film due to be released in 22 months. It is expected that the game will be available to buy two months after the film's release, by which time it will be possible to judge the popularity of the film with a high degree of certainty. However, at present, there is considerable uncertainty about whether the film, and therefore the game, is likely to be successful. Although MMC would pay for the exclusive rights to develop and sell the game now, the directors are of the opinion that they should delay the decision to produce and market the game until the film has been released and the game is available for sale.

Exhibit 2: New project details

MMC has forecast the following end of year cash flows for the four-year sales period of the game.

Year	1	2	3	4
Cash flows ($ million)	25	18	10	5

MMC will spend $7 million at the start of each of the next two years to develop the game and the gaming platform, and to pay for the exclusive rights to develop and sell the game. Following this, the company will require $35 million for production, distribution and marketing costs at the start of the four-year sales period of the game.

It can be assumed that all the costs and revenues include inflation. The relevant cost of capital for this project is 11% and the risk-free rate is 3.5%. MMC has estimated the likely volatility of the cash flows at a standard deviation of 30%.

13 Furlion Co (Mar/Jun 2016, amended) (49 mins)

(a) Assess, showing all relevant calculations, whether Furlion Co should proceed with the significant opportunity. Discuss the assumptions made and other factors which will affect the decision of whether to establish a plant in Naswa.

The Black–Scholes pricing (BSOP) model may be used, where appropriate. A BSOP spreadsheet is available on the ACCA practice platform to complete the relevant calculations. **(14 marks)**

(b) Discuss the possibility of the Naswan Government obtaining funding for further land reclamation from the World Bank, referring specifically to the International Development Association. **(6 marks)**

 BPP

Professional marks will be awarded for the demonstration of skill in analysis and evaluation, scepticism and commercial acumen in your answer. **(5 marks)**

(Total = 25 marks)

Exhibit 1: Furlion Co

Furlion Co manufactures heavy agricultural equipment and machinery which can be used in difficult farming conditions. Furlion Co's chief executive has been investigating a significant opportunity in the country of Naswa, where Furlion Co has not previously sold any products. The government of Naswa has been undertaking a major land reclamation programme and Furlion Co's equipment is particularly suitable for use on the reclaimed land. Because of the costs and other problems involved in transporting its products, Furlion Co's chief executive proposes that Furlion Co should establish a plant for manufacturing machinery in Naswa. He knows that the Naswan government is keen to encourage the development of sustainable businesses within the country.

Exhibit 2: Financial forecasts

Initial calculations suggest that the proposed investment in Naswa would have a negative net present value of $1.01 million. However, Furlion Co's chief executive believes that there may be opportunities for greater cash flows in future if the Naswan government expands its land reclamation programme. The government at present is struggling to fund expansion of the programme out of its own resources and is looking for other funding. If the Naswan government obtains this funding, the chief executive has forecast that the increased demand for Furlion Co's products would justify $15 million additional expenditure at the site of the factory in three years' time. The expected net present value for this expansion is currently estimated to be $0.

It can be assumed that all costs and revenues include inflation. The relevant cost of capital is 12% and the risk-free rate is 4%. The chief executive has estimated the likely volatility of cash flows at a standard deviation of 30%.

14 Tisa Co (June 2012, amended)   (49 mins)

(a) Provide a reasoned estimate of the cost of capital that Tisa Co should use to calculate the net present value of the two processes. Include all relevant calculations. **(8 marks)**

(b) Calculate the internal rate of return (IRR) and the modified internal rate of return (MIRR) for Process Omega. Given that the IRR and MIRR of Process Zeta are 26.6% and 23.3% respectively, recommend which process, if any, Tisa Co should proceed with and explain your recommendation. **(8 marks)**

(c) Elfu Co has estimated an annual standard deviation of $800,000 on one of its other projects, based on a normal distribution of returns. The average annual return on this project is $2,200,000.

Estimate the project's value at risk (VaR) at a 99% confidence level for 1 year and over the project's life of 5 years. Explain what is meant by the answers obtained. The standardised value for a 99% confidence level is 2.33 standard deviations. **(4 marks)**

Professional marks will be awarded for the demonstration of skill in analysis and evaluation, scepticism and commercial acumen in your answer. **(5 marks)**

(Total = 25 marks)

Exhibit 1: Tisa Co

Tisa Co is considering an opportunity to produce an innovative component which, when fitted into motor vehicle engines, will enable them to utilise fuel more efficiently. The component can be manufactured using either process Omega or process Zeta. Although this is an entirely new line of business for Tisa Co, it is of the opinion that developing either process over a period of four years

and then selling the production rights at the end of four years to another company may prove lucrative.

The annual after-tax cash flows for each process are as follows:

Exhibit 2: Process Omega and Process Zeta

Process Omega

Year	0	1	2	3	4
After-tax cash flows ($'000)	(3,800)	1,220	1,153	1,386	3,829

Process Zeta

Year	0	1	2	3	4
After-tax cash flows ($'000)	(3,800)	643	546	1,055	5,990

Tisa Co has 10 million 50c shares trading at 180c each. Its loans have a current value of $3.6 million and an average after-tax cost of debt of 4.50%. Tisa Co's capital structure is unlikely to change significantly following the investment in either process.

Exhibit 3: Elfu Co

Elfu Co manufactures electronic parts for cars including the production of a component similar to the one being considered by Tisa Co. Elfu Co's equity beta is 1.40, and it is estimated that the equivalent equity beta for its other activities, excluding the component production, is 1.25. Elfu Co has 400 million 25c shares in issue trading at 120c each. Its debt finance consists of variable rate loans redeemable in seven years. The loans paying interest at base rate plus 120 basis points have a current value of $96 million. It can be assumed that 80% of Elfu Co's debt finance and 75% of Elfu Co's equity finance can be attributed to other activities excluding the component production. Both companies pay annual corporation tax at a rate of 25%. The current base rate is 3.5% and the market risk premium is estimated at 5.8%.

15 Tippletine (Mar/Jun 2018, amended)   (49 mins)

(a) Calculate the adjusted present value for the investment on the basis that it is financed by the subsidised loan and conclude whether the project should be accepted or not. Show all relevant calculations.   **(15 marks)**

(b) Discuss the issues which Tippletine Co's shareholders who are not directors would consider if its directors decided that the new investment should be financed by the issue of convertible loan notes on the terms suggested.

   Note. You are not required to carry out any calculations when answering part (b).   **(5 marks)**

Professional marks will be awarded for the demonstration of skill in analysis and evaluation, scepticism and commercial acumen in your answer.   **(5 marks)**

(Total = 25 marks)

Exhibit 1: Tippletine Co

Tippletine Co is based in Valliland. It is listed on Valliland's stock exchange but only has a small number of shareholders. Its directors collectively own 45% of the equity share capital.

Tippletine Co's growth has been based on the manufacture of household electrical goods. However, the directors have taken a strategic decision to diversify operations and to make a major investment in facilities for the manufacture of office equipment.

 BPP

Exhibit 2: Details of investment

The new investment is being appraised over a four-year time horizon. Revenues from the new investment are uncertain and Tippletine Co's finance director has prepared what she regards as cautious forecasts.

Year	1	2	3	4
Operating cash flows before tax	($7 million)	$12.5 million	$13.225 million	$13.834 million

The new investment will require immediate expenditure on facilities of $30.6 million. Tax allowable depreciation will be available on the new investment at an annual rate of 25% reducing balance basis. It can be assumed that there will either be a balancing allowance or charge in the final year of the appraisal. The finance director believes the facilities will remain viable after four years, and therefore a realisable value of $13.5 million can be assumed at the end of the appraisal period.

The new facilities will also require an immediate initial investment in working capital of $3 million. Working capital requirements will increase by the rate of inflation for the next three years and any working capital at the start of Year 4 will be assumed to be released at the end of the appraisal period.

Tippletine Co pays tax at an annual rate of 30%. Tax is payable with a year's time delay. Any tax losses on the investment can be assumed to be carried forward and written off against future profits from the investment.

Predicted inflation rates are as follows:

Year	1	2	3	4
	8%	6%	5%	4%

Exhibit 3: Financing the investment

Tippletine Co has been considering two choices for financing all of the $30.6 million needed for the initial investment in the facilities:

- A subsidised loan from a government loan scheme, with the loan repayable at the end of the four years. Issue costs of 4% of the gross finance would be payable. Interest would be payable at a rate of 30 basis points below the risk-free rate of 2.5%. In order to obtain the benefits of the loan scheme, Tippletine Co would have to fulfil various conditions, including locating the facilities in a remote part of Valliland where unemployment is high.

- Convertible loan notes, with the subscribers for the notes including some of Tippletine Co's directors. The loan notes would have issue costs of 4% of the gross finance. If not converted, the loan notes would be redeemed in six years' time. Interest would be payable at 5%, which is Tippletine Co's normal cost of borrowing. Conversion would take place at an effective price of $2.75 per share. However, the loan note holders could enforce redemption at any time from the start of Year 3 if Tippletine Co's share price fell below $1.50 per share. Tippletine Co's current share price is $2.20 per share.

Issue costs for the subsidised loan and convertible loan notes would be paid out of available cash reserves. Issue costs are not allowable as a tax-deductible expense.

In initial discussions, the majority of the board favoured using the subsidised loan. The appraisal of the investment should be prepared on the basis that this method of finance will be used. However, the chairman argued strongly in favour of the convertible loan notes, as, in his view, operating costs will be lower if Tippletine Co does not have to fulfil the conditions laid down by the government of Valliland. Tippletine Co's finance director is sceptical, however, about whether the other shareholders would approve the issue of convertible loan notes on the terms suggested. The directors will decide which method of finance to use at the next board meeting.

Other information

Humabuz Co is a large manufacturer of office equipment in Valliland. Humabuz Co's geared cost of equity is estimated to be 10.5% and its pre-tax cost of debt to be 5.4%. These estimates are based on a capital structure comprising $225 million 6% irredeemable bonds, trading at $107 per $100, and 125 million $1 equity shares, trading at $3.20 per share. Humabuz Co also pays tax at an annual rate of 30% on its taxable profits.

16 Robson (Mar/Jun 2021, amended)   (49 mins)

The following **exhibits** provide information relevant to the question.

(1)   Robson Co and project information

(2)   Further information on project finance

This information should be used to answer the question **requirements** within your chosen **response option(s)**.

Required

(a)   Calculate the adjusted present value of the investment and recommend whether the project should be accepted or not.   **(13 marks)**

(b)   Discuss the factors the capital providers, excluding the bank, will consider before deciding whether or not to approve the funding decision for Robson Co's investment in a new manufacturing plant.   **(7 marks)**

Professional marks will be awarded for the demonstration of skill in analysis and evaluation, scepticism and commercial acumen in your answer.   **(5 marks)**

(Total = 25 marks)

Exhibit 1: Robson Co and project information

Robson Co is a food manufacturer with a portfolio of well-known brands. The founding directors retain a significant minority shareholding in the company and continue to serve on the board following a successful listing ten years ago. After obtaining the listing, Robson Co's gearing ratio increased significantly above the sector average as the result of a poorly timed expansion strategy, mainly financed by debt. Earnings became increasingly volatile, and the debt burden triggered a decline in the company's financial performance. The board responded to these problems five years ago by pursuing a debt-reduction turnaround strategy, which has been financed by a series of rights issues and asset disposals.

Even though this strategy successfully reduced the gearing ratio, which is now equal to the industry average, the share price remains depressed due to competitive pressures within the industry. The company's credit rating has recently been downgraded once again. Robson Co's chief executive officer (CEO) has identified an opportunity to relocate the manufacturing plant and develop a state-of-the-art automated production line, which will reduce the underlying cost base and be a source of competitive advantage.

Project information

Robson Co's finance director has prepared estimates of the free cash flows generated by the project, based on a four-year time horizon:

Year	0	1	2	3	4
	$m	$m	$m	$m	$m
Free cash flows		20.9	20.6	28.7	104.6

The investment cost is $120m, which Robson Co's CEO proposes to finance as follows:

	$m
Disposal of existing manufacturing plant	20
Rights issue	10
Subsidised loan, 3.5% annual interest rate	40
Bank loan, 9% annual interest rate	50
Total	**120**

The bank loan is repayable in equal annual instalments over four years. Issue costs of 2% are payable on gross external financing and are not allowable for corporation tax. Issue costs are payable out of available cash reserves. The finance director has asked you to ignore underwriting costs relating to the rights issue.

Additional information

Robson Co's current asset beta is 1.222. The risk-free rate is 3% and the market risk premium is 9%. The CEO expects the business risk of the company to remain unchanged as a result of the investment.

Corporation tax is payable at an annual rate of 20%.

Exhibit 2: Further information on project finance

The board discussed the financing of the project at a recent meeting. Robson Co's corporate bankers have already approved the funding decision for the $50m bank loan but the finance director is concerned about the following capital providers:

External shareholders

The last rights issue took place 18 months ago and there were two others in the previous five years. A group of shareholders have formed an action group to exert pressure on the board for more drastic change. This included a campaign to replace the CEO, which was only narrowly avoided when the shareholders voted at the most recent annual general meeting. The CEO is optimistic about the prospects of a rights issue but suggested underwriting the issue to reduce the risk of failure.

Subsidised loan provider

The government funds the subsidised loan programme to boost job creation in the economically deprived northern region of the country, which is where the new automated manufacturing plant is to be located. Although the loan has yet to be approved, the chief executive is optimistic about the outcome of their application. One feature of the loan programme is that it is open to applicants without assets available to provide security although other restrictions may be imposed. This is relevant to Robson Co since surplus assets were disposed of during the turnaround strategy and those which remain will be used to secure the new bank loan.

17 Toltuck (Mar/Jun 2017, amended)   (49 mins)

(a) Calculate the valuation and yield to maturity of Toltuck Co's $100 bond under its old and new credit ratings. **(10 marks)**

(b) Discuss the factors which may have affected the credit rating of Toltuck Co published by the credit agency, and the impact of the fall in Toltuck Co's credit rating on its ability to raise financial capital. **(10 marks)**

Professional marks will be awarded for the demonstration of skill in analysis and evaluation and commercial acumen in your answer. **(5 marks)**

(Total = 25 marks)

Exhibit 1: Toltuck Co

Toltuck Co is a listed company in the building industry which specialises in the construction of large commercial and residential developments. Toltuck Co had been profitable for many years, but has just incurred major losses on the last two developments which it has completed in its home country of Arumland. These developments were an out-of-town retail centre and a major residential development. Toltuck Co's directors have blamed the poor results primarily on the recent recession in Arumland, although demand for the residential development also appears to have been adversely affected by it being located in an area which has suffered serious flooding over the last two years.

As a result of returns from these two major developments being much lower than expected, Toltuck Co has had to finance current work-in-progress by a significantly greater amount of debt finance, giving it higher gearing than most other construction companies operating in Arumland. Toltuck Co's directors have recently been alarmed by a major credit agency's decision to downgrade Toltuck Co's credit rating from AA to BBB. The directors are very concerned about the impact this will have on the valuation of Toltuck Co's bonds and the future cost of debt.

Exhibit 2: Credit rating and bond finance

The following information can be used to assess the consequences of the change in Toltuck Co's credit rating.

Toltuck Co has issued an 8% bond, which has a face or nominal value of $100 and a premium of 2% on redemption in three years' time. The coupon on the bond is payable on an annual basis.

The government of Arumland has three bonds in issue. They all have a face or nominal value of $100 and are all redeemable at par. Taxation can be ignored on government bonds. They are of the same risk class and the coupon on each is payable on an annual basis. Details of the bonds are as follows:

Bond	Redeemable	Coupon	Current market value $
1	1 year	9%	104
2	2 years	7%	102
3	3 years	6%	98

Credit spreads, published by the credit agency, are as follows (shown in basis points):

Rating	1 year	2 years	3 years
AA	18	31	45
BBB	54	69	86

Exhibit 3: Toltuck's shareholder base

Toltuck Co's shareholder base can be divided broadly into two groups. The majority of shareholders are comfortable with investing in a company where dividends in some years will be high, but there will be low or no dividends in other years because of the cash demands facing the business. However, a minority of shareholders would like Toltuck Co to achieve at least a minimum dividend each year and are concerned about the company undertaking investments which they regard as very speculative.

18 Tonpantau (December 2022)　　　　　　　　　　　(49 mins)

The following **exhibits** provide information relevant to the question:

(1)　Tonpantau Co proposed investment

(2)　Details of investment

This information should be used to answer the question **requirements** within your chose **response option(s)**.

Required

(a)　Evaluate the financial acceptability of the proposed investment.　　　　**(12 marks)**

(b)　Discuss, with reference to Tonpantau Co's proposed investment:

- how real options build on traditional net present value analysis when evaluating investment decisions; and

- the problems with incorporating and valuing real options. Your answer should make specific reference to the Black–Scholes model.

　　　　　　　　　　　　　　　　　　　　　　　　　　　　　　　(8 marks)

Professional marks will be awarded for the demonstration of skill in analysis and evaluation, scepticism, and commercial acumen in your answer.　　　　　**(5 marks)**

　　　　　　　　　　　　　　　　　　　　　　　　　　　　(Total = 25 marks)

Exhibit 1: Tonpantau Co proposed investment

Tonpantau Co is a publishing company, currently publishing mathematics and business studies texts and online study material for schools. The company is considering entering new markets in these subject areas. Initially, it will produce material for mathematics degree courses, but then it plans to produce material for other university courses and professional qualifications.

Tonpantau Co's directors feel that the decision to invest being made in phases, and the possibility of not pursuing the investment further if sales of the mathematics material are disappointing, are significant. However, they are unsure how to incorporate these factors into the investment appraisal. Tonpantau Co's directors are also uncertain about whether its closest competitors have any plans to enter these new markets, or how its competitors will react if Tonpantau Co is successful in its new markets.

Exhibit 2: Details of investment

Tonpantau Co's board has set a four-year time horizon for consideration of the investment, based on its current plans for producing the new material. Planned capital expenditure on this investment will be as follows:

Year	1	2	3
	$000	$000	$000
Planned capital expenditure	20,000	20,000	12,000

In addition, total working capital required at the start of each year will be as follows:

Year	1	2	3	4
	$000	$000	$000	$000
Working capital required	3,000	3,450	4,000	3,800

Working capital is expected to be fully released at the end of year 4.

Forecast pre-tax profits for the investment are stated below. They are stated AFTER the deduction of tax-allowable depreciation, which is equal to accounting depreciation.

Year	1	2	3	4
	$000	$000	$000	$000
Tax-allowable depreciation	2,600	5,200	6,700	6,700
Pre-tax profits	8,700	11,600	15,200	15,500

Tax is payable at 20% in the year in which profits are made.

Bodfari Co is a company which produces mathematics and business studies material for university and professional exam courses. Bodfari Co's debt/equity ratio is 25:75 and its equity beta is 1.60. Tonpantau Co's debt/equity ratio is 40:60.

The current risk-free rate is 4.25% and the market risk premium can be assumed to be 5.5%. For the purposes of estimating the cost of capital, it can be assumed that the beta of debt is zero. Tonpantau Co's debt consists of a 6% bond, which has a nominal value of $100 and a premium of 4% on redemption in four years' time. The coupon on the bond is payable on an annual basis.

The annual spot rate curve for the bond is as follows:

1 year	4.33%
2 year	5.15%
3 year	5.93%
4 year	6.58%

 BPP

19 Vogel (June 2014, amended)   (49 mins)

(a)   Discuss two possible actions Vogel Co could take to reduce the risk that the acquisition of Tori Co fails to increase shareholder value and comment on possible reasons why Vogel Co may have switched from a strategy of organic growth to one of growing by acquiring companies.

(6 marks)

(b)   Estimate, showing all relevant calculations, the maximum premium Vogel Co could pay to acquire Tori Co, explaining the approach taken and any assumptions made.   **(14 marks)**

Professional marks will be awarded for the demonstration of skill in analysis and evaluation, scepticism and commercial acumen in your answer.

(5 marks)

(Total = 25 marks)

Exhibit 1: Vogel Co

Vogel Co, a listed engineering company, manufactures large-scale plant and machinery for industrial companies. Until ten years ago, Vogel Co pursued a strategy of organic growth. Since then, it has followed an aggressive policy of acquiring smaller engineering companies, which it feels have developed new technologies and methods, which could be used in its manufacturing processes. However, it is estimated that only between 30% and 40% of the acquisitions made in the last ten years have successfully increased the company's shareholder value.

Potential acquisition

Vogel Co is currently considering acquiring Tori Co, an unlisted company, which has three departments. Department A manufactures machinery for industrial companies, Department B produces electrical goods for the retail market, and the smaller Department C operates in the construction industry. Upon acquisition, Department A will become part of Vogel Co, as it contains the new technologies which Vogel Co is seeking, but Departments B and C will be unbundled, with the assets attached to Department C sold and Department B being spun off into a new company called Ndege Co.

Exhibit 2: Financial information

Given below are extracts of financial information for the two companies for the year ended 30 April 20X4.

	Vogel Co	Tori Co
	$m	$m
Sales revenue	790.2	124.6
Profit before depreciation, interest and tax (PBDIT)	244.4	37.4
Interest	13.8	4.3
Depreciation	72.4	10.1
Pre-tax profit	158.2	23.0
Non-current assets	723.9	98.2
Current assets	142.6	46.5
7% unsecured bond	–	40.0
Other non-current and current liabilities	212.4	20.2
Share capital (50c/share)	190.0	20.0
Reserves	464.1	64.5

Share of current and non-current assets and profit of Tori Co's three departments:

	Department A	Department B	Department C
Share of current and non-current assets	40%	40%	20%
Share of PBDIT and pre-tax profit	50%	40%	10%

Exhibit 3: Other information

(1) It is estimated that for Department C, the realisable value of its non-current assets is 100% of their book value, but its current assets' realisable value is only 90% of their book value. The costs related to closing Department C are estimated to be $3 million.

(2) The funds raised from the disposal of Department C will be used to pay off Tori Co's other non-current and current liabilities.

(3) The 7% unsecured bond will be taken over by Ndege Co. It can be assumed that the current market value of the bond is equal to its book value.

(4) At present, around 10% of Department B's PBDIT come from sales made to Department C.

(5) Ndege Co's cost of capital is estimated to be 10%. It is estimated that in the first year of operation Ndege Co's free cash flows to firm will grow by 20%, and then by 5.2% annually thereafter.

(6) The tax rate applicable to all the companies is 20%, and Ndege Co can claim 10% tax-allowable depreciation on its non-current assets. It can be assumed that the amount of tax-allowable depreciation is the same as the investment needed to maintain Ndege Co's operations.

(7) Vogel Co's current share price is $3 per share and it is estimated that Tori Co's price/earnings (P/E) ratio is 25% higher than Vogel Co's P/E ratio. After the acquisition, when Department A becomes part of Vogel Co, it is estimated that Vogel Co's P/E ratio will increase by 15%.

(8) It is estimated that the combined company's annual after-tax earnings will increase by $7 million due to the synergy benefits resulting from combining Vogel Co and Department A.

20 Selorne (September 2018, amended) (49 mins)

(a)

    (i) Estimate the equity value of the combined company and the expected additional value arising from the combination of Selorne Co and Chawon Co. **(5 marks)**

    (ii) Estimate the share of the gain from the combination created for Chris Chawon and the share of the gain created for Selorne Co's shareholders and comment on your results. **(6 marks)**

(b) Discuss the factors which may prevent the forecast synergies from being achieved. **(4 marks)**

(c) Discuss the factors which Selorne Co's board will consider when determining which source or sources of finance are chosen to finance a possible cash bid for the share capital of Chawon Co. **(5 marks)**

Professional marks will be awarded for the demonstration of skill in analysis and evaluation, scepticism and commercial acumen in your answer. **(5 marks)**

(Total = 25 marks)

Exhibit 1: Selorne Co and Chawon Co

Selorne Co

Selorne Co is one of the biggest removal companies in Pauland, offering home and business removals. It has a number of long-term contracts with large businesses, although it has not won any new major contracts in the last two years. Selorne Co is listed on Pauland's stock market for smaller companies. Selorne Co is financed by a mixture of equity and short and long-term debt, but its gearing level is below the average for its sector.

Selorne Co has four executive directors, who each own 20% of the company's share capital, with the other 20% owned by external shareholders. Selorne Co has paid a constant dividend since it has been listed and its share price has risen slightly over the last three years.

Selorne Co is based in a number of the large cities and towns in Pauland and owns the majority of the sites where it is located. Many of its employees have worked for the company for a long time. Drivers of the lorries used by Selorne Co are required to have a special, heavy vehicles licence. Salary levels at Selorne Co are relatively high compared with other companies in the sector.

Chawon Co

Selorne Co is currently considering making a bid for Chawon Co, an unlisted company specialising in distribution and delivery services. Chawon Co is owned 100% by its founder, Chris Chawon. Chawon Co has built up a portfolio of small contracts over time. It has made unsuccessful bids for two larger contracts over the last 12 months, the bids being rejected primarily because Chawon Co was not felt to be big enough to be able to guarantee the level of service required.

Chawon Co is based in many of the same cities and towns where Selorne Co is located, although Chawon's premises are all rented. The drivers of Chawon's vehicles do not require a heavy vehicles licence. Chawon Co has a few long-serving employees who are mostly centre managers. Most of its drivers and staff, however, stay at Chawon Co for only a short time. Salary levels are low, although Chawon Co pays high levels of overtime and high bonuses if target profit levels are achieved. Chawon Co is highly geared, leading to recent media speculation about its financial viability.

 BPP

Exhibit 2: Terms of bid for Chawon Co

In initial discussions about the acquisition, Chris Chawon indicated that he would prefer the consideration to be a share-for-share exchange, the terms being one Chawon Co share for five Selorne Co shares.

Chawon Co has 2 million $1 shares in issue, and Selorne Co has 50 million $0.50 shares in issue.

Each Selorne Co share is currently trading at $6.50 giving a total market value of 50m shares × $6.50 = $325m, which is a multiple of 8 of its free cash flow to equity. The multiple of 8 can be assumed to remain unchanged if the acquisition takes place.

Chawon Co's free cash flow to equity is currently estimated at $7 million, with an expected annual growth rate of 3%, and it is expected to generate a return on equity of 15%. Chris Chawon expects that the total free cash flows to equity of the combined company will increase by $5 million due to synergy benefits. He believes that Selorne Co will be able to win more contracts because it is larger and because it will be diversifying the services which it offers. He also believes that significant operational synergies can be achieved, pointing out the time Selorne Co drivers spend idle during the winter months when removal activity is traditionally lower. Chris Chawon believes that he can achieve the synergies if he is given management responsibility for the operational reorganisation, including dealing with the staff employment and retention issues. Chris Chawon thinks that synergies could also be achieved in central administration and in premises costs.

The chief executive and the finance director of Selorne Co are in favour of bidding for Chawon Co. However, one of the other executive directors is opposed to the bid. He is sceptical about the level of synergies which can be achieved and does not want Chris Chawon to be brought into the management of Selorne Co. He suggests that if the bid is to go ahead, it should be a cash offer rather than a share exchange. Selorne Co's chief executive has responded that Chris Chawon is likely to ask for a higher equivalent price if the purchase is for cash.

Exhibit 3: Financing the bid for Chawon Co

Selorne Co's finance director has pointed out that Selorne Co will need additional funding if Chawon Co is purchased for cash. He has suggested that there may be a number of possible sources of finance:

- A rights issue
- A fixed rate, long-term, bank loan
- A three-year, unsecured, mezzanine loan facility
- Convertible debt, with conversion rights being exercisable in five years' time

21 Kerrin (Sep/Dec 2019, amended)   (49 mins)

(a) Discuss possible sources of financial synergy arising from Kerrin Co's acquisition of Danton Co and comment on the finance director's concern that synergy is often overestimated, including any steps which could be taken by Kerrin Co's board to address this problem.

(7 marks)

(b) Advise the directors on a suitable share-for-share exchange offer which meets the criteria specified by Danton Co's shareholders and calculate the effect of the cash and share-for-share offers on the post-acquisition wealth of both Kerrin Co's and Danton Co's shareholders.

(13 marks)

Professional marks will be awarded for the demonstration of skill in analysis and evaluation, scepticism and commercial acumen in your answer.   (5 marks)

(Total = 25 marks)

Exhibit 1: Kerrin Co

A new client has approached you for advice on a potential acquisition. Kerrin Co is a consumer electronics manufacturer and retailer. The company obtained a listing eight years ago with the

founders retaining a 20% stake in the business. Whilst Kerrin Co had previously experienced rapid growth in earnings before tax, problems arose soon after the listing as competition intensified. Although the company remains profitable, annual growth has declined significantly and is currently 3%.

The board is concerned by the lack of future growth opportunities. The current share price reflects these concerns, trading well below the offer price of eight years ago. In response, the directors have decided to invest in a market development strategy for future growth, utilising significant cash reserves to acquire companies in other areas of the country where competition is less intense. The board has identified a potential target, Danton Co.

Danton Co

Danton Co is a privately-owned consumer electronics company, established ten years ago. Significant unrelieved losses were incurred in the early years of development, although the company is now profitable and achieving growth in earnings before tax of 6% per year. However, cash reserves are low. Access to capital has acted as a severe constraint on Danton Co's reinvestment potential throughout this period. The founders and their families own 60% of the shares with the balance held by a venture capitalist organisation, which acquired its equity stake around six years ago.

Exhibit 2: Acquisition information

Kerrin Co's board is keen to ensure that Danton Co's founders remain as directors after the acquisition and the company has sufficient cash reserves to purchase Danton Co outright.

Early discussions between the directors of both companies suggest Danton Co's shareholders would approve a cash offer of $13.10 per share. As an alternative, the board is considering a share-for-share exchange to fund the acquisition in order to preserve cash for future acquisitions and dividend payments. Recent mergers have attracted an acquisition premium of around 25%–30% and Danton Co's directors indicated their shareholders would be expecting a premium towards the higher end of this scale for a share-for-share offer. Kerrin Co has therefore asked you to design a share-for-share offer scheme which will allow for a 30% acquisition premium. You have been provided with extracts from the latest financial statements for both companies.

Extracts from the most recent financial statements

	Kerrin Co	Danton Co
	$m	$m
Operating profit	448.6	201.8
Earnings before tax	381.9	116.3

Exhibit 3: Additional financial information

The book value of Kerrin Co's $0.50 ordinary shares is $375 million. These shares are currently trading at $5.28 and the finance director expects the price earnings (PE) ratio to increase by 10% if the acquisition proceeds.

Danton Co upgraded its main manufacturing facility during the previous year and expects to make annual pre-tax cost savings of $2.5 million from the start of the current financial year. The book value of Danton Co's $0.25 ordinary shares is $35 million. Based on an analysis of companies of a comparable size and cost structure, it is estimated that Danton Co's PE ratio is 20% higher than Kerrin Co's current PE ratio.

Kerrin Co's chief executive officer estimates annual pre-tax revenue and cost synergies of $15.2 million to arise as a result of the acquisition. In addition, the finance director anticipates annual pre-tax financial synergies of $5.3 million, although she insists this is a cautious estimate after reading an article on recent merger and acquisition activity where post-acquisition synergies have either been overestimated or failed to materialise.

The rate of corporation tax relevant to both companies is 20%.

22 Louieed (Mar/Jun 2016, amended) (49 mins)

(a) Discuss the advantages and disadvantages of the acquisition of Tidded Co from the viewpoint of Louieed Co. **(6 marks)**

(b) Calculate, and comment on, the funding required for the acquisition of Tidded Co and the impact on Louieed Co's earnings per share and gearing, for each of the three options given above.

Note. Up to 10 marks are available for the calculations. **(14 marks)**

Professional marks will be awarded for the demonstration of skill in analysis and evaluation, scepticism and commercial acumen in your answer. **(5 marks)**

(Total = 25 marks)

Exhibit 1: Louieed Co and Tidded Co

Louieed Co

Louieed Co, a listed company, is a major supplier of educational material, selling its products in many countries. It supplies schools and colleges and also produces learning material for business and professional exams. Louieed Co has exclusive contracts to produce material for some examining bodies. Louieed Co has a well-defined management structure with formal processes for making major decisions.

Although Louieed Co produces online learning material, most of its profits are still derived from sales of traditional textbooks. Louieed Co's growth in profits over the last few years has been slow and its directors are currently reviewing its long-term strategy. One area in which they feel that Louieed Co must become much more involved is the production of online testing materials for exams and to validate course and textbook learning.

Bid for Tidded Co

Louieed Co has recently made a bid for Tidded Co, a smaller listed company. Tidded Co also supplies a range of educational material, but has been one of the leaders in the development of online testing and has shown strong profit growth over recent years. All of Tidded Co's initial five founders remain on its board and still hold 45% of its issued share capital between them. From the start, Tidded Co's directors have been used to making quick decisions in their areas of responsibility. Although listing has imposed some formalities, Tidded Co has remained focused on acting quickly to gain competitive advantage, with the five founders continuing to give strong leadership.

Louieed Co's initial bid of five shares in Louieed Co for three shares in Tidded Co was rejected by Tidded Co's board.

Exhibit 2: New bid proposal

There has been further discussion between the two boards since the initial offer was rejected and Louieed Co's board is now considering a proposal to offer Tidded Co's shareholders two shares in Louieed Co for one share in Tidded Co or a cash alternative of $22.75 per Tidded Co share. It is expected that Tidded Co's shareholders will choose one of the following options:

(1) To accept the two shares for one share offer for all the Tidded Co shares;

(2) To accept the cash offer for all the Tidded Co shares; or

(3) 60% of the shareholders will take up the two shares for one share offer and the remaining 40% will take the cash offer.

In the case of the third option being accepted, it is thought that three of the company's founders, holding 20% of the share capital in total, will take the cash offer and not join the combined company. The remaining two founders will probably continue to be involved in the business and be members of the combined company's board.

Impact of the merger

Louieed Co's Finance Director has estimated that the merger will produce annual post-tax synergies of $20 million. He expects Louieed Co's current price/earnings (P/E) ratio to remain unchanged after the acquisition.

Exhibit 3: Financial information

Extracts from most recent accounts

Extracts from the two companies' most recent accounts are shown below:

	Louieed	Tidded
	$m	$m
Profit before finance cost and tax	446	182
Finance costs	(74)	(24)
Profit before tax	372	158
Tax	(76)	(30)
Profit after tax	296	128
Issued $1 nominal shares (m)	340	90
Other financial information		
P/E ratios, based on most recent accounts	14	15.9
Long-term liabilities (market value) ($m)	540	193
Cash and cash equivalents ($m)	220	64

The tax rate applicable to both companies is 20%.

Assume that Louieed Co can obtain further debt funding at a pre-tax cost of 7.5% and that the return on cash surpluses is 5% pre-tax.

Assume also that any debt funding needed to complete the acquisition will be reduced instantly by the balances of cash and cash equivalents held by Louieed Co and Tidded Co.

23 Makonis (December 2013, amended)   (49 mins)

(a) Estimate the additional equity value created by combining Nuvola Co and Makonis Co, based on the free cash flows to firm method. Comment on the results obtained.   **(12 marks)**

(b) Estimate the impact on Makonis Co's shareholders wealth if the bid proceeds on the revised basis (ie a 50% premium is paid), and discuss how the proposal to increase the premium from 30% to 50% could be financed.   **(8 marks)**

Professional marks will be awarded for the demonstration of skill in analysis and evaluation, and commercial acumen in your answer.   **(5 marks)**

(Total = 25 marks)

Exhibit 1: Makonis Co

Makonis Co, a listed company producing motor cars, wants to acquire Nuvola Co, an engineering company involved in producing innovative devices for cars. Makonis Co is keen to incorporate some of Nuvola Co's innovative devices into its cars and thereby boost sales revenue.

Exhibit 2: Financial information for Makonis Co and Nuvola Co

The following financial information is provided for the two companies:

	Makonis Co	Nuvola Co
Current share price	$5.80	$2.40
Number of issued shares (m)	210	200
Equity beta	1.2	1.2
Asset beta	0.9	1.2

Exhibit 3: Further information on combining the two companies

It is thought that combining the two companies will result in several benefits. Free cash flows to firm of the combined company will be $216 million in current value terms, but these will increase by an annual growth rate of 5% for the next four years, before reverting to an annual growth rate of 2.25% in perpetuity. In addition to this, combining the companies will result in cash synergy benefits of $20 million per year, for the next four years. These synergy benefits are not subject to any inflationary increase and no synergy benefits will occur after the fourth year. The debt to equity ratio of the combined company will be 40:60 in market value terms and it is expected that the combined company's cost of debt will be 4.55%.

The corporation tax rate is 20%, the current risk-free rate of return is 2% and the market risk premium is 7%. It can be assumed that the combined company's asset beta is the weighted average of Makonis Co's and Nuvola Co's asset betas, weighted by their current market values.

Details of offer

Makonis Co has offered to acquire Nuvola Co through a mixed offer of one of its shares for two Nuvola Co shares plus a cash payment, such that a 30% premium is paid for the acquisition. Nuvola Co's equity holders feel that increasing the cash payment so that a 50% premium is paid, would be more acceptable. Makonis Co has sufficient cash reserves if the premium is 30%, but not if it is 50%.

24 Hav (June 2013, amended)   (49 mins)

(a) Distinguish between the different types of synergy and discuss possible sources of revenue synergy based on the above scenario.   (6 marks)

(b) Based on the two different opinions expressed by Hav Co and Strand Co, calculate the maximum acquisition premium payable in each case.   (7 marks)

(c) Calculate the percentage premium per share that Strand Co's shareholders will receive under each acquisition payment method and justify, with explanations, which payment method would be most acceptable to them.   (7 marks)

Professional marks will be awarded for the demonstration of skill in analysis and evaluation, scepticism and commercial acumen in your answer.   (5 marks)

(Total = 25 marks)

Exhibit 1: Hav Co and Strand Co

Hav Co

Hav Co is a publicly listed company involved in the production of highly technical and sophisticated electronic components for complex machinery. It has a number of diverse and popular products, an active research and development department, significant cash reserves and a highly talented management who are very good in getting products to market quickly.

 BPP

A new industry that Hav Co is looking to venture into is biotechnology, which has been expanding rapidly and there are strong indications that this recent growth is set to continue. However, Hav Co has limited experience in this industry. Therefore, it believes that the best and quickest way to expand would be through acquiring a company already operating in this industry sector.

Strand Co

Strand Co is a private company operating in the biotechnology industry and is owned by a consortium of business angels and company managers. The owner-managers are highly skilled scientists who have developed a number of technically complex products but have found it difficult to commercialise them. They have also been increasingly constrained by the lack of funds to develop their innovative products further.

Discussions have taken place about the possibility of Strand Co being acquired by Hav Co. Strand Co's managers have indicated that the consortium of owners is happy for the negotiations to proceed. If Strand Co is acquired, it is expected that its managers would continue to run the Strand Co part of the larger combined company.

Strand Co is of the opinion that most of its value is in its intangible assets, comprising intellectual capital. Therefore, the premium payable on acquisition should be based on the present value to infinity of the after-tax excess earnings the company has generated in the past three years, over the average return on capital employed of the biotechnological industry. However, Hav Co is of the opinion that the premium should be assessed on synergy benefits created by the acquisition and the changes in value, due to the changes in the price-to-earnings (PE) ratio before and after the acquisition.

Exhibit 2: Financial information

Given below are extracts of financial information for Hav Co for 20X3 and Strand Co for 20X1, 20X2 and 20X3:

	Hav Co	Strand Co	Strand Co	Strand Co
Year ended 30 April	20X3	20X3	20X2	20X1
	$m	$m	$m	$m
Earnings before tax	1,980	397	370	352
Non-current assets	3,965	882	838	801
Current assets	968	210	208	198
Share capital ($0.25/share)	600	300	300	300
Reserves	2,479	183	166	159
Non-current liabilities	1,500	400	400	400
Current liabilities	354	209	180	140

The current average PE ratio of the biotechnology industry is 16.4 times, and it has been estimated that Strand Co's PE ratio is 10% higher than this. However, it is thought that the PE ratio of the combined company would fall to 14.5 times after the acquisition. The annual after-tax earnings will increase by $140m due to synergy benefits resulting from combining the two companies.

Both companies pay tax at 20% per year and Strand Co's annual cost of capital is estimated at 7%. Hav Co's current share price is $9.24 per share. The biotechnology industry's pre-tax return on capital employed is currently estimated to be 20% per year.

Exhibit 3: Form of payment

Hav Co has proposed to pay for the acquisition using one of the following methods:

- A cash offer of $5.72 for each Strand Co share; or

- A cash offer of $1.25 for each Strand Co share plus one $100 3% convertible bond for every $5 nominal value of Strand Co shares. In six years, the bond can be converted into 12 Hav Co shares or redeemed at nominal value.

25 Propleis and Adictcan (December 2022)   (49 mins)

The following **exhibits** provide information relevant to the question:

(1)   Propleis Co and Adictcan Co

(2)   Acquisition valuation

This information should be used to answer the question **requirements** within your chosen **response option(s)**.

Required

(a)   Estimate:

- the equity value of the combination of Propleis Co and Adictcan Co; and
- the benefits which would be gained by Propleis Co's shareholders from the acquisition

(10 marks)

(b)   Discuss the assumptions made in the calculations in (a), including whether the expected synergies are likely to be achieved. **(6 marks)**

(c)   Explain the actions which Propleis Co's board can take to ensure that the companies are integrated successfully and synergies are realised. **(4 marks)**

Professional marks will be awarded for the demonstration of skill in analysis and evaluation, scepticism and commercial acumen in your answer. **(5 marks)**

(Total = 25 marks)

Exhibit 1: Propleis Co and Adictcan Co

Propleis Co and Adictcan Co are two listed publishing companies. The main focus of both companies is publishing magazines, although they also publish a limited number of books linked to the magazines.

Propleis Co publishes property and lifestyle magazines, Adictcan Co publishes magazines covering professional sports. Both companies publish a combination of magazines which have been established in recent years and some of which have been published for much longer.

Propleis Co has an in-house team of staff writers and editors who are responsible for content. Most are young and tend to stay for a limited time before moving on to other publishing jobs. Adictcan Co has a team of in-house writers and editors for each magazine, who are specialists in the sport which their magazines cover, and who in some cases have worked for the magazines for many years. Currently, successful sports stars also write for Adictcan Co's magazines. Adictcan Co's board has given the managerial and writing teams of the most successful magazines considerable autonomy in determining the content and development of their magazines.

Both companies have an online presence in addition to publishing paper copies of their magazines. Electronic subscribers for both companies can access some content which is only available online. Whereas Propleis Co has won awards for its online presence and e-marketing, Adictcan Co's website has been criticised for looking old-fashioned, with the main appeal of its online offering being the high quality of the writing of the content which is only available online.

Propleis Co is planning to make a takeover bid for Adictcan Co and has contacted Adictcan Co's board. Propleis Co's board believes that the acquisition could provide synergies, particularly in the areas of online presence, marketing and cross-selling, and also savings in staff, administration and paper costs.

Exhibit 2: Acquisition valuation

The current market value of Propleis Co's equity is $620m and of Adictcan Co's equity is $340m.

Adictcan Co's board has indicated that its shareholders will expect a premium of 20% above its current equity value. Propleis Co's board feels that its shareholders will also expect a gain of at least 20% of the current equity value of their shares from the acquisition.

 BPP

Propleis Co wishes to estimate the equity values of this acquisition with the free cash flow to firm method, using the following information:

- Expected sales revenue in the first year when the companies are combined of $720m (the sum of the sales revenue of the two companies for the most recent financial year), and an expected sales growth rate in each of years 2 to 4 of 8%.

- Expected post-tax operating cash flows in each of years 1 to 4 of 14% of sales revenue.

- The company requires additional investment in non-current assets of $25m in year 1 and $0.30 for every $1 increase in sales revenue in each of years 2 to 4.

- After year 4, an expected annual growth rate of the company's free cash flows to firm of 4% for the foreseeable future.

- Assume a cost of capital of 10%.

- The target debt/equity ratio of the combined company is 1:3.

CORPORATE RECONSTRUCTION AND REORGANISATION

Questions in this part of the Exam Practice kit mainly cover Section D of the syllabus , the subject of Chapters 14–15 of the BPP Course Book for AFM.

26 Flufftort (Sep/Dec 2015, amended)   (49 mins)

(a)

    (i)   Prepare a projected statement of financial position as at 30 June 20X6, on the assumption that Gupte VC exercises its rights and Gupte VC's shares are repurchased and cancelled by Flufftort Co.   **(4 marks)**

    (ii)   Prepare a projected statement of financial position as at 30 June 20X6 on the assumption that the proposed refinancing and investment take place.   **(4 marks)**

(b)   Evaluate whether the suggested refinancing scheme is likely to be agreed by all finance providers.   **(12 marks)**

Professional marks will be awarded for the demonstration of skill in analysis and evaluation, and commercial acumen in your answer.   **(5 marks)**

(Total = 25 marks)

Exhibit 1: Flufftort Co

Five years ago the Patel family invested in a new business, Flufftort Co, which manufactures furniture. Some family members became directors of Flufftort Co, others have not been actively involved in management. A venture capital firm, Gupte VC, also made a 20% investment in Flufftort Co. A representative of Gupte VC was appointed to Flufftort Co's board. Flufftort Co also took out a long-term 8.5% bank loan.

Sales have generally been disappointing. As a result, members of the Patel family have been reluctant to invest further in Flufftort Co. Over the last year Gupte VC has taken a tougher attitude towards Flufftort Co. Gupte VC pressurised Flufftort Co to pay a dividend of $2 million for the year ended 30 June 20X5. Gupte VC has also said that if Flufftort Co's financial results do not improve, Gupte VC may exercise its right to compel Flufftort Co to buy back its shares at par on 30 June 20X6.

However, Flufftort Co's most recent product, the Easicushion chair, has been a much bigger success than expected. In order to produce enough Easicushion chairs to affect its results substantially, Flufftort Co will need to make significant expenditure on manufacturing facilities and additional working capital.

Exhibit 2: Financial statement extracts

EXTRACTS FROM STATEMENT OF PROFIT OR LOSS FOR YEAR ENDED 30 JUNE 20X5 AND FORECAST STATEMENT OF PROFIT OR LOSS FOR YEAR ENDED 30 JUNE 20X6

	20X5	20X6 forecast
	$m	$m
Operating profit	8.0	6.0
Finance cost	(3.0)	(3.0)
Profit before tax	5.0	3.0
Tax on profits (20%)	(1.0)	(0.6)
Profit for the period	4.0	2.4
Dividends	(2.0)	–
Retained earnings	2.0	2.4

Note. The forecast statement of profit or loss for the year ended 30 June 20X6 is not affected by the proposed investment. This can be assumed only to affect results after 30 June 20X6. The figure shown for retained earnings in the 20X6 forecast can be assumed to be the net increase in cash for the year ended 30 June 20X6.

SUMMARISED STATEMENT OF FINANCIAL POSITION AS AT 30 JUNE 20X5

	$m
Assets	
Non-current assets	69.0
Current assets excluding cash	18.0
Cash	7.6
Total assets	94.6
Equity and liabilities	
Share capital ($1 shares)	50.0
Retained earnings	2.6
Total equity	52.6
Long-term liabilities	
8.5% bank loan	30.0
9% loan note	5.0
Total long-term liabilities	35.0
Current liabilities	7.0
Total liabilities	42.0
Total equity and liabilities	94.6

Exhibit 3: Further notes

(1) 55% of shares are owned by the members of the Patel family who are directors, 25% by other members of the Patel family and 20% by Gupte VC.

(2) The bank loan is secured on the non-current assets of Flufftort and is due for repayment on 31 December 20X9. The loan is subject to a covenant that the ratio of equity to non-current liabilities should be greater than 1.3 on a book value basis. Flufftort has also been granted an overdraft facility of up to $5 million by its bank.

(3) The loan note is held by Rajiv Patel, a member of the Patel family who is not a director. The loan note is unsecured, is subordinated to the bank loan and has no fixed date for repayment.

(4) If no finance is available for investment in manufacturing facilities, non-current assets, current assets excluding cash, the bank loan, loan note and current liabilities can be assumed to be the same at 30 June 20X6 as at 30 June 20X5.

However, the chief executive and finance director of Flufftort Co intend to propose that the company should be refinanced to fund the expanded production of the Easicushion chair. They have not yet consulted anyone else about their proposals.

Details of the proposed refinancing are as follows:

(1) The members of the Patel family who are directors would subscribe to an additional 15 million $1 shares at par.

(2) Gupte VC would subscribe to an additional 20 million $1 shares at par.

(3) The 8.5% bank loan would be renegotiated with the bank and the borrowing increased to $65 million, to be repaid on 30 June 20Y2. The expected finance cost of the loan would be 10% per year, so the finance costs will be $6.5 million per year.

(4) Rajiv Patel's loan note would be replaced by 5 million $1 shares.

(5) The refinancing would mean non-current assets would increase to $125 million, current assets other than cash would increase to $42 million and current liabilities would increase to $12 million.

(6) Operating profits would be expected to increase to $20 million in the first full year after the facilities are constructed (year ended 30 June 20X7) and $25 million in the second year (year ended 30 June 20X8). No dividends would be paid for these two years, as cash surpluses would be used for further investment as required. Tax on company profits can be assumed to remain at 20%.

27 Newimber (Mar/Jun 2019, amended)   (49 mins)

(a) Discuss the advantages and disadvantages of demerging the sportswear division into a new company.   **(4 marks)**

(b) Estimate the change in the weighted average cost of capital of Newimber Co if the demerger of the sportswear division takes place; and the valuation of Poynins Co using free cash flows, based on the information and assumptions given. Briefly discuss your results.   **(12 marks)**

(c) Discuss the factors which may determine the policies Poynins Co should adopt for communication of information to its shareholders and other significant stakeholders.
                                                                                (4 marks)

Professional marks will be awarded for the demonstration of skill in analysis and evaluation, scepticism and commercial acumen in your answer.   **(5 marks)**

                                                                    (Total = 25 marks)

Exhibit 1: Newimber Co

Newimber Co is a listed company which has always manufactured formal clothing for adults and children. It obtained a listing ten years ago after years of steady growth. 70% of shares in the

 **BPP**

company are owned by its directors or their relatives, with the remaining 30% owned by external investors, including institutional investors.

Sportswear division

Eight years ago it set up a division to manufacture sportswear. This investment has been very successful and the sportswear division now accounts for 40% of total group revenue, having grown much quicker than the original formal clothing division.

Newimber Co's board has given divisional management at the sportswear division more authority over time, although the board has continued to make major policy and investment decisions relating to the division. Initially, relations between Newimber Co's board and management of the sportswear division were good, but there have been problems over the last couple of years. The sportswear division's management has been frustrated by the board's refusal to approve their recent investment plans on the grounds that they were too risky. In order to achieve operational efficiencies, the sportswear division's management would also like to pursue stricter policies for managing operational staff and suppliers than Newimber Co's board has so far allowed.

Exhibit 2: Restructuring

A few months ago, the management of the sportswear division approached Newimber Co's board with a proposal for a management buyout of the sportswear division. However, the price the sportswear division's management was able to offer was insufficient to persuade Newimber Co's board to sell the sportswear division to them.

Newimber Co's board has subsequently decided that the sportswear division should be demerged into a new company, Poynins Co. The shareholders and proportion of shares held would be the same for Poynins Co as it currently is for Newimber Co. The sportswear division's senior management team would become the board of Poynins Co and Poynins Co would seek an immediate listing on the same stock exchange as Newimber Co.

Exhibit 3: Financial information

The market capitalisation of Newimber Co's share capital is currently $585 million. Newimber Co also currently has $200 million 5.9% loan notes. The loan notes are redeemable in five years' time at a premium of 5%. Newimber Co's equity beta is currently estimated at 1.4. Newimber Co's current cost of equity is 11.8% and its current before-tax cost of debt is 4.5%.

The asset beta of the formal clothing division is estimated to be 1.21. The weighting in estimating Newimber Co's overall asset beta is 60% for the formal clothing division to 40% for the sportswear division. The debt beta can be assumed to be zero.

In return for 40% of the issued share capital of Newimber Co, its current shareholders will receive 100% of the issued share capital of Poynins Co, corresponding to the assets and liabilities being transferred. The shares in Newimber Co which shareholders have given up will be cancelled. After the demerger, Newimber Co's new market capitalisation can be assumed to be $351 million. Poynins Co will have no long-term debt, the liability for the $200 million loan notes remaining with Newimber Co.

The current risk-free rate of return is estimated to be 3.4%. The market risk premium is estimated to be 6%. A tax rate of 28% is applicable to all companies.

The sportswear division's managers believe that its free cash flows (after taking into account tax and any required capital spending) will increase to the following once Poynins Co has been listed:

Year	1	2	3
	$m	$m	$m
Free cash flows	12.4	16.9	22.7

From year 4 onwards the free cash flow growth is forecast to slow to 3% per year.

28 Hanwood (Sep/Dec 2021, amended) (49 mins)

The following **exhibits** provide information relevant to the question:

(1) Hanwood Shoes Co

(2) Sale of children's shoes division

(3) Impact and consequences of sale

(4) Hanwood Shoes Co's SOFP

This information should be used to answer the question **requirements** within your chosen **response option(s)**.

Required

(a) Calculate the expected sales price of the children's shoes division and demonstrate its impact on Hanwood Shoe Co's statement of financial position and forecast earnings per share.

(13 marks)

(b) Discuss whether Hanwood Shoes Co's investors are likely to be satisfied with the proposed sale of the children's shoes division and its consequences for profits and funding. **(7 marks)**

Professional marks will be awarded for the demonstration of skill in analysis and evaluation, scepticism and commercial acumen in your answer. **(5 marks)**

(Total = 25 marks)

Exhibit 1: Background

Hanwood Shoes Co started trading 40 years ago, manufacturing and selling children's shoes in shops. The shoes have been of higher quality than shoes produced by its competitors, although also more expensive. School shoe sales in particular have been a consistent large generator of cash, helping to fund the company's expansion.

About 15 years ago, Hanwood Shoes Co started manufacturing and selling adults' shoes. Hanwood Shoes Co's adults' shoes are currently sold at a higher profit margin than children's shoes. Adults' shoe sales now generate the majority of Hanwood Shoes Co's profits. The adults' shoes sold are a mixture of formal types with a long lifespan and some fashionable shoes. The inventory turnover period for adults' shoes is, on average, significantly higher than for children's shoes.

Hanwood Shoes Co is organised on the basis of two separate divisions for children's and adults' shoes. Its shops sell either children's shoes or adults' shoes, but not both. Hanwood Shoes Co also sells adult shoes to other retailers.

Five years ago, Hanwood Shoes Co restructured its cost base. It moved production of children's shoes to new facilities in its home country and outsourced the production of adults' shoes to foreign suppliers. However, Hanwood Shoes Co's board now predicts that profits from children's shoes will increase at a slower rate than adults' shoes. It expects that in the next few years, a greater share of the children's shoes market will be taken by companies with a lower cost base.

Hanwood Shoes Co's board is aware that it must convince investors that any major strategic changes it makes will result in an increase in earnings per share. Investors will also consider a change in earnings per share against any change in the business risk profile of the company.

Exhibit 2: Proposed sale of a division

Hanwood Shoes Co's board wishes to improve the company's cash position for two reasons. First, loan notes of $175m nominal value are due to be redeemed in just over a year's time. The board is unwilling to seek renewed loan funding because the terms would not be favourable and some investors have expressed concern about gearing levels. Second, Hanwood Shoes Co has recently been slow to pay some of its suppliers of adults' shoes. One major supplier recently delayed delivery of shoes to Hanwood Shoes Co until it was paid for previous deliveries.

Hanwood Shoes Co's chief executive proposed that the company should in future only sell adults' shoes and should sell the children's shoes division. He believed from industry contacts that at least

 BPP

three children's clothing manufacturers, looking to expand their product range, would be interested. The finance director suggested that the proceeds from the sale of the division could first be used to pay off the loan notes. It would then be used to increase cash held and thus improve liquidity. The remaining proceeds would be invested in the adults' shoes division to improve earnings per share.

Exhibit 3: Financial information

(1) The sales price of the children's shoes division will be the sum of the present value of predicted future free cash flows. The discount rate to be used is 10%.

(2) The predicted after-tax free cash flows of the children's shoes division ($m) are as follows:

Year	1	2	3	4
	76	81	85	88

(3) The predicted after-tax profits of the children's shoes division in Year 1 can be assumed to be $76m. The total after-tax profits for Hanwood Shoes Co for Year 1 if the children's shoe division is not sold is predicted to be $217m.

(4) After Year 4, free cash flows for the children's shoes division should be assumed to increase at a rate of 3.5% per year.

(5) The proceeds received for selling the children's shoes division would be used first to pay off the 9% loan notes. Part of the remaining amount from the sales proceeds will be held as part of current assets, so that the current ratio increases to 1.4. The rest of the sale proceeds will be invested in non-current assets.

(6) The profit on the sale of the children's shoes division should be taken directly to reserves.

(7) The non-current assets of the children's shoes division can be assumed to be $608m and the current assets can be assumed to be $349m.

(8) Additional investment in non-current assets is expected to earn an 18% pre-tax return and additional investment in current assets is expected to earn a 6% pre-tax return.

(9) Tax is payable at an annual rate of 20% on profits.

Exhibit 4: Hanwood Shoes Co's current statement of financial position

	$m
Assets	
Non-current assets	1,200
Current assets	909
Total assets	2,109
Equity and liabilities	
Called-up share capital ($1 shares)	50
Reserves	737
Total equity	787
Non-current liabilities	
9% loan notes	175
7% loan notes	145
Bank loans	108
Total non-current liabilities	428
Current liabilities	894
Total equity and liabilities	2,109

29 Bento (June 2015, amended)   (49 mins)

(a) Distinguish between an MBO and an MBI. Discuss the relative benefits and drawbacks to Okazu Co if it is disposed through an MBO instead of an MBI.   **(4 marks)**

(b) Estimate, showing all relevant calculations, whether the restrictive covenant imposed by Dofu Co is likely to be met.   **(10 marks)**

(c) Use the dividend valuation model to estimate the value of the new MBO, and briefly discuss, whether or not the MBO would be beneficial for Dofu Co and Okazu Co's senior management team.   **(6 marks)**

Professional marks will be awarded for the demonstration of skill in analysis and evaluation, scepticism and commercial acumen in your answer.   **(5 marks)**

(Total = 25 marks)

Exhibit 1: Bento Co

In order to raise funds for future projects, the management of Bento Co, a large manufacturing company, is considering disposing of one of its subsidiary companies, Okazu Co, which is involved in manufacturing rubber tubing. It is considering undertaking the disposal through a management buyout (MBO) or a management buy-in (MBI). Bento Co wants $60 million from the sale of Okazu Co.

Recent financial statements

Given below are extracts from the most recent financial statements for Okazu Co:

BPP

YEAR ENDING 30 APRIL

	20X5
	$'000
Total non-current assets	40,800
Total current assets	12,300
Total assets	53,100
Equity	24,600
Non-current liabilities	16,600
Current liabilities:	
Trade and other payables	7,900
Bank overdraft	4,000
Total current liabilities	11,900
Total equity and liabilities	53,100

YEAR ENDING 30 APRIL

	20X5
	$'000
Sales revenue	54,900
Operating profit	12,200
Finance costs	1,600
Profit before tax	10,600
Taxation	2,120
Profit for the year	8,480

Notes relating to financial statements

(1) Current assets, non-current assets and the trade and other payables will be transferred to the new company when Okazu Co is sold. The bank overdraft will be repaid by Bento Co prior to the sale of Okazu Co.

(2) With the exception of the bank overdraft, Bento Co has provided all the financing to Okazu Co. No liabilities, except the trade and other payables specified above, will be transferred to the new company when Okazu Co is sold.

(3) It is estimated that the market value of the non-current assets is 30% higher than the book value and the market value of the current assets is equivalent to the book value.

(4) The group finance costs and taxation are allocated by Bento Co to all its subsidiaries in pre-agreed proportions.

Exhibit 2: Financing

Okazu Co's senior management team has approached Dofu Co, a venture capital company, about the proposed MBO. Dofu Co has agreed to provide leveraged finance for a 50% equity stake in the new company on the following basis:

- $30 million loan in the form of an 8% bond on which interest is payable annually, based on the loan amount outstanding at the start of each year. The bond will be repaid on the basis of fixed equal annual payments (constituting of interest and principal) over the next four years.

- $20 million loan in the form of a 6% convertible bond on which interest is payable annually. Conversion may be undertaken on the basis of 50 equity shares for every $100 from the beginning of Year 5 onwards.

- 5,000,000 $1 equity shares for $5,000,000.

Okazu Co's senior management will contribute $5,000,000 for 5,000,000 $1 equity shares and own the remaining 50% of the equity stake.

As a condition for providing the finance, Dofu Co will impose a restrictive covenant that the new company's gearing ratio will be no higher than 75% at the end of its first year of operations, and then fall to no higher than 60%, 50% and 40% at the end of Year 2 to Year 4 respectively. The gearing ratio is determined by the book value of debt divided by the combined book values of debt and equity.

Exhibit 3: Forecast growth after the MBO

After the MBO, it is expected that earnings before interest and tax will increase by 11% per year and annual dividends of 25% on the available earnings will be paid for the next four years. It is expected that the annual growth rate of dividends will reduce by 60% from Year 5 onwards following the MBO. The new company will pay tax at a rate of 20% per year. The new company's cost of equity has been estimated at 12%.

30 Charborough Co (March / June 2022, amended)   (49 mins)

The following exhibits provide information relevant to the question:

(1) Introduction – Charborough Co – including an alternative suggestion from a non-executive director

(2) Sale of coffee shops

(3) CC's statement of financial position

(4) Other information

This information should be used to answer the question requirements within your chosen response option(s).

Required

(a) (i)   Calculate the expected sale price of the coffee shops.   **(4 marks)**

    (ii) Calculate the impact of the sale of the coffee shops on CC's:

- forecast statement of financial position;

- forecast earnings per share; and

- weighted average cost of capital.

                                              (9 marks)

(b) Evaluate the arguments for and against the decision to sell the coffee shops.   **(7 marks)**

Professional marks will be awarded for the demonstration of skill in analysis and evaluation, scepticism and commercial acumen in your answer.   **(5 marks)**

                                              (Total = 25 marks)

Exhibit 1: Introduction – Charborough Co

Charborough Co (CC) was established 20 years ago offering high-quality coffee at a reasonable price. As well as offering takeaway coffees, CC marketed its coffee shops as being comfortable places in which to spend time and meet friends. For most of its life, CC's coffee shops have outperformed its competitors and CC was able to obtain a listing six years ago.

Most of the funds obtained from the listing were used to buy a struggling fast-food chain and rebrand it as a fruit juice bar chain. The fruit juice bar chain and coffee shops are now separate divisions within CC.

 BPP

The fruit juice bars offer a mix of drinks and salads with flavours from around the world; the appearance of the bars reflecting its global influences. This chain has been successful in terms of attracting fashionable young customers but has required considerable investment. Up until recently, much of this investment has come from surpluses generated by CC's coffee shops. However, the growth in the profits of the coffee shops has slowed in the last two years. Customer and media comment has suggested that CC's coffee shops now need significant refurbishment expenditure.

Competition in the coffee shop sector has led to some mergers between rival chains. CC has just received an enquiry from a competitor about whether it would be interested in selling its coffee shops. CC's board is likely to accept a reasonable offer for its coffee shops, as it believes the juice bars offer more prospects for future growth in profits. A large cash inflow from the sale of the coffee shops would fund further expansion of the juice bars, and refurbishment and upgrading of existing juice bars over the next few years.

Exhibit 2: Sale of coffee shops

The sales price of the coffee shops will be the sum of the present value of predicted future free cash flows:

(1) The predicted after-tax profits of the coffee shop ($m) are as follows:

Year	1	2	3	4
	296	328	360	388

The after-tax profits of CC (including the profits on the coffee shops) can be assumed to be $658m in year 1, if the coffee shops are not sold. These amounts can be assumed to be equal to after-tax cash flows.

(2) Capital investment in the coffee shops can be assumed to be $60 million in year 1. In the second to fourth years, capital investment each year will increase by $0.50 per $1 increase in after-tax profits.

(3) After year 4, free cash flows for the coffee shops should be assumed to increase at 3–5% per year for the foreseeable future.

(4) The discount rate to be used should be the current weighted average cost of capital, which is 10%.

Exhibit 3: CC's statement of financial position

	A	B	C	D
1	CC's current statement of financial position (including fruit juice bars and coffee shops)			
2		$m		
3	**Assets**			
4	Non-current assets	6,625		
5	Current assets	535		
6	**Total assets**	7,160		
7	**Equity and liabilities**			
8	Called-up share capital	500		
9	Retained earnings	2,930		
10	Total equity	3,430		
11	Non-current liabilities			
12	9% loan notes	1,700		
13	Bank loans	1,575		
14	Total non-current liabilities	3,275		
15	Current liabilities	455		
16	**Total equity and liabilities**	7,160		

Exhibit 4: Other information

(1) The proceeds received from selling the coffee shops would be used first to pay off the 9% loan notes. The remaining amount would be invested in enhancement expenditure on the non-current assets of the juice bars. The investment in the non-current assets in the juice bars would be expected to earn a 17% pre-tax return.

(2) The current net book value of the non-current assets of the coffee shops can be assumed to be $3,350m. The profit on the sale of the coffee shops would be taken directly to retained earnings.

(3) The figures for current assets and liabilities can be assumed to remain the same when the coffee shops are sold.

(4) The overall pre-tax cost of debt is currently 8%. It can be assumed to fall to 7% when the 9% loan notes are redeemed.

(5) CC currently has 500 million $1 shares in issue. These are currently trading at $8 per share. This is expected to rise by 5% as a result of the sale of the coffee shops and the improved prospects for the juice bars.

(6) The asset beta for the juice bars can be assumed to be 0.7.

(7) Tax is payable at an annual rate of 25% on profits.

(8) The current risk-free rate is 4% and the return on the market portfolio is 11%.

31 Felinhen Co (September 2022) (49 mins)

The following exhibits provide information relevant to the question.

(1) Felinhen Co

(2) Valuation of woodcraft business

This information should be used to answer the question requirements within your chosen response option(s).

Required

(a) Calculate the valuation of the woodcraft business in the three projected scenarios. **(9 marks)**

(b) Based on part (a):

- Discuss the possible courses of action Felinhen Co's board could take regarding the woodcraft business;

- Discuss other possible courses of action that Felinhen Co's board may consider; and

- Recommend what the course of action should be.

(11 marks)

Professional marks will be awarded for the demonstration of skill in analysis and evaluation, scepticism and commercial acumen in your answer. **(5 marks)**

(Total = 25 marks)

Exhibit 1: Felinhen Co

Felinhen Co is a company which carries out agricultural and woodland management. Felinhen Co also has a wholly owned retail subsidiary, Counwood Co, with the boards of the two companies having the same directors. Counwood Co runs two businesses:

The first business is countryside stores that sell outdoor clothing and accessories.

The second is the woodcraft business. This sells furniture and other products made of wood. The wood is sourced from woodlands managed by Felinhen Co. The wood is made into furniture and other products in craft centres and sold in woodcraft shops, both owned by Counwood Co.

The craft centres are staffed by skilled craftsmen assisted by apprentices. There are some online sales of the products sold in the countryside stores, but woodcraft products are not currently sold online.

The Felinhen Co group will have to make significant investment expenditure over the next few years. Profits from the woodcraft business have declined in recent years, and in the year just ended, the woodcraft business made its first operating loss. Felinhen Co's board believes that, without additional investment, there is a significant risk that the woodcraft business will continue to make losses over the next few years. As the board also wants the Felinhen Co group to have greater focus on its core activity of agricultural and woodland management, it initially decided to close all the woodcraft shops and craft centres.

However, the proposals have faced significant opposition due to the loss of jobs and adverse media coverage. A group of shop employees, backed by a couple of wealthy 'business angels' and a crowdfunding campaign, have offered to buy out the woodcraft business. The consideration offered, based on recent years' results and the funding available, is $3m.

Felinhen Co's board has asked the group's finance director to consider three valuations which relate to the three projected scenarios and are based on:

- Net proceeds from closing all the craft centres and woodcraft shops and selling their assets individually;

- Expected free cash flows if the craft centres were kept open, the woodcraft shops closed, and the products made in the craft centres were sold in the countryside stores and online; and

- Expected free cash flows if the craft centres and woodcraft shops stayed open and necessary investment was made in them. This scenario will provide a comparison to the offer made by the buy-out group. Investing in the craft centres and woodcraft shops is not an option which Felinhen Co's board is currently considering.

Exhibit 2: Valuation of woodcraft business

Financial data

- **Close all the craft centres and woodcraft shops and sell their assets individually**

Counwood Co's most recent summary statement of financial position

	$000
Assets	
Non-current assets	5,820
Current Assets	1,750
Total assets	7,570
Equity and liabilities	
Share capital	20
Retained funds	6,580
Current liabilities	970
Total equity and liabilities	7,570

The net assets of the woodcraft business can be assumed to be 60% of Counwood Co's total net assets. The realisable value of the woodcraft shops and craft centres can be assumed to be 75% of the woodcraft business's net assets, taking into account the costs of closure.

- **Close the woodcraft shops, keep the craft centres open and sell the products made in the craft centres in the countryside stores and online**

Assume that there would be an immediate net cash inflow of $800,000, taking account of asset sales, shop closure costs and necessary investment.

Forecast figures are as follows:

Year	1	2	3	4	5
	$000	$000	$000	$000	$000
After-tax profits	470	494	516	536	558
Additional Investment	100	120	135	145	150

Assume that additional investment for each year is equal to depreciation in that year. From year 6 onwards, after-tax profits and additional investment would be expected to be the same amount as in year 5 for the foreseeable future.

Assume a cost of capital of 12%.

- **Keep all the craft centres and woodcraft shops open and make the necessary investment in them**

Assume that there would need to be an immediate investment of $600,000.

Forecast figures are as follows:

 BPP

Year	1	2	3
	$000	$000	$000
After-tax profits	380	420	440
Depreciation	170	190	200
Additional Investment	300	250	210

From year 4 onwards, the annual growth rate of free cash flows would be expected to be 3% for the foreseeable future.

Assume a cost of capital of 12%.

TREASURY AND ADVANCED RISK MANAGEMENT TECHNIQUES

The questions in this part of the Exam Practice kit mainly cover Section E of the AFM syllabus, the subject of Chapters 11–13 of the BPP Course Book.

32 Gogarth (Mar/Jun 2021, amended) (49 mins)

The following **exhibits** provide information relevant to the question.

(1) Gogarth Co's currency risk management

(2) Board queries about risk management

This information should be used to answer the question **requirements** within your chosen **response option(s)**.

Required

(a) Advise Gogarth Co on, and recommend, an appropriate hedging strategy for its US$ cash flows on 31 August. Include relevant calculations. **(15 marks)**

(b) Discuss the role of Gogarth Co's treasury function in relation to the management of economic risk in relation to foreign exchange. **(5 marks)**

Professional marks will be awarded for the demonstration of skill in analysis and evaluation, and commercial acumen in your answer. **(5 marks)**

(Total = 25 marks)

Exhibit 1: Gogarth Co's currency risk management

Gogarth Co is an electrical equipment manufacturer, based in Malaysia, looking to develop its operations abroad. One of its biggest sales markets is the USA and Gogarth Co also imports components from the USA. Gogarth Co regularly hedges transactions in foreign currencies.

It is currently 1 May. On 31 August, Gogarth Co is due to pay $14,500,000 to an American supplier and receive $37,400,000 from an American customer.

The following quotations have been obtained:

Exchange rates (quoted as US dollar per Malaysian Ringgit US$/MR1)

Spot	0.2355–0.2358
Four months forward	0.2370–0.2374

Currency futures (contract size MR500,000, futures price quoted as US$/MR1)

	Futures price
June	0.2366
September	0.2378

Currency options (contract size MR500,000, exercise price quoted as US$/MR1, premium: US cents/MR1)

Exercise price	Calls June	Calls September	Puts June	Puts September
0.2368	0.11	0.14	0.19	0.23

Futures and options contracts mature at the month end. The number of contracts to be used should be rounded to the nearest whole number in calculations. If the amount cannot be hedged using an exact number of futures or options contracts, the amount unhedged or over-hedged

should be hedged using the forward market. For the purposes of the calculations, it should be assumed that the options are exercised.

Exhibit 2: Board queries about risk management

The head of Gogarth Co's treasury function gave a presentation about the treasury function and what it does to manage foreign exchange risk at the last board meeting.

A new non-executive director has stated that he understands what the treasury function does in relation to the management of transaction risk, but is unclear on the treasury function's role in the management of economic risk.

33 Adverane (Mar/Jun 2018, amended)   (49 mins)

(a) Advise Adverane Co on, and recommend, an appropriate hedging strategy for the US$ cash flows it is due to receive from, or pay to, Elted Co.   **(9 marks)**

(b)

    (i) Calculate the inter-group transfers which are forecast to take place.   **(7 marks)**

    (ii) Discuss the advantages of multilateral netting by a central treasury function within the Adverane Group.   **(4 marks)**

Professional marks will be awarded for the demonstration of skill in analysis and evaluation, and commercial acumen in your answer.   **(5 marks)**

(Total = 25 marks)

Exhibit 1: Adverane Group

The Adverane Group is a multinational group of companies, with its headquarters in Switzerland. The Adverane Group consists of a number of fully owned subsidiaries and Elted Co, an associate company based in the USA, in which Adverane Group owns 30% of the ordinary equity share capital. Balances owing between the parent, Adverane Co, and its subsidiaries, and between subsidiaries, are settled by multilateral netting. Transactions between the parent and Elted Co are settled separately.

Transactions with Elted Co

Adverane Co wishes to hedge transactions with Elted Co which are due to be settled in four months' time in US$. Adverane Co will owe Elted Co US$3.7 million for a major purchase of supplies and Elted Co will owe Adverane Co US$10.15 million for non-current assets. Adverane Group's treasury department is considering whether to use money markets or exchange-traded currency futures for hedging.

Annual interest rates available to Adverane Co:

	Investing rate	Borrowing rate
Switzerland	2.7%	3.9%
USA	2.5%	3.7%

Exhibit 2: Exchange traded currency futures

Contract size CHF125,000, price quotation US$ per CHF1

Three-month expiry: 1.1213

Six-month expiry: 1.1204

Exhibit 3: Netting

The balances owed to and owed by members of Adverane Group when netting is to take place are as follows:

Owed by	Owed to	Local currency (m)
Adverane (Switzerland)	Bosha (Eurozone)	CHF15.90
Adverane (Switzerland)	Diling (Brazil)	CHF4.46
Bosha (Eurozone)	Cogate (USA)	€24.89
Bosha (Eurozone)	Diling (Brazil)	€18.57
Cogate (USA)	Adverane (Switzerland)	US$27.08
Cogate (USA)	Diling (Brazil)	US$5.68
Diling (Brazil)	Adverane (Switzerland)	BRL38.80
Diling (Brazil)	Bosha (Eurozone)	BRL51.20

Spot rates are currently as follows:

	CHF	€	US$	BRL
1 CHF =	1.0000	0.9347–0.9369	1.1196–1.1222	3.1378–3.1760

The group members will make settlement in Swiss francs. Spot mid-rates will be used in calculations. Settlement will be made in the order that the company owing the largest net amount in Swiss francs will first settle with the company owed the smallest net amount in Swiss francs.

Note. CHF is Swiss Franc, € is Euro, US$ is United States dollar and BRL is Brazilian Real.

34 Nutourne (December 2018, amended) (49 mins)

(a) Evaluate which of the exchange-traded derivatives would give Nutourne Co the higher receipt, considering scenarios when the options are and are not exercised. **(12 marks)**

(b) Discuss why Nutourne Co may prefer to use exchange-traded derivatives rather than over-the-counter derivatives to hedge foreign currency risk. **(3 marks)**

(c) Explain to the non-executive director how the mark-to-market process would work for the CHF futures, including the significance of the data supplied by the treasury department. Illustrate your explanation with calculations showing what would happen on the first day, using the data supplied by the treasury department. **(5 marks)**

Professional marks will be awarded for the demonstration of skill in analysis and evaluation, and commercial acumen in your answer. **(5 marks)**

(Total = 25 marks)

Exhibit 1: Nutourne Co

Nutourne Co is a company based in the USA, supplying medical equipment to the USA and Europe.

It is 30 November 20X8. Nutourne Co's treasury department is currently dealing with a sale to a Swiss customer of CHF12.3 million which has just been agreed, where the customer will pay for the equipment on 31 May 20X9. The treasury department intends to hedge the foreign exchange risk on this transaction using traded futures or options as far as possible. Any amount not hedged by a futures or option contract will be hedged on the forward market.

 **BPP**

Exhibit 2: Exchange rate information

Spot and forward exchange rates (quoted as US$/CHF 1)

Spot	1.0292–1.0309
Three months forward	1.0327–1.0347
Six months forward	1.0358–1.0380

Currency futures (contract size CHF125,000, futures price quoted as US$ per CHF1)

	Futures price
December	1.0318
March	1.0345
June	1.0369

Currency options (contract size CHF125,000, exercise price quotation US$ per CHF1, premium: US cents per CHF1)

	Calls			Puts		
Exercise price	*December*	*March*	*June*	*December*	*March*	*June*
1.0375	0.47	0.50	0.53	0.74	0.79	0.86

Futures and options contracts mature at the month end.

Exhibit 3: Non-executive director's comments

A new non-executive director has recently been briefed about the work of the treasury department and has a number of questions about hedging activities. He wants to understand why Nutourne Co prefers to use exchange-traded derivatives for hedging instead of using over-the-counter options.

The non-executive director has also heard about the mark-to-market process and wants to understand the terminology involved, and how the process works, using the transaction with the Swiss customer as an example. The treasury department has supplied relevant information to answer his query. The contract specification for the CHF futures contract states that an initial margin of US$1,450 per contract will be required and a maintenance margin of US$1,360 per contract will also be required. The tick size on the contract is US$0.0001 and the tick value is US$12.50. You can assume that on the first day when Nutourne Co holds the futures contracts, the loss per contract is US$0.0011.

35 Frongoch Co (March / June 2022, amended)   (49 mins)

The following exhibits provide information relevant to the question:

(1)   Frongoch Co hedging a payment

(2)   Alternative exchange rate scenarios

This information should be used to answer the question requirements within your chosen response option(s).

Required

(a)   Recommend, on financial grounds, a hedging strategy for the €18,250,000 payment using the market data available on 1 March (exhibit 1) and assuming the options are exercised. Assume basis diminishes to zero at contract maturity at a constant rate, based on monthly intervals.   **(9 marks)**

(b)   Evaluate the impact on the results of using the three hedging instruments being considered if the rates and futures prices are as per scenarios (i) and (ii) on 1 August (exhibit 2).   **(7 marks)**

(c)   Explain what is meant by basis and basis risk and discuss the impact of basis risk on the hedging decision being considered in (a) and (b).   **(4 marks)**

Professional marks will be awarded for the demonstration of skill in analysis and evaluation, scepticism and commercial acumen in your answer.   **(5 marks)**

(Total = 25 marks)

Exhibit 1: Frongoch Co hedging a payment

Frongoch Co is an American company, with a centralised treasury function based in the US. Today's date is 1 March. Frongoch Co's treasury team is currently looking at hedging a payment of €18,250,000 to a German supplier, which Frongoch Co is due to make on 1 August. The following market data have been obtained.

Exchange rates (quoted as US$ per €1)

Spot as at 1 March 1.1483 – 1.1497

Five months forward 1.1528 – 1.1544

Currency futures (contract size €125,000, price quoted as US$ per €1)

September 1.1560

Currency options (contract size €125,000, exercise price quoted as US$ per €1, premium: US cents per €1)

	Calls			Puts		
Exercise price	March	June	September	March	June	September
1.1540	0.54	0.61	0.69	0.79	0.90	1.02

Futures and options contracts mature at the month end.

Exhibit 2: Alternative exchange rate scenarios

The treasury team has also been asked to consider two scenarios for what the exchange rates could be on 1 August, and also the significance of basis risk in deciding how the risk should be hedged. The scenarios are as follows:

Scenario (i)

Exchange rates (quoted as US$ per €1)

Spot as at 1 August 1.1519 – 1.1534

Five months forward 1.1565 – 1.1581

Currency futures (contract size €125,000, price quoted as US$ per €1)

September 1.1552

Scenario (ii)

Exchange rates (quoted as US$ per €1)

Spot as at 1 August 1.1532 – 1.1549

Five months forward 1.1566 – 1.1584

Currency futures (contract size €125,000, price quoted as US$ per €1)

September 1.1563

 **BPP**

36 Lough Co (September 2022)　　　　　　　　　　　(49 mins)

The following exhibits provide information relevant to the question.

(1) Lough Co

(2) Payment to supplier in Swedish krona

(3) Treasury function

This information should be used to answer the question requirements within your chosen response option(s).

Required

(a) Calculate the impact on intra-group cash flows if Lough Co and its three subsidiaries use multilateral netting to settle outstanding balances. Briefly explain the main advantage of a multilateral netting system.　　　　　　　　　**(9 marks)**

(b) Evaluate which of the methods suggested by Lough Co's treasury manager would minimise the payment to the Swedish supplier in five months' time.　　　**(4 marks)**

(c) Explain how a centralised treasury department assists with Lough Co's cost reduction strategy and discuss the advantages of the finance director's proposal to decentralise the treasury function.　　　　　　　　　　　　　**(7 marks)**

Professional marks will be awarded for the demonstration of skill in analysis and evaluation, scepticism and commercial acumen in your answer.　　　**(5 marks)**

(Total = 25 marks)

Exhibit 1: Lough Co

Lough Co is a holding company based in the United States. Lough Co's treasury department centrally manages financial risk on behalf of the company's subsidiaries, many of which are based abroad. Multilateral netting is used to settle intra-group balances. Spot mid-rates are used for the purposes of multilateral netting and the United States dollar (USD) is the base currency.

The following cash flows are due between Lough Co and three of its subsidiary companies. The subsidiaries are Fitz Co, based in the United Kingdom (currency GBP), Gahana Co, based in India (currency INR) and Adalar Co, based in Turkey (currency TRY).

Owed by	Owed to	Amount (m)
Lough Co	Gahana Co	INR3,447.70
Lough Co	Adalar Co	TRY126.20
Fitz Co	Lough Co	USD75.75
Fitz Co	Gahana Co	INR333.13
Fitz Co	Adalar Co	TRY256.29
Gahana Co	Fitz Co	GBP34.08
Gahana Co	Adalar Co	TRY135.52
Adalar Co	Lough Co	USD12.80

The following spot mid-rate quotations have been obtained:

	GBP/USD 1	INR/USD 1	TRY/USD 1
Spot	0.7070	72.4000	7.2235

Settlements are made in the order that the company owing the largest net amount in USD settles with the company owed the smallest net amount in USD.

Exhibit 2: Payment to supplier in Swedish krona

Lough Co makes regular payments to a supplier based in Sweden. Sweden's currency is the Swedish Krona (SEK). The next payment is for SEK125m and is due in five months' time. The treasury manager is concerned about the exposure to transaction risk and is considering hedging the payment using either the forward or money markets based on the following data:

Exchange rates; quoted as SEK per USD 1

Spot	8.4458–8.4924
Five months forward	8.5308–8.5778

Annual interest rates available to Lough Co

	Investing	Borrowing
United States	1.5%	2.2%
Sweden	2.1%	3.1%

Exhibit 3: Treasury function

Lough Co operates in a highly competitive industry which is undergoing a process of structural adjustment. A wave of merger and acquisition activity has led to consolidation within the industry as companies seek to maximise economies of scale. This has resulted in a decline in Lough Co's profitability over the last few years. Faced with these developments, the new chief executive officer intends to implement a cost reduction strategy to improve the company's competitive position.

As part of a company-wide restructuring, Lough Co's directors are due to discuss the future of the treasury function at the next board meeting. The finance director is in favour of restructuring the treasury function due to ongoing problems and has highlighted these in a recent briefing note to the board. For example, there have been delays in approving the finance required for new projects, which meant Gahana Co missed out on an excellent investment opportunity. The main reason for these delays is the complexity of the information required for the approvals process at head office.

Another example of the type of problem experienced by subsidiaries occurred when the plan to float Adalar Co on the local stock exchange had to be abandoned due to a lack of interest from investors even though significant expenditure had already been incurred. There are also concerns about the high turnover of staff in senior management roles across many of Lough Co's subsidiaries due to the lack of delegation of authority. The finance director believes a decentralised treasury function would help to avoid these problems.

37 Buryecs (Mar/Jun 2017, amended)   (49 mins)

(a) Discuss the advantages and drawbacks of using the currency swap to manage financial risks associated with the franchise in Wirtonia.   **(4 marks)**

(b)

    (i) Calculate the annual percentage interest saving which Buryecs Co could make from using a currency swap, compared with borrowing directly in Wirtonia, demonstrating how the currency swap will work.   **(4 marks)**

    (ii) Evaluate, using net present value, the financial acceptability of Buryecs Co operating the rail franchise under the terms suggested by the government of Wirtonia and calculate the gain or loss in € from using the swap arrangement.   **(8 marks)**

 **BPP**

(c) Calculate the results of hedging the receipt of $7,500 million using the OTC currency option and briefly comment on whether the OTC currency option would be a better method of hedging this receipt than a currency swap.

(4 marks)

Professional marks will be awarded for the demonstration of skill in analysis and evaluation, scepticism and commercial acumen in your answer.

(5 marks)

(Total = 25 marks)

Exhibit 1: Buryecs

Buryecs Co is an international transport operator based in the Eurozone which has been invited to take over a rail operating franchise in Wirtonia, where the local currency is the dollar ($). Previously this franchise was run by a local operator in Wirtonia but its performance was unsatisfactory and the government in Wirtonia withdrew the franchise.

Buryecs Co will pay $5,000 million for the rail franchise immediately. The government has stated that Buryecs Co should make an annual income from the franchise of $600 million in each of the next three years. At the end of the three years the government in Wirtonia has offered to buy the franchise back for $7,500 million if no other operator can be found to take over the franchise.

Today's spot exchange rate between the Euro and Wirtonia $ is €0.1430 = $1. The predicted inflation rates are as follows:

Year	1	2	3
Eurozone	6%	4%	3%
Wirtonia	3%	8%	11%

Assume a discount rate of 14%.

Exhibit 2: Currency swap

Buryecs Co's finance director has contacted its bankers with a view to arranging a currency swap, since he believes that this will be the best way to manage financial risks associated with the franchise. The swap would be for the initial fee paid for the franchise, with a swap of principal immediately and in three years' time, both these swaps being at today's spot rate. Buryecs Co's bank would charge an annual fee of 0.5% in € for arranging the swap. Buryecs Co would take 60% of any benefit of the swap before deducting bank fees, but would then have to pay 60% of the bank fees.

Relevant borrowing rates are:

	Buryecs Co	Counterparty
Eurozone	4.0%	5.8%
Wirtonia	Wirtonia bank rate + 0.6%	Wirtonia bank rate + 0.4%

Exhibit 3: Currency option

In order to provide Buryecs Co's board with an alternative hedging method to consider, the finance director has obtained the following information about over-the-counter (OTC) options in Wirtonia $ from the company's bank.

The exercise price quotation is in Wirtonia $ per €1, premium is % of amount hedged, translated at today's spot rate.

Exercise price	Call options	Put options
7.75	2.8%	1.6%

38 Lurgshall (Mar/Jun 2019, amended)   (49 mins)

(a) Compare the results of hedging the $84 million, using the options and the swap, with the results already obtained using the forward rate agreement and futures, and comment on the results. Show all relevant calculations, including how the interest rate swap would work.

Note. Up to 4 marks are available for discussion.   (15 marks)

(b) Criticise the views of the chief executive about the work carried out by the treasury department and the staff required to do this work.   (5 marks)

Professional marks will be awarded for the demonstration of skill in analysis and evaluation, scepticism and commercial acumen in your answer.   (5 marks)

(Total = 25 marks)

Exhibit 1: Lurgshall Co

Lurgshall Co is a listed electronics company. Lurgshall Co has recently appointed a new chief executive, who has a number of plans to expand the company. The chief executive also plans to look carefully at the costs of all departments in Lurgshall Co's head office, including the centralised treasury department.

The first major investment which the chief executive will oversee is an investment in facilities to produce application-specific components. To finance the planned investment, it is likely that Lurgshall Co will have to borrow money.

Exhibit 2: Hedging information

It is now 1 May. At present, it seems that Lurgshall Co will need to borrow $84 million on 1 September for a period of six months, though both the amount and the period of borrowing are subject to some uncertainty. The treasurer plans to borrow the funds at a variable rate of central bank base rate plus 50 basis points. The central bank base rate is currently 4.5% but is expected to rise by up to 0.6% between now and 1 September.

So far, the possibility of hedging a rise in central bank base rate of 0.6% using a forward rate agreement or September $ futures has been investigated. The results of the calculations for these instruments were as follows:

4–10 Forward rate agreement from Birdam Bank: 5.38%

Three-month traded September $ futures: 5.36%

Lurgshall Co's treasurer also wants to consider using options on futures to hedge loans.

Although Lurgshall Co has not previously used swaps for hedging purposes, the treasurer has asked Birdam Bank to find a counterparty for a potential swap arrangement.

Relevant information about options and swaps is as follows:

Options

The current price for three-month $ September futures, $2 million contract size is 95.05. The price is quoted in basis points at 100 – annual % yield.

Options on three-month September $ futures, $2 million contract size, option premiums are in annual %

September calls	Strike price	September puts
0.132	95.25	0.411

It can be assumed that futures and options contracts are settled at the end of each month. Basis can be assumed to diminish to zero at contract maturity at a constant rate, based on monthly time intervals. It can also be assumed that there is no basis risk and there are no margin requirements.

 BPP

Swap

Birdam Bank has found a possible counterparty to enter into a swap with Lurgshall Co. The counterparty can borrow at an annual floating rate of central bank base rate + 1.5% or a fixed rate of 6.1%. Birdam Bank has quoted Lurgshall Co a notional fixed rate of 5.6% for it to borrow. Birdam Bank would charge a fee of 10 basis points to each party individually to act as the intermediary of the swap. Both parties would share equally the potential gains from the swap contract.

Exhibit 3: Chief executive's views

Lurgshall Co's new chief executive has made the following comments:

> I understand that the treasury department has a number of day-to-day responsibilities, including investing surplus funds for the short-term liquidity management and hedging against currency and interest rates. However, these tasks could all be carried out by the junior, less experienced, members of the department. I do not see why the department needs to employ experienced, expensive staff, as it does not contribute to the strategic success of the company.

39 Wardegul (Sep/Dec 2017, amended)   (49 mins)

(a) Recommend a hedging strategy for the D27,000,000 investment, based on the hedging choices which treasury staff are considering, if interest rates increase by 1.1% or decrease by 0.6%. Support your answer with appropriate calculations and discussion.   **(17 marks)**

(b) Discuss the advantages of operating treasury activities through regional treasury functions compared with each country having a separate treasury function.   **(3 marks)**

Professional marks will be awarded for the demonstration of skill in analysis and evaluation, and commercial acumen in your answer.   **(5 marks)**

(Total = 25 marks)

Exhibit 1: Wardegul Co

Wardegul Co, a company based in the Eurozone, has expanded very rapidly over recent years by a combination of acquiring subsidiaries in foreign countries and setting up its own operations abroad. Wardegul Co's board has found it increasingly difficult to monitor its activities and Wardegul Co's support functions, including its treasury function, have struggled to cope with a greatly increased workload. Wardegul Co's board has decided to restructure the company on a regional basis, with regional boards and appropriate support functions. Managers in some of the larger countries in which Wardegul Co operates are unhappy with reorganisation on a regional basis, and believe that operations in their countries should be given a large amount of autonomy and be supported by internal functions organised on a national basis.

Exhibit 2: Hedging information

Assume it is now 1 October 20X7. The central treasury function has just received information about a future transaction by a newly acquired subsidiary in Euria, where the local currency is the dinar (D). The subsidiary expects to receive D27,000,000 on 31 January 20X8. It wants this money to be invested locally in Euria, most probably for five months until 30 June 20X8.

Wardegul Co's treasury team is aware that economic conditions in Euria are currently uncertain. The central bank base rate in Euria is currently 4.2% and the treasury team believes that it can invest funds in Euria at the central bank base rate less 30 basis points. However, treasury staff have seen predictions that the central bank base rate could increase by up to 1.1% or fall by up to 0.6% between now and 31 January 20X8.

Wardegul Co's treasury staff normally hedge interest rate exposure by using whichever of the following products is most appropriate:

- Forward rate agreements (FRAs)
- Interest rate futures
- Options on interest rate futures

Treasury function guidelines emphasise the importance of mitigating the impact of adverse movements in interest rates. However, they also allow staff to take into consideration upside risks associated with interest rate exposure when deciding which instrument to use.

A local bank in Euria, with which Wardegul Co has not dealt before, has offered the following FRA rates:

4–9:   5.02%

5–10:   5.10%

The treasury team has also obtained the following information about exchange traded Dinar futures and options:

Three-month D futures, D500,000 contract size

Prices are quoted in basis points at 100 − annual % yield:

December 20X7:	94.84
March 20X8:	94.78
June 20X8:	94.66

Options on three-month D futures, D500,000 contract size, option premiums are in annual %

| | Calls | | | | Puts | |
December	March	June	Strike price	December	March	June
0.417	0.545	0.678	94.25	0.071	0.094	0.155
0.078	0.098	0.160	95.25	0.393	0.529	0.664

It can be assumed that futures and options contracts are settled at the end of each month. Basis can be assumed to diminish to zero at contract maturity at a constant rate, based on monthly time intervals. It can also be assumed that there is no basis risk and there are no margin requirements.

40 Daikon (June 2015, amended)   (49 mins)

(a) Based on the two hedging choices available to Daikon Co and the initial assumptions given above, draft a response to the CEO's request made in the first paragraph of the question.

(11 marks)

(b) Discuss the impact on Daikon Co of each of the three further issues given in Exhibit 3. As part of the discussion, include the calculations of the daily impact of the mark-to-market closing prices on the transactions specified by the CEO.

(9 marks)

Professional marks will be awarded for the demonstration of skill in analysis and evaluation, and commercial acumen in your answer.

(5 marks)

(Total = 25 marks)

Exhibit 1: Daikon Co

For a number of years Daikon Co has been using forward rate agreements to manage its exposure to interest rate fluctuations. Recently its chief executive officer (CEO) attended a talk on using exchange-traded derivative products to manage risks. She wants to find out by how much the extra cost of the borrowing detailed below can be reduced, when using interest rate futures and options on interest rate futures to manage the interest rate risk. She asks that detailed

 BPP

calculations for each of these two derivative products be provided and a reasoned recommendation be made.

Exhibit 2: Hedging information

Daikon Co is expecting to borrow $34,000,000 in five months' time. It expects to make a full repayment of the borrowed amount in 11 months' time. Assume it is 1 June 20X5 today. Daikon Co can borrow funds at central bank base rate plus 70 basis points. The central bank base rate is currently 3.6%, but Daikon Co expects that interest rates may increase by as much as 80 basis points in five months' time.

The following information and quotes from an appropriate exchange are provided on central bank base rate-based $ futures and options.

Three-month $ December futures are currently quoted at 95.84. The contract size is $1,000,000, the tick size is 0.01% and the tick value is $25.

Options on three-month $ futures, $1,000,000 contract, tick size 0.01% and tick value $25. Option premiums are in annual %

December calls	Strike price	December puts
0.541	95.50	0.304
0.223	96.00	0.508

It can be assumed that settlement for both the futures and options contracts is at the end of the month; that basis diminishes to zero at a constant rate until the contract matures and time intervals can be counted in months; that margin requirements may be ignored; and that if the options are in-the-money, they will be exercised at the end of the hedge instead of being sold.

Exhibit 3: Further issues

In the talk, the CEO was informed of the following issues:

(1) Futures contracts will be marked to market daily. The CEO wondered what the impact of this would be if 50 futures contracts were bought at 95.84 on 1 June and 30 futures contracts were sold at 95.61 on 3 June, based on the $ December futures contract given above. The closing settlement prices are given below for four days:

Date	Settlement price
1 June	95.84
2 June	95.76
3 June	95.66
4 June	95.74

(2) Daikon Co will need to deposit funds into a margin account with a broker for each contract they have opened, and this margin will need to be adjusted when the contracts are marked to market daily.

(3) It is unlikely that option contracts will be exercised at the end of the hedge period unless they have reached expiry. Instead, they are more likely to be sold and the positions closed.

41 Fitzharris (Sep/Dec 2020, amended)   (49 mins)

(a) Calculate, in percentage terms, the results of the hedging strategies that are being considered for the $48m loan, if the central bank base rate increases to 4.1% or falls to 3.3%. Your calculations should demonstrate the rates at which payments between counterparties should be made.   **(12 marks)**

(b) Comment on the results of your calculations in (a) and discuss the advantages for Fitzharris Co of interest rate swaps compared with traded collars. **(4 marks)**

(c) Discuss how the delta value of an option could be used in determining the number of contracts purchased. **(4 marks)**

Professional marks will be awarded for the demonstration of skill in analysis and evaluation, and commercial acumen in your answer. **(5 marks)**

(Total = 25 marks)

Exhibit 1: Fitzharris Co

Fitzharris Co is a large construction company. Its treasury department uses a variety of derivatives regularly to manage interest rate and commodity price risk.

Exhibit 2: Transaction to be hedged

Today's date is 1 August. Fitzharris Co plans to borrow an amount of $48m on 1 December, to finance a major construction project, for a period of up to three years. Its treasury department has decided to hedge the risk associated with this borrowing, as there is some uncertainty about how interest rates will move over the rest of this year. The current central bank base rate is 3.7%, but predictions in the media suggest that it could rise or fall by 0.4% by 1 December. Fitzharris Co can currently borrow funds at a floating rate of central bank base rate plus 50 basis points.

Fitzharris Co's treasury department is considering hedging the interest rate risk by using:

(1) An interest rate swap arranged through Fitzharris Co's bank

(2) A collar on options on interest rate futures

Swap

Fitzharris Co's bank has found a possible counterparty for a swap with Fitzharris Co. The counterparty can borrow at an annual floating rate of base rate plus 130 basis points, or a fixed rate of 4.8%. Fitzharris Co's bank has quoted it a nominal fixed rate of 4.6% for it to borrow. The bank would charge a fee of five basis points to each party individually to act as the intermediary of the swap. Both parties would share equally the potential gains from the swap.

Collar

Options on three-month December $ futures, $1,000,000 contract size, option premiums are in annual %

Strike price	Calls	Puts
96.25	0.198	
95.75		0.211

The current three-month $ futures price for December futures is 95.85.

Futures and options contracts are assumed to be settled at the end of each month. Basis is assumed to diminish to zero at contract maturity at a constant rate, based on monthly time intervals. It is also assumed that there is no basis risk and there are no margin requirements.

Exhibit 3: Delta value

A member of Fitzharris's treasury team has suggested that if option contracts are purchased to hedge against the interest rate movements, then the number of contracts purchased should be determined by a hedge ratio based on the delta value of the option.

 BPP

42 Keshi (December 2014, amended)   (49 mins)

(a) Based on the two hedging choices Keshi Co is considering, recommend a hedging strategy for the $18,000,000 borrowing. Support your answer with appropriate calculations and discussion.   (15 marks)

(b) Discuss the key differences between a Salam contract, under Islamic finance principles, and futures contracts and briefly comment on the implications of this issue for the structure of Keshi's treasury department.   (5 marks)

Professional marks will be awarded for the demonstration of skill in analysis and evaluation, and commercial acumen in your answer.   (5 marks)

(Total = 25 marks)

Exhibit 1: Keshi Co

Keshi Co is a large multinational company with a number of international subsidiary companies. A centralised treasury department manages Keshi Co and its subsidiaries' borrowing requirements, cash surplus investment and financial risk management. Financial risk is normally managed using conventional derivative products such as forwards, futures, options and swaps.

Exhibit 2: Hedging information

Assume it is 1 December 20X4 today and Keshi Co is expecting to borrow $18,000,000 on 1 February 20X5 for a period of seven months. It can either borrow the funds at a variable rate of central bank base rate plus 40 basis points or a fixed rate of 5.5%. The central bank base rate is currently 3.8% but Keshi Co feels that this could increase or decrease by 0.5% over the coming months due to increasing uncertainty in the markets.

The treasury department is considering whether or not to hedge the $18,000,000, using either exchange-traded March options or over-the-counter swaps offered by Rozu Bank.

The following information and quotes for $ March options are provided from an appropriate exchange. The options are based on three-month $ futures and $1,000,000 contract size and option premiums are in annual %.

March calls	Strike price	March puts
0.882	95.50	0.662
0.648	96.00	0.902

Option prices are quoted in basis points at 100 minus the annual percentage yield and settlement of the options contracts is at the end of March 20X5. The current basis on the March futures price is 44 points and it is expected to be 33 points on 1 January 20X5, 22 points on 1 February 20X5 and 11 points on 1 March 20X5.

Rozu Bank has offered Keshi Co a swap on a counterparty variable rate of central bank base rate plus 30 basis points or a fixed rate of 4.6%, where Keshi Co receives 70% of any benefits accruing from undertaking the swap, prior to any bank charges. Rozu Bank will charge Keshi Co 10 basis points for the swap.

Exhibit 3: Other information

Keshi Co's chief executive officer believes that a centralised treasury department is necessary in order to increase shareholder value, but Keshi Co's new chief financial officer (CFO) thinks that having decentralised treasury departments operating across the subsidiary companies could be more beneficial. The chief financial officer thinks that this is particularly relevant to the situation which Suisen Co, a company owned by Keshi Co, is facing.

Suisen Co operates in a country where most companies conduct business activities based on Islamic finance principles. It produces confectionery products including chocolates. It wants to use Salam contracts instead of commodity futures contracts to hedge its exposure to price fluctuations of cocoa. Salam contracts involve a commodity which is sold based on currently

agreed prices, quantity and quality. Full payment is received by the seller immediately, for an agreed delivery to be made in the future.

43 Pault (Sep/Dec 2016, amended)   (49 mins)

(a)

    (i)   Using the current annual spot yield curve rates as the basis for estimating forward rates, calculate the amounts Pault Co expects to pay or receive each year under the swap (excluding the fee of 25 basis points).   **(6 marks)**

    (ii) Calculate Pault Co's interest payment liability for Year 1 if the yield curve rate is 4.5% or 2.9%, and comment on your results.   **(6 marks)**

(b) Advise the chairman on the current value of the swap to Pault Co and the factors which would change the value of the swap.   **(4 marks)**

(c) Advise the non-director on the possible problems with the swap, as requested in Exhibit 3.   **(4 marks)**

Professional marks will be awarded for the demonstration of skill in analysis and evaluation, scepticism and commercial acumen in your answer.   **(5 marks)**

(Total = 25 marks)

Exhibit 1: Pault Co

Pault Co is currently undertaking a major programme of product development. Pault Co has made a significant investment in plant and machinery for this programme. Over the next couple of years, Pault Co has also budgeted for significant development and launch costs for a number of new products, although its finance director believes there is some uncertainty with these budgeted figures, as they will depend upon competitor activity amongst other matters.

Exhibit 2: Financing issues

Pault Co issued floating rate loan notes, with a face value of $400 million, to fund the investment in plant and machinery. The loan notes are redeemable in ten years' time. The interest on the loan notes is payable annually and is based on the spot yield curve, plus 50 basis points.

Pault Co's finance director has recently completed a review of the company's overall financing strategy. His review has highlighted expectations that interest rates will increase over the next few years, although the predictions of financial experts in the media differ significantly.

The finance director is concerned about the exposure Pault Co has to increases in interest rates through the loan notes. He has therefore discussed with Millbridge Bank the possibility of taking out a four-year interest rate swap. The proposed terms are that Pault Co would pay Millbridge Bank interest based on an equivalent fixed annual rate of 4.847%. In return, Pault Co would receive from Millbridge Bank a variable amount based on the forward rates calculated from the annual spot yield curve rate at the time of payment minus 20 basis points. Payments and receipts would be made annually, with the first one in a year's time. Millbridge Bank would charge an annual fee of 25 basis points if Pault Co enters the swap.

The current annual spot yield curve rates are as follows:

Year	1	2	3	4
Rate	3.70%	4.25%	4.70%	5.10%

Exhibit 3: Concerns raised

A number of concerns were raised at the recent board meeting when the swap arrangement was discussed.

 **BPP**

- Pault Co's chairman wondered what the value of the swap arrangement to Pault Co was, and whether the value would change over time.
- One of Pault Co's non-executive directors has queried the swap arrangement, and has asked for a brief outline of possible problems with the swap.

44 Brandon (Sep/Dec 2021, amended)   (49 mins)

The following **exhibits** provide information relevant to the question:

(1)   Brandon Co

(2)   Transaction to be hedged

This information should be used to answer the question **requirements** within your chosen **response option(s)**.

Required

(a)   Explain how the functional areas of a treasury department could add value to Brandon Co's restructuring plans and for each functional area, discuss the advantages of a centralised treasury department.   **(6 marks)**

(b)   Recommend a hedging strategy for the $36m loan based on the hedging choices the treasury manager is considering, if the central bank base rate increases to 6.6%. Support your answer with appropriate calculations.

    Note. Up to 3 marks are available for discussion.   **(14 marks)**

Professional marks will be awarded for the demonstration of skill in analysis and evaluation, and commercial acumen in your answer.   **(5 marks)**

(Total = 25 marks)

Exhibit 1: Background

Brandon Co is a holding company, operating a small chain of luxury department stores in city centre locations throughout the eurozone. Under the existing structure, the stores are grouped into a number of regional subsidiaries, each with their own head office and treasury function. The board plans to undertake a restructuring exercise in response to a significant decline in revenue over recent years. This will involve closing unprofitable stores within the eurozone whilst expanding into other more profitable locations worldwide. The proposal represents a significant expansion for the company and will be financed by a combination of debt and equity.

The restructuring is due to be discussed at the upcoming board meeting, including the possibility of centralising the treasury function.

Exhibit 2: Financing requirements

Assume today's date is 1 November. Brandon Co's treasury manager predicts a short-term loan of $36m will be required next year on 31 January to fund an investment in non-current assets as part of the overseas expansion. The loan will be repaid on 31 May.

Brandon Co can borrow at the central bank base rate plus 40 basis points. The central bank base rate is currently 5.7%. Interest rates have been relatively volatile over the last few years and the finance director is concerned that the central bank could increase the base rate to 6.6% between now and 31 January in response to expectations about inflationary pressures within the economy. Recent media reports have also speculated on the possibility of a reduction in the base rate.

Hedging

Brandon Co's treasury manager is considering the following hedging possibilities with the objective of minimising exposure to interest rate risk:

- Forward rate agreements (FRAs)
- Interest rate futures

- Options on interest rate futures

The following data is available for each of the above:

FRAs

The following FRA rates are available:

3–4	5.82%
3–7	5.90%
4–8	5.99%

Three-month $ futures, $500,000 contract size

Prices are quoted in basis points at 100 – annual % yield.

December	94.07
March	93.95
June	93.82

Options on three-month $ futures, $500,000 contract size, option premiums are in annual %

	Calls			Puts		
Strike price	December	March	June	December	March	June
93.75	0.168	0.238	0.323	0.025	0.087	0.163

Assume futures and options contracts are settled at the end of each month. Basis is assumed to diminish to zero at contract maturity at a constant rate, based on monthly time intervals. It is also assumed that there is no basis risk and there are no margin requirements.

45 Lirio (Mar/Jun 2016, amended)   (98 mins)

(a) With reference to purchasing power parity, explain how exchange rate fluctuations may lead to economic exposure.   **(4 marks)**

(b) Prepare a discussion paper, including all relevant calculations, for the BoD of Lirio Co which:

   (i)   Estimates Lirio Co's dividend capacity as at 28 February 20X7, prior to investing in the large project   **(8 marks)**

   (ii) Advises Lirio Co on, and recommends, an appropriate hedging strategy for the euro (€) receipt it is due to receive in three months' time from the sale of the equity investment
                                                                                    (14 marks)

   (iii) Using the information on dividends provided in the question, and from (b)(i) and (b)(ii) above, assesses whether or not the project would add value to Lirio Co   **(7 marks)**

   (iv) Discusses the issues of proposed methods of financing the project which need to be considered further   **(7 marks)**

Professional marks will be awarded for the demonstration of skill in communication, analysis and evaluation, scepticism and commercial acumen in your answer.   **(10 marks)**

                                                                            (Total = 50 marks)

Exhibit 1: Lirio Co

Lirio Co is an engineering company which is involved in projects around the world. It has been growing steadily for several years and has maintained a stable dividend growth policy for a number of years now. The board of directors (BoD) is considering bidding for a large project which requires a substantial investment of $40 million. It can be assumed that the date today is 1 March 20X6.

The BoD is proposing that Lirio Co should not raise the finance for the project through additional debt or equity. Instead, it proposes that the required finance is obtained from a combination of funds received from the sale of its equity investment in a European company and from cash flows generated from its normal business activity in the coming two years. As a result, Lirio Co's current capital structure of 80 million $1 equity shares and $70 million 5% bonds is not expected to change in the foreseeable future.

The BoD has asked the company's treasury department to prepare a discussion paper on the implications of this proposal. The following information on Lirio Co has been provided to assist in the preparation of the discussion paper.

Exhibit 2: Expected income and cash flow commitments prior to undertaking the large project for the year to the end of February 20X7

Lirio Co's sales revenue is forecast to grow by 8% next year from its current level of $300 million to $324 million, and the operating profit margin is expected to be 15% of sales revenue. It is expected that Lirio Co will have the following capital investment requirements for the coming year, before the impact of the large project is considered:

(1) A $0.10 investment in working capital for every $1 increase in sales revenue;

(2) An investment equivalent to the amount of depreciation to keep its non-current asset base at the present productive capacity. The current depreciation charge already included in the operating profit margin is 25% of the non-current assets of $50 million;

(3) A $0.20 investment in additional non-current assets for every $1 increase in sales revenue; and

(4) $8 million additional investment in other small projects.

In addition to the above sales revenue and profits, Lirio Co has one overseas subsidiary – Pontac Co, from which it receives dividends of 80% on profits. Pontac Co produces a specialist tool which it sells locally for $60 each. It is expected that it will produce and sell 400,000 units of this specialist tool next year. Each tool will incur variable costs of $36 per unit and total annual fixed costs of $4 million to produce and sell.

Lirio Co pays corporation tax at 25% and Pontac Co pays corporation tax at 20%. In addition to this, a withholding tax of 8% is deducted from any dividends remitted from Pontac Co. A bi-lateral tax treaty exists between the countries where Lirio Co is based and where Pontac Co is based. Therefore, corporation tax is payable on profits made by subsidiary companies, but full credit is given for corporation tax already paid.

It can be assumed that receipts from Pontac Co are in $ equivalent amounts and exchange rate fluctuations on these can be ignored.

Exhibit 3: Sale of equity investment in the European country

It is expected that Lirio Co will receive euro (€) 20 million in three months' time from the sale of its investment. The € has continued to remain weak, while the $ has continued to remain strong through 20X5 and the start of 20X6. The financial press has also reported that there may be a permanent shift in the €/$ exchange rate, with firms facing economic exposure. Lirio Co has decided to hedge the € receipt using one of currency forward contracts, currency futures contracts or currency options contracts.

Exhibit 4: Hedging information

The following exchange contracts and rates are available to Lirio Co.

	Per €1
Spot rates	$1.1585–$1.1618
Three-month forward rates	$1.1559–$1.1601

Currency futures (contract size $125,000, quotation: € per $1)

March futures   €0.8638

June futures   €0.8656

Currency options (contract size $125,000, exercise price quotation € per $1, premium € per $1)

	Calls	Calls	Puts	Puts
Exercise price	March	June	March	June
0.8600	0.0255	0.0290	0.0267	0.0319

It can be assumed that futures and options contracts expire at the end of their respective months.

Exhibit 5: Dividend history, expected dividends and cost of capital, Lirio Co

Year to end of February	20X3	20X4	20X5	20X6
Number of $1 equity shares in issue ('000)	60,000	60,000	80,000	80,000
Total dividends paid ($'000)	12,832	13,602	19,224	20,377
Dividends per share ($)	0.214	0.227	0.240	0.255

It is expected that dividends will grow at the historic rate, if the large project is not undertaken.

 **BPP**

Expected dividends and dividend growth rates if the large project is undertaken:

Year to end of February 20X7	Remaining cash flows after the investment in the $40 million project will be paid as dividends.
Year to end of February 20X8	The dividends paid will be the same amount as the previous year.
Year to end of February 20X9	Dividends paid will be $0.31 per share.
In future years from February 20X9	Dividends will grow at an annual rate of 7%.

Lirio Co's cost of equity capital is estimated to be 12%.

46 Chrysos (Mar/Jun 2017, amended) (98 mins)

(a) Explain what a reverse takeover involves and discuss the relative advantages and disadvantages to a company, such as Chrysos Co, of obtaining a listing through a reverse takeover as opposed to an initial public offering (IPO). **(7 marks)**

(b) Prepare a report for the board of directors of Chrysos Co which includes:

  (i) An extract of the financial position and an estimate of Chrysos Co's value to the equity holders, after undertaking the restructuring programme. **(18 marks)**

  (ii) An explanation of the approach taken and assumptions made in estimating Chrysos Co's value to the equity holders, after undertaking the restructuring programme. **(5 marks)**

  (iii) A discussion of the impact of the restructuring programme on Chrysos Co and on the venture capital organisations. **(10 marks)**

Professional marks will be awarded for the demonstration of skill in communication, analysis and evaluation, scepticism and commercial acumen in your answer. **(10 marks)**

(Total = 50 marks)

Exhibit 1: Chrysos Co

The eight-member board of executive directors (BoD) of Chrysos Co, a large private, unlisted company, is considering the company's long-term business and financial future. The BoD is considering whether or not to undertake a restructuring programme. This will be followed a few years later by undertaking a reverse takeover to obtain a listing on the stock exchange in order to raise new finance. However, a few members of the BoD have raised doubts about the restructuring programme and the reverse takeover, not least the impact upon the company's stakeholders. Some directors are of the opinion that an initial public offering (IPO) would be a better option when obtaining a listing compared to a reverse takeover.

Chrysos Co was formed about 15 years ago by a team of five senior equity holders who are part of the BoD and own 40% of the equity share capital in total; 30 other equity holders own a further 40% of the equity share capital but are not part of the BoD; and a consortium of venture capital organisations (VCOs) own the remaining 20% of the equity share capital and have three representatives on the BoD. The VCOs have also lent Chrysos Co substantial debt finance in the form of unsecured bonds due to be redeemed in ten years' time.

Exhibit 2: Chrysos's business units

Chrysos Co has two business units: a mining and shipping business unit, and a machinery parts manufacturing business unit. The mining and shipping business unit accounts for around 80% of Chrysos Co's business in terms of sales revenue, non-current and current assets, and payables. However, it is estimated that this business unit accounts for around 75% of the company's

operating costs. The smaller machinery parts manufacturing business unit accounts for the remaining 20% of sales revenue, non-current and current assets, and payables; and around 25% of the company's operating costs.

Exhibit 3: Recent financial statements (extracts)

The following figures have been extracted from Chrysos Co's most recent financial statements:

Profit before depreciation, interest and tax for the year to 28 February 20X7

	$m
Sales revenue	16,800
Operating costs	(10,080)
Profit before depreciation, interest and tax	6,720

Financial position as at 28 February 20X7

	$m
Non-current assets	
Land and buildings	7,500
Equipment	5,400
Current assets	
Inventory	1,800
Receivables	900
Total assets	15,600
Equity	
Share capital ($1 par value per share)	1,800
Reserves	5,400
Non-current liabilities	
4.50% unsecured bonds 20Y6 (from the VCOs)	4,800
Other debt	1,050
Current liabilities	
Payables	750
Bank overdraft	1,800
Total equity and liabilities	15,600

Exhibit 4: Corporate restructuring programme

The purpose of the restructuring programme is to simplify the company's gearing structure and to obtain extra funding to expand the mining and shipping business in the future. At present, Chrysos Co is having difficulty obtaining additional funding without having to pay high interest rates.

Machinery parts manufacturing business unit

The smaller machinery parts manufacturing business unit will be unbundled either by having its assets sold to a local supplier for $3,102 million after its share of payables have been paid or the smaller machinery parts manufacturing business unit will be unbundled through a management buy-out by four managers. In this case, it is estimated that its after-tax net cash flows will increase by 8% in the first year only and then stay fixed at this level for the foreseeable future. The cost of capital related to the smaller business unit is estimated to be 10%. The management buy-

out team will pay Chrysos Co 70% of the estimated market value of the smaller machinery parts manufacturing business unit.

Mining and shipping business unit

Following the unbundling of the smaller machinery parts manufacturing business unit, Chrysos Co will focus solely on the mining and shipping business unit, prior to undertaking the reverse takeover some years into the future.

As part of the restructuring programme, the existing unsecured bonds lent by the VCOs will be cancelled and replaced by an additional 600 million $1 shares for the VCOs. The VCOs will pay $400 million for these shares. The bank overdraft will be converted into a 15-year loan on which Chrysos Co will pay a fixed annual interest of 4.50%. The other debt under non-current liabilities will be repaid. In addition to this, Chrysos Co will invest $1,200 million into equipment for its mining and shipping business unit and this will result in its profits and cash flows growing by 4% per year in perpetuity.

Exhibit 5: Additional financial information

Chrysos Co aims to maintain a long-term capital structure of 20% debt and 80% equity in market value terms. Chrysos Co's finance director has assessed that the 4.50% annual interest it will pay on its bank loan is a reasonable estimate of its long-term cost of debt, based on the long-term capital structure above.

Although Chrysos Co does not know what its cost of capital is for the mining and shipping business unit, its finance director has determined that the current ungeared cost of equity of Sidero Co, a large quoted mining and shipping company, is 12.46%. Chrysos Co's finance director wants touse Sidero Co's ungeared cost of equity to calculate its cost of capital for the mining and shipping business unit.

The annual corporation tax rate on profits applicable to all companies is 18% and it can be assumed that tax is payable in the year incurred. All the non-current assets are eligible for tax allowable depreciation of 12% annually on the book values. The annual reinvestment needed to keep operations at their current levels is equivalent to the tax allowable depreciation.

47 Conejo (Sep/Dec 2017, amended)   (98 mins)

(a) Discuss the possible reasons for the finance director's suggestions that Conejo Co could benefit from higher levels of debt with respect to risk, from protection against acquisition bids, and from tax benefits.

(6 marks)

(b) Prepare a report for the board of directors of Conejo Co which:

(i) Estimates, and briefly comments on, the change in value of the current bond and the coupon rate required for the new bond, as requested by the CFO;   (6 marks)

(ii) Estimates the Macaulay duration of the new bond based on the interest payable annually and face value repayment, and the Macaulay duration based on the fixed annual repayment of the interest and capital, as suggested by the CEO; and   (6 marks)

(iii) Estimates the impact of the two proposals, on how the funds may be used, on next year's forecast earnings, forecast financial position, forecast earnings per share and on forecast gearing.   (11 marks)

(iv) Using the estimates from (b)(i), (b)(ii) and (b)(iii), discusses the impact of the proposed financial reconstruction and the proposals on the use of funds on:

• Conejo Co;

• Possible reaction(s) of credit rating companies and on the expected credit migration, including the suggestion made by the CEO; and

• Conejo Co's debt holders.

(11 marks)

Professional marks will be awarded for the demonstration of skill in communication, analysis and evaluation, scepticism and commercial acumen in your answer. **(10 marks)**

(Total = 50 marks)

Exhibit 1: Conejo Co

Conejo Co is a listed company based in Ardilla and uses the $ as its currency. The company was formed around 20 years ago and was initially involved in cybernetics, robotics and artificial intelligence within the information technology industry. At that time due to the risky ventures Conejo Co undertook, its cash flows and profits were very varied and unstable.

Around ten years ago, it started an information systems consultancy business and a business developing cyber security systems. Both these businesses have been successful and have been growing consistently. This in turn has resulted in a stable growth in revenues, profits and cash flows. The company continues its research and product development in artificial intelligence and robotics, but this business unit has shrunk proportionally to the other two units.

Just under eight years ago, Conejo Co was successfully listed on Ardilla's national stock exchange, offering 60% of its share capital to external equity holders, whilst the original founding members retained the remaining 40% of the equity capital. The company remains financed largely by equity capital and reserves, with only a small amount of debt capital. Due to this, and its steadily growing sales revenue, profits and cash flows, it has attracted a credit rating of A from the credit rating agencies.

Exhibit 2: Capital structure considerations

At a recent board of directors (BoD) meeting, the company's chief financial officer (CFO) argued that it was time for Conejo Co to change its capital structure by undertaking a financial reconstruction, and be financed by higher levels of debt. As part of her explanation, the CFO said that Conejo Co: is now better able to bear the increased risk resulting from higher levels of debt finance; would be better protected from predatory acquisition bids if it was financed by higher levels of debt; and could take advantage of the tax benefits offered by increased debt finance.

She also suggested that the expected credit migration from a credit rating of A to a credit rating of BBB, if the financial reconstruction detailed below took place, would not weaken Conejo Co financially.

Exhibit 3: Financial reconstruction

The BoD decided to consider the financial reconstruction plan further before making a final decision. The financial reconstruction plan would involve raising $1,320 million ($1.32 billion) new debt finance consisting of bonds issued at their face value of $100. The bonds would be redeemed in five years' time at their face value of $100 each. The funds raised from the issue of the new bonds would be used to implement one of the following two proposals:

- Either buy back equity shares at their current share price, which would be cancelled after they have been repurchased; or
- Invest in additional assets in new business ventures.

 **BPP**

Exhibit 4: Conejo Co, financial information

EXTRACT FROM THE FORECAST FINANCIAL POSITION FOR NEXT YEAR

	$m
Non-current assets	1,735
Current assets	530
Total assets	2,265
Equity and liabilities	
Share capital ($1 per share par value)	400
Reserves	1,700
Total equity	2,100
Non-current liabilities	120
Current liabilities	45
Total liabilities	165
Total liabilities and capital	2,265

Conejo Co's forecast after-tax profit for next year is $350 million and its current share price is $11 per share.

The non-current liabilities consist solely of 5.2% coupon bonds with a face value of $100 each, which are redeemable at their face value in three years' time. These bonds are currently trading at $107.80 per $100. The bond's covenant stipulates that should Conejo Co's borrowing increase, the coupon payable on these bonds will increase by 37 basis points.

Conejo Co pays tax at a rate of 15% per year and its after-tax return on the new investment is estimated at 12%.

Exhibit 5: Other financial information

Current government bond yield curve

Year	1	2	3	4	5
	1.5%	1.7%	1.9%	2.2%	2.5%

Yield spreads (in basis points)

	1 year	2 years	3 years	4 years	5 years
A	40	49	59	68	75
BBB	70	81	94	105	112
BB	148	167	185	202	218

The finance director wants to determine the percentage change in the value of Conejo Co's current bonds, if the credit rating changes from A to BBB. Furthermore, she wants to determine the coupon rate at which the new bonds would need to be issued, based on the current yield curve and appropriate yield spreads given above.

Conejo Co's chief executive officer (CEO) suggested that if Conejo Co paid back the capital and interest of the new bond in fixed annual repayments of capital and interest through the five-year life of the bond, then the risk associated with the extra debt finance would be largely mitigated. In

this case, it was possible that credit migration, by credit rating companies, from A rating to BBB rating may not happen. He suggested that comparing the duration of the new bond based on the interest payable annually and the face value in five years' time with the duration of the new bond where the borrowing is paid in fixed annual repayments of interest and capital could be used to demonstrate this risk mitigation.

48 Chikepe (Mar/Jun 2018, amended)   (98 mins)

(a) Compare and contrast the reasons for the opinions held by Director A and by Director B, and discuss the types of synergy benefits which may arise from the acquisition strategy suggested by Director B.   (7 marks)

(b) Discuss how using real options methodology in conjunction with net present value could help establish a more accurate estimate of the potential value of companies, as suggested by Director C.   (4 marks)

(c) Prepare a report for the board of directors of Chikepe Co which:

   (i)   Estimates the current equity value of Foshoro Co;   (5 marks)

   (ii) Estimates the equity value arising from combining Foshoro Co with Chikepe Co;
                                                                               (11 marks)

   (iii) Evaluates whether the acquisition of Foshoro Co would be beneficial to Chikepe Co's shareholders and discusses the limitations of the valuation method used in (c)(i) and (c)(ii) above.   (7 marks)

(d) Discuss how the mandatory bid rule and the principle of equal treatment protects shareholders in the event of their company facing a takeover bid, and briefly discuss the effectiveness of defensive measures against hostile takeovers such as the disposal of crown jewels.   (6 marks)

Professional marks will be awarded for the demonstration of skill in communication, analysis and evaluation, scepticism and commercial acumen in your answer.   (10 marks)

(Total = 50 marks)

Exhibit 1: Chikepe

Chikepe Co is a large, listed company operating in the pharmaceutical industry, with a current market value of equity of $12,600 million and a debt-to-equity ratio of 30:70, in market value terms. Institutional investors hold most of its equity shares. The company develops and manufactures antibiotics and anti-viral medicines. Both the company and its products have an established positive reputation among the medical profession, and its products are used widely. However, its rate of innovation has slowed considerably in the last few years and it has fewer new medical products coming into the market.

Exhibit 2: Acquisition strategy

At a recent meeting of the board of directors (BoD), it was decided that the company needed to change its current strategy of growing organically to one of acquiring companies, in order to maintain the growth in its share price in the future. The members of the BoD had different opinions on the type of acquisition strategy to pursue.

Director A was of the opinion that Chikepe Co should follow a strategy of acquiring companies in different business sectors. She suggested that focusing on just the pharmaceutical sector was too risky and acquiring companies in different business sectors will reduce this risk.

Director B was of the opinion that Director A's suggestion would not result in a reduction in risk for shareholders. In fact, he suggested that this would result in agency related issues with Chikepe Co's shareholders reacting negatively and as a result, the company's share price would fall. Instead, Director B suggested that Chikepe Co should focus on its current business and acquire

 **BPP**

other established pharmaceutical companies. In this way, the company will gain synergy benefits and thereby increase value for its shareholders.

Director C agreed with Director B but suggested that Chikepe Co should consider relatively new pharmaceutical companies, as well as established businesses. In her opinion, newer companies might be involved in research and development of innovative products, which could have high potential in the future. She suggested that using real options methodology with traditional investment appraisal methods such as net present value could help establish a more accurate estimate of the potential value of such companies.

The company has asked its finance team to prepare a report on the value of a potential target company, Foshoro Co, before making a final decision.

Exhibit 3: Foshoro Co

Foshoro Co is a non-listed pharmaceutical company established about ten years ago. Initially Foshoro Co grew rapidly, but this rate of growth slowed considerably three years ago, after a venture capital equity backer exited the company by selling its stake back to the founding directors. The directors had to raise substantial debt capital to buy back the equity stake. The company's current debt to equity ratio is 60:40. This high level of gearing means that the company will find it difficult to obtain funds to develop its innovative products in the future.

The following financial information relates to Foshoro Co:

Extract from the most recent statement of profit or loss

	$m
Sales revenue	878.1
Profit before interest and tax	192.3
Interest	78.6
Tax	22.7
Profit after tax	91.0

In arriving at the profit before interest and tax, Foshoro Co deducted tax allowable depreciation and other non-cash expenses totalling $112.0 million. It requires a cash investment of $98.2 million in non-current assets and working capital to continue its operations at the current level.

Over the past three years Foshoro Co's profits and cash flows have grown steadily by an average of 3% per year. It is likely that this growth rate will continue for the foreseeable future if Foshoro Co is not acquired by Chikepe Co. Foshoro Co's cost of capital has been estimated at 10%.

Exhibit 4: Combined company: Chikepe Co and Foshoro Co

Once Chikepe Co acquires Foshoro Co, it is predicted that the combined company's sales revenue will be $4,200 million in the first year, and its operating profit margin on sales revenue will be 20% for the foreseeable future.

After the first year, the sales revenue is expected to grow at 7% per year for the following three years. It is anticipated that after the first four years, the growth rate of the combined company's free cash flows will be 5.6% per year.

The combined company's tax allowable depreciation is expected to be equivalent to the amount of investment needed to maintain the current level of operations. However, as the company's sales revenue increases over the four-year period, the combined company will require an additional investment in assets of $200 million in the first year and then $0.64 per $1 increase in sales revenue for the next three years.

It can be assumed that the asset beta of the combined company is the weighted average of the individual companies' asset betas, weighted in proportion of the individual companies' value of equity. It can also be assumed that the capital structure of the combined company remains at Chikepe Co's current capital structure level, a debt-to-equity ratio of 30:70. Chikepe Co pays interest on borrowings at a rate of 5.3% per year.

Chikepe Co estimates that it will be able to acquire Foshoro Co by paying a premium of 30% above its estimated equity value to Foshoro Co's shareholders.

Exhibit 5: Other financial information

	Equity beta	Asset beta
Chikepe Co	1.074	0.800
Foshoro Co	2.090	0.950

The current annual government borrowing base rate is 2% and the annual market risk premium is estimated at 7%.

Both companies pay tax at an annual rate of 20%.

Chikepe Co estimates equity values in acquisitions using the free cash flow to firm method.

Exhibit 6: Future acquisitions

The BoD agreed that in the future it is likely that Chikepe Co will target both listed and non-listed companies for acquisition. It is aware that when pursuing acquisitions of listed companies, the company would need to ensure that it complied with regulations such as the mandatory bid rule and the principle of equal treatment to protect shareholders. The BoD is also aware that some listed companies may attempt to defend acquisitions by employing anti-takeover measures such as the disposal of crown jewels.

 BPP

49 Washi (September 2018, amended) (98 mins)

(a) Discuss how investing in overseas projects may enable Washi Co to gain competitive advantage over its competitors, who only invest in domestic projects. **(5 marks)**

(b) Prepare a report for the board of directors of Washi Co which:

(i) Estimates the expected amount of JPY receivable under each hedge choice and the additional debt finance needed to fund the Airone project for the preferred hedge choice; **(12 marks)**

(ii) Estimates the net present value of the Airone project in Japanese yen, based on the end of year one being the start of the project (Year 0); **(9 marks)**

(iii) Evaluates the preferred hedge choice made, the debt finance needed and whether the Airone project should be undertaken, considering both financial and non-financial factors. **(8 marks)**

(c) Washi Co's chief operations officer (COO) has suggested that it would be more beneficial for the company to let its major subsidiary companies have their own individual treasury departments, instead of having one centralised treasury department for the whole company.

Required

Discuss the validity of the COO's suggestion. **(6 marks)**

Professional marks will be awarded for the demonstration of skill in communication, analysis and evaluation, scepticism and commercial acumen in your answer. **(10 marks)**

(Total = 50 marks)

Exhibit 1: Washi Co

Washi Co is a large, unlisted company based in Japan and its local currency is the Japanese Yen (JPY). It manufactures industrial equipment and parts. Initially Washi Co's customers consisted of other Japanese companies, but over the last 12 years it has expanded into overseas markets and also sources its materials from around the world. The company's board of directors (BoD) believes that the strategy of overseas investments, through subsidiary companies, branches and joint ventures, has directly led to the company's substantial increase in value in the past few years.

Exhibit 2: Proposed investment

Washi Co's BoD is considering investing in a project based in Airone, whose currency is the Airone Rand (ARD). It believes that the project will be an important addition to the company's portfolio of investments, because Washi Co does not currently have a significant presence in the part of the world where Airone is located. It is intended that the project will commence in one year's time. Details of the project are given below.

Exhibit 3: Funding and hedging information

Washi Co intends to finance the project through proceeds from an agreed sale of a small European subsidiary, with any remaining funding requirement being met by additional debt finance issued in Japanese Yen. The company is due to receive the proceeds from the sale of a European subsidiary company in six months' time and it will then invest these funds in short-dated Japanese treasury bills for a further six months before they are needed for the project. Washi Co has a centralised treasury department, which hedges expected future cash flows against currency fluctuations.

The agreed proceeds from the sale of the European subsidiary company receivable in six months' time are Euro (EUR) 80 million. The BoD is concerned about a negative fluctuation in EUR/JPY rate between now and in six months when the EUR 80 million will be received. Therefore, it has asked Washi Co's treasury department to hedge the expected receipt using one of currency forwards, currency futures or exchange traded currency options. Washi Co's treasury department has obtained the following information:

	JPY per EUR 1	ARD per EUR 1
Spot	129.2–132.4	92.7–95.6
Six-month forward rate	125.3–128.6	

Currency futures (contract size EUR 125,000, quotation JPY per EUR 1)

Four-month expiry	126.9
Seven-month expiry	125.2

Currency options (contract size EUR 125,000, exercise price quotation: JPY per EUR 1, premium quotation: JPY per EUR 1)

At an exercise price of JPY 126.0 per EUR 1

	Four-month expiry	Seven-month expiry
Calls	2.3	2.6
Puts	3.4	3.8

Annualised yield on short-dated Japanese treasury bills = 1.20%

Airone's annual inflation rate is 9% currently, but has fluctuated markedly in the last five years. The Japanese annual inflation rate is 1.5% and has been stable for many years.

Exhibit 4: Airone project financial estimates

A member of Washi Co's finance team has produced the following estimates of the Airone project which is expected to last for four years. The estimates are based on the notes given below but not on the further information. The estimates have been checked and verified independently for their numerical accuracy.

All figures are in ARD millions.

Project year	0	1	2	3	4
Sales revenue		13,000	30,800	32,300	4,500
Costs		(10,200)	(24,200)	(24,500)	(3,200)
Tax allowable depreciation		(1,000)	(1,000)	(1,000)	(1,000)
Pre-tax profits		1,800	5,600	6,800	300
Tax at 15%		(270)	(840)	(1,020)	(45)
Tax allowable depreciation		1,000	1,000	1,000	1,000
Working capital	(400)				400
Investment in buildings	(5,750)				
Investment in machinery	(4,000)				
Cash flows in ARD	(10,150)	2,530	5,760	6,780	1,655

BPP

Notes (incorporated into the estimates above):

Notes.

1   The estimates are based on using the end of the first year, when the project commences, as the start of the project (Year 0). The numbers are given in ARD million.

2   The total investment required for the project is ARD 10,150 million and separated into buildings, machinery and working capital in the table above. The machinery is eligible for tax allowable depreciation on a straight-line basis and the working capital is redeemable at the end of the project.

3   The impact of inflation has been incorporated into the sales revenue and cost figures, at Airone's current annual inflation figures.

4   Corporation tax has been included based on Airone's annual rate of 15%. The tax is payable in the year that the tax liability arises.

Exhibit 5: Further information (not incorporated into the estimates above):

(1)   Undertaking the Airone project will result in lost sales for Washi Co. These sales would have generated a pre-tax contribution of JPY 110 million in the first year of the project, rising by the Japanese rate of inflation in the following Years 2 to 4 of the project.

(2)   The Airone project costs include components which are made in Japan by Washi Co and would be imported to the Airone project. The pre-inflation revenues generated from the sale of the components are estimated to be as follows:

In JPY millions

Project year	1	2	3	4
Components revenue	1,200	2,400	2,500	300

These revenues are expected to increase by the Japanese inflation rate in Years 2 to 4 of the project. The contribution which Washi Co expects to earn on these components is 25% of revenue.

(3)   The Japanese annual corporation tax rate is 30% and tax is payable in the year that the tax liability arises. A bilateral tax treaty exists between Japan and Airone, which permits offset of overseas tax against any Japanese tax liability on overseas earnings.

(4)   Washi Co's finance department has estimated a cost of capital of 12% to be used as a discount rate for the project.

50   Opao (Dec 2018, amended)   (98 mins)

(a)   Explain what portfolio restructuring and organisational restructuring involve, and discuss possible reason(s) why the change in the type of shareholders may have made Opao Co change from being a conglomerate to one focusing on just two business sectors.   **(4 marks)**

(b)   Prepare a report for the board of directors of Opao Co which:

(i)   Estimates the value of equity of Opao Co and of Tai Co before the acquisition, and of the combined company after the acquisition;   **(10 marks)**

(ii)   Estimates the percentage gain in value for each Opao Co share and Tai Co share, under each of the cash, the share-for-share, and the mixed offers; and   **(12 marks)**

(iii)   Evaluates the likely reaction of Opao Co's and Tai Co's shareholders to the acquisition offers.   **(7 marks)**

(c)   Following the MBI, the BoD of Burgut Co announced that its intention was to list the company on a recognised stock exchange within seven years. The BoD is discussing whether to obtain the listing through an initial public offering (IPO) or through a reverse takeover, but it does not currently have a strong preference for either option.

Required

Distinguish between an IPO and a reverse takeover, and discuss whether an IPO or a reverse takeover would be an appropriate method for Burgut Co to obtain a listing. **(7 marks)**

Professional marks will be awarded for the demonstration of skill in communication, analysis and evaluation, scepticism and commercial acumen in your answer. **(10 marks)**

(Total = 50 marks)

Exhibit 1: Opao Co

Around seven years ago, Opao Co, a private conglomerate company involved in many different businesses, decided to obtain a listing on a recognised stock exchange by offering a small proportion of its equity shares to the public. Before the listing, the company was owned by around 100 shareholders, who were all closely linked to Opao Co and had their entire shareholding wealth invested in the company. However, soon after the listing these individuals started selling their shares in Opao Co, and over a two-year period after the listing, its ownership structure changed to one of many diverse individual and institutional shareholders.

As a consequence of this change in ownership structure, Opao Co's board of directors (BoD) commenced an aggressive period of business reorganisation through portfolio and organisational restructuring. This resulted in Opao Co changing from a conglomerate company to a company focusing on just two business sectors: financial services and food manufacturing. The financial press reported that Opao Co had been forced to take this action because of the change in the type of its shareholders. The equity markets seem to support this action, and Opao Co's share price has grown strongly during this period of restructuring, after growing very slowly initially.

Opao Co recently sold a subsidiary company, Burgut Co, through a management buy-in (MBI), although it also had the option to dispose of Burgut Co through a management buy-out (MBO).

Opao Co is now considering acquiring Tai Co and details of the proposed acquisition are as follows:

Exhibit 2: Proposed acquisition of Tai Co

Tai Co is an unlisted company involved in food manufacturing. Opao Co's BoD is of the opinion that the range of products produced by Tai Co will fit very well with its own product portfolio, leading to cross-selling opportunities, new innovations, and a larger market share. The BoD also thinks that there is a possibility for economies of scale and scope, such as shared logistic and storage facilities, giving cost saving opportunities. This, the BoD believes, will lead to significant synergy benefits and therefore it is of the opinion that Opao Co should make a bid to acquire Tai Co.

Exhibit 3: Financial information related to Opao Co, Tai Co and the combined company

Opao Co

Opao Co has 2,000 million shares in issue and are currently trading at $2.50 each.

Tai Co

Tai Co has 263 million shares in issue and the current market value of its debt is $400 million. Its most recent profit before interest and tax was $132.0 million, after deducting tax allowable depreciation and non-cash expenses of $27.4 million. Tai Co makes an annual cash investment of $24.3 million in non-current assets and working capital. It is estimated that its cash flows will grow by 3% annually for the foreseeable future. Tai Co's current cost of capital is estimated to be 11%.

Combined company

If Opao Co acquires Tai Co, it is expected that the combined company's sales revenue will be $7,351 million in the first year and its annual pre-tax profit margin on sales will be 15.4% for the foreseeable future. After the first year, sales revenue will grow by 5.02% every year for the next three years. It can be assumed that the combined company's annual depreciation will be equivalent to the investment required to maintain the company at current operational levels. However, in order to increase the sales revenue levels each year, the combined company will

require an additional investment of $109 million in the first year and $0.31 for every $1 increase in sales revenue for each of the next three years.

After the first four years, it is expected that the combined company's free cash flows will grow by 2.4% annually for the foreseeable future. The combined company's cost of capital is estimated to be 10%. It expected that the combined company's debt to equity level will be maintained at 40:60, in market value terms, after the acquisition has taken place.

Both Opao Co and Tai Co pay corporation tax on profits at an annual rate of 20% and it is expected that this rate will not change if Opao Co acquires Tai Co. It can be assumed that corporation tax is payable in the same year as the profits it is charged on.

Exhibit 4: Possible acquisition price offers

Opao Co's BoD is proposing that Tai Co's acquisition be made through one of the following payment methods:

- A cash payment offer of $4.40 for each Tai Co share; or
- Through a share-for-share exchange, where a number of Tai Co shares are exchanged for a number of Opao Co shares, such that 55.5% of the additional value created from the acquisition is allocated to Tai Co's shareholders and the remaining 44.5% of the additional value is allocated to Opao Co's shareholders; or
- Through a mixed offer of a cash payment of $2.09 per share and one Opao Co share for each Tai Co share. It is estimated that Opao Co's share price will become $2.60 per share when such a mixed offer is made.

Similar acquisitions in the food manufacturing industry have normally attracted a share price premium of between 15% and 40% previously.

51 Talam (Mar/Jun 2019, amended) (98 mins)

(a) Discuss how incorporating real options into net present value decisions may help Talam Co with its investment appraisal decisions. **(5 marks)**

(b) Prepare a report for the board of directors (BoD) of Talam Co which:

(i) Estimates, showing all relevant calculations, the net present value of the Uwa Project before considering the offer from Honua Co and the Jigu Project; **(12 marks)**

(ii) Addresses the requests made by the finance director about asset value for the Jigu project and estimated value of the offer from Honua Co using the real options method; and **(7 marks)**

(iii) Assesses whether the Uwa Project should be undertaken, using the results from, and discussing the assumptions made in, the calculations in (b)(i) and (b)(ii) above. **(8 marks)**

(c) Discuss the impact on Talam Co and its aims arising from the possible sustainability and ethical issues relating to biodegradable drones and advise on how these issues may be addressed. **(8 marks)**

Professional marks will be awarded for the demonstration of skill in communication, analysis and evaluation, scepticism and commercial acumen in your answer. **(10 marks)**

Note. In the exam a Black-Scholes spreadsheet model will be available to input the variable into.

(Total = 50 marks)

Exhibit 1: Talam Co

Talam Co, a listed company, aims to manufacture innovative engineering products which are environmentally friendly and sustainable. These products have been highly marketable because of their affordability. Talam Co's mission statement also states its desire to operate to the highest

ethical standards. These commitments have meant that Talam Co has a very high reputation and a high share price compared to its competitors.

Talam Co is considering a new project, the **Uwa Project**, to manufacture drones for use in the agricultural industry, which are at least 50% biodegradable, at competitive prices. The drones will enable farmers to increase crop yields and reduce crop damage. Manufacture of drones is a new business area for Talam Co. The project is expected to last for four years.

Talam Co will also work on the **Jigu Project** (a follow-on project to the Uwa Project) to make 95%+ biodegradable drones. It is expected that the Jigu Project will last for a further five years after the Uwa Project has finished. If the Uwa Project is discontinued or sold sooner than four years, the Jigu Project could still be undertaken after four years.

Exhibit 2: Uwa Project

The following number of drones are expected to be produced and sold:

Year	1	2	3	4
Number of drones produced and sold	4,300	19,200	35,600	25,400

In the first year, for each drone, it is expected that the selling price will be $1,200 and the variable costs will be $480. The total annual direct fixed costs will be $2.7m. After the first year, the selling price is expected to increase by 8% annually, the variable costs by 4% annually and the fixed costs by 10% annually, for the next three years. Training costs are expected to be 200% of the variable costs in Year 1, 60% in Year 2, and 10% in each of Years 3 and 4. There is substantial uncertainty about the drones produced and sold, and Talam Co estimates the project to have a standard deviation of 30%.

At the start of every year, the Uwa Project will need working capital. In the first year, this will be 20% of sales revenue. In subsequent years, the project will require additional or a reduction in working capital of 10% for every $1 increase or decrease in sales revenue respectively. The working capital is expected to be fully recovered when the Uwa Project ceases.

The Uwa Project will need $35m of machinery to produce the drones at the start of the project. Tax allowable depreciation is available on the machinery at 15% per year on a straight-line basis. The machinery is expected to be sold for $7m (post-inflation) at the end of the project. Talam Co makes sufficient profits from its other activities to take advantage of any tax loss relief. Tax is paid in the year it falls due.

Honua Co's offer

Honua Co, whose main business is drone production, has approached Talam Co with an offer to buy the Uwa Project in its entirety from Talam Co for $30m at the start of the third year of the project's life. Talam Co's finance director has requested that the value of Honua Co's offer is estimated using the real options method.

Additional information

Both Honua Co and Talam Co pay corporation tax at an annual rate of 20%. Talam Co has estimated Uwa Project's and Jigu Project's risk-adjusted cost of capital at 11%, based on Honua Co's asset beta. Talam Co believes that the central bank base rate, which is currently 2.30%, provides a good estimate of the risk-free rate of interest.

Exhibit 3: Jigu Project as a real option

Talam Co estimates that Jigu Project's cash flows are highly uncertain, and its standard deviation is 50%. It is estimated that $60m will be required at the start of the project in four years' time. Using conventional net present value, Talam Co's best estimate is that net present value will be $10m at the start of the project.

The following figures were estimated for the Jigu Project using the real options method.

Asset value (Pa) = $46.1m (to nearest 100,000)

Exercise price (Pe) = $60m

Exercise date (t) = 4 years

 **BPP**

Risk-free rate (r) = 2.30%

Volatility (s) = 50%

Call option value: $15.3m

It can be assumed that the call option value is accurate.

Talam Co's finance director wants to know how the asset value of $46.1m has been estimated.

Exhibit 4: Biodegradable drones and related issues

At a recent trade show, the biodegradable drones attracted considerable interest from organisations worldwide. Nevertheless, some expressed concern about the drone price, which they felt was too high.

Talam Co estimates that even a modest reduction in each drone's price would make the projects unprofitable. Therefore, the operations director suggested that costs could be reduced if drone components were produced in Dunia, a country where Talam Co already gets some of its other products made.

However, the public relations director brought up an issue concerning Dunia. He said that several companies in Dunia, which Talam Co trades with, employ young teenage children. These companies pay the education fees for the teenagers, and the companies argued that stopping this practice would harm the teenagers' families financially.

52 Okan (Sep/Dec 2019, amended)   (98 mins)

(a) Prepare a report for the board of directors (BoD) of Okan Co which:

    (i)   Estimates the minimum amount of debt borrowing Okan Co would require.   **(4 marks)**

    (ii) Estimates:

        (1)   Project Alpha's and Project Beta's base case NPV, in six months' time, before considering the financing side effects;   **(11 marks)**

        (2)   Project Alpha's and Project Beta's APV, in six months' time; and   **(6 marks)**

        (3)   Project Alpha's duration based on its base case present values of cash flows;

                                                      (2 marks)

                                                  (19 marks)

    (iii) Evaluates and justifies which project Okan Co should choose, basing the decision on the factors Okan Co considers to be important. The evaluation should include a discussion of the assumptions made.   **(7 marks)**

(b) Discuss why Okan Co's subsidiary company may be exposed to economic risk (economic exposure) and how it may be managed.   **(4 marks)**

(c) Discuss how each category of risk, in terms of severity and frequency, may be managed.
                                                       (6 marks)

Professional marks will be awarded for the demonstration of skill in communication, analysis and evaluation, scepticism and commercial acumen in your answer.   **(10 marks)**

(Total = 50 marks)

Exhibit 1: Okan Co

Okan Co, a large, listed company located in Yasailand (which uses the currency Y$), manufactures engines and engine parts.

It is considering whether or not to invest in one of two new four-year projects: Project Alpha or Project Beta. Details of both projects are given separately. Previously, Okan Co has used relevant risk-adjusted discount rates to calculate the net present value (NPV) of projects. However, the finance director believes that calculating adjusted present values (APV) of projects would be more appropriate. Okan Co wants to base its decision on which project to invest in; the returns

generated by the projects; the projects' risk as measured by their project durations; and important non-financial aspects. Both projects are due to commence in six months' time.

Exhibit 2: Funding for projects Alpha and Beta

Project Alpha or Project Beta will each require the same amount of initial funding of Y$50,000,000.

Proceeds from the sale of a factory based in Europe in six months' time, for Euro (€)10,000,000, will provide part of the funding and the balance will be financed by debt borrowing.

Okan Co expects to hedge the €10,000,000 using either forward markets or money markets. The following information is available on these markets:

Exhibit 3: Information for hedging

Foreign exchange rates

	Y$/€1
Spot	2.5210–2.5862
Six months forward	2.5462–2.6121

Bank interest rates

	Investing	Borrowing
Yasailand	2.40%	5.00%
Eurozone	1.05%	2.20%

The balance of funding raised by domestic debt borrowing will be through a four-year subsidised loan on which interest is payable at 2.1%, although Okan Co's normal borrowing rate is 5%. Issue costs related to raising this finance will be 3% of the gross proceeds.

Exhibit 4: Project Alpha details

Project Alpha's base case NPV and APV in six months' time when the project will commence should be estimated using the following information.

The sales revenues and production costs related to Project Alpha in six months' time, before any annual price or cost increases, are estimated as follows:

Year	1	2	3	4
Sales revenue (Y$ 000s)	15,750	28,350	47,250	23,100
Production cost (Y$ 000s)	6,120	10,710	21,420	8,160

It is expected that the sales price will increase at an annual inflation rate of 10%. Domestic production costs are likely to increase at Yasailand's annual inflation rate.

In addition to the above, components will be imported from the UK (currency £), at the following current cost:

Year	1	2	3	4
Component costs (£ 000s)	1,200	1,800	3,700	1,400

The costs of components from the UK are fixed and not subject to inflation.

The funds of Y$50,000,000 for Project Alpha will be used to purchase plant and equipment needed for manufacturing purposes. Tax allowable depreciation is available on the value of the plant and equipment at 25% per year on a reducing balance basis, with a balancing allowance or

charge applicable at the end of the project. The plant and equipment is expected to be sold for Y$10,000,000 (post-inflation) at the end of the project.

At the start of every year, Project Alpha will require working capital. In the first year this will be 10% of the estimated Year 1 sales revenue. In subsequent years, the project will require an increase or a reduction in working capital of 15% for every $1 increase or decrease in sales revenue respectively. The working capital is expected to be fully released when Project Alpha ceases.

The expected spot exchange rate between the Y$ and the £, in six months' time, is expected to be Y$3.03 per £1. The annual inflation rates are currently 2% in the UK and 4% in Yasailand. It can be assumed that these inflation rates will not change for the foreseeable future.

The cost of capital for appraising the base case net present value of Project Alpha is 10%. Okan Co pays tax at an annual rate of 20%. Tax is payable in the same year as the profits it is based on. Okan Co makes sufficient profits from its other activities to take advantage of any tax loss relief.

Exhibit 5: Project Beta details

Given below are Project Beta's base case present values, based on the project start date in six months' time, discounted at the project's relevant risk-adjusted all-equity financed discount rate:

Year	1	2	3	4
Present values (Y$ 000s)	8,450	19,360	22,340	4,950

It can be assumed that any working capital requirements for Project Beta are included in the annual cash flows.

Project Beta's duration has been calculated as 2.43 years, based on its base case present values.

Exhibit 6: Economic risk and risk categories

One of Okan Co's subsidiary companies in Yasailand, which produces and sells all its products domestically, has still found that it is exposed to economic risk (economic exposure). The directors of the subsidiary believe that this is because Yasailand's government has maintained comparatively higher interest rates, even though the inflation in Yasailand is now under control.

Okan Co categorises the risks inherent in its projects according to the severity of their impact and the frequency of their occurrence, as follows: (i) severe and frequent; (ii) not severe but frequent; (iii) severe but not frequent; and (iv) neither severe nor frequent.

53 Westparley (Mar/Jun 2020, amended)   (98 mins)

(a) Discuss the behavioural factors which may have led to businesses such as Matravers Tech being valued highly. **(5 marks)**

(b) Prepare a report for the board of directors of Westparley Co which:

(i) Compares the additional value which Westparley Co believes can be generated from the sale of Matravers Tech based on the P/E ratio, with that of the projected present value of its future free cash flows; **(4 marks)**

(ii) Calculates the weighted average cost of capital for the combined company; **(5 marks)**

(iii) Estimates the total value which Westparley Co's shareholders will gain from the acquisition of Matravers Co; and **(10 marks)**

(iv) Assesses the strategic and financial value to Westparley Co of the acquisition, including a discussion of the estimations and assumptions made. **(11 marks)**

(c) Briefly discuss the factors which may determine how the offer for Matravers Co will be financed. **(5 marks)**

Professional marks will be awarded for the demonstration of skill in communication, analysis and evaluation, scepticism and commercial acumen in your answer. **(10 marks)**

(Total = 50 marks)

Exhibit 1: Westparley Co

Westparley Co is a listed retailer, mainly selling food and small household goods. It has outperformed its competitors over the last few years as a result of providing high quality products at reasonable prices, and also having a stronger presence online. It has kept a control on costs, partly by avoiding operating large stores on expensive city centre sites. Instead, it has had smaller stores on the edge of cities and towns, and a limited number of larger stores on convenient out-of-town sites, aiming at customers who want their journeys to shops to be quick. One of its advertising slogans has been: 'We are where you want us to be.'

Westparley Co's share price has recently performed better than most companies in the retail sector generally. Share prices in the retail sector have been relatively low as a result of poor results due to high competition, large fixed cost base and high interest rates. The exception has been shares in retailers specialising in computer and high-technology goods. These shares appear to have benefited from a boom generally in share prices of high-technology companies. Some analysts believe share prices of many companies in the high-technology sector are significantly higher than a rational analysis of their future prospects would indicate.

Exhibit 2: Matravers Co

Westparley Co has identified the listed retailer Matravers Co as an acquisition target, because it believes that Matravers Co's shares are currently undervalued and part of Matravers Co's operations would be a good strategic fit for Westparley Co.

Matravers Co operates two types of store:

Matravers Home mainly sells larger household items and home furnishings. These types of retailer have performed particularly badly recently and one major competitor of Matravers Home has just gone out of business. Matravers Home operates a number of city centre sites but has a much higher proportion of out-of-town sites than its competitors.

Matravers Tech sells computers and mobile phones in much smaller outlets than those of Matravers Home.

Extracts from Matravers Co's latest annual report are given below:

	$m
Pre-tax profit	1,950
Long-term loan	6,500
Share capital ($1 shares)	5,000

The share of pre-tax profit between Matravers Home and Matravers Tech was 80:20.

The current market value of Matravers Co's shares is $12,500m and its debt is currently trading at its book value. Westparley Co believes that it will have to pay a premium of 15% to Matravers Co's shareholders to buy the company.

Westparley Co intends to take advantage of the current values attributed to businesses such as Matravers Tech by selling this part of Matravers Co at the relevant sector price earnings ratio of 18, rather than a forecast estimate of Matravers Tech's present value of future free cash flows of $4,500m.

The company tax rate for both companies is 28% per year.

Exhibit 3: Post-acquisition cost of capital

The post-acquisition cost of capital of the combined company will be based on its cost of equity and cost of debt. The asset beta post-acquisition can be assumed to be both companies' asset betas weighted in proportion to their current market value of equity.

BPP

Westparley Co has 4,000 million $1 shares in issue, currently trading at $8.50 giving a market value of $34,000m. It has $26,000m debt in issue, currently trading at $105 per $100 nominal value giving a market value of $27,300m. Its equity beta is 1.02.

Matravers Co's asset beta is 0.75. The current market value of Matravers Co's shares is $12,500m and its long-term loan is currently trading at its book value of $6,500m.

The risk-free rate of return is estimated to be 3.5% and the market risk premium is estimated to be 8%.

The pre-tax cost of debt of the combined company is expected to be 9.8%. It can be assumed that the debt:equity ratio of the combined company will be the same as Westparley Co's current debt:equity ratio in market values.

The company tax rate for both companies is 28% per year.

Exhibit 4: Plans for Matravers Co

The offer for Matravers Co will be a cash offer. Any funding required for this offer will be a mixture of debt and equity. Although for the purposes of the calculation it has been assumed that the overall mix of debt and equity will remain the same, the directors are considering various plans for funding the purchase which could result in a change in Westparley Co's gearing.

As soon as it acquires all of Matravers Co's share capital, Westparley Co would sell Matravers Tech as it does not fit in with Westparley Co's strategic plans and Westparley Co wishes to take advantage of the large values currently attributed to high-technology businesses. Westparley Co would then close Matravers Home's worst-performing city centre stores. It anticipates the loss of returns from these stores would be partly compensated by higher online sales by Matravers Co, generated by increased investment in its online operations. The remaining city centre stores and all out-of-town stores would start selling the food and household items currently sold in Westparley Co's stores, and Westparley Co believes that this would increase profits from those stores.

Westparley Co also feels that reorganising Matravers Co's administrative functions and using increased power as a larger retailer can lead to synergies after the acquisition.

Exhibit 5: Post-acquisition details

Once Matravers Tech has been sold, Westparley Co estimates that sales revenue from the Matravers Home stores which remain open, together with the online sales from its home business, will be $43,260m in the first year post-acquisition, and this figure is expected to grow by 3% per year in years 2 to 4.

The profit margin before interest and tax is expected to be 6% of sales revenue in years 1 to 4.

Tax allowable depreciation is assumed to be equivalent to the amount of investment needed to maintain existing operations. However, an investment in assets (including working capital) will be required of $630m in year 1. In years 2 to 4, investment in assets each year will be $0.50 of every $1 increase in sales revenue.

After four years, the annual growth rate of free cash flows is expected to be 2% for the foreseeable future.

As well as the free cash flows from Matravers Co, Westparley Co expects that post-tax synergies will arise from its planned reorganisation of Matravers Co as follows in the next three years:

Year	1	2	3
	$m	$m	$m
Free cash flows	700	750	780

The current market value of Matravers Co's shares is $12,500m and its debt is currently trading at its book value of $6,500m.

54 Chakula (Mar/Jun 2021, amended) (98 mins)

The following **exhibits** provide information relevant to the question.

(1) Introduction – about Chakula Co, the demerger of Kawa Co and Lahla Co a prospective buyer of Kawa Co

(2) Areas for further clarification – requested by Lahla Co

(3) Capital structure details – for all companies

(4) Kawa Co as a demerged company

(5) Acquisition of Kawa Co by Lahla Co

This information should be used to answer the question **requirements** within your chosen **response option(s)**.

Required

(a) Explain why a regulatory framework related to mergers and acquisitions is necessary to protect the interests of shareholders and other stakeholders. **(5 marks)**

(b) Discuss the two theoretical propositions, as raised by Lahla Co's board of directors (BoD), in relation to a company's capital structure. **(6 marks)**

(c) Prepare a report for the BoD of Lahla Co which:

  (i) Estimates the value of each Kawa Co share if it is demerged and listed as an independent company; **(8 marks)**

  (ii) Estimates:

   • the additional equity value created when combining Lahla Co and Kawa Co;

   • the percentage gain to each of Lahla Co's and Kawa Co's shareholder group under each payment method;

   • the impact on Lahla Co's capital structure under each payment method; and

   (12 marks)

  (iii) Evaluates the financial and other factors that both Lahla Co's shareholders and Kawa Co's shareholders would consider prior to agreeing to the acquisition, and the impact on Lahla Co's capital structure under each payment method. **(9 marks)**

Professional marks will be awarded for the demonstration of skill in communication, analysis and evaluation, scepticism and commercial acumen in your answer. **(10 marks)**

(Total = 50 marks)

Exhibit 1: Introduction

Chakula Co is a large, listed company involved in two business sectors. Its main business is in the production of food and drink for supermarkets and other large traders. It also owns a chain of coffee shops nationwide. Chakula Co's board of directors (BoD) thinks that the company is undervalued and is of the opinion that it should focus on the rapid innovation taking place in the food and drink production sector.

Therefore, Chakula Co's BoD has decided to unbundle the coffee shops' business into a company called Kawa Co. Chakula Co will then either demerge Kawa Co through a spin-off or sell Kawa Co. Chakula Co will then turn its full focus on its remaining business of food and drink production. Initially, Chakula Co's shareholders will own Kawa Co on the basis of owning one Kawa Co share for every Chakula Co share owned by them.

Lahla Co is a large unlisted company controlled by 20 shareholders who all have a significant stake in the business. Lahla Co owns a number of hotels around the country and is looking to diversify into the coffee retail business. Lahla Co has approached Chakula Co about the possibility of purchasing Kawa Co. Lahla Co will finance the purchase either through a cash-only offer or a share-for-share offer.

 BPP

If Kawa Co is demerged, it will be listed on the stock exchange as an independent company. Chakula Co is unsure whether to sell Kawa Co to Lahla Co or to demerge it into an independent company.

Exhibit 2: Areas for further clarification

Further clarification has been sought by Lahla Co's BoD on the following two areas:

(1) Lahla Co's chief executive officer (CEO) has determined that a regulatory framework in the area of mergers and acquisitions is designed to protect the interests of shareholders and other stakeholders. She wants to find out why there is a need for a regulatory framework.

(2) The acquisition of Kawa Co will be a major investment for Lahla Co and its BoD has concerns about how the acquisition will be financed. The BoD has heard that there are several theories explaining the capital structure of a company, including the following two propositions:

- A company should maximise its debt financing; and

- Too much debt can be harmful to a company and there needs to be a balance between equity and debt financing.

Exhibit 3: Capital structure details

Extracts from Chakula Co's financial statements are as follows:

	$m
Assets less current liabilities	5,010
Financed by:	
Share capital (nominal value $0.50 per share)	1,000
Reserves	1,180
Non-current liabilities: Loan notes A (nominal value $100 per loan note)	2,470
Non-current liabilities: Loan notes B (nominal value $100 per loan note)	360

Chakula Co's shares are trading at $2.45 each. The estimated equity value of Kawa Co is $1,200m.

Chakula Co's loan notes A currently have a total market value of $2,100m. Loan notes B currently have a total market value of $400m. After the unbundling, loan notes B will be serviced by Kawa Co and loan notes A will remain with Chakula Co, with the post-tax cost of debt for loan notes B expected to be 3.52%. It is expected that Kawa Co will maintain its capital structure after the unbundling.

Lahla Co's debt to equity ratio is estimated to be 40:60 in equivalent market value terms and it has 1,200 million shares in issue.

The cost of equity for Kawa Co is estimated to be 13.51%.

All companies pay corporation tax at a rate of 20% per year and tax is payable in the same year as the profits it is based on.

Exhibit 4: Kawa Co as a demerged company

The following estimated information will be applicable to Kawa Co if it is demerged.

Chakula Co's sales revenue is $4,500m currently, of which 20% is attributable to Kawa Co. It is estimated that after Kawa Co is demerged, its annual sales revenue growth rate will be 6% and the profit margin before interest and tax will be 21% of sales revenue, for each of the next four years. It can be assumed that the current tax allowable depreciation will remain equivalent to the amount of investment needed to maintain the current level of operations, but that Kawa Co will require an additional investment in assets of $0.25 for every $1 increase in sales revenue.

After the initial four years, the annual growth rate of the company's free cash flows is expected to be 2.5% for the foreseeable future.

Exhibit 5: Acquisition of Kawa Co by Lahla Co

The following estimated information applies to the acquisition of Kawa Co by Lahla Co, if Kawa Co is acquired.

The average price to earnings (PE) ratio for the hotel industry is 15:61, however, Lahla Co's PE ratio is estimated to be 10% lower than this.

Extracts from the current statements of profit or loss applicable to Lahla Co and Kawa Co are as follows:

	Lahla Co	Kawa Co
	$m	$m
Profit before interest and tax	305.0	161.2
Interest	(91.2)	(14.8)
Tax 20%	(42.8)	(29.3)
Profit after tax	171.0	117.1

After the acquisition, it is expected that the PE ratio of the combined company will be the midpoint between the two individual companies' PE ratios. The annual after-tax profits will increase by $62m due to combining the two companies.

Lahla Co has proposed to pay for acquiring Kawa Co either through a cash offer of $0.66 for a Kawa Co share, or one Lahla Co share for every three Kawa Co shares. Lahla Co will borrow the money needed to pay for the acquisition.

55 Zhichi (Sep/Dec 2021, amended)   (98 mins)

The following **exhibits** provide information relevant to the question:

(1)   Zhichi Co policy failures

(2)   New project discount rate

(3)   New project cash flows

(4)   Financing the new project

(5)   Future project funding

This information should be used to answer the question **requirements** within your chosen **response option(s)**.

Required

(a)   Discuss and justify the actions Zhichi Co should take to address the two financial strategy policy failures.   **(6 marks)**

(b)   Prepare a report for the board of directors (BoD) of Zhichi Co which:

   (i)   Estimates an appropriate discount rate to use to determine the net present value of the new project based on all-equity finance;   **(6 marks)**

   (ii)   Estimates the net present value of the new project, assuming that it is all-equity financed;   **(9 marks)**

   (iii)   Estimates the adjusted present value of the new project;   **(7 marks)**

   (iv)   Evaluates whether the new project should be undertaken, and:

   •   discusses the assumptions made in the estimates above;

   •   discusses whether the adjusted present value method would be more appropriate than the conventional net present value method to evaluate the new project.

                                                                                                                    (8 marks)

 BPP

(c) Compare and contrast whether Zhichi Co should raise future funding through new debt finance or through asset securitisation. **(4 marks)**

Professional marks will be awarded for the demonstration of skill in communication, analysis and evaluation, scepticism and commercial acumen in your answer. **(10 marks)**

(Total = 50 marks)

Exhibit 1: Zhichi Co policy failures

Zhichi Co is a large, listed engineering company involved in the development and manufacture of environmentally friendly products for businesses worldwide. Until a few years ago, the value of its shares had been increasing steadily and it regularly outperformed its main rivals. However, more recently its shares have been underperforming and many financial analysts are recommending that Zhichi Co shares should be sold. Zhichi Co's investors are becoming increasingly concerned.

The analysis concluded that this underperformance was due to two policy failures in the company's financial strategy, as follows:

- Zhichi Co has used a fixed discount rate of 10% to assess all investment projects for some years now. None of the company's senior management can remember why this rate was chosen; and

- Zhichi Co has continually funded new investment projects using equity finance and the analysis concluded that this financing strategy sent the wrong signals to investors.

Exhibit 2: New project discount rate

Zhichi Co is considering a new project to manufacture environmentally friendly motor scooters which are fully carbon neutral. This is a diversification into a new business area for Zhichi Co in which it has no previous experience. Zhichi Co's chief financial officer is of the opinion that Zhichi Co should determine an appropriate discount rate for the project based on an initial assumption that the project will be all-equity financed.

Liyu Co would be a competitor to Zhichi Co as it manufactures environmentally friendly motor scooters, as well as equipment for wind farms. Approximately 60% of Liyu Co's business is manufacturing motor scooters and the remaining 40% is manufacturing wind farm equipment.

Given below is the most recent financial information relating to Liyu Co.

Share capital ($0.25 nominal value)	$20,000,000
Reserves	$27,436,000
Market value of equity	$172,000,000
Market value of debt	$48,260,000
Equity beta	1.20

Sanwenyu Co is involved in the manufacture of equipment for wind farms. It has estimated its cost of equity as 15.4%, and it is financed 20% by debt and 80% by equity in market value terms.

The estimated risk-free rate is 4.8% and the market risk premium is 8%. The corporation tax rate applicable to all the companies is 20%.

Exhibit 3: New project cash flows

Zhichi Co expects the new project manufacturing environmentally friendly motor scooters to last for four years. The project will require an immediate expenditure of $70m for plant and machinery. After the project ends in four years' time, it is anticipated that the project will be sold for $42m, inclusive of any inflationary increase.

The following estimates of revenues and costs, relating directly to the project, have been made:

- In the first year, sales revenue is expected to be $10m and then increase to $40m in year two. In the final two years of the project, sales revenue will grow by 20% each year.

- Costs are estimated at 120% of sales revenue for the first year and 80% of sales revenue for the second year before reducing to 40% of sales revenue for each of the final two years.

Substantial initial working capital of $10m will be required at the start of year one of the project. Subsequently, working capital of 15% of sales revenue for that year will be required at the start of years two to four. Any remaining working capital will be released at the end of the project.

Zhichi Co pays corporation tax of 20% every year. Tax is payable with a year's time delay and any tax losses from the project are set against the company's profits from other projects. Tax allowable depreciation is available on the expenditure on the plant and machinery for the project at an annual rate of 15% on a reducing balance basis. It is anticipated that the plant and machinery will have a realisable value of $20m at the end of the project, and this realisable value is included in the project's estimated sale price of $42m.

Exhibit 4: Financing the new project

Due to the positive environmental nature of the new project, Zhichi Co can obtain the entire funding for the project through a loan at a subsidised interest rate of 180 basis points lower than the estimated risk-free rate of 4.8%. Zhichi Co's normal borrowing rate is 6%. Zhichi Co has decided that the project should be entirely funded through the subsidised loan.

Issue costs, which need to be paid, are anticipated to be 3% of the gross finance. Issue costs are not allowable as a tax-deductible expense.

Given that the new project is to be funded by the subsidised loan, Zhichi Co's chief financial officer is of the opinion that the adjusted present value of the project would be more appropriate than the conventional net present value, based on a risk-adjusted cost of capital, to evaluate the project. However, he cannot explain why this should be the case.

Exhibit 5: Future project funding

Zhichi Co's board of directors (BoD) is considering whether to raise funds for forthcoming projects either through new debt finance or through asset securitisation.

In addition to its manufacturing business, Zhichi Co receives rental income on some of its factory premises and its plant and machinery which it hires to other companies. The BoD is of the opinion that it should securitise this rental income.

56 Prysor Co (March / June 2022)   (98 mins)

The following exhibits provide information relevant to the question:

(1) Prysor Co's investment in Elan

(2) Investment appraisal details

(3) Campaign For Fair Production

This information should be used to answer the question requirements within your chosen response option(s).

Required

(a) Explain the role of the World Trade Organisation and assess the implications for Prysor Co of the free trade agreement between Elan and Marteg in the context of the World Trade Organisation's requirements.   **(4 marks)**

(b) Prepare a report for the board of directors of Prysor Co which:

(i)   Evaluates the financial acceptability of the investment in Elan;   **(14 marks)**

(ii) Discusses the assumptions made with respect to the calculations in (b)(i) above;

                    (4 marks)

(iii) Calculates:

- The investment's duration; **(2 marks)**

- The % change in initial selling price required for the investment to have a zero net present value, based on sales revenue; **(6 marks)**

(8 marks)

(iv) Discusses the significance of, and concerns with, the calculations in (b)(iii) above; **(5 marks)**

(c) Discuss the factors that may determine the extent to which Prysor Co adopts the Campaign for Fair Production's charter in developing its framework for investment policy. **(5 marks)**

Professional marks will be awarded for the demonstration of skill in communication, analysis and evaluation, scepticism and commercial acumen in your answer. **(10 marks)**

(Total = 50 marks)

Exhibit 1: Prysor Co's investment in Elan

Prysor Co is a multinational company, based in the country of Marteg (currency M$). Prysor Co's board is considering establishing a subsidiary in the country of Elan (currency ED) to manufacture and sell a new model of mobile phone. Elan has free trade agreements in place with a number of countries, including Marteg and trades on World Trade Organisation terms with other countries.

Exhibit 2: Investment appraisal details

Prysor Co's board has specified a four-year time horizon for the investment in Elan, though the subsidiary may operate for longer. The board would also consider an offer for the subsidiary as a going concern.

Expected sales units and revenue of the phone are as follows:

Year	1	2	3	4
Sales units	50,000	65,000	83,000	90,000
Sales revenue (ED000)	8,000	10,920	14,641	16,670

These sales revenue figures have been calculated using the assumption that Prysor Co will charge a unit selling price of ED160 in year 1 and increase the unit selling price by 5% per year in years 2 to 4.

The new phone will require a component made in Marteg and charged at a transfer price of M$7 per unit in year 1. The transfer price will increase by the annual rate of inflation in Marteg each year in years 2 to 4. The parent company will achieve a pre-tax contribution of 35% on sales of the component to the subsidiary in Elan.

Investment in the new phone is likely to mean the loss of future sales of an existing phone. If the new product is manufactured, the pre-tax contribution lost from the sales of the existing phone would be expected to be M$400,000 in year 1, increasing by the annual rate of inflation in Marteg each year in years 2 to 4.

Other costs of the project are forecast to be as follows, after taking into account inflation:

Year	1	2	3	4
	ED000	ED000	ED000	ED000
Other costs	3,508	4,934	6,230	6,685

The immediate investment in non-current assets will be ED14,460,000. The realisable value of non-current assets at the end of year 4 is expected to be ED3,400,000, assuming that the subsidiary is not sold as a going concern and its assets are sold individually. Tax allowable depreciation is deductible from taxable profits in the first three years of the investment, as follows:

Year	1	2	3
	ED000	ED000	ED000
Tax allowable depreciation	3,615	2,711	2,033

A balancing allowance of ED2,701,000 can be assumed to be available at the end of year 4, on the basis of the forecast net realisable value of the assets.

Prysor Co will pay tax at an annual rate of 20% in Elan on its profits in that country. However, it will be exempt from any impact of taxation in Elan in the first two years of operating there. All post-tax cash flows will be remitted to Prysor Co in Marteg. Prysor Co pays tax on profits at an annual rate of 30% in Marteg. A bi-lateral tax treaty exists between Elan and Marteg. Under its terms, Prysor Co will be assumed to have paid tax at an annual rate of 20% in Elan in all four years. Tax in both countries is payable in the year in which the tax liability arises.

Prysor Co is of the opinion that it has sufficient working capital and that no further working capital will be needed for the project.

Predicted inflation rates in the two countries are as follows:

Year	1	2	3	4
Elan	6%	4%	3%	3%
Marteg	10%	9%	8%	7%

The current exchange rate is ED2.6000 = M$1. Using purchasing power parity theory, the following exchange rates have been forecast:

Year	1	2	3	4
ED/M$1	2.5055	2.3906	2.2799	2.1947

A discount rate of 14% should be used to assess the investment.

Sensitivity analysis and duration

Prysor Co's directors are particularly concerned with the sensitivity of the results of the investment appraisal if the initial selling price has to be lower to establish the phone in its market. The directors are also wondering how long it will take for the investment to contribute value. Prysor Co's finance director has suggested that this should be measured by the investment's duration.

Exhibit 3: Campaign For Fair Production

Recent improvement in Elan's economic position has been partly due to investment from foreign companies. The Campaign For Fair Production (CFFP), a global lobbying organisation seeking better treatment of workers and local communities, has claimed that foreign companies currently investing in Elan have adopted a number of unethical practices there.

The CFFP has called for all foreign investors in Elan to go beyond their legal responsibilities there and adopt the CFFP's charter. The charter includes requirements to increase wages steadily, provide appropriate education for employees, keep the adverse impacts on the local environment to a minimum and prohibit the use of child labour. The charter also requires companies to disclose how they are meeting its requirements. The CFFP is likely to call for boycotts of companies which fail to agree to its charter and continue to follow unethical practices in Elan.

Prysor Co's board will consider whether to agree to the CFFP's charter as part of its appraisal of investing in Elan. As Prysor Co may also invest in production facilities in other countries in the longer term, the board will consider whether the charter ought to be part of the framework for developing the company's future investment policies.

 BPP

Prysor Co has a good reputation and produces a published statement of corporate responsibility. Prysor Co is keen to maintain its reputation.

57 Para Fuels (September 2022)   (98 mins)

The following exhibits provide information relevant to the question:

(1)   Para Fuels Co, production facility replacement

(2)   Traditional technology: Investment A

(3)   New technology: Investment B

(4)   Comments made at the BoD meeting

This information should be used to answer the question requirements within your chosen response option(s).

Required

(a)   Explain why Para Fuels Co might include the value of the potential offer from Kero Innovations Co, when considering Investment B.   **(4 marks)**

(b)   Prepare a report for the Board of Directors (BoD) of Para Fuels Co which:

   (i)   Calculates the estimated net present value of Investment A (traditional technology)
                                                                                  (9 marks)

   (ii)   Calculates:

   • The estimated net present value of Investment B (new technology) before taking account of the potential offer from Kero Innovations Co; and

   • the estimated net present value of Investment B (new technology) after taking account of the potential offer from Kero Innovations Co
                                                                                  (9 marks)

   (iii) Based on financial grounds, recommends whether Investment A or Investment B should be undertaken and discusses the assumptions made in the calculations. This should be done prior to discussing the comments made at the BoD meeting.   **(7 marks)**

   (iv)   Discusses the comments made at the BoD meeting and suggests how Para Fuels Co may wish to proceed if the new technology is adopted.   **(11 marks)**

Professional marks will be awarded for the demonstration of skill in communication, analysis and evaluation, scepticism and commercial acumen in your answer.   **(10 marks)**

                                                                        (Total = 50 marks)

Exhibit 1: Para Fuels Co

Para Fuels Co produces paraffin from crude oil, which is refined for use as jet fuel. For many years, Para Fuels was a private company but it listed three years ago and now has a wide range of diverse shareholders, including institutional investors.

Para Fuels Co has a number of production facilities and one of these is coming to the end of its productive life. Para Fuels Co's board of directors (BoD) is considering two alternatives. The first one is replacing this production facility with a new one, which will be modern and largely environmentally friendly. This facility will continue to produce paraffin from crude oil and is based on traditional technology.

The second alternative is based on converting household waste into paraffin, using new technology which has the potential to dramatically reduce environmental damage caused by air traffic. The BoD thinks it may be beneficial to convert the production facility based on this new alternative instead. There is a lot of uncertainty surrounding this investment. A competitor, Kero Innovations Co, has suggested that it may purchase the new alternative production facility at the end of the first three years of the investment.

Details of the production based on both the traditional technology (Investment A) and the new alternative technology (Investment B) are given in the following exhibits. It is anticipated that both Investment A and Investment B will have a useful life of 25 years. Para Fuels Co's cost of capital has been estimated at 12%.

Exhibit 2: Traditional technology: Investment A

The following information relates to investment A where Para Fuels Co continues to produce paraffin from crude oil, using traditional technology.

The initial investment in the production facility will be $14m. Tax allowable depreciation is available on the production facility at an annual rate of 25% reducing balance in years 1 to 3. At the end of year 4, any remaining written down value can be written off as a balancing adjustment. As with production facilities of this nature, there will be no residual value after the 25-year project life because of substantial decommissioning costs.

Sales revenue in year 1 is expected to be $12.75m and this is expected to increase by 5% per year in each of the years 2 to 4.

Production costs are expected to be $5.25m in year 1. The pre-inflation amounts for years 2 to 4 are given below, as are the annual inflationary rates for production costs in each of years 2 to 4:

Year	2	3	4
Pre-inflation amount	$6.20m	$7.10m	$8.00m
Annual inflationary rate	6%	7%	8%

It is anticipated that working capital of 10% of sales revenue will be needed in years 1 to 4, at the start of each year, and that no additional working capital will be needed in years 5 to 25. At the end of 25 years, it is expected that the working capital will be required for the decommissioning costs and will not be released.

Para Fuels Co pays tax at a rate of 20% on profits in the year in which the tax liability occurs. Tax on losses is refunded in the year in which the loss occurs.

An estimate has been made of the discounted value of post-tax cash flows for years 5 to 25. This totals $5.40m at the start of year 5.

Exhibit 3: New technology: Investment B

Currently, the new technology used to convert household waste into paraffin is expensive to set up and run, although set-up and running costs are expected to reduce once this technology becomes established. The initial set-up costs for the Investment B production facility using the new technology are estimated to be $34.6m.

Due to high costs and lower revenues initially, the after-tax free cash flows generated by this investment are expected to be $1.4m in year 1. These are expected to increase by 40% in each of years 2 and 3. In year 4, when costs reduce and revenues increase, the after-tax free cash flows are expected to be twice as much as the year 3 amount.

Due to a high level of uncertainty with Investment B, it is expected that the annual after-tax free cash flows from years 5 to 25 will remain the same as year 4. It is possible that this is an underestimate and, in the future, more realistic amounts can be determined. The annuity factor for the 12% cost of capital and based on a useful life of 25 years is 7.843.

Kero Innovations Co has suggested it may offer to purchase Investment B, at the start of year 4 for $27m. Due to the uncertainties surrounding this investment, the cash flows are expected to vary by a standard deviation of as much as 40%. The risk-free rate of return is estimated to be 5%.

Exhibit 4: Comments made at the BoD meeting

Para Fuels Co's BoD met to discuss adopting the new technology, for its production facility replacement, based on converting household waste into paraffin. The following comments were made at the meeting:

- The company's chief executive officer (CEO) gave an enthusiastic talk about the need for Para Fuels Co to fulfil its environmental, social and governance (ESG) responsibilities. The chief marketing officer (CMO) pointed out that it is likely that airlines around the world will face increasing pressure on their ESG agendas and, in particular, how they are helping to protect the environment. However, the CMO also said that airlines will need to ensure that this type of jet fuel is safe to use.

- The chief financial officer (CFO) was more cautious. She pointed to the fact that there is no binding contract with Kero Innovations Co. She also said that while Para Fuel Co's shareholders would be supportive of the company pursuing an environmental agenda, the majority of shareholders will be concerned if that led to a significant negative impact on the corporate value. The CFO reminded the BoD that although only one production facility needs to be replaced very soon, more will need to be replaced after two years.

- Nevertheless, the CFO suggested that if this new technology becomes established and produces jet fuel which is safe to use, Para Fuels Co will get the benefit of being one of the first companies to adopt the new technology for the production facility. This could be advantageous in terms of cost reduction and revenue maximisation.

58 Fondir (December 2022)   (98 mins)

The following **exhibits** provide information relevant to the question:

(1) Fondir Co, risk management – includes details on communication

(2) Receipt from Lothil

(3) Short-term investment

This information should be used to answer the question **requirements** within your chosen **response option(s)**.

Required

(a) Explain the exposure Fondir Co faces with respect to the falling sales revenue from Italy and suggest how this exposure could be managed.   **(6 marks)**

(b) Prepare a report for the Board of Directors (BoD) of Fondir Co which:

   Required

   (i) Calculates the amounts receivable in $ from Lothil in four months' time, using the over-the-counter (OTC) forward rate and the OTC option;   **(7 marks)**

   (ii) Calculates the interest return in $ of the cash flows from Lothil when futures contracts are used to hedge the interest rate fluctuations of 0.5%. Calculations should include the number of futures contracts needed and the gain or loss in the futures market in $;   **(9 marks)**

   (iii) Comments on the results obtained in (b)(i) and (ii), and addresses the queries raised by the BoD with respect to alternative methods to hedge the receipt and the margin requirements;   **(9 marks)**

   (iv) Discusses if it would be beneficial for Fondir Co to manage its financial risks, and whether or not the company should communicate its risk management approach to its stakeholders.   **(9 marks)**

Professional marks will be awarded for the demonstration of skill in communication, analysis and evaluation, scepticism and commercial acumen in your answer.   **(10 marks)**

(Total = 50 marks)

Exhibit 1: Fondir Co, risk management – includes details on communication

Fondir Co, based in the USA (currency $), is involved in the production and sale of high-quality foods under its popular brand called 'Delibeli'. Initially, its products were mainly aimed at the USA

market, but increasingly the products are sold internationally to North and South America and to Europe. This rapid growth has meant that Fondir Co is expanding its production facilities and receiving its revenues in a variety of currencies.

Fondir Co has developed robust systems to manage its operational risks, but so far it has not managed its financial risk from currency and interest rate fluctuations. Fondir Co's board of directors (BoD), on the whole, is supportive of the opinion that the company's financial risks should be managed using derivative products, and the company's approach to risk management should be communicated to its main stakeholder groups including shareholders, managers, lenders and employees.

Fondir Co's marketing director questioned whether these and other financial risks should be managed at all. He suggested that the costs of managing such risks would outweigh the benefits derived from the management of these risks, and therefore would be disadvantageous for the company.

Fondir Co's finance director (FD) argued that although many risks can be managed using derivatives, some risks were harder to manage. She gave the Italian market as an example, where direct competitors from France and Germany have successfully penetrated the Italian market. As a result, Fondir Co has found that its sales revenue from the Italian market has been falling and the FD suggests that this is due to the weakening of the Euro (€) (the Italian currency) against the $. The FD is of the opinion that this relative weakening of the € is likely to continue for some time and cannot be managed through the use of derivative instruments.

Exhibit 2: Receipt from Lothil

Fondir Co sells its products to companies and customers based in Lothil, a country based in Europe, whose currency is the Lothil Lira (LL). It is expecting a receipt of LL357m in four months' time, on 1 May. Although there are no exchange-traded derivative products available for hedging the Lothil Lira, Fondir Co has access to two over-the-counter (OTC) derivative products.

The first is a four-month forward rate agreed today, based on the Lothil annual base rate of 6% plus 60 basis points and the USA annual base rate of 3.3% less 30 basis points. The spot exchange rate between Lothil and the USA is LL84.00/$1.

The second is an OTC $ call or put option with an exercise price of LL84.00. The premium for the call option is LL4.00 per $1 and for the put option it is LL3.00 per $1. The option premium is payable at the commencement of the option contract, and Fondir Co would borrow the money needed for the premium using its overdraft facility. The company pays interest on its overdraft at an annual rate of 5.4%.

The BoD wants to know how the currency exposure of this receipt can be managed using the two instruments above, and also whether it is possible to hedge this using alternative methods and not derivative instruments.

Exhibit 3: Short-term investment

Fondir Co will choose the more financially beneficial hedging instrument to hedge the cash receipt from Lothil. Once the cash has been received in four months' time, on 1 May and exchanged into $, it will be invested for a further five months before the cash is needed elsewhere. Fondir Co's BoD wants to know how interest rate futures can be used to hedge against an increase or decrease of 0.5% in the base rate. Fondir Co can invest funds on a short-term basis at the USA base rate (which is currently 3.3%) less 30 basis points.

The following information is provided for June futures:

The three-month $ futures contracts have a contract size of $500,000. The June futures contract price of 96.10 is quoted in terms of basis points at 100 − annual % yield.

In the calculations the following can be assumed:

- Settlement of the futures contracts is at the end of the month;
- Basis diminishes to zero at contract maturity, based on monthly time intervals;
- There is no basis risk;
- Margin requirements can be ignored.

 **BPP**

The BoD has heard that dealing with futures can be expensive because of margin requirements. They want to know what margins are and whether or not dealing with futures is expensive because of this.

BPP

Answers

1 Cadnam

Course Book references

Dividend policy is mainly covered in Chapters 1 and 16, other ratio analysis is covered in Chapter 2.

Top tips

Planning time at the question is crucial, the clues in the scenario help in the hardest part of the question (part (b)) because they implied the use of share price analysis and dividend analysis to analyse historic performance and performance relative to another company. Discussion points would then be based on this analysis, which broadly shows slowing profit growth (worse than rivals), far higher and rising dividend payouts, worsening affordability vs dividend capacity, falling share price growth and lower than rivals in the past two years.

Easy marks

In part (a) and the first part of part (b), the calculations should be easy as long as you show clear workings for your calculations.

ACCA examining team's comments

Discussion about ethical issues was generally unsatisfactory. Many candidates did not refer to the scenario that suggested low pay to workers in the company could be an ethical issue in the light of the government's enquiry into low pay. Few candidates discussed the questionable ethics behind the statement made by the directors that they were confident the dividend increase could be maintained despite knowing about uncertainty surrounding future income prospects.

Marking guide		Marks
(a) Interest	1	
Tax	1	
Investment in additional assets	2	
Depreciation	1	
Maximum		5
(b) Calculations		
Growth in PAT	1	
Growth in dividends	1	
Residual profit	2	
Growth in share price	1	
Calculations maximum 4 marks		
Discussion maximum 4 marks		
Dividends	3	
Share price	2	
Maximum		8
(c) Dividend policy statement	4	
Directors' remuneration	4	
Marks Available		8

 BPP

ANSWERS

Maximum	<u>7</u>

Professional skills

Analysis and Evaluation

- Appropriate use of the data to determine suitable calculations to understand each company's dividend policy

- Appropriate use of the data to support discussion and draw appropriate conclusions on Cadnam Co's dividend policy

- Demonstration of ability to consider relevant factors applicable to each company's situation

Commercial acumen

- Effective use of examples and/or practical considerations related to the context to illustrate points being made relating to the discussion of dividend policy and directors pay.

Scepticism

- Effective challenge and critical assessment of the information and assumptions provided in relation to dividend policy and remuneration policies.

- Effective challenge of evidence and assumptions supplied with respect to the analysts' views.

- Demonstration of ability to consider all relevant factors applicable to the decisions made.

Maximum	<u>5</u>
Total	<u>25</u>

(a) **Dividend capacity**

	$m
Operating profit	2,678
Less: Interest (8% × $10,250m)	(820)
Less: Taxation (30% × ($2,678m − $820m))	(557)
Less: Investment in additional assets (25% × 0.03 × $2,678m / (1.03 × 0.02))	
Calculated as 25% of the increase in sales revenue of $3,900m (see below):	
20X5 revenue = 20X5 profit ÷ 0.02 = [2,678 (20X6 profit) ÷ 1.03] ÷ 0.02 = 130,000	
20X6 revenue = 2,678 ÷ 0.02 = 133,900 ∴ increase in revenue = 3,900	(975)
Forecast dividend capacity	<u>326</u>

(b) **Growth in profit after tax**

	Geometric mean annual growth rate
	%
Cadnam	4.6
Holmsley	7.2

Geometric mean is the average compound growth over three years between 20X5 and 20X2 and is calculated as: [(value in 20X5 divided by 20X2 value) ^ (1/time period)] minus 1.

For example, Cadnam = [(1,580 / 1,380) ^ (1/3)] − 1 = 0.046 or 4.6%

Growth in dividends

	Geometric mean annual growth rate
	%
Cadnam	10.1
Holmsley	5.3

Geometric mean is the average compound growth over three years between 20X5 and 20X2. For example Cadnam = [(1,020/765)^(1/3)] – 1 = 0.101 or 10.1%

Residual profit (after tax-profit for the year – dividend – new investment)

	20X2	20X3	20X4	20X5
	$m	$m	$m	$m
Cadnam	333	338	41	(304)
Holmsley	330	375	419	486

Growth in share price

	Geometric mean annual growth rate
	%
Cadnam	5.6
Holmsley	5.6

Geometric mean is the average compound growth over three years between 20X5 and 20X2. For example Cadnam = [(5.75/4.88)^(1/3)] – 1 = 0.056 or 5.6%

Comments

Dividends

Both companies have shown fairly consistent increases over the last three years, with Cadnam Co's dividends increasing at around 10% each year, and Holmsley Co's dividends increasing at around 5% over the last three years. However, Holmsley Co's policy appears to be sustainable at present, whereas it is doubtful whether Cadnam Co's policy is sustainable.

Holmsley Co has managed to increase dividends, gradually also increasing investment in additional assets, profits and residual profits.

In order to maintain its rate of dividend increase, however, Cadnam Co has had to pay out an increasing proportion of earnings each year (as its profits are increasing at a slower rate than its dividends). In 20X5, Cadnam Co's residual profits became negative, and the dividend capacity calculation for 20X6 suggests that a much lower level of dividends would be appropriate.

Share price

The average increase for both companies over the last four years has been the same. However, the percentage increases over the last two years for Holmsley Co has been higher than for Cadnam Co. This suggests that the market has placed more significance on the higher percentage growth in Holmsley Co's after-tax profits than in Cadnam Co's higher percentage growth in dividends, maybe seeing this as an indication that Holmsley Co's strategy has been more successful and is more likely in future to deliver higher share price growth.

(c) **Dividend policy**

One possible question is whether the statement in the annual report fairly reflects the likely future dividend policy of Cadnam Co. The report gives the impression that the current dividend policy will be sustained, whereas the figures suggest that this may not be the case. If the policy proves not to be sustainable, it would suggest a failure either of integrity (if the

directors made a statement with a high risk that it would not be true) or due care (that they failed to take into account indicators which suggested their policy is not sustainable). The directors may be questioned by the auditors about whether this statement is true and fair.

There is also the question of balancing the interests of different stakeholders. To some degree, criticism of rises in dividend and director remuneration levels versus increases in employee salary levels could be said to be a matter of opinion.

However, the fact that there is a government enquiry into low pay in the sector suggests that pay levels are lower than society deems desirable. The force of the criticisms may be enhanced by the statements which Cadnam Co has made about developing an integrated reporting approach. Integrated reporting is not just about extra details in the annual report, but also reflects an underlying policy of carrying out business which includes responsiveness to the needs of different stakeholders.

The dividend capacity figures may also call into question whether Cadnam Co's board is taking excessive risks. Does paying out increasing dividends in future mean that the company is likely to have inadequate resources to sustain its business, and may be jeopardising the interests of lenders and employees as well as stakeholders? Certainly, there appear to be doubts about maintenance of future income levels with a number of contracts coming up for renewal and terms possibly being tightened by clients. Clients may be doubtful about renewing contracts if Cadnam Co's solvency appears doubtful.

Directors' remuneration

The directors' remuneration packages also raise concerns.

Comparison with Holmsley Co shows that salary, which is not dependent on performance, is a more significant element of the remuneration packages at Cadnam Co than Holmsley Co. Both companies have bonuses which depend to some degree on performance.

However, Cadnam Co's directors are also rewarded by loyalty bonuses, which again do not depend on performance but staying with the company. Holmsley Co has a share option scheme in place, which would seem to reward longer-term good performance, although it cannot be determined how significant a part of remuneration share options will be. Cadnam Co's remuneration scheme appears only to reward short-term profitability, possibly meaning that the directors may neglect the longer-term success and possibly even viability of the company.

2 Chithurst

Course Book references

Dividend policy is covered in Chapters 1 and 16. Valuing a firm using the dividend valuation model is covered in Chapter 8.

Top tips

In part (a), the key is to spend time analysing the actual policies being followed, not in righting generalised answers on the relevance or irrelevance of dividend policies in general. A similar question was set in June 2013.

Easy marks

Part (b) should have been easier because of the clear instructions as to the nature of the analysis that was required.

Marking guide		Marks
(a) Benefits of dividend policy – 1–2 marks for each company		5
Drawbacks of dividend policy – 2–3 marks for each company		6
Calculations – Dividend payout ratios – 1 mark per company		3

Other calculations	2
Marks Available	16
Maximum	14
(b) Comments on valuation of each company, max 2 marks per company	
(max 3 marks for valuation calculation(s))	6
Maximum	6

Professional skills

Analysis and Evaluation

- Appropriate use of the data to determine suitable calculations
- Appropriate use of the data to support discussion and draw appropriate conclusions
- Demonstration of reasoned judgement when considering key matters
- Demonstration of ability to consider relevant factors applicable to Chithurst Co's situation

Scepticism

- Effective challenge of information and assumptions supplied and, techniques carried out to support a valuation
- Demonstration of ability to consider all relevant factors applicable to the decisions made by Chithurst Co

Commercial acumen

- Effective use of examples and/or calculations from the scenario information and other practical considerations related to the context to illustrate points being made relating to dividend policy
- Recognition of external constraints and opportunities as necessary

Maximum	5
Total	25

(a) **Dividend payout ratio**

	Chithurst Co	Eartham Co	Iping Co
	%	%	%
20X2	42.9	40.0	46.7
20X3	41.3	(150.0)	19.3
20X4	35.1	40.0	33.1
20X5	34.0	40.0	31.8

Residual profit (after-tax profit for the year – dividend – new investment)

	Chithurst Co	Eartham Co	Iping Co
	$m	$m	$m
20X2	26	27	3
20X3	18	(40)	7
20X4	38	24	4
20X5	43	43	6

Chithurst Co's policy

Benefits

Chithurst Co's policy provides shareholders with a stable, predictable income each year. As profits have grown consistently, dividend cover has increased, which suggests that, for now, dividend levels are sustainable. These are positive signals to the stock market.

Drawbacks

Chithurst Co's dividend policy is unpopular with some of its shareholders. They have indicated a preference for dividend levels to bear a greater relation to profit levels. Although they are still in a minority and cannot force the directors to pay more dividends, they are now possibly a significant minority. Ultimately, Chithurst Co's share price could fall significantly if enough shareholders sell their shares because they dislike the dividend policy.

The dividend policy may also have been established to meet the financial needs of the shareholders when Chithurst Co was unquoted. However, it is now difficult to see how it fits into Chithurst Co's overall financial strategy. The greater proportion of funds retained does not appear to be linked to the levels of investment Chithurst Co is undertaking. Chithurst Co's shareholders may be concerned that best use is not being made of the funds available. If there are profitable investments which Chithurst Co could be making but is not doing so, then Chithurst Co may find it more difficult in future to sustain the levels of profit growth. Alternatively, if profitable investments do not exist, some shareholders may prefer to have funds returned in the form of a special dividend or share repurchase.

Eartham Co

Benefits

For three out of four years, Eartham Co has been paying out dividends at a stable payout ratio. This may be attractive to some investors, who have expectations that the company's profits will keep increasing in the longer term and wish to share directly in increases in profitability.

The year when Eartham Co's dividend payout ratio differed from the others was 20X3, when Eartham Co made a loss. A dividend of $15 million was paid in 20X3, which may be a guaranteed minimum. This limits the downside risk of the dividend payout policy to shareholders, as they know they will receive this minimum amount in such a year.

Drawbacks

Although shareholders are guaranteed a minimum dividend each year, dividends have been variable. Eartham Co's shareholders may prefer dividends to increase at a steady rate which is sustainable over time, even if this rate is lower than the rate of increase in some years under the current policy.

If Eartham Co had another poor year of trading like 20X3, shareholders' expectations that they will be paid a minimum dividend may mean that cash has to be earmarked to pay the minimum dividend, rather than for other, maybe better, uses in the business.

Having a 'normal' dividend policy results in expectations about what the level of dividend will be. Over time Eartham Co's managers may be reluctant to change to a lower payout ratio because they fear that this will give shareholders an adverse signal. Even if its directors maintain a constant ratio normally, shareholders may question whether the proportion of funds being retained is appropriate or whether a higher proportion could be paid out as dividends.

Eartham Co appears to be linking investment and dividend policy by its normal policy of allocating a constant proportion of funds for dividends and therefore a constant proportion of funds to invest. However, the actual level of new investments does not seem to bear much relation to the proportion of funds put aside for investment. When deciding on investments, the directors would also take into account the need to take advantage of opportunities as they arise and the overall amount of surplus funds built up over the years, together with the other sources of external finance available.

Iping Co

Benefits

Iping Co seems to have adopted a residual dividend policy, which links investment and dividend decisions. The strategy appears to be to make investments if they offer sufficient return to increase long-term company value and only pay dividends if there are no more profitable investments. They are assuming that internal funds are cheaper than external funds, or maybe Iping Co cannot raise the funds required from external sources.

The policy is likely to appeal to shareholders who are more concerned with capital growth than short-term income.

Drawbacks

Dividend payments are totally unpredictable, as they depend on the investment choices. Shareholders cannot rely on having any dividend income in a particular year.

Many shareholders may be prepared to sacrifice dividends for a while in order for funds to be available for investment for growth. However, at some point they may consider that Iping Co is well established enough to be able to maintain a consistent dividend policy as well as invest sufficiently for future growth.

(b) **Use of dividend valuation model**

Chithurst Co

Valuation = 33/0.11 = $300m

Chithurst Co's market capitalisation of $608 million is considerably in excess of the valuation suggested by the dividend valuation model. This may suggest that investors have some positive expectations about the growth of the company which is not picked up in the dividend growth model which assumes that dividend growth will continue to be zero.

However, the lower market capitalisation compared with the other two companies and the smaller increase in share price suggest that investors have higher expectations of long-term growth from Eartham Co and Iping Co.

Eartham Co

Three-year growth rate = $\sqrt[3]{(48/38)} - 1 = 8.1\%$

Valuation using three-year growth rate = 48 (1 + 0.081)/(0.14 − 0.081) = $879m

Eartham Co's market capitalisation is closer to the valuation suggested by the dividend growth model compared to Chithurst, probably because the dividend growth model is modelling some growth.

The higher market capitalisation, together with the recent increase in share price, suggests that Eartham Co's shareholders have an optimistic view of its ability to sustain growth and indicates confidence in the directors' strategy, including the investments they have made.

Iping Co

Three-year growth rate = $\sqrt[3]{(42/35)} - 1 = 6.3\%$

Valuation using three-year growth rate = 42 (1 + 0.063)/(0.12 − 0.063) = $783.3m

The larger increase in share price compared with the other two companies suggests that Iping Co's investors expect its investments to produce high long-term returns and hence are presumably satisfied with its dividend policy.

3 Chawan

Marking guide	Marks	
(a) Explanation of a dark pool network	3	
Explanation of why Chawan Co may want to use one	2	
Marks Available	5	
Maximum		4
(b) Investor ratios	4	
Other ratios	2	
Trends and other calculations	4	
Note. Maximum 5 marks if only ratio <u>calculations</u> provided		
Discussion of company performance over time	3	
Discussion of company performance against competitors	3	
Discussion of actual returns against expected returns	2	
Discussion of need to maintain portfolio and alternative investments	2	
Discussion of future trends and expectations	2	
Discussion of takeover rumour and action as a result	2	
Other relevant discussion/commentary	2	
Marks Available	26	
Maximum		16

Professional skills

Analysis and Evaluation

- Appropriate use of the data to determine suitable calculations to support the disposal decision
- Appropriate use of the data to support discussion and draw appropriate conclusions
- Appraisal of information objectively to make a commercial recommendation

Scepticism

- Effective challenge of information and assumptions supplied and, techniques carried out to support the disposal decision

Commercial acumen

- Effective use of examples and/or practical considerations related to the context to illustrate points being made relating to disposing of the shares.

Maximum   <u>5</u>

Total   <u><u>25</u></u>

(a) A dark pool network allows shares to be traded anonymously, away from public scrutiny. No information on the trade order is revealed prior to it taking place. The price and size of the order are only revealed once the trade has taken place. Two main reasons are given for dark pool networks: first they prevent the risk of other traders moving the share price up or down; and second they often result in reduced costs because trades normally take place at the mid-price between the bid and offer; and because broker-dealers try to use their own private pools, thereby saving exchange fees.

Chawan Co's holding in Oden Co is 27 million shares out of a total of 600 million shares, or 4.5%. If Chawan Co sold such a large holding all at once, the price of Oden Co shares may fall temporarily and significantly, and Chawan Co may not receive the value based on the current price. By utilising a dark pool network, Chawan Co may be able to keep the price of the share largely intact, and possibly save transaction costs.

Although the criticism against dark pool systems is that they prevent market efficiency by not revealing bid-offer prices before the trade, proponents argue that in fact market efficiency is maintained because a large sale of shares will not move the price down artificially and temporarily.

(b) **Ratio calculations**

Focus on investor ratios

Oden Co	20X2	20X3	20X4	20X5
Earnings per share		$0.27	$0.24	$0.12
Price to earnings ratio		9.3	10.0	18.3
Gearing ratio (debt/(debt + equity))		37.6%	36.9%	37.1%
Interest cover (operating profit/finance costs)		9.5	7.5	3.5
Dividend yield	7.1%	7.2%	8.3%	6.8%
Travel and leisure (T&L) sector				
Price to earnings ratio	11.9	12.2	13.0	13.8
Dividend yield	6.6%	6.6%	6.7%	6.4%

Other calculations

Oden Co sales revenue annual growth rate average between 20X3 and 20X5 =

$$\left(\frac{1,185}{1,342}\right)^{1/2} - 1 = -6.0\%$$

Between 20X4 and 20X5 = (1,185 − 1,335)/1,335 = −11.2%.

Share price changes	20X2–20X3	20X3–20X4	20X4–20X5
Oden Co	19.0%	–4.0%	–8.3%
T&L sector	15.8%	–2.3%	12.1%

Oden Co

Return to shareholders (RTS)	20X3	20X4	20X5
Dividend yield	7.2%	8.3%	6.8%
Share price gain	19.0%	–4.0%	–8.3%
Total	26.2%	4.3%	–1.5%

Average: 9.7%

Required return (based on capital asset pricing model (CAPM))	13.0%	13.6%	16.0%

Average: 14.2%

T&L sector (RTS)	20X3	20X4	20X5
Dividend yield	6.6%	6.7%	6.4%
Share price gain	15.8%	–2.3%	12.1%
Total shareholder return	22.4%	4.4%	18.5%

Average: 15.1%

Required return (based on CAPM)	12.4%	13.0%	13.6%

Average: 13.0%

Tutorial note. Dividend yield, when calculated as part of total shareholder return, is normally calculated as current dividend ÷ **closing** share price of the **previous** year. This is not the case in the calculations shown here because the closing share price is not given (the share price given is the average share price for the year) but a calculation based on the previous year share price would be acceptable in the exam.

Discussion

The following discussion compares the performance of Oden Co over time to the T&L sector and against expectations, in terms of it being a sound investment. It also considers the wider aspects which Chawan Co should take account of and the further information which the company should consider before coming to a final decision.

In terms of Oden Co's performance between 20X3 and 20X5, it is clear from the calculations above that the company is experiencing considerable financial difficulties. Profit margins have fallen and so has the earnings per share (EPS). While the amount of gearing appears fairly stable, the interest cover has deteriorated. The reason for this is that borrowing costs have increased at the same time as operating profit is declining. The share price has decreased over the three years as well and in the last year so has the dividend yield. This would indicate that the company is unable to maintain adequate returns for its investors (please also see below).

Although Oden Co has tried to maintain a dividend yield which is higher than the sector average, its price/earnings (P/E) ratio has been lower than the sector average between 20X3 and 20X4. It does increase significantly in 20X5, but this is because of the large fall in the EPS, rather than an increase in the share price. This could be an indication that there is less confidence in the future prospects of Oden Co, compared to the rest of the T&L sector. This is further corroborated by the higher dividend yield which may indicate that the company has fewer value-creating projects planned in the future. Finally, whereas the T&L sector's average share price seems to have recovered strongly in 20X5, following a small fall in 20X4, Oden

Co's share price has not followed suit and the decline has gathered pace in 20X5. It would seem that Oden Co is a poor performer within its sector.

This view is further strengthened by comparing the actual returns to the required returns based on the capital asset pricing model (CAPM). Both the company and the T&L sector produced returns exceeding the required return in 20X3 and Oden Co experienced a similar decline to the sector in 20X4. However, in 20X5, the T&L sector appears to have recovered but Oden Co's performance has worsened. This has resulted in Oden Co's actual average returns being significantly below the required returns between 20X2 and 20X5.

Taking the above into account, the initial recommendation is for Chawan Co to dispose of its investment in Oden Co. However, there are three important caveats which should be considered before the final decision is made.

The first caveat is that Chawan Co should look at the balance of its portfolio of investments. A sale of $58 million worth of equity shares within a portfolio total of $360 million may cause the portfolio to become unbalanced and for unsystematic risk to be introduced into the portfolio. Presumably, the purpose of maintaining a balanced portfolio is to virtually eliminate unsystematic risk by ensuring that it is well diversified. Chawan Co may want to reinvest the proceeds from the sale of Oden Co (if it decides to proceed with the disposal) in other equity shares within the same sector to ensure that the portfolio remains balanced and diversified.

The second caveat is that Chawan Co may want to look into the rumours of a takeover bid of Oden Co and assess how realistic it is that this will happen. If there is a realistic chance that such a bid may happen soon, Chawan Co may want to hold onto its investment in Oden Co for the present time. This is because takeover bids are made at a premium and the return to Chawan Co may increase if Oden Co is sold during the takeover.

The third caveat is that Chawan Co may want to consider Oden Co's future prospects. The calculations above are based on past performance between 20X2 and 20X5 and indicate an increasingly poor performance. However, the economy is beginning to recover, albeit slowly and erratically. Chawan Co may want to consider how well placed Oden Co is to take advantage of the improving conditions compared to other companies in the same industrial sector.

If Chawan Co decides that none of the caveats materially affect Oden Co's poor performance and position, then it should dispose of its investment in Oden Co.

4 High K

Course Book references

Analysis of financial strategy is covered in Chapter 2 of the Course Book.

Easy marks

The ratio analysis required here should have been a source of easy marks.

Examining team's comments

The performance of candidates who attempted this question was good. Sometimes candidates merely stated that a ratio/trend was increasing or decreasing, without attempting to address why this may be happening.

Marking guide	Marks
(a) **Ratios** (max 50% for calculations)	
Profitability	2
Liquidity	1
Solvency	2

(b) 1 mark per relevant point

Professional skills

Analysis and Evaluation

- Appropriate use of the data to determine suitable calculations to evaluate High K's performance
- Appropriate use of the data to support discussion and draw appropriate conclusions
- Appraisal of information objectively to make a commercial assessment

Scepticism

- Effective challenge of information and assumptions supplied and, techniques carried out to support the appraisal

Commercial acumen

- Effective use of examples and/or practical considerations related to the context to illustrate points being made relating to financing and performance appraisal.

Maximum	5
Total	**25**

(a) Profitability

Revenues from the different types of store and online sales have all increased this year, despite a drop in store numbers. The increase in revenue this year may be largely due, however, to the government-induced pre-election boom in consumer expenditure, which appears unlikely to be sustained. Because the split of profits is not given, it is impossible to tell what has been the biggest contributor to increased profit. Profit as well as revenue details for different types of store would be helpful, also profit details for major product lines.

Improvements in return on capital employed derive from increases in profit margins and asset turnover.

The improvements in gross margins may be due to increased pressure being put on suppliers, in which case they may not be sustainable because of government pressure.

The asset turnover shows an improvement which partly reflects the increase in sales. There have been only limited movements in the portfolio of the larger stores last year. The fall in non-current assets suggests an older, more depreciated, asset base. If there is no significant investment, this will mean a continued fall in capital employed and improved asset turnover. However, in order to maintain their appeal to customers, older stores will need to be refurbished and there is no information about refurbishment plans. Information about recent impairments in asset values would also be helpful, as these may indicate future trading problems and issues with realising values of assets sold.

Liquidity

The current ratio has improved, although the higher cash balances have been partly reflected by higher current liabilities. The increase in current liabilities may be due to a deliberate

policy of taking more credit from suppliers, which the government may take measures to prevent. Being forced to pay suppliers sooner will reduce cash available for short-term opportunities.

Gearing

The gearing level in 20Y6 is below the 20Y4 level, but it would have fallen further had a fall in debt not been partly matched by a fall in High K Co's share price. It seems surprising that High K Co's debt levels fell during 20Y6 at a time of lower interest rates. Possibly lenders were (rightly) sceptical about whether the cut in central bank lending rate would be sustained and limited their fixed rate lending. Interest cover improved in 20Y6 and will improve further if High K Co makes use of revolving credit facilities. However, when High K Co's loans come up for renewal, terms available may not be as favourable as those High K Co has currently.

Investors

The increase in after-tax profits in 20Y5 and 20Y6 has not been matched by an increase in share price, which has continued to fall. The price/earnings ratio has been falling from an admittedly artificially high level, and the current level seems low despite earnings and dividends being higher. The stock market does not appear convinced by High K Co's current strategy. Return to shareholders in 20Y6 has continued to rise, but this has been caused by a significant % increase in dividend and hence increase in dividend yield. The continued fall in share price after the year end suggests that investors are sceptical about whether this increase can be maintained.

Revenue analysis

Town centre stores

High K Co has continued to close town centre stores, but closures have slowed recently and revenue increased in 20Y6. This suggests High K Co may have selected wisely in choosing which stores to keep open, although Dely Co believes there is no future for this type of store. Arguably though, town centre stores appeal to some customers who cannot easily get to out-of-town stores. Town centre stores may also be convenient collection points for customers using online click and collect facilities.

Convenience stores

High K Co has invested heavily in these since 20X3. The figures in 20Y4 suggest it may have over-extended itself or possibly suffered from competitive pressures and saturation of the market. The 20Y6 results show an improvement despite closures of what may have been the worst-performing stores. The figures suggest Dely Co's decision to close its convenience stores may be premature, possibly offering High K Co the opportunity to take over some of its outlets. Maintaining its convenience store presence would also seem to be in line with High K Co's commitment to be responsive to customer needs. Profitability figures would be particularly helpful here, to assess the impact of rental commitments under leases.

Out-of-town stores

Although the revenue per store for out-of-town stores has shown limited improvement in 20Y6, this is less than might have been expected. The recent consumer boom would have been expected to benefit the out-of-town stores particularly, because expenditure on the larger items which they sell is more likely to be discretionary expenditure by consumers which will vary with the business cycle. Where Dely Co sites its new out-of-town stores will also be a major issue for High K Co, as it may find some of its best-performing stores face more competition. High K Co again may need to consider significant refurbishment expenditure to improve the look of these stores and customer experience in them.

Online sales

Online sales have shown steady growth over the last few years, but it is difficult to say how impressive High K Co's performance is. Comparisons with competitors would be particularly important here, looking at how results have changed over the years compared with the level of investment made. It is also impossible to tell from the figures how much increases in online sales have been at the expense of store sales.

Conclusion

If High K Co's share price is to improve, investors need it to make some sort of definite decision about strategy the way its competitors have since its last year end. What the chief executive has been saying about flexibility and keeping a varied portfolio has not convinced investors. If High K Co is to maintain its competitive position, it may well have no choice but to make a significant further investment in online operations. Possibly as well it could review where its competitor is closing convenience stores, as it may be able to open, with limited investment, new stores in locations with potential.

However, it also must decide what to do about the large out-of-town stores, as their performance is already stagnating and they are about to face enhanced competition. High K Co will also need to determine its dividend policy, with maybe a level of dividend which is considered the minimum acceptable to shareholders allowed for in planning cash outflows.

Appendix

Profitability	20Y4	20Y5	20Y6
Gross profit %	4.33	5.07	6.19
Operating profit %	0.87	1.70	2.91
Asset turnover (sales revenue/(total assets – current liabilities))	2.36	2.42	2.53
Return on capital employed % (operating profit % × asset turnover)	2.05	4.11	7.36
Liquidity			
Current ratio	0.84	1.29	1.69
Solvency			
Gearing (non-current liabilities/(non-current liabilities + share capital)) using market values of share capital	37.6	36.8	32.5
Interest cover	1.63	3.54	7.12
Investors			
Dividend cover	0.35	1.29	1.71
Price/earnings ratio	54.46	12.15	5.52
Return to shareholders			
Dividend yield %	5.30	6.36	10.60
Share price gain/(loss) %	(9.00)	(5.65)	(3.29)
Total	(3.70)	0.71	7.31
Revenue/store ($m)			
Town centre	31.91	33.05	33.93
Convenience	5.41	5.66	5.99
Out-of-town	46.45	46.16	46.46

Note. Credit will be given for alternative relevant calculations and discussion. Candidates are not expected to complete all of the calculations or evaluation above to obtain the available marks.

(b) High K Co has not raised any equity finance over the last five years. Its falling share price means that a new share issue may not be successful. It may not only need debt finance to be renewed, but additional funding to be obtained.

High K Co intends to make more use of revolving credit facilities, which it need not draw on fully, rather than loans, which will mean that its finance costs are lower than on ordinary debt. However, these facilities are likely to be at floating rates, so if the government increases the central bank rate significantly, they could come at significant cost if High K Co decides to utilise them fully.

Finance costs on new debt, whatever form it takes, may therefore be significant and lower interest cover. High K Co may have to investigate selling some of the stores it owns either outright or on a sale or leaseback basis.

5 Tillinton

Course Book references

Analysis of financial strategy is covered in Chapter 2 of the Course Book.

Easy marks

The ratio analysis required here should have been a source of easy marks. Part (b) is also relatively straightforward in terms of applying knowledge of behavioural finance theory.

Examining team's comments

Every candidate should have aimed for the 10 marks available on the calculations as they are relatively easily earned. As only a mark is typically awarded for a ratio calculation, candidates who calculated well in excess of 10 ratios have done extra work without gaining more calculation marks. Equally, some answers produced only a few ratios or did not examine the full trend. Doing so, meant they obtained fewer marks than were available here. It is also disappointing to see answers which used the wrong formulae to calculate basic ratios particularly, the return on capital employed, asset turnover, current ratio, gearing and price/earnings. Or mixed up dividend yield with payout ratio. These ratios and their interpretation are considered as assumed knowledge from the applied skills level.

Answers which interpreted and discussed the ratios calculated with reference to the question scenario and provided insight scored high marks. However, all too often, answers earned very few or no marks for the evaluation aspect as they merely described the increases and/or decreases in ratios and trends over the three-year period without further analysis.

In part (b) candidates were asked to discuss how behavioural factors may have affected the company's higher than expected share price. There were some excellent answers suggesting that these candidates may have read the AFM technical article published on this topic area.

Marking guide	Marks
(a) **Ratios** (max 50% for calculations)	
Profitability	3
Liquidity	1
Solvency	2
Investor	3
Discussion	
Profitability	4
Liquidity	2
Solvency	2
Investor	2
Conclusion	2

Maximum		16

(b) Up to 2 marks per relevant point

Maximum		4

Professional skills

Analysis and Evaluation

*   Appropriate use of the data to determine suitable calculations to evaluate Tillinton Co's performance and business prospects

*   Appropriate use of the data to support discussion and draw appropriate conclusions

*   Demonstration of reasoned judgement when considering key matters for Tillinton Co

*   Demonstration of ability to consider relevant factors applicable to Tillinton Co's situation

Commercial acumen

*   Effective use of examples and/or calculations from the scenario information and other practical considerations related to the context to illustrate points being made.

*   Recognition of external constraints and opportunities as necessary

*   Recommendations are practical and plausible in the context of Tillinton Co's situation

Scepticism

*   Effective challenge and critical assessment of the information and assumptions provided in relation to assessing Tillinton's performance and prospects

*   Effective challenge of evidence and assumptions supplied with respect to the Chief Executive's statement

Maximum		5
Total		25

(a) **Profitability**

Tillinton Co's chief executive is correct in saying that the absolute increase in revenue and gross profits on all products was greater in 20X3 than 20X2, but the % increase in revenue was smaller on all products, and the % increase in gross profit on toys was also lower. The % increase on the electronic toys shows the biggest fall, possibly indicating greater competition.

The improvements in operations mentioned by the chief executive seem to have maintained gross and operating profit margins and resulted in the absolute overall increases in gross and operating profits. However, this aspect of performance is almost all attributable to Tillinton Co's older products. The gross profit on electronic toys has hardly increased and the gross profit margin has fallen over the last two years. Although the margin remains higher than on the other products, even the 20X3 margin may not be sustainable. If competitors are starting to catch up with Tillinton Co, then the profit margin on the current range of electronic toys may continue to fall in future years, as prices fall to maintain market share.

Despite the emphasis on developing the products, the revenue generated by electronic toys is still below the revenue generated by non-electronic toys.

Asset turnover and return on capital employed have risen significantly over the last two years. However, part of the reason for the 20X3 increases was the significant increase in current liabilities. The further amount of investment which the chief executive appears to be contemplating suggests that asset turnover and return on capital employed may fall in future years, particularly if profit margins on electronic toys cannot be sustained.

Liquidity

The figures for other current assets seem to support the chief executive's contention that working capital is being managed better, as other current assets are falling as revenue and gross profits are rising.

However, the fall of the current ratio from 1.52 to 0.64 is significant, and the biggest reason for the fall in 20X3 was the large increase in current liabilities. Cash balances have remained at a low level, despite higher revenues and profit. Possibly there is now a bank overdraft, which could have contributed to the significant increase in finance costs between 20X2 and 20X3. It would seem that cash reserves have been exhausted by the combination of investment in non-current assets and the payments to finance providers (both interest and dividends), and Tillinton Co is more dependent on short-term liability finance. Slowdown in any product area, particularly electronic toys, may result in significant liquidity problems.

Solvency

Gearing has fallen over the last two years, but this is due to share price increases which may not be sustainable. If book values rather than market values are used to calculate gearing, the fall in gearing is much smaller. More information is needed about an additional $30 million in long-term loans. Although costs on these may be higher than on its current loans, this would not account for all the increase in finance costs. As discussed above, Tillinton Co may be making use of overdraft finance. The fact that current liabilities have increased much more than non-current liabilities could be an indication that Tillinton Co is having problems raising all the longer term loan finance which it requires.

The figures suggest that Tillinton Co's board needs to review future financing carefully if the company wants to make further investment in electronic products. At some stage, the board will have to consider raising further finance, either through an issue of shares or through selling off parts of its operations.

Investor ratios

Both earnings and dividends per share have risen since 20X1, which could help explain the significant increase in share price. Dividend cover has remained around 2.0 despite an increase in earnings. Although dividends have increased, dividend yield has fallen since 20X1. The increase in total shareholder return is due solely to the increases in share price, which have also resulted in the price-earnings ratio increasing in 20X3. The current rate of share price increase does not appear to be warranted by the most recent results and may be partly due to generous dividend levels, which may not be sustainable if more cash is required for investment.

Conclusion

Despite the chief executive's optimistic message in the annual report, the benefits from the electronic toys development may be short-lived. There appears to be a mismatch between investment, dividend and financing policies. As discussed, margins on current products may fall further and there is no guarantee that margins on new electronic toys or other products will be higher if competition generally is increasing.

Further significant investment in electronic toys or other goods may be difficult to finance. Increased reliance on short-term finance is clearly not sustainable, but obtaining more debt may be problematic, particularly if gearing levels rise as share prices fall. Tillinton Co seems reluctant to take advantage of high share price levels to issue equity capital. This, plus the increase in dividends, may indicate Tillinton Co's board is unwilling to risk upsetting shareholders, despite the large increases in share price. The chief executive may be right in saying that funds may have to be obtained by selling off one of the other parts of the business, but revenue and profits from the older products may be more sustainable. An increased concentration on electronic products may be a high-risk strategy. Possibly, if investors become less positive towards the electronic goods sector, they may realise this, resulting in an increase in cost of capital and a fall in share price.

Note. Credit will be given for relevant, alternative approaches to the calculations and discussion.

 **BPP**

Appendix

	20X1	20X2	20X3
Profitability			
% increase in revenue		18.1	17.0
Gross profit %	27.5	27.6	27.6
% increase in gross profit		18.4	17.1
Operating profit %	14.8	15.4	15.7
% increase in operating profit		22.9	19.0
Asset turnover (revenue/(total assets − current liabilities))	0.65	0.73	0.81
Return on capital employed %			
(operating profit % × asset turnover)	9.6	11.2	12.7
Liquidity			
Current ratio	1.52	1.15	0.64
Solvency			
Gearing % (non-current liabilities/(non-current			
liabilities + market value of share capital))	29.4	25.8	22.0
Gearing % (non-current liabilities/(non-current			
liabilities + book value of share capital + reserves))	43.3	43.0	42.2
Interest cover	4.5	5.0	4.5
Investors			
Dividend cover (earnings per share / dividends per share)	1.98	2.10	2.01
Market price per $0.50 share	2.76	3.49	4.44
Price/earnings ratio (price / earnings per share)	18.4	18.4	21.1
Dividend yield % (dividend per share/share price)	2.72	2.58	2.36
Share price gain/(loss) %	<u>10.40</u>	<u>26.45</u>	<u>27.22</u>
Total shareholder return %	13.12	29.03	29.58

Note. Credit will be given for alternative, relevant, calculations and discussion. Candidates will not be expected to complete all the calculations above to obtain full marks.

(b) Tillinton Co's shares may be overvalued because share prices generally are too high. The situation may be a stock market bubble. Share prices have been rising consistently recently and this could be encouraging investors to buy more shares, further increasing share prices.

The bubble could be more localised. Tillinton Co seems to be positioning itself as much in terms of producing technologically advanced electronic products as manufacturing toys. The electronic goods sector may be more likely than other sectors to attract investors on the basis of future profit potential, with investors possibly following a herd instinct, investing because others have been investing in the expectation of future gains.

Possibly, investors are more persuaded by the chairman's confident language and future promises than they are by the concerns the figures suggest. They may also be paying excessive attention to the most recent set of results, rather than seeing them in the context of whether they can be sustained in the future.

If investors are attempting to make a valuation, they could prefer using a model which confirms what they believe the shares are worth (confirmation bias), rather than one which gives a more reliable indication of value. As discussed above, shareholders may be basing

their estimates of value on the recent increases in dividend, even though it may be doubtful whether this is sustainable.

6 Arthuro

Marking guide	Marks	
(a) Calculation of operating profit, interest and domestic tax	2	
Depreciation	1	
Profit on disposal of non-current assets and cash from disposal	2	
Investment in new non-current assets	2	
Investment in working capital	1	
Calculation of dividend remittance from Bowerscots	1	
Calculation of additional tax payable on Bowerscots profits	1	
Comment	1	
Marks Available	11	
Maximum		10
(b) (i) Benefits of new policy	3	
Problems of new policy	3	
Marks Available	6	
Maximum		5
(ii) Agency problems	4	
Solutions to problems	4	
Marks Available	8	
Maximum		5

Marking guide

Professional skills

Analysis and Evaluation

- Appropriate use of the data to determine suitable calculations to forecast Arthuro's dividend capacity
- Appropriate use of the data to support discussion and draw appropriate conclusions
- Demonstration of reasoned judgement when considering key matters for Arthuro Co
- Demonstration of ability to consider relevant factors applicable to Arthuro Co's situation

Commercial acumen

- Effective use of examples and/or calculations from the scenario information and other practical considerations related to the context to illustrate points being made relating to the remittances decision
- Recognition of external constraints and opportunities as necessary

Scepticism

- Effective challenge and critical assessment of the information and assumptions provided in relation to dividend and agency issues.
- Demonstration of ability to consider all relevant factors applicable to the decisions made.

	Marks
Maximum	5
Total	**25**

(a) Forecast dividend capacity is as follows:

	$'000
Operating profit (20% × 1.04 × $520m)	108,160
Less: Interest (8% × $135m)	(10,800)
Less: Taxation (30% × ($108.16m – $10.8m))	(29,208)
Add: Depreciation	30,000
Less: Profit on disposal of NCA	(5,900)
Add: Cash received on disposal of NCA (W1)	16,300
Less: Investment in new NCA (W2)	(44,800)
Less: Investment in working capital (15% × 0.04 × $520m)	(3,120)
Add: Dividend remittance from Bowerscots Co (W3)	34,200
Less: Additional tax on Bowerscots Co's profits (10% × $45m)	(4,500)
Forecast dividend capacity	90,332

There are 120m shares in issue after the rights issue so the potential dividend per share is $90.332m / 120m = $0.75 per share. This is just sufficient to maintain the level of dividend at $0.74 per share.

Workings

1   **Disposal of non-current assets**

	$'000
Profit on disposal	5,900
Cost	35,000
Less: Depreciation	(24,600)
Cash received on disposal	16,300

2   **Investment in non-current assets**

	$'000
Net book value at end of most recent year (start of 'normal' year)	110,000
Less: Depreciation in 'normal' year	(30,000)
Less: Net book value of assets disposed ($35m – $24.6m)	(10,400)
Net book value before investment in non-current assets	69,600
Required level of non-current assets ($110m × 1.04)	114,400
Investment in non-current assets	44,800

3   **Dividend remittance from Bowerscots**

	$'000
Profit before tax	45,000
Less: Tax at 20%	(9,000)
Profit after tax	36,000
Remitted to Arthuro Co (36,000 × 0.95)	34,200

(b) (i)   **Benefits of policy**

The change of policy appears to be viable. Arthuro Co would have had some slack if it had not undertaken the rights issue. The new policy takes up this slack and effectively tops up the amount required with an increase in dividends.

The new policy appears to ensure that Arthuro Co will have sufficient funds to pay the required level of dividends and fulfil its own investment requirements. It will mean that Bowerscots Co has less retained funds available for investment, but Arthuro Co's investment opportunities may be more profitable.

Problems with policy

Arthuro Co is now close to taking all of Bowerscots Co's post-tax earnings as dividends. Only a limited fall in Bowerscots Co's earnings would be needed for its dividends not to be enough to sustain Arthuro Co's dividend level. A fall could easily happen given the highly competitive environment in which Bowerscots Co operates. If Arthuro Co wanted to increase its dividends over time, it could not do so by receiving extra dividends from Bowerscots Co.

As mentioned, an increase in dividend will leave Bowerscots Co's management with less retained earnings to invest. The amount of investment they can undertake with the reduced funds available may be insufficient to sustain earnings levels and hence dividends for Arthuro Co.

The tax regime between the two countries means that the group will suffer more tax. The amount of additional tax payable by Arthuro Co on Bowerscots Co's profits will remain unchanged, but the increase in dividends will mean an increase in withholding tax, for

ANSWERS

which Arthuro Co will receive no credit. Given the lower tax rate in Owlia, for tax purposes higher retained earnings for Bowerscots Co would be preferable, possibly with funds loaned to Arthuro Co rather than paid as dividends.

(ii) **Agency problems**

An agency situation arises between Arthuro Co's board (the principal) and Bowerscots Co's management (the agent). The proposals are likely to involve agency costs.

The policy limits the discretion of Bowerscots Co's management by restricting the amounts of retained funds available. However, this seems an inefficient way of exercising closer control, with agency costs including the increased liability for withholding tax. If Arthuro Co's board has concerns about Bowerscots Co's management, it would be better to make changes in the management team.

Even if Arthuro Co's board has confidence in Bowerscots Co's management team, it may nevertheless wish to oversee Bowerscots Co more closely, given the dependence of its dividend capacity on the amount received from the subsidiary. Again, increased supervision will involve increased agency costs in terms of time spent by Arthuro Co's management.

Bowerscots Co's management may feel that the new policy threatens their remuneration, as the limited funds available for investment will adversely affect the company's ability to maintain its profit levels. The managers may seek to join competitors, disrupting Bowerscots Co's management, jeopardising its ability to achieve its profit forecasts.

Resolving agency problems

Ways of motivating Bowerscots Co's management include making their remuneration less dependent on Bowerscots Co's results, for example, allowing them share options in Arthuro Co. If more of their remuneration depends on the group's results, Bowerscots Co's management may be happier with the suggested arrangement if they feel it will benefit the group. However, this motivational effect will be limited if Bowerscots Co's management feels that the group results are not influenced much by what they do.

Alternatively, a greater proportion of Bowerscots Co's management's remuneration could be by methods which are not dependent on its results, for example, increased salary or better benefits. However, by weakening the link between results and remuneration, it lessens their incentive to strive to produce the results needed to maintain the required level of dividend.

The decision-making on investments at group level may also have to change. Bowerscots Co will, under the new policy, have insufficient funds for major investments. Its management team should have the opportunity to make a case for retaining a greater percentage of funds, as they may have better investment opportunities than those available to the parent.

7 Lamri

Course Book references

Dividend capacity is covered in Chapter 1, and transfer pricing is covered in Chapter 16.

Top tips

The bulk of the marks relate to calculations in this question therefore it is important to show all your workings. However, there is a lot to do for 14 marks so try to identify shortcuts where you can – for example, the cash from domestic activities both prior to and subsequent to the implementation of the proposal is the same so there is no need to calculate this twice.

Don't be afraid to state what you might think is the obvious. There are marks available for identifying the irrelevance of adjusting for depreciation so make sure you mention your reasons for not including this calculation.

In part (b) it is important to recognise that the implementation of the proposal would result in a shortfall in dividend capacity (don't forget to uplift existing dividend by 8%). By recognising this issue, you can then make suggestions as to how the problem can be overcome.

Easy marks

There are several easy marks to be gained in part (a) – for example, calculating operating profit, interest and tax.

Examining team's comments

This question required a logical and systematic approach as a lot was being asked (particularly in part (a)). Good attempts at part (a) achieved high marks but sometimes the answers were not appropriately structured which resulted in mixed-up answers. Few appropriate answers were received for part (b) and mostly reflected the disorganised approach to part (a).

Marking guide	Marks	
(a) Calculation of operating profit, interest and domestic tax	3	
Calculation of investments in working capital and non - current assets (including correct treatment of depreciation)	3	
Calculation of dividend remittance before new policy implementation	2	
Calculation of additional tax payable on Magnolia profits before new policy implementation	1	
Calculation of dividend remittance after new policy implementation	3	
Calculation of additional tax payable on Magnolia profits after new policy implementation	1	
Dividend capacity	1	
Maximum		14
(b) Concluding comments and explanation of reason	2	
Possible actions (1 mark per suggestion)	4	
Maximum		6

Professional skills

Analysis and Evaluation

- Appropriate use of the data to determine suitable calculations
- Appropriate use of the data to support discussion and draw appropriate conclusions
- Demonstration of reasoned judgement when considering key matters for Lamri Co
- Demonstration of ability to consider relevant factors applicable to Lamri Co's situation

Commercial acumen

- Effective use of examples and/or calculations from the scenario information and other practical considerations related to the context to illustrate points being made relating to the transfer pricing decision
- Recognition of external constraints and opportunities as necessary

Scepticism

- Demonstration of ability to consider all relevant factors applicable to the decisions made.

Maximum		5
Total		25

 BPP

(a) Dividend capacity

Prior to implementing TE's proposal

	$m
Operating profit (30% of $80m)	24.00
Less interest (8% of $35m)	(2.80)
Profit before tax	21.20
Less tax (28%)	(5.94)
Profit after tax	15.26
Less investment in working capital [15% of (20/120 × $80m)]	(2.00)
Less investment in non-current assets [25% of (20/120 × $80m)]	(3.33)
Less investment in new project	(4.50)
Cash flow from domestic activities	5.43
Overseas subsidiaries dividend remittances (W1)	3.16
Less tax paid on Magnolia's profits [(28 – 22)% of $5.40m]	(0.32)
Dividend capacity	8.27

> **Tutorial note.** There is no need to add back depreciation to obtain cash flow as the investment that amounts to the total depreciation charged will cancel out this calculation. The effect is therefore neutral.

After implementing TE's proposal

	$m
Cash flows from domestic activities (see above)	5.43
Overseas subsidiaries dividend remittances (W2)	2.71
Additional tax on Magnolia's profits (6% of $3.12m)	(0.19)
Dividend capacity	7.95

Workings

1 Overseas subsidiaries dividend remittances prior to TE's proposal

	Magnolia $m	Strymon $m
Sales revenue	15.00	5.70
Less variable costs	(2.40)	(3.60)
Less transferred costs	(5.70)	0
Less fixed costs	(1.50)	(2.10)
Operating profit	5.40	0
Less tax	(1.19)	0
Profit after tax	4.21	0
Remitted to Lamri	(3.16)	0
Retained in company	1.05	0

2　*Overseas subsidiaries dividend remittances after implementing TE's proposal*

	Magnolia	Strymon
	$m	$m
Sales revenue	15.00	7.98
Less variable costs	(2.40)	(3.60)
Less transferred costs	(7.98)	0
Less fixed costs	(1.50)	(2.10)
Operating profit	3.12	2.28
Less tax	(0.69)	(0.96)
Profit after tax	2.43	1.32
Remitted to Lamri	(1.82)	(0.89)
Withholding tax		(0.10)
Retained in company	0.61	0.33

(b) **Comments on impact of TE's proposal**

If the proposal is implemented, Lamri's dividend capacity will fall from $8.27 million to $7.95 million. Whilst the dividend capacity prior to implementation of the proposal exceeds the dividend to be paid ($7.5m × 1.08 = $8.1m), the proposal would lead to a shortfall in dividend capacity. The shortfall arises due to the high tax rate paid on Strymon's profits that Lamri cannot obtain credit for. Not only does Lamri lose the withholding tax on the remittances (10%), it is also paying an additional 14% in corporation tax (42% − 28%).

There are several ways in which the problem of this relatively small shortfall could be overcome. Lamri might consider reducing the growth rate of its dividends to a level that would be covered by the dividend capacity of $7.95 million. However, this might send adverse signals to the market given that a steady 8% growth has been maintained over the last few years.

Another alternative would be to borrow the shortfall. This may not be a popular option if Lamri wishes to avoid increasing its borrowings, particularly to fund dividend payments. Given that it would have to borrow to fund current shortfalls, there is a possibility that this problem would continue in the future, leading to even greater borrowings or the potential of having to reduce dividend growth.

Lamri might wish to consider postponing the project to a later date but the potential impact on company business would have to be evaluated. We are told in the scenario that a number of projects are in the pipeline for the future. Therefore, postponing a current investment may not be feasible without impacting on future investments.

The final possibility would be to ask for a higher remittance from Strymon or Magnolia. The main problem with this would be the potential negative impact on morale of the subsidiaries' managers if they are required to pay over greater proportions of their profits (which may affect any profit-related benefits they may have).

8 Moonstar

Marking guide

	Marks	
(a) Calculation of receivable	1	
Loan note amounts attributable to the A, B and C tranches	1	
Impact of swap	2	
Calculation of interest payable on interest for tranches A-, B- and C-rated tranches	3	
Estimation of return to subordinated certificates	1	
Comments and calculation relating to sensitivity	3	
Maximum		11
(b) Benefits of securitisation	4	
Risks associated with securitisation	3	
Marks Available	7	
Maximum		5
(c) Explanation/discussion of suitability of Mudaraba contract	3	
Discussion of bank's views	2	
Marks Available	5	
Maximum		4

Professional skills

Analysis and Evaluation

- Appropriate use of the data to determine suitable calculations in relation to the securitisation proposals
- Appropriate use of the data to support discussion and draw appropriate conclusions
- Demonstration of reasoned judgement when considering key matters for Moonstar Co
- Demonstration of ability to consider relevant factors applicable to the situation

Commercial acumen

- Effective use of examples and/or calculations from the scenario information and other practical considerations related to the context to illustrate points being made relating to the financing decision
- Recognition of external constraints and opportunities as necessary

Scepticism

- Effective challenge and critical assessment of the information and assumptions provided in relation to risk faced by investors.
- Demonstration of ability to consider all relevant factors applicable to the decisions made.

Maximum	$\underline{5}$
Total	$\underline{\underline{25}}$

(a) An annual cash flow account compares the estimated cash flows receivable from the property against the liabilities within the securitisation process. The swap introduces leverage into the arrangement.

Cash flow receivable	$m	*Cash flow payable*	$m
$200m × 11%	$\underline{22.00}$	A-rated loan notes	
Less service charge	(0.20)	Pay $108m (W1) × 11% (W2)	11.88
		B-rated loan notes	
		Pay $27m (W1) × 12%	3.24
		C-rated loan notes	
		Pay $27m (W1) × 13%	$\underline{3.51}$
	$\underline{21.80}$		$\underline{18.63}$
		Balance to the subordinated certificates	$\underline{3.17}$

Workings

1 **Loan notes**

		$m
A	$200m × 0.9 × 0.6	108
B	$200m × 0.9 × 0.15	27
C	$200m × 0.9 × 0.15	27

2 **Swap**

	$m
Pay fixed rate under swap	$\underline{9.5\%}$
Pay floating rate	base rate + 1.5%
Receive floating rate under swap	$\underline{\text{(base rate)}}$
Net payment	$\underline{11\%}$

The holders of the certificates are expected to receive $3.17 million on $18 million, giving them a return of 17.6%. If the cash flows are 5% lower than the non-executive director has predicted, annual revenue received will fall to $20.90 million, reducing the balance available for the subordinated certificates to $2.07 million, giving a return of 11.5% on the subordinated certificates, which is below the returns offered on the B- and C-rated loan notes. The point at which the holders of the certificates will receive nothing and below which the holders of the C-rated loan notes will not receive their full income will be an

BPP

annual income of $18.83 million (a return of 9.4%), which is 14.4% less than the income that the non-executive director has forecast.

(b) **Benefits**

The finance costs of the securitisation may be lower than the finance costs of ordinary loan capital. The cash flows from the commercial property development may be regarded as lower risk than Moonstar Co's other revenue streams. This will impact upon the rates that Moonstar Co is able to offer borrowers.

The securitisation matches the assets of the future cash flows to the liabilities to loan note holders. The non-executive director is assuming a steady stream of lease income over the next ten years, with the development probably being close to being fully occupied over that period.

The securitisation means that Moonstar Co is no longer concerned with the risk that the level of earnings from the properties will be insufficient to pay the finance costs. Risks have effectively been transferred to the loan note holders.

Risks

Not all of the tranches may appeal to investors. The risk-return relationship on the subordinated certificates does not look very appealing, with the return quite likely to be below what is received on the C-rated loan notes. Even the C-rated loan note holders may question the relationship between the risk and return if there is continued uncertainty in the property sector.

If Moonstar Co seeks funding from other sources for other developments, transferring out a lower risk income stream means that the residual risks associated with the rest of Moonstar Co's portfolio will be higher. This may affect the availability and terms of other borrowing.

It appears that the size of the securitisation should be large enough for the costs to be bearable. However, Moonstar Co may face unforeseen costs, possibly unexpected management or legal expenses.

(c) A Mudaraba contract would involve the bank providing capital for Moonstar Co to invest in the development. Moonstar Co would manage the investment which the capital funded. Profits from the investment would be shared with the bank, but losses would be solely borne by the bank. A Mudaraba contract is essentially an equity partnership, so Moonstar Co might not face the threat to its credit rating which it would if it obtained ordinary loan finance for the development. A Mudaraba contract would also represent a diversification of sources of finance. It would not require the commitment to pay interest that loan finance would involve.

Moonstar Co would maintain control over the running of the project. A Mudaraba contract would offer a method of obtaining equity funding without the dilution of control which an issue of shares to external shareholders would bring. This is likely to make it appealing to Moonstar Co's directors, given their desire to maintain a dominant influence over the business.

The bank would be concerned about the uncertainties regarding the rental income from the development. Although the lack of involvement by the bank might appeal to Moonstar Co's directors, the bank might not find it so attractive. The bank might be concerned about information asymmetry – that Moonstar Co's management might be reluctant to supply the bank with the information it needs to judge how well its investment is performing.

9 Fernhurst

Course Book references

Investment appraisal methods are covered in Chapter 3.

Top tips

In part (a) time management will be important, there are a lot of calculations to do (tax, inflation, working capital, duration) and it will be important to clearly lays these out so that a marker can follow your calculations and so that you avoid making careless mistakes. Move on if a particular calculation is proving to be time consuming.

Easy marks

Parts (b) and (c) are opportunities to score strongly. Part (b) asked for a calculation (and discussion) of the sensitivity of the project to a reduction in the selling price. Good exam technique could have been employed here to deal with the only area of complexity (the 15% chance of negative cash flows in Year 1) as a brief discussion point in your answer. Part (c) required a discussion of the meaning and significance of NPV; this allowed candidates to identify the important of risk and uncertainty in investment appraisal.

Marking guide	Marks
(a) Sales revenue	1
Variable costs	1
Fixed costs	1
Tax-allowable depreciation	1
Tax payable	1
Working capital	2
NPV of project	1
Comment on NPV	1
Duration calculation	2
Comment on duration	1
	12
(b) Reduction in selling price	2
Discussion	3
Marks Available	5
Maximum	4
(c) Significance of net present value	2
Shareholders' attitude to the longer and shorter term	3
Marks Available	5
Maximum	4

Professional skills

Analysis and Evaluation

- Appropriate use of the data to determine suitable calculations to support the investment decision
- Appropriate use of the data to support discussion and draw appropriate conclusions

 **BPP**

- Demonstration of reasoned judgement when considering key matters for Fernhurst Co

Scepticism

- Effective challenge of evidence and assumptions supplied with respect to the non-executive director's comment.
- Effective challenge of assumptions used to forecast revenue and costs for the investment in Milland

Maximum	5
Total	**25**

(a)

	1	2	3	4
	$'000	$'000	$'000	$'000
Sales revenue (W1)	13,250	16,695	22,789	23,928
Variable costs (W2)	(5,788)	(7,292)	(9,954)	(10,452)
Contribution	7,462	9,403	12,835	13,476
Marketing expenditure	(1,500)			
Fixed costs	(900)	(945)	(992)	(1,042)
Tax-allowable depreciation (W3)	(3,200)	(2,560)	(2,048)	(8,192)
Taxable profits/(losses)	1,862	5,898	9,795	4,242
Taxation (25%)	(466)	(1,475)	(2,449)	(1,061)
Add back tax-allowable depreciation	3,200	2,560	2,048	8,192
Cash flows after tax	4,596	6,983	9,394	11,373
Initial investment				
Working capital (W4)	(41)	(53)	(56)	1,175
Cash flows	4,555	6,930	9,338	12,548
Discount factor	0.901	0.812	0.731	0.659
Present values	4,104	5,627	6,826	8,269

Present value 24,826

Subtracting the cash outflows at time 0 ($16,000 for non-current assets and $1,025 for working capital) gives the project NPV:

$24,826 – $16,000 – $1,025 = **$7,801**

The net present value (NPV) is positive, which indicates the project should be undertaken.

Alternative approach using spreadsheet functionality:

Alternatively, the present value of the cash flows from time 1–4 can be calculated using the =NPV spreadsheet function. Either method is acceptable, but the spreadsheet function gives a slightly more precise answer and, with practice, should be quicker to use in the exam.

The spreadsheet extract shown in the following section shows the =NPV formula being applied using the cost of capital of 11%.

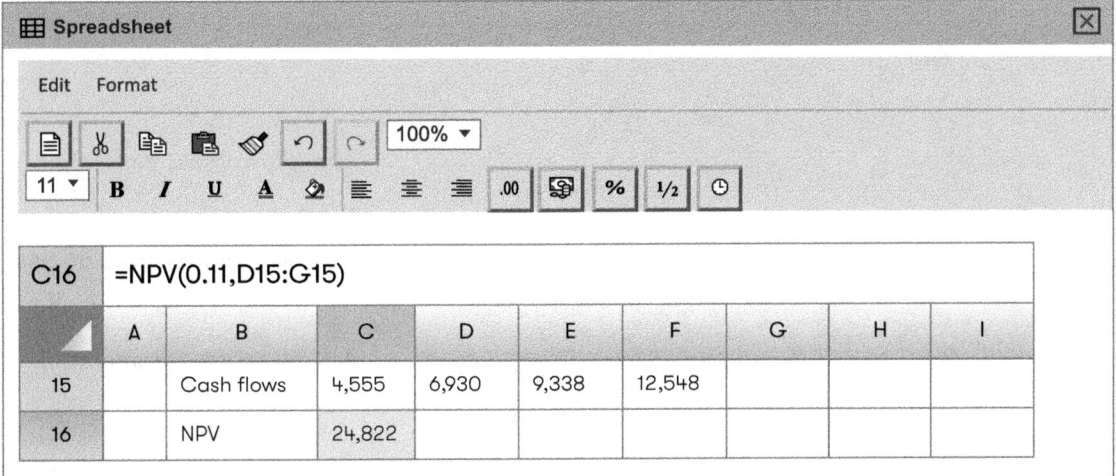

C16	=NPV(0.11,D15:G15)								
◢	A	B	C	D	E	F	G	H	I
15		Cash flows	4,555	6,930	9,338	12,548			
16		NPV	24,822						

Note that the NPV function assumes that the first cash flow is in one year's time, so you then have to subtract the time 0 cash outflows as before to give the project NPV as:

$24,822 – $16,000 – $1,025 = **$7,797**

Workings

1 **Sales revenue**

Year		$'000
1	132,500 × $100	13,250
2	132,500 × $100 × 1.05 × 1.2	16,695
3	132,500 × $100 × 1 .05^2 × 1.2 × 1.3	22,789
4	132,500 × $100 × 1.05^3 × 1.2 × 1.3	23,928

Note. These calculations can be embedded in a spreadsheet cell and do not need to be written out in full.

2 **Variable costs**

Year		$'000
1	132,500 × $43.68	5,788
2	132,500 × $43.68 × 1.05 × 1.2	7,292
3	132,500 × $43.68 × 1.05^2 × 1.2 × 1.3	9,954
4	132,500 × $43.68 × 1.05^3 × 1.2 ×1.3	10,452

3 Tax-allowable depreciation

Year		$'000
		16,000
1	Tax-allowable depreciation	(3,200)
		12,800
2	Tax-allowable depreciation	(2,560)
		10,240
3	Tax-allowable depreciation	(2,048)
		8,192
4	Balancing allowance	(8,192)
		0

4 Working capital

Year		$'000	Change in working capital
0	1,025		1,025
1	1,025 × 1.04	1,066	41
2	1,066 × 1.05	1,119	53
3	1,119 × 1.05	1,175	56
4	reduce to zero	0	(1,175)

The change in cash flow is based on the change in working capital, an increase in working capital causes a cash outflow and vice-versa.

Duration

Present value of inflows = NPV of project + outlay in Time 0 = 7,801 + 17,025 = **24,826**

Year	1	2	3	4
Present value (PV) $'000	4,104	5,627	6,826	8,269
PV × year	4,104	11,254	20,478	33,076

Duration = (4,104 + 11,254 + 20,478 + 33,076) / 24,286 = 2.78 years

The **project duration** is a measure of the **average time over which this project delivers its value,** ie it is the equivalent of a project that delivers 100% of its (present value) cash inflows in 2.78 years' time.

Alternative calculation:

Year	1	2	3	4
Present value (PV) $'000	4,104	5,627	6,826	8,269
Percentage of total PV	16.5%	22.7%	27.5%	33.3%

Duration = (1 × 0.165) + (2 × 0.227) + (3 × 0.275) + (4 × 0.333) = 2.78 years

(b) Reduction in selling price

The post-tax value of the sales revenue can be quickly calculated as approximately $43,434,000 by copying the sales revenue data from the previous NPV and applying the NPV function again, as shown here:

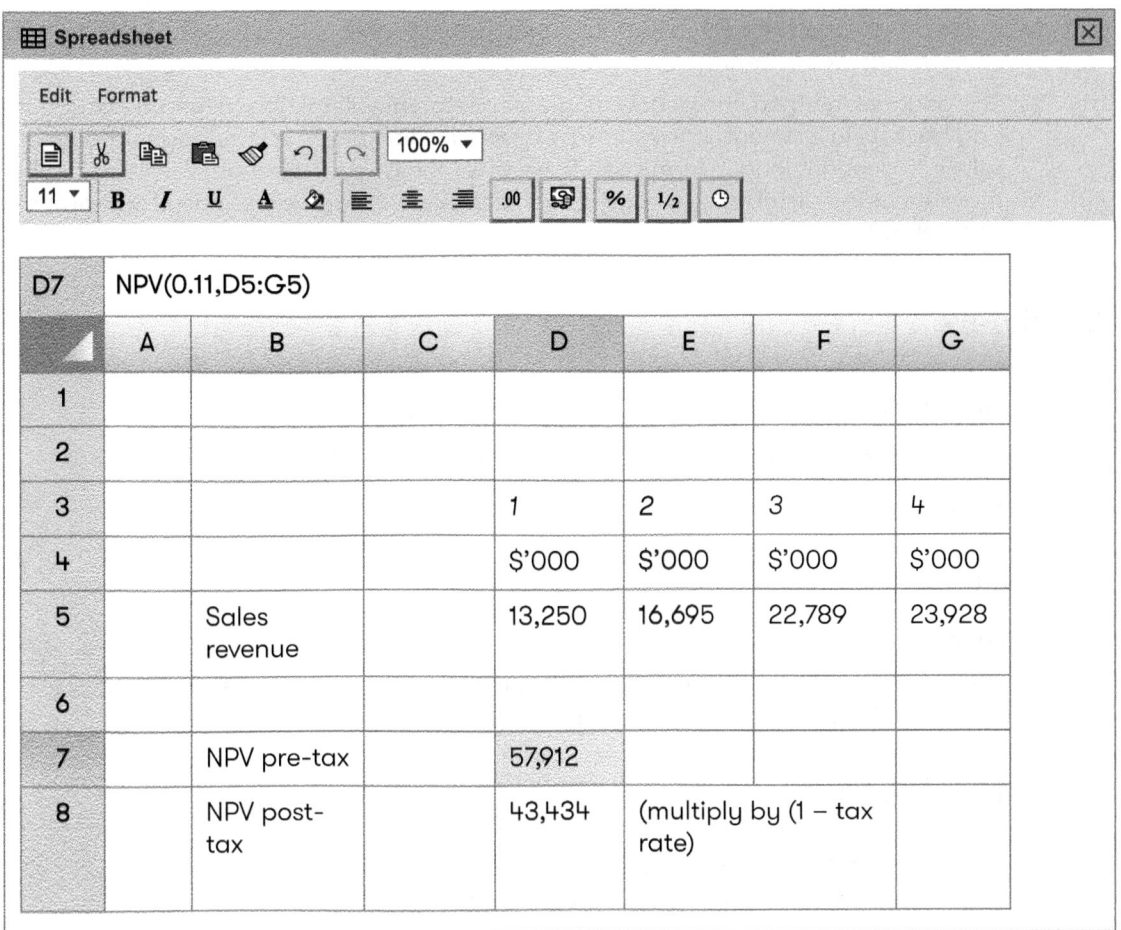

Spreadsheet

Edit   Format

D7   NPV(0.11,D5:G5)

	A	B	C	D	E	F	G
1							
2							
3				1	2	3	4
4				$'000	$'000	$'000	$'000
5		Sales revenue		13,250	16,695	22,789	23,928
6							
7		NPV pre-tax		57,912			
8		NPV post-tax		43,434	(multiply by (1 – tax rate)		

The reduction in selling price for the project NPV to fall to zero = 7,801/43,434 = 18.0%

Fernhurst Co would appear to have some scope to reduce the price in order to guarantee the success of the product launch. It would be useful to know whether the finance director's views on the success of the product would change if the product was launched at a lower price. There may be scope to launch at a price which is more than 18.0% lower than the planned launch price, and increase the sales price subsequently by more than the rate of inflation if the launch is a success.

If the directors are unwilling to reduce the price, then their decision will depend on whether they are willing to consider other ways of mitigating a failed launch or take a chance that the product will make a loss and be abandoned. They will take into account both the probability (15%) of the loss and the magnitude (at least $1,000,000 but possibly higher).

Presumably the finance director's assessment of the probability of a loss is based more on doubts about the demand level rather than the level of costs, as costs should be controllable. Possibly Fernhurst Co's directors may consider a smaller-scale launch to test the market, but then Fernhurst Co would still be left with expensive facilities if the product were abandoned. The decision may therefore depend on what alternative uses could be made of the new facilities.

(c) The non-executive director has highlighted the importance of long-term maximisation of shareholders' wealth. The NPV is the most important indicator of whether an investment is likely to do that.

However, investors are not necessarily concerned solely with the long term. They are also concerned about short-term indicators, such as the annual dividend which the company can sustain. They may be concerned if the company's investment portfolio is weighted towards projects which will produce good long-term returns, but limited returns in the near future.

Risk will also influence shareholders' views. They may prefer investments where a higher proportion of returns are made in the shorter term, if they feel that longer-term returns are

 **BPP**

much more uncertain. The NPV calculation itself discounts longer-term cash flows more than shorter-term cash flows.

The payback method shows how long an investment will take to generate enough returns to pay back its investment. It favours investments which pay back quickly, although it fails to take into account longer-term cash flows after the payback period. Duration is a better measure of the distribution of cash flows, although it may be less easy for shareholders to understand.

10 Riviere

Course Book references

Project appraisal is covered in Chapter 3. Free trade areas are covered in Chapter 16.

Top tips

Make sure that you answer parts (a) and (c) in full – there are two aspects to both of these questions.

Easy marks

There are some easy marks to be gained in parts (a) and (c) for some straightforward discussion points; ensure where possible that these relate to the scenario.

Marking guide	Marks	
(a) Discussion of the EU as a free trade area	3	
Discussion of the possible benefits to Riviere Co	3	
Marks Available	6	
Maximum		4
(b) Calculation of IRR	1	
Calculation of MIRR	1	
Standard deviation calculations	1	
Value at risk calculations	2	
Discussion of merits of NPV and MIRR	3	
Explanation of VaR		
Recommendation	2	
Maximum		10
(c) Discussion of possible legal risks	4	
Discussion of how to deal with these	4	
Marks Available	8	
Maximum		6

Professional skills

Analysis and Evaluation

- Appropriate use of the data to support discussion and draw appropriate conclusions for Project Drugi

- Demonstration of reasoned judgement when considering key matters for Riviere Co

- Demonstration of ability to consider relevant factors applicable to Riviere Co's situation

- Identification of further analysis, which could be carried out to enable an appropriate recommendation to be made.

- Appraisal of information objectively to make a recommendation

Scepticism

- Effective challenge of information and assumptions supplied and, techniques carried out to support an investment decision and evaluation of risk
- Demonstration of ability to consider all relevant factors applicable to the decisions made by Riviere Co

Commercial acumen

- Effective use of examples and/or calculations from the scenario information and other practical considerations related to the context to illustrate points being made relating to risk management
- Recognition of external constraints and opportunities as necessary
- Recommendations are practical and plausible in the context of Riviere Co's situation

Maximum	5
Total	25

(a) **A free trade area** like the EU aims to remove barriers to trade and allow **freedom of movement** of production resources such as capital and labour within the EU. The EU also has a **common legal structure** across all member countries and tries to **limit any discriminatory practice** against companies operating in these countries.

The EU also erects **common external trade barriers** to trade against countries which are not member states.

Riviere Co may benefit from operating within the EU in a number of ways.

It may be protected from non-EU competition because companies outside the EU may find it **difficult to enter the EU** markets due to barriers to trade.

A common legal structure should ensure that the standards of food quality and packaging apply equally across all the member countries. This will **reduce compliance costs** for Riviere, which may be an important issue for a small company with limited financial resources.

Having access to capital and labour within the EU may make it easier for the company to set up branches inside the EU, if it wants to. The company may also be able to access any grants which are available to companies based within the EU.

(b) **Project Drugi internal rate of return (IRR)**

Net present value (NPV): €2,293,000 approximately using a cost of capital of 10%

Time	0	1	2	3	4	5
Cash flows (€'000)	(11,840)	1,230	1,680	4,350	10,240	2,200
Try 20%	1.0	0.833	0.694	0.579	0.482	0.402
Present value	(11,840)	1,025	1,166	2,519	4,936	884

NPV = €(1,310,000)

IRR = 10% + 2,293/(2,293 + 1,310) × 10% approximately = **16.4%**

Alternative approach using spreadsheet functionality:

Alternatively, the internal rate of return can be calculated using the =IRR spreadsheet function. Either method is acceptable, but the spreadsheet function gives a more precise answer and, with practice, should be much quicker to use in the exam.

The spreadsheet extract shown in the following section shows the =IRR formula being applied:

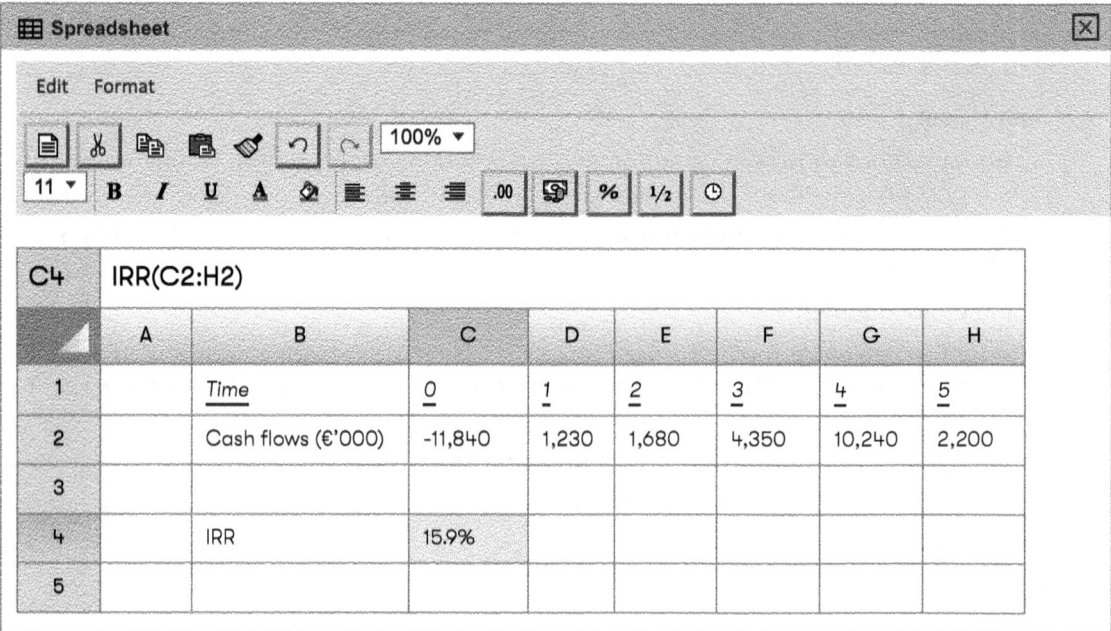

Modified internal rate of return (MIRR)

Total present values (PVs) of inflows from Time 1 to 5 at 10% discount rate = outlay + NPV of project = €11,840,000 + €2,293,000 = €14,133,000

MIRR (using formula provided) =

$$\left[\frac{PV_r}{PV_i}\right]^{1/n} \times (1 + r_e) - 1$$

MIRR =

$$\left[\frac{14,133}{11,840}\right]^{1/5} \times (1 + 0.1) - 1 = 14\%$$

Alternative approach using spreadsheet functionality:

Alternatively, the modified internal rate of return can be calculated using the =MIRR spreadsheet function. Either method is acceptable, but the spreadsheet function, with practice, should be quicker to use in the exam.

The spreadsheet extract shown in the following section shows the =MIRR formula being applied:

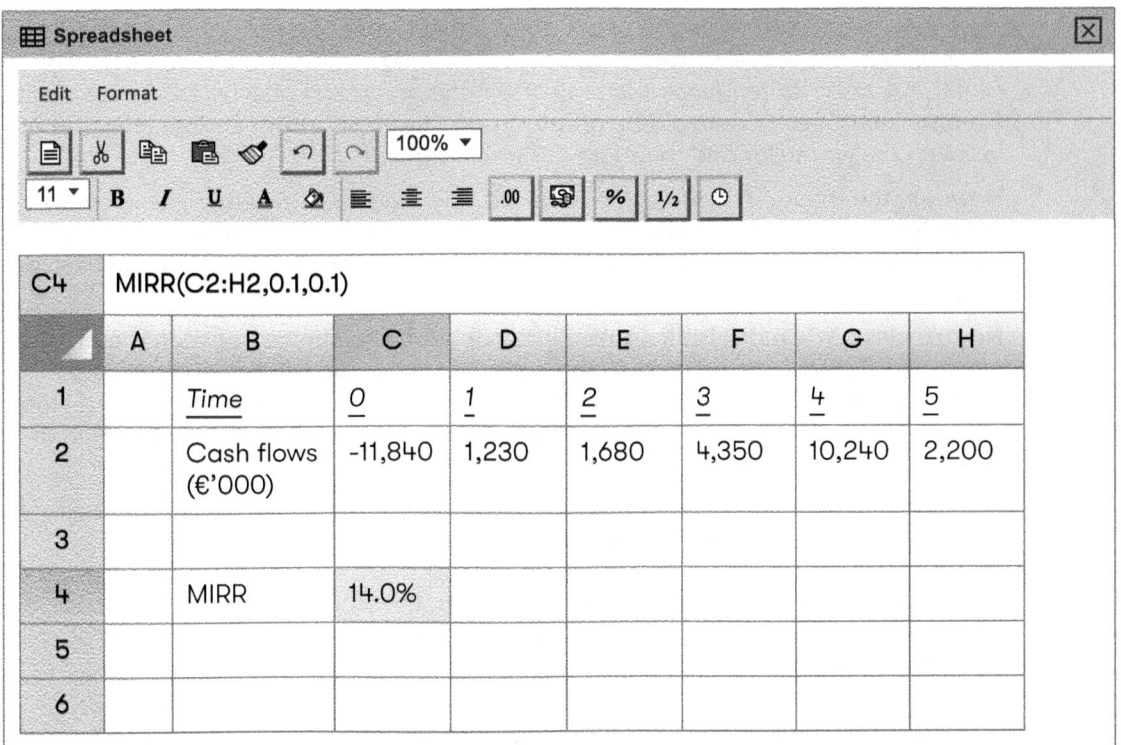

Spreadsheet

Edit   Format

C4	MIRR(C2:H2,0.1,0.1)						
	A	B	C	D	E	F	G	H
1		*Time*	0	1	2	3	4	5
2		Cash flows (€'000)	-11,840	1,230	1,680	4,350	10,240	2,200
3								
4		MIRR	14.0%					
5								
6								

Value at risk (VaR)

A 95% confidence level requires the annual present value VaR to be less than 1.645 standard deviations below the mean.

A 90% confidence level requires the annual present value VaR to be less than 1.282 standard deviations below the mean.

95%, 5-year present value VaR = $400,000 × 1.645 × square root of 5 (since it is a 5-year project) = approx. **€1,471,000**

90%, 5-year present value VaR = $400,000 × 1.282 × square root of 5 (since it is a 5-year project) = approx. approx. **€1,147,000**

	Privi	Drugi
NPV (10%)	€2,054,000	€2,293,000
IRR	17.6%	16.4%
MIRR	13.4%	14.0%
VaR (over the project's life)		
95% confidence level	€1,103,500	€1,471,000
90% confidence level	€860,000	€1,147,000

The IRR for project Privi is higher. However, where projects are mutually exclusive, the **IRR can give an incorrect answer.** One reason for this is that the IRR assumes that returns are reinvested at the internal rate of return, whereas NPV and the MIRR assume that they are reinvested at the cost of capital (discount rate) which in this case is 10%. The cost of capital is a more realistic assumption as this is the minimum return required by investors in a company.

The NPV and the MIRR both indicate that project Drugi would create more value for Riviere Co.

Therefore, based purely on cash flows, **project Drugi should be accepted due to the higher NPV and MIRR, as they give the theoretically correct answer of the value created.**

The VaR provides an indication of the potential riskiness of a project. For example, if Riviere Co invests in project Drugi then it can be 95% confident that the PV will not fall by more than €1,471,000 over its life. Hence the project will still produce a positive NPV. However, there is a 5% chance that the loss could be greater than €1,471,000. With project Privi, the potential loss in value is smaller and therefore it is less risky.

However, the theory of value at risk is based on a normal distribution, which assumes that virtually all possible outcomes will be within three standard deviations of the mean and that success and failure are equally likely. The logic of this may be questionable for a one-off project.

Nevertheless, when risk is also taken into account, the choice between the projects is not clear cut and depends on Riviere Co's attitude to risk and return. Project Drugi gives the higher potential NPV but is riskier, whereas project Privi is less risky but gives a smaller NPV. This is before taking into account additional uncertainties such as trading in an area in which Riviere Co is not familiar.

It is therefore recommended that Riviere Co should only proceed with project Drugi if it is willing to accept the higher risk and uncertainty.

> **Tutorial note.** From the September 2024 exam, the standardised values associated with confidence levels will be given in exam questions as normal distribution tables will not be provided in the exam.

(c) There are a number of possible **legal risks** which Riviere Co may face:

(1) The countries where the product is sold may have **different legal regulations** on food preparation, quality and packaging.

(2) The legal regulations may be more lax in countries outside the EU but Riviere Co needs to be aware that **complying only with the minimum standards may impact its image negatively overall**, even if they are acceptable in the countries concerned.

(3) There may be **trade barriers**, eg **import quotas** in the countries concerned which may make it difficult for Riviere Co to compete.

(4) The legal system in some countries **may not recognise the trademarks** or production patents which the company holds on its packaging and production processes. This may enable competitors to copy the food and the packaging.

(5) Different countries may have different regulations regarding **product liability** from poorly prepared and/or stored food which cause harm to consumers.

Possible mitigation strategies:

(1) Riviere Co needs to undertake sufficient **research** into the countries' **current laws** and regulations to ensure that it complies with the standards required. It may even want to ensure that it exceeds the required standards to ensure that it maintains its reputation.

(2) Riviere Co needs to ensure that it also keeps abreast of **potential changes** in the law. It may also want to ensure that it complies with best practice, even if it is not the law yet. Often current best practices become enshrined in future legislation.

(3) Strict **contracts** need to be set up between Riviere Co and any agents it uses to transport and sell the food. These could be followed up by **regular checks** to ensure that the standards required are maintained.

Note. Credit will be given for alternative, relevant discussion for parts (a) and (c).

11 Hathaway

Marking guide		Marks	
(a) (i) Contribution		2	
Fixed costs		1	
Tax (including tax allowable)		2	
NPV		$\underline{1}$	
			6
(ii) Expected NPV		$\underline{2}$	
			2
(iii) Alternative option NPV		2	
Decision outcome		$\underline{1}$	
			3
(iv) Decision		2	
Comments		$\underline{3}$	
			5
(b) Post-completion audit:			
Rationale		2	
Benefits		$\underline{3}$	
Marks Available		5	
Maximum			$\underline{4}$

Professional skills

Analysis and Evaluation

- Appropriate use of the data to determine suitable calculations to support the investment decision
- Appropriate use of the data to support discussion and draw appropriate conclusions
- Demonstration of reasoned judgement
- Demonstration of ability to consider relevant factors
- Identification of further analysis, which could be carried out to enable an appropriate recommendation to be made.

Scepticism

- Effective challenge of information and assumptions provided by the chief engineer

Commercial acumen

- Effective use of examples and/or calculations from the scenario information and other practical considerations related to the context to illustrate points being made

- Recognition of external constraints such as regulatory approval and opportunities as necessary

Maximum	$\underline{5}$
Total	$\underline{\underline{25}}$

(a)   (i)   **Net present value (NPV):** All figures are in $ms unless otherwise indicated

Year	1	2	3	4	5
Contribution (w1)		15.00	16.07	17.21	18.43
Fixed costs		(8.70)	(8.96)	(9.23)	(9.51)
Tax allowable depreciation		(2.40)	(2.40)	(2.40)	(2.40)
Balancing adjustment					(2.40)
Taxable profits		3.90	4.71	5.58	4.12
Taxation (20%)		(0.78)	(0.94)	(1.12)	(0.82)
Add back depreciation		2.40	2.40	2.40	4.80
Investment cost	(12.00)				
Cash flows	(12.00)	5.52	6.17	6.86	8.1
Discount factors (12%)	0.893	0.797	0.712	0.636	0.567
NPV	(10.72)	4.40	4.39	4.36	4.59
	7.02				

(Alternatively, this can be calculated using the =NPV function to work out the value of the cash flows from time 1-5)

Working

Working 1 (W1): Contribution

Year	2	3	4	5
Volume (000s)	3.00	3.15	3.31	3.47
Contribution per unit ($000s)	5.00	5.10	5.20	5.31
Contribution ($m)	15.00	16.07	17.21	18.43

(ii)   **Incorporating finance director's objections**

- Expected NPV of chief engineer's proposal:
- PV of years 2–5 = $17.74m
- 60% PV of years 2–5 = $10.64m
- Expected PV of years 2–5 = (0.8 × $17.74m + 0.2 × $10.64m) = $16.32m
- Expected NPV = $16.32m – $10.72m = $5.6m

(iii) **Alternative option NPV**

- Annuity factor (12%, t2 – t8) = 4.968 – 0.893 = 4.075
- PV of years 2–8 = 4.075 × $3.43m = $13.98m
- NPV = $13.98m – $10.72m = $3.26m
- Therefore, it is more beneficial to follow the chief engineer's proposal.

(iv) **Apply for regulatory approval or sell**

Next, consider decision to sell to Gepe Co now or continue with application for regulatory approval.

NPV of sale to Gepe Co now = $4.3m

Expected NPV = 0.7 × $5.6m + 0.3 × (0.893 × $1.0m) = $4.19m

Therefore, more beneficial to sell immediately to Gepe Co.

Recommendation:

Immediate sale to Gepe Co for $4.3 million.

Comments

Based on the chief engineer's assumptions, the project generates a positive NPV of $7.02 million and should therefore be accepted in preference to the option to sell the concept for $4.3 million. On the other hand, when the finance director's objections are incorporated into the appraisal, the expected NPV is only $4.19 million and should therefore be rejected in favour of the option to sell.

It should be noted that the expected NPV of $4.19 million is an average. In other words, it is the average NPV if the project is carried out repeatedly which may not be useful in the case of a one-off development opportunity. Based on the calculations above, there is a 30% chance that the NPV will be only $893,000, which may pose a risk the directors are not prepared to take. The directors' attitude to risk will be an important factor in the final decision.

Furthermore, the analysis largely depends upon the values of the probabilities prescribed, the range of possible outcomes and the accuracy of the revenue and cost assumptions. Sensitivity analysis may be useful in testing the impact of variations in each of these variables on the final outcome.

(b) A post-completion audit is an objective, after the fact, appraisal of all phases of the capital investment process regarding a specific project. Each project is examined from conception until as much as a few years after it has become operational. It examines the rationale behind the initial investment decision, including the strategic fit, and the efficiency and effectiveness of the outcome. The key objective is to improve the appraisal and implementation of future capital investment projects by learning from past mistakes and successes.

An effective post-completion audit may have identified the reasons behind the failure of Hathaway Co's project kappa to achieve its forecast revenues. By comparing the actual project outcome with the original projections, an audit will examine whether the benefits claimed prior to approval ever materialise.

The audit is not an academic exercise; an effective audit would identify failings and help Hathaway Co learn from past mistakes as well replicate its successes. Project kappa's principal failing seems to be the inaccuracy of the revenue assumptions. An audit would establish the reasons behind that failing and identify ways in which this can be addressed. For example, it is possible the initial assumptions failed to predict future competitor actions or the full range of potential economic scenarios. In this way, Hathaway Co's managers benefit by learning how to appraise investment proposals more accurately and implement them more efficiently than before.

Note. *Credit will be given for alternative and valid discursive comments*

 BPP

12 MMC

Marking guide

	Marks
(a) Value of project without considering option to delay decision and conclusion	2
Current price variable (P_a) for Black–Scholes formula	1
Additional cost (P_e) for Black–Scholes formula	2
Other variables for Black–Scholes formula	1
Value of option to delay decision	1
Revised value of project and conclusion	2
Maximum	9
(b) 1 to 2 marks per well-explained point	
Maximum	6
(c) 1 to 2 marks per well-explained point	
Maximum	5

Professional skills

Analysis and Evaluation

- Demonstration of reasoned judgement when considering key matters for MMC Co

- Demonstration of ability to consider relevant factors applicable to MMC's situation

Scepticism

- Effective challenge of information and assumptions supplied (particularly in the relation to the Black–Scholes option pricing model) and, techniques carried out to support an investment decision

- Demonstration of ability to consider all relevant factors applicable to the decisions made by MMC Co

Commercial acumen

- Effective use of examples and/or calculations from the scenario information and other practical considerations related to the context to illustrate points being made relating to capital rationing
- Recognition of external constraints and opportunities as necessary

Maximum	$\underline{5}$
Total	$\underline{\underline{25}}$

(a) **Financial impact of option to delay**

First of all we calculate the present value (PV) of the project without the option to delay.

Year	0	1	2	3	4	5	6
	$m	$m	$m	$m	$m	$m	$m
Cash flows	(7.0)	(7.0)	(35.0)	25.0	18.0	10.0	5.0
Discount factor (11%)	1.000	0.901	0.812	0.731	0.659	0.593	0.535
DCF	(7.0)	(6.31)	(28.42)	18.28	11.86	5.93	2.68

NPV = $(2.98)m

Without the option to delay the project would be rejected.

Option to delay – use the Black–Scholes model to value this option

Using the BSOP spreadsheet provided in the exam is the quickest approach here:

The variables needed to complete the model are:

P_a = current value of the project (that is the PV of its cash inflows)

= $18.28m + $11.86m + $5.93m + $2.68m

= $38.75m

P_e = 'exercise price' of the project (that is, the cost of production etc that can be delayed)

= $35m

t = exercise date (that is, when the exercise price is paid) = 2 years

r = risk-free rate = 3.5%

s = standard deviation = 0.3

These should be input to the spreadsheet provided, in row 3 as shown.

The spreadsheet then completes the calculations, as shown.

BPP

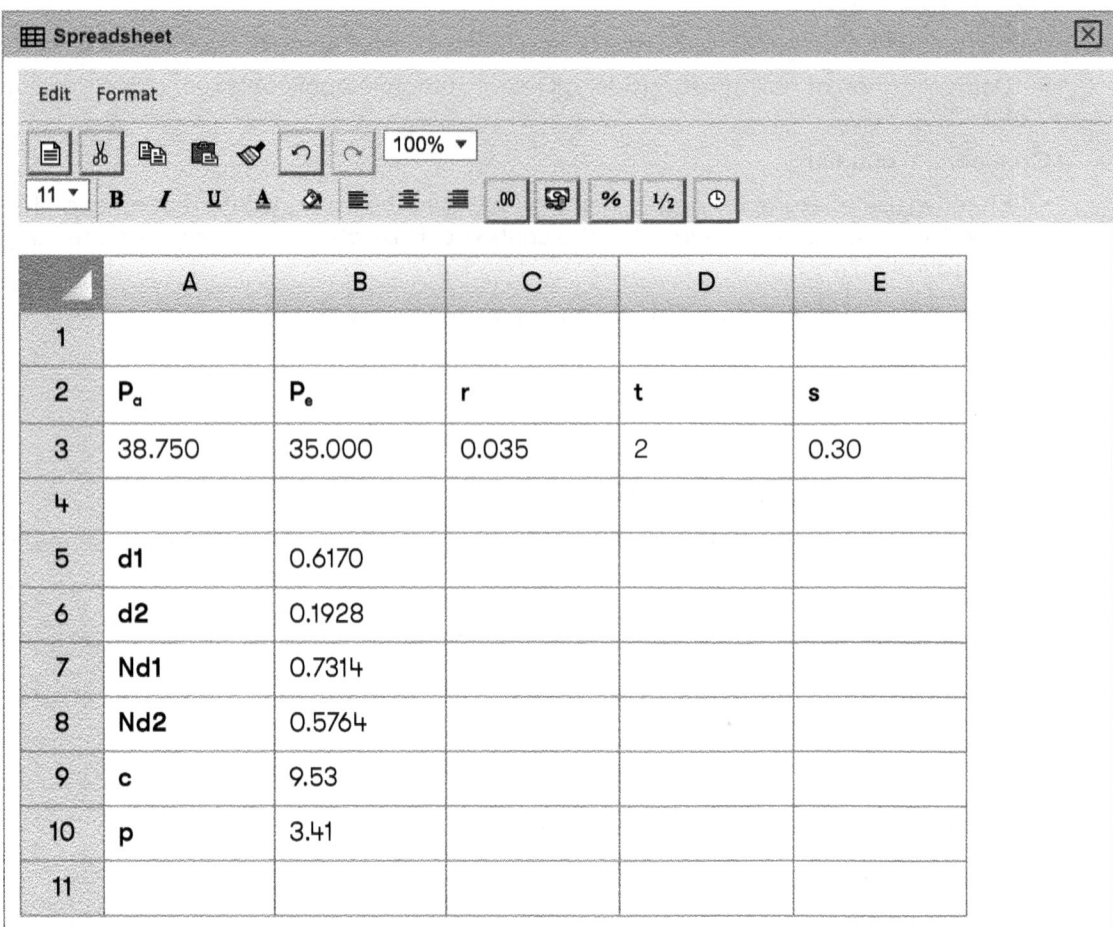

	A	B	C	D	E
1					
2	P_a	P_e	r	t	s
3	38.750	35.000	0.035	2	0.30
4					
5	d1	0.6170			
6	d2	0.1928			
7	Nd1	0.7314			
8	Nd2	0.5764			
9	c	9.53			
10	p	3.41			
11					

The value of the option to delay, which is a call option, is therefore $9.53m.

Total value of project = $9.53m – $2.98m = $6.55m

The project would therefore be accepted with the option to delay included.

(b) **Implications of the results**

The option to delay the project gives management time to consider and monitor the potential investment before committing to its execution. This extra time will allow management to assess the popularity of similar launches and also to monitor competition. The success of the film will be heavily reliant on the marketing campaign launched by the film's promoters prior to its release – management will be able to monitor the extent of this campaign before committing to an expensive (and potentially unsuccessful) project.

However, the calculations of the value of the option to delay are subject to several limiting assumptions, primarily the volatility of the cash flows. The value of the option to delay ($9.127 million) is not an exact figure but rather an **indication** of how much management would value the opportunity to delay. The result shows that management should not dismiss the project immediately, despite the current negative NPV.

There may be other options embedded within the project. The technology used to develop the game may be used for other projects in the future (option to **redeploy**). Alternatively, the project could lead to follow-on projects if the film is successful enough to generate sequels.

(c) The value of the option depends on the following variables.

- **The price of the security**

A decrease in the price of the security will mean that a call option becomes **less valuable**. Exercising the option will mean purchasing a security that has a lower value.

- **The exercise price of the option**

A decrease in the exercise price will mean that a call option becomes **more valuable**; the profit that can be made from exercising the option will have increased.

- **Risk-free rate of return**

A decrease in the risk-free rate will mean that a call option becomes **less valuable**. The purchase of an option rather than the underlying security will mean that the option holder has spare cash available which can be invested at the risk-free rate of return. A decrease in that rate will mean that it becomes less worthwhile to have spare cash available, and hence to have an option rather than having to buy the underlying security.

- **Time to expiry of the option**

A decrease in the time of expiry will mean that a call option becomes **less valuable**, as the time premium element of the option price has been decreased.

- **Volatility of the security price**

A decrease in volatility will mean that a call option becomes **less valuable**. A decrease in volatility will decrease the chance that the security price will be above the exercise price when the option expires.

13 Furlion Co

Course Book references

The Black–Scholes model and its use in the valuation of real options are covered in Chapter 4, and the World Bank is covered in Chapter 16.

Top tips

A number of articles on the Black–Scholes model were published on the ACCA website in the lead up to these exams, so make sure you are checking the ACCA website for recently published articles.

If you have studied – and are comfortable with – the valuation of real options using the Black–Scholes model, part (a) of this question should be relatively straightforward. The main issues you have to deal with are recognising that you are dealing with real options rather than traded options and appreciating that the option to delay is a call option.

Part (a) is a straightforward application of the Black–Scholes model. Make sure you make clear to the marker the value you are attaching to each of the components of the formulae being used. Remember to deal with the discussion areas of the question too – an easy thing to forget in the midst of large calculations!

Part (b) should be fairly brief. A couple of points about the role and limitations of the World Bank (and the International Development Association) are all that is needed.

Easy marks

Discussion of the limitations of Black–Scholes and other factors to be taken into account in part (a).

Marking guide	Marks
(a) Current price variable (Pa) in BSOP formula	2
Other variables in BSOP formula	2
Value of the option to expand decision	1
Revised value of projects and comments	3
Assumptions	3
Other factors	3
	14

 **BPP**

(b) Role of World Bank 1

     Usefulness of World Bank as a source of finance 2

     Role of IDA 1

     Usefulness of IDA as a source of finance .... <u>2</u>

                                                       <u>6</u>

Professional skills

Analysis and Evaluation

- Appropriate use of the data to use in the Black–Scholes Option Pricing model
- Appropriate use of the data to support discussion and draw appropriate conclusions
- Demonstration of reasoned judgement when considering key matters for Furlion Co
- Demonstration of ability to consider relevant factors applicable to Furlion Co's situation
- Appraisal of information objectively to make a recommendation

Scepticism

- Effective challenge of evidence and assumptions supplied with respect to the managers views on real option valuation
- Demonstration of ability to consider all relevant factors applicable to the decisions made by Furlion Co

Commercial acumen

- Effective use of examples and/or calculations from the scenario information and other practical considerations related to the context to illustrate points being made
- Recognition of external constraints and opportunities as necessary

Maximum .... <u>5</u>

Total .... <u><u>25</u></u>

(a) **Value of option to expand** – use the Black–Scholes model to value this option

    Using the BSOP spreadsheet provided in the exam is the quickest approach here:

    The variables needed to complete the model are:

    s = volatility = 30%

    P_a = current price (value of project including option exercise price) = $15m × 0.712 = $10.68m

    P_e = Exercise price (capital expenditure) = $15 million

    t = Exercise date = 3 years

    r = Risk-free rate = 4%

    These should be input to the spreadsheet provided, in row 3 as shown.

The spreadsheet then completes the calculations, as shown.

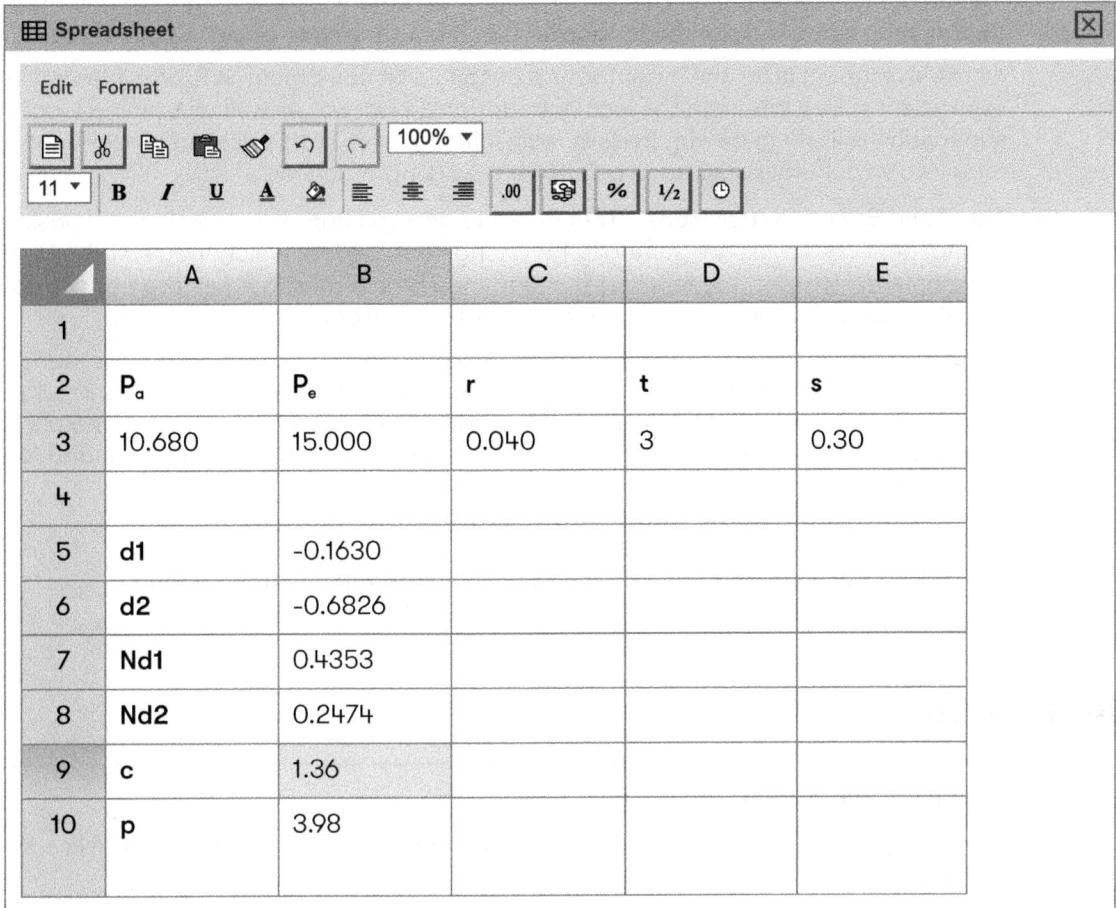

	A	B	C	D	E
1					
2	P_a	P_e	r	t	s
3	10.680	15.000	0.040	3	0.30
4					
5	d1	-0.1630			
6	d2	-0.6826			
7	Nd1	0.4353			
8	Nd2	0.2474			
9	c	1.36			
10	p	3.98			

The option to expand is valued as a call option, it is worth $1.36m

Overall value = $1.36m – $1.01m = $0.35m

The investment has a positive net present value, so should be accepted on those grounds. Furlion Co should also consider the value of an abandonment option if results turn out to be worse than expected or a delay option if it wants to see how the reclamation programme is going to continue.

Assumptions made and other factors

Using real options for decision making has limitations. Real options are built around uncertainties surrounding future cash flows, but real option theory is only useful if management can respond effectively to these uncertainties as they evolve.

The Black–Scholes model for valuing real options has a number of assumptions which may not be true in practice. It assumes that there is a market for the underlying asset and the volatility of returns on the underlying asset follows a normal distribution. The model also assumes perfect markets, a constant risk-free interest rate and constant volatility.

Furlion Co will also consider expectations about the future of the land reclamation programme. Has the programme been as quick and as effective as the Naswan government originally expected? Furlion Co will also want to consider how the programme will be affected by the amount of funding the government obtains and any conditions attached to that funding.

Furlion Co may also wish to consider whether its investment of this type will be looked on favourably by the Naswan government and whether tax or other concessions will be available. These may come with conditions, given the government's commitment to a sustainable economy, such as the way production facilities operate or the treatment of employees.

Given that this is a market which may expand in the future, Furlion Co should also consider the reaction of competitors. This may be a market where establishing a significant presence quickly may provide a significant barrier if competitors try to enter the market later.

As the investment is for the manufacture of specialist equipment, it is possible that there is insufficient skilled labour in the local labour pool in Naswa. As well as training local labour, supervision is likely to be required, at least initially, from staff based in other countries. This may involve cultural issues such as different working practices.

(b) The World Bank provides loans, often direct to governments, on a commercial basis, for capital projects. Loans are generally for a long-term period, which may suit the Naswan government. However, the terms of the loan may be onerous; not just the finance costs but the other conditions imposed on the scope of the projects.

Given the circumstances of the investment, Naswa may be able to obtain assistance from the International Development Association, which is part of the World Bank. This provides loans on more generous terms to the poorest countries. However, it is designed for countries with very high credit risk which would struggle to obtain funding by other means, and Naswa may not be eligible.

 Videos can be viewed by accessing your ebook version on VitalSource.

---

14 Tisa Co

Course Book references

Investment appraisal is covered in Chapter 3, and a risk-adjusted cost of capital is covered in Chapter 6.

Top tips

For part (a) you need to calculate the weighted average cost of capital (WACC). This can be done by estimating the project's asset beta, then using Tisa Co's capital structure to estimate the equity beta, then calculate the WACC.

Part (c) requires an understanding of how to calculate VaR, but you could still get marks from the explanations of what the figures mean even if you have not calculated them correctly.

For part (b) do not neglect the requirement to explain the recommendation you have made.

Examining team's comments

In part (a) most candidates made a reasonably good attempt at determining the cost of capital, although few candidates were able to calculate the asset beta of other activities and therefore the component asset beta. A small number of candidates used an average of equity and debt weightings and, where this was done correctly, appropriate credit was given. Many responses did not give reasons for the approach taken and thereby did not achieve some relatively easy marks.

Few responses calculated the annual and five-year VaR figures in part (c), and very few provided explanations of the values obtained.

Marking guide	Marks
(a) Reasoning behind cost of capital calculation	2
Calculation of component asset beta	3
Calculation of component equity beta, and K_e and WACC	3
	8
(b) Calculation of IRR for Process Omega	3

Calculation of MIRR for Process Omega	1
Resolution and advice	$\underline{4}$
	8
(c) Annual and five-year VaR	2
Explanation	$\underline{2}$
	$\underline{4}$

Professional skills

Analysis and Evaluation

- Appropriate use of the data to determine suitable calculations
- Appropriate use of the data to support discussion and draw appropriate conclusions
- Demonstration of reasoned judgement when considering key matters for Tisa Co

Commercial acumen

- Effective use of examples and/or calculations from the scenario information and other practical considerations related to the context to illustrate points being made relating to the investment decision
- Recommendations on which process Tisa Co should proceed with are practical and plausible

Scepticism

- Effective challenge of information and assumptions supplied and, techniques carried out to support any investment decision
- Demonstration of ability to consider all relevant factors applicable to the decisions made by Tisa Co

Maximum	$\underline{5}$
Total	$\underline{\underline{25}}$

(a) Use the information for Elfu Co to estimate the component project's asset beta. Then use Tisa Co's capital structure to estimate the project's equity beta and WACC. It is assumed that the beta of debt is zero.

Elfu Co MV_e = $1.20 × 400m shares = $480m

Elfu Co MV_d = $96 million

Elfu Co portfolio asset beta = 1.40 × $480m/($480m + $96m × (1 – 0.25)) = 1.217

Elfu Co asset beta of other activities = 1.25 × $360m/($360m + $76.8m × (1 – 0.25)) = 1.078

1.217 = component asset beta × 0.25 + 1.078 × 0.75

Component asset beta = (1.217 – (1.078 × 0.75))/0.25 = 1.634

Component equity beta based on Tisa Co capital structure

1.634 × [($18m + $3.6m × 0.75)/$18m] = 1.879

Using CAPM

K_e = 3.5% + 1.879 × 5.8% = 14.40%

WACC = (14.40% × $18m + 4.5% × $3.6m)/($18m + $3.6m) = 12.75%, say 13%

Using this WACC assumes that the capital structure will not change significantly as a result of the investment, which we are told is the case.

BPP

ANSWERS

(b) **Process Omega**

Year	Cash flow	Discount factor 13%	PV	Discount factor 20%	PV
	$'000		$'000		$'000
0	(3,800)	1.000	(3,800)	1.000	(3,800)
1	1,220	0.885	1,080	0.833	1,016
2	1,153	0.783	903	0.694	800
3	1,386	0.693	960	0.578	801
4	3,829	0.613	2,347	0.482	1,846
			1,490		663

IRR is approximately 13% + (1,490/(1,490 – 663)) × (20% – 13%) = 25.6%

> **Tutorial note.** You are unlikely to have used these exact discount rates, in which case you may reach a different conclusion in the discussion part of this question. As long as your conclusion is based on your calculations you will gain credit, whichever discount rates have been used.

Alternative approach using spreadsheet functionality:

Alternatively, the internal rate of return can be calculated using the =IRR spreadsheet function. Either method is acceptable, but the spreadsheet function gives a more precise answer and, with practice, should be quicker to use in the exam.

The spreadsheet extract shown in the following section shows the =IRR formula being applied:

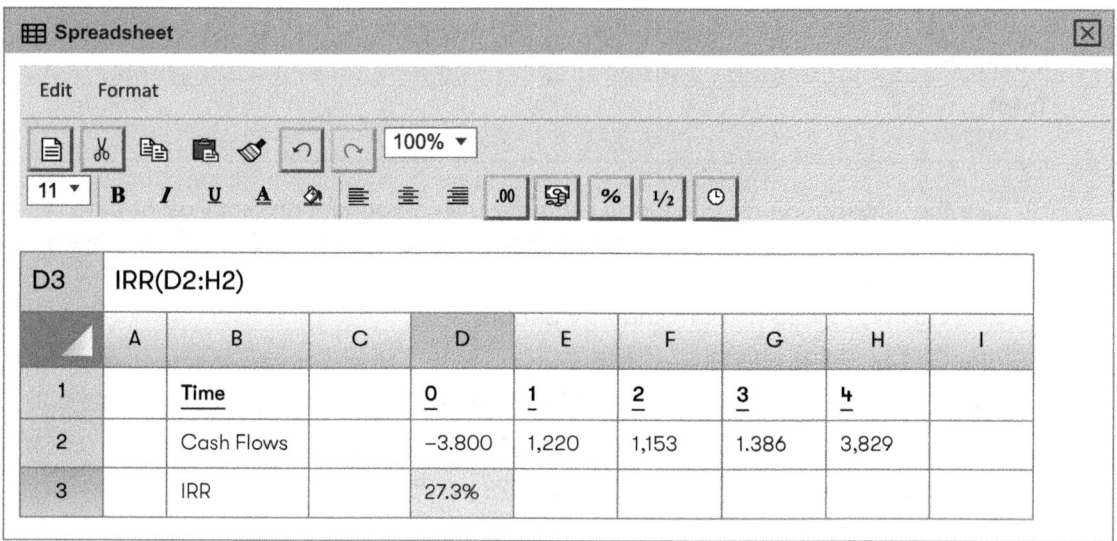

MIRR

MIRR =

$$\left[\frac{PV_r}{PV_i}\right]^{1/n} \times (1 + r_e) - 1$$

PV of investment phase = 3,800

PV of return phase = 3,800 + NPV of 1,490 = 5,290

MIRR =

$$\left[\frac{5,290}{3,800}\right]^{1/4} \times (1 + 0.13) - 1$$

= 0.227 or **22.7%**

Alternative approach using spreadsheet functionality:

Alternatively, the modified internal rate of return can be calculated using the =MIRR spreadsheet function. Either method is acceptable, but the spreadsheet function gives a slightly more precise answer and, with practice, should be quicker to use in the exam.

The spreadsheet extract shown in the following section shows the =MIRR formula being applied:

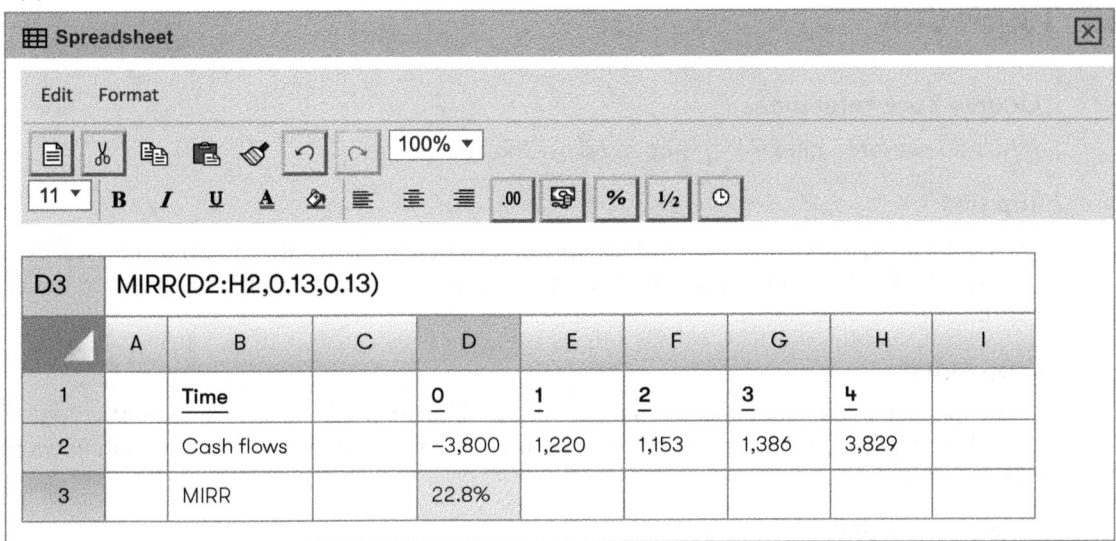

	A	B	C	D	E	F	G	H	I
		D3	MIRR(D2:H2,0.13,0.13)						
1		Time		0	1	2	3	4	
2		Cash flows		−3,800	1,220	1,153	1,386	3,829	
3		MIRR		22.8%					

Discussion

IRR assumes that positive cash flows are **reinvested and earn a return at the same rate as the project's IRR**. The MIRR assumes that positive cash flows are reinvested at the cost of capital. The assumption is more **reasonable** and the result produced is consistent with the net present value.

Therefore, basing the recommendation on the MIRR method, process Zeta should be adopted as it delivers a higher return than Omega (22.8%) and also delivers a return above the risk-adjusted cost of capital of 13%.

However, the difference between the two projects is not significant and it could reasonably be noted that Zeta depends more on its cash flows in time 4 than project Omega does. This reliance on a cash flow which could be assumed to be highly uncertain would mean that Omega could be recommended in preference to Zeta.

[other conclusions are possible here]

(c) A 99% confidence level requires the VaR to be less than 2.33 standard deviations below the mean.

Annual VaR = 2.33 × $800,000 = $1,864,000

Five-year VaR = $1,864,000 × $5^{0.5}$ = $4,168,031

This means that Elfu Co can be 99% confident that the cash flows will not fall by more than $1,864,000 in any one year or $4,168,031 in total over the five-year period.

This implies 99% certainty sure that the returns will be at least ($2,200,000 − $1,864,000) = $336,000 each year.

The company can also be 99% sure that the total five-year returns will be at least ($11,000,000 − $4,168,031) = $6,831,969. There is only a 1% chance that the returns will be less than $336,000 each year or $6,831,969 in total.

However, the theory of value at risk is based on a normal distribution, which assumes that virtually all possible outcomes will be within three standard deviations of the mean and that success and failure are equally likely. The logic of this may be questionable for a one-off project.

Value at risk is also based around the calculation of a standard deviation and this may be hard to estimate in reality since it is based on forecasting the possible spread of the results of a project around an average.

> **Tutorial note.** From the September 2024 exam, the standardised values associated with confidence levels will be given in exam questions as normal distribution tables will not be provided in the exam.

15 Tippletine

Course Book references

Adjusted present value (APV) is covered in Chapter 6.

Top tips

For part (a)(i) you have to know which formula to use to calculate the ungeared cost of equity. It is the MM Proposition 2 formula for ungearing a cost of equity which is given to you in the exam.

Easy marks

There are numerous easy marks to be picked up in part (a)(i) in the net present value calculations, although care will need to be taken over the timing of the tax cash flows because of the one-year delay.

Examining team's comments

Part (a) required candidates to undertake an investment appraisal using the adjusted present value technique, where the loan that might be used to finance the investment had significant financing side effects. Most candidates scored reasonable marks on this part.

Part (b) required candidates to discuss an alternative form of loan finance (convertible loan notes) that could be used to fund the investment. This part was often omitted and generally was not well-answered when attempted, highlighting a number of weaknesses in student performance. There was a lack of knowledge with candidates failing to discuss important features of convertible loan finance, such as a company needing to have sufficient money to redeem the notes if necessary.

Candidates also failed to respond to the question verb 'discuss', which generally requires some coverage of both advantages and disadvantages. Few answers said anything about the advantages of the convertible loan notes. Many answers failed to examine the terms from the shareholders' viewpoint, as the question required.

Marking guide	Marks
(a) Tax allowable depreciation	1
Taxation	2
Working capital	2
Discount factor & base case NPV	2
Issue costs	1
Tax shield on loan	2
Subsidy	1
Tax shield on subsidy	1

Adjusted present value	1	
Comments and conclusion	2	
		15

(b) 1–2 marks per point

Maximum ... 5

Professional skills

Analysis and Evaluation

- Appropriate use of the data to determine suitable calculations to appraise the investment using APV
- Appropriate use of the data to support discussion and draw appropriate conclusions
- Demonstration of reasoned judgement when considering key matters for Tippletine Co
- Demonstration of ability to consider relevant factors applicable to Tippletine Co's situation

Scepticism

- Effective challenge and critical assessment of the information and assumptions provided in relation to convertible debt
- Effective challenge of evidence and assumptions supplied with respect to the chairman's view on financing
- Effective challenge of information and assumptions supplied and, techniques carried out to support any investment decision
- Demonstration of ability to consider all relevant factors applicable to the decisions made by Tippletine Co

Commercial acumen

- Effective use of examples and/or calculations from the scenario information and other practical considerations related to the context to illustrate points being made relating to investment and financing
- Recognition of external constraints and opportunities as necessary
- Recommendations are practical and plausible in the context of Tippletine Co's situation

Maximum ... 5

Total ... 25

(a)

Year	0	1	2	3	4	5
	$'000	$'000	$'000	$'000	$'000	$'000
Cash flow before tax		(7,000)	12,500	13,225	13,834	
Taxation (W1)					(310)	(4,328)
Investment	(30,600)				13,500	
Working capital (W2)	(3,000)	(240)	(194)	(172)	3,606	
Cash flows	(33,600)	(7,240)	12,306	13,053	30,630	(4,328)
Discount factor 9% (W3)	1.000	0.917	0.842	0.772	0.708	0.650
Discounted cash flows	(33,600)	(6,639)	10,362	10,077	21,686	(2,813)
Base case NPV	(927)					

Alternative approach using spreadsheet functionality:

Alternatively, the present value of the cash flows from time 1–5 can be calculated using the =NPV spreadsheet function. Either method is acceptable, but the spreadsheet function gives a slightly more precise answer and, with practice, should be quicker to use in the exam.

The spreadsheet extract shown in the following section shows the =NPV formula being applied using the cost of capital of 9%.

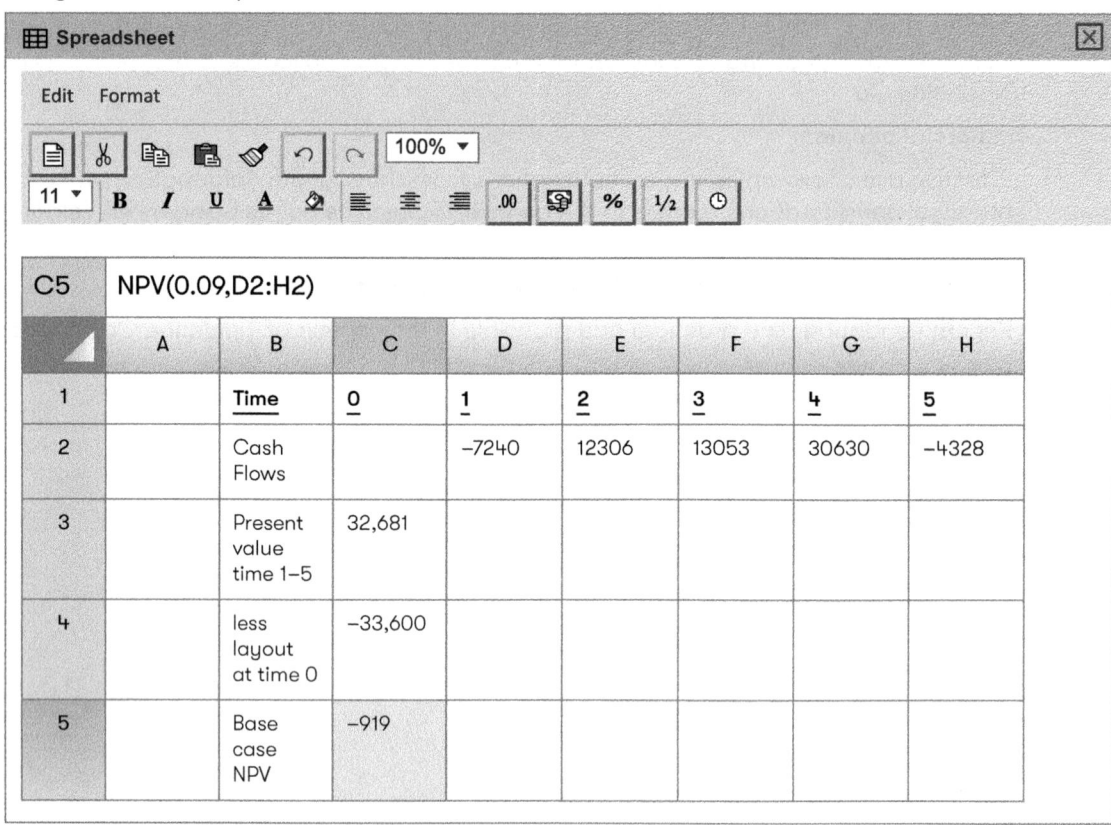

Note. that the NPV function assumes that the first cash flow is in one year's time, so you then have to subtract the time 0 cash outflows as before to give the project NPV

 **BPP**

Workings

1 Taxation

Year	TAD = Tax-allowable depreciation	Balance
		$'000
	Investment	30,600
1	TAD 25% reducing balance	(7,650)
		22,950
2	TAD 25% reducing balance	(5,738)
		17,212
3	TAD 25% reducing balance	(4,303)
		12,909
4	Balancing charge	591
		13,500

Year	1	2	3	4
	$'000	$'000	$'000	$'000
Cash flow before tax	(7,000)	12,500	13,225	13,834
Tax-allowable depreciation	(7,650)	(5,738)	(4,303)	591
Adjusted cash flow	(14,650)	6,762	8,922	14,425
Offset against previous losses		(14,650)	(7,888)	
Losses carried forward	(14,650)	(7,888)		
Taxable cash flow			1,034	14,425
Taxation at 30%			310	4,328
Year			4	5

2 Working capital

Year	1	2	3	4
	$'000	$'000	$'000	$'000
	3,000 × 0.08 = 240	(3,000 + 240) × 0.06 = 194	(3,000 + 240 + 194) × 0.05 = 172	3,000 + 240 + 194 + 172 = 3,606

3 Ungeared cost of equity

Humabuz Co

MV debt = $225m × 1.07 = $240.8m

MV equity = 125m × $3.20 = $400m

Ungeared cost of equity

$k_e = k_e^i + (1 - t)(k_e^i - k_d) V_d/V_e$

$10.5\% = k_e^i + (1 - 0.3)(k_e^i - 5.4\%)(240.8/400)$

$10.5\% + 2.28\% = 1.42 k_e^i$

$k_e^i = 9\%$

4 *Issue costs*

Gross finance required: ($30,600,000/0.96) = $31,875,000

Debt issue costs: $31,875,000 × 0.04 = $1,275,000

5 *Tax shield on loan*

Use PV of an annuity (PVA) for years 2–5 at 5% (assume 5% is cost of debt).

Note. The risk-free rate of 2.5% could also be used for discounting.

Subsidised loan: $30,600,000 × (0.025 − 0.003) × 0.3 × (4.329 − 0.952) = $682,000

6 *Subsidy*

Benefit = $30,600,000 × (0.05 − 0.022) × 3.546 = $3,038,000

Tax relief lost = $30,600,000 × (0.05 − 0.022) × 0.3 × (4.329 − 0.952) = $868,000

7 *Financing side effects*

	$'000
Issue costs (W4)	(1,275)
Tax shield on loan (W5)	682
Subsidy benefit (W6)	3,038
Tax relief lost on subsidy benefit (W6)	(868)
Total benefit of financing side effects	1,577

Conclusion

If base case net present value is used, the project has a negative net present value of $927,000, and on that basis should be rejected. However, the financing side effects add $1,577,000 to the value of the project, giving a positive adjusted present value of $650,000. On that basis the project should be accepted.

The revenues from the project appear to be uncertain and the realisable value at the end of the project may be optimistic. It would be useful to have an indication of the range of outcomes and an idea of the probability that the project will have a negative APV.

(b) Advantages of convertible loan notes

The investors may be happy that directors are demonstrating their commitment to the company by subscribing to convertible loan notes. The conversion rights mean that these directors will benefit if the share price increases, aligning their interests with shareholders.

The conversion terms also mean that the loan notes will not necessarily have to be repaid in a few years' time. This may be significant if Tippletine Co does not have the cash available for redemption then.

Drawbacks of convertible loan notes

The convertible loan notes would be treated as debt, increasing Tippletine Co's gearing, which may concern the other shareholders. The interest on the convertible loan notes will be payable before dividends and may leave less money for distribution to shareholders. Shareholders may doubt whether the higher interest burden on the convertible loan notes, compared with the subsidised loan, is compensated for by the lower costs of Tippletine Co not having to fulfil the government's requirements.

The other shareholders may be concerned by the interest rate on the convertible notes being Tippletine Co's normal cost of borrowing. The option to convert is an advantage for convertible loan note holders. They would often effectively pay for this option by receiving a lower rate of interest on the loan notes.

Shareholders would want to assess how likely conversion would be – that is, how likely it would be that the share price will rise above $2.75. The option to convert may also change the balance of shareholdings, giving the directors who held the notes a greater percentage of

share capital and possibly more influence over Tippletine Co. The other shareholders may be unhappy with this.

The shareholders may also have reservations about the loan note holders having the option to redeem if Tippletine Co's share price is low. This reduces the risk of providing the finance from the loan note holders' viewpoint. However, if the share price is low, Tippletine Co's financial results and cash flows may be poor and it may struggle to redeem the loan notes. Shareholders may also be concerned that there is no cap the other way, allowing Tippletine Co to force conversion if the share price reaches a high enough level.

Note. Credit will be given for alternative relevant discussion.

16 Robson

Course Book references

Project appraisal using adjusted present value is mainly covered in Chapter 6.

Easy marks

There are easy numerical marks in part (a) if you read the question carefully and produce the required analysis. There is no need to complete the hardest part of the question accurately to score a pass mark. [The main technical difficulty here was in calculation the annual interest on a bank loan that was being repaid in equal amounts over a four-year period.]

Examining team's comments

Vague generalised statements will receive little if any credit in this type of question. However, answers that were specific in terms of which capital provider they related to and the practical scenario were rewarded generously here. The examiner's comments gave an example of the following statement which was awarded 2 marks:

"The subsidised loan provider would need to consider whether an automated plant is going to fulfil the government's job creation objective and whether the skills exist in that part of the country to run such a plant".

Marking guide		Marks
(a) Base case	1	
Ungeared cost of equity	1	
Issue costs	1	
Tax shield on subsidised loan	2	
Tax shield on bank loan	4	
Subsidy benefit	1	
Adjusted present value	1	
Recommendations	2	
Maximum		13
(b) Shareholders (eg fund availability, control, track record)	5	
Subsidised loan provider (eg job creation, default risk, covenants)	4	
Marks Available	9	
Maximum		7

Professional skills

Analysis and Evaluation

- Appropriate use of the data to determine suitable calculations
- Appropriate use of the data to support discussion and draw appropriate conclusions

- Appraisal of information objectively to make a recommendation

Scepticism

- Demonstration of ability to consider all relevant factors applicable to the decisions made by the capital providers

Commercial acumen

- Effective use of examples and/or practical considerations related to the context to illustrate points being made relating to capital providers

	Marks
Maximum	5
Total	25

(a) **Project cash flows:** All figures are in $m

Year	0	1	2	3	4
Cash flows	(120.0)	20.9	20.6	28.7	104.6
Discount factors – 14% (w1)	1.000	0.877	0.769	0.675	0.592
Present values	(120.0)	18.3	15.8	19.4	61.9

Base case net present value = ($4.6m)

Base case net present value is negative and on this basis should therefore be rejected.

Financing side effects: All figures are in $m

Issue costs (w2)	(2.0)
Tax shield on subsidised loan (w3)	0.9
Tax shield on bank loan (w4)	2.0
Subsidy benefit (w5)	5.7
Total benefit of financing side effects	6.6

Recommendation

The adjusted present value of the project is $2.0m and so the project should be accepted.

Workings

1 ***Ungeared cost of equity***

$\beta_a = 1.222$

$K_{eu} = r_f + \beta_a (r_m - r_f) = 0.03 + (1.222 \times 0.09) = 14\%$

2 ***Issue costs***

$100m \times 0.02 = \$2,000,000$

Note. Issue costs are payable out of cash reserves, so the finance does not need to be grossed up.

3 ***Tax shield on subsidised loan***

Annuity factor (9%, 4 years) = 3.240

$40m \times 0.035 \times 0.20 \times 3.240 = \$907,200$

Note. The risk-free rate would also be acceptable as a discount rate.

BPP

4 *Tax shield on bank loan*

Annual repayment = $50m / 3.240 = $15,432,098

Year	1	2	3	4
	$ 000	$ 000	$ 000	$ 000
Opening balance	50,000	39,068	27,152	14,164
Interest at 9%	4,500	3,516	2,444	1,275
Repayment	(15,432)	(15,432)	(15,432)	(15,432)
Closing balance	39,068	27,152	14,164	7
Tax relief on interest (20%)	900	703	489	255
Discount factor (9%)	0.917	0.842	0.772	0.708
Present value	825	592	378	181

Total present value = $1,976,000

5 *Subsidy benefit*

Subsidy benefit = $40m × (0.09 − 0.035) × 0.80 × 3.240 = $5,702,400

(b) **Factors each capital provider may consider**

External shareholders

The chief executive's optimism regarding the rights issue may be misplaced. Robson Co's shareholders may question the need for another rights issue so soon after the last one. Nor may they have the funds available to take up their rights, particularly when there has been a series of fund raising exercises in the last six years. Whilst in theory the shareholders are able to sell their rights, this would mean accepting a dilution in their voting power, which may not be acceptable. Therefore, it is possible a rights issue could fail. Even if Robson Co has the issue underwritten, failure of the rights issue would have an adverse impact on Robson Co's share price and the market's confidence in the board.

Shareholders may question the logic behind the new project and whether the forecast results can be delivered. They may need reassurance that lessons from the past have been learnt. The underwriting costs have been ignored in the financial appraisal even though these are likely to be significant and may prove fatal to the final outcome, particularly when the project's APV is quite marginal at $2m.

The loan will mean that Robson Co's gearing once again exceeds the average and shareholders will require higher returns to compensate for the increase in financial risk. The shareholders may question whether the commitment to service and repay the new loans may mean that Robson Co will have difficulty paying an acceptable level of dividend.

Subsidised loan provider

The subsidised loan programme provides capital for investment with the objective of boosting employment in a deprived part of the country. Since the funds ultimately originate from the taxpayer, the government is accountable for any funding decisions made. Robson Co's ability to service and ultimately repay the debt is therefore paramount. Robson Co's credit rating provides an assessment of the probability of default and the recent downgrade may cause concern. Even though Robson Co is unable to provide assets for security, the directors may still be faced with other covenants, for example restrictions on dividends or further borrowing which may upset shareholders.

The subsidy means demand for such loans is likely to be high and the selection criteria difficult so it is unlikely that the outcome is a foregone conclusion in the way Robson Co's CEO suggests. Based on the information provided it is unclear whether the new project would meet those selection criteria. Although Robson Co's new project is to be located in an area targeted for regeneration, it remains the case that the objective of the move is to automate

BPP

ANSWERS

the production line. Whilst jobs may still be created in a deprived area, net job creation nationwide is still likely to be negative. Whether such a policy would be attractive to the government, or the taxpayer, remains to be seen.

Note. Credit will be given for alternative and valid comments.

17 Toltuck

Marking guide	Marks	
(a) Government yield curve	2	
Toltuck Co spot-curve old and new	2	
Bond valuation – old and new	3	
Yield to maturity – old and new	3	
		10
(b) Financial factors	4	
Other factors (eg country, industry, management)	4	
Impact: 1–2 marks per issue	5	
Limit marks for (b) to 4 marks in total if answer does not mention Toltuck Co's position		
Maximum		10

Professional skills

Analysis and Evaluation

- Appropriate use of the data to determine suitable calculations to value the bond and calculate the yield to maturity under both credit ratings
- Demonstration of reasoned judgement when considering key matters for Toltuck Co
- Demonstration of ability to consider relevant factors applicable to Toltuck Co's situation

Commercial acumen

- Effective use of examples and/or calculations from the scenario information and other practical considerations related to the context of Toltuck Co and the factors that may have affected its credit rating.

	Marks
Maximum	5
Total	**25**

(a) The government yield curve can be estimated from the data available:

Bond 1: $104 = $109/(1 + r_1)$

$r_1 = ($109/$104) - 1 = 4.81\%$

Bond 2: $102 = $7/1.0481 + $107/(1 + r_2)^2$

$r_2 = [107/(102 - 6.68)]^{1/2} - 1 = 5.95\%$

Bond 3: $98 = $6/1.0481 + $6/1.0595^2 + $106/(1 + r_3)^3$

$r_3 = [106/(98 - 5.72 - 5.35)]^{1/3} - 1 = 6.83\%$

Year	Govt yield curve	Spread old rating	Toltuck Co spot old rating	Spread new rating	Toltuck Co spot new rating
	%	%	%	%	%
1	4.81	0.18	4.99	0.54	5.35
2	5.95	0.31	6.26	0.69	6.64
3	6.83	0.45	7.28	0.86	7.69

Valuation of bond under old credit rating

Year	Payment	Discount factor	Discounted cash flow
	$		$
1	8	$1/1.0499$	7.62
2	8	$1/1.0626^2$	7.09
3	110	$1/1.0728^3$	89.09
Bond valuation			103.80

Valuation of bond under new credit rating

Year	Payment	Discount factor	Discounted cash flow
	$		$
1	8	$1/1.0535$	7.59
2	8	$1/1.0664^2$	7.03
3	110	$1/1.0769^3$	88.08
Bond valuation			102.70

Yield to maturity under old credit rating

Year	Payment	Discount factor	Discounted cash flow	Discount factor	Discounted cash flow
	$	8%	$	7%	$
0	(103.80)	1.000	(103.80)	1.000	(103.80)
1–3	8.00	2.577	20.62	2.624	20.99
3	102.00	0.794	80.99	0.816	83.23
			(2.19)		0.42

Using IRR approach, yield to maturity = 7 + ((0.42/(2.19 + 0.42)) × (8 − 7)) = 7.16%

BPP

Yield to maturity under new credit rating

Year	Payment	Discount factor	Discounted cash flow	Discount factor	Discounted cash flow
	$	8%	$	7%	$
0	(102.70)	1.000	(102.70)	1.000	(102.70)
1–3	8.00	2.577	20.62	2.624	20.99
3	102.00	0.794	80.99	0.816	83.23
			(1.09)		1.52

Using IRR approach, yield to maturity = 7 + ((1.52/(1.09 + 1.52)) × (8 − 7)) = 7.58%

Market value of $100 bond has fallen by $1.10 and the yield to maturity has risen by 0.42%.

(b) **Factors which may have affected the credit rating of Toltuck Co published by the credit agency**

The credit agency will have taken the following criteria into consideration when assessing Toltuck C's credit rating:

Country

Toltuck Co's debt would not normally be rated higher than the credit ratings of its country of origin, Arumland. Therefore, the credit rating of Arumland should normally be at least AA. The rating will also have depended on Toltuck Co's standing relative to other companies in Arumland. The credit agency may have reckoned that Toltuck Co's recent poor results have weakened its position.

Industry

The credit agency will have taken account of the impact of the recession on property construction companies generally in Arumland. Toltuck Co's position within the industry compared with competitors will also have been assessed. If similar recent developments by competitors have been more successful, this is likely to have had an adverse impact on Toltuck Co's rating.

Management

The credit agency will have made an overall assessment of management and succession planning at Toltuck Co. It will have looked at business and financing strategies and planning and controls. It will also have assessed how successful the management has been in terms of delivering financial results. The credit agency may have believed the poor returns on recent developments show shortcomings in management decision-making processes and it may have rated the current management team poorly.

Financial

The credit agency will have analysed financial results, using measures such as return on capital employed. The agency will also have assessed possible sources of future earnings growth. It may have been sceptical about prospects, certainly for the short term, given Toltuck Co's recent problems.

The credit agency will also have assessed the financial position of Toltuck Co, looking at its gearing and working capital management, and considering whether Toltuck Co has enough cash to finance its needs. The agency will also have looked at Toltuck Co's relationship with its bankers and its debt covenants, to assess how flexible its sources of finances are if it comes under stress. It may well have been worried about Toltuck Co's gearing being higher than the industry average and concerned about the high levels of cash it needs to finance operations. It will also have assessed returns on developments-in-progress compared with commitments to repay loans. Greater doubt about Toltuck Co's ability to meet its commitments is likely to have been a significant factor in the fall in its rating.

The agency will also have needed reassurance about the quality of the financial information it was using, so it will have looked at the audit report and accounting policies.

 BPP

Impact of the fall in Toltuck Co's credit rating on its ability to raise financial capital

Toltuck Co may not have increased problems raising debt finance if debtholders do not react in the same way as the credit rating agency. They may attach different weightings to the criteria which they use. They may also come to different judgements about the quality of management and financial stability. Debtholders may believe that the recent problems Toltuck Co has had generating returns may be due more to external factors which its management could not have controlled.

However, it is probable that the fall in Toltuck Co's credit rating will result in it having more difficulty raising debt finance. Banks may be less willing to provide loans and investors less willing to subscribe for bonds. Even if debt finance is available, it may come with covenants restricting further debt or gearing levels. This will mean that if Toltuck Co requires substantial additional finance, it is more likely to have to make a rights issue or issue new equity on the stock market. Shareholders may be faced with the choice of subscribing large amounts for new capital or having their influence diluted. This may particularly worry the more cautious shareholders.

Even if Toltuck Co can obtain the debt it needs, the predicted increase in yield to maturity may be matched by debtholders demanding a higher coupon rate on debt. This will increase finance costs, and decrease profits and earnings per share, with a possible impact on share price. It will also mean that fewer funds are available for paying dividends. Toltuck Co has been faced with difficult decisions on balancing investment expenditure versus paying dividends and these difficulties may well increase.

Additional debt may have other restrictive covenants. They may restrict Toltuck Co's buying and selling of assets, or its investment strategy. Restrictions on Toltuck Co's decisions about the developments it undertakes may impact adversely on shareholder returns.

Loan finance or bonds will also come with repayment covenants. These may require Toltuck Co to build up a fund over time which will be enough to redeem the debt at the end of its life. Given uncertainties over cash flows, this commitment to retain cash may make it more difficult to undertake major developments or pay an acceptable level of dividend.

18 Tonpantau

Course Book references

For part (a), the idea of a project-specific cost of capital is mainly covered in Chapter 6, while real options (part b) are covered in Chapter 4.

Top Tips

When writing a discussion answer candidates should aim to make one point per mark available, although there is quite often up to two marks if the point is developed well.

When making a discussion point it is important to make use of the scenario which is provided. So, in part (b) you should include in your answer a reference to the real options apparently available to Tonpantau Co. Ignoring the scenario also makes it especially hard to earn professional marks.

Examining Team comments

The Examining Team noted in part (a) that 'Candidates who get stuck at some point in their calculations must not be afraid of making assumptions and then carrying on. As previously stated, a significant number of candidates calculated the value of the bond but could not then calculate the cost of the bond. Those with good exam technique simply stated an assumed cost of debt and proceeded to calculate a WACC using this. In this way they only lost 2 technical marks'.

		Marks
(a)	Taxation	1
	Tax-allowable depreciation	1
	Working capital	1
	Net present value	1
	Asset beta	1
	Equity beta	1
	Cost of equity	1
	Valuation of bond	2
	Cost of debt	2
	Weighted average cost of capital	1
		12
(b)	Real options show value of flexibility	2
	Option to expand	2
	Option to withdraw/abandon	2
	Problems with using real options	3
	Marks Available	9
	Maximum	8

Professional skills marks

Analysis and evaluation

- Appropriate use of the data to determine suitable calculations
- Appropriate use of the data to support discussion, draw appropriate conclusions and design appropriate responses
- Identification of omissions from the analysis, or further analysis, which could be carried out to enable an appropriate decision/recommendation to be made

Scepticism

- Effective challenge of information, evidence and assumptions supplied and techniques carried out to support key facts and/or decisions
- Demonstration of the ability to probe into the reasons for issues and problems, including the identification of missing information or additional information, which would be required to challenge conclusions or recommendations which have already been reached

Commercial acumen

- Effective use of examples from the scenario information and other practical considerations related to the context to illustrate points being made

Maximum		5
Total		25

(a)

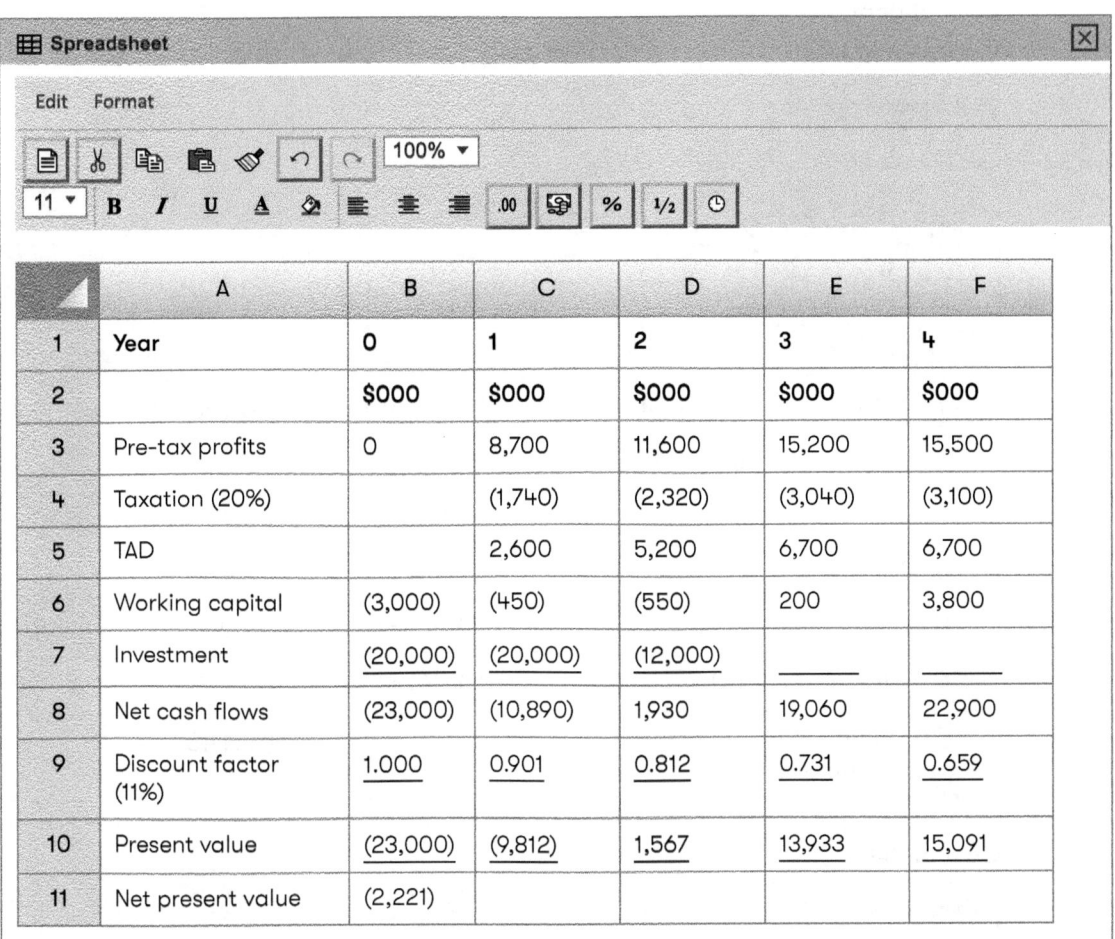

	A	B	C	D	E	F
1	Year	0	1	2	3	4
2		$000	$000	$000	$000	$000
3	Pre-tax profits	0	8,700	11,600	15,200	15,500
4	Taxation (20%)		(1,740)	(2,320)	(3,040)	(3,100)
5	TAD		2,600	5,200	6,700	6,700
6	Working capital	(3,000)	(450)	(550)	200	3,800
7	Investment	(20,000)	(20,000)	(12,000)		
8	Net cash flows	(23,000)	(10,890)	1,930	19,060	22,900
9	Discount factor (11%)	1.000	0.901	0.812	0.731	0.659
10	Present value	(23,000)	(9,812)	1,567	13,933	15,091
11	Net present value	(2,221)				

The project has a negative present value, so on the basis of the calculations should not be undertaken.

Working

Cost of equity

Use Bodfari Co's information to estimate the asset beta of the investment. Assume the beta of debt is zero.

Asset beta = 1.60 × 75/(75 + 25 × (1 – 0.2)) = 1.263

Tonpantau Co's equity beta is based on its capital structure:

Equity beta = 1.263 x (60 + 40 × (1 – 0.2))/60 = 1.937

Using CAPM k_e = 4.25% + (1.937 x 5.5%) = 14.90%

Cost of debt

Valuation of bond

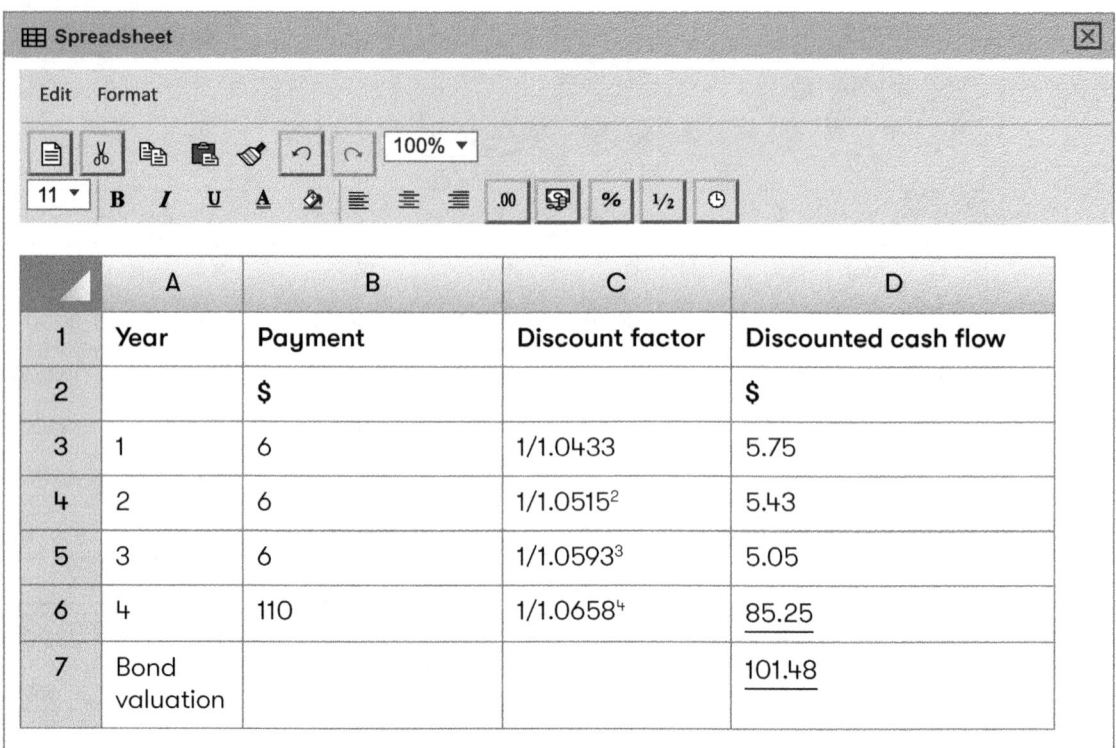

Spreadsheet

	A	B	C	D
1	Year	Payment	Discount factor	Discounted cash flow
2		$		$
3	1	6	$1/1.0433$	5.75
4	2	6	$1/1.0515^2$	5.43
5	3	6	$1/1.0593^3$	5.05
6	4	110	$1/1.0658^4$	85.25
7	Bond valuation			101.48

Cost of debt

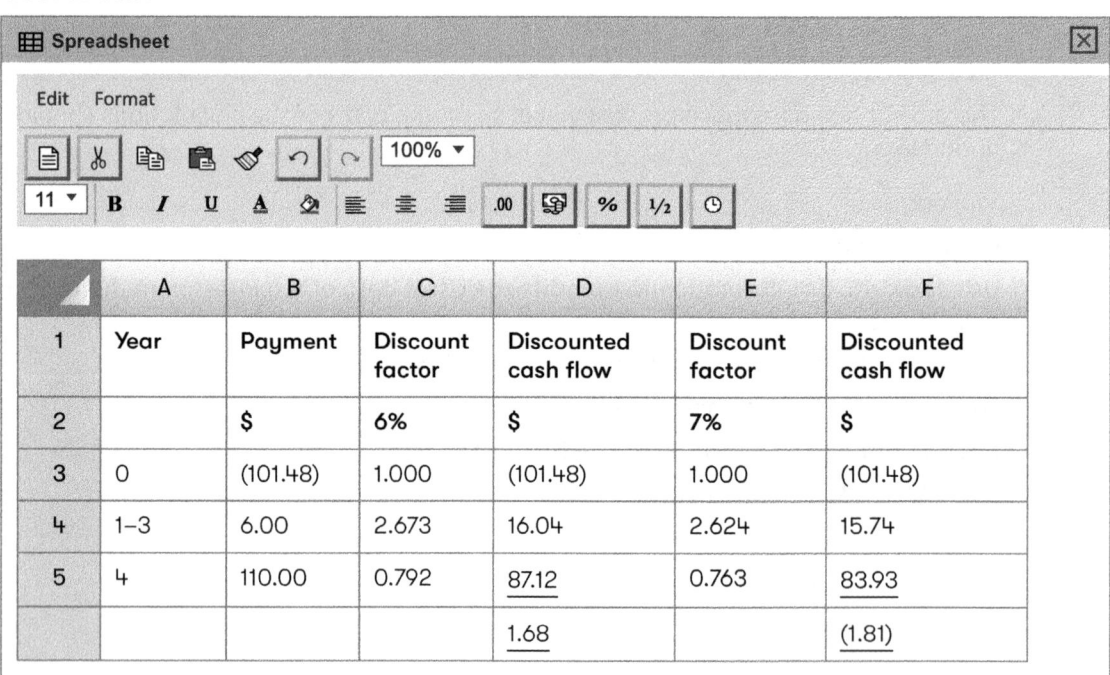

Spreadsheet

	A	B	C	D	E	F
1	Year	Payment	Discount factor	Discounted cash flow	Discount factor	Discounted cash flow
2		$	6%	$	7%	$
3	0	(101.48)	1.000	(101.48)	1.000	(101.48)
4	1–3	6.00	2.673	16.04	2.624	15.74
5	4	110.00	0.792	87.12	0.763	83.93
				1.68		(1.81)

Using IRR approach, cost of debt = 6 + [(1.68/(1.68 + 1.81)) x (7 – 6)] = 6.48%

Alternative method

Alternatively, the internal rate of return can be calculated using the =IRR spreadsheet function. Either method is acceptable, but the spreadsheet function gives a more precise answer and, with practice, should be much quicker to use in the exam.

 BPP

The spreadsheet extract shown in the following section shows the =IRR formula being applied:

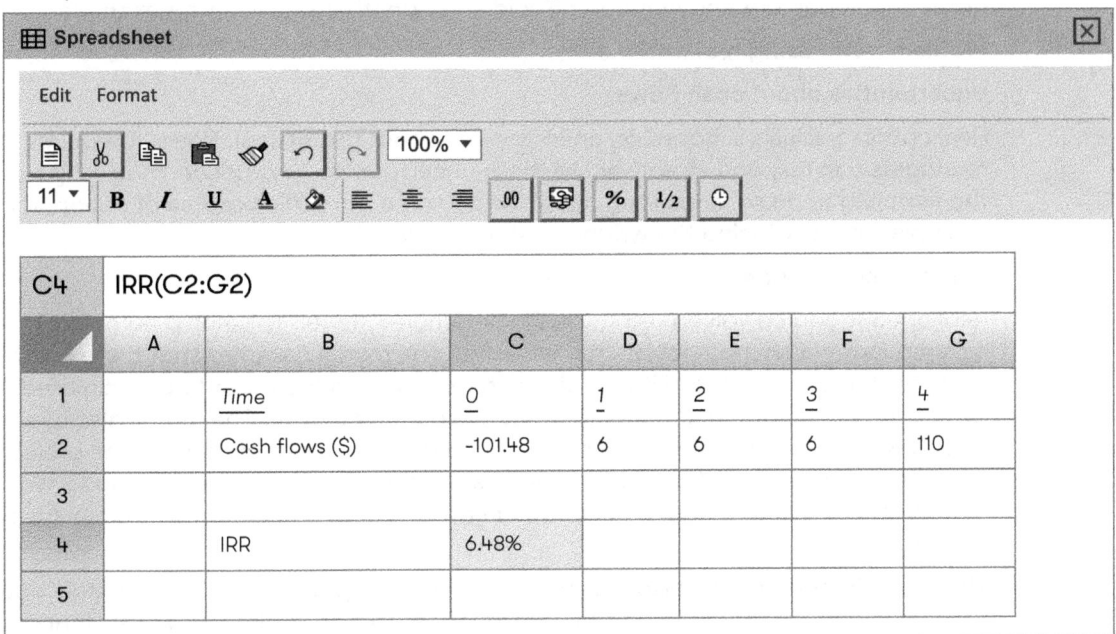

WACC

WACC = [(60/(60 + 40)) x 14.90%] + [(40/(60 + 40)) x 6.48% x (1 – 0.2)] = 11.01%, say 11%

(b)

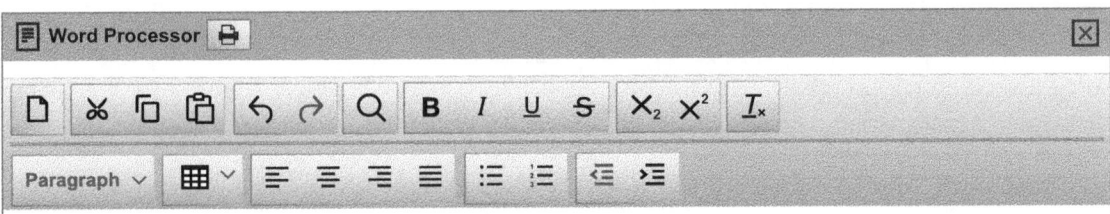

Use of real options

Real options provide an additional perspective on net present value calculations in situations of uncertainty. Ordinary net present calculations involve deciding immediately and irrevocably whether to undertake an investment. Real option theory can help when a decision does not have to be made on a now or never basis. The theory is useful when a decision can be made and then changed or where there may be additional opportunities which can be exploited once an initial decision has been made to undertake an investment.

Real option models calculate the added value of the flexibility which a company has where it has a choice and time to decide. This flexibility is incorporated as the time value of the option, which is additional to the intrinsic value of the investment opportunity. The value of the real option will increase when the uncertainty relating to the underlying asset increases, given that the option has an unlimited upside but a limited downside.

Tonpantau Co

Real options are relevant to Tonpantau Co as it has potential to expand its current investment or abandon it. It can decide after year 0 to produce more products than planned, giving it the chance to increase the intrinsic value of the overall investment. The option to expand is a call option. The initial investment is the premium required to expand and the exercise price is the value of the additional investment over and above what is planned.

Because the investment is phased over two years, Tonpantau Co also may have the opportunity to withdraw from (abandon) the project if initial sales are disappointing. The option to withdraw will be exercised if the salvage/liquidation value on abandonment exceeds the value of the net cash flows being forgone. The option would effectively be a

put option. The option's value will be influenced by whether there is value in the intellectual property already created, if it can be sold on to another publisher for example.

Problems with using real options

Uncertainties about cash flows

Real option analysis is based on uncertainties about future cash flows. It requires that managers can respond effectively to these uncertainties. In practice, they may not have the flexibility to do so, once they have decided on a particular course of action, for example, commissioning the writing of study material.

Black–Scholes model

Real options can be valued using the Black-Scholes model. This has a number of assumptions which may not be true in reality. The model assumes that there is sufficient data available for the volatility of returns for the underlying asset to be estimated accurately and that the underlying asset has a market value. The model also assumes a constant risk-free interest rate, constant volatility and a perfect market. The project's cash flows are assumed to follow a lognormal distribution. The Black-Scholes model was designed for valuing financial options rather than options in physical investments such as training material.

The Black–Scholes model also assumes that the real option is a European-style option which can only be exercised on the date when the option expires. However, Tonpantau Co may make the decision to expand or contract its product range at any time over the next few years, meaning that the option is more representative of an American-style option which can be exercised before expiry. The model may thus underestimate the true value of the option for Tonpantau Co.

 BPP

19 Vogel

Course Book references

Acquisitions are covered in Chapters 8 and 10.

Easy marks

You should be able to pick up some relatively straightforward marks in part (a).

Examining team's comments

In part (b) there was little coherent presentation and structure to the answer, with many numbers and calculations presented in a haphazard manner. This approach did not gain many marks as it was not clear where the answer was heading and gave little confidence that the candidate knew what they were doing.

Marking guide		Marks
(a)	2 marks per point for discussing risk	4
	1 mark per point for commenting on strategy	2
	Maximum	6
(b)	Cash gained from sales of Department C assets	1
	Calculation of free cash flows for Ndege Co	2
	Calculation of present values of Ndege Co cash flows and value	2
	Vogel Co P/E ratios before and after acquisition	2
	Tori Co P/E ratio and value	1
	Value created from combining Department A with Vogel Co	1
	Maximum premium payable	1
	Approach taken	2
	Assumptions made	3
	Marks Available	15
	Maximum	14

Professional skills

Analysis and Evaluation

- Appropriate use of the data to determine suitable calculations to establish the maximum premium Vogel Co should pay
- Appropriate use of the data to support discussion and draw appropriate conclusions
- Demonstration of reasoned judgement when considering key matters for Vogel Co
- Demonstration of ability to consider relevant factors applicable to Vogel Co's situation
- Appraisal of information objectively to make a recommendation

Scepticism

- Effective challenge and critical assessment of the information and assumptions provided in relation to the acquisition
- Demonstration of ability to consider all relevant factors applicable to the decisions made

BPP

Commercial acumen

- Effective use of examples and/or calculations from the scenario information and other practical considerations related to the context to illustrate points being made relating to Vogel Co

- Recognition of external constraints and opportunities in relation to the proposed acquisition

- Recommendations are practical and plausible in the context of Vogel Co's situation

Maximum	5
Total	25

(a) Since Vogel Co has a poor track record of adding value from its acquisitions it needs to review recent acquisitions to understand why they have not added value, ie it should do a post-audit of these acquisitions.

Vogel Co should also ensure that the valuation is based on reasonable input figures and that proper due diligence of the perceived benefits is undertaken prior to the offer being made. Often it is difficult to get an accurate picture of the target when looking at it from the outside. Vogel Co needs to ensure that it has sufficient data and information to enable a thorough and sufficient analysis to be undertaken.

The sources of synergy need to be properly assessed to ensure that they are achievable and to identify what actions Vogel Co needs to undertake to ensure their achievement. Targets should be set for all areas of synergy and responsibility for achieving these targets should be clearly allocated to members of Vogels' senior management team.

The non-executive directors should play a crucial role in ensuring that acquisitions are made to enhance the value for the shareholders. Procedures need to be established to ensure that the acquisition is not overpaid. Vogel Co should determine the maximum premium it is willing to pay and not go beyond that figure. Research indicates that often too much is paid to acquire a company and the resultant synergy benefits are not sufficient to cover the premium paid. Often this is the result of the management of the acquiring company wanting to complete the deal at any cost, because not completing the deal may be perceived as damaging to both their own, and their company's, reputation.

Vogel Co needs to ensure that it has proper procedures in place to integrate the staff and systems of the target company effectively, and also to recognise that such integration takes time. Vogel Co may decide instead to give the target company a large degree of autonomy and thus make integration less necessary; however, this may result in a reduction in synergy benefits.

Vogel Co should also have strategies in place to retain key staff in the companies that it is acquiring – these people need to be identified at an early stage and given assurances over their role and responsibilities post-acquisition. Vogel Co should also be mindful that its own and the acquired company's staff and management need to integrate and ensure a good working relationship between them.

Note. Only two suggestions were asked for.

Vogel Co may have switched from a strategy of organic growth to one of growth by acquisition because acquiring a company to gain access to new products, markets, technologies and expertise will almost certainly be quicker and may be less costly than developing these internally.

Horizontal acquisitions may help Vogel Co eliminate key competitors and thereby reduce rivalry and possible overcapacity in its industry; they may also have enabled Vogel Co to take advantage of economies of scale and to compete against large rivals.

Vertical acquisitions may help Vogel Co to secure the supply chain and maximise returns from its value chain.

Furthermore, organic growth, especially into a new area, would need managers to gain knowledge and expertise of an area or function, which they are not currently familiar with.

Note. Credit will be given for alternative relevant comments.

(b) **Approach taken**

The maximum premium payable is equal to the maximum additional benefit created from the acquisition of Tori Co, with no increase in value for the shareholders of Vogel Co. It should be noted that the shareholders of Vogel Co would probably not approve of the acquisition if they do not gain from it, but certainly they would not approve a bid in excess of this.

The additional benefit can be estimated as the sum of the cash gained (or lost) from selling the assets of Department C, spinning off Department B and integrating Department A, less the sum of the values of Vogel Co and Tori Co as separate companies.

Estimation of cash gained from selling the assets of Department C:

Non-current assets = (20% × \$98.2m) = \$19.64m

Current assets = (20% × \$46.5m × 0.9) = \$8.37m

Liabilities and closure costs = (\$20.2 + \$3m) = \$23.2m

Total = \$19.64m + \$8.37m − \$23.2m = **\$4.81m**

Value created from spinning off Department B into Ndege Co

Free cash flow of Ndege Co	\$m
Current share of PBDIT (0.4 × \$37.4m)	14.96
Less PBIT attributable to Department C (10% × 14.96)	(1.50)
Less tax-allowable depreciation (0.4 × 98.2 × 0.10)	(3.93)
Profits before tax	9.53
Tax (20%)	(1.91)
Free cash flows	7.62

Value of Ndege Co =

Present value of \$7.62 million free cash flow growing at 20% in the first year and discounted at 10%:

\$7.62m × 1.2 × 0.909 = \$8.31m

Add present value of cash flows from Year 2 onwards:

(\$9.14m × 1.052)/(0.1 − 0.052) × 0.909 = \$182.11m

Less bond taken over by Ndege = \$40 million

Value to shareholders of Ndege Co = 8.31 + 182.11 − 40 = $150.42m

Current values

Vogel Co's current value = \$3 × 380m = $1,140m

Vogel Co, profit after tax = \$158.2m × 0.8 = $126.56m

Vogel Co, P/E ratio before acquisition = \$1,140.0m/\$126.56m = 9.01 say 9

Vogel Co, P/E ratio after acquisition = 9 × 1.15 = 10.35

Tori Co, P/E ratio before acquisition = 9 × 1.25 = 11.25

Tori Co post-tax profit = \$23m × 0.8 = \$18.4m

Tori Co's current value = 11.25 × \$18.4m = $207.0m

Value created from combined company

Post-acquisition 50% of Tori's earnings will remain after the disposal of Department C and the spin-off of Department B. So earnings will become:

$126.56m + (0.5 × $18.4m) + $7m synergy) = $142.76m

So the combined company should be worth the P/E of 10.35 × $142.76m = $1,477.57m.

Maximum premium =

	$m
Value of combined firm	1,477.57
Value of Ndege	150.42
Value for disposal of C	4.81
Less current value ($1,140m + $207.0m)	1,347.00
	285.80

Assumptions

Based on the calculations given above, it is estimated that the value created will be $285.80 million.

However, Vogel Co needs to assess whether the numbers it has used in the calculations and the assumptions it has made are reasonable. For example, Ndege Co's future cash flows seem to be growing without any additional investment in assets and Vogel Co needs to establish whether or not this is reasonable. It also needs to establish how the increase in its P/E ratio was determined after acquisition. Perhaps sensitivity analysis would be useful to show the impact on value changes, if these figures are changed. Given its poor record in generating value previously, Vogel Co needs to pay particular attention to these figures.

20 Selorne

Course Book references

Acquisitions are covered in Chapters 8-10 of the Course Book.

Examining team's comments

In part (a)(i), common mistakes in the weaker attempts included getting the number of shares wrong for Selorne Co, mixing up free cash flow to equity with equity value and adding the two together, and miscalculating the additional value created.

Part (a)(ii) the majority of candidates answered this question part quite poorly probably because there were no standard valuation models to apply.

Part (b) candidates who described the various types of synergies available and how they could be achieved, received limited or no marks as they did not answer the question asked. Answers which scored high marks made good use of the scenario in the question and provided suggestions to explain why the synergy estimates might not be reliable.

In part (c), candidates received no marks when they compared the choice between a cash payment and a share-for-share exchange for the bid, as it is irrelevant to the question requirement. Secondly, it is disappointing to read in some answers which described that a rights issue would dilute the existing shareholders' control. Dilution of control would only happen if the said shareholders do not subscribe to their rights shares.

			Marks	
(a)	(i)	Valuation of Chawon Co	2	
		Valuation of Salorne Co's FCFE	1	
		Valuation of combined company	1	
		Additional value created	1	
				5
	(ii)	Value per share combined company	1	
		Value of Chawon's shareholding in combined company	1	
		Share of gain created for Chawon	1	
		Share of gain for Selorne's shareholders	1	
		Comments	2	
				6
(b)	Up to 2 marks per relevant point discussed, discussion must relate to Selorne to obtain 2 marks for a point		3	
	Problems with achieving synergies		3	
	Marks Available		6	
	Maximum			4
(c)	Up to 2 marks per relevant factor discussed			
	Maximum			5

Professional skills

Analysis and Evaluation

- Appropriate use of the data to determine suitable calculations to value the combined entity
- Appropriate use of the data to support discussion and draw appropriate conclusions
- Demonstration of reasoned judgement when considering key matters for Selorne Co
- Demonstration of ability to consider relevant factors applicable to Selorne Co's situation
- Appraisal of information objectively to make a recommendation

Scepticism

- Effective challenge and critical assessment of the information and assumptions provided in relation to synergies
- Effective challenge of evidence and assumptions supplied with respect to the director's view on synergy
- Demonstration of ability to consider all relevant factors applicable to the decisions made by Selorne Co

Commercial acumen

- Effective use of examples and/or calculations from the scenario information and other practical considerations related to the context to illustrate points being made relating to the acquisition
- Recognition of external constraints and opportunities as necessary

	Marks
Maximum	5
Total	25

(a) (i) Selorne Co current equity value = 50m shares × $6.50 = $325m

Chawon Co current equity value = $7m × 1.03/(0.15 − 0.03) = $60.1m

Selorne Co free cash flow to equity = $325m/8 = $40.6m

Combined company valuation = ($40.6m + $7m + $5m) × 8 = $420.8m

Additional value created = $420.8m − $325m − $60.1m = $35.7m

(ii) Chris Chawon will hold 2m × 5 = 10m shares in combined company

Value per share in combined company = $420.8m/(50m + 10m) = $7.01

Value of Chris Chawon's shareholding = 10m × $7.01 = $70.1m

Gain created for Chris Chawon = $70.1m − $60.1m = $10m

Gain created for Selorne Co shareholders = $35.7m − $10m = $25.7m

Chris Chawon will have a 16.7% (10m/(50m + 10m)) shareholding in the combined company but 28.0% ($10m/$35.7m) of the gain on the combination will be attributable to him. Shareholders who are doubtful about the merger may question whether this is excessive, as possibly Chawon Co's desire to sell is being prompted by the company struggling to remain solvent.

(b) A significant problem may be lack of unity at the top of the company. Selorne Co's directors are not all keen on the acquisition and this may spill over into being unable to agree on a clear post-acquisition plan. If lack of unity at board level becomes apparent to staff, it may be difficult to achieve unity at employee level.

Chris Chawon's role in the combined company may also make synergies difficult to achieve. He will have a significant shareholding and a place on the board, so it will be difficult for him not to be involved. Possibly he has the abilities and desire to achieve changes in operational practices which other board members lack. However, if Chris is given the leading role he requires, there may be a change in management style which may upset long-serving Selorne Co staff. Some may leave, jeopardising the continuity which seems to have been an important part of Selorne Co's success.

Another reason for possible problems with staff is the differing remuneration arrangements. Selorne Co's staff may have stayed with the company because both their job prospects and their remuneration have been safe. Attempts to change their employment conditions may lead to resistance and employee departures. Ex-Chawon Co employees who have been with the company for a while may expect salaries to be increased to be more in line with Selorne Co's employees, particularly if bonus arrangements become less generous.

The success of the acquisition may also depend on how well the staff of the two businesses integrate. Integration may be difficult to achieve. Many of Chawon Co's staff will not have the necessary licence to drive the Selorne Co lorries and may not wish to go through the process of obtaining this licence. Selorne Co drivers may be reluctant to drive the smaller vehicles. Staff sticking to what they have been used to driving is likely to prolong a 'them and us' culture.

(c) **Availability**

Although the finance director has identified possible sources of finance, there is no guarantee that they will necessarily be available. The success of a rights issue may well depend on the willingness and ability of the director-shareholders to subscribe. It may be difficult to find others willing to take up the directors' rights if they do not subscribe, as the directors' unwillingness may be seen as indicating a lack of confidence in the business. A rights issue may also take longer to arrange than other methods, which may be significant if Selorne Co needs the finance quickly to complete the acquisition.

Obtaining a bank loan or mezzanine finance may be difficult if Selorne Co takes on Chawon Co's debt and is viewed as too highly geared as a result. The success of a convertible debt issue may depend on the terms, also how possible subscribers view the future prospects of Selorne Co and the marketability of the shares.

Cost

Cost will be another significant factor. The cost of equity will normally be viewed as higher anyway than the cost of debt. Issue costs of equity are likely to be higher than those of debt. As Selorne Co's share price is stable, its current external shareholders appear content with the dividends paid, so there does not appear to be pressure to increase them. In any case, the board is not required to pay dividends every year.

Fixed interest cost on the bank loan may become a burden if interest rates fall, but the cost can be forecast with certainty. Because the mezzanine finance is unsecured, it is likely to have a higher interest cost than the bank loan. The rights of conversion to shares attaching to the convertible debt will mean a lower rate can be set for this, but the cost will depend on how appealing the possibility of conversion is. Again, the finance cost of debt will depend on the finance providers' attitude towards the increased debt burden resulting from the acquisition of Chawon Co.

Director preferences

The choice will also be determined by Selorne Co's board's attitude to gearing as well as how the possible finance providers view the company's gearing level. The board may feel that Selorne Co has reached, or exceeded, the gearing level which it would regard as desirable by taking on Chawon Co's debt. If this is the case, the board would have to use equity finance. The board may also be influenced by how gearing is likely to change over time. Over the next few years gearing may fall as Selorne Co makes profits and (hopefully) its share price increases. Chawon Co's debt may be repaid and not replaced. The convertible debt and mezzanine finance will also not be long-term sources of debt finance.

Control of Selorne Co

Selorne Co's board decision may also be determined by the implications of the different sources of finance for control of the company. The directors' control of the company will not be diminished if a rights issue is used and they take up their rights. An issue of shares arising from the convertible debt would change the balance of shareholdings, so the directors would have to decide how significant this would be. Mezzanine finance may also offer conversion rights, but possibly these could only be exercised if Selorne Co defaulted, which the board may view as unlikely.

Using a bank loan will have no impact on share capital, but the bank may impose restrictions which the directors are unwilling to bear, particularly if high gearing is an issue. These conditions could include restrictions on the sale of assets, limitations of dividends, or requiring accounting figures, for example, liquidity or solvency ratios, not to go beyond certain levels.

Mix of finance

Ultimately the board may also consider the possibility of a mix of finance. The offer could be backed by a core of equity finance from a rights issue, but if Selorne Co has to pay a higher price than expected, the difference could be made up by mezzanine finance.

Note. Credit will be given for alternative, relevant answers.

21 Kerrin

Course Book references

Business valuations are covered in Chapters 8-10.

Top tips

Careful planning is required before starting your calculations. A sensible approach in part (b) (the main part of the question) is:

(1) Identify the value of the acquired company (Danton) using the information on P/E ratios given and then increasing by 30% to reflect the return required.

(2) Identify the post-acquisition value of the combined entity using the information on P/E ratios given.

(3) Calculate the percentage of this that would be owned by the acquired company Danton, then the balance is the percentage owned by Kerrin.

(4) Kerrin's 750 million shares = the percentage owned by Kerrin so the total number of shares can be estimated to determine the extra shares needed to be offered for Danton. This gives the terms of the share for share exchange.

 BPP

The impact on shareholder wealth can be assessed by comparing the pre and post-acquisition values of each company.

There is quite a lot of thinking required here, but once a sensible approach is established the numbers are fairly straightforward.

Easy marks

Discussion marks in part (a) may have presented some opportunities for easy marks (but see examining team's comments below).

ACCA examining team's comments

For part (a) candidates often discussed non-financial synergies such as revenue and cost synergies which were not asked for. These candidates did not read the question carefully and thus wasted their time, as no marks were given for such a discussion. Whilst the majority of candidates agreed that synergies were often overestimated, they did not discuss the reasons why synergies may be overestimated. Candidates must read the question requirements carefully to ensure they are addressing the question which has been set. The element of the requirement on preventative measures that a company may take to avoid overestimating synergies was generally well answered.

Marking guide		Marks	
(a)	Financial synergies	5	
	Overestimation of synergies	3	
	Proposed steps	2	
	Marks Available	10	
	Maximum		7
(b)	Kerrin PE ratio	2	
	Danton valuation	2	
	Post-acquisition valuation	3	
	Share-for-share offer terms	2	
	Advice	1	
	Impact on shareholder wealth	3	
			13

Professional skills

Analysis and Evaluation

- Appropriate use of the data to determine suitable calculations
- Appropriate use of the data to support discussion and draw appropriate conclusions
- Demonstration of reasoned judgement when considering key matters for Kerrin Co
- Demonstration of ability to consider relevant factors applicable to Kerrin Co's situation
- Appraisal of information objectively to make a valid recommendation

Scepticism

- Effective challenge and critical assessment of the information and assumptions provided
- Effective challenge of evidence and assumptions supplied with respect to the finance director's view on synergy
- Demonstration of ability to consider all relevant factors applicable to the decisions made by Kerrin Co

Commercial acumen

- Effective use of examples and/or calculations from the scenario information and other practical considerations related to the context to illustrate points being made

 BPP

- Recognition of external constraints and opportunities as necessary
- Recommendations are practical and plausible in the context of Kerrin Co's situation

    Note. Credit will be given for alternative and valid comments.

Maximum   5

Total   25

(a) Financial synergies

Many acquisitions are justified on the basis that the combined organisation will be more profitable or grow at a faster rate than the companies operating independently. The expectation is that the acquisition will generate higher expected cash flows or a lower cost of capital, creating value for shareholders. The additional value created is known as synergy, the sources of which can be categorised into three types: revenue, cost and financial synergies.

Based on the scenario, there are a number of possible sources of financial synergy. As a private company, Danton Co is experiencing a funding constraint whereas Kerrin Co has significant cash reserves but limited growth opportunities. The combination of the two can create additional value since Danton Co may be able to utilise Kerrin Co's cash resources to fund its expansion in a way which would not have been possible otherwise, leading to an increase in the expected cash flows.

Assuming both companies' cash flows are less than perfectly correlated, those of the combined company will be less volatile than the individual companies operating independently. This reduction in volatility enables the combined company to borrow more and possibly cheaper financing than would otherwise have been possible. This increase in debt capacity, and therefore the present value of the tax shield, increases the value of the combined company in the form of a lower cost of capital.

Further benefits may arise if Kerrin Co is able to utilise Danton Co's unrelieved tax losses. Whilst Danton is no longer loss making and could offset these tax losses independently, the combined company may be able to obtain tax relief earlier, since the acquisition increases the availability of profits against which carried forward tax losses can be offset. The present value of the tax saved will therefore be greater in the combined company.

If both companies were publicly traded, there would be no benefit from diversification, since investors are capable of diversifying at a lower cost and with greater ease than the company. However, Danton Co is privately owned and the shareholders are therefore exposed to diversifiable unsystematic risk. Therefore the acquisition may lead to potential diversification and risk reduction benefits. The reduction in the cost of the capital increases the value of the combined company.

Overestimation of synergy value

There is evidence that bidding companies often overestimate the value of synergy arising from a potential acquisition with the result that companies pay too much for their target. When this happens, there is destruction in wealth for the bidding company's shareholders. There are a number of possible explanations for this problem.

First, merger and acquisition activity tends to be driven by the availability of cheap credit. At the peak of a wave of activity, there may be competition for targets, thereby increasing acquisition premiums.

Second, conflicts of interest may lead to a biased evaluation process. Deal advisers such as investment banks earn a large proportion of their fees from mergers and acquisitions. Their advice on whether an acquisition makes sense is potentially biased if they do not look after their clients' interests.

Third, management overconfidence may explain why this occurs. Acquiring companies may overestimate the acquisition synergy and/or underestimate the time it will take to deliver.

Management may then be reluctant to admit mistakes when the facts change, even when there is still time to back out of a deal. Agency costs may also be a factor if managers are more interested in pursuing personal goals than maximising shareholder wealth.

Finally, there may be difficulties integrating the companies due to different work cultures and conflicts of interest.

Steps to address this problem

Kerrin Co's board needs to plan for synergy and take active steps to ensure that it is delivered. This responsibility needs to be allocated to someone who can ensure spare cash is utilised to invest in new growth opportunities, that tax losses are offset as efficiently as possible and that the combined company avails itself of cheaper financing. Companies which allocate this responsibility and monitor and review performance tend to be more successful in creating value. In order to avoid any bias, the deal advisers who stand to profit from an acquisition need to be separate from the evaluation process. Effective due diligence ensures the financial documents which form the basis of a valuation are scrutinised and inspected.

(b)

    (1)   Identify the value of the acquired company (Danton):

        Danton's P/E ratio:

        Future maintainable earnings (FME) = ($381.9) × 0.8 = $305.5m

        Kerrin Co number of shares = 375m/ $0.5 = 750m

        Kerrin EPS = $305.5m / 750 = $0.4073

        Price earnings (PE) ratio = $5.28/ 0.4073 = 12.96

        Danton's estimated P/E ratio = 12.96 × 1.2 = 15.55

        Danton Co future maintainable earnings:

        = ($116.3m + $2.5m) × 0.8 = $95.0m

        Danton's post-acquisition value:

        Danton Co pre-acquisition PE valuation = 15.55 × $95m = $1,477.3m

        Value increased by 30% post-acquisition = 1,477.3m × 1.3 = $1920.5m

    (2)   Identify the post-acquisition value of the combined entity using the information on P/E ratios given.

        Pre-tax value of synergies = $15.2m + $5.3m = $20.5m

        Post-tax value of synergies = $20.5m × (1-0.2) = $16.4m

        Combined Co future maintainable earnings = $305.5m (Kerrin) + $95m (Danton) + $16.4m (synergies) = $416.9m

        Combined Co PE ratio 12.96 × 1.1 = 14.3

        Combined Co post-merger valuation = 14.3 × $416.9m = $5,961.7m

    (3)   Calculate the percentage of this that would be owned by the acquired company Danton, then the balance is the percentage owned by Kerrin.

        The percentage of the post merger value that would be owned by Danton can be calculated as (1920.5/5961.7= 32.21%) and the balance (67.79%) is therefore, the percentage owned by Kerrin.

    (4)   Kerrin's 750 million shares = the percentage owned by Kerrin so the total number of shares can be estimated to determine the extra shares needed to be offered for Danton. This gives the terms of the share for share exchange

Given that Kerrin has 750 million shares and that this is 67.79% of the total, then the total number of shares must be 750m/0.6779 = 1, 106.4m shares, so an extra 356.4 million shares need to be offered for Dantons 140 million shares (35m/$0.25 = 140m).

This gives the terms of the share for share exchange as approximately 2.55 Kerrin shares per Danton share (calculated as 356.4 / 140). Using an offer of 2.55 Kerrin shares means that Dantons' shareholders would own 2.55 × 140m = 357 million shares.

Impact on shareholder wealth

	Kerrin Co	Danton Co
	$m	$m
Pre-acquisition valuation	3,960.0	1,477.3
Cash offer	(5.28 × 750m)	
Danton Co shareholders cash received: $13.10 × 140m shares		1,834.0
Kerrin Co post-acquisition equity valuation: $5,961.7m less acquisition cost of $1,834.0m	4,127.7	
Increase in shareholder wealth	4.2%	24.1%
Share-for-share offer		
Post-acquisition value		
Kerrin Co: (750/1,110) × $5,961.7	4,028.2	
Danton Co (357/1,110) × $5,961.7		1,917.4
Increase in shareholder wealth	1.7%	29.8%

The terms of the share-for-share offer meet the criteria specified by Danton Co's directors.

Note. Credit will be given for alternative valid approaches.

22 Louieed

Course Book references

Chapter 9 covers strategic issues and, acquisitions, and Chapter 10 covers financing issues.

Top tips

In part (a) ensure you use the clues in the scenario to discuss the pros and cons of the acquisition.

In part (b), for 14 marks, it is very important to answer the question (which does not require a valuation so there would be no marks for providing one) and for answering the whole question. For example, answers that only answered the first aspect of the question (on finance required) would only have scored two marks.

Easy marks

Candidates who focused on the simpler bids (pure cash and pure paper) would have been able to access most of the marks in part (b).

Marking guide	Marks
(a) Reasons for acquisition	3
Reasons against acquisition	3
	6
(b) Funding of bid: 1 mark for cash option, 1 mark for mixed option	2
Earnings per share: 1 mark for share-for-share option, 2 marks for cash option, 2 marks for mixed option	5

Gearing: 1 mark for each option	3
Comments	5
Marks Available	15
Maximum	14

Professional skills

Analysis and Evaluation

- Appropriate use of the data to determine suitable calculations for the financing proposals
- Demonstration of reasoned judgement when considering key matters for Louieed Co
- Demonstration of ability to consider relevant factors applicable to Louieed Co's situation

Commercial acumen

- Effective use of examples and/or calculations from the scenario information and other practical considerations related to the context to illustrate points being made relating to the acquisition
- Recognition of external constraints and opportunities as necessary

Scepticism

- Effective challenge and critical assessment of the information and assumptions provided in relation to the acquisition.
- Demonstration of ability to consider all relevant factors applicable to the decisions made.

Maximum	5
Total	25

(a) **Advantages of the acquisition**

Louieed Co and Tidded Co appear to be a good strategic fit for a number of reasons. Louieed Co appears to have limited potential for further growth. Acquiring Tidded Co, a company with better recent growth, should hopefully give Louieed Co the impetus to grow more quickly.

Acquiring a company which has a specialism in the area of online testing will give Louieed Co capabilities quicker than developing this function in-house. If Louieed Co does not move quickly, it risks losing contracts to its competitors.

Acquiring Tidded Co will give Louieed Co access to the abilities of some of the directors who have led Tidded Co to becoming a successful company. They will provide continuity and hopefully will help integrate Tidded Co's operations successfully into Louieed Co. They may be able to lead the upgrading of Tidded Co's existing products or the development of new products which ensures that Louieed Co retains a competitive advantage.

It appears that Tidded Co's directors now want to either realise their investment or be part of a larger company, possibly because it will have more resources to back further product development. If Louieed Co does not pursue this opportunity, one of Louieed Co's competitors may purchase Tidded Co and acquire a competitive advantage itself.

There may also be other synergistic benefits, including savings in staff costs and other savings, when the two companies merge.

Disadvantages of the acquisition

It is not known what the costs of developing in-house capabilities will be. Although the process may be slower, the costs may be less and the process less disruptive to Louieed Co than suddenly adding on Tidded Co's operations.

It is not possible to tell which of Tidded Co's directors are primarily responsible for its success. Loss of the three directors may well represent a significant loss of its capability. This will be

enhanced if the three directors join a competitor of Louieed Co or set up in competition themselves.

There is no guarantee that the directors who remain will fit into Louieed Co's culture. They are used to working in a less formal environment and may resent having Louieed Co's way of operating imposed upon them. This could result in departures after the acquisition, jeopardising the value which Tidded Co has brought.

Possibly Tidded Co's leadership in the online testing market may not last. If competitors do introduce major advances, this could mean that Tidded Co's current growth is not sustainable.

(b) **Funding of bid**

    (1)   No extra finance will be required if all Tidded Co's shareholders take up the share offer.

    (2)   All Tidded Co's shareholders take up cash offer

Cash required = 90m × $22.75 = $2,048m

Extra debt finance required = $2,048m − $220m − $64m = $1,764m

    (3)   60% share-for-share offer, 40% cash offer

Cash required = 40% × 90m × $22.75 = $819m

Extra debt finance required = $819m − $220m − $64m = $535m

Impact of bid on earnings per share (EPS)

    (1)   Louieed Co's EPS prior to acquisition = $296m/340 = $0.87

All Tidded Co's shareholders take up share offer

Number of shares after acquisition = 340m + (90m × 2) = 520m

EPS after acquisition = ($296m + $128m + $20m)/520m = $0.85

    (2)   All Tidded Co's shareholders take up cash offer

Number of shares after acquisition = 340 million

EPS after acquisition = ($296m + $128m + $20m − $11.36m − $105.84m)/340m = $0.96

$105.84 million is the post-tax finance cost on the additional loan finding required of $1,764 million. Therefore $1,764m × 7.5% × 80% = $105.84m.

$11.36m is the post-tax opportunity cost of lost interest on the cash and cash equivalents surpluses of the two companies of $220m + $64m = $284m. Therefore $284m × 5% × 80% = $11.36m.

    (3)   60% share-for-share offer, 40% cash offer

Number of shares after acquisition 340m + (90m × 2 × 0.6) = 448m

EPS after acquisition = ($296m + $128m + $20m − $11.36m − $32.1m)/448m = $0.89

$32.1 million is the post-tax finance cost on the additional loan funding required of $535 million. Therefore $535m × 7.5% × 80% = $32.1m.

Impact of bid on gearing (using market values)

Louieed Co's gearing (debt/(debt + equity)) prior to bid = 540/(540 + (340 × 12.19)) = 11.5%

    (1)   All Tidded Co's shareholders take up share offer

Debt/(Debt + equity) after bid = (540 + 193)/(540 + 193 + (520 × $0.85 × 14)) = 10.6%

    (2)   All Tidded Co's shareholders take up cash offer

Debt/(Debt + equity) after anticipated bid = (540 + 193 + 1,764)/(540 + 193 + 1,764 + (340 × $0.96 × 14)) = 35.3%

    (3)   60% share-for-share offer, 40% cash offer

Debt/(Debt + equity) after bid = (540 + 193 + 535)/(540 + 193 + 535 + (448 × $0.89 × 14)) = 18.5%

 **BPP**

ANSWERS

Comments

The calculations suggest that:

- if Tidded Co's shares are acquired on a share-for-share exchange on the terms required by its shareholders, Louieed Co's shareholders will suffer a fall in EPS attributable to them from $0.87 to $0.85. If the P/E ratio does not change (as suggested) then this will result in a fall in shareholder wealth.

- issuing extra shares will lead to a dilution of the power of Louieed Co's existing shareholders. If all of Tidded Co's shareholders take up the share-for-share offer, they will hold around one-third of the shares of the combined company (180m/520m) and this may be unacceptable to Louieed Co's shareholders.

- if the forecast for the 60% take-up of the offer is correct, even by combining the cash flows of the two companies, the new company will have insufficient funds to be able to pay all the shareholders who are expected to take up the cash offer. Further finance will be required.

- there is also no guarantee that the forecast of 40% of the shareholders taking up the cash offer is correct. If all five of the major shareholders decide to realise their investment rather than just two, this will increase the cash required by $512 million (25% × $22.75 × 90m), for example.

- gearing will increase if loan finance is needed to finance the cash offer. If the mixed share and cash offer is taken up in the proportions stated, the gearing level of the combined company will increase from 11.5% to 18.5%. Current shareholders may not be particularly concerned about this. However, if all or most of the share capital is bought for cash, the gearing level of the combined company will be significantly greater, at a maximum of 35.3%, than Louieed Co's current gearing. This may be unacceptable to current shareholders and could mean an increase in the cost of equity, because of the increased risk, and also possibly an increase in the cost of debt, assuming in any case that debt finance at the maximum level required will be available. To guard against this risk, Louieed Co's board may want to limit the cash offer to a certain percentage of share value.

 Videos can be viewed by accessing your ebook version on VitalSource.

23 Makonis

Course Book references

Acquisitions are covered in Chapters 8 and 10.

Top tips

For part (a) make sure that you both state **and** discuss your assumptions; often candidates only stated their assumptions but did not discuss them.

Examining team's comments

In part (a) common errors included not converting the asset beta into the equity beta; deducting tax from the free cash flows; growing cash flows from the wrong year; and not recognising that the debt value has to be deducted from the value of the company to find the value attributable to equity holders.

Marking guide	Marks
(a) Market values of Makonis Co and Nuvola Co	1
Combined company asset beta	1
Combined company equity beta	1

Combined company value: Years 1 to 4	3
Combined company value: Years 5 to perpetuity	1
Combined company value: value to equity holders and additional value	2
Comment	2
	12

(b) Impact on Makonis Co's equity holders if the premium paid to Nuvola Co's equity holders is 50% 2

Discussion of how Makonis Co would pay the high premium (1 mark for quantifying the extra required) 6

8

Professional skills

Analysis and Evaluation

- Appropriate use of the data to determine suitable calculations
- Demonstration of reasoned judgement when considering key matters for Makonis Co
- Demonstration of ability to consider relevant factors applicable to Makonis Co's situation

Commercial acumen

- Effective use of examples and/or calculations from the scenario information and other practical considerations related to the context to illustrate points being made relating to the acquisition
- Recognition of external constraints and opportunities as necessary

Maximum 5

Total 25

(a) **Combined company, cost of capital**

Asset beta

(1.2 × 480 + 0.9 × 1,218) / (480 + 1,218) = 0.985

Equity beta

0.985 × (60 + 40 × 0.8) / 60 = 1.51

Cost of equity

2% + 1.51 × 7% = 12.57%

Cost of capital

12.57% × 0.6 + 4.55% × 0.8 × 0.4 = 9.00%

Combined company equity value

Year	1	2	3	4
	$m	$m	$m	$m
Free cash flows before synergy (growing at 5%)	226.80	238.14	250.05	262.55
Synergies	20.00	20.00	20.00	20.00
Free cash flows	246.80	258.14	270.05	282.55
PV of free cash flows at 9%	226.42	217.27	208.53	200.17

Note. The present value (PV) figures are slightly different if discount table factors are used, instead of formulae. Full credit will be given if discount tables are used to calculate PV figures.

Total PV of cash flows (Years 1 to 4) = $852.39 million

 **BPP**

Total PV of cash flows (Years 5 to perpetuity) = 262.55 × 1.0225/(0.09 – 0.0225) × (1.09 to the power of – 4) = $2,817.51m

Total value to firm = $3,669.90m

Value attributable to equity holders = $3,669.90m × 0.6 = $2,201.94m

The current value of Makonis is $5.80 × 210m = $1,218 million.

The value of Nuvola is $2.40 × 200m = $480 million.

Additional value created from the combined company = $2,201.94m – ($1,218m + $480m) = $2,201.94m – $1,698.00m = **$503.94m** (or 29.7%)

Although the equity beta and therefore the risk of the combined company is more than Makonis Co on its own, probably due to Nuvola Co's higher business risk (reflected by the higher asset beta), overall the benefits from growth in excess of the risk-free rate and additional synergies have led to an increase in the value of the combined company of just under 30% when compared to the individual companies' values.

However, a number of assumptions have been made in obtaining the valuation, for example the assumption of growth of cash flows in perpetuity and whether this is realistic or not. It may be appropriate to undertake sensitivity analysis to determine how changes in the variables would impact on the value of the combined company, and whether the large increase in value is justified.

(b) If 50% premium is paid to Nuvola Co's equity holders, they will receive = 50% × $480m = $240m of the additional value created.

Makonis Co's equity holders will receive about $263.94 million ($503.94m – $240m) ie over 50% of the available gain. This amounts to 21.7% (263.94/1,218) of its current value.

Hence, Makonis Co's equity holders will still benefit substantially from the takeover.

An extra 20% premium amounts to $480m × 0.2 = $96m.

Makonis Co needs to determine how it is going to acquire the additional funds and the implications from this.

For example, it could borrow the money required for the additional funds, but taking on more debt may affect the cost of capital and therefore the value of the company.

It could raise the funds by issuing more equity shares, but this may not be viewed in a positive light by the current equity holders.

Makonis Co may decide to try to offer a higher proportion of its shares in the share-for-share exchange instead of paying cash for the additional premium. However, this will affect its equity holders and dilute their equity holding further. Even the current proposal to issue 100 million new shares will mean that Nuvola Co's equity holders will own just under one-third of the combined company and Makonis Co's shareholders would own just over two-thirds of the combined company.

Makonis Co should also consider what Nuvola Co's equity holders would prefer. They may prefer less cash and more equity due to their personal tax circumstances but, in most cases, cash is preferred by the target firm's equity holders.

24 Hav

Marking guide	Marks
(a) Distinguish between different synergies	2
Evaluating possible revenue synergies	3
Concluding comments	1
	6
(b) Average earnings and capital employed	1
Average capital employed	1
After-tax premium	1
PV of premium (excess earnings)	1
Hav Co and Strand Co values	1
Combined company value	1
Value created/premium (P/E method)	1
	7
(c) Strand Co, value per share	1
Cash offer premium (%)	1
Cash and bond offer premium (%)	2
Explanation and justification	3
	7

Professional skills

Analysis and Evaluation

- Appropriate use of the data to determine suitable calculations
- Appropriate use of the data to support discussion and draw appropriate conclusions on the maximum acquisition price premium payable.

- Appraisal of information objectively to make a recommendation on preferred payment method

Scepticism

- Effective challenge and critical assessment of the information and assumptions provided in relation to the valuations

Commercial acumen

- Effective use of examples and/or practical considerations related to the context to illustrate points being made relating to synergies or payment methods

Maximum	5
Total	25

(a) An acquisition creates synergy benefits when the value of the combined entity is more than the sum of the two companies' values. Synergies can be separated into three types: revenue synergies which result in higher revenues for the combined entity, higher return on equity and a longer period when the company is able to maintain competitive advantage; cost synergies which result mainly from reducing duplication of functions and related costs, and from taking advantage of economies of scale; financial synergies which result from financing aspects such as the transfer of funds between group companies to where it can be utilised best, or from increasing debt capacity.

Revenue synergies are perhaps where the greatest potential for growth comes from but are also more difficult to identify, quantify and enact. Good post-acquisition planning is essential for these synergies to be realised but they can be substantial and long-lasting. In this case, Hav Co's management can help market Strand Co's products more effectively by using their sales and marketing talents resulting in higher revenues and longer competitive advantage. Research and development activity can be combined to create new products using the technologies in place in both companies, and possibly bringing innovative products to market quicker. The services of the scientists from Strand Co will be retained to drive innovation forward, but these need to be nurtured with care since they had complete autonomy when they were the owners of Strand Co.

The main challenge in ensuring long-lasting benefits is not only ensuring accurate identification of potential synergies but putting into place integration processes and systems to gain full benefit from them. This is probably the greater challenge for management, and, when poorly done, can result in failure to realise the full value of the acquisition. Hav Co needs to be aware of this and make adequate provisions for it.

Note. Credit will be given for alternative relevant comments and suggestions

(b) **Maximum premium based on excess earnings method**

Average pre-tax earnings: (397 + 370 + 352)/3 = $373.0m

Average capital employed: [(882 + 210 − 209) + (838 + 208 − 180) + (801 + 198 − 140)]/3 = $869.3m

Excess annual value/annual premium = 373m − (20% × $869.3m) = $199.1m

After-tax annual premium = $199.1m × 0.8 = $159.3m

PV of annual premium (assume perpetuity) = $159.3m/0.07 = $2,275.7m

According to this method, the maximum premium payable is $2,275.7m in total.

Maximum premium based on price-to-earnings (PE) ratio method

Strand Co estimated PE ratio = 16.4 × 1.10 = 18.0

Strand Co profit after tax: $397m × 0.8 = $317.6m

Hav Co profit after tax = $1,980m × 0.8 = $1,584.0m

Hav Co, current value = $9.24 × 2,400 shares = $22,176.0m

Strand Co, current value = $317.6m × 18.0 = $5,716.8m

Combined company value = ($1,584m + $317.6m + $140.0m) × 14.5 = $29,603.2m

Maximum premium = $29,603.2m −($22,176.0m + $5,716.8) = $1,710.4m

(c) Strand Co, current value per share = $5,716.8m/1,200m shares = $4.76 per share

Maximum premium % based on PE ratio = $1,710.4m/$5,716.8m × 100% = 29.9%

Maximum premium % based on excess earnings = $2,275.7m/$5,716.8m × 100% = 39.8%

Cash offer: premium (%)

($5.72 −$4.76)/$4.76 × 100% = 20.2%

Cash and bond offer: premium (%)

Each share has a nominal value of $0.25, therefore $5 is $5/$0.25 = 20 shares

Bond value = $100/20 shares = $5 per share

Cash payment = $1.25 per share

Total = $6.25 per share

Premium percentage = ($6.25 −$4.76)/$4.76 = 31.3%

On the basis of the calculations, the cash together with bond offer yields the highest return; in addition to the value calculated above, the bonds can be converted to 12 Hav Co shares, giving them a price per share of $8.33 ($100/12). This price is below Hav Co's current share price of $9.24, and therefore the conversion option is already in-the-money. It is probable that the share price will increase in the 10-year period and therefore the value of the convertible bond should increase. A bond also earns a small coupon interest of $3 per $100 a year. The 31.3% return is the closest to the maximum premium based on the excess earnings method and more than the maximum premium based on the PE ratio method. It would seem that this payment option transfers more value to the owners of Strand Co than the value created based on the PE ratio method.

However, with this option Strand Co shareholders only receive an initial cash payment of $1.25 per share compared to $5.72 per share for the cash payment method. This may make it the more attractive option for the Hav Co shareholders as well, and although their shareholding will be diluted under this option, it will not happen for some time.

The pure cash offer gives an immediate and definite return to Strand Co's shareholders, but is also the lowest offer and may also put a significant burden on Hav Co having to fund so much cash, possibly through increased debt.

It is likely that Strand Co's shareholder/managers, who will continue to work within Hav Co, will accept the mixed cash and bond offer. They, therefore, get to maximise their current return and also potentially gain when the bonds are converted into shares. Different impacts on shareholders' personal taxation situations due to the different payment methods might also influence the choice of method.

It should also be noted that the maximum premiums calculated have used what appears to be subjective adjustments to a PE ratio, or the assumption that annual excess earnings will occur in perpetuity. Neither of these may hold in reality, which would affect the maximum premium payable.

BPP

25 Propleis and Adictcan

Marking guide	Marks
(a) Sales revenue years 1–4	1
Post-tax operating cash flows years 1–4	1
Capital investment years 1–4	1
Combined company total value years 1–4	1
Combined company value after first four years	2
Combined company market value of equity	1
Evaluation of benefit to Propleis Co's shareholders	3
	10
(b) Assumptions	
(Points can include cost of capital assumptions, free cash flows assumptions, inclusion of acquisition costs)	4
Synergies	
	4

(Points can include possible supply and administration synergies, some scope for marketing synergies, limited scope for staff synergies, staff synergies depend on retaining staff)

Marks Available 8

Maximum 6

(c) 1 mark per suggestion

(Points can include investigation of Adictcan Co, communication to staff about key issues, flexible plan, Adictcan Co integrated into strategy)

<u>4</u>

Professional skills marks

Analysis and evaluation

- Appropriate use of the data to determine suitable calculations
- Appropriate use of the data to support discussion, draw appropriate conclusions and design appropriate responses
- Identification of omissions from the analysis, or further analysis, which could be carried out to enable an appropriate decision/recommendation to be made

Scepticism

- Effective challenge of information and assumptions supplied and techniques carried out to support key facts and/or decisions

Commercial acumen

- Effective use of examples and/or calculations from the scenario information and other practical considerations related to the context to illustrate points being made
- Recognition of possible consequences of past and future actions and decisions, for example, when exercising certain choices

Maximum <u>5</u>

Total <u>25</u>

(a) **Free cash flows years 1–4**

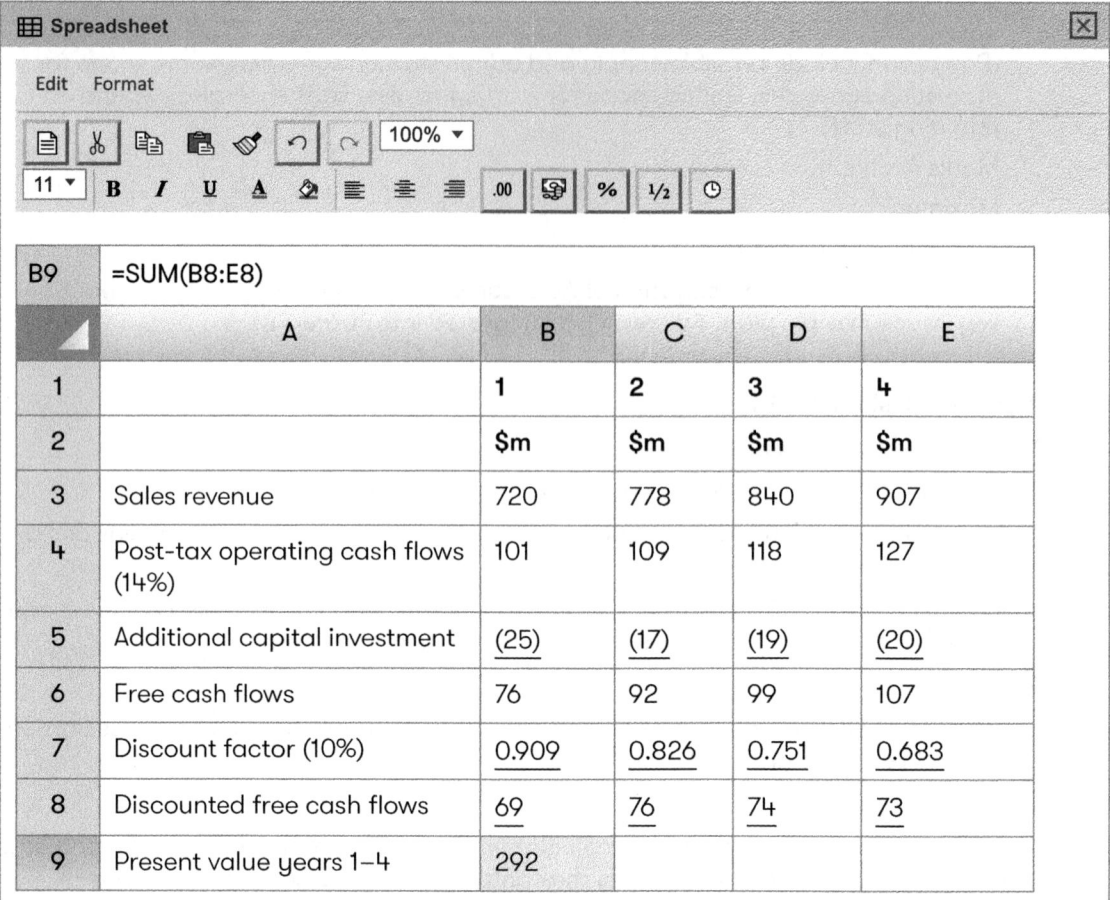

B9	=SUM(B8:E8)				
	A	B	C	D	E
1		1	2	3	4
2		$m	$m	$m	$m
3	Sales revenue	720	778	840	907
4	Post-tax operating cash flows (14%)	101	109	118	127
5	Additional capital investment	(25)	(17)	(19)	(20)
6	Free cash flows	76	92	99	107
7	Discount factor (10%)	0.909	0.826	0.751	0.683
8	Discounted free cash flows	69	76	74	73
9	Present value years 1–4	292			

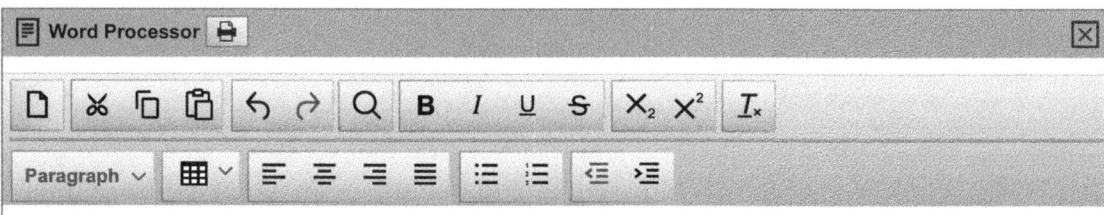

The present value of the cash flows after year 4 = ($107m × 1.04)/(0.1 − 0.04) × 0.683 = $1,267m

The estimated market value of the combined company is therefore $292m (see spreadsheet) + $1,267m = $1,559m.

The equity value of the combined company is estimated as 75% (since the debt:equity ratio is 1:3 then debt: debt + equity = 1:4) × $1,559m = $1,169m.

So the synergy benefits by combining the two companies = $1,169m − ($620m + $340m) = $209m.

The premium payable to Adictcan Co shareholders is 20% × $340m = $68m

So the balance of synergy benefits going to Propleis Co's shareholders = $209m − $68m = $141m.

As a percentage of current value of Propleis this is: $141m/$620m × 100% = 22.7%.

The valuation suggests that if Propleis Co pays the acquisition price required, its shareholders will gain more than the required 20% gain ($124m) on the value of their shares, fulfilling their requirements.

 **BPP**

(b)

Assumptions

The value of the equity in the merged company is currently $17m higher than required ($141m compared to $124m) by Propleis Co's shareholders and their expectations would not be fulfilled if the equity value of the merged company was lower by more than this amount, suggesting the need for sensitivity analysis of the figures or analysis of scenarios with detailed assumptions.

It is assumed that the sales growth rate, margins, the taxation rate and incremental capital investment can be determined accurately and remain constant. Whether Propleis Co's proposals, particularly for marketing Adictcan Co's titles, can maintain the sales growth rate of 8% from Year 2 until Year 4 may be doubtful. The profit margin may change as integration progresses and may depend on volume of sales. The incremental capital investment may be underestimated, due to developments in the technology used in online publishing.

A growth rate of free cash flows after year 4 is also assumed to be maintainable in perpetuity, which may be unrealistic, even though some of the magazines have a long history. Information on long-term market trends is needed to assess this figure.

No indication is given of the reason for the choice of cost of capital of 10%. If the 10% is the weighted average cost of capital, that assumes that there will be no change in the finance and business risks and the same capital structure will be maintained, which requires confirmation.

Costs of acquisition are assumed to be estimated fairly. Due diligence will be needed to confirm that there are no further hidden costs which need to be considered in the valuation. Costs associated with combining the two companies, for example, IT integration costs and HR costs including redundancy, may have been under-estimated.

Synergies

Assumptions about the synergies which will be gained will underpin the free cash flow estimates. Synergies in some areas appear to be realistic. Buying paper in greater quantities could lead to bulk discounts, and there may well be some savings from removing duplication of administration functions.

Other synergies may be more difficult to achieve. Adopting Propleis Co's methods of e-marketing may give Adictcan Co greater reach and a more appealing online presence. However, cross-selling between the two groups of magazines may be limited by their appealing to differing readerships. The appeal of Adictcan Co's titles appears to be primarily based on their specialist content, which would not be affected by changes resulting from the acquisition. The differing subject matter of the two companies' magazines would mean there was little or no opportunity to share common content.

There would also seem to be limited opportunity to realise synergies regarding publishing staff. Adictcan Co's business has been based on the expertise of its staff and Propleis Co's staff may need to develop knowledge of the sports to be able to work on Adictcan Co's titles. Staffing issues may represent the biggest barrier to sufficient value being gained from the acquisition. If Adictcan Co's staff dislike the environment of the merged company, they may leave, and the best staff may easily find jobs at competitor titles.

(c)

Integration and realisation of synergies is most likely to happen if first Propleis Co can make a thorough investigation of Adictcan Co and possible sources of synergy. The investigation should identify key personnel whom Propleis Co would wish to retain and should also cover staff remuneration and redundancy provisions. IT needs to be thoroughly reviewed, to understand if there are barriers in the way of integration.

Communication with Adictcan Co's staff throughout the acquisition process is an important aspect of trying to minimise staff turnover. Initially, staff are likely to be fearful for their jobs and require reassurance that they will be retained; Propleis Co also needs to make decisions early on about aspects of the business which are important to staff. These include matters relating to organisation and culture, in particular how much autonomy staff will continue to be given and areas where there is likely to be greater central direction, for example, online presence. Propleis Co also needs to communicate to key staff what opportunities and incentives they will be offered by the merged company. As current sports stars can be means of attracting readers to magazines, Propleis Co also needs to take steps to retain them as writers.

A flexible plan will be needed for the acquisition process and for integrating Adictcan Co's business into Propleis Co. Propleis Co's management needs to spend sufficient time in making sure the plan achieves its objectives. Development of the magazines acquired also needs to be included as an important part of Propleis Co's longer-term strategic planning.

26 Flufftort

Course Book references

Financial reconstruction is covered in Chapter 14.

Easy marks

You should be able to pick up some relatively easy marks in part (b). This required an evaluation of the acceptability of the financing scheme to all parties. There were up to two marks per well-explained point. This should have picked up the breach of a loan covenant in part (a)(i) as well as issues relating to control and risk.

Examining team's comments

In part (a), it is worth reminding candidates that occasionally, as in this part of the question, there are marks available for relatively straightforward calculations without needing to apply complex techniques.

Marking guide			Marks
(a) (i)	SOFP if shares purchased and cancelled		
	Cash and other assets	2	
	Equity	1	
	Liabilities	1	
			4
(ii)	SOFP if full refinancing takes place		
	Cash and other assets	2	
	Equity	1	
	Liabilities	1	
			4
(b)	Up to 2 marks for each well-discussed point		
	Maximum		12

Professional skills

Analysis and Evaluation

- Appropriate use of the data to determine suitable calculations
- Appropriate use of the data to support discussion and draw appropriate conclusions
- Demonstration of reasoned judgement when considering key matters
- Demonstration of ability to consider relevant factors applicable to Flufftort Co's situation
- Identification of further analysis, which could be carried out to enable an appropriate recommendation to be made.
- Appraisal of information objectively to make a recommendation

Commercial acumen

- Effective use of examples and/or calculations from the scenario information and other practical considerations related to the context to illustrate points being made relating to Flufftort
- Recognition of external constraints and opportunities as necessary

 BPP

- Recommendations are practical and plausible in the context of Flufftort Co's situation

	Marks
Maximum	5
Total	25

(a) (i) **Statement of financial position (SOFP) if Gupte VC shares are purchased by Flufftort Co and cancelled**

	$m
Assets	
Non-current assets	69
Current assets excluding cash	18
Cash	–
Total assets	87
Equity and liabilities	
Share capital	40
Retained earnings	5
Total equity	45
Long-term liabilities	
Bank loan	30
Loan note	5
Total long-term liabilities	35
Current liabilities	7
Total liabilities	42
Total equity and liabilities	87

(ii) **SOFP if full refinancing takes place**

	$m
Assets	
Non-current assets	125
Current assets excluding cash	42
Cash (balancing figure)	5
Total assets	172
Equity and liabilities	
Share capital	90
Retained earnings	5
Total equity	95
Long-term liabilities	
Bank loan	65
Loan note	–
Total long-term liabilities	65
Current liabilities	12
Total liabilities	77
Total equity and liabilities	172

(b) **Current situation**

Initial product developments have not generated the revenues required to sustain growth. The new Easicushion chair appears to offer Flufftort Co much better prospects of commercial success. At present, however, Flufftort Co does not have the resources to make the investment required.

Purchase of Gupte VC's shares

In the worst case scenario, Gupte VC will demand repayment of its investment in a year's time. The calculations in (a) show the financial position in a year's time, assuming that there is no net investment in non-current assets or working capital, the purchase of shares is financed solely out of cash reserves and the shares are cancelled. Repayment by this method would mean that the limits set out in the covenant would be breached (45/35 = 1.29) and the bank could demand immediate repayment of the loan.

The directors can avoid this by buying some of Gupte VC's shares themselves, but this represents money which is not being put into the business. In addition, the amount of shares which the directors would have to purchase would be greater if results, and therefore reserves, were worse than expected.

Financing the investment

The calculations in (a) show that the cash flows associated with the refinancing would be enough to finance the initial investment. The ratio of equity to non-current liabilities after the refinancing would be 1.46 (95/65), in line with the current limits in the bank's covenant. However, financing for the subsequent investment required would have to come from surplus cash flows.

Shareholdings

The disposition of shareholdings will change as follows:

	Current shareholdings		Shareholdings after refinancing	
	m	%	m	%
Directors	27.5	55.0	42.5	47.2
Other family members	12.5	25.0	12.5	13.9
Gupte VC	10.0	20.0	30.0	33.3
Loan note holder	-	-	5.0	5.6
	50.0	100.0	90.0	100.0

Gupte VC's percentage shareholding will rise from 20% to 33.3%, enough possibly to give it extra rights over the company. The directors' percentage shareholding will fall from 55% to 47.2%, which means that collectively they no longer have control of the company. The percentage of shares held by family members who are not directors falls from 25% to around 19.5%, taking into account the conversion of the loan note. This will mean, however, that the directors can still maintain control if they can obtain the support of some of the rest of the family.

Position of finance providers

The refinancing has been agreed by the chief executive and finance director. At present, it is not clear what the views of the other directors are, or whether the $15 million contributed by directors will be raised from them in proportion to their current shareholdings. Some of the directors may not be able to, or wish to, make a significant additional investment in the company. On the other hand, if they do not, their shareholdings, and perhaps their influence within the company, will diminish. This may be a greater concern than the board collectively losing control over the company, since it may be unlikely that the other shareholders will combine to outvote the board.

The other family shareholders have not been actively involved in Flufftort Co's management out of choice, so a reduction in their percentage shareholdings may not be an issue for them. They may have welcomed the recent dividend payment as generating a return on their investment. However, as they appear to have invested for the longer term, the new investment appears to offer much better prospects in the form of a capital gain on listing or buyout than an uncertain flow of dividends. The new investment appears only to have an upside for them in the sense that they are not being asked to contribute any extra funding towards it.

Rajiv Patel is unlikely to be happy with the proposed scheme. He is exchanging a guaranteed flow of income for an uncertain flow of future dividends sometime after 20X8. On the other hand, his investment may be jeopardised by the realisation of the worst case scenario, since his debt is subordinated to the bank's debt.

The most important issue from Gupte VC's viewpoint is whether the extra investment required is likely to yield a better outcome than return of its initial investment in a year's time. The plan that no dividends would be paid until after 20X8 is a disadvantage. On the other hand, the additional investment seems to offer the only prospect of realising a substantial gain by Flufftort Co being either listed or sold. The arrangement will mean that Gupte VC may be able to exercise greater influence over Flufftort Co, which may provide it with a greater sense of reassurance about how Flufftort Co is being run. The fact that Gupte VC has a director on Flufftort Co's board should also give it a clear idea of how successful the investment is likely to be.

The bank will be concerned about the possibility of Flufftort Co breaching the covenant limits and may be concerned whether Flufftort Co is ultimately able to repay the full amount without jeopardising its existence. The bank will be concerned if Flufftort Co tries to replace loan finance with overdraft finance. The refinancing provides reassurance to the bank about gearing levels and a higher rate of interest. The bank will also be pleased that the level of interest cover under the refinancing is higher and increasing from 2.0 in 20X6 to 3.1 ($20m /

$6.5m) in 20X7 and 3.8 ($25m / 6.5) in 20X8). However, it will be concerned about how Flufftort Co finances the additional investment required if cash flows from the new investment are lower than expected. In those circumstances Flufftort Co may seek to draw on its overdraft facility.

Conclusion

The key players in the refinancing are Gupte VC, the bank and the directors other than the chief executive and the finance director. If they can be persuaded, then the scheme has a good chance of being successful. However, Rajiv Patel could well raise objections. He may be pacified if he retains the loan note. This would marginally breach the current covenant limit (90/70 = 1.29), although the bank may be willing to overlook the breach as it is forecast to be temporary. Alternatively, the refinancing would mean that Flufftort Co just had enough spare cash initially to redeem the loan note, although it would be more dependent on cash surpluses after the refinancing to fund the additional investment required.

27 Newimber

Marking guide	Marks	
(a) Advantages of demerger	3	
Disadvantages of demerger	3	
Marks Available	6	
Maximum		4
(b) Market value of debt	2	
Pre merger WACC	1	
New equity beta and cost of equity of Newimber	1	
New WACC Newimber	1	
Pre-merger asset beta	1	
Ponyins beta	1	
Ponyins WACC	1	
Discounted free cash flows Ponyins years 1 to 3	1	
Discounted free cash flows Ponyins year 4 onwards	2	
Discussion	2	
Maximum		12
(c) 1–2 per relevant point		
		4

Professional skills

Analysis and Evaluation

- Appropriate use of the data to determine suitable calculations to value Poyins Co
- Appropriate use of the data to support discussion and draw appropriate conclusions
- Demonstration of reasoned judgement when considering key matters
- Demonstration of ability to consider relevant factors

Scepticism

- Effective challenge and critical assessment of the information and assumptions provided by the sportswear division's managers

Commercial acumen

- Effective use of examples and/or calculations from the scenario information and other practical considerations related to the context to illustrate points being made relating to the MBO
- Recognition of external constraints and opportunities as necessary

Maximum	<u>5</u>
Total	<u>25</u>

(a) **Advantages of demerger**

If the managers of the sportswear division's belief that they can run the division better without the interventions of senior management at Newimber Co is well-founded, the business may be able to achieve operational efficiencies and increases in value.

The new company is not tied to the financial commitments associated with the formal clothing division in terms of finance cost and loan repayment. Its management will have the ability to determine the finance structure which best suits the new business.

Newimber Co's shareholders will continue to own both companies. If shareholders are concerned about the diversification of their portfolio, this will remain unchanged.

The demerger may allow Newimber Co's management team to focus on the formal clothing division. They should not need to spend time dealing with disagreements with the sportswear division's management team.

Disadvantages of demerger

There will be legal costs associated with the demerger, such as the cost of obtaining a listing for the new company arising out of the sportswear division. Also setting up the new company and establishing the new structure looks likely to take up significant management time. This may mean that neither company is focused on external opportunities and challenges for some time, maybe impacting results and competitive position.

Both the new companies may suffer adverse effects through being smaller entities. Economies of scale may be lost and the companies may find it less easy to raise new finance. Looking at the position across both companies in total, distributable profits may fall because of a rise of overheads, as each company will need its separate infrastructure and service departments.

The current arrangement may frustrate the management of the sportswear division, but the command structure is clear. Once the director-shareholders of Newimber Co merely become shareholders of the new company, they will not be able to intervene actively in its management and overrule its management team. Agency problems may arise if these shareholders have different attitudes to risk to Poynins Co's board or different views on the importance of short-term versus long-term objectives.

(b) **Current WACC Newimber Co**

k_e is 11.8% and k_d is 4.5%

Annuity factor 4.5% for 5 years = $1 - (1 + 0.045)^{-5}/0.045 = 4.390$

Loan value per $100 = ($5.90 × 4.390) + ($105.00 × 1.045^{-5}) = $110.16 MVd = $110.16/100 × $200m = $220m

WACC = ((585 × 11.8%) + (220 × 4.5% × 0.72))/805 = 9.5%

New WACC Newimber Co

MVe is $351 million

β_e = 1.21 ((351 + (220 (1 − 0.28)/351) = 1.76 k_e = 3.4% + (1.76 × 6%) = 14.0%

WACC = ((351 × 14.0%) + (220 × 4.5% × 0.72))/571 = 9.9%, an increase of 0.4%

WACC Poynins Co

Current β_a of Newimber Co = 1.4(585/(585 + (220 (1 − 0.28))) = 1.10

β Poynins Co = (1.10 − (0.6 × 1.21))/0.4 = 0.935

WACC Poynins Co = 3.4% + (0.935 × 6%) = 9.0%

Free cash flows Poynins Co

Year	1	2	3
	$m	$m	$m
Free cash flows	12.4	16.9	22.7
Discount factor (9%)	0.917	0.842	0.772
Discounted cash flows	11.4	14.2	17.5

Discounted free cash flows Years 1 to 3 = $43.1 million

Discounted post-tax cash flows Year 4 onwards

= ($22.7m (1 + 0.03)/0.09 − 0.03) = $389.7m × 0.772 = $300.8m

Poynins Co's valuation = $43.1m + $300.8m = $343.9m

> **Tutorial note.** Alternatively the M&M formula for the cost of equity can be used to ungear and regear the cost of equity of Newimber.

Discussion

If the managers' estimates of the sportswear division's future free cash flows are realistic, then the valuation using free cash flows ($343.9m) exceeds the current valuation ($585m − $351m = $234m).

The valuation is dependent upon achieving ambitious growth targets in Years 1 to 3, particularly given the loss of economies of scale discussed above. The board and shareholders of Newimber Co would want details about the assumptions behind these figures, particularly as growth after that is only assumed to be 3%. The valuation is also dependent upon the investment figures being accurate, so directors and shareholders would again need more detail of these so that they can decide whether the extra investment is likely to generate the increased cash flows predicted.

They would also want to determine how the managers of the sportswear division plan to fund the investments, particularly if initial operating cash flows are not as high as expected.

The restructuring will lead to a marginal increase in the WACC of Newimber Co, as its financial risk increases with more gearing. The directors may be worried that Newimber Co's credit rating will fall.

(c) **Requirement for business review**

The directors of Poynins Co will have to fulfil the same statutory and listing requirements as Newimber Co currently fulfils. These are likely to include the requirements for a business review.

Investors are likely to be particularly interested in how future strategies for Poynins Co may differ from those which have been pursued recently. They are also likely to want to know about attitudes to risk management and risk management policies, as the new company appears to be likely to be more risk-seeking than the old division. They will also want to know about changes in finance policy, particularly if dividend policies are likely to differ.

Communication with stakeholders

Poynins Co's directors are likely to communicate with major shareholders on a regular basis; more than once a year. These will include the director-shareholders actively involved in Newimber Co and external investors. Poynins Co's directors will need to ensure that what they communicate keeps both sets of shareholders happy if the two groups have different priorities.

Poynins Co's directors will also have to be mindful of the need to communicate what their plans are to other important stakeholders. Employees and suppliers are particularly important here, as Poynins Co's board has plans for operational efficiencies. Employees may be interested in being informed about changes in working conditions. Attempts to impose tougher conditions on employees without communication or consultation may lead to employee departures or other disruptions. Suppliers will be interested in changes to payment arrangements. Suppliers may be concerned anyway about dealing with a new, smaller company, so may seek to impose shorter credit periods or lower credit limits if they do not have sufficient information.

Note. Credit will be given for alternative, valid comments.

28 Hanwood

Course Book references

Business re-organisations and financial reconstructions are covered in Chapters 14 and 15.

Easy marks

There are easy numerical marks in part (a) if you read the question carefully and produce the required analysis. There is no need to complete the hardest part of the question (the current asset adjustment) accurately to score a pass mark.

Marking guide	Marks
(a) PV of free cash flows Years 1–4	2
PV of free cash flows Year 5 onwards	2
Revised statement of financial position	4
Revised eps	5
	13
(b) Up to 2 marks per relevant point	
(relevant points can include need to sell, timing, amount, less diversification, alternative strategies, impact on eps impact on funding)	
Maximum	7

Professional skills marks:

Analysis and Evaluation

- Appropriate use of the data to determine suitable calculations

- Appropriate use of the data to support discussion and draw appropriate conclusions
- Appraisal of information objectively to make a recommendation

Scepticism

- Demonstration of ability to consider all relevant factors applicable to the decisions made by the capital providers

Commercial acumen

- Effective use of examples and/or practical considerations related to the context to illustrate points being made relating to capital providers

Maximum	<u>5</u>
Total	<u><u>25</u></u>

(a) **Proceeds from sales of children's shoes division**

Year	1	2	3	4
	$m	$m	$m	$m
Free cash flows	76	81	85	88
Discount factor 10%	<u>0.909</u>	<u>0.826</u>	<u>0.751</u>	<u>0.683</u>
Present value	<u>69</u>	<u>67</u>	<u>64</u>	<u>60</u>
Present value	260			

Growth rate year 5 onwards = 3.5%

Present value in year 5 onwards = ($88m × 1.035/ (0.10 − 0.035) × 0.683 = $957m

Total present value = $260m + $957m = $1,217m

This is the assumed sales value.

Impact on statement of financial position ($m)

Profit on sale = $1,217m − $608m − $349m = $260m

This impacts reserves as stated in the question.

Current assets adjustment

Currents assets of $909m (now)

Decrease by value of current assets in children's shoes = $349m

Final working capital = $894m current liabilities × 1.4 = $1,252m

Increase in working capital = $1,252m − ($909m − $349m) = $692m

Non-current assets adjustment

The balance of the sales proceeds is invested in **non-current assets** after investing in working capital and repaying the 9% loan note:

= $1,217m − $692m − $175m = $350m

	Original	Sales	Adjustments	Final
	$m	$m	$m	$m
Assets				
Non-current assets	1,200	(608)	350	942
Current assets	909	(349)	692	1,252
Total assets	2,109			2,194
Equity and liabilities				
Called-up share capital	50			50
Reserves	737	260		997
Total equity	787			1,047
Non-current liabilities				
9% loan notes	175		(175)	0
7% loan notes	145			145
Bank loans	108			108
Total non-current liabilities	428			253
Current liabilities	894			894
Total equity and liabilities	2,109			2,194

Impact on eps ($m)

	Current forecast	Revised forecast
Predicted post tax profits	217	217
Less: Profits from children's shoes		(76)
Add: Interest saved, net of tax ($175m × 9% × (1 − 0.2))		13
Add: Return on additional non-current assets ($350m × 18% × (1 − 0.2))		50
Add: Return on additional current assets ($692m × 6% × (1 − 0.2))		33
Adjusted profits	217	237
Number of shares	50m	50m
Adjusted eps	$4.34	$4.74

(b) **Sale**

Investors may query the need for the sale at this time. Although the board expects the children's shoes market to become more competitive in a few years' time, this has not yet happened. Investors may wonder if a better sales price could be obtained in a few years' time with a few more years' growth. Although some investors are concerned about gearing, a sale to reduce debt funding may seem to be a forced sale, and investors may ask whether alternative strategies could resolve the problems.

Investors may also wonder why Hanwood Shoes Co is not exploring the possibility of selling the production facilities (if sale proceeds equalled net book value, that would be enough to pay off the 9% loan notes). Hanwood Shoes Co could then use the same outsourcing business model for producing children's shoes which it does for adults' shoes.

Investors may also be concerned whether Hanwood Shoes Co is achieving best value from the sale if the company is going to be selling the division at $1,217m. Assuming a higher growth rate (perhaps by taking the geometric average of growth over the next four years) would give a higher selling price. Hanwood Shoes Co could also be expected to ask for a premium on the sale, given that a number of companies looking to develop their sales of children's shoes may be interested. That said, the cash flows in the calculation are taken to infinity, which is optimistic.

Investors would also wonder about the decreased diversification that the sale would mean. Although adults' shoes achieve higher margins than children's shoes, they may need more investment to maintain their position, and the appeal of fashionable ranges may be uncertain. Children's school shoes have been a reliable cash generator. Ultimately also, the investors may feel that they are investing in a smaller company, given the decrease in the non-current base and range of products, and may want to invest elsewhere in a company offering better growth prospects.

Profits

The forecast increase in earnings per share is 9.2%, but investors will question whether the assumptions on which the forecast is based are optimistic. They will also take into account the risks of the business being less diversified as it will solely be selling adult shoes. However, part of the increase in profits is a fall in the commitment to paying interest, which investors may view positively if they are concerned about gearing.

Funding

The sale will help fund an improvement in the gearing of the company. The funds will not only be available to pay off the 9% loan notes immediately, they could also be used to pay off the bank loan and/or the other loan notes in time, or reduce trade payables as they may be being used as a source of short-term funding. However, investors might also wonder how future investment in adults' shoe shops would be funded, particularly if future sales did not meet current expectations. Current lenders may have placed restrictions on Hanwood Shoes Co seeking new borrowing from other sources. If Hanwood Shoes Co was able to seek additional loan capital, it would have a smaller non-current asset base to offer as security, which may affect lenders' attitudes.

29 Bento

Marking guide	Marks
(a) Distinguish between an MBI and an MBO	2
Discuss the relative benefits and drawbacks	4

 **BPP**

Marks Available	6	
Maximum		4
(b) Annual annuity on 8% bond	1	
Split between interest and capital repayment	2	
Operating profit for the first 4 years	1	
Finance costs	2	
Tax and dividend payable for the first 4 years (1 mark each)	2	
Book values of debt and equity in Years 1 to 4	2	
Gearing and concluding comment	2	
Marks Available	12	
Maximum		10
(c) Valuation method)	3	
Discussion (1 to 2 marks per point)	4	
Marks Available	7	
Maximum		6

Professional skills

Analysis and Evaluation

- Appropriate use of the data to determine suitable calculations to assess if the restrictive covenants will be met and to value the new MBO
- Appropriate use of the data to support discussion and draw appropriate conclusions
- Demonstration of reasoned judgement when considering key matters

Commercial acumen

- Effective use of examples and/or calculations from the scenario information and other practical considerations related to the context to illustrate points being made
- Recognition of external constraints and opportunities as necessary

Scepticism

- Demonstration of ability to consider all relevant factors applicable to the decisions made.

Maximum		5
Total		**25**

(a) An MBO involves the purchase of a business by the management team running that business. Hence, an MBO of Okazu Co would involve the takeover of that company from Bento Co by Okazu Co's current management team. However, an MBI involves purchasing a business by a management team brought in from outside the business.

The benefits of an MBO relative to an MBI to Okazu Co are that the existing management is likely to have detailed knowledge of the business and its operations. Therefore they will not need to learn about the business and its operations in a way which a new external management team may need to. It is also possible that an MBO will cause less disruption and resistance from the employees when compared to an MBI. If Bento Co wants to continue doing business with the new company after it has been disposed of, it may find it easier to work with the management team which it is more familiar with. The internal management team may be more focused and have better knowledge of where costs can be reduced and sales revenue increased, in order to increase the overall value of the company.

The drawbacks of an MBO relative to an MBI to Okazu Co may be that the existing management may lack new ideas to rejuvenate the business. A new management team, through their skills and experience acquired elsewhere, may bring fresh ideas into the business. It is also possible that the management of Bento Co and Okazu Co have had disagreements in the past and the two teams may not be able to work together in the future if

they need to. Finally, the financing deal that has been proposed by Dofu for the MBO may not be acceptable to Okazu because it would result in Dofu becoming the majority shareholder in the new company.

(b) Annuity (8%, 4 years) = 3.312

Annuity payable per year on loan = $30,000,000/3.312 = $9,057,971

Interest payable on convertible loan, per year = $20,000,000 × 6% = $1,200,000

Annual interest on 8% bond

Year end	1	2	3	4
	$'000	$'000	$'000	$'000
Opening loan balance	30,000	23,342	16,151	8,385
Interest at 8%	2,400	1,867	1,292	671
Annuity	(9,058)	(9,058)	(9,058)	(9,058)
Closing loan balance	23,342	16,151	8,385	(2)*

* The loan outstanding in Year 4 should be zero. The small negative figure is due to rounding.

Estimate of profit and retained earnings after MBO

Year end	1	2	3	4
	$'000	$'000	$'000	$'000
Operating profit	13,542	15,032	16,686	18,521
Finance costs	(3,600)	(3,067)	(2,492)	(1,871)
Profit before tax	9,942	11,965	14,194	16,650
Taxation	(1,988)	(2,393)	(2,839)	(3,330)
Profit for the year	7,954	9,572	11,355	13,320
Dividends	(1,989)	(2,393)	(2,839)	(3,330)
Retained earnings	5,965	7,179	8,516	9,990

Estimate of gearing

Year end	1	2	3	4
	$'000	$'000	$'000	$'000
Book value of equity	15,965*	23,144	31,660	41,650
Book value of debt	43,342	36,151	28,385	20,000
Gearing	73%	61%	47%	32%
Covenant	75%	60%	50%	40%
Covenant breached?	No	Yes	No	No

* The book value of equity consists of the sum of the 5,000,000 equity shares which Dofu Co and Okazu Co's senior management will each invest in the new company (total 10,000,000), issued at their nominal value of $1 each, and the retained earnings from Year 1. In subsequent years the book value of equity is increased by the retained earnings from that year.

The gearing covenant is forecast to be breached in the second year only, and by a marginal amount. It is forecast to be met in all the other years. It is unlikely that Dofu Co will be too concerned about the covenant breach.

BPP

(c) **Dividend valuation model**

Year	Dividend	DF (12%)	PV
	$'000		$'000
1	1,989	0.893	1,776
2	2,393	0.797	1,907
3	2,839	0.712	2,021
4	3,330	0.636	2,118
Total			7,822

Annual dividend growth rate, Years 1 to 4 = $(3,330/1,989)^{(1/3)} - 1 = 18.7\%$

Annual dividend growth rate after Year 4 = 7.5% [40% × 18.7%]

Value of dividends after Year 4 = ($3,330,000 × 1.075)/(0.12 − 0.075) × 0.636 = $50,594,000 approximately

Based on the dividend valuation model, the value of the equity in the new company is approximately: $7,822,000 + $50,594,000 = $58,416,000

It can be argued that if the future growth potential of the company is represented by the dividend valuation model, then the price of $60 million asked for by Bento does not seem excessive, ie it is the right ball park and may bring benefit to both management teams.

However, the dividend valuation model can produce a large variation in results if the model's variables are changed by even a small amount. Therefore, the basis for estimating the variables should be examined carefully to judge their reasonableness, and sensitivity analysis applied to the model to demonstrate the impact of the changes in the variables. The value of the future potential of the new company should also be estimated using alternative valuation methods including free cash flows and price/earnings methods.

In addition, Okazu Co's management may be concerned that, if the convertible bond is converted into equity shares, Dofu Co would become the majority shareholder in the new company. This may not be acceptable to them but may add to the attraction from Dofu Co's management team viewpoint.

Note. Credit will be given for alternative, relevant discussion for parts (a) and (c).

30 Charborough Co

Course Book references

Business reorganisation is covered in Chapter 15.

Top Tips

This question presents a lot of work for the candidate to do, although none of it is especially complicated. With this type of time-pressured question it is especially important that you do not waste time making points that are either (i) not really relevant to the scenario or (ii) are not sufficiently detailed to be given credit. For example, in part (b) it would not be sufficient to say that the sale of the division may damage a company's reputation without explaining why this might be the case.

Marking guide		Marks	
(a) (i) PV of free cash flows Years 1–4		2	
PV of free cash flows Year 5 onwards		2	
			4
(ii) Revised statement of financial position		3	
Revised EPS		3	
Revised WACC			
Equity beta – juice bars		1	
Revised cost of equity – juice bars		1	
Revised WACC		1	
			9
(b) Factors in favour of sale		4	
(discussion may include conflict between investment requirements, cash for juice bar investment, maximising proceeds, lower WACC)			
Factors against sale		4	
(discussion may include business no longer diversified, exceeding shareholders' risk profile, coffee bars being lower risk, juice bar forecasts being optimistic)			
Marks Available		8	
Maximum			7

Professional skills marks

Analysis and Evaluation

- Appropriate use of the data to determine suitable calculations
- Appropriate use of the data to support discussion and draw appropriate conclusions
- Appraisal of information objectively to make a recommendation

Scepticism

- Effective challenge of information supplied to support key facts and/or decisions
- Demonstration of ability to consider relevant factors applicable to discussing a diversification strategy

Commercial acumen

- Recommendations are practical and plausible in the context of the company's situation

 BPP

- Effective use of examples from the scenario information and other practical considerations related to the context to illustrate points being made

Maximum   5

Total   25

(a) (i)   **Proceeds from sales of coffee shops**

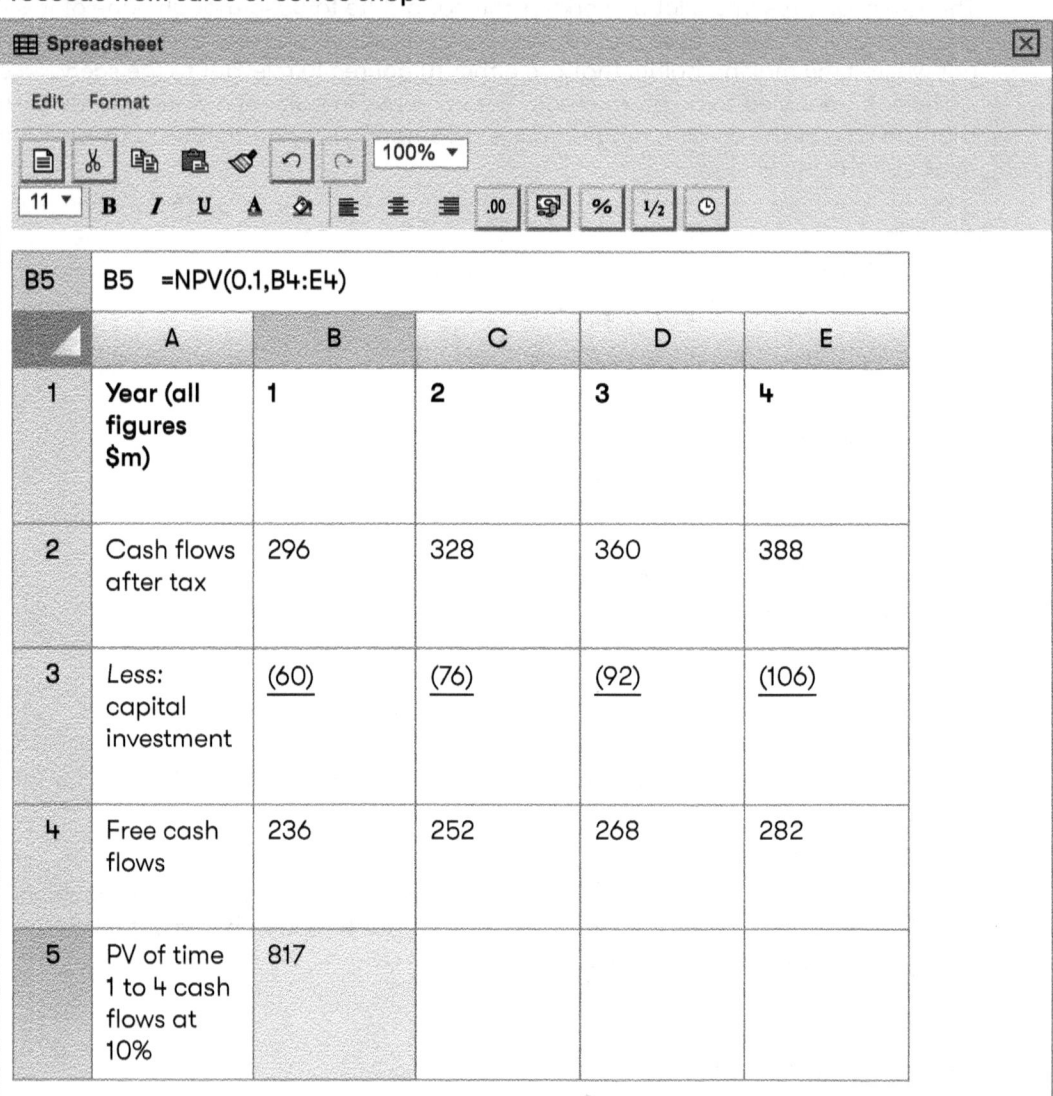

Present value in Year 5 onwards = $282m x 1.035 / (0.10 − 0.035) x 0.683 = $3,067m

Total present value = $817m + $3,067m = $3,884m

BPP

(ii) Impact on statement of financial position

Profit on sale = $3,884m − $3,350m = $534m

Non-current asset investment = $3,884m − $1,700m = $2,184m

Assets	Original	Sales	Adjustments	Final
	$m	$m	$m	$m
Non-current assets	6,625	(3,350)	2,184	5,459
Current assets	535	3,884	(3,884)	535
Total assets	7,160			5,994
Equity and liabilities				
Called-up share capital	500			500
Retained earnings	2,930	534		3,464
Total equity	3,430			3,964
Non-current liabilities				
9% loan notes	1,700		(1,700)	
Bank loans	1,575			1,575
Total non-current liabilities	3,275			1,575
Current liabilities	455			455
Total equity and liabilities	7,160			5,994

Impact on eps

	Current forecast	Revised forecast
	$m	$m
Predicted post tax profits	658	658
Less: profits from coffee shops		(296)
Add: interest saved, net of tax ($1,700 × 9% × (1 − 0.25))		115
Add: return on additional non-current assets ($2,184 × 17% × (1 − 0.25))		278
Adjusted profits	658	755
Number of shares	500 million	500 million
Adjusted eps	$1.32	$1.51

Impact on WACC

Equity beta

V_e = 500 million × $8 × 1.05 = $4,200m

V_d = $1,575m

β_e = 0.7(4,200 + 1,575 (1 − 0.25))/4,200 = 0.897

Revised cost of equity

k_e = 4 + (11 − 4)0.897 = 10.28%

Revised WACC

WACC = 10.28(4,200/(4,200 + 1,575)) + 7(1 − 0.25) (1,575/(4,200 + 1,575)) = 8.91%

(b)

Arguments in favour of the sale

Cash surpluses generated by the coffee shops have for some time provided funds for the investment in the juice bars, but it appears that that period may be coming to an end. The growth in the cash flows from the coffee shops has slowed down. The shops themselves require more investment, potentially creating a conflict between the two businesses for future investment.

The sale now of the coffee shops will provide a significant injection of cash into the juice bar business. This can aid the rapid expansion which Charborough Co's (CC's) board desires, and this expansion could mean scale savings in cost.

Selling the coffee shops now when there is interest from a competitor to buy them may result in a better outcome than waiting. Although no premium is added to the free cash flows to arrive at the sales price, the assumptions about the rate of increase of free cash flows may be optimistic given the level of competition. Delaying the sale may show this to be the case.

The sale of the coffee shops and repayment of the debt will also lead to a lower weighted average cost of capital. Being able to focus on one business rather than two will simplify management of CC's business.

Arguments against the sale

The sale will mean that CC is no longer diversified into two businesses. In theory, shareholders should be able to achieve diversification themselves by adjusting their portfolio, but in practice transaction costs and other issues may mean they do not want to do this.

As well as reduced diversification, the juice bars may have too much business risk for the shareholders' risk profile. Although CC has developed a successful niche, more competitors may well enter this niche. Although the juice bars may currently be seen as fashionable, fashions can change and even significant expenditure updating the look of the juice bars may not be enough to stop consumers going elsewhere. If the juice bars start making lower returns, this will lead to less cash being available for further investment, resulting in the juice bars becoming less appealing.

By contrast, investors may believe that the coffee shops have lower business risk because they are less subject to changes in fashion. Maintaining demand for takeaway coffee may be primarily about getting the combination of price and quality right. Investment in the coffee shops may offer better longer-term returns than continued high investment in the juice bars.

These doubts suggest that the assumptions behind the calculations may be optimistic. CC may not be able to achieve the desired sales price, lowering the funds available for investment in the juice bars. The 17% pre-tax return (12.75% post-tax) on investment in the juice bars may be optimistic. If the return on the additional expenditure on the juice bars is lower than the return earned by the coffee shops, earnings per share will fall.

 Videos can be viewed by accessing your ebook version on VitalSource.

 **BPP**

31 Felinhen Co

Marking guide	Marks
(a) Sale of individual assets (breakup basis)	1
Close woodcraft shops and keep craft centres open	
Not including depreciation and additional investment	1
Present value of free cash flows years 1–5	1
Present value of free cash flows year 6 onwards	1
Carry on current business and invest	
Depreciation	1
Additional investment	1
Present value of free cash flows years 1–3	1
Present value of free cash flows year 4 onwards	2
	9
(b) Up to 2 marks per valid point made	
Sale of individual assets	3
Close woodcraft shops and keep craft centres open	3
Sale to buy-out group	3
Other courses of action	3
Recommendation	1
	11

Professional skills marks

Analysis and evaluation

- Appropriate use of the data to determine suitable calculations
- Appropriate use of the data to support discussion, draw appropriate conclusions and design appropriate responses
- Identification of omissions from the analysis, or further analysis, which could be carried out to enable an appropriate decision/recommendation to be made

Scepticism

- Effective challenge of information, evidence and assumptions supplied and techniques carried out to support key facts and/or decisions

- Effective challenge and critical assessment of the information, evidence and assumptions provided, including identification of contradictory evidence, and ongoing questioning of the reliability of the information/evidence provided/gathered

Commercial acumen

- Recommendations are practical and plausible in the context of Felinhen Co's situation
- Effective use of examples and/or calculations from the scenario information and other practical considerations related to the context to illustrate points being made

Maximum

$\underline{5}$

Total

$\underline{\underline{25}}$

(a) **Scenario 1**

Sale of individual assets

Realisable value = 60% × 75% × ($7,570,000 − $970,000) = $2,970,000

Scenario 2

Close woodcraft shops and keep craft centres open

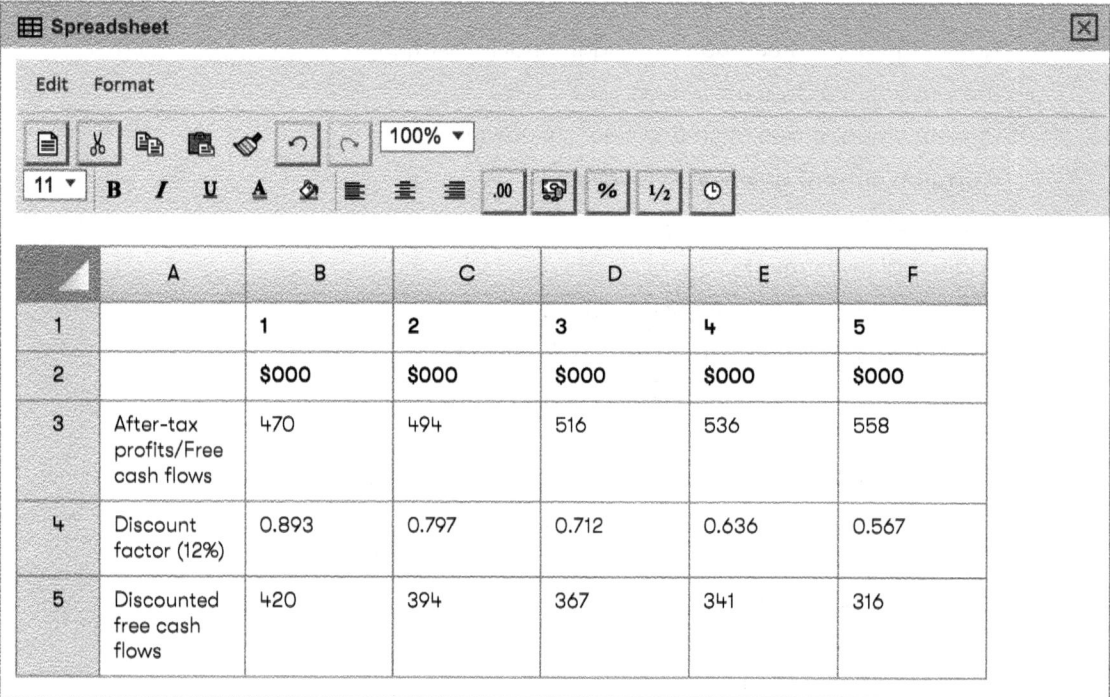

	1	2	3	4	5
	$000	$000	$000	$000	$000
After-tax profits/Free cash flows	470	494	516	536	558
Discount factor (12%)	0.893	0.797	0.712	0.636	0.567
Discounted free cash flows	420	394	367	341	316

Present value of free cash flows Years 1 to 5 = $1,838,000

Present value of free cash flows Year 6 onwards = ($558,000/0.12) x 0.567 = $2,637,000

Total valuation = $800,000 + $1,838,000 + $2,637,000 = $5,275,000

No adjustment is made for additional investment as it equals depreciation.

Scenario 3

Carry on current business and invest

Year	1	2	3
	$000	$000	$000
After-tax profits	380	420	440
Add: Depreciation	170	190	200
Less: Additional investment	(300)	(250)	(210)
Free cash flows	250	360	430
Discount factor (12%)	0.893	0.797	0.712
Discounted free cash flows	223	287	306

Present value of free cash flows Years 1 to 3 = $816,000

Present value of free cash flows Year 4 onwards = ($430,000 × 1.03)/(0.12 – 0.03) × 0.712 = $3,504,000

Total valuation = $816,000 + $3,504,000 – $600,000 = $3,720,000

(b) **Sale of individual assets**

The value achieved by selling off the assets on an individual basis should be regarded as a floor value for the woodcraft business. The figures for the realisable value of the assets may be uncertain, possibly being more or less than forecast.

This option does have the advantage of bringing in a quick cash receipt, which can help to fund the investment expenditure which Felinhen Co has to make. If Felinhen Co is adopting a strategy of focusing on core activities, the sale makes its situation simpler and frees up management time which would have been required for the woodcraft business. However, if the woodcraft business could become profitable again, selling it off in this way represents the loss of a potential future income stream. The realisable value of the assets is also lower than the value of the other strategies being considered, meaning it is questionable whether it is the best option for Felinhen Co.

This option is also likely to have the biggest reputation risk, as shown already by the adverse media coverage.

Close woodcraft shops and keep craft centres open

This policy offers a smaller quick cash receipt than the sale of all the individual assets, although again the amount would be dependent on the realisable value of the assets sold.

Long term, however, this option appears to offer the highest value for Felinhen Co. The future profit figures will, however, be subject to some uncertainties. It is questionable how well the products would sell in other locations. There is no information about how successful online selling has been for the countryside store products and the products being sold are much bulkier, suggesting the need for investment in vehicles and higher distribution costs. The valuation is dependent on the assumption that the business carries on in perpetuity, which may be unrealistic. There is also no justification given for the cost of capital.

This option would keep the craft centres open, mitigating the reputation risk. The board would have to consider the more complicated logistics of trading the wood products in the ways proposed. Additional storage facilities may be required, given that the woodcraft shops would no longer be available to store items. There is also the logistical problem of countryside stores having to accommodate much larger items such as furniture, limiting the products which can be displayed.

Sale to buy-out group

The sale at the price offered again is a quick cash receipt.

The price offered of $3m is not far above the forecast income from selling the assets of the business individually, which should be regarded as the lowest acceptable price for the

woodcraft business. It is possible that the individual assets could sell for more than expected and the total receipt might be higher than the current offer from the buy-out team. However, it appears to be certain that Felinhen Co would receive the $3m if it accepts the buy-out group's offer, whereas it may not achieve the $3m if the assets are sold individually.

The calculation for carrying on the business and investing gives an indication of the potential of the woodcraft business if the required investment is made in it, and it is 24% higher than the offer made by the buy-out group. However, the same comments as above apply to carrying on the value to perpetuity and using a cost of capital which has not been justified. The valuation suggested by the calculation may well not be acceptable to the purchasers. Their plans for the business may be based on different and less optimistic assumptions, indicating their lower valuation of $3m is realistic. If the forecast cash flows are realistic, that would suggest that the woodcraft business still could have significant longer-term value for Felinhen Co, even if significant immediate expenditure is needed.

Selling the woodcraft business as a whole would also not involve Felinhen Co having to take decisions about shutting shops and craft centres, avoiding the risk to its reputation.

Other options

The decision is based on the woodcraft business making a loss in a single year, after a number of years of profitability. It appears that the decision to close or sell the business may be premature. Given that it is forecast to make profits with further investment, there may be a possibility that it could make profits even without this investment in the coming year, although there has been a decline in profits prior to making the loss. Felinhen Co's board should certainly consider the possibility of letting the woodcraft business operate for at least another year. It is questionable whether that would be a riskier strategy than any of the others proposed.

The board should also consider partial implementation of some of the options stated. The valuation calculation indicates that keeping the craft centres and shops open and investing in them has a significantly lower value than just keeping the craft centres open. However, the board could consider just shutting the worst-performing shops. If the most profitable shops were kept open and investment was made in them, then, as well as making a positive contribution, they could also act as a showcase for the products and a collection hub for online sales.

The woodcraft shops' profitability might be improved, and a potential extra sales outlet opened, if some of the products currently sold in the countryside stores were also sold in the woodcraft shops.

Felinhen Co's board has generally not considered the links and any synergies between the two businesses. Arguably, also, if it wanted to focus on its agricultural and woodland management, it should analyse the possibility of divesting of all of Counwood Co and not just its woodcraft business.

Recommendation

The sale of the business to the buy-out group would provide immediate funds for other required purposes and appears to be a marginally better option than selling the assets individually. It would also mean that Felinhen Co did not suffer the negative publicity through closing the craft centres and shops. Although just keeping the craft centres open and selling their products elsewhere may be a better long-term financial option, the financial and operational uncertainties are likely to be too great for the board to tolerate and also would not result in the desired focus of activities.

Felinhen Co's board should negotiate with the buy-out group to try to obtain a higher price than offered, though they should consider settling for a lower price than suggested by the valuation of $3,720,000, which may be over-optimistic.

32 Gogarth

Course Book references

Currency risk management is covered in Chapter 12.

Top tips

Read the question requirements carefully, marks are only available in part b for discussing economic risk, not other types of risk.

Examining team's comments

The ACCA examiner's report noted that 'In a question of this nature there are generally 3–4 marks available for advice and recommendations following the calculations. These marks can be earned quickly and easily and candidates must ensure that they do this. At present many candidates are not earning these marks. Candidates are assured that even if their calculations are not correct, they can still earn credit so long as their recommendation is consistent with their calculations'.

Marking guide		Marks
(a) Netting of receipt and payment	1	
Forward contract	1	
Futures		
Buy/Sept/No of contracts	1	
Lock in rate	2	
Expected receipt	1	
Receipt from under/over hedge	1	
Options		
Number of contracts	1	
Premium	2	
Forward hedge	1	
Outcome	1	
Discussion	$\underline{4}$	
Marks Available	16	
Maximum		15
(b) Understanding of economic risk	1	
Up to 2 marks for each well-developed point		
(points could include identification of cash flows affected, identification of influences on exchange rate, role in implementing economic risk management, role in advising on economic risk management)	$\underline{5}$	
Marks Available	6	
Maximum		$\underline{5}$

Professional skills

Analysis and Evaluation

- Appropriate use of the data to determine suitable calculations
- Appropriate use of the data to support discussion and draw appropriate conclusions

- Appraisal of information objectively to make a hedging recommendation

Commercial acumen

- Effective use of examples and/or practical considerations related to the context to illustrate points being made relating to hedging the transaction or economic risk

Maximum   5

Total   25

(a)

The net receipt is $22,900,000 (see workings).

Forward contract

The receipts from a forward contract would be MR96,461,668.

Futures

193 September contracts to buy MR are required (see workings).

This leaves a small amount of over-hedged currency which can be hedged at the forward rate, giving a net receipt of MR96,461,603.

Note. Alternatively, the futures outcome could also be calculated as MR96,461,668 which is calculated by applying the effective futures rate to the actual transaction ($22,900,000/0.2374 = MR96,461,668). This is very slightly less accurate because it does not recognise the impact of over/under hedging. However, it avoids spending time analysing this issue, which is not likely to have a material impact on decision-making. This approach is **much quicker to calculate** and would lose a maximum of 1 mark.

Options

193 September call option contracts to buy MR would need to be purchased.

This leaves a small amount of under-hedged currency which can be hedged at the forward rate, giving the outcome of MR96,131,887 (assuming the options are exercised).

Recommendations

The forward contract gives a marginally higher receipt than the futures.

Futures would be subject to basis risk, the risk that the difference between the futures price and spot rate does not decrease linearly towards the maturity of futures. This means that the receipt may be uncertain. Futures also require a margin payment, an initial payment of cash into a margin account operated by the futures exchange, with further payments if losses are made on contracts.

Options give a lower receipt, because of the need to pay a premium. Gogarth Co may consider options if it considers there is a chance that the dollar will be in a stronger position against the Malaysian ringgit than suggested by the forward rate, or if one or other transaction is likely to fall through.

Overall, Gogarth Co should choose the forward contract as it offers the marginally higher receipt and is not subject to basis risk.

Note. Other valid recommendations could be made.

Workings (shown in a spreadsheet)

Net receipt

$37,400,000 − $14,500,000 = $22,900,000

Forward contract

$22,900,000/0.2374 = MR96,461,668

Futures

Basis

Assume that basis reduces to zero at contract maturity in a linear fashion.

Opening basis with 5 months to end of future

= 0.2378 (future) − 0.2358 (spot) = 0.0020

Closing basis on 31 August with 1 month remaining

= 0.0020 × 1/5 = 0.0004

Effective futures rate = Opening future − closing basis

= 0.2378 − 0.0004 = **0.2374**

Number of contracts

= $22,900,000/0.2374/MR500,000 = 192.9, say 193

Amount over-hedged

= (500,000 × 193 × $0.2374) − $22,900,000 = $9,100 paid at the forward rate = $9,100/0.2370
= MR38,397

Outcome

	MR
Futures (500,000 × 193)	96,500,000
Payment on forward market	(38,397)
	96,461,603

Options

Number of contracts

= $22,900,000/0.2368/MR500,000 = 193.4 contracts, approximately 193 contracts

Premium

= 193 × $0.0014 × 500,000 = $135,100

Premium in MR, translated at spot rate = $135,100/0.2355 = MR573,673

Amount under-hedged

= $22,900,000 − (193 × 500,000 × $0.2368) = $48,800

Translated at forward rate = $48,800/0.2374 = MR205,560

Outcome, assuming options are exercised

	MR
Options (500,000 × 193)	96,500,000
Receipt on forward market	205,560
Premium	(573,673)
	96,131,887

(b) Economic risk is the longer-term risk that the present value of future cash flows may be increased or reduced by exchange rate movements. The treasury function will be involved in

the development of longer-term responses, as the derivatives the treasury function will use for hedging of short-term exchange risk will not be appropriate.

Risk analysis

The treasury function needs to identify the cash flows that may be affected by exchange rate movements. These may not just include transactions with overseas customers and suppliers. Home market sales can also be affected if, for example, the currency of the country where a foreign competitor is based weakens against the ringgit and the competitor can then afford to charge cheaper ringgit prices.

The treasury function must also identify the factors affecting exchange rate movements in the longer term and assess what their impact is likely to be. This could include predicted movements; for example, changes in the economic cycle, and also the impact of sudden economic shocks. The treasury function will need to assess the impact of these exchange rate movements on Gogarth Co. This will include consideration of the other impacts that the factors affecting exchange rates will have; for example, a change in interest rate policy affecting demand for electrical equipment directly as well as influencing exchange rate levels.

Risk management

The treasury function will be particularly involved in determining funding policy in the context of the need to manage economic risk. One aspect of economic risk management is matching any assets held in a foreign country with a loan in that country's currency. The treasury function will determine the suitability of borrowing abroad and the best possible arrangement if foreign currency loans are required.

Economic risk can also be managed by diversifying customer, supplier and operational bases and changing pricing policy. The treasury function will be involved in assessing the possible impacts of policy changes. However, the decisions will be taken in the context of operational considerations, such as supplier management, and wider strategic considerations, such as scope of operations.

33 Adverane

> ### Course Book references
>
> Currency hedging is covered in Chapter 11 (netting) and Chapter 12.
>
> ### Top tips
>
> For part (a) you have to use your time efficiently given the marks available – a short-cut approach to futures calculations is essential here.
>
> ### Easy marks
>
> There are numerous easy marks to be picked up in part (b) for calculating and discussing netting.
>
> ### Examining team's comments
>
> Many candidates spent far too long on this question to the detriment of the rest of the exam. Good time management, an ability to work under pressure and making a reasonable attempt at all the requirements of all the questions are the key ingredients for success.
>
> Part (a) required candidates to determine a hedging strategy, having been given the choice of money market hedging and traded futures. A few candidates wasted time by not netting off the amounts owed and owing. Many candidates remembered how to carry out money market hedging, although a number treated the amount to be hedged as if it was a payment, not a receipt. Likewise, a number of candidates scored well on the futures hedging part of the question. A surprisingly common error was that candidates did not say clearly that the company should buy futures – this should have been an easy mark. Some candidates also adjusted the calculation of the number of contracts by the time period of the hedge – this adjustment is made in interest rate futures calculations, not currency futures calculations.

There were a number of versions of the basis calculation, although many candidates did calculate basis correctly.

Part (b)(i) required multilateral netting calculations for subsidiaries operating in a number of countries with different currencies. Most candidates used a systematic approach and gained the majority of marks for this part. The main weakness was failing to follow the instructions given in the question scenario. A few candidates did not use the spot mid-rate to translate amounts, as the scenario required.

Part (b)(ii) asked for a discussion of the advantages of multilateral netting. Candidates tended to focus on lower transaction costs and hedging implications, with few considering the availability of more advantageous exchange rates and central treasury administration being easier. Some candidates focused on the words 'central treasury function' and produced the lists they had learnt of the advantages and disadvantages of treasury centralisation, which was not what the question required.

Marking guide	Marks	
(a) Calculation of net US$ receipt	1	
Money market hedge	2	
Futures		
Buy futures	1	
Predicted futures rate based on basis reduction	2	
Expected receipt	1	
Number of contracts	1	
Conclusion	2	
Marks Available	10	
Maximum		9
(b) (i) CHF amounts owed and owing	2	
Totals owed and owing	2	
Net amounts owed	1	
Payments and receipts	2	
		7
(ii) Advantages – 1 mark each		
Maximum		4

Professional skills

Analysis and Evaluation

- Appropriate use of the data to determine suitable calculations to appraise an appropriate hedging strategy
- Appropriate use of the data to support discussion and draw appropriate conclusions
- Demonstration of reasoned judgement when considering key matters for Adverane
- Demonstration of ability to consider relevant factors applicable to Adverane's situation

Commercial acumen

Effective use of examples and/or calculations from the scenario information and other practical considerations related to the context to illustrate points being made relating to hedging and netting.

Maximum	5
Total	25

(a)

Adverane Co will have a net dollar receipt of $6,450,000 (see workings) in four months' time and needs to hedge against the Swiss Franc strengthening.

Money market

Borrowing in US$s and investing into CHF gives a receipt of CHF5,728,714 (see workings).

Futures

Buying 46 Swiss Franc futures (using six-month futures contracts) gives an outcome of approximately CHF5,753,791. There is a small inaccuracy in the calculations as they do not consider the impact of the hedged amount, however the unhedged amount is very small here and the impact will be immaterial.

On the basis that futures give the higher expected receipt, they should be chosen, but Adverane Co should assess whether basis risk is likely to be significant, ie the risk that the future rate may not change over time in the way that is predicted.

The futures contracts will also require a payment of an upfront margin (a deposit), so Adverane will need to ensure that it can cope with the cash flow implications of using a futures hedge. However, no cash flow problems have been mentioned.

Adverane Co should also consider, as regards money market hedging, that CHF receipts could be used to pay off any existing CHF loans or for other investment purposes, in which case the benefit to Adverane Co could be greater than hedging using futures.

Using the money market borrowing rate (which would be saved), this would have the effect of changing final step in the money market hedge outcome to CHF5,677,615 × (1 + [0.039/3]) = CHF5,751,424.

This increases the attractiveness of the money market hedge, although the futures outcome is still better.

Therefore, on balance, the futures contract is recommended.

Workings (shown in a spreadsheet)

Net receipt = $10,150,000 − $3,700,000 = $6,450,000

Money market

Borrow sufficient US$ now to match to receipt in 4 months:

US$6,450,000/(1 + [0.037/3]) = US$6,371,419

Convert into CHF at spot rate:

US$6,371,419/1.1222 = CHF5,677,615

Invest in CHF for 4 months:

CHF 5,677,615 × (1 + [0.027/3]) = **CHF 5,728,714**

Futures

Basis

Assume that basis reduces to zero at contract maturity in a linear fashion.

Opening basis with six months to expiry of future = future − spot = 1.1204 − 1.1222 = −0.0018

In four months' time, there are two months until the expiry of the future, so the closing basis is estimated as −0.0018 × 2/6 = −0.0006.

 BPP

Effective rate

The effective futures rate is therefore opening future − closing basis

= 1.1204 − −0.0006 = 1.1210.

Expected receipt using the effective rate = $6,450,000/1.1210 = **CHF 5,753,791**

Number of contracts = CHF5,753,791/125,000 = 46.03 contracts, approximately 46 contracts

(b) (i) Use mid-spot rates to translate amounts.

Owed by	Owed to	Local currency (m)	CHF (m)
Adverane (Switzerland)	Bosha (Eurozone)	CHF15.90	15.90
Adverane (Switzerland)	Diling (Brazil)	CHF4.46	4.46
Bosha (Eurozone)	Cogate (USA)	€24.89	26.60
Bosha (Eurozone)	Diling (Brazil)	€18.57	19.84
Cogate (USA)	Adverane (Switzerland)	US$27.08	24.16
Cogate (USA)	Diling (Brazil)	US$5.68	5.07
Diling (Brazil)	Adverane (Switzerland)	BRL38.80	12.29
Diling (Brazil)	Bosha (Eurozone)	BRL51.20	16.22

Owed to   *Owed by*

	Adverane (Switzerland)	Bosha (Eurozone)	Cogate (USA)	Diling (Brazil)	Total
	CHFm	CHFm	CHFm	CHFm	CHFm
Adverane (Switzerland)			24.16	12.29	36.45
Bosha (Eurozone)	15.90			16.22	32.12
Cogate (USA)		26.60			26.60
Diling (Brazil)	4.46	19.84	5.07		29.37
Owed by	(20.36)	(46.44)	(29.23)	(28.51)	
Owed	36.45	32.12	26.60	29.37	
Net	16.09	(14.32)	(2.63)	0.86	

Under the terms of the arrangement, Bosha, the company with the largest debt, will pay Diling, the company with the smallest amount owed to it, CHF0.86 million. Bosha will pay Adverane CHF13.46 million and Cogate will pay Adverane CHF2.63 million.

(ii) The advantage of using a central treasury for multilateral netting is that the central treasury can coordinate the information about inter-group balances.

• There will be a smaller number of foreign exchange transactions; three transactions instead of eight without netting. This will mean lower commission and transmission costs.

• There will be less loss of interest through money being in transit.

• The foreign exchange rates available may be more advantageous as a result of large transaction sizes resulting from consolidation.

• The netting arrangements should make cash flow forecasting easier in the group.

 **BPP**

ANSWERS

34 Nutourne

Marking guide		Marks
(a) Futures		
Sell futures now	1	
Number of contracts	1	
Forward hedge	1	
Predicted futures rate using basis	1	
Overall expected receipt	1	
Options		
Purchase June put	1	
Premium	1	
Overall expected receipt	1	
Calculation of when option is a better choice	2	
Comments	2	
		12
(b) Reasons for using exchange-traded derivatives compared to OTC – 1 mark per point		
Maximum		3
(c) Significance of initial and maintenance margins	2	
Mark-to-market explanation	1	
Numerical illustration using Nutourne Co's figures	3	
Marks Available	6	
Maximum		5

Professional skills

Analysis and Evaluation

- Appropriate use of the data to determine suitable calculations to evaluate the proposed hedging strategies

- Appropriate use of the data to support discussion and draw appropriate conclusions

- Demonstration of reasoned judgement when considering key matters for Nutourne
- Demonstration of ability to consider relevant factors applicable to Nutourne's situation

Commercial acumen

- Effective use of examples and/or calculations from the scenario information and other practical considerations related to the context to illustrate points being made relating to hedging

Maximum   5

Total   25

(a)

Nutourne Co will have a Swiss Franc receipt of CHF 12.3 million in six months' time and needs to hedge against the dollar strengthening.

Futures

Nutourne would sell 98 June Swiss futures contracts, resulting in an outcome of $12,740,340 (see workings), assuming that basis reduces to zero at contract maturity in a linear fashion.

Options contract

Nutourne Co would purchase 98 CHF June put options.

Assuming the options are exercised this results in an outcome of $12,655,815.

The options would give the higher receipt if they were not exercised and the spot rate moved sufficiently in Nutourne Co's favour. If Nutourne Co allowed the option to lapse, it would obtain the same receipt as under the futures if the US$/CHF spot rate was US$1.0444 = CHF1 (see workings).

Comments

If the options are exercised, the futures would give the higher receipt. The options give a lower receipt because of the premium which Nutourne Co has to pay. The futures will be subject to the risk that basis (the difference between the futures price and the spot price) may not decrease linearly as the futures approach maturity, as assumed in the above calculations. This will mean that the hedge of the CHF 12,250,000 is imperfect, and the receipt may be unpredictable despite a futures hedge being taken out.

The options can also be allowed to lapse if for some reason the contract is not completed. If this happens, Nutourne Co will only have to settle the forward contract.

Workings (provided in a spreadsheet)

Futures

No. of contracts = CHF12,300,000/125,000 = 98.4, say 98, hedging CHF12,250,000

Remainder to be hedged on the forward market is CHF12,300,000 – CHF12,250,000 = CHF 50,000

Receipt = CHF50,000 × 1.0358 = $51,790

Calculation of futures price

Estimate from opening June futures rate of 1.0369, with seven months to expiry; this means that opening basis is 0.0077 (since the future is above the current spot of 1.0292 by this amount). At the end of May, with only one month until expiry this basis should fall to 1/7 × 0.0077 = 0.0011.

Effective futures rate = opening futures rate − closing basis

= 1.0369 − 0.0011 = 1.0358

Expected receipt

= CHF12,250,000 × 1.0358 = $12,688,550

Outcome

	$
Futures	12,688,550
Remainder on forward market	51,790
	12,740,340

Or

Applying the effective futures rate of 1.0358 to the actual amount of CHF 12,300,000 gives 12,300,000 × 1.0358 = $12,740,340

Options contract

Amount not hedged, hedged by forward contract CHF translated as $51,790 as before.

Assuming the options are exercised:

	$
Receipt (W1)	12,709,375
Premium (W2)	(105,350)
Forward contract	51,790
	12,655,815

Workings

1   **Receipt**

CHF125,000 × 98 × 1.0375 = $12,709,375

2   **Premium**

1.0375 options = 98 × 125,000 × 0.0086 = $105,350

The options would give the higher receipt if they were not exercised and the spot rate moved sufficiently in Nutourne Co's favour. If Nutourne Co allowed the option to lapse, it would obtain the same receipt as under the futures if the US$/CHF spot rate was x, such that

12,688,550 = 12,250,000x − 105,350

12,250,000x = 12,688,550 + 105,350

so that x is US$1.0444 = CHF1.

(b)   One of the main reasons why the treasury function uses exchange-traded derivatives is that the contracts can be bought and sold as required which means that it is easier to adjust the hedging position if required.

Also, because the markets are regulated by an exchange, counterparty risk (the risk of the other party to the transaction defaulting) should be minimised.

Exchange traded derivatives can also be exercised over a period of time, while OTC derivatives are normally exercisable on a specific date. This adds to the attractiveness of exchange traded options if there is uncertainty about the timing of the actual transaction.

(c) The mark-to-market process begins with Nutourne Co having to deposit an amount (the initial margin) in a margin account with the futures exchange when it takes out the futures. The margin account will remain open as long as the futures are open. The profit or loss on the futures is calculated daily and the margin account is adjusted for the profit or loss.

The maintenance margin is the minimum balance which has to be maintained on the margin account.

If the losses on the futures are so large that the balance on the margin account is less than the maintenance margin, then the futures exchange will make a demand (a margin call) for an extra payment (the variation margin) to increase the balance on the account back to the maintenance margin.

The complexity of managing this process is one of the limitations of exchange traded derivatives.

In the example, initial margin = $1,450 × 98 = $142,100

Maintenance margin = $1,360 × 98 = $133,280

Loss in ticks = 0.0011/0.0001 = 11

Total loss = 11 ticks × $12.50 × 98 = $13,475

Balance on margin account = $142,100 − $13,475 = $128,625

This is less than the maintenance margin, so Nutourne Co would have to deposit an extra ($133,280 − $128,625) = $4,655 (the variation margin) to bring the balance on the margin account up to the maintenance margin.

Alternative solution

In some exchanges, a variation margin may be required to increase the balance on the account back to its initial margin level. Therefore, in this case, the variation margin amount would be $13,475 (ie $142,100 − $128,625).

35 Frongoch Co

Course Book references

Currency hedging is covered in Chapter 12.

Top Tips

The key issue in most currency hedging questions is to get **the basics** right. Here, it is vital that you correctly identify **which side of the spread to use** (care is needed here as the exchange rate is quoted to the Euro) and also **which type** of futures and options contracts to use.

In part (c) 2 easy marks are available for defining basis and basis risk.

Marking guide	Marks	
(a) Forward contract	1	
Futures		
Buy September futures	1	
Predicted futures price	1	
Number of contracts	1	
Outcome	1	
Options		
Purchase September call	1	
Premium	1	
Outcome	1	
Recommendation	1	
		9
(b) Forward contract stays the same under both scenarios	1	
New option result when spot rate = 1.1534 and option is not exercised	1	
Options result stays the same when spot rate = 1.1549	1	
Futures result stays the same when spot rate = 1.1534 and futures price = 1.1552	1	
New futures result when spot rate = 1.1549 and futures price = 1.1563	2	
Evaluation of impact of basis risk on hedging methods	1	
Maximum		7
(c) Definition of basis	1	
Definition of basis risk	1	
Further discussion in relation to Frongoch Co	3	
Marks Available	5	
Maximum		4

Professional skills marks

Analysis and Evaluation

- Appropriate use of the data to determine suitable calculations
- Appropriate use of the data to support discussion and draw appropriate conclusions
- Appraisal of information objectively to make a recommendation

Scepticism

- Effective challenge of information supplied to support key facts and/or decisions
- Demonstration of ability to consider relevant factors applicable to hedging options

Commercial acumen

- Recommendations are practical and plausible in the context of the company's situation
- Effective use of examples from the scenario information and other practical considerations related to the context to illustrate points being made

Maximum	5
Total	25

(a) Forward contract

€18,250,000 x 1.1544 $/€ = $21,067,800

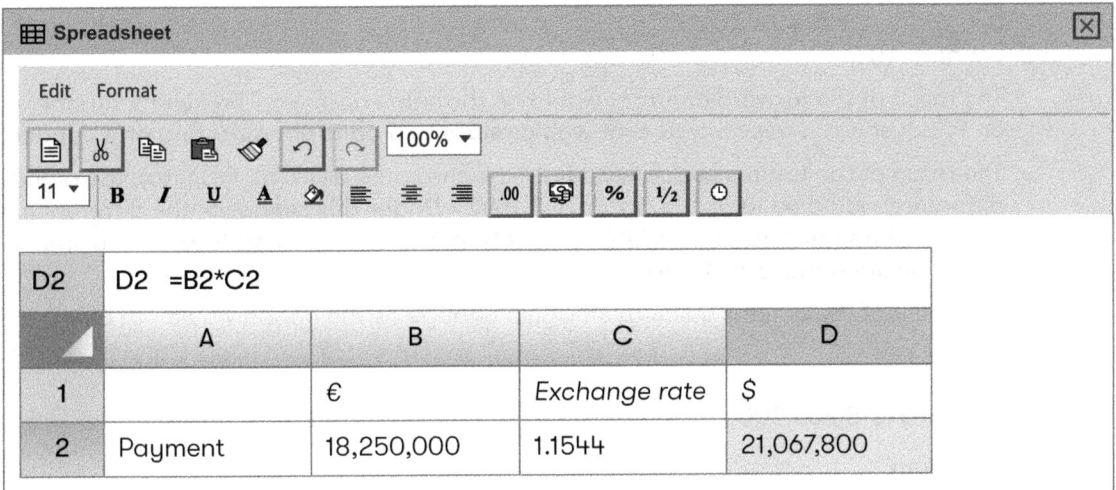

Futures

Buy € September futures.

Basis

Assume that basis reduces to zero at contract maturity in a linear fashion.

Opening basis = future - spot = 1.1560 − 1.1497= 0.0063 with 7 months to end of future contract

Predicted closing basis = 0.0063 × 2/7 as 2 months of the future remains = 0.0018.

Effective futures price ($/€) = Opening future − closing basis = 1.1560 − 0.0018 = 1.1542

Alternatively, the predicted futures price ($/€) = 1.1497 + ([1.1560 − 1.1497] × 5/7) = 1.1542

Number of contracts = €18,250,000 / €125,000 = 146

Outcome

Futures (€125,000 x 146 x 1.1542 $/€) = $21,064,150

Alternatively, futures outcome = €18,250,000 x effective rate of 1.1542 $/€ = $21,064,150

Options

Purchase € September call options Number of contracts = 146 as above

Premium = 146 x 0.0069 $/€ x 125,000 = $125,925

Outcome, assuming options are exercised

	$
Options (€125,000 x 146 x 1.1540 $/€)	21,060,500
Premium	125,925
	21,186,425

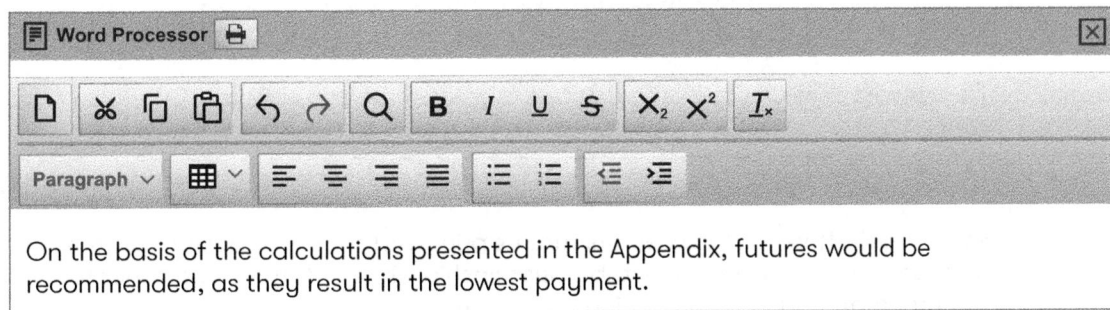

On the basis of the calculations presented in the Appendix, futures would be recommended, as they result in the lowest payment.

(b) **Scenario (i)**

The result of the forward contract would be the same as in (a). The five-month forward rate on 1 August is not relevant, as that **would relate to a contract maturing on 1 January.**

The result of the futures hedge would also be the same as in (a). From (a), the predicted basis difference would be 18 points (1.1560 – 1.1542). **Under this scenario, the difference would also be 18 points (1.1552 – 1.1534) so the effective rate (opening future – closing basis) would be unchanged at 1.1542.**

The result of the options calculation would change as the option would not be exercised.

	$
Options (€18,250,000 x 1.1534)	21,049,550
Premium	125,925
	21,175,475

Scenario (ii)

The result of the forward contract would be the same as in (a), as discussed in Scenario (i).

The result of the options would be the same as in (a). The options would be exercised as the spot rate is greater than the **exercise price.**

The result of the futures hedge would be different from (a). The expected gap between the spot rate and futures price would **be 14 basis points (1.1563 – 1.1549) so the effective rate (opening future – closing basis) would be:**

Effective futures price ($/€) = Opening future – closing basis = 1.1560 – 0.0014 = 1.1546

Outcome = €18,250,000 x effective rate of 1.1546 $/€ = $21,071,450

This would make the hedge less effective by $7,300 compared to the outcome in scenario (i) of $21,064,150.

Alternative working for futures 1 August

1 August

	$/€
Pay spot rate	1.1549
Buy € futures	1.1560
(Sell € futures)	(1.1563)
	1.1546

Net cost $/€ 1.1546 x €18,250,000 = $21,071,450

(c)

Basis is the difference between the futures price and spot rate. Basis risk is the risk that the spot rate will not have a predictable relationship with the futures price prior to the futures contract maturing and basis being zero.

It is assumed in (a) that the basis will decrease in a linear fashion towards zero as the futures approach maturity, so that it will be 18 points at 1 August. However, in the scenario

in (b)(ii), the linear relationship has not held, and basis is only 14 points, resulting in a less effective hedge and greater cost. This could happen due to short-term factors, such as currency supply issues. Short-term factors could also have meant that basis is greater than 18 points.

The consequence of basis risk is that the net payment may not be fixed or predictable using futures contracts. In the scenario being analysed in (b)(ii), assuming incorrectly that basis will decrease linearly will mean that futures are chosen when forward contracts, which are not subject to basis risk, would give the best result. However, the financial consequences of basis risk are still likely to be much smaller than the possible losses if the payment was not hedged.

36 Lough Co

Top Tips

Treasury management (including netting) is covered in Chapter 11 of the Course Book, and currency risk management is covered in Chapter 12.

Examining team's comments

To demonstrate the skill of scepticism, candidates were expected to adopt a questioning approach in a way that would lead to effective challenges of the information provided in the scenario. A small number of candidates used the data in exhibit two, which predicted a depreciation of the Swedish krona relative to the dollar, to question whether there was a need to hedge the payment at all. This was an excellent example of scepticism being demonstrated.

Marking guide		Marks
(a) USD amounts owing and owed	2	
Totals owing and owed	2	
Net amounts owing and owed	1	
Settlement transactions	2	
Main advantage	2	
		9
(b) Forward	1	
Money market	2	
Advice	2	
		4
(c) Cost reduction strategy, eg economies of scale, expertise, bulk borrowing and internal cash transfers	4	
Finance director's proposal, eg responsiveness, staff motivation, awareness of local conditions and cost benefit analysis	4	
		7

Professional skills marks

Analysis and evaluation

- Appropriate use of the data to determine suitable calculations
- Appropriate use of the data to support discussion and draw appropriate conclusions
- Appraisal of information objectively to make a recommendation

Scepticism

- Effective challenge of information, evidence and assumptions supplied and techniques carried out to support key facts and/or decisions

 **BPP**

- Demonstration of ability to consider all relevant factors, including Lough Co's cost reduction strategy, applicable to a given course of action

Commercial acumen

- Effective use of examples and/or calculations from the scenario information and other practical considerations related to the context to illustrate points being made

Maximum   5

Total   25

(a)

Owed by	Owed to	Amount (m)	Amount (USD m)
Lough Co	Gahana Co	INR3,447.70	47.62
Lough Co	Adalar Co	TRY126.20	17.47
Fitz Co	Lough Co	USD75.75	75.75
Fitz Co	Gahana Co	INR333.13	4.60
Fitz Co	Adalar Co	TRY256.29	35.48
Gahana Co	Fitz Co	GBP34.08	48.20
Gahana Co	Adalar Co	TRY135.52	18.76
Adalar Co	Lough Co	USD12.80	12.80

Owed by (amounts in USD m)

	Lough Co	Fitz Co	Gahana Co	Adalar Co	Total
Owed to					
Lough Co		75.75		12.80	88.55
Fitz Co			48.20		48.20
Gahana Co	47.62	4.60			52.22
Adalar Co	17.47	35.48	18.76		71.71
Owed by	(65.09)	(115.83)	(66.96)	(12.80)	
Owed to	88.55	48.20	52.22	71.71	
Net amount	23.46	(67.63)	(14.74)	58.91	

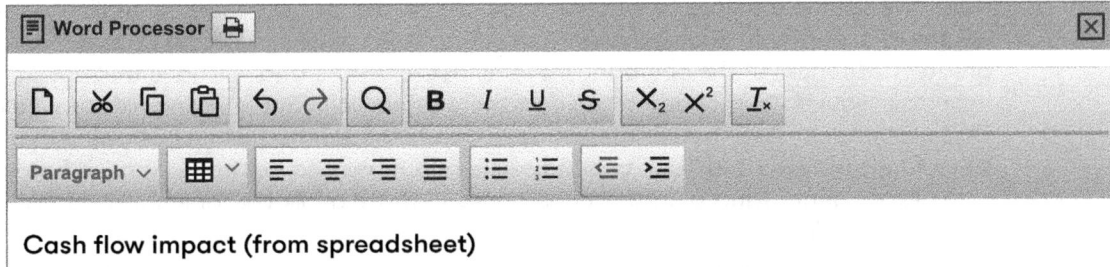

Cash flow impact (from spreadsheet)

Fitz Co pays USD23.46m to Lough Co and then USD44.17m to Adalar Co.

Gahana Co pays USD14.74m to Adalar Co.

Main advantage of multilateral netting

Multilateral netting is not technically a method of managing exposure to foreign exchange risk. It is a cost saving mechanism, which enables Lough Co to minimise the number of settlement transactions by netting off intra-group balances before settlement is made. This will significantly reduce the transaction costs associated with intra-group settlements in a way that is congruent with the chief executive officer's (CEO's) new cost reduction strategy.

(b)

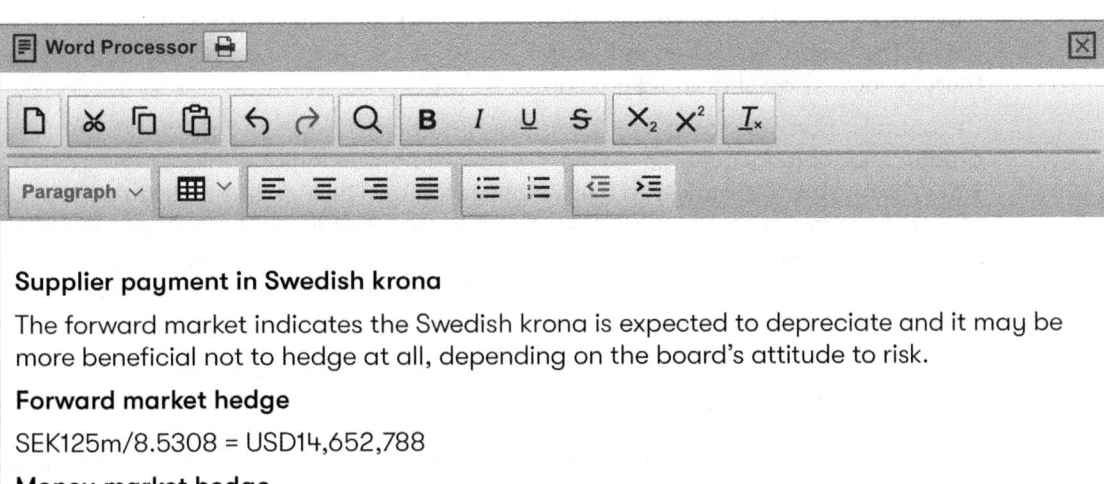

Supplier payment in Swedish krona

The forward market indicates the Swedish krona is expected to depreciate and it may be more beneficial not to hedge at all, depending on the board's attitude to risk.

Forward market hedge

SEK125m/8.5308 = USD14,652,788

Money market hedge

Deposit: SEK125m/(1 + [0.021 × 5/12]) = SEK123,915,737

Convert: SEK123,915,737/8.4458 = USD14,671,877

Borrow: USD14,671,877 x (1 + [0.022 x 5/12]) = USD14,806,368

Both hedging methods result in a fixed payment. The forward market hedge minimises the payment whilst also being administratively less complex and would therefore be the preferred choice.

(c)

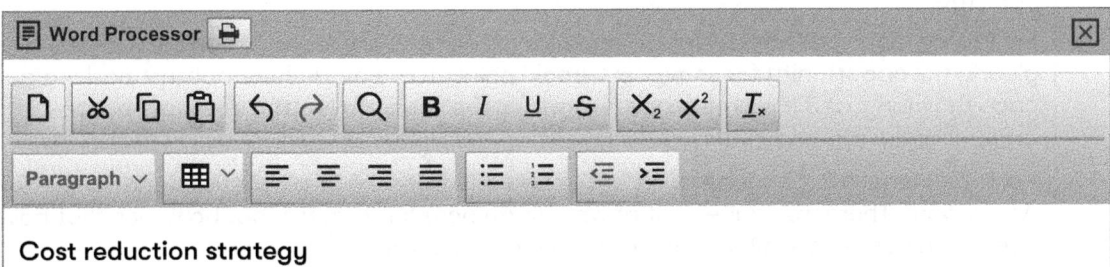

Cost reduction strategy

The centralised treasury function contributes to Lough Co's cost reduction strategy by exploiting significant economies of scale, therefore reducing average costs and increasing shareholder value. Scale economies avoid the unnecessary duplication of skills across the group and concentrate the expertise required within a central department. If Lough Co

decentralises the treasury function it would be much more expensive to replicate the same degree of expertise in each subsidiary. A centralised treasury will also have a much greater awareness of the company's overall risk exposure and will have the resources and expertise required to manage those risks more effectively. Scale economies reduce Lough Co's cost of debt since better interest rates can be negotiated when borrowing in bulk and since funds are remitted back to head office and managed centrally, surplus funds will also attract better rates of interest compared to those available for smaller deposits managed locally.

Another benefit is that funds can also be transferred internally from subsidiaries with spare cash resources to the subsidiaries which need them, which avoids the unnecessary expense of raising finance on the external market. In addition, as seen in the scenario, a centralised treasury is able to undertake multilateral netting, which reduces the costs associated with hedging.

Finance director's proposal

The disadvantages of a centralised treasury department are highlighted in the finance director's briefing note. As evidenced by the experience of Lough Co's Indian subsidiary, decision making may take too long to be effective when the treasury is centralised. Local managers would be able to respond much more quickly to local developments and may have avoided the delay in funding and hence the missed opportunity experienced by Gahana Co. More autonomous decision making would also increase staff motivation and may help to avoid the current problems with staff turnover which have been experienced across the group. Increased motivation improves Lough Co's profit-making potential, thereby increasing shareholder value.

Decentralisation delegates decision making authority to those individuals who have a greater feel for local conditions. The low take-up of the initial public offering (IPO) in Turkey is another example of a missed opportunity. The lack of attention paid to the needs of local investors seems to have been a major contributory factor to that failure. A decentralised treasury function would have been able to build relationships with potential investors and would have had a greater understanding of their needs without incurring the unnecessary expense associated with a failed IPO.

The finance director's suggestion to decentralise the treasury would have avoided many of the problems which have been experienced by Lough Co's subsidiaries but seems incongruent with the CEO's new cost reduction strategy. However, the problems experienced by Lough Co's centralised treasury are also incurring significant costs. In the absence of further information, the board will need to weigh up the costs and benefits of both treasury structures before making a final decision.

37 Buryecs

Course Book references

Foreign currency hedging is covered in Chapter 12.

Top tips

Part (a), 6 marks, this asked for an analysis of the pros and cons of currency swaps. There was clearly the opportunity for some 'text-book' points to be made here but the marking guide caps the marks at 3 if no reference is made to the scenario (eg the swap did not cover the full amount of the currency inflows).

Part (b)(i) required a brief analysis of the benefits from the swap and explanation of how it would work. There was quite a lot of work to do here for 4 marks, but no issues that have not been seen before in similar interest rate swap questions.

Part (b)(ii) required an NPV analysis of the project. This required a careful projection of future exchange rates using PPP theory and recognising that exchange rates were being quoted to 1 unit of the foreign currency.

Part (c) was an assessment of the outcome of using an OTC option contract. It would have been sensible to assess this against the swap but most of the marks were available for simple showing the outcome of the option contract. Care had to be taken here to understand the currency the option contracts were in and whether calls or puts were needed.

A similar question was set in June 2011.

Examining team comments

In part (c) a large number of candidates showed a lack of understanding when they chose call instead of put options. Many attempted to treat the currency options as if they were exchange traded when they were not. Finally, few candidates discussed whether the currency option is a preferred hedging method to a currency swap, hence many missed out on the marks allocated to this part of the question.

Marking guide		Marks
(a) Advantages	3	
Disadvantages	3	
Limit marks for (a) to 2 marks in total if answer does not mention Buryecs Co's situation		
Marks Available	6	
Maximum		4
(b) (i) Recognition that swap gives advantage	1	
Swap mechanism	2	
Net benefit after bank charges	1	
		4
(ii) Exchange rates	2	
Correct translation of amounts swapped	1	
Correct translation of other amounts	1	
Net present value	1	
Gain in € from the swap of the initial fee amount	1	
Comments	3	
Marks Available	9	
Maximum		8
(c) Put option	1	
$7.75 option calculations	2	
Comments	1	
		4

Professional skills

Analysis and Evaluation

- Appropriate use of the data to determine suitable calculations
- Appropriate use of the data to support discussion and draw appropriate conclusions
- Demonstration of reasoned judgement
- Demonstration of ability to consider relevant factors
- Identification of further analysis, which could be carried out to enable an appropriate recommendation to be made.
- Appraisal of information objectively to make a recommendation

 BPP

Scepticism

- Effective challenge of information and assumptions supplied and, techniques carried out to support any risk management and investment decision

- Demonstration of ability to consider all relevant factors applicable to the decisions made

Commercial acumen

- Effective use of examples and/or calculations from the scenario information and other practical considerations related to the context to illustrate points being made

- Recognition of external constraints and opportunities as necessary

- Recommendations are practical and plausible

Maximum $\underline{5}$

Total $\underline{\underline{25}}$

(a) The currency swap will involve Buryecs Co taking out a loan in € and making an arrangement with a counterparty in Wirtonia, which takes out a loan in $. Buryecs Co will pay the interest on the counterparty's loan and vice versa.

Advantages

Payment of interest in $ can be used to match the income Buryecs Co will receive from the rail franchise, reducing foreign exchange risk.

Buryecs Co will be able to obtain the swap for the amount it requires and may be able to reverse the swap by exchanging with the other counterparty. Other methods of hedging risk may be less certain. The cost of a swap may also be cheaper than other methods of hedging, such as options.

The swap can be used to change Buryecs Co's debt profile if it is weighted towards fixed-rate debt and its directors want a greater proportion of floating rate debt, to diversify risk and take advantage of probable lower future interest rates.

Drawbacks

The counterparty may default. This would leave Buryecs Co liable to pay interest on the loan in its currency. The risk of default can be reduced by obtaining a bank guarantee for the counterparty.

The swap may not be a worthwhile means of hedging currency risk if the exchange rate is unpredictable. If it is assumed that exchange rates are largely determined by inflation rates, the predicted inflation rate in Wirtonia is not stable, making it more difficult to predict future exchange rates confidently. If the movement in the exchange rate is not as expected, it may turn out to have been better for Buryecs Co not to have hedged.

Buryecs Co is swapping a fixed rate commitment in the Eurozone for a floating rate in Wirtonia. Inflation is increasing in Wirtonia and there is a risk that interest rates will increase as a result, increasing Buryecs Co's finance costs.

The swap does not hedge the whole amount of the receipt in Year 3. Another method will have to be used to hedge the additional receipt from the government in Year 3 and the receipts in the intervening years.

If the government decides to impose exchange controls in Wirtonia, Buryecs Co may not be able to realise the receipt at the end of Year 3, but will still have to fulfil the swap contract.

(b) (i)

	Buryecs Co	Counterparty	Interest rate benefit
Eurozone	4.0%	5.8%	1.8%
Wirtonia	Bank rate + 0.6%	Bank rate + 0.4%	0.2%
Gain on swap (60:40)	1.2%	0.8%	2.0%
Bank fee (60:40)	(0.3%)	(0.2%)	(0.5%)
Gain on swap after bank fee	0.9%	0.6%	1.5%

The swap arrangement will work as follows:

	Buryecs Co	Counterparty
Buryecs Co borrows at	4.0%	
Counterparty borrows at		Bank rate + 0.4%
Swap		
Counterparty receives		(Bank rate)
Buryecs Co pays	Bank rate	
Counterparty pays		4.6%
Buryecs Co receives	(4.6%)	
Advantage	120 basis points	80 basis points
Net result	Bank rate – 0.6%	5.0%

After paying the 30 point basis fee, Buryecs Co will effectively pay interest at the bank rate – 0.3% and benefit by 90 basis points or 0.9%. The counterparty will effectively pay interest at 5.2% and benefit by 60 basis points or 0.6%.

(ii) Using the purchasing power parity formula to calculate exchange rates:

$S_1 = S_0 \times (1 + h_c)/(1 + h_b)$

Year	1	2	3
	0.1430 × 1.06/1.03 = 0.1472	0.1472 × 1.04/1.08 = 0.1417	0.1417 × 1.03/1.11 = 0.1315

At Year 3, $5,000 million will be exchanged at the original spot rate as per the agreement and the remaining inflows will be exchanged at the Year 3 rate.

Year	0	1	2	3
	$m	$m	$m	$m
Initial fee	(5,000)			
Payment at end of franchise				7,500
Annual income		600	600	600
Year 0 Exchange rate	0.1430			
Years 1–3 Exchange rates		0.1472	0.1417	0.1315

ANSWERS

	€m	€m	€m	€m
Swap translated at 0.1430	(715)			715
Amount not covered by swap (7,500 – 5,000) translated at 0.1315				329
Annual income		88	85	79
Cash flows in home country	(715)	88	85	1,123
Discount factor 14%	1.000	0.877	0.769	0.675
Present value	(715)	77	65	758

The net present value of the project is €185 million, indicating that it should go ahead. However, the value is dependent on the exchange rate, which is worsening for the foreign income. If there are also uncertainties about the variability of returns during the three years, the directors may consider the project to be in excess of their risk appetite and decline the opportunity.

As a result of the exchange rates on the initial fee being fixed at the year 0 spot rate, Buryecs Co has gained $5,000m × (0.1430 – 0.1315) × 0.675 = €39m.

(c) Receipt using swap arrangement = €715m + €329m = €1,044m

Predicted exchange rate at Year 3 is €0.1315 = $1 or $7.6046 = €1

Options

Buy $ put options as receiving $.

$7.75 exercise price

Do not exercise

Net receipt = €986m – (1.6% × $7,500m × 0.1430) = €969m

The $7.75 option gives a worse result than the swap even before the premium is deducted, because of the exchange rate being fixed on the swap back of the original amount paid. These calculations do not take into account possible variability of the finance costs associated with the swap, caused by swapping into floating rate borrowing.

38 Lurgshall

                Marks

(a) Options

Buy put options	1
Number of contracts	1
Basis calculations	1
Premium calculation	1
Exercise option?	1
Impact of interest rate increase	1
Swaps	
Comparative advantage and recognition of benefit	2
Initial decision to borrow floating by Lurgshall & fixed by counterparty	1
Swap impact	2
Net benefit after charges	1
Comments	$\underline{4}$
Marks Available	16
Maximum	15

(b) 1–2 marks per relevant point $\underline{5}$

                                                 $\underline{\underline{5}}$

Professional skills

Analysis and Evaluation

- Appropriate use of the data to determine suitable calculations for each hedging technique
- Appropriate use of the data to support discussion and draw appropriate conclusions
- Appraisal of information objectively to make a hedging recommendation

Scepticism

- Effective challenge of evidence and assumptions supplied with respect to the chief executive's view on the treasury department

Commercial acumen

- Effective use of examples and/or practical considerations related to the context to illustrate points being made relating to hedging the transaction or treasury discussion

Maximum $\underline{5}$

Total $\underline{\underline{25}}$

(a) Options

Buy put options as need to hedge against a rise in interest rates.

Number of contracts required: $84,000,000/$2,000,000 × 6/3 = 84

Total basis = futures price 4.95% – 4.50% current rate (1 May) = 0.45%

Unexpired basis on 1 September = 0.45 × 1/5 = 0.09

Expected futures rate if rates rise by 0.6% = 4.5% + 0.6% + 0.09% = 5.19%

Exercise %	4.75%
Futures %	5.19%
Exercise?	Yes
Gain in %	0.44%

	%
Interest paid (4.5% + 0.6% + 0.5%)	5.6
Gain from options	(0.44)
Premium	0.411
Net payment	5.571%

Effective in $ annual interest rate

$84m × 0.05571 × 6/12 = $2,339,820

Alternative options calculations

Buy put options as need to hedge against a rise in interest rates.

Number of contracts required: $84,000,000/$2,000,000 × 6/3 = 84

Total basis = current price (1 May) – futures price = (100 – 4.50) – 95.05 = 0.45

Unexpired basis on 1 September = 0.45 × 1/5 = 0.09

Expected futures price = 100 – 5.1 – 0.09 = 94.81

Exercise price	95.25
Futures price as above	94.81
Exercise?	Yes
Gain in basis points	44

	$
Interest paid ($84,000,000 × 5.6% × 6/12)	2,352,000
Gain from options	
0.0044 × $2,000,000 × 3/12 × 84	(184,800)
Premium	
0.00411 × $2,000,000 × 3/12 × 84	172,620
Net payment	2,339,820
Effective annual interest rate	
2,339,820/84,000,000 × 12/6	= 5.57%

Swaps

	Lurgshall Co	Counterparty	Interest rate differential
Fixed rate	5.60%	6.10%	0.50%
Floating rate	base rate + 0.50%	base rate + 1.50%	1.00%

Lurgshall Co has an advantage in borrowing at both fixed and floating rates, but the floating rate advantage is larger. Gain % for Lurgshall Co = 50% (1 – 0.5 – 0.2) = 0.15

	Lurgshall Co	Counterparty
Rate without swap	(5.60%)	(base rate + 1.50%)
Benefit	0.15%	0.15
Net result	(5.45%)	(base rate + 1.35%)
Swap Borrows at	(base rate + 0.50%)	(6.10)
Lurgshall Co pays	(4.85%)	4.85%
Counterparty pays	base rate	(base rate)
Bank fee	(0.10%)	(0.10%)
Net result	(5.45%)	(base rate + 1.35%)

Comments

The swap gives a result which is marginally worse than the forward rate agreement and the futures. The options give a worse result than the other choices.

Risks which might be considered include counterparty risk for the forward rate agreement and swap. Using Birdam Bank should mean that this risk is low for forward rate agreements, and also for swaps, assuming that the bank bears the risk of the counterparty defaulting.

Basis risk should be considered for the traded futures. Here, because the differences between the instruments are small, a failure to estimate basis accurately may mean that futures are chosen when they do not offer the lowest borrowing cost. For the swaps, if Lurgshall Co swaps into fixed rate debt, it faces the market risk of an unexpected fall in interest rates.

Other factors to consider include the possibility that rates will increase rather less than forecast, meaning that the option would not be exercised and at some point would be the lowest cost choice. The length of time of the swap also needs to be considered. Although it commits Lurgshall Co to the fixed rate, if the borrowing turns out to be longer than the six months, the swap may provide a better time match than the other hedging opportunities.

(b) The chief executive appears to underestimate the degree of knowledge required for day-to-day work. Less experienced staff may be able to arrange borrowing if the lender has already been chosen or, for example, arrange forward rate agreements to be used if they are prescribed.

However, if judgement is required as to, for example, which lender or hedging instrument to use, using less experienced staff may mean that a sub-optimal decision is taken. Poor decisions may result in opportunity costs, for example, not using the lender who gives the best deal or being committed to a fixed forward rate agreement when an option would have allowed the business to take advantage of favourable rate movements. These opportunity costs may not be as clear as the salary costs of experienced staff.

As the business operates internationally, the treasury department will need to monitor financial market conditions and exchange rates, and other issues which may be significant such as political developments. Because of their previous experiences, longer-serving staff are more likely to appreciate the implications of developments and whether treasury policies and decisions need to change in response to changes in risk. Senior staff are also needed to manage the work of less experienced staff to prevent or mitigate the effect of mistakes which may be costly.

Experienced staff are also needed to establish overall guidelines and policies for treasury activities. Their judgement will be required to establish principles which will mean that actions taken by staff are in line with the risk appetite of the business and are sufficiently prudent from the viewpoint of risk management. Experienced staff will also have greater knowledge of law, accounting standards and tax regulations, which can help the business avoid penalties and perhaps structure its dealings so that it can, for example, minimise the level of tax paid.

The chief executive has plans for a major expansion of the business, involving significant investment and financing decisions. Advice from experienced treasury staff will be invaluable in supporting the decisions required. If Lurgshall Co is planning a major acquisition, the treasury function can provide advice on the structure of consideration and financing implications. If, as here, a major investment is being contemplated, experienced staff can advise on translating views on risk into a relevant cost of capital, which will help ensure that the financial appraisal of the investment is realistic.

 Videos can be viewed by accessing your ebook version on VitalSource.

---

39 Wardegul

Course Book references

Interest rate risk and hedging are covered in Chapter 13.

Top tips

If you are familiar with interest rate hedging using derivatives, this should be a relatively straightforward question. Use the BPP proforma for setting up futures and options to ensure you do not forget any of the steps.

In part (b) read the question and its requirements carefully; in this question, many candidates misread the question and answered it in terms of national or global functions, some without even mentioning regional functions, which was asked for in the question. These answers indicated the question had not been properly understood, and candidates mistakenly reproduced their textbook knowledge of centralised (global) versus decentralised (country) treasury functions instead of applying their knowledge to the question asked.

Easy marks

Part (a) is a commonly examined area, offering an opportunity to show your knowledge of this area.

Examining team's comments

Part (a) Some candidates omitted to identify which hedging instruments they had chosen for example, a buy vs sell futures or a put vs call options, making it difficult for markers to award marks. A number of candidates omitted to discuss their results and/or make a recommendation meaning that they could not be awarded these marks.

Marking guide	Marks
(a) Impact of FRA for rate increase and decrease	2
Selection of March futures and options	1
Number of contracts	1
Basis calculation	1
Impact of interest rate increase/decrease with futures	3
Buy call options	1
Premium calculations	1
Exercise options?	1
Impact of interest rate increase/decrease with options	3

Discussion	3
Maximum	17

(b) Regional functions compared with national functions: 1 mark per point

Maximum	3

Professional skills

Analysis and Evaluation

- Appropriate use of the data to determine suitable calculations to evaluate the proposed hedging strategies
- Appropriate use of the data to support discussion and draw appropriate conclusions
- Appraisal of information objectively to make a hedging recommendation

Commercial acumen

- Effective use of examples and/or practical considerations related to the context to illustrate points being made relating to hedging the transaction or treasury discussion

Maximum	5
Total	**25**

(a) **Forward rate agreement**

FRA 5.02% (4–9) since the investment will take place in four months' time for a period of five months.

If interest rates increase by 1.1% to 5.3%

	D
Investment return 5.0% × 5/12 × D27,000,000	562,500
Payment to bank (5.3% – 5.02%) × 5/12 × D27,000,000	(31,500)
Net receipt	531,000
Effective annual interest rate 531,000/27,000,000 × 12/5	4.72%

If interest rates fall by 0.6% to 3.6%

	D
Investment return 3.3% × 5/12 × D27,000,000	371,250
Receipt from bank (5.02% – 3.6%) × 5/12 × D27,000,000	159,750
Net receipt	531,000
Effective annual interest rate as above	4.72%

Futures

Go long in the futures market, as the hedge is against a fall in interest rates. Use March contracts, as investment will be made on 31 January.

Number of contracts = D27,000,000/D500,000 × 5 months/3 months = 90 contracts

Basis

Current price (1 October) – futures price = basis

(100 – 4.20) – 94.78 = 1.02

Unexpired basis on 31 January = 2/6 × 1.02 = 0.34

BPP

If interest rates increase by 1.1% to 5.3%

	D
Investment return as above	562,500
Expected futures price: 100 − 5.3 − 0.34 = 94.36	
Loss on the futures market: (0.9436 − 0.9478) × D500,000 × 3/12 × 90	(47,250)
Net return	515,250
Effective annual interest rate 515,250/27,000,000 × 12/5	4.58%

If interest rates fall by 0.6% to 3.6%

	D
Investment return as above	371,250
Expected futures price: 100 − 3.6 − 0.34 = 96.06	
Profit on the futures market: (0.9606 − 0.9478) × D500,000 × 3/12 × 90	144,000
Net receipt	515,250
Effective annual interest rate as above	4.58%

Options on futures

Buy call options as need to hedge against a fall in interest rates. As above, 90 contracts required.

If interest rates increase by 1.1% to 5.3%

Exercise price	94.25	95.25
Futures price as above	94.36	94.36
Exercise?	Yes	No
Gain in basis points	11	0
	D	D
Investment return (as above)	562,500	562,500
Gain from options (0.0011 × 500,000 × 3/12 × 90)	12,375	0
Premium		
0.00545 × D500,000 × 3/12 × 90	(61,313)	
0.00098 × D500,000 × 3/12 × 90		(11,025)
Net return	513,562	551,475
Effective interest rate		
513,562/27,000,000 × 12/5	4.56%	
551,475/27,000,000 × 12/5		4.90%

If interest rates fall by 0.6% to 3.6%

Exercise price	94.25	95.25
Futures price as above	96.06	96.06
Exercise?	Yes	Yes
Gain in basis points	181	81
Investment return (as above)	371,250	371,250
Gain from options		
Gain from options: 0.0181 × D500,000 × 3/12 × 90	203,625	
Gain from options: 0.0081 × D500,000 × 3/12 × 90		91,125
Premium as above	(61,313)	(11,025)
Net return	513,562	451,350
Effective interest rate		
513,562/27,000,000 × 12/5	4.56%	
451,350/27,000,000 × 12/5		4.01%

Alternative presentation of calculations:

Forward rate agreement:

FRA 5.02% (4–9) since the investment will take place in four months' time and last for five months.

Possible scenarios:	Rates rise by 1.1%	Rates fall by 0.6%
Base rate (now = 4.2%)	5.3%	3.6%
Return on investment (Base − 0.3%)	5.0%	3.3%
Impact of FRA (5.02% vs Base)	(0.28%)	1.42%
Net outcome as %	4.72%	4.72%
In Ds (% × D27,000,000 × 5/12)	531,000	531,000

Futures agreement:

March contracts to buy at 94.78 or 5.22% (100 − 94.78) are needed to cover to the start of the investment (31 January). The number of contracts required will be D27m/D0.5m contract size × 5 months (investment term) divided by 3 months (contract term) = 90.

Opening basis on 1 Oct: future − base = 5.22% − 4.20% = 1.02% with six months to expiry of March future.

Estimated closing basis on 31 January = 1.02% × 2/6 = 0.34% with two months to expiry of March future.

So if rates rise to a base rate of 5.3% the estimated futures price is 5.3% + 0.34% = 5.64%.

If rates fall to a base rate of 3.6% the estimated futures price is 3.6% + 0.34% = 3.94%.

 **BPP**

Possible scenarios:	Rates rise by 1.1%	Rates fall by 0.6%
Base rate (now = 4.2%)	5.3%	3.6%
Return on investment (Base − 0.3%)	5.0%	3.3%
Impact of Future:		
Opening rate 1 Oct (to receive)	5.22%	5.22%
Closing rate 31 January (to pay)	5.64%	3.94%
Net outcome on future	(0.42%)	1.28%
Overall net outcome (actual + future)	4.58%	4.58%
In Ds (% × D27,000,000 × 5/12)	515,250	515,250

Options agreement:

March call options at 5.75% (94.25) or 4.75% (95.25) can be chosen. There is an argument for either, this solution illustrates the outcome if 4.75% is chosen, which is the rate closest to the current base rate and provides compensation if interest rates fall at a lower premium compared to the 5.75% rate. Again 90 contracts will be needed, and contracts are closed out against the futures price on 31 January.

Possible scenarios:	Rates rise by 1.1%	Rates fall by 0.6%
Base rate (now = 4.2%)	5.3%	3.6%
Return on investment (Base − 0.3%)	5.0%	3.3%

Impact of Future:

	Rates rise by 1.1%	Rates fall by 0.6%
Call option rate 1 Oct	4.75%	4.75%
Closing rate 31 January (to pay)	5.64%	3.94%
Net outcome on future	Do not exercise	0.81%
Premium	(0.098)%	(0.098)%
Outcome (actual + option− premium)	4.902%	4.012%
In Ds (% × D27,000,000 × 5/12)	551,475	451,350

Discussion

The forward rate agreement gives the highest guaranteed return. If Wardegul Co wishes to have a certain cash flow and is primarily concerned with protecting itself against a fall in interest rates, it will most likely choose the forward rate agreement. The 95.25 option gives a better rate if interest rates rise, but a significantly lower rate if interest rates fall, so if Wardegul Co is at all risk averse, it will choose the forward rate agreement.

This assumes that the bank which Wardegul Co deals with is reliable and there is no risk of default. If Wardegul Co believes that the current economic uncertainty may result in a risk that the bank will default, the choice will be between the futures and the options, as these are guaranteed by the exchange. Again the 95.25 option may be ruled out because it gives a much worse result if interest rates fall to 3.6%. The futures give a marginally better result than the 94.25 option in both scenarios but the difference is small. If Wardegul Co feels there is a possibility that interest rates will be higher than 5.41%, the point at which the 94.25 option would not be exercised, it may choose this option rather than the future.

(b) Organising treasury activities on a regional basis would be consistent with what is happening in the group overall. Other functions will be organised regionally. A regional treasury function may be able to achieve synergies with them and also benefit from information flows being organised based on the regional structure.

If, as part of a reorganisation, some treasury activities were to be devolved outside to a bank or other third party, it would be simpler to arrange for a single provider on a regional basis than arrange for separate providers in each country.

A regional function will avoid duplication of responsibilities over all the countries within a region. A regional function will have more work to do, with maybe a greater range of activities, whereas staff based nationally may be more likely to be under-employed. There may be enough complex work on a regional basis to justify employing specialists in particular treasury areas which will enhance the performance of the function. It may be easier to recruit these specialists if recruitment is done regionally rather than in each country.

Regional centres can carry out some activities on a regional basis which will simplify how funds are managed and mean less cost than managing funds on a national basis. These include pooling cash, borrowing and investing in bulk, and netting of foreign currency income and expenditure.

Regional centres could in theory be located anywhere in the region, rather than having one treasury function based in each country. This means that they could be located in the most important financial centres in each region or in countries which offered significant tax advantages.

From the point of view of Wardegul Co's directors and senior managers, it will be easier to enforce common standards and risk management policies on a few regional functions than on many national functions with differing cultures in individual countries.

40 Daikon

Marking guide	Marks	
(a) Additional interest cost	1	
Contract types	1	
Number of contracts and remaining basis	2	
Futures calculations	1	
Options calculations	4	
Comments and conclusion	3	
Marks Available	12	
Maximum		11
(b) Marked to market calculations	3	
Impact of daily marked to market	3	
Impact of margin requirements	3	
Impact of selling options instead of exercising	3	

Marks Available	12
Maximum	<u>9</u>

Professional skills

Analysis and Evaluation

- Appropriate use of the data to determine suitable calculations to appraise the proposed hedging strategies
- Appropriate use of the data to support discussion and draw appropriate conclusions
- Appraisal of information objectively to make a hedging recommendation

Commercial acumen

- Effective use of examples and/or practical considerations related to the context to illustrate points being made relating to hedging the transaction

Maximum	<u>5</u>
Total	<u><u>25</u></u>

(a) Borrowing period is 6 months (11 months – 5 months).

Current borrowing cost = $34,000,000 × 6 months/12 months × 4.3% = $731,000

Borrowing cost if interest rates increase by 80 basis points (0.8%) = $34,000,000 × 6/12 × 5.1% = $867,000

Additional cost = $136,000 [$34,000,000 × 6/12 × 0.8%]

Using futures to hedge

Need to hedge against a rise in interest rates, therefore go short (contracts to sell) in the futures market.

Borrowing period is 6 months

No. of contracts needed = $34,000,000/$1,000,000 × 6 months/3 months = 68 contracts.

Basis

Current price (on 1 June 20X5) – futures price = total basis

(100 – 3.6) – 95.84 = 0.56

Unexpired basis (at beginning of November) = 2/7 × 0.56 = 0.16

Assume that interest rates increase by 0.8% (80 basis points) to 4.4%

Expected futures price = 100 – 4.4 – 0.16 = 95.44 (or 100 – 95.44 = 4.56%)

Gain on the futures market = (95.84 – 95.44) × $25 × 68 = $68,000 (or 4.56% closing future – 4.16% opening future = 0.4%)

Net additional cost = ($136,000 – $68,000) $68,000 (or 0.8% – 0.4% gain on future = 0.4%)

Using options on futures to hedge

Need to hedge against a rise in interest rates, therefore buy put options. As before, 68 put option contracts are needed ($34,000,000/$1,000,000 × 6 months/3 months).

Assume that interest rates increase by 0.8% (80 basis points) to 4.4%

	95.50	96.00
Exercise price	95.50	96.00
Futures price	95.44	95.44
Exercise?	Yes	Yes
Gain in basis points	6	56
Gain on options		
6 × $25 × 68	$10,200	
56 × $25 × 68		$95,200
Premium		
30.4 × $25 × 68	$51,680	
50.8 × $25 × 68		$86,360
Option benefit/(cost)	$(41,480)	$8,840
Net additional cost		
($136,000 + $41,480)	$177,480	
($136,000 − $8,840)		$127,160

Alternative solution (shown in %)

	%	%
Borrow	−5.1	−5.1
Opening	4.5	4.0
Closing	4.56	4.56
	0.06	0.56
Premium	−0.304	−0.508
NET	−5.344	−5.048
Extra vs 4.3%	−1.044	−0.748
	(0.01044 × $34m × 6/12)	(0.00748 × $34m × 6/12)
In $s	**−177,480**	**−127,160**

Based on the assumption that interest rates increase by 80 basis points in the next five months, the futures hedge would lower the additional cost by the greatest amount and is significantly better than the options hedge.

In addition to this, futures fix the amount which Daikon Co is likely to pay, assuming that there is no basis risk. The benefits accruing from the options are lower, with the 95.50 option increasing the overall cost. This is due to the high premium costs. However, if interest rates do not increase and actually reduce, then the options provide more flexibility because they do not have to be exercised when interest rates move in the company's favour. But the movement will need to be significant before the cost of the premium is covered.

On that basis, on balance, it is recommended that hedging using futures is the best choice as they will probably provide the most benefit to Daikon Co.

However, it is recommended that the points made in part (b) are also considered before a final conclusion is made.

(b) **Mark to market: Daily settlements**

2 June: 8 basis points (95.76 – 95.84) × $25 × 50 contracts = $10,000 loss

3 June: 10 basis points (95.66 – 95.76) × $25 × 50 contracts + 5 basis points (95.61 – 95.66) × $25 × 30 contracts = $16,250 loss

[Alternatively: 15 basis points (95.61 – 95.76) × $25 × 30 contracts + 10 basis points (95.66 – 95.76) × $25 × 20 contracts = $16,250 loss]

4 June: 8 basis points (95.74 – 95.66) × $25 × 20 contracts = $4,000 profit

Both mark to market and margins are used by markets to reduce (eliminate) the risk of non-payment by purchasers of the derivative products if prices move against them.

Mark to market closes all the open deals at the end of each day at that day's settlement price, and opens them again at the start of the following day. The notional profit or loss on the deals is then calculated and the margin account is adjusted accordingly on a daily basis. The impact on Daikon Co is that if losses are made, then the company may have to deposit extra funds with its broker if the margin account falls below the maintenance margin level. This may affect the company's ability to plan adequately and ensure it has enough funds for other activities. On the other hand, extra cash accruing from the notional profits can be withdrawn from the broker account if needed.

Each time a market-traded derivative product is opened, the purchaser needs to deposit a margin (initial margin) with the broker, which consists of funds to be kept with the broker while the position is open. As stated above, this amount may change daily and would affect Daikon Co's ability to plan for its cash requirements, but also open positions require that funds are tied up to support these positions and cannot be used for other purposes by the company.

The value of an option prior to expiry consists of time value, and may also consist of intrinsic value if the option is in-the-money. If an option is exercised prior to expiry, Daikon Co will only receive the intrinsic value attached to the option but not the time value. If the option is sold instead, whether it is in-the-money or out-of-the-money, Daikon Co will receive a higher value for it due to the time value. Unless options have other features, like dividends, attached to them, which are not reflected in the option value, they would not normally be exercised prior to expiry.

41 Fitzharris

Course Book references

Interest rate hedging is covered in Chapter 13 and delta hedging is covered in Chapter and 11.

Top tips

Part (a). A complication here is that a swap would cover the whole period of the loan whilst a collar would only cover a short initial period unless it was rolled forward. Under exam conditions it is best to ignore this and prepare some standard % calculations, this issue can then be raised in the discussion part of this question.

Part (b). A comment should be brief — here it was only worth 1 mark. The discussion should compare the two forms of hedging and not just list all of the general pros and cons of collars and swaps. The key point is that these instruments have to be compared to each other.

Marking guide	Marks
(a) **Swaps**	
Comparative advantage of 0.6%	1
Initial decision to borrow floating by Fitzharris Co and fixed by counterparty	1
Advantage of 0.25% per party after the bank fee	1
Suitable swap rates	1

 BPP

Final rate to be paid by Fitzharris Co	1	
Collars		
Number of contracts	1	
Basis calculation	1	
Buy put and sell call options	1	
Premium calculation	1	
Exercise options?	2	
Impact of interest rate increase/decrease with collars	$\underline{2}$	
Marks Available	13	
Maximum		12
(b) Comment on calculations	1	
Advantages of swaps compared with collars (advantages could include flexibility, longer time period, certainty of finance costs, comparative advantage)	$\underline{4}$	
Marks Available	5	
Maximum		4
(c) 1 to 2 marks per well explained point.		
		$\underline{4}$

Professional skills

Analysis and Evaluation

- Appropriate use of the data to determine suitable calculations to evaluate the proposed hedging strategies
- Appropriate use of the data to support discussion and draw appropriate conclusions
- Appraisal of information objectively to make a hedging recommendation

Commercial acumen

Effective use of examples and/or practical considerations related to the context to illustrate points being made relating to hedging the transaction

Maximum	$\underline{5}$
Total	$\underline{\underline{25}}$

(a) **Swap**

	Fitzharris Co	Counterparty	Interest rate differential
Fixed rate	4.60%	4.80%	0.20%
Floating rate	Base rate + 0.50%	Base rate + 1.30%	0.80%

Fitzharris Co has an advantage in borrowing at both fixed and floating rates, but the floating rate advantage is larger.

Gain % for Fitzharris Co = 50% (0.8 – 0.2 – 0.1) = 0.25

	Fitzharris Co	Counterparty
Rate without swap	(4.60%)	(Base rate + 1.30%)
Benefit	0.25%	0.25%
Net result	(4.35%)	(Base rate + 1.05%)
Swap		
Borrows at	(Base rate + 0.50%)	(4.80%)
Fitzharris Co pays	(3.80%)	3.80%
Counterparty pays	Base rate	(Base rate)
Bank fee	(0.05%)	(0.05%)
Net result	(4.35%)	(Base rate + 1.05%)

Collar

Buy December put options at 95.75 for 0.211 and sell December call options at 96.25 for 0.198

Number of contracts = ($48,000,000/$1,000,000) × (36 months/3 months) = 576**

Basis = Current price (1 August) – futures price

(100 – 3.70) – 95.85 = 0.45

Unexpired basis on 1 December = 1/5 × 0.45 = 0.09

Premium = (0.00211 – 0.00198) = 0.013%

If base rate rises by 0.4% to 4.1%

Futures price = 100 – 4.1 – 0.09 = 95.81

	Buy put	Sell call
Exercise price	95.75	96.25
Futures price	95.81	95.81
Exercise?*	No	No
Loss in basis points	–	–

*The put option is not exercised, because Fitzharris Co can sell the futures at the futures market price of 95.81 rather than the option exercise price of 95.75. The call option is not exercised, as the option holder can buy the futures at the lower futures market price of 95.81 rather than the exercise price of 96.25.

	%
Borrowing cost (4.1% + 0.5%)	4.600
Premium	0.013
Total payment	4.613

If base rate falls by 0.4% to 3.3%

Futures price = 100 – 3.3 – 0.09 = 96.61

	Buy put	Sell call
Exercise price	95.75	96.25
Futures price	96.61	96.61
Exercise?*	No	Yes
Loss in basis points	–	36

* The put option is not exercised, as by not exercising the option Fitzharris Co can sell the futures at the higher futures market price of 96.61 rather than the lower exercise price of 95.75. The call option is exercised, because the option holder can buy the futures at the option exercise price of 96.25 rather than the futures market price of 96.61.

	%
Borrowing cost (3.3% + 0.5%)	3.800
Loss on options (0.0036 × 100)	0.360
Premium	0.013
Effective annual interest rate	4.173

> **Tutorial note.** It is possible to justify a range of different hedging periods for this situation. Any justified hedging period from the four-month period of uncertainty, outlined in the question, up to 36 months was awarded credit. It was recognised that in reality a collar for 36 months would not happen and instead there would be a rolling series of hedges.
>
> Answers which calculated costs in dollar amounts based on their number of contracts and then calculated an effective annual rate, were also eligible for full credit.

(b) **Comment**

The calculations do not give a clear indication of which strategy should be chosen. The swap gives a better result if base rate rises by 0.4%, the options if base rate falls by 0.4%. The decision may be determined by whether the company views a rise or fall in interest rates as being more likely, or how it views the advantages and disadvantages of the strategies.

Advantages of swaps

As swaps are over-the counter arrangements, they can be arranged in any size. The amount covered by collars based on traded options is determined by the size of the option contract. There may be over and under hedging.

The traded options available may last for a short period, perhaps up to two years, less maybe than the period of the loan. Swaps can be arranged for a much longer period.

Fitzharris Co is swapping here a commitment to pay a variable rate of interest that is uncertain with a guaranteed fixed rate of interest. This allows Fitzharris Co to forecast finance costs on the loan with certainty. The net payments on the collar will depend on how interest rates move.

Unlike collars, swaps make use of the principle of comparative advantage. Fitzharris Co can borrow in the market where the best deal is available to it.

(c) The delta value measures the extent to which the value of a derivative instrument, such as an option, changes as the value of its underlying asset changes. For example, a delta of 0.8 would mean that a company would need to purchase 1.25 option contracts (1/0.8) to hedge against a rise in price of an underlying asset of that contract size, known as the hedge ratio. This is because the delta indicates that when the underlying asset increases in value by $1, the value of the equivalent option contract will increase by only $0.80.

The option delta is equal to N(d1) from the Black-Scholes option pricing formula. This means that the delta is constantly changing when the volatility or time to expiry change. Therefore, even when the delta and hedge ratio are used to determine the number of option contracts needed, this number needs to be updated periodically to reflect the new delta.

42 Keshi

Marking guide	Marks	
(a) Buy put options and number of contracts	1	
Future prices if interest rates rise or fall	1	
Option contract calculations for any exercise price	3	
Second set of option calculations if provided	1	
Swap and resulting advantage	2	
Swap impact	2	
Effective borrowing rate	2	
Discussion and recommendation	4	
Marks Available	16	
Maximum		15
(b) 1–2 marks per well-explained point	4	
Comment on implication for treasury department structure	1	
		5

Professional skills

Analysis and Evaluation

- Appropriate use of the data to determine suitable calculations to evaluate the proposed hedging strategies
- Appropriate use of the data to support discussion and draw appropriate conclusions
- Appraisal of information objectively to make a hedging recommendation

Commercial acumen

- Effective use of examples and/or practical considerations related to the context to illustrate points being made relating to hedging the transaction

Maximum	5
Total	**25**

(a) **Options**

Keshi needs to hedge against a rise in interest rates, therefore it needs to buy **put options**.

Keshi Co needs 42 March put option contracts ($18,000,000/$1,000,000 × 7 months/3 months).

Basis

Current March futures price − spot price = total basis = 44 basis points as at 1 December

Unexpired basis as at 1 February = 22 **or 0.22% (given in the question)**

If 95.50 options (ie 4.5%) are used:

	Rates fall − 0.5%	Rates rise + 0.5%
	%	%
Base rate (currently 3.8%)	3.3	4.3
Borrowing rate for Keshi	3.7	4.7
Closing future base rate + basis of 0.22%	3.52	4.52
Exercise option at 4.5%?	No	Yes
Premium	(0.662)	(0.662)
Option gain/(loss)		0.02
Net effective annual interest rate	**4.362%**	**5.342**
	(3.7 + 0.662)	(4.7 + 0.662 − 0.02)

Alternative solution:

Expected futures price on 1 February if interest rates increase by 0.5% = 100 − (3.8 + 0.5) − 0.22 = 95.48

Expected futures price on 1 February if interest rates decrease by 0.5% = 100 − (3.8 − 0.5) − 0.22 = 96.48

If interest rates increase by 0.5% to 4.3%

Exercise price 95.50

Futures price 95.48

Exercise?   Yes

Gain in basis points 2

Underlying cost of borrowing

4.7% × 7/12 × $18,000,000 = $493,500

Gain on options

0.0002 × $1,000,000 × 3/12 × 42 = $2,100

Premium

0.00662 × $1,000,000 × 3/12 × 42 = $69,510

Net cost $560,910

Effective interest rate **5.342%** (560,910 / 18,000,000 × 12/7)

If interest rates decrease by 0.5% to 3.3%

Exercise price 95.50

Futures price 96.48

Exercise?   No

Underlying cost of borrowing

3.7% × 7/12 × $18,000,000 = $388,500

Premium $69,510

Net cost $458,010

 **BPP**

Effective interest rate **4.362%** (458,010 / 18,000,000 × 12/7)

Using swaps

Keshi will want to swap into fixed rate finance in order to hedge the risk of interest rates rising. With this type of swap the outcome will be as follows:

	Keshi Co
No swap:	(5.5%)
Swap:	
Loan	(base rate + 0.4%)
Fixed rate paid	(4.6%)
Floating rate received	base rate + 0.3%
Net cost pre-fee	(4.7%)
Total gain (5.5 vs 4.7)	0.8%
Gain to Keshi (70% of 0.8)	0.56%
Outcome pre-fees (5.5 − 0.56)	4.94%
Outcome post-fees (4.94 + 0.1)	**5.04%**

Discussion and recommendation

Under each choice the interest rate cost to Keshi Co will be as follows:

	Doing nothing	95.50 option	Swap
If rates increase by 0.5%	4.7% floating; 5.5% fixed	5.342%	5.04%
If rates decrease by 0.5%	3.7% floating; 5.5% fixed	4.362%	5.04%

Borrowing at the floating rate and undertaking a **swap** effectively fixes the rate of interest at 5.04% for the loan, which is **significantly lower than the market fixed rate of 5.5%**.

On the other hand, **doing nothing** and borrowing at the floating rate minimises the interest rate at 4.7%, against the next best choice which is the swap at 5.04% if interest rates increase by 0.5%. And, should interest rates decrease by 0.5%, then doing nothing and borrowing at a floating rate of 3.7% minimises cost, compared to the next best choice which is the 95.50 option.

On the face of it, **doing nothing and borrowing at a floating rate seems to be the better choice** if interest rates increase or decrease by a small amount, but if interest rates increase substantially then this choice will no longer result in the lowest cost.

The swap minimises the variability of the borrowing rates, while doing nothing and borrowing at a floating rate maximises the variability. If Keshi Co wants to eliminate the risk of interest rate fluctuations completely, then it should borrow at the floating rate and swap it into a fixed rate.

(b) Islamic principles stipulate the need to avoid uncertainty and speculation. In the case of Salam contracts, payment for the commodity is made at the start of the contract. The buyer and seller of the commodity know the price, the quality and the quantity of the commodity and the date of future delivery with certainty. Therefore, **uncertainty and speculation** are avoided.

On the other hand, futures contracts are marked to market daily and this could lead to uncertainty in the amounts received and paid every day. Furthermore, **standardised futures contracts have fixed expiry dates and predetermined contract sizes.**

This may mean that the underlying position is not hedged or covered completely, leading to limited speculative positions even where the futures contracts are used entirely for hedging purposes.

Finally, only a few commodity futures contracts are offered to cover a range of different quality grades for a commodity, and therefore price movement of the futures market may not be completely in line with the price movement in the underlying asset.

By decentralising Keshi Co's treasury function to its subsidiary companies, each subsidiary company may be better placed to take **local regulations and customs** into consideration. An example is the case of Suisen Co's need to use Salam contracts instead of conventional derivative products which the centralised treasury department may use as a matter of course.

Note. Credit will be given for alternative, relevant discussion in part (b).

43 Pault

> **Course Book references**
>
> Chapter 13 for interest rate hedging, Chapter 14 for debt-equity swaps.
>
> **Top tips**
>
> It is important to read articles produced by the examining team, this question was covered by an article that was published in the lead up to the September exam. It is important not to panic with this type of question, for example part (a)(ii) required the evaluation of a swap after 1 year; this did not require anything from (a)(i) and should have been accessible even to candidates that had struggled with (a)(i).
>
> **Easy marks**
>
> Part (b), 4 marks – required advice on the factors influencing the value of a swap. Part (c), 9 marks – required a discussion of the advantages and disadvantages of simply continuing with floating rate finance compared to using a swap. This was well answered and was the easiest, and most important part of the question.

Marking guide

			Marks
(a)	(i)	Gross amount payable by Pault Co	1
		Calculation of forward rates	3
		Basis point reduction	1
		Net amounts receivable or payable each year	1
			6
	(ii)	Yield interest calculations	5
		Comment on interest payment liability	1
			6
(b)	Up to 2 marks per point		
	Maximum		4
(c)	Drawbacks (up to 2 marks per relevant point)		
	Maximum		4

Professional skills

Analysis and Evaluation

- Appropriate use of the data to determine suitable calculations to evaluate the swap
- Appropriate use of the data to support discussion and draw appropriate conclusions

Scepticism

- Effective challenge of evidence and assumptions supplied with respect to the chairman and non-executive's view on the swap

Commercial acumen

- Effective use of examples and/or practical considerations related to the context to illustrate points being made relating to the swap

Maximum	5
Total	**25**

(a)   (i)   Gross amount of annual interest paid by Pault Co to Millbridge Bank = 4.847% × $400m = $19.39m.

Gross amounts of annual interest receivable by Pault Co from Millbridge Bank, based on Year 1 spot rates and Years 2–4 forward rates:

Year

1   0.0350 × $400m = $14m

2   0.0460 × $400m = $18.4m

3   0.0541 × $400m = $21.64m

4   0.0611 × $400m = $24.44m

Working

Year 2 forward rate: $(1.0425^2/1.037) - 1 = 4.80\%$

Year 3 forward rate: $(1.0470^3/1.0425^2) - 1 = 5.61\%$

Year 4 forward rate: $(1.0510^4/1.0470^3) - 1 = 6.31\%$

Rates are reduced by 20 basis points in calculation.

At the start of the swap, Pault will expect to pay or receive the following net amounts at each of the next four years:

Year

1       $14m – $19.39m = $(5.39m) payment

2       $18.4m – $19.39m = $(0.99m) payment

3       $21.64m – $19.39m = $2.25m receipt

4       $24.44m – $19.39m = $5.05m receipt

(ii)   **Interest payment liability**

	Impact %	Yield interest 2.9% $m	Yield interest 4.5% $m
Borrow at yield interest + 50 bp	(Yield + 0.5)	(13.60)	(20.00)
Receive yield – 20 bp	Yield – 0.2	10.80	17.20
Pay fixed 4.847%	(4.847)	(19.39)	(19.39)
Bank fee – 25 bp	(0.25)	(1.00)	(1.00)
	(5.797)	(23.19)	(23.19)

The interest payment liability will be $23.19 million, whatever the yield interest, as the receipt and payment are based on the yield curve net of interest rate fluctuations.

(b) At the start of the contract, the value of the swap will be zero. The terms offered by Millbridge Bank equate the discounted value of the fixed rate payments by Pault Co with the variable rate payments by Millbridge Bank.

However, the value of the swap will not remain at zero. If interest rates increase more than expected, Pault Co will benefit from having to pay a fixed rate and the value of the swap will increase. The value of the swap will also change as the swap approaches maturity, with fewer receipts and payments left.

However, the swap is for a shorter period than the loan and thus allows Pault Co to reconsider the position in four years' time. It may choose to take out another swap then on different terms, or let the arrangement lapse and pay floating rate interest on the loan, depending on the expectations at that time of future interest rates.

(c) **Disadvantages of swap arrangement**

The swap represents a long-term commitment at a time when interest rates appear uncertain. It may be that interest rate rises are lower than expected. In this case, Pault Co will be committed to a higher interest rate and its finance costs may be higher than if it had not taken out the finance arrangements. Pault Co may not be able to take action to relieve this commitment if it becomes clear that the swap was unnecessary.

On the basis of the expected forward rates, Pault Co will not start benefiting from the swap until Year 3. Particularly during Year 1, the extra commitment to interest payments may be an important burden at a time when Pault Co will have significant development and launch costs.

Pault Co will be liable for an arrangement fee. However, other methods of hedging which could be used will have a cost built into them as well.

44 Brandon

Course Book references

Interest rate risk management is covered in Chapter 13.

Top tips

Read the question requirements carefully; marks are only available in part (a) for discussing how centralising would add value to the company for a specific aspect of the treasury function.

Examining team's comments

The ACCA Examiner's comments noted that 'a small number of candidates scored very high marks in the more complicated parts of this requirement but still struggled to pass overall, simply because they had ignored the need for a recommendation (losing the marks that were available for discussion) and/or instructions on how to set up the futures and options hedges.'

Marking guide		Marks
(a) Functional areas (eg liquidity management, currency management, funding and corporate finance)		3
Advantages of centralised treasury (eg netting off, expertise, pooling, strategic oversight and dividend policy)		3
Maximum		6
(b) FRA		1
Go short on March futures		1
Number of contracts		1
Basis		1

Impact of interest rate increase with futures	2
Buy March puts	1
Premium calculation	1
Exercise	1
Impact of interest rate increase on options	2
Discussion	3
Maximum	14

Professional skills marks (examples)

Analysis and Evaluation

- Appropriate use of the data to determine suitable calculations
- Appropriate use of the data to support discussion and draw appropriate conclusions
- Appraisal of information objectively to make a hedging recommendation

Commercial acumen

- Effective use of examples and/or practical considerations related to the context to illustrate points being made relating to centralising the treasury function

Maximum	5
Total	25

(a) There are a number of ways the functional areas of a treasury department could add value to Brandon Co's expansion plans.

Liquidity management

As Brandon Co expands, the increase in the volume of transactions across the group will require a greater emphasis on liquidity management, including the need to support Brandon Co's working capital requirement. A centralised treasury department could add value by netting off subsidiaries' debit and credit balances, which would reduce the number of transactions and hence transaction costs.

Currency management

The expansion outside the eurozone introduces foreign exchange risk into the group and the need to manage the impact of currency flows on Brandon Co's earnings and shareholder value. Effective currency management, including the use of derivatives, can have a significant impact on shareholder value for companies with overseas assets. A centralised treasury department will have the resources to employ experts with the knowledge required to manage these risks. It would also be possible to employ techniques across the group, such as matching income earned by one subsidiary with expenditure by another subsidiary in the same currency, reducing risk and the need for external hedging methods.

Funding

The treasury department will play a role in sourcing the appropriate debt instruments and matching maturities to the time horizon of the investment as well as managing the relationship with lenders. A centralised treasury department could add value by pooling funding requirements across the group to achieve better rates by borrowing in bulk.

Corporate finance

The corporate finance function would undertake the equity issue(s) to raise part of the funds required for the overseas expansion and be involved with the strategic decision-making such as formulating a dividend policy which meets the needs of shareholders. A centralised treasury department would have the appropriate level of oversight of Brandon Co's group activities to provide operational, strategic and corporate finance advice to enhance value. It

can advise on short-term investment strategies, evaluate subsidiary performance and manage Brandon Co's financial structure to minimise the cost of capital.

(b) **FRAs**

FRA rate 5.90% (3–7) since the funds will be required in three months' time for a period of four months.

If central bank rate increases to 6.6%

	%
Interest payment: (6.6% + 0.4%)	7.0
Receipt from bank: (6.6% – 5.9%)	(0.7)
Net borrowing cost	6.3

Cost in $s = 0.063 × 4/12 × $36,000,000 = $756,000

Alternative solution:

	$
Interest payment: (6.6% + 0.4%) × 4/12 × $36,000,000	840,000
Receipt from bank: (6.6% – 5.9%) × 4/12 × $36,000,000	(84,000)
Net borrowing cost	756,000
Effective annual interest rate: 756,000/36,000,000 × 12/4	6.3%

Futures

Hedge against an increase in interest rates, therefore go short (contract to sell) in futures market. Use March contracts, as funds will be required on 31 January.

Number of contracts = $36,000,000/$500,000 × 4 months/3 months = 96 contracts

Basis

Future rate – Spot rate (1 November) = basis

(100 – 93.95)% – 5.7% = 0.35%

There is a 5-month period between 1 November and the end of the March futures contract.

Unexpired basis on 31 January = 2/5 × 0.35 = 0.14%

Alternative solution:

Future price – Spot price (1 November) = basis

(100 – 5.70) – 93.95 = 0.35

Unexpired basis on 31 January = 2/5 × 0.35 = 0.14

If central bank rate increases to 6.6%

	%
Interest payment as above	7.0
Expected futures rate: 6.6 + 0.14 = 6.74	
Profit on the futures market: (6.05% opening vs 6.74% closing)	(0.69)
Net borrowing cost	6.31

Cost in $s = 0.0631 × 4/12 × $36,000,000 = $757,200

This can also be calculated as opening futures rate – closing basis = 6.05 – 0.14 = 5.91% which gives the effective lock-in rate. Then add the premium above the base rate paid by Brandon Co of 0.4% = 5.91% + 0.4% = 6.31%

BPP

ANSWERS

Alternative solution

	$
Interest payment as above	840,000
Expected futures price: 100 − 6.6 − 0.14 = 93.26	
Profit on the futures market: (0.9395 − 0.9326) × $500,000 × 3/12 × 96	(82,800)
Net borrowing cost	757,200
Effective annual interest rate: 757,200/36,000,000 ×12/4	6.31%

Options on interest rate futures

Buy March put options to hedge against an increase in interest rates. As above, 96 contracts are required.

Premium = 0.087% or 0.00087 × $500,000 × 3/12 × 96 = $10,440

If central bank base rate increases to 6.6%

	%
Interest payment as above	7.0
Profit on options	(0.49)
Premium	0.087
Net borrowing cost	6.597
Cost in $s = 0.06597 × 4/12 × $36,000,000 = $791,640	

Alternative solution

	Buy put
Exercise price	93.75
Expected futures price, as above	93.26
Exercise?	Yes
Gain in basis points	49

	$
Interest payment as above	840,000
Profit on options 0.0049 × $500,000 × 3/12 × 96	(58,800)
Premium	10,440
Net borrowing cost	791,640
Effective annual interest rate: 791,640/36,000,000 × 12/4	6.60%

Advice

The forward rate agreement and futures market provide broadly similar results. The outcome of the forward rate agreement hedge is marginally lower and may be the preferred choice. In theory, both methods provide a fixed interest payment and a certain cash outflow but futures contracts are subject to basis risk and margin requirements.

If the central bank rate increases to 6.6%, the option is the least attractive hedging method due to the expensive premium. Unlike forward rate agreements and futures contracts, however, options do not have to be exercised and allow Brandon Co to benefit from upside potential if the central bank base rate falls. Treasury staff would need to assess the likelihood and amount of a possible reduction in interest rates when assessing the viability of the option.

If the board is to achieve its objective of minimising risk exposure, the certain cash flow associated with the forward rate agreement will be more attractive than the variable outcome associated with the options.

 **BPP**

45 Lirio

Course Book references

Purchasing power parity theory is covered in chapter 5. Dividend capacity is covered in Chapter 16. Currency hedging is covered in Chapter 12.

Top tips

Where a 50-mark question covers a wide range of syllabus areas, as here, you need to focus on maximising your marks in the areas that you can do and not get too distracted by the areas that you find more difficult.

Part (a) – as is often the case, the 50-mark question starts with a basic area, here requiring an explanation of purchasing power parity theory.

Part (b)(i) required an assessment of the dividend capacity of the company. This is a topic that has been examined before.

Part (b)(ii) asked for assessment of the outcome of a currency hedge using either forwards, futures or options. This required a careful analysis of the appropriate part of the 'spread' to use and recognition that the $ was the contract currency for the futures and options contracts. Apart from this, the calculations here have been tested many times in previous exam sittings.

In part (b)(iii) the question gave information about the impact of the project on the pattern of future dividends. This suggested the use of the dividend valuation model (DVM) to establish the value of the company before and after the project to see if the project would 'add value'. Those candidates who realised that the DVM was needed scored well here. However, in general this part of the question was poorly done because candidates were not able to see the need for DVM.

Part (b)(iv) asked for a discussion of the proposed methods of financing the project.

This could have been satisfactorily answered by using the details provided in the scenario.

The implication of the changing patterns of dividend (given in the question) resulting from the project is that a cut in the dividend was being considered to finance the project. However, many candidates missed this and therefore failed to discuss the potential impact of the project on dividend policy. This was the key issue in this part of the question.

Easy marks

There were easier marks in many elements of this compulsory question (part (a), some of (b)(i), (b)(ii), some of (b)(iv) and the presentation marks in part (b)). Targeting these easier marks is an essential element in exam technique for AFM.

Marking guide		Marks
(a) Up to 2 marks per well-explained point		
Maximum		4
(b) (i) Appendices 1 and 1.1		
Interest paid		1
Tax paid for normal activities		1
Investment in working capital		1
Investment in additional non-current assets		1
Correct treatment of depreciation		1

Cash flows remitted from Pontac Co	2
Additional tax payable	1
	8

(ii) Appendix 2

Amount received based on forward contracts	1
Correctly identifying long contracts and purchasing call options	1
Expected futures price based on linear narrowing of basis	1
Amount received based on futures contracts	1
Recognition of small over-hedge when using futures contracts	1
Option contracts or futures contracts purchased	1
Premium paid in dollars	1
Amount received based on options contracts	2
1–2 marks for each well-discussed point	4
Reasonable recommendation	1
	14

(iii) Appendix 3 and project assessment

Estimate of dividend growth rate (prior to project undertaken)	1
Estimate of corporate value (prior to project undertaken)	1
Annual dividend per share after transfer of funds to project	2
Estimate of value after project is undertaken	2
Concluding comments on project assessment	1
	7

(iv) Discussion of issues

Limitations of method used	2
Signalling impact of change in dividend policy	2
Clientele impact of change in dividend policy	3
Rationale for not considering debt or equity	4
Other relevant discussion points	3
Maximum	7

Professional skills

Communication

- General format and structure (use of headings/sub-headings and an introduction)
- Style, language and clarity (appropriate layout and tone of report response, presentation of calculations, appropriate use of the tools)
- Effectiveness of communication (answer is relevant, specific rather than general and focused to the requirement)
- Adherence to the details of the proposal in the scenario

Analysis and Evaluation

- Appropriate use of the data to determine suitable calculations
- Appropriate use of the data to support discussion and draw appropriate conclusions

Scepticism

- Effective challenge of information and assumptions supplied and, techniques carried out to support any investment decision
- Demonstration of ability to consider all relevant factors

 **BPP**

Commercial acumen

- Effective use of examples and/or calculations from the scenario information and other practical considerations related to the context to illustrate points being made

- Recognition of external constraints and opportunities as necessary

$\underline{10}$

Total

$\underline{\underline{50}}$

(a) Purchasing power parity (PPP) predicts that the exchange rates between two currencies depend on the relative differences in the rates of inflation in each country. Therefore, if one country has a higher rate of inflation compared to another, then its currency is expected to depreciate over time. However, according to PPP the 'law of one price' holds because any weakness in one currency will be compensated by the rate of inflation in the currency's country (or group of countries, in the case of the euro).

Economic exposure refers to the degree by which a company's cash flows are affected by fluctuations in exchange rates. It may also affect companies which are not exposed to foreign exchange transactions, due to actions by international competitors.

If PPP holds, then companies may not be affected by exchange rate fluctuations, as lower currency value can be compensated by the ability to raise prices due to higher inflation levels. This depends on markets being efficient.

However, a permanent shift in exchange rates may occur, not because of relative inflation rate differentials, but because a country (or group of countries) lose their competitive positions.

In such cases, where a company receives substantial amounts of revenue from companies based in countries with relatively weak economies, it may find that it is facing economic exposure and its cash flows decline over a long period of time.

(b) **Discussion paper to the BoD, Lirio Co**

Discussion paper compiled by:

Date:

Purpose of the discussion paper

The purpose of this discussion paper is:

(1) To consider the implications of the BoD's proposal to use funds from the sale of its equity investment in the European company and from its cash flows generated from normal business activity over the next two years to finance a large project, instead of raising funds through equity and/or debt

(2) To assess whether or not the project adds value for Lirio Co or not

Background information

The funds needed for the project are estimated at $40,000,000 at the start of the project. $23,118,000 of this amount is estimated to be received from the sale of the equity investment (Appendices 2 and 3). This leaves a balance of $16,882,000 (Appendix 3), which will be obtained from the free cash flows to equity (the dividend capacity) of $21,642,000 (Appendix 1) expected to be generated in the first year. However, this would leave only $4,760,000 available for dividend payments in the first year, meaning a cut in expected dividends from $0.27/share to $0.0595/share (Appendix 3). The same level of dividends will be paid in the second year as well.

Project assessment

Based on the dividend valuation model, Lirio Co's market capitalisation, and therefore its value, is expected to increase from approximately $360 million to approximately $403 million, or by just under 12% (Appendix 3). This would suggest that it would be beneficial for the project to be undertaken.

Possible issues

(1) The dividend valuation model is based on a number of factors such as: an accurate estimation of the dividend growth rate, a non-changing cost of equity and a predictable future dividend stream growing in perpetuity. In addition to this, it is expected that the sale of the investment will yield €20,000,000 but this amount could increase or reduce in the next three months. The dividend valuation model assumes that dividends and their growth rate are the sole drivers of corporate value, which is probably not accurate.

(2) Although the dividend irrelevancy theory proposed by Modigliani and Miller suggests that corporate value should not be affected by a corporation's dividend policy, in practice changes in dividends do matter for two main reasons. First, dividends are used as a signalling device to the markets and unexpected changes in dividends paid and/or dividend growth rates are not generally viewed positively by them. Changes in dividends may signal that the company is not doing well and this may affect the share price negatively.

(3) Second, corporate dividend policy attracts certain groups of shareholders or clientele. In the main this is due to personal tax reasons. For example, higher rate taxpayers may prefer low dividend payouts and lower rate taxpayers may prefer higher dividend payouts. A change in dividends may result in the clientele changing and this changeover may result in excessive and possibly negative share price volatility.

(4) It is not clear why the BoD would rather not raise the required finance through equity and/or debt. The BoD may have considered increasing debt to be risky. However, given that the current level of debt is $70 million compared to an estimated market capitalisation of $360 million (Appendix 3), raising another $40 million through debt finance will probably not result in a significantly higher level of financial risk. The BoD may have been concerned that going into the markets to raise extra finance may result in negative agency type issues, such as having to make proprietary information public, being forced to give extra value to new equity owners, or sending out negative signals to the markets.

Areas for further discussion by the BoD

Each of these issues should be considered and discussed further by the BoD. With reference to point (i), the BoD needs to discuss whether the estimates and the model used are reasonable in estimating corporate value or market capitalisation. With reference to points (ii) and (iii), the BoD needs to discuss the implications of such a significant change in the dividend policy and how to communicate Lirio Co's intention to the market so that any negative reaction is minimised. With reference to point (iv), the BoD should discuss the reasons for any reluctance to raise finance through the markets and whether any negative impact of this is perhaps less than the negative impact of points (ii) and (iii).

Appendix 1: Expected dividend capacity prior to large project investment

	$'000
Operating profit (15% × $324m))	48,600
Less interest (5% of $70m)	(3,500)
Less taxation (25% × ($48.6m − 3.5m))	(11,275)
Less investment in working capital ($0.10 × (0.08 × $300m))	(2,400)
Less investment in additional non-current assets ($0.20 × (0.08 × $300m))	(4,800)
Less investment in projects	(8,000)
Cash flows from domestic operations	18,625
Cash flows from Pontac Co's dividend remittances (see Appendix 1.1)	3,297
Additional tax payable on Pontac Co's profits (5% × $5.6m)	(280)
Dividend capacity	21,642

Appendix 1.1: Dividend remittances expected from Pontac Co

	$'000
Total contribution $24 × 400,000 units	9,600
Less fixed costs	(4,000)
Less taxation (20% × $5.6m)	(1,120)
Profit after tax	4,480
Remitted to Lirio Co (80% × $4.48m × 92%)	3,297

Appendix 2: Euro (€) investment sale receipt hedge

Lirio Co can use one of forward contracts, futures contracts or option contracts to hedge the € receipt.

Forward contract

Since it is a € receipt, the 1.1559 rate will be used.

€20,000,000 × 1.1559 = $23,118,000

Futures contracts

Go long to protect against a weakening € and use the June contracts to hedge as the receipt is expected at the end of May 20X6 or beginning of June 20X6 (in three months' time).

Opening basis = futures rate – spot rate

Here the June futures rate (per $) is 0.8656 and the March spot rate (per $) = 1 / 1.1585 = 0.8632.

So opening basis is 0.8656 – 0.8632 = 0.0024

There are four months to the expiry of the June futures contract so we can assume that when the futures contracts are closed out, one month before expiry, then ¼ of this basis will remain. So closing basis is estimated as 0.0024 × ¼ = 0.0006.

The effective futures rate can be estimated as opening futures rate – closing basis

> **Tutorial note.** Other methods are possible.
>
> Here this gives 0.8656 – 0.0006 = 0.8650.
>
> Expected receipt = €20,000,000/0.8650 = $23,121,387
>
> Number of contracts bought = $23,121,387/$125,000 = approximately 185 contracts (resulting in a very small over-hedge and therefore not material)
>
> **(Full credit will be given where the calculations are used to show the correction of the over-hedge using forwards.)**

Option contracts

Purchase the June call option to protect against a weakening € and because receipt is expected at the end of May 20X6 or beginning of June 20X6.

Exercise price is 0.86, therefore expected receipt is €20,000,000/0.8600 = $23,255,814

Contracts purchased = $23,255,814/$125,000 = 186.05, say 186

Amount hedged = $125,000 × 186 = $23,250,000

Premium payable = 186 × 125,000 × 0.0290 = €674,250

Premium in $ = €674,250 × 1.1618 = $783,344

Amount not hedged = €20,000,000 – (186 × 125,000 × 0.8600) = €5,000

Use forward contracts to hedge €5,000 not hedged. €5,000 × 1.1559 = $5,780

(Full credit will be given if a comment on the under-hedge being immaterial and therefore not hedged is made, instead of calculating the correction of the under-hedge.)

Total receipts = $23,250,000 + $5,780 – $783,344 = $22,472,436

Advice and recommendation

Hedging using options will give the lowest receipt at $22,472,436 from the sale of the investment, while hedging using futures will give the highest receipt at $23,127,387, with the forward contracts giving a receipt of $23,118,000.

The lower receipt from the option contracts is due to the premium payable, which allows the option buyer to let the option lapse should the € strengthen. In this case, the option would be allowed to lapse and Lirio Co would convert the € into $ at the prevailing spot rate in three months' time. However, the € would need to strengthen significantly before the cost of the option is covered. Given market expectation of the weakness in the € continuing, this is not likely to be the case.

Although futures and forward contracts are legally binding and do not have the flexibility of option contracts, they both give higher receipts. Hedging using futures gives the higher receipt, but futures require margin payments to be made upfront and contracts are marked to market daily. In addition to this, the basis may not narrow in a linear fashion and therefore the amount received is not guaranteed. All these factors create uncertainty in terms of the exact amounts of receipts and payments resulting on a daily basis and the final receipt.

On the other hand, when using forward contracts to hedge the receipt exposure, Lirio Co knows the exact amount it will receive. It is therefore recommended that Lirio Co use the forward markets to hedge the expected receipt.

Note. It could be argued that in spite of the issues when hedging with futures, the higher receipt obtained from using futures markets to hedge means that they should be used. This is acceptable as well.

Appendix 3: Estimate of Lirio Co's value based on the dividend valuation model

If the large project is not undertaken and dividend growth rate is maintained at the historic level

Dividend history

Average dividend per share growth rate = $(0.255/0.214)^{1/3} - 1 = 1.0602$ (or say 6%)

Expected dividend in February 20X7 = $0.255 × 1.06 = $0.270

Lirio Co, estimate of value if large project is not undertaken =

$0.270/(0.12 − 0.06) = $4.50 per share or $360 million market capitalisation

If the large project is undertaken

Funds required for project	$40,000,000
Funds from sale of investment (Appendix 2)	$23,118,000
Funds required from dividend capacity cash flows	$16,882,000
Dividend capacity funds before transfer to project (Appendix 1)	$21,642,000
Dividend capacity funds left after transfer	$4,760,000
Annual dividend per share after transfer	$0.0595
Annual dividend paid (end of February 20X7 and February 20X8)	$0.0595
Dividend paid (end of February 20X9)	$0.3100
New growth rate	7%

Lirio Co, estimate of value if large project is undertaken =

$0.0595 × 1.12^{-1} + $0.0595 × 1.12^{-2} + $0.3100 × 1.12^{-3} + [$0.3100 × 1.07/(0.12 − 0.07)] × 1.12^{-3} = $5.04 per share or $403 million market capitalisation.

Note. A discussion paper can take many formats. The answer provides one possible format. Credit will be given for alternative and sensible formats; and for relevant approaches to the calculations and commentary.

46 Chrysos

Marking guide	Marks	
(a) Explanation of what a reverse takeover involves	2	
Advantages (up to 2 marks per well explained advantage)	4	
Disadvantages (up to 2 marks per well explained disadvantage)	4	
Marks Available	10	
Maximum		7
(b) (i) Extract of financial position after restructuring programme	5	
Appendix 1		
Manufacturing business unit unbundled through an MBO		
Estimate of cash flows	3	
Estimate of amount payable to ChrysosCo	2	
Selection of higher value unbundling option	1	
Appendix 2		
Chrysos Co, cost of equity	1	
Chrysos Co, cost of capital	1	
Appendix 3		
Estimate of cash flows	3	
Estimate of equity value	2	
		18

			Marks
(ii)	Explanation of approach taken	2	
	Explanation of assumptions made (up to 2 marks per assumption)	4	
	Maximum		5
(iii)	**Appendix 4**		
	Value from increased ownership	1	
	Additional value	1	
	Discussion of restructuring programme on the VCOs	4	
	Discussion of restructuring programme on Chrysos Co	5	
	Maximum		10

Professional skills

Communication

- General report format and structure (use of headings/sub-headings and an introduction)
- Style, language and clarity (appropriate layout and tone of report response, presentation of calculations, appropriate use of the tools)
- Effectiveness of communication (answer is relevant, specific rather than general and focused to the requirement)
- Adherence to the details of the proposal in the scenario

Analysis and Evaluation

- Appropriate use of the data to determine suitable calculations to value Chrysos Co
- Appropriate use of the data to support discussion and draw appropriate conclusions
- Demonstration of reasoned judgement when considering key matters for Chrysos Co
- Identification of further analysis, which could be carried out to enable an appropriate recommendation to be made.
- Demonstration of ability to consider relevant factors applicable to Chrysos Co's choices

Scepticism

- Effective challenge and critical assessment of the information and assumptions provided in relation to the valuation
- Effective challenge of information and assumptions supplied and, techniques carried out to support the valuation decision
- Demonstration of ability to consider all relevant factors applicable to the decisions made by Chrysos Co

Commercial acumen

- Effective use of examples and/or calculations from the scenario information and other practical considerations related to the context to illustrate points being made
- Recognition of external constraints and opportunities as necessary
- Recommendations are practical and plausible in the context of Chrysos Co's situation

Maximum		10
Total		50

ANSWERS

(a) A reverse takeover enables a private, unlisted company, like Chrysos Co, to gain a listing on the stock exchange without needing to go through the process of an initial public offering (IPO). The private company merges with a listed 'shell' company. The private company initially purchases equity shares in the listed company and takes control of its board of directors. The listed company then issues new equity shares and these are exchanged for

 BPP

equity shares in the unlisted company, thereby the original private company's equity shares gain a listing on the stock exchange. Often the name of the listed company is also changed to that of the original unlisted company.

Advantages relative to an IPO

(1)   An IPO can take a long time, typically between one and two years, because it involves preparing a prospectus and creating an interest among potential investors. The equity shares need to be valued and the issue process needs to be administered. Since with the reverse takeover shares in the private company are exchanged for shares in the listed company and no new capital is being raised, the process can be completed much quicker.

(2)   An IPO is an expensive process and can cost between 3% and 5% of the capital being raised due to involvement of various parties, such as investment banks, law firms, etc, and the need to make the IPO attractive through issuing a prospectus and marketing the issue. A reverse takeover does not require such costs to be incurred and therefore is considerably cheaper.

(3)   In periods of economic downturn, recessions and periods of uncertainty, an IPO may not be successful. A lot of senior managerial time and effort will be spent, as well as expenditure, with nothing to show for it. On the other hand, a reverse takeover would not face this problem as it does not need external investors and it is not raising external finance, but is being used to gain from the potential benefits of going public by getting a listing.

Disadvantages relative to an IPO

(1)   The 'shell' listed company being used in the reverse takeover may have hidden liabilities and may be facing potential litigation, which may not be obvious at the outset. Proper and full due diligence is necessary before the process is started. A company undertaking an IPO would not face such difficulties.

(2)   The original shareholders of the listed company may want to sell their shares immediately after the reverse takeover process has taken place and this may affect the share price negatively. A lock-up period during which shares cannot be sold may be necessary to prevent this.

Note. An IPO may need a lock-up period as well, but this is not usually the case.

(3)   The senior management of an unlisted company may not have the expertise and/or understanding of the rules and regulations which a listed company needs to comply with. The IPO process normally takes longer and is more involved, when compared to a reverse takeover. It also involves a greater involvement from external experts. These factors will provide the senior management involved in an IPO, with opportunities to develop the necessary expertise and knowledge of listing rules and regulations, which the reverse takeover process may not provide.

(4)   One of the main reasons for gaining a listing is to gain access to new investor capital. However, a smaller, private company which has become public through a reverse takeover may not obtain a sufficient analyst coverage and investor following, and it may have difficulty in raising new finance in future. A well-advertised IPO will probably not face these issues and find raising new funding to be easier.

(b)   **Report to the board of directors (BoD), Chrysos Co**

This report provides extracts from the financial position and an estimate of the value of Chrysos Co after it has undertaken a restructuring programme. It also contains an explanation of the process used in estimating the value and of the assumptions made. Finally, the report discusses the impact of the restructuring programme on the company and on venture capital organisations.

It is recommended that the manufacturing business unit is unbundled through a management buy-out, rather than the assets being sold separately, and it is estimated that Chrysos Co will receive $3,289 million from the unbundling of the manufacturing business unit (Appendix 1). This amount is recorded as a cash receipt in the extract of the financial position given below.

Extract of Chrysos Co's financial position following the restructuring programme

	$m
Non-current assets	
Land and buildings (80% × $7,500m)	6,000
Equipment ((80% × $5,400m) + $1,200m)	5,520
Current assets	
Inventory (80% × $1,800m)	1,440
Receivables (80% × $900m)	720
Cash ($3,289m + $400m − $1,200m − $1,050m)	1,439
Total assets	15,119
Equity	
Share capital ($1,800 + $600m)	2,400
Reserves **	10,319
Non-current liabilities	
Bank loan	1,800
Current liabilities	
Payables (80% × $750m)	600
Total equity and liabilities	15,119

** Balancing figure

Estimate of Chrysos Co's equity value following the restructuring programme

It is estimated that Chrysos Co's equity value after the restructuring programme has taken place will be just over $46 billion (Appendix 3).

Process undertaken in determining Chrysos Co's equity value

The corporate value is based on a growth rate of 4% on cash flows in perpetuity, which are discounted at Chrysos Co's cost of capital (Appendix 2). The cash flows are estimated by calculating the profit before depreciation and tax of the unbundled firm consisting of just the mining and shipping business unit and then deducting the depreciation and taxation amounts from this.

The bank loan debt is then deducted from the corporate value to estimate the value of the firm which is attributable to the equity holders (Appendix 3).

Assumptions made in determining Chrysos Co's equity value

It is assumed that Sidero Co's ungeared cost of equity is equivalent to Chrysos Co's ungeared cost of equity, given that they are both in the same industry and therefore face the same business risk. Modigliani and Miller's Proposition 2 is used to estimate Chrysos Cos's restructured cost of equity and cost of capital.

It is assumed that deducting depreciation and tax from the profit before depreciation, interest and tax provides a reasonably accurate estimate of the free cash flows (Appendix 3). Other adjustments such as changes in working capital are reckoned to be immaterial and therefore not considered. Depreciation is not added back because it is assumed to be the same as the capital needed for reinvestment purposes.

It is assumed that the cash flows will grow in perpetuity. The assumption of growth in perpetuity may be over-optimistic and may give a higher than accurate estimate of Chrysos Co's equity value.

BPP

Note. Credit will be given for alternative and relevant assumptions.

Impact of the restructuring programme on Chrysos Co and on the venture capital organisations (VCOs)

By acquiring an extra 600 million equity shares, the proportion of the VCOs' equity share capital will increase to 40% ((600m + 20% × 1,800)/(1,800 + 600)) from 20%. Therefore, the share of the equity value the VCOs will hold in Chrysos Co will increase by $9,229 million, which is 77.5% more than the total of the value of bonds cancelled and extra payment made (Appendix 4). As long as the VCOs are satisfied that the equity value of Chrysos Co after the restructuring programme has been undertaken is accurate, the value of their investment has increased substantially. The VCOs may want undertake a feasibility study on the annual growth rate in cash flows of 4% and the assumption of growth in perpetuity. However, the extent of additional value created seems to indicate that the impact for the VCOs is positive.

By cancelling the VCOs' unsecured bonds and repaying the other debt in non-current liabilities, an opportunity has been created for Chrysos Co to raise extra debt finance for future projects. Based on a long-term capital structure ratio of 80% equity and 20% debt, and a corporate value of $47,944 million (Appendix 3), this equates to just under $9,600 million of possible debt finance which could be accessed. Since the bank loan has a current value of $1,800 million, Chrysos Co could raise just under an extra $7,800 million debt funding and it would also have $1,439 million in net cash available from the sale of the machinery parts manufacturing business unit.

Chrysos Co's current value has not been given and therefore it is not possible to determine the financial impact of the equity value after the restructuring has taken place on the company as a whole. Nevertheless, given that the company has access to an extra $7,800 million debt funding to expand its investment into new value-creating projects, it is likely that the restructuring programme will be beneficial. However, it is recommended that the company tries to determine its current equity value and compares this with the proposed new value. A concern may be that both the five senior equity holders' group and the 30 other equity holders group's proportion of equity shares will reduce to 30% from 40% each, as a result of the VCOs acquiring an additional 600 million shares. Both these shareholder groups need to be satisfied about the potential negative impact of these situations against the potential additional benefits accruing from the restructuring programme, before the company proceeds with the programme.

Conclusion

The restructuring programme creates an opportunity for Chrysos Co to have access to extra funding and additional cash for investment in projects in the future. The VCOs are likely to benefit financially from the restructuring programme as long as they are satisfied about the assumptions made when assessing the value created. However, Chrysos Co will need to ensure that all equity holder groups are satisfied with the change in their respective equity holdings.

Report compiled by:

Date:

Note. Credit will be given for alternative and relevant points.

Appendices

Appendix 1: Unbundling the manufacturing business unit

Option 1: Sale of assets

Net proceeds to Chrysos Co from net sale of assets of the manufacturing business unit are $3,102 million.

Option 2: Management buy-out

	$m
Sales revenue (20% × $16,800m)	3,360
Operating costs (25% × 10,080m)	(2,520)
Profit before depreciation, interest and tax	840
Depreciation (12% × 20% × ($7,500m + $5,400m))	(310)
	530
Tax (18% × $530m)	(95)
Cash flows	435

Estimated value = ($435m × 1.08)/0.10 = $4,698m

Amount payable to Chrysos Co = 70% × $4,698m = $3,289m

The option to unbundle through a management buy-out (option 2) is marginally better for Chrysos Co and it will opt for this.

Appendix 2: Calculation of cost of equity and cost of capital

Chrysos Co, estimate of cost of equity (Ke) and cost of capital (CoC)

Ke = 12.46% + [0.82 × (12.46% − 4.5%) × (0.2/0.8)]

Ke = 14.09%

CoC = 0.8 × 14.09% + 0.2 × 4.5% × 0.82 = 12.01, say 12%

Appendix 3: Estimate of value

	$m
Sales revenue (80% × $16,800m)	13,440
Costs prior to depreciation, interest and tax (75% × 10,080m)	(7,560)
Profit before depreciation and tax	5,880
Depreciation (12% × ($6,000m + $5,520m))	(1,382)
	4,498
Tax (18% × $4,498m)	(810)
Cash flows	3,688

Cost of capital to be used in estimating Chrysos Co's value is 12% (Appendix 2)

Estimated corporate value = ($3,688m × 1.04)/(0.12 − 0.04) = $47,944m

Estimated equity value = $47,944m − $1,800m = $46,144m

Note. It is also acceptable to calculate cash flows after interest payment and use the cost of equity to estimate the equity value based on cash flows to equity instead of cash flows to firm.

Appendix 4: Value created for VCOs

Value attributable to the VCOs = 40% × $46,144m = $18,458m

Value from increased equity ownership (this has doubled from 20% to 40%)

50% × $18,458m = $9,229m

Value of unsecured bonds foregone by the VCOs = $4,800m

Additional capital invested by the VCOs = $400m

Total of additional capital invested and value of bonds forgone = $5,200m

Additional value = ($9,229m − $5,200m)/$5,200m = 77.5% (or $4,029m)

 **BPP**

47 Conejo

Marking guide		Marks	
(a)	Being able to bear higher levels of financial risk	3	
	Better protection from predatory takeover bids	3	
	Taxation benefit of higher levels of debt finance	2	
	Marks Available	8	
	Maximum		6
(b) (i)	**Appendix 1**		
	Conejo Co's yield curve based on BBB rating	1	
	Bond value based on BBB rating and spot yieald rates	1	
	Comment on reason for virtually no change in value	1	
	Calculation of the coupon rate of the new bond	2	
	Comment on coupon rate	1	
			6
(ii)	**Appendix 2**		
	Duration based on annual coupon and balloon payment of $100 in Year 5	2	
	Amount of fixed annual repayments of capital and interest	2	
	Duration based on annual equivalent payments	2	
			6
(iii)	**Appendix 3**		
	Financial position, Proposal 1	3	
	Financial position, Proposal 2	3	
	Interest payable on additional new debt finance	1	
	Interest payable on higher coupon for current debt finance	1	
	Return on additional investment	1	
	Gearing calculations	1	
	Earnings per share calculations	1	
			11
(iv)	Discussion in report		
	Impact on Conejo Co	6	

Credit migration, credit rating agencies and CEO's opinion	6
Impact on Conejo Co's debt holders: current and new	3
Maximum	11

Professional skills

Communication

- General report format and structure (use of headings/sub-headings and an introduction)
- Style, language and clarity (appropriate layout and tone of report response, presentation of calculations, appropriate use of the tools)
- Effectiveness of communication (answer is relevant, specific rather than general and focused to the requirement)
- Adherence to the details of the proposal in the scenario

Analysis and Evaluation

- Appropriate use of the data to determine suitable calculations
- Appropriate use of the data to support discussion and draw appropriate conclusions
- Demonstration of reasoned judgement when considering key matters for Conejo Co
- Identification of further analysis, which could be carried out to enable an appropriate recommendation to be made.
- Demonstration of ability to consider relevant factors applicable to Conejo Co's choices

Scepticism

- Demonstration of ability to consider all relevant factors applicable to the decisions made by Conejo Co

Commercial acumen

- Effective use of examples and/or calculations from the scenario information and other practical considerations related to the context to illustrate points being made
- Recognition of external constraints and opportunities as necessary
- Recommendations are practical and plausible in the context of Conejo Co's situation

Maximum	10
Total	**50**

(a) Increasing the debt finance of a company relative to equity finance increases its financial risk, and therefore the company will need to be able to bear the consequences of this increased risk. However, companies face both financial risk, which increases as the debt levels in the capital structure increase, and business risk, which is present in a company due to the nature of its business.

In the case of Conejo Co, it could be argued that as its profits and cash flows have stabilised, the company's business risk has reduced, in contrast to early in its life, when its business risk would have been much higher due to unstable profits and cash flows. Therefore, whereas previously Conejo Co was not able to bear high levels of financial risk, it is able to do so now without having a detrimental impact on the overall risk profile of the company. It could therefore change its capital structure and have higher levels of debt finance relative to equity finance.

The predatory acquisition of one company by another could be undertaken for a number of reasons. One possible reason may be to gain access to cash resources, where a company which needs cash resources may want to take over another company which has significant cash resources or cash generative capability. Another reason may be to increase the debt capacity of the acquirer by using the assets of the target company. Where the relative level

 BPP

of debt finance is increased in the capital structure of a company through a financial reconstruction, like in the case of Conejo Co, these reasons for acquiring a company may be diminished. This is because the increased levels of debt would probably be secured against the assets of the company and therefore the acquirer cannot use them to raise additional debt finance, and cash resources would be needed to fund the higher interest payments.

Many tax jurisdictions worldwide allow debt interest to be deducted from profits before the amount of tax payable is calculated on the profits. Increasing the amount of debt finance will increase the amount of interest paid, reducing the taxable profits and therefore the tax paid. Modigliani and Miller referred to this as the benefit of the tax shield in their research into capital structure, where their amended capital proposition demonstrated the reduction in the cost of capital and increase in the value of the firm, as the proportion of debt in the capital structure increases.

(b) **Report to the board of directors (BoD), Conejo Co**

Introduction

This report discusses whether the proposed financial reconstruction scheme which increases the amount of debt finance in Conejo Co would be beneficial or not to the company and the main parties affected by the change in the funding, namely the equity holders, the debt holders and the credit rating companies. Financial estimates provided in the appendices are used to support the discussion.

Impact on Conejo Co

Benefits to Conejo Co include the areas discussed in part (a) above and as suggested by the CFO. The estimate in Appendix 3 assumes that the interest payable on the new bonds and the extra interest payable on the existing bonds are net of the 15% tax. Therefore, the tax shield reduces the extra amount of interest paid. Further, it is likely that because of the large amount of debt finance which will be raised, the company's assets would have been used as collateral. This will help protect the company against hostile takeover bids. Additionally, Proposal 2 (Appendix 3) appears to be better than proposal 1, with a lower gearing figure and a higher earnings per share figure. However, this is dependent on the extra investment being able to generate an after-tax return of 12% immediately. The feasibility of this should be assessed further.

Conejo Co may also feel that this is the right time to raise debt finance as interest rates are lower and therefore it does not have to offer large coupons, compared to previous years. Appendix 1 estimates that the new bond will need to offer a coupon of 3.57%, whereas the existing bond is paying a coupon of 5.57%.

The benefits above need to be compared with potential negative aspects of raising such a substantial amount of debt finance. Conejo Co needs to ensure that it will be able to finance the interest payable on the bonds and it should ensure it is able to repay the capital amount borrowed (or be able to re-finance the loan) in the future. The extra interest payable (Appendix 3) will probably not pose a significant issue given that the profit after tax is substantially more than the interest payment. However, the repayment of the capital amount will need careful thought because it is significant.

The substantial increase in gearing, especially with respect to Proposal 1 (Appendix 3), may worry some stakeholders (eg shareholders) because of the extra financial risk. However, based on market values, the level of gearing may not appear so high. The expected credit migration from A to BBB seems to indicate some increase in risk, but it is probably not substantial.

The BoD should also be aware of, and take account of, the fact that going to the capital markets to raise finance will require Conejo Co to disclose information, which may be considered strategically important and could impact negatively on areas where Conejo Co has a competitive advantage.

Conejo may also be concerned about the additional restrictive covenants which will result from the extra debt finance, and the extent to which these covenants will restrict the financial flexibility of Conejo Co when undertaking future business opportunities.

Reaction of credit rating companies

Credit ratings assigned to companies and to borrowings made by companies by credit rating companies depend on the probability of default and recovery rate. A credit migration from A to BBB means that Conejo Co has become riskier in that it is more likely to default and bondholders will find it more difficult to recover their entire loan if default does happen. Nevertheless, the relatively lower increase in yield spreads from A to BBB, compared to BBB to BB, indicates that BBB can still be considered a relatively safe investment.

Duration indicates the time it takes to recover half the repayments of interest and capital of a bond, in present value terms. Duration measures the sensitivity of bond prices to changes in interest rates. A bond with a higher duration would see a greater fluctuation in its value when interest rates change, compared to a bond with a lower duration.

Appendix 2 shows that a bond which pays interest (coupon) and capital in equal annual instalments will have a lower duration. This is because a greater proportion of income is received earlier and income due to be received earlier is less risky. Therefore, when interest rates change, this bond's value will change by less than the bond with the higher duration.

The CEO is correct that the bond with equal annual payments of interest and capital is less sensitive to interest rate changes, but it is not likely that this will be a significant factor for a credit rating company when assigning a credit rating.

A credit rating company will consider a number of criteria when assigning a credit rating, as these would give a more appropriate assessment of the probability of default and the recovery rate. These criteria include, for example, the industry within which the company operates, the company's position within that industry, the company's ability to generate profits in proportion to the capital invested, the amount of gearing, the quality of management and the amount of financial flexibility the company possesses. A credit rating company will be much less concerned about the manner in which a bond's value fluctuates when interest rates change.

Impact on debt holders

Although the current debt holders may be concerned about the extra gearing which the new bonds would introduce to Conejo Co, Appendix 1 shows that the higher coupon payments which the current debt holders will receive would negate any fall in the value of their bonds due to the credit migration to BBB rating from an A rating.

Given that currently Conejo Co is subject to low financial risk, and probably lower business risk, it is unlikely that the current and new debt holders would be overly concerned about the extra gearing. The earnings figures in Appendix 3 also show that the after-tax profit figures provide a substantial interest cover and therefore additional annual interest payment should not cause the debt holders undue concern either.

The current and new debt holders would be more concerned about Conejo Co's ability to pay back the large capital sum in five years' time. However, a convincing explanation of how this can be achieved or a plan to roll over the debt should allay these concerns.

The current and new debt holders may be concerned that Conejo Co is not tempted to take unnecessary risks with the additional investment finance, but sensible use of restrictive covenants and the requirement to make extra disclosures to the markets when raising the debt finance should help mitigate these concerns.

Conclusion

Overall, it seems that the proposed financial reconstruction will be beneficial, as it will provide opportunities for Conejo Co to make additional investments and/or an opportunity to reduce equity capital, and thereby increasing the earnings per share. The increased gearing may not look large when considered in terms of market values. It may also be advantageous to undertake the reconstruction scheme in a period when interest rates are low and the credit migration is not disadvantageous.

However, Conejo Co needs to be mindful of how it intends to repay the capital amount in five years' time, the information it will disclose to the capital markets and the impact of any negative restrictive covenants.

ANSWERS

Report compiled by:

Date

Appendices:

Appendix 1: Change in the value of the current bond from credit migration and coupon rate required from the new bond (Question (b)(i))

Spot yield rates (yield curve) based on BBB rating

1 year	2.20%
2 year	2.51%
3 year	2.84%
4 year	3.25%
5 year	3.62%

Bond value based on BBB rating

$\$5.57 \times 1.0220^{-1} + \$5.57 \times 1.0251^{-2} + \$105.57 \times 1.0284^{-3} = \$107.81$

Current bond value = $107.80

Although the credit rating of Conejo Co declines from A to BBB, resulting in higher spot yield rates, the value of the bond does not change very much at all. This is because the increase in the coupons and the resultant increase in value almost exactly matches the fall in value from the higher spot yield rates.

Coupon rate required from the new bond

Take R as the coupon rate, such that:

$(\$R \times 1.0220^{-1}) + (\$R \times 1.0251^{-2}) + (\$R \times 1.0284^{-3}) + (\$R \times 1.0325^{-4}) + (\$R \times 1.0362^{-5}) + (\$100 \times 1.0362^{-5}) = \$100$

4.5665R + 83.71 = 100

R = $3.57

Coupon rate for the new bond is 3.57%.

If the coupon payments on the bond are at a rate of 3.57% on the face value, it ensures that the present values of the coupons and the redemption of the bond at face value exactly equals the bond's current face value, based on Conejo Co's yield curve.

Appendix 2: Macaulay durations (Question (b)(ii))

Macaulay duration based on annual coupon of $3.57 and redemption value of $100 in Year 5:

$[(\$3.57 \times 1.0220^{-1} \times 1 \text{ year}) + (\$3.57 \times 1.0251^{-2} \times 2 \text{ years}) + (\$3.57 \times 1.0284^{-3} \times 3 \text{ years}) + (\$3.57 \times 1.0325^{-4} \times 4 \text{ years}) + (\$103.57 \times 1.0362^{-5} \times 5 \text{ years})]/\$100$

= [3.49 + 6.79 + 9.85 + 12.57 + 433.50]/100 = 4.7 years

Macaulay duration based on fixed annual repayments of interest and capital:

Annuity factor: (3.57%, 5 years) = $(1 - 1.0357^{-5})/0.0357$ = 4.51 approximately

Annual payments of capital and interest required to pay back new bond issue = $100/4.51 = $22.17 per $100 bond approximately

$[(\$22.17 \times 1.0220^{-1} \times 1 \text{ year}) + (\$22.17 \times 1.0251^{-2} \times 2 \text{ years}) + (\$22.17 \times 1.0284^{-3} \times 3 \text{ years}) + (\$22.17 \times 1.0325 - 4 \times 4 \text{ years}) + (\$22.17 \times 1.0362^{-5} \times 5 \text{ years})]/\$100$

= [21.69 + 42.20 + 61.15 + 78.03 + 92.79]/100 = 3.0 years

Alternative presentation of duration calculations:

(Discount factors are based on the interest rates shown in previous presentation)

Based on annual rate of 3.57% and redemption in Year 5:

Time	1	2	3	4	5	Total
$	3.57	3.57	3.57	3.57	103.57	
df	0.978	0.952	0.919	0.880	0.837	
PV	3.5	3.4	3.3	3.1	86.7	100.0
% PV	0.04	0.03	0.03	0.03	0.87	1.0
% × year	0.04	0.06	0.09	0.12	4.35	**4.7**

Based on fixed annual repayments of interest and capital:

	1	2	3	4	5	Total
$	22.17	22.17	22.17	22.17	22.17	Total
df	0.978	0.952	0.919	0.880	0.837	
PV	21.7	21.1	20.4	19.5	18.6	101.3
% PV	0.22	0.21	0.20	0.20	0.19	1.0
% × year	0.22	0.42	0.60	0.80	0.95	**3.0**

Appendix 3: Forecast earnings, financial position, earnings per share and gearing (Question (b)(iii)) Adjustments to forecast earnings

Amounts in $m	Current	Proposal 1	Proposal 2
Forecast after-tax profit	350.00	350.00	350.00
Interest payable on additional borrowing (based on a coupon rate of 3.57%)			
3.57% ×$1,320m × (1 − 0.15)		(40.06)	(40.06)
Additional interest payable due to higher coupon			
0.37% × $120m × (1 − 0.15)		(0.38)	(0.38)
Return on additional investment (after tax)			
12% × $1,320m			158.40
Adjusted profit after tax	350.00	309.56	467.96

Forecast financial position

Amounts in $m	Current	Proposal 1	Proposal 2
Non-current assets	1,735.00	1,735.00	3,055.00
Current assets	530.00	489.56	647.96
Total assets	2,265.00	2,224.56	3,702.96
Equity and liabilities			
Share capital ($1 per share par value)	400.00	280.00	400.00
Reserves	1,700.00	459.56	1,817.96
Total equity	2,100.00	739.56	2,217.96
Non-current liabilities	120.00	1,440.00	1,440.00
Current liabilities	45.00	45.00	45.00
Total liabilities	165.00	1,485.00	1,485.00
Total liabilities and capital	2,265.00	2,224.56	3,702.96
Gearing % (non-current liabilities/equity)	5.7%	194.7%	64.9%
Earnings per share (in cents)			
(Adjusted profit after tax/no. of shares)	87.5c	110.6c	117.0c

Note. If gearing is calculated based on non-current liabilities/(non-current liabilities + equity) and/or using market value of equity, instead of as above, then this is acceptable as well.

Proposal 1

Additional interest payable is deducted from current assets, assuming it is paid in cash and this is part of current assets. Reserves are also reduced by this amount. (Other assumptions are possible.)

Shares repurchased as follows: $1 × 120m shares deducted from share capital and $10 × 120m shares deducted from reserves. $1,320 million, consisting of $11 × 120m shares, added to non-current liabilities.

Proposal 2

Treatment of additional interest payable is as per Proposal 1.

Additional debt finance raised, $1,320 million, is added to non-current liabilities and to non-current assets, assuming that all this amount is invested in non-current assets to generate extra income.

It is assumed that this additional investment generates returns at 12%, which is added to current assets and to profits (and therefore to reserves).

(Explanations given in notes are not required for full marks, but are included to explain how the figures given in Appendix 3 are derived.)

Note. Credit will be given for alternative relevant presentation of financial positions and discussion.

48 Chikepe

Marking guide		Marks
(a) Compare and contrast the two directors' opinions	5	
Discussion of types of synergy benefits	5	
Marks Available	10	
Maximum		7
(b) 1–2 marks per point		
Maximum		4

 BPP

(c) (i) **(Appendix 1)**

Exclude interest from free cash flows	1
Estimate of free cash flows	2
Estimate of Foshoro Co's value	1
Estimate of equity value of Foshoro Co	1
	5

(ii) **(Appendix 2)**

Combined company asset beta	1
Combined company equity beta	1
Combined company cost of equity	1
Combined company cost of capital	1
Combined company sales revenue (or operating profits) (Years 1 to 4)	1
Combined company taxation amounts (Years 1 to 4)	1
Combined company additional asset investment (Years 1 to 4)	1
Combined company total value (Years 1 to 4)	1
Combined company value after first four years	1
Combined company total market value	1
Combined company market value of equity	1
	11

(iii) **(Discussion in report and Appendix 3)**

Evaluation of benefit to Chikepe Co shareholders	4
Discussion of the limitations of the valuation method used	4
Maximum	7

(d) Discussion of mandatory-bid rule and principle of equal treatment | 4 |

Discussion of effectiveness of disposal of crown jewels | 2 |

| | 6 |

Professional skills

Communication

- General report format and structure (use of headings/sub-headings and an introduction)
- Style, language and clarity (appropriate layout and tone of report response, presentation of calculations, appropriate use of the tools)
- Effectiveness of communication (answer is relevant, specific rather than general and focused to the requirement)
- Adherence to the details of the proposal in the scenario

Analysis and Evaluation

- Appropriate use of the data to determine suitable calculations to evaluate the acquisition
- Appropriate use of the data to support discussion and draw appropriate conclusions
- Demonstration of ability to consider relevant factors for Chikepe

Scepticism

- Effective challenge of information and assumptions supplied and, techniques carried out to support any investment decision
- Effective challenge of evidence and assumptions supplied with respect to the director's view on strategy
- Demonstration of ability to consider all relevant factors applicable to the decisions made by Chikepe

Commercial acumen

- Effective use of examples and/or calculations from the scenario information and other practical considerations related to the context to illustrate points being made

- Recognition of external constraints and opportunities as necessary

                  <u>10</u>

Total   <u>50</u>

(a) Director A's focus is on reducing the risk in the business through diversification and thereby increasing its value. A strategy of risk diversification resulting in greater value can work in situations where the equity holders are exposed to both unsystematic and systematic risks, for example, when their investment is concentrated in one company. In such situations, the shareholders would be subject to unsystematic risk and diversification would reduce this risk.

In the case of Chikepe Co, this is unlikely to be the case, as a large proportion of shares are owned by institutional shareholders, and it is likely that their investment portfolios are already well-diversified and therefore they are not exposed to unsystematic risk. Further diversification will be of no value to them. In fact, it may be construed that managers are only taking this action for their own benefit, as they may be closely tied to the company and therefore be exposed to total risk (both unsystematic and systematic risks). This may then become a source of agency-related conflict between the management and the shareholders.

However, diversification overseas into markets which have some barriers to entry might reduce both systematic and unsystematic risks as well.

Director B, on the other hand, seems to be suggesting that Chikepe Co should focus on its core business and increase value through identifying areas of synergy benefits. It may be the case that Chikepe Co's management and directors are well placed to identify areas where the company can gain value by acquiring companies with potential synergy benefits.

The types of synergy benefits, which may arise in established pharmaceutical companies, can include:

(1) Identifying undervalued companies, where the management is not effective in unlocking the true value of company. By replacing the existing management, Chikepe Co may be able to unlock the value of the company.

(2) Acquiring companies which have strategic assets or product pipelines. Chikepe Co may be well-placed to identify companies which have a number of product pipelines, which those companies are not exploiting fully. By acquiring such companies, Chikepe Co may be able to exploit the product pipelines.

(3) Through acquisitions, Chikepe Co may be able to exploit economies of scope by eliminating process duplication, or economies of scale where its size may enable it to negotiate favourable terms.

(4) Foshoro Co may benefit if Chikepe Co acquires it because it is struggling to raise funding for its innovative products. Chikepe Co is an established company but has few new product innovations coming in the future. Therefore, it may have spare cash resources which Foshoro Co may be able to utilise.

Note. Credit will be given for alternative valid discussion.

(b) Traditional investment appraisal methods such as net present value assume that an investment needs to be taken on a now or never basis, and once undertaken, it cannot be reversed. Real options take into account the fact that in reality, most investments have within them certain amounts of flexibility, such as whether or not to undertake the investment immediately or to delay the decision; to pursue follow-on opportunities; and to cancel an investment opportunity after it has been undertaken. Where there is increasing uncertainty and risk, and where a decision can be changed or delayed, this flexibility has value, known as the time value of an option.

 BPP

Net present value captures just the intrinsic value of an investment opportunity, whereas real options capture both the intrinsic value and the time value, to give an overall value for an opportunity. When a company still has time available to it before a decision needs to be made, it may have opportunities to increase the intrinsic value of the investment through the strategic decisions it makes.

Investing in new companies with numerous potential innovative product pipelines may provide opportunities for flexibility where decisions can be delayed and the intrinsic value can be increased through strategic decisions and actions taken by the company. Real options try to capture the value of this flexibility within companies with innovative product pipelines, whereas net present value does not.

(c) **Report to the board of directors (BoD), Chikepe Co**

Introduction

This report evaluates whether the acquisition of Foshoro Co would be beneficial to Chikepe Co's shareholders by estimating the additional equity value created from the synergies resulting when the two companies are combined. The market values of equity of the two companies as separate entities are considered initially and then compared with the equity value of the two companies together. The free cash flow to firm valuation method is used to estimate the values of the companies and the limitations of this method are discussed.

The market value of equity of Chikepe Co is given as $12,600 million.

Based on the free cash flow to firm valuation method:

- The current market value of equity of Foshoro Co is estimated at $986 million (Appendix 1); and (Appendix 1); and

- The market value of equity of the combined company is estimated at $14,993 million (Appendix 2).

Therefore, the additional market value of equity arising from synergy benefits when the two companies are combined is estimated at $1,407 million (Appendix 3), which is then split between Foshoro Co's shareholders receiving $296 million (a 30% premium) and Chikepe Co's shareholders receiving the balance of $1,111 million, which is approximately 8.8% excess over the original equity value (Appendix 3).

However, the valuation method used has a number of limitations, as follows:

(1) The values of both Foshoro Co and the combined company are based on estimations and assumptions, for example:

    (i) Foshoro Co's future growth rate of free cash flows is based on past growth rates and it is assumed that this will not change in the future.

    (ii) It is not explained how Foshoro Co's cost of capital is estimated/calculated. Such an estimate may be more difficult to make for private companies.

    (iii) The assumption of perpetuity is made when estimating the values of Foshoro Co and the combined company, and this may not be valid.

(2) The basis for the synergy benefits, such as higher growth rates of sales revenue and profit margins, needs to be explained and justified. It is not clear how these estimates have been made.

(3) Whereas it may be possible to estimate the asset beta of a listed company such as Chikepe Co, it may be more difficult to provide a reasonable estimate for the asset beta of Foshoro Co. Therefore, the estimate of the cost of capital of the combined company may not be accurate.

(4) The costs related to the acquisition process would need to be factored in.

Therefore, whereas the free cash flow method of estimating corporate values is theoretically sound, using it in practice to estimate values is open to errors and judgements.

Conclusion

The valuations indicate that Chikepe Co's shareholders would benefit from the acquisition of Foshoro Co and the value of their shares should increase by 8.8%. However, the method used to estimate the value created makes a number of estimates and assumptions. It is therefore

recommended that a range of valuations is made under different assumptions and estimates, through a process of sensitivity analysis, before a final decision is made. As well as this, the limitations of the valuation method used should be well understood and taken into account.

Report compiled by:

Date

APPENDICES:

Appendix 1 (Part (c)(i)): Foshoro Co, estimate of current value

Cost of capital = 10%

Growth rate of profits and free cash flows = 3%

Free cash flow to firm (FCFF) = PBIT + non-cash expenses − additional cash investment − tax

FCFF = $192.3m + $112.0m − $98.2m − (20% × $192.3m) = $167.6m

Foshoro Co, estimated value = ($167.6m × 1.03)/(0.10 − 0.03) = $2,466.1m

Current estimated market value of equity of Foshoro Co = $2,466.1m × 40% = $986.4m, say $986m approximately.

Appendix 2 (Part (c)(ii)): Estimate of value created from combining Chikepe Co and Foshoro Co

Asset beta of combined company = (0.800 × $12,600m + 0.950 × $986.4m)/($12,600m + $986.4m) = 0.811

Equity beta of combined company = 0.811 × (0.70 + 0.30 × 0.80)/0.70 = 1.089

Cost of equity, combined company = 2% + 1.089 × 7% = 9.6% approx.

Cost of capital, combined company = 9.6% × 0.7 + 5.3% × 0.3 × 0.8 = 8% approx.

Combined company, free cash flows and value computation ($ millions)

Sales growth rate, Years 2 to 4 = 7% per year; operating profit margin = 20%

Year	1	2	3	4
Sales revenue	4,200	4,494	4,809	5,146
Operating profit	840	899	962	1,029
Less tax (20%)	(168)	(180)	(192)	(206)
Less additional investment in assets	(200)	(188)	(202)	(216)
Free cash flows	472	531	568	607
PV of free cash flows (8%)	437	455	451	446

	$m
Present value (first four years)	1,789
Present value (after four years)	
607 × 1.056/(0.08 − 0.056) × 0.735	19,630
Estimated market value of the combined company	21,419

Market value of equity of the combined company = 70% × $21,419m = $14,993m

Appendix 3: Synergy benefits and their distribution

Additional market equity value created by combining the two companies

$14,993m − ($12,600m + $986m) = $1,407m

Therefore, synergy benefits resulting from combining the two companies: $1,407 million

Premium payable to Foshoro Co shareholders: 30% × $986m = $296m

 BPP

Balance of synergy benefits going to Chikepe Co's shareholders: $1,111 million

As a percentage of current value: $1,111m/$12,600m × 100% = 8.8%

(d) Both the mandatory bid rule and the principle of equal treatment are designed to protect minority shareholders, where an acquirer has obtained a controlling interest of the target company. The mandatory bid rule provides minority shareholders with the opportunity to sell their shares and exit the target company at a specified fair share price. This price should not be lower than the highest price paid for shares, which have already been acquired within a specified period. The principle of equal treatment requires the acquiring company to offer the same terms to minority shareholders as were offered to the earlier shareholders from whom the controlling interest was acquired. Both these regulatory devices are designed to ensure that the minority shareholders are protected financially and are not exploited by the acquirer.

The purpose of the disposal of crown jewels is to make the target company unattractive to the acquirer. Disposal of crown jewels involves selling the target company's most valuable assets, and therefore making the target company less attractive to the acquirer. The effectiveness of this type of defence tactic can be limited, as the company's management would need its shareholders to authorise such moves. Shareholders may not be willing to do this as they normally get premiums on their shares during takeover battles. Additionally, disposing of key strategic assets could substantially weaken a company's competitive advantage and therefore its future potential. Such action may be detrimental to the company and therefore shareholders would probably not approve that course of action.

49 Washi

> **Course Book references**
>
> International investment appraisal is covered in Chapter 5, and currency hedging is covered in Chapter 13.
>
> **Examining team's comments**
>
> Part (b) On futures hedging, many candidates omitted to identify whether futures contracts were to be sold or bought at the start of the hedge. Quite a few candidates incorrectly hedged using call options instead of put options. A large majority of candidates made no attempt to calculate the proceeds from the six-month investment of the JPY receivable which would reduce the additional debt finance needed, thus receiving no marks for this part. The main difficulty that many candidates encountered was calculating the ARD/JPY spot cross rates from the given JPY/EUR and ARD/EUR spot exchange rates and then forecasting ARD/JPY exchange rates using purchasing power parity. These spot cross rates and forecast exchange rates are then used to convert the initial investment amount in ARD currency to JPY currency to determine the debt finance required as well as for the investment appraisal in part (c)(ii).
>
> Common mistakes in the answers include not showing workings for the exchange rates produced, therefore no 'own figure rule' (OFR) marks could be awarded if the exchange rates were wrong; not labelling the currencies making it difficult for markers to identify the exchange rate referred to in the calculation; cross rates incorrectly calculated and purchasing power parity wrongly applied in forecasting the ARD/JPY exchange rates.
>
> Part (c) required candidates to discuss the validity of decentralising the one treasury department for the whole group into individual treasury departments for the major subsidiary companies. Most candidates demonstrated a good understanding in contrasting the benefits of both centralised and individual treasury departments and scored high marks. Answers which focussed only on the benefits of decentralisation or centralisation of the treasury function scored limited marks.

Marking guide

	Marks
(a) 1–2 marks per valid point	
Maximum	5
(b) (i) (Appendix 1)	
Amount to be received based on forward rate	1
Decision to go short on futures	1
Estimate of futures rate in six months based on basis	1
Amount to be received based on futures market	1
Decision to purchase put options	1
Premium payable	1
Amount to be received based on options market	1
Decision: select appropriate hedge instrument	1
JPY receivable following further six months of investment	1
Estimate of current cross rate(s)	1
Estimate of ARD/JPY rate in one year's time	1
Debt borrowing required	1
	12
(ii) (Appendix 2)	
Estimate of future ARD/JPY rates	1
Lost contribution	1

		Marks	
	Tax saving on lost contribution	1	
	Contribution from sales of components	2	
	Tax on contribution from components sales	2	
	Additional tax payable in Japan	2	
	Present values and net present value	1	
			9
(iii)	**(Report on project and funding evaluation)**		
	Evaluation of hedge choice and debt finance required	4	
	Evaluation of Airone project	4	
	Conclusion	2	
	Marks Available	10	
	Maximum		8
(c)	Benefits of a centralised treasury department	4	
	Benefits of decentralised treasury departments	3	
	Marks Available	7	
	Maximum		6

Professional skills

Communication

- General report format and structure (use of headings/sub-headings and an introduction)
- Style, language and clarity (appropriate layout and tone of report response, presentation of calculations, appropriate use of the tools)
- Effectiveness of communication (answer is relevant, specific rather than general and focused to the requirement)

Analysis and Evaluation

- Appropriate use of the data to determine suitable calculations
- Appropriate use of the data to support discussion and draw appropriate conclusions
- Identification of further analysis, which could be carried out to enable an appropriate recommendation to be made.
- Demonstration of ability to consider relevant factors applicable to Washi Co's choices

Scepticism

- Effective challenge of information and assumptions supplied and, techniques carried out to support any investment decision

Commercial acumen

- Effective use of examples and/or calculations from the scenario information and other practical considerations related to the context to illustrate points being made
- Recognition of external constraints and opportunities as necessary

	Marks
Maximum	10
Total	50

(a) Washi Co may want to invest in overseas projects for a number of reasons which result in competitive advantage for it, for example:

Investing overseas may give Washi Co access to new markets and/or enable it to develop a market for its products in locations where none existed before. Being involved in marketing

and selling products in overseas markets may also help it gain an understanding of the needs of customers, which it may not have had if it merely exported its products.

Investing overseas may give Washi Co easier and cheaper access to raw materials it needs. It would therefore make good strategic sense for it to undertake the overseas investment.

Investing in projects internationally may give Washi Co access to cheaper labour resources and/or access to expertise which may not be readily available in Japan. This could therefore lead to reduction in costs and give Washi Co an edge against its competitors.

Closer proximity to markets, raw materials and labour resources may enable Washi Co to reduce its costs. For example, transportation and other costs related to logistics may be reduced if products are manufactured close to the markets where they are sold.

Risk, such as economic risk resulting from long-term currency fluctuations, may be reduced where costs and revenues are matched and therefore naturally hedged.

Washi Co may increase its reputation because it is based in the country within which it trades leading to a competitive edge against its rivals.

International investments might reduce both the unsystematic and systematic risks for Washi Co if its shareholders only hold well diversified portfolios in domestic markets, but not internationally.

Note. Credit will be given for alternative valid areas of discussion.

(b) **Report to the board of directors (BoD), Washi Co**

Introduction

This report evaluates whether or not Washi Co should invest in the Airone project and the amount of debt finance required of JPY 3,408.6 million (Appendix 1) to fund the project. The evaluation considers both the financial and the non-financial factors.

Evaluation of the preferred hedge choice and debt finance required

The income from the sale of the European subsidiary is maximised when futures contracts are used. Therefore, these are chosen as Washi Co will borrow the least amount of debt finance as a result. However, compared to the forward contract, futures are marked-to-market daily and require a margin to be placed with the broker. This could affect Washi Co's liquidity position. The assumption has been made that basis reduces proportionally as the futures contracts approach expiry, but there is no guarantee that this will be the case. Therefore, basis risk still exists with futures contracts. Although forward contracts give a smaller return, there is no basis risk and margin requirements. However, they do contain a higher risk of default as they are not market traded. Options give the lowest return but would give Washi Co the flexibility of not exercising the option should the Euro strengthen against the Yen.

Although the EUR 80 million receipt from the sale of the subsidiary has been agreed, there may be a risk that the sale may fall through and/or the funds or some proportion of the funds are not received. Washi Co may need to assess and factor in this risk, however small it may be.

The amount of interest on deposit is based on the current short-dated Japanese treasury bills and the estimate of the borrowing requirement is computed from the predicted exchange rate between ARD and JPY in a year's time, based on the purchasing power parity. Both these estimates could be inaccurate if changes occur over the coming months. Although insufficient information is provided for a financial assessment, Washi Co should explore the possibility of converting the EUR into ARD immediately on receipt and keeping it in an ARD bank account until needed, instead of first converting EUR into JPY and then into ARD.

Using debt finance to make up any shortfall in the funding requirement may be appropriate for Washi Co given that it is an unlisted company and therefore access to other sources of funding may be limited. Nevertheless, Washi Co should assess how the extra borrowing would affect any restrictive covenants placed on it and the impact on its cost of capital. Since the amount seems to be small in the context of the project as a whole, this may not be a major problem.

Washi Co should also explore whether or not investing in the Airone project restricts its ability to fund other projects or affects its ability to continue normal business activity, especially if Washi Co is facing the possibility of hard capital rationing.

Evaluation of the Airone project

The net present value of the Airone project is estimated to be JPY (457) million (Appendix 2). Given the negative net present value, the initial recommendation would be to reject the project. However, given that the result is marginal, Washi Co should consider the following factors before rejecting the project.

At present, Washi Co does not have a significant presence in the part of the world where Airone is located. Taking on the project may make good strategic sense and provide a platform for Washi Co to establish its presence in that part of the world.

Furthermore, once Washi Co has established itself in Airone, it may be able to develop further opportunities and new projects. The value of these follow-on options has not been incorporated into the financial assessment. Washi Co should explore the possibility of such opportunities and their possible value.

The financial assessment ends abruptly at the end of the four years. No indication is given on what would happen to the project thereafter. It may be sold as a going concern or, if closed, its land and assets may be sold. The cash flows from these possible courses of action need to be incorporated into the assessment, and these could make the project worthwhile.

A number of assumptions and estimates would have been made in the financial assessment. For example, the rate of inflation used for future figures is the current rate and the tax rate used is the current rate, these may well change in the coming years. Therefore, it is best to undertake sensitivity analysis and produce a number of financial assessments before making any firm commitment to proceed with the project or deciding to reject it.

Conclusion and recommendation

The income from the sale of the European subsidiary is maximised when futures contracts are used, but Washi Co should weigh this against the benefits and drawbacks of all hedging instruments before making a final decision.

Although the project is currently giving a negative net present value, rejecting it at the outset is premature. A number of factors, discussed above, need to be considered and assessed before a final decision is made. Sensitivity analysis would be very helpful in this respect.

Finally, Washi Co should consider alternative uses for the funding which will be dedicated to the project. These alternative uses for the finance need to be considered before any decision is made, especially if Washi Co is facing the possibility of hard capital rationing.

Report compiled by:

Date

APPENDICES:

Appendix 1 (Part (c)(i)): Japanese Yen receivable from sale of European subsidiary under each hedging choice and the additional debt finance needed to fund the Airone project

Forward rate

Since it is a EUR receipt, the lock-in rate of JPY125.3 per EUR will be used.

Expected receipt from sale: EUR 80m × 125.3 = JPY 10,024m

Futures contracts

The futures contracts need to show a gain when the Euro depreciates against the Yen, therefore a short position is needed, using the seven-month contracts. It is assumed that basis will depreciate proportionally to the time expired.

Effective futures rate

Assume that basis reduces to zero at contract maturity in a linear fashion.

Opening basis with 7 months to end of future = 125.2 (future) − 129.2 (spot) = −4

Closing basis on completion of actual transaction with 1 month remaining for the future = −4 × 1/7 = −0.6

Effective futures rate = Opening future - closing basis = 125.2 − −0.6 = 125.2 + 0.6 = 125.8

Number of contacts sold = EUR 80,000,000/EUR 125,000 = 640 contracts

Expected receipt from sale: EUR 125,000 × 640 × 125.8 = JPY 10,064m

The outcome could also be calculated by converting the expected receipt **using the effective rate**. This would give EUR 80 million × 125.8 = JPY 10,064 million.

Options contracts

640 seven-month put options contracts will be purchased to protect against a depreciation of Euro.

If options are exercised:

EUR 125,000 × 640 × 126 = JPY 10,080m

Premium payable = JPY 3.8 × 125,000 × 640 = JPY 304m

Net income = JPY 10,080m − JPY 304m = JPY 9,776m

Conclusion

Futures contracts give the highest receipt and will, therefore, be used to hedge the expected Euro receipt.

Receipt invested

Invested for further six months till needed for the Airone project.

JPY 10,064m × (1 + (0.012/2)) = JPY 10,124.4m

Spot cross rates: 0.70 − 0.74 ARD per JPY 1

[92.7/132.4 = 0.70 and 95.6/129.2 = 0.74]

Expected ARD/JPY conversion spot rate in 12 months = 0.70 × 1.09/1.015 = 0.75

Additional debt finance needed to fund Airone project

Investment amount required = ARD 10,150m/0.75 = JPY 13,533m

Debt finance required = JPY 13,533m − JPY 10,124.4m = JPY 3,408.6m

Appendix 2 (Part (c)(ii): Airone project net present value

Project year	0	1	2	3	4
Cash flows in ARD (millions)	(10,150)	2,530	5,760	6,780	1,655
Future exchange rate ARD/JPY (W1)	0.75	0.81	0.87	0.93	1.00
In JPY million					
Project year	0	1	2	3	4
Cash flows	(13,533)	3,123	6,621	7,290	1,655
Lost contribution		(110)	(112)	(113)	(115)
Tax saving on lost contribution (30%)		33	34	34	35
Contribution: components (W2)		300	609	644	79
Tax on components cont. (30%)		(90)	(183)	(193)	(24)
Additional tax payable (15%) (W3)		(333)	(966)	(1,097)	(45)
Net cash flows	(13,533)	2,923	6,003	6,565	1,585
Present value (discounted at 12%)	(13,533)	2,610	4,784	4,674	1,008

Expected net present value is JPY (457)m

ANSWERS

Workings

1 **Predicted future exchange rate (ARD/JPY)**

Project year	0	1	2	3	4
	0.70 × 1.09/1.015	0.75 × 1.09/1.015	0.81 × 1.09/1.015	0.87 × 1.09/1.015	0.93 × 1.09/1.015
Exchange rate ARD/JPY	0.75	0.81	0.87	0.93	1.00

2 **Components contribution**

Project year	1	2	3	4
In JPY millions				
Components revenue (post inflation)	1,200	2,436	2,576	314
Contribution (25%)	300	609	644	79

3 **Additional tax payable**

Project year	1	2	3	4
Pre-tax profits (ARD m)	1,800	5,600	6,800	300
Additional tax payable at 15% (JPY m)	1,800/0.81 × 0.15 = 333	5,600/0.87 × 0.15 = 966	6,800/0.93 × 0.15 = 1,097	300/1.0 × 0.15 = 45

(c) It is difficult to conclude definitively whether a centralised treasury department is beneficial or not in all circumstances and for all companies. It depends on each company itself and the circumstances it faces. Washi Co should take this into account before making a final decision.

Benefits of a centralised treasury department

Having a centralised treasury management function avoids the need to have many bank accounts and may therefore reduce transactions costs and high bank charges.

Large cash deposits may give Washi Co access to a larger, diverse range of investment opportunities and it may be able to earn interest on a short-term basis, to which smaller cash deposits do not have access. On the other hand, if bulk borrowings are required, it may be possible for Washi Co to negotiate lower interest rates, which it would not be able to do on smaller borrowings.

A centralised treasury function can offer the opportunity for Washi Co to match income and expenditure and reduce the need for excessive risk management, and thereby reduce costs related to this.

A centralised treasury management department could hire experts, which smaller, diverse treasury management departments may not have access to.

A centralised treasury function may be better able to access what is beneficial for Washi Co as a whole, whereas local treasury functions may lead to dysfunctional behaviour.

Benefits of separate (decentralised) treasury departments

It could be argued that decentralised treasury departments are better able to match and judge the funding required with the need for asset purchases for investment purposes on a local level. Therefore, they may be able to respond quicker when opportunities arise and so could be more effective and efficient.

Individual departments within a subsidiary may have better relationships with the treasury departments of that subsidiary and are therefore able to present their case without lengthy bureaucratic delays.

Ultimately, the benefits may be implicit rather than explicit. Having decentralised treasury departments may make the subsidiary companies' senior management and directors more empowered and have greater autonomy. This in turn may increase their levels of motivation, as they are more in control of their own future, resulting in better decisions being made.

50 Opao

Marking guide	Marks	
(a) Explanation of portfolio restructuring and organisational restructuring	2	
Discussion of reason(s) for change in business focus	2	
		4
(b) (i) **(Appendix 1)**		
Equity value of Opao Co	1	
Tai Co, free cash flow to firm	2	
Estimate of value of Tai Co	1	
Estimate of equity value of Tai Co	1	
Combined company, free cash flows	2	
Value of combined company, Years 1 to 4	1	
Value of combined company, after Year 4	1	
Equity value of combined company	1	
		10
(ii) **(Appendix 2)**		
Cash offer, percentage gain, Tai Co	1	
Cash offer, percentage gain, Opao Co	2	
Share-for-share offer, share of additional value	1	
Share-for-share offer, Opao Co share value	1	
Share-for-share offer, total shares allocated to Tai Co	1	

Share-for-share offer, 2 Opao Co shares for 1 Tai Co share	1
Share-for-share offer, percentage gain, Tai Co	1
Share-for-share offer, percentage gain, Opao Co	1
Mixed offer, percentage gain, Tai Co	1
Mixed offer, percentage gain, Opao Co	2
	12

(iii) **(Report on proposed acquisition)**

Evaluation: Opao Co	4
Evaluation: Tai Co	4
Marks Available	8
Maximum	7

(c) Explanation of difference between an IPO and reverse takeover — 3

Discussion of using an IPO or reverse takeover to obtain a listing — 5

Marks Available — 8

Maximum — 7

Professional skills

Communication

- General report format and structure (use of headings/sub-headings and an introduction)
- Style, language and clarity (appropriate layout and tone of report response, presentation of calculations, appropriate use of the tools)
- Effectiveness of communication (answer is relevant, specific rather than general and focused to the requirement)
- Adherence to the details of the proposal in the scenario

Analysis and Evaluation

- Appropriate use of the data to determine suitable calculations to support the acquisition offer
- Appropriate use of the data to support discussion and draw appropriate conclusions
- Demonstration of reasoned judgement when considering key matters for Opao Co and Tai Co
- Demonstration of ability to consider relevant factors
- Identification of further analysis, which could be carried out to enable an appropriate recommendation to be made.
- Appraisal of information objectively

Scepticism

- Demonstration of ability to consider all relevant factors applicable to the decisions made

Commercial acumen

- Effective use of examples and/or calculations from the scenario information and other practical considerations related to the context to illustrate points being made
- Recognition of external constraints and opportunities as necessary
- Recommendations are practical and plausible in the context of Opao Co's situation

Maximum — 10

Total — 50

 BPP

(a) Portfolio restructuring involves the acquisition of companies, or disposals of assets, business units and/or subsidiary companies through divestments, demergers, spin-offs, MBOs and MBIs. Organisational restructuring involves changing the way a company is organised. This may involve changing the structure of divisions in a business, business processes and other changes such as corporate governance.

The aim of either type of restructuring is to increase the performance and value of the business.

Opao Co, in going from a conglomerate business to one focusing on just two business areas, can be seen as restructuring its portfolio, as businesses and assets that are not part of financial services and food manufacturing are disposed of, and businesses focusing on these areas are acquired. Financial markets may take the view that focusing on food manufacturing and financial services has enabled Opao Co's senior management to concentrate on areas in which they have expertise. Whereas other businesses in which the senior management are not experts are disposed of. This activity leads to the maximisation of business value.

Shareholders are interested in maximising returns from their investments, which companies achieve through maximizing business value, whilst minimising the risks inherent in their investment activity. Shareholders who are closely linked to a particular business do not hold diversified investment portfolios, and therefore benefit from diversification of risk undertaken by a company, investing in many different areas. On the other hand, institutional shareholders and other shareholders, who hold diversified portfolios, would not benefit from a company undertaking risk management through diversification by becoming a conglomerate. Instead, such companies would increase value by focusing on areas in which they have relative expertise, as Opao Co seems to do. So Opao Co's changing owner clientele has forced it to change its overall strategy. This strategy change was implemented through portfolio restructuring.

(b) **Report to the board of directors (BoD), Opao Co**

Introduction

This report provides an estimate of the additional value created if Opao Co were to acquire Tai Co, and the gain for each company's shareholders based on a cash offer, a share-for-share offer and a mixed offer. It evaluates the likely reaction of the two companies' shareholders to each payment method.

Summary of the estimates from the appendices

From Appendix 1

Opao Co equity value pre-acquisition: $5,000 million

Tai Co equity value pre-acquisition: $1,000 million

Combined company equity value post-acquisition: $6,720 million

From Appendix 2

Therefore, additional value based on synergy benefits is $720m or 12% ($720m/$6,000m)

Estimated percentage gain in value

	Opao Co	Tai Co
Cash offer	11.2%	15.8%
Share-for-share offer	6.4%	40.0%
Mixed offer	9.7%	23.4%

Likely reactions

Tai Co's shareholders are likely to consider all the offers made, because they all fall within the range of premiums paid in previous acquisitions of 15% to 40%. The cash offer is at the lower end of the range, the share-for-share offer at the top end of the range and the mixed offer in between. It is likely that Tai Co's shareholders will be more attracted to the share-for-share

offer as it maximises their return. However, this offer is reliant on the fact that the expected synergy benefits will be realised and Tai Co will probably need to analyse the likelihood of this. Cash payment, although much lower, gives a certainty of return. The mixed offer provides some of the certainty of a cash payment, but also offers a higher return compared to the cash offer. This return is roughly in the middle of the premium range. It may therefore prove to be the better option for Tai Co's shareholders.

Opao Co's shareholders benefit less from the acquisition compared to Tai Co's shareholders. In each case, they get less than the additional value created of 12%, with the cash payment offering the highest return of 11.2%, which is just below the 12% overall return. The share-for-share offer gives the least return at just over half (6.4%) of the overall return of 12%. Nevertheless, with this option, cash is retained within Opao Co and can be used for other value creating projects. Opao Co's shareholders may also prefer the mixed offer, because the return they are expecting to receive is between the cash and share-for-share offers. Also, less cash resources are used compared to the cash offer, and they still benefit from a significant proportion of the additional value created.

Conclusion

Based on the benefits accruing to both sets of shareholders, it is not possible to conclusively say that one method of acquisition payment would be acceptable to both sets of shareholders. However, both sets of shareholders may be persuaded that the mixed offer provides a reasonable compromise between the wholly cash and the wholly share-for-share prices. Given that synergy benefits are shared (even if not equally), both companies' share prices should increase if the acquisition proceeds, as long as the estimates when estimating the valuations are reasonably accurate.

Report compiled by:

Date

APPENDICES:

Appendix 1 (Part (c)(i)):

Equity value of Opao Co prior to acquisition

$2.50/share × 2,000m shares = $5,000m

Equity value of Tai Co prior to acquisition

Free cash flows to firm = $132.0m + $27.4m − $24.3m − ($132.0m × 0.2) = $108.7m

Company value = $108.7m × 1.03/(0.11 − 0.03) = $1,399.5m, say $1,400m

Equity value = $1,400m − $400m = $1,000m

Equity value of combined company post acquisition

All amounts in $ millions

Year	1	2	3	4
Sales revenue (5.02% growth, yrs 2 to 4)	7,351	7,720	8,108	8,515
Pre-tax profit (15.4% of sales revenue)	1,132	1,189	1,249	1,311
Less: Tax (20%)	(226)	(238)	(250)	(262)
Less: Additional investment ($0.31 per $1, yrs 2 to 4)	(109)	(114)	(120)	(126)
Free cash flows	797	837	879	923
Present value of free cash flows (10%)	724	691	660	630

Combined company value: years 1 to 4 = $2,705 million

Combined company value: after year 4 = 923 × 1.024/(0.1 − 0.024) × 1.1^{-4} = $8,494m

Total combined company value = $11,199 million

Equity value (60% × $11,199m) = $6,719.4m, say $6,720 million

Appendix 2 (Part (c)(ii): Percentage gains for Tai Co and Opao Co shareholders under each payment method

Estimate of additional value created from acquisition due to synergy benefits

$6,720m − ($5,000m + $1,000m) = $720m

Tai Co, value per share = $1,000m/263m shares = $3.80/share approx.

Cash offer

Tai Co shareholders, percentage gain

($4.40 − $3.80)/$3.80 = $0.60/$3.80 = 15.8%

Opao Co shareholders, percentage gain

Amount of additional value created going to Tai Co shareholders = $0.60 × 263m shares = $157.8m

Amount of additional value created going to Opao Co shareholders = $720m − $157.8m = $562.2m

As a percentage = ($562.2m/2,000m shares)/$2.50 = 11.2%

Share-for-share offer

Share of additional value to Tai Co shareholders = $720m × 0.555 = $399.6m

Share of additional value to Opao Co shareholders = $720m × 0.445 = $320.4m

Opao Co equity value after acquisition = $5,320.4 million

Opao Co, estimated share price after acquisition = $5,320.4m/2,000m shares = $2.66/share

Opao Co shares to be allocated to Tai Co shareholders = ($1,000m + $399.6m)/$2.66 = 526m shares approximately

Therefore, share-for-share offer will be 2 Opao Co shares for 1 Tai Co share (526/263 = 20)

Tai Co shareholders, percentage gain

($2.66 × 2 shares − $3.80 × 1 share)/($3.80 × 1 share) = 40%

Opao Co shareholders, percentage gain

($2.66 − $2.50)/$2.50 = 6.4%

Mixed offer

Tai Co shareholders, percentage gain

(($2.60 + $2.09) − $3.80)/$3.80 = $0.89/$3.80 = 23.4%

Opao Co shareholders, percentage gain

Amount of additional value going to Tai Co shareholders = $0.89 × 263m = $234.1m

Amount of additional value created going to Opao Co shareholders = $720m − $234.1m = $485.9m

As a percentage = ($485.9m/2,000m shares)/$2.50 = 9.7%

> **Tutorial note.** Credit would also be given for using the post-acquisition price provided in the question to analyse the impact on Opao Co's shareholders with the mixed offer.

(c) The initial public offering (IPO) is the conventional way to obtain a listing where a company issues and offers shares to the public. When doing this, the company will follow the normal procedures and processes required by the stock exchange regarding a new issue of shares and will comply with the regulatory requirements.

Undertaking a reverse takeover enables a company to obtain a listing without going through the IPO process. The BoD of Burgut Co would initially take control of a 'shell' listed company by buying some shares in that company and taking over as its BoD. The 'shell' listed company was probably a normal listed company previously, but is no longer trading. New equity shares in the listed company would then be exchanged for Burgut Co's shares, with the external appearance that the listed company has taken over Burgut Co. But in reality Burgut Co has now effectively got a listing, having taken control of the listed company

previously. Normally, the name of the original listed company would then be changed to Burgut Co.

Compared with an IPO, the main benefits of undertaking a reverse takeover are that it is cheaper, takes less time and ensures that Burgut Co will obtain a listing on a stock exchange. An IPO can cost between 3% and 5% of the capital being raised because it involves investment banks, lawyers, and other experts. A marketing campaign and issuing a prospectus are also needed to make the offering attractive and ensure shares to the public do get sold. A reverse takeover does not need any of these and therefore avoids the related costs. The IPO process can typically take one or two years to complete due to hiring the experts, the marketing process and the need to obtain a value for the shares. Additionally, the regulatory process and procedures of the stock exchange need to be complied with. With a reverse takeover, none of these are required and therefore the process is quicker. Finally, there is no guarantee that an IPO will be successful. In times of uncertainty, economic downturn or recession, it may not attract the attention of investors and a listing may not be obtained. With reverse takeover, because the transaction is an internal one, between two parties, it will happen and Burgut Co will be listed.

However, obtaining a listing through a reverse takeover can have issues attached to it. The listed 'shell' company may have potential liabilities which are not transparent at the outset, such as potential litigation action. A full due diligence of the listed company should be conducted before the reverse takeover process is started. The IPO process is probably better at helping provide the senior management of Burgut Co with knowledge of the stock exchange and its regulatory environment. The involvement of experts and the time senior management need to devote to the listing process will help in this regard. Due to the marketing effort involved with an IPO launch, it will probably have an investor following, which a reverse takeover would not. Therefore, a company which has gone through an IPO would probably find it easier to raise extra funds, whilst a company which has gone through a reverse takeover may find it more difficult to raise new funding.

Overall, neither option of obtaining a listing has a clear advantage over the other. The choice of listing method depends on the company undertaking the listing and the purpose for which it is doing so.

Note. Credit will be given for alternative valid areas of discussion.

51 Talam

Course Book references

Advanced investment appraisal and real options are covered in Chapters 2 and 4 respectively. Sustainability and ethical issues are covered in Chapter 1.

Top tips

It is important to take time to get to grips with what is being required with this question, and it is vital to allocate time to planning to make sure that the requirements are fully understood before you start writing. This is especially important with this question.

Easy marks

There are numerous easy marks to be picked up in the discussion parts (a) and (c) of this question. However, you will need to apply your knowledge to the scenario to score well and not simply repeat technical knowledge (see Examining Team comments below). Also, the first part of the calculations was a standard NPV and should have been, and was, handled well.

Examining team's comments

Surprisingly, part (a) was not done very well. Only a minority of candidates considered the full range of discursive points. Many answers simply stated the different kinds of real options, such as the option to expand, delay a decision or discontinue, and then went on to mention that real options were helpful in situations where there was flexibility in making the decisions. Very

---

few responses then progressed to discuss how this could be incorporated into investment decisions, and whether or not real options were helpful.

In part (b)(iii) some candidates did little in the way of an assessment and/or just listed the assumptions but did not discuss them.

In part (c) few responses considered the full range of strategic commercial interests which a company would consider.

Marking guide	Marks

(a) 1–2 marks per well-explained comment

5

5

(b) (i) (Appendix 1)

Sales revenue	2
Variable costs	2
Fixed costs	1
Training costs	2
Tax	2
Working capital	2
Uwa project NPV	1

12

(ii) (Appendix 2)

Jigu project underlying asset value	2
Honua Co Offer: exercise price	1
Honua Co Offer: underlying asset value	2
Honua Co Offer: other variables used in option calculation	1
Honua Co Offer: choose put value	1

7

(iii) Initial assessment of value of the Uwa project — 3

Up to 2 marks per well discussed assumption (max 3 marks if assumptions relating to real options are not discussed) — 6

Marks Available — 9

Maximum — 8

(c) Discussion of the issues — 5

Discussion of how the issues may be addressed — 5

Marks Available — 10

Maximum — 8

Professional skills

Communication

- General report format and structure (use of headings/sub-headings and an introduction)
- Style, language and clarity (appropriate layout and tone of report response, presentation of calculations, appropriate use of the tools)
- Effectiveness of communication (answer is relevant, specific rather than general and focused to the requirement)

Analysis and Evaluation

- Appropriate use of the data to determine suitable calculations to support the investment decision

- Appropriate use of the data to support discussion and draw appropriate conclusions
- Identification of further analysis, which could be carried out to enable an appropriate recommendation to be made.
- Demonstration of ability to consider relevant factors applicable to Talam Co's choices

Scepticism

- Effective challenge of information and assumptions supplied and, techniques carried out to support any investment decision

Commercial acumen

- Effective use of examples and/or calculations from the scenario information and other practical considerations related to the context to illustrate points being made in respect of options and sustainability/ethics
- Recognition of external constraints and opportunities as necessary

Maximum   <u>10</u>

Total $\underline{\underline{50}}$

(a) When making decisions following investment appraisals of projects, net present value assumes that a decision must be made immediately or not at all, and once made, it cannot be changed. Real options, on the other hand, recognise that many investment appraisal decisions have some flexibility.

For example, decisions may not have to be made immediately and can be delayed to assess the impact of any uncertainties or risks attached to the projects. Alternatively, once a decision on a project has been made, to change it, if circumstances surrounding the project change. Finally, to recognise the potential future opportunities, if the initial project is undertaken, like the Jigu Project.

Real options give managers choices when making decisions about whether or not to undertake projects, by estimating the value of this flexibility or choice. Real options take into account the time available before a decision on a project has to be made, as well as taking into account the risks and uncertainties attached to the project. It uses these factors to estimate an additional value which can be attributable to the project. Real options view risks and uncertainties as opportunities, where upside outcomes can be exploited, and a company has the option to disregard any downside impact.

By incorporating the value of any real options available into an investment appraisal decision, Talam Co will be able to assess the full value of a project.

(b) **Report to Talam Co Board**

Introduction

This report assesses whether or not the Uwa Project should be undertaken based on its value from an initial net present value (NPV) calculation, and then taking into account the options provided by the offer from Honua Co and the Jigu Project. As part of the assessment, a discussion of the assumptions and their impact on the assessment is provided.

Assessment

The value of the Uwa Project based on just the initial NPV is a small negative amount of $(6,000) approximately (Appendix 1). This would indicate that the project is not worth pursuing, although the result is very marginal. The offer from Honua Co, and the Jigu Project, using the real options method, gives an estimated value of $17.71m (Appendix 2), which is positive and substantial. This indicates that the Uwa Project should be undertaken.

Assumptions

The following assumptions have been made when calculating the values in Appendices 1 and 2.

(1) Since the Uwa Project is in a different industry to Talam Co's current activities, the project-specific, risk-adjusted cost of capital of 11% based on Honua Co's asset beta is used. It is assumed that Honua Co's asset beta would provide a good approximation of the business risk inherent in drone production.

(2) It is assumed that all the variables used to calculate the values of the projects in Appendices 1 and 2 are correct and accurate. Furthermore, it is assumed all the variables such as inflation rates, tax rates, interest rates and volatility figures remain as forecast through the period of each project. It is also assumed that the time periods related to the projects and the offer from Honua is accurate and/or reasonable.

(3) The Black-Scholes option pricing (BSOP) model is used to estimate the real option values of the Jigu Project and the Honua Co offer. The BSOP model was developed for financial products and not for physical products, on which real options are applied. The BSOP model assumes that a market exists to trade the underlying project or asset without restrictions, within frictionless financial and product markets.

(4) The BSOP model assumes that the volatility or risk of the underlying asset can be determined accurately and readily.

Whereas for traded financial assets this would most probably be reasonable, as there is likely to be sufficient historical data available to assess the underlying asset's volatility, this is probably not going to be the case for real options. For large, one-off projects, there would be little or no historical data available. Volatility in such situations would need to be estimated using simulation models, such as the Monte-Carlo simulation, with the need to ensure that the model is developed accurately and the data input used to generate outcomes reasonably reflects what is likely to happen in practice.

(5) The BSOP model assumes that the real option is a European-style option which can only be exercised on the date when the option expires. In some cases, it may make more strategic sense to exercise an option earlier. The real option is more representative of an American-style option which can be exercised before expiry. Therefore, the BSOP model may underestimate the true value of an option.

(6) Real options models assume that any contractual obligations involving future commitments made between parties will be binding and will be fulfilled. For example, it is assumed that Honua Co will fulfil its commitment to purchase the project from Talam Co at the start of the third year for $30 million and there is therefore no risk of non-fulfilment of that commitment.

(7) The BSOP model does not take account of behavioural anomalies which may be displayed by managers when making decisions.

Conclusion

The initial recommendation is that the Uwa Project should be undertaken when the offer from Honua Co and going ahead with the Jigu Project are included. Taken together, these result in a significant positive NPV. However, one or more of the above assumptions may not apply and therefore NPV value is not a 'correct' value. Instead, the appendices provide indicative value, which can be attached to the flexibility of a choice of possible future actions that are embedded with the Uwa Project and indicate that it should be undertaken.

Report compiled by:

Date

Note. Credit will be given for alternative valid discussion comments.

APPENDICES:

Appendix 1

(Part (b)(i)):

Net present value computation of the Uwa Project before incorporating the offer from Honua Co and the financial impact of the Jigu Project. All figures are in $000s.

Year	0	1	2	3	4
Sales revenue (W1)		5,160	24,883	49,840	38,405
Less:					
Variable costs (W2)		2,064	9,581	18,476	13,716
Fixed costs		2,700	2,970	3,267	3,594
Tax allowable depreciation (TAD) (W3)		5,250	5,250	5,250	12,250
Training costs		4,128	5,749	1,848	1,372
Cash flows before tax		(8,982)	1,333	20,999	7,473
Tax (W3)		1,796	(267)	(4,200)	(1,495)
Add back TAD (W3)		5,250	5,250	5,250	12,250
Working capital	(1,032)	(1,972)	(2,496)	1,144	4,356
Machinery purchase and sale	(35,000)				7,000
Net cash flows	(36,032)	(3,908)	3,820	23,193	29,584
Present value of cash flows (discounted at 11%)	(36,032)	(3,521)	3,100	16,959	19,488

Approximate NPV = $(6,000)

Tutorial note. The present value of the cash flows from time 1–4 can be calculated using the =NPV spreadsheet function. This is shown in the following spreadsheet extract:

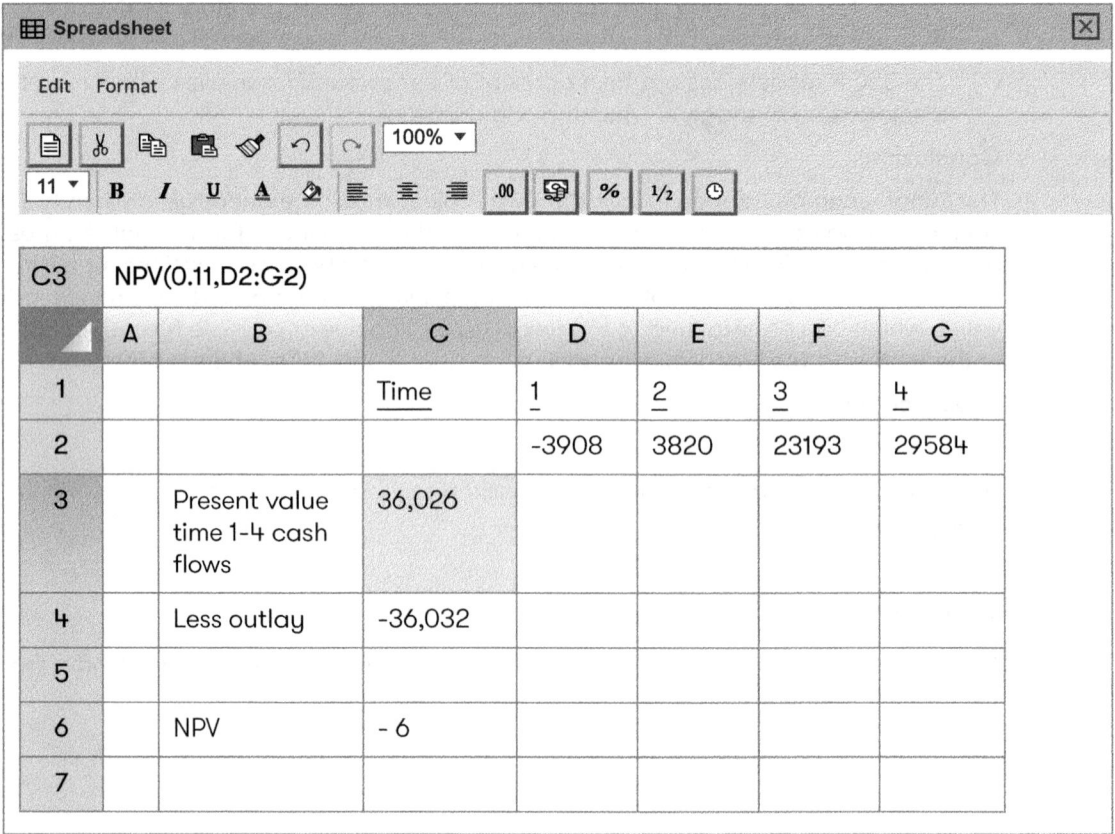

Spreadsheet							⊠
Edit Format							
C3	NPV(0.11,D2:G2)						
	A	B	C	D	E	F	G
1			Time	1	2	3	4
2				-3908	3820	23193	29584
3		Present value time 1-4 cash flows	36,026				
4		Less outlay	-36,032				
5							
6		NPV	- 6				
7							

 BPP

Note that the NPV function assumes that the first cash flow is in one year's time, so you then have to subtract the time 0 cash outflows to obtain the project's NPV.

Workings

1 Sales revenue

Year	1	2	3	4
Units produced and sold	4,300	19,200	35,600	25,400
Selling price ($) (inflated at 8%)	1,200	1,296	1,400	1,512
Sales revenue ($000s)	5,160	24,883	49,840	38,405

2 Variable costs

Year	1	2	3	4
Units produced and sold	4,300	19,200	35,600	25,400
Variable costs per unit ($) (inflated at 4%)	480	499	519	540
Total variable costs ($000s)	2,064	9,581	18,476	13,716

3 Tax

Year	1	2	3	4
Straight-line $35,000 × 0.15 = $5,250				
Written down value (WDV) start year	35,000	29,750	24,500	19,250
WDV end year (written down to scrap value)	29,750	24,500	19,250	(7,000)
Balancing allowance				12,250

Appendix 2

(Part (b)(ii):

Jigu Project:

Asset value

Asset value of Jigu Project of $46.1m is estimated as present value of future cash flows related to the project:

$70m × 1.11^{-4}$, where $70m = $60m + $10m.

Honua Co offer, initial variables used:

Asset value (P$_a$) = $16,959,000 + $19,488,000 = $36,447,000 (cash flows foregone)

Exercise price (P$_e$) = $30m

Exercise date (t) = 2 years

Risk-free rate (r) = 2.30%

Volatility (s) = 30%

BPP

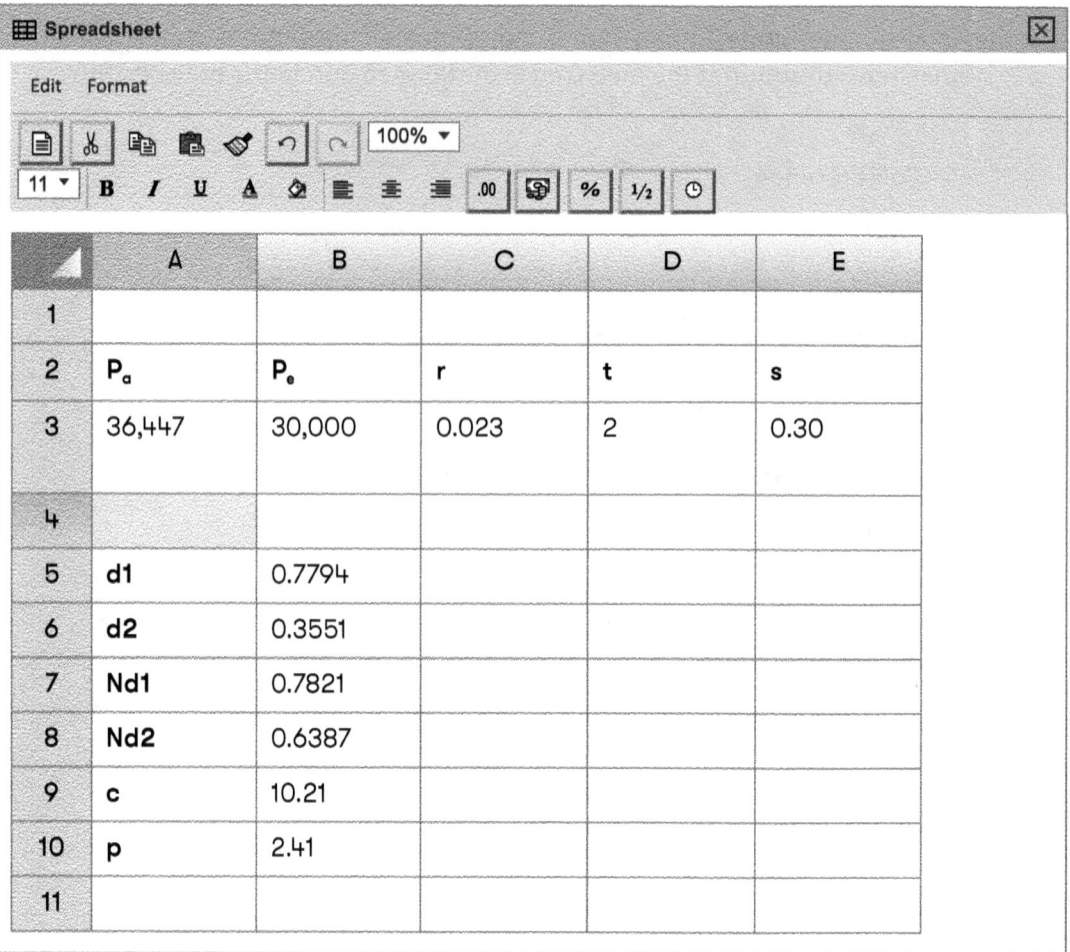

	A	B	C	D	E
1					
2	P_a	P_e	r	t	s
3	36,447	30,000	0.023	2	0.30
4					
5	d1	0.7794			
6	d2	0.3551			
7	Nd1	0.7821			
8	Nd2	0.6387			
9	c	10.21			
10	p	2.41			
11					

Value of put = $2.41m

Estimated total value arising from the two real options

Value of Jigu Project: $15.3m

Value of Honua Co's offer: $2.41m

Estimated total value from the two real options: $2.41m + $15.3m = $17.71m

(c) The overarching issue is that of conflict between the need to satisfy shareholders and the financial markets, and Talam Co's stated aims of bringing affordable environmentally friendly products to market and maintaining high ethical standards. This overarching issue can be broken down into smaller related issues.

Producing profitable products will presumably result in positive NPV projects, thus ensuring a continued strong share price performance. This should satisfy the markets and shareholders. However, if the products cannot be sold at a reasonable selling price because some farmers are not able to afford the higher prices, then this may compromise Talam Co's aim of bringing environmentally friendly products to market and making them affordable.

A possible solution is to lower production costs by shifting manufacturing to locations where such costs are lower. Talam Co's BoD thus considered the move to Dunia to lower production costs. This presumably would allow Talam Co to reduce prices and make the drones more affordable, but at the same time ensure that the projects result in positive NPVs. However, the issue here is that supplier companies in Dunia, whom Talam Co trades with, use young teenage children as part of their workforce. This may impact negatively on Talam Co's stated aim of maintaining high ethical standards. In fact, Talam Co may need to rethink its links with companies it trades with in Dunia entirely. Otherwise there is a real risk that Talam Co could suffer from long-term loss of reputation, and this may cause substantial and sustained financial damage to the company.

 BPP

Talam Co may decide that maintaining its share price and its reputation should take the highest priority and therefore it may reach a decision that the best way to address the issue(s) is to not try to reduce costs, and to withdraw from Dunia completely. But this would prevent many agriculturalists from taking advantage of the biodegradable drones. Therefore, Talam Co may want to explore alternative ways to meet all the aims.

Talam Co could consider moving to another location, if this was feasible. It is not known from the narrative whether or not viable alternatives are available, but Talam Co would need to ensure that possible alternative locations would have the infrastructure to produce the components at the same or lower costs. Talam Co may also want to consider the softer issues; for example, it will want a good working relationship and network in the new locations, which it has with the companies in Dunia. These may need to be developed and would take time, and probably incur additional costs.

For these reasons, Talam Co may decide to explore the existing production facilities in Dunia further. It is possible that the supplier companies are not exploiting the young teenage children but are supporting their education and their families in a positive way. Stopping the relationship may jeopardise this support. Talam Co would need to investigate the working conditions of the children and the manner in which they are rewarded and supported. It may want to consult the guardians of the young teenage children and see if there are other feasible solutions. For example, could the guardians be employed instead of the young teenage children or are they already engaged in alternative employment?

After all factors are considered, Talam Co may conclude that the best way to achieve all its aims is to continue in Dunia and also have the production of drone components located there. If this is the case and young teenage children continue to be employed there, then Talam Co would need a sustained public relations campaign to defend its position and demonstrate how it ensures that the teenage children have not been exploited, but are gainfully employed and receiving a good education to help them progress in life.

 Videos can be viewed by accessing your ebook version on VitalSource.

Note. Credit will be given for alternative valid discussion comments.

52 Okan

(a) **(Appendix 1)**

Forward market hedge	1	
Money markets hedge	2	
Minimum borrowing required	1	
Maximum		

    (i)   **(Appendix 2a)**

Sales revenue	1	
Production costs	1	
Component costs	3	
Tax	2	
Working capital	2	
Project Alpha base case NPV	1	
Project Beta base case NPV	1	
		4

    (ii)   **(Appendix 2b)**

Issue costs	1	
Annual tax shield	1	
Annual subsidy	1	
Present value of tax shield and subsidy	1	
Project Alpha adjusted present value	1	
Project Beta adjusted present value	1	
(Appendix 2c)		
Project Alpha duration	2	
		19

    (iii)   Discussion of the assumptions made   4

               Evaluation and justification   3

               Maximum   7

(b) Explanation of economic risk faced by Okan Co   3

      Discussion of management of economic risk   2

      Marks Available   5

      Maximum   4

(c) Discussion of management of each of the four risk categories (Maximum 2 marks per risk category discussed. Maximum of 5 marks if not all categories discussed)

      Maximum   6

Professional skills

Communication

- General report format and structure (use of headings/sub-headings and an introduction)
- Style, language and clarity (appropriate layout and tone of report response, presentation of calculations, appropriate use of the tools)
- Effectiveness of communication (answer is relevant, specific rather than general and focused to the requirement)
- Adherence to the details of the proposal in the scenario

Analysis and Evaluation

- Appropriate use of the data to determine suitable calculations to support the investment and financing decisions
- Appropriate use of the data to support discussion and draw appropriate conclusions
- Demonstration of reasoned judgement when considering key matters
- Demonstration of ability to consider relevant factors
- Identification of further analysis, which could be carried out to enable an appropriate recommendation to be made.
- Appraisal of information objectively to make a recommendation

Scepticism

- Effective challenge and critical assessment of the information and assumptions provided in relation to APV
- Demonstration of ability to consider all relevant factors applicable to the decisions made by Okan Co

Commercial acumen

- Effective use of examples and/or calculations from the scenario information and other practical considerations related to the context to illustrate points being made
- Recognition of external constraints and opportunities as necessary
- Recommendations are practical and plausible in the context of Okan Co's situation

	<u>10</u>
Total	<u><u>50</u></u>

(a) **Report to the board of directors (BoD), Okan Co**

Introduction

This report evaluates, and provides a justification and decision on, whether Okan Co should pursue Project Alpha or Project Beta, based on the important factors identified by the company, namely the returns generated by the projects, the projects' risks and non-financial aspects.

Evaluation

Financing

Using forward markets to hedge the expected receipt in six months' time results in the higher receipt equalling Y$25,462,000 approximately. If the money markets hedge is used the receipt is Y$25,234,936 (Appendix 1).

Using forward markets to hedge the expected receipt would therefore minimise the amount of debt borrowing. However, the amount receivable from the money markets hedge is based on the annual bank investment rate available to Okan Co of 2.4%.

Okan Co may be able to use the funds borrowed to generate a higher return than the bank investment, and therefore using money markets to undertake the hedge may be financially advisable. Okan Co should investigate any opportunities for higher income but based on the current results, the forward market hedge is recommended to minimise the amount of debt finance needed.

Minimum amount of debt borrowing required is Y$24,538,000 approximately.

Project returns and risk

	Project Alpha	Project Beta
Base case net present value (NPV) (in six months' time)	Y$5,272,000 (Appendix 2a)	Y$5,100,000 (Appendix 2a)
Adjusted present value (APV)	Y$6,897,218 (Appendix 2b)	Y$6,725,218 (Appendix 2b)
Project duration	3.04 years (Appendix 2c)	2.43 years (given)

Project Alpha's and Project Beta's base case NPVs and APVs are similar to each other, with Project Alpha expected to yield a small amount in excess to the yield expected from Project Beta. However, Project Beta's project duration is significantly lower.

This is because a higher proportion of Project Beta's cash flows come earlier in the project's life, compared to Project Alpha.

There is more certainty to earlier cash flows and this is reflected in the lower duration for Project Beta. Project Beta's risk is lower than Project Alpha.

In estimating the base case NPV and APV for Project Alpha, it is assumed that the cash flows are known with reasonable certainty and the inflation rates will not change during the life of the project. It is also assumed that the future exchange rate between the Y$ and the £ will change in accordance with the purchasing power parity differential. Furthermore, it is assumed that the prices and costs related to Project Alpha will increase in line with inflation during the six months before the project starts. For Project Alpha, it is assumed that the initial working capital requirement is funded by the company and not from the funds raised from the subsidised loan, similar to the assumption made for Project Beta. However, for both projects, Okan Co needs to consider, and take account of, the opportunity costs related to this.

In terms of the Project Alpha's discount rate, it is assumed that the given discount rate accurately reflects the business risk of the project.

Whilst this level of detail is not provided for Project Beta, it is assumed that similar assumptions will have been made for Project Beta as well. In the case of both projects, Okan Co should assess the accuracy or reasonableness of the assumptions, and if necessary, conduct sensitivity analysis to observe how much the projects' values change if input variables are altered.

 Notwithstanding the assumptions and caveats made above, it would appear that Project Beta would be preferable to Project Alpha, given that it has a similar APV but a significantly lower risk.

Nevertheless, there may be good strategic reasons why Okan Co may select Project Alpha over Project Beta. For example, these reasons may include providing access to new markets, enabling Okan Co to erect barriers to entry against competitors or looking at follow-on opportunities as possible real options.

Justification

Due to the substantially lower risk (as measured by the project duration) and similar APV, it is recommended that Project Beta be selected by Okan Co. It is also recommended that forward markets are used to hedge the income expected in six months' time to part fund the project. This would minimise the debt borrowing needed.

However, this decision is predicated on the fact that the implications of the assumptions and the wider strategic reasons discussed above have been carefully considered by Okan Co.

Report compiled by:

Date

Note. Credit will be given for alternative and valid evaluative comments.

Appendices:

Appendix 1 (Part (b)(i)):

Expected receipt in six months' time, using forward markets:

  €10,000,000 × 2.5462 = Y\$25,462,000

Expected receipt in six months' time, using money markets:

  €10,000,000/(1 + 0.022/2) = €9,891,197

  €9,891,197 × 2.5210 = Y\$24,935,708

Y\$24,935,708 × (1 + 0.024/2) = Y\$25,234,936

Minimum amount of debt borrowing Okan Co would require:

Y\$50,000,000 – Y\$25,462,000 = Y\$24,538,000

Appendix 2a (Part (b)(ii)): Projects Alpha and Beta, base case net present value, in six months' time

Base case net present value before considering financing side effects. All figures are in Y\$000s.

Year	0	1	2	3	4
Sales revenue (W1)		17,325	34,304	62,890	33,821
Less:					
Production costs (W2)		(6,365)	(11,584)	(24,095)	(9,546)
Component costs (W3)		(3,708)	(5,670)	(11,877)	(4,578)
Cash flows before tax		7,252	17,050	26,918	19,697
Tax (W4)		1,050	(1,535)	(3,977)	(1,721)
Working capital	(1,733)	(2,547)	(4,288)	4,360	4,208
Plant purchase and sale	(50,000)				10,000
Net cash flows	(51,733)	5,755	11,227	27,301	32,184
Base case present value of cash flows (discounted at 10%)	(51,733)	5,232	9,279	20,512	21,982

Approximate, base case net present value (NPV) of Project Alpha = Y\$5,272,000.

Base case net present value (NPV) of Project Beta = Y\$(8,450,000 + 19,360,000 + 22,340,000 + 4,950,000) – Y\$50,000,000 = Y\$ 5,100,000

Workings

1 *Sales revenue*

Year	1	2	3	4
Pre-inflated revenues (Y\$ 000s)	15,750	28,350	47,250	23,100
Inflation	× 1.1^1	× 1.1^2	× 1.1^3	× 1.1^4
Post-inflated revenues (Y\$ 000s)	17,325	34,304	62,890	33,821

2 Production costs

Year	1	2	3	4
Pre-inflated production costs (Y$ 000s)	6,120	10,710	21,420	8,160
Inflation	× 1.04^1	× 1.04^2	× 1.04^3	× 1.04^4
Post-inflated production costs (Y$ 000s)	6,365	11,584	24,095	9,546

Component costs are not inflated, but future exchange rates are based on purchasing power parity (PPP).

3 Component cost

Year	1	2	3	4
PPP multiplier	3.03 × 1.04/1.02	3.09 × 1.04/1.02	3.15 × 1.04/1.02	3.21 × 1.04/1.02
Forecast Y$ per £1	3.09	3.15	3.21	3.27
Component cost (£)	1,200	1,800	3,700	1,400
Component cost (Y$)	3,708	5,670	11,877	4,578

4 Tax

Year	1	2	3	4
Cash flows before tax	7,252	17,050	26,918	19,697
Tax allowable depreciation	(12,500)	(9,375)	(7,031)	(11,094)
Taxable cash flows	(5,248)	7,675	19,887	8,603
Tax payable (20%)	(1,050)	1,535	3,977	1,721

Appendix 2b (Part (b)(ii)): Projects Alpha and Beta, adjusted present value (APV), in six months' time

Issue costs = 3/97 × Y$24,538,000 = Y$758,907

Annual tax shield = 2.1% × Y$24,538,000 × 20% = Y$103,060

Annual interest saved on subsidised loan = 2.9% × Y$24,538,000 × 80% = Y$569,282

Annuity factor, Years 1 to 4 at 5% interest = 3.546

Present value of the tax shield and loan subsidy benefit = (Y$103,060 + Y$569,282) × 3.546 = Y$2,384,125

Project Alpha APV	Y$
Base case NPV of Project Alpha (Appendix 2a)	5,272,000
Issue costs	(758,907)
Present value of the tax shield and loan subsidy benefit	2,384,125
APV	6,897,218

Project Beta APV	Y$
Base case NPV of Project Beta (Appendix 2a)	5,100,000
Issue costs	(758,907)
Present value of the tax shield and loan subsidy benefit	2,384,125
APV	6,725,218

Appendix 2c (Part (b)(ii)): Project Alpha's duration based on its base case present values of cash flows Project Alpha

Year	1	2	3	4
PVs × years	5,232,000 × 1 = 5,232,000	9,279,000 × 2 = 18,558,000	20,512,000 × 3 = 61,536,000	21,982,000 × 4 = 87,928,000

Total PVs × time = 173,254,000 approximately

Total PVs = 57,005,000 approximately

Project Alpha duration = 173,254,000/57,005,000 = 3.04 years

(b) **Explanation of why the subsidiary company may be exposed to economic risk and how it may be managed**

Companies face economic exposure when their competitive position is affected due to macroeconomic factors such as changes in currency rates, political stability, or changes in the regulatory environment. Long-term economic exposure or economic shocks can cause a permanent shift in the purchasing power and other parity conditions. Normally, companies face economic exposure when they trade internationally. However, even companies which do not trade internationally nor rely on inputs sourced internationally may still face economic exposure.

In the case of Okan Co's subsidiary company, economic risk may have occurred because interest rates have been kept at a high level, causing the original parity conditions to break down. High interest rates will be attractive to international investors, as they can get higher returns and higher rates may lead to the Y$ becoming stronger relative to other currencies. This in turn would allow international competitors to produce goods more cheaply than the subsidiary company and thereby enhance their competitive position relative to the subsidiary company.

Managing economic exposure is difficult due to its long-lasting nature and because it can be difficult to identify. Financial instruments, such as derivatives, and money markets cannot normally be used to manage such risks. Okan Co's subsidiary company can try tactics such as borrowing in international or eurocurrency markets, sourcing input products from overseas suppliers and ultimately shifting production facilities overseas. None of these are easy or cheap and can expose the company to new types of risks. Okan Co would also need to assess that any action it takes to manage economic risk fits into its overall risk management strategy.

(c) **How each category or risk may be managed**

Risks which fall into the severe and frequent category need immediate attention, as they could threaten the company's survival or derail its long-term strategy. The aim here would be to reduce the severity of the risks and the frequency with which they occur quickly. It may mean avoiding certain actions or abandoning certain projects, even if they could be profitable in the long term. Where a company has a real option and does not need to take action which will result in high frequency and high severity of risk, it may prefer to wait and see what happens.

Where the frequency of risks occurring is high but their impact is not severe, action needs to be taken so that such risks do not become severe in the future. For example, the company could put systems into place to detect these risks early and plans to deal with them if they do occur. Where the same kind of risks occur often, the company may decide to have set processes for dealing with them. For example, where there is a loss of relatively unskilled staff, the company may decide to replace staff quickly with casual workers, but also have appropriate training facilities in place.

If there are risks which are severe but only happen occasionally or infrequently, the company should try to insure against these. Contingency plans could also be put into place to mitigate the severity. For example, if the consequences of IT failure are high when a business decides to move to a new system, it could put appropriate contingencies into place. These may

BPP

include secondary backup IT systems or initially trialling the new system on a few business units before undertaking a complete role out.

Risks which are neither severe, nor frequent, should be monitored and kept under review, but no significant action should be taken. It is possible that any significant action would incur costs which would likely be higher than the benefits derived from eliminating such risks. Monitoring such risks will ensure that should they move out of this category into the more severe/frequent categories, the company can start to take appropriate action.

Note. Credit will be given for alternative and valid explanatory and discussion comments.

53 Westparley

Course Book references

Business valuations are covered in Chapters 8, 9 and 10.

Easy marks

There are numerous easy marks to be picked up in parts (b)(i) and (b)(ii) of this question.

Examining team's comments

In part (a), a significant number of candidates ignored the behavioural aspect and restricted their discussion to purely rational factors underpinning corporate valuations, often at great length. A more careful reading of the requirement and scenario, both of which emphasised the behavioural aspect, would have avoided this problem.

In part (b)(iv) some candidates wasted significant amounts of time, listing each of the variables in turn and commenting on their accuracy or the assumption that they would remain constant without discussing the validity or reliability of these assumptions in more detail. Such an approach scored very few marks.

A substantial minority of candidates did not address the requirement for a report format and hence failed to earn some relatively easy marks. Too many reports ignored the need for a conclusion which restricted the number of professional marks that could be awarded. A small number of candidates wasted significant amounts of time writing lengthy introductory paragraphs that added very little to the report.

Marking guide		Marks
(a) 1–2 marks per relevant point (examples may include asking price, opportunity to purchase and information available is positive, herd instinct, following fashion and confirmation bias)		
Maximum		5
(b) (i) Share of pre-tax profit	1	
After-tax profit	1	
Proceeds from sell-off	1	
Comparison with free cash flow valuation	1	
		4
(ii) Westparley Co asset beta	1	
Combined company asset beta	1	
Combined company equity beta	1	
Combined company cost of equity	1	
Combined company cost of capital	1	
		5

		Marks	
(iii)	Sales revenue	1	
	Profit before interest and tax	1	
	Tax	1	
	Additional capital investment	1	
	PV of free cash flows years 1–4	1	
	PV of free cash flows year 5 onwards	1	
	Present value of synergies	2	
	Premium payable	1	
	Value attributable to Westparley Co's shareholders	1	
			10
(iv)	Strategic value	4	
	Financial value	3	
	Estimations made	4	
	Assumptions made	4	
	Marks Available	15	
	Maximum		11

(c) 1–2 marks per relevant point (examples may include available security, available tax relief, shareholder attitude to debt, industry norms)

5

Professional skills

Communication

- General report format and structure (use of headings/sub-headings and an introduction)
- Style, language and clarity (appropriate layout and tone of report response, presentation of calculations, appropriate use of the tools)
- Effectiveness of communication (answer is relevant, specific rather than general and focused to the requirement)
- Adherence to the details of the proposal in the scenario

Analysis and Evaluation

- Appropriate use of the data to determine suitable calculations
- Appropriate use of the data to support discussion and draw appropriate conclusions
- Demonstration of reasoned judgement when considering key matters for Westparley Co
- Demonstration of ability to consider relevant factors applicable to Westparley Co's situation
- Identification of further analysis, which could be carried out to enable an appropriate recommendation to be made.
- Appraisal of information objectively to make a recommendation

Scepticism

- Effective challenge and critical assessment of the information and assumptions provided
- Demonstration of ability to consider all relevant factors applicable to the decisions made

Commercial acumen

- Effective use of examples and/or calculations from the scenario information and other practical considerations related to the context to illustrate points being made
- Recognition of external constraints and opportunities as necessary
- Recommendations are practical and plausible in the context of Westparley Co's situation

| Maximum | 10 |
| **Total** | 50 |

(a) **Individual business**

A number of behavioural factors, to do with the individual company as well as the sector as a whole, may lead to Matravers Tech being valued higher than appears to be warranted by rational analysis of its future prospects. One possible factor is the asking price, even if it is not a fair one, may provide a reference point which significantly influences the purchaser's valuation of the business.

The fact that Matravers Tech is available for purchase may help raise its price. Purchasers may see this as a rare opportunity to buy an attractive business in this retail sector. This will be made more likely if investors have loss aversion bias, a desire to buy Matravers Tech now because otherwise the opportunity will be lost.

Matravers Tech being offered for sale will mean that information about the company, showing it in a positive light, will be available for purchasers. This could result in availability bias, investors taking particular note of this information because they can readily obtain it, rather than other information which may be more difficult or costly to find.

Sector

There are a number of possible behavioural reasons why share prices in this sector appear generally higher than rational analysis indicates. One is the herd instinct, investing in the sector because other investors have also been buying shares, not wishing to make judgements independently of other investors.

The herd instinct may be generated by previous share price movements. Investors may believe once prices start rising in the sector, they will continue to do so indefinitely.

Following fashion may also be a factor. Fund managers who wish to give the impression that they are actively managing their portfolio by making regular changes to it, may have a preference for companies which appear up to date and are currently popular. This may be linked to an expectation that sales of technologically advanced goods are likely to generate high returns.

There is also confirmation bias, the idea that investors will pay attention to evidence which confirms their views that the sector is a good one in which to invest, and ignore evidence which contradicts their beliefs. In the past, technology companies have been valued using methods which support the beliefs of investors that they are of high value, rather than traditional methods, such as cash flow analysis, which suggest a lower business value is more realistic.

(b) **Report to the board of directors, Westparley Co**

This report evaluates whether the acquisition of Matravers Co would be beneficial to Westparley Co's shareholders by estimating the future value generated by Matravers Co (ie Matravers Home currently), the proceeds from selling Matravers Tech and the additional value created from synergies immediately after the companies are combined.

Strategic fit

The strategic case for taking over the business appears to be strongest for the out-of-town stores and the online business. The acquisition would provide an additional out-of-town presence for Westparley Co. Better usage in the out-of-town stores could generate higher returns. Having the food and home businesses on the same site could generate some cross-sales between the two. Possibly combining the two companies' online presence and investing further could mean Matravers Home benefiting from the factors which have driven strong performance by Westparley Co.

Taking over the city centre stores, even the successful ones, seems to have less strategic logic, however. Westparley Co would be taking on a high cost burden. The success of the food business in city centres is doubtful, as food shops sited there will be less convenient for customers who do not live in the city centres, and Westparley Co has marketed itself as being easily accessible for customers. There is, perhaps, wider incompatibility between the two businesses. The food business is characterised by quick shopping for often a limited number of items, whereas purchases in the home business, particularly of larger items, are likely to take longer and site convenience be less of an issue.

Financial aspects

Based on the predictions for future cash flows and required premiums from Matravers Co's shareholders, the acquisition would add value to Westparley Co's shareholders, if, and only if, the excess value on selling Matravers Tech and the synergies are both largely achieved. Together they add up to $2,400m ($558m + $1,842m) compared with total added value of $1,897m. There are questions about the estimates for these figures and also the estimates for the future free cash flows of the current Matravers Home business.

Synergies

Most of the additional value is due to synergies and it is difficult to see how the synergies are calculated. There is likely to be scope for some administrative savings. However, operational cost synergies appear less obvious as the two companies are operating in different retail sectors. Any synergy figures will also have to take account of costs in achieving synergies, such as store closure costs, and also commitments such as leases which may be a burden for some time. Synergies may also not be achieved because of lack of co-operation by staff or problems integrating the two businesses.

Current Matravers Home business

The suggested increase in cash flows appears doubtful for a number of reasons. If stores being closed are making positive cash flow contributions, these will have to be replaced. Whether they can be is doubtful given the problems in this part of the retail sector. It may be a more profitable use of store space to have an area for food sales, but the food sales generated in Matravers Co's shops may take business from Westparley Co's existing shops. Similarly, increased online sales may be at the expense of sales in stores.

Sale of Matravers Tech

There is no indication of how interested buyers will be in the business. The industry price-earnings (P/E) ratio used may be an average which does not reflect Matravers Tech's circumstances. It would be better to find a P/E ratio for a proxy company with similar financial and business risk. As Matravers Tech would not be listed, this would suggest a discount to the P/E ratio should be applied. Since also Westparley Co has an estimate of future free cash flow, potential buyers may be able to come up with their own estimates and base the price they are prepared to pay on their estimates.

Other assumptions

One important assumption is the 15% premium expected to be required by Matravers Co's shareholders. Other assumptions made in the calculations include operating profit margin and tax rates remaining constant and cash flows being assumed to increase to perpetuity. Incremental capital investment is assumed to be accurate. It is assumed that the cost of debt will remain unchanged and that the asset beta, cost of equity and cost of debt can be determined accurately. Given all the assumptions, Westparley Co should carry out sensitivity analysis using different assumptions and obtaining a range of values.

Conclusion

On the assumptions made, the acquisition appears to add financial value for the shareholders of Westparley Co. However, the figures are subject to a significant number of uncertainties and the strategic logic for buying the whole Matravers business appears unclear. On balance, Westparley Co may want to consider a more limited acquisition of just the out-of-town stores if these are available, as their acquisition appears to make better strategic sense.

Report compiled by:

Date

Appendix 1 Estimate of additional value created from sell-off of Matravers Tech (b)(i)

Share of pre-tax profit = 20% × $1,950m = $390m

After-tax profit = $390m × (1 – 0.28) = $281m

Proceeds from sell-off based on P/E ratio = $281m × 18 = $5,058m

Excess value from sell-off = $5,058m – $4,500m = $558m

Appendix 2 Estimate of combined company cost of capital (b)(ii)

Matravers Co asset beta = 0.75

Westparley Co asset beta

Market value of debt = 1.05 × $26,000m = $27,300m

Market value of equity = 4,000 million × $8.50 = $34,000m

Asset beta = 1.02 × (34,000)/(34,000 + (27,300 × 0.72)) = 0.65

Combined company, asset beta

Market value of Matravers Co equity = $12,500m

Asset beta = ((0.75 × 12,500) + (0.65 × 34,000))/(12,500 + 34,000) = 0.68

Equity beta = 0.68 ((34,000 + (27,300 × 0.72))/34,000) = 1.07

Combined company cost of equity = 3.5% + (1.07 × 8%) = 12.1%

Combined company cost of capital = ((34,000 × 12.1%) + (27,300 × 9.8% × 0.72))/(34,000 + 27,300) = 9.9%, say 10%

Appendix 3 Estimate of the value created for Westparley Co's shareholders (b)(iii)

Cash flows, years 1 to 4

Year	1	2	3	4
	$m	$m	$m	$m
Sales revenue	43,260	44,558	45,895	47,272
Profit before interest and tax	2,596	2,673	2,754	2,836
Tax	(727)	(748)	(771)	(794)
Additional capital investment	(630)	(649)	(669)	(689)
Free cash flows	1,239	1,276	1,314	1,353
Discount factor	0.909	0.826	0.751	0.683
Present value of free cash flows	1,126	1,054	987	924

Present value years 1 to 4 = $4,091m

Present value year 5 onwards (($1,353m × 1.02)/(0.1 – 0.02)) × 1.10^{-4} = $11,781m

Total present value = $4,091m + $11,781m = $15,872m

 BPP

Synergies

Year	1	2	3
	$m	$m	$m
Free cash flows	700	750	780
Discount factor	0.909	0.826	0.751
Present value of cash flows	636	620	586

Present value of synergies = $1,842m

Amount payable for Matravers Co's shares = $12,500m × 1.15 = $14,375m

Value attributable to Matravers Co's investors = $14,375m + $6,500m = $20,875m

Value attributable to Westparley Co shareholders = present value of cash flows + proceeds from sell-off + value of synergies − value to Matravers Co's investors

= $15,872m + $5,058m + $1,842m − $20,875m = $1,897m

(c) **Directors' preferences**

Directors may be concerned about too high a burden of payment to finance providers, in terms of cost or ultimately repayment of debt. They may not wish to commit the company to conditions imposed by finance providers.

By contrast, they may be concerned about how a change in the shareholder base as a result of a share issue may impact upon their own position. Directors may also be concerned about the impression given by their choice of finance. It may be seen as a sign of a lack of confidence by directors that Westparley Co can sustain its current share price.

Costs and cash flows

Gearing decisions may not just be determined by their own preferences but by external conditions or constraints. Choosing more debt could lower the overall cost of capital, due to lower cost and tax relief, making investments such as Matravers Co appear more profitable.

Against that, higher levels of debt mean increased finance cost commitments, even though Westparley Co may need further cash for investment in stores. This may be an important concern if interest rates are high.

Availability

The availability of finance may also be a significant issue, particularly if an acquisition has to be completed quickly. An equity issue may take time to arrange and require shareholder approval. Sufficient debt finance may be difficult to obtain if lenders feel that Westparley Co already has significant commitments to debt finance providers.

The timescale over which finance is available may be significant. Westparley Co may seek longer-term finance if existing debt finance is due to be repaid soon or if significant cash is needed for short-term investment, not just in Matravers Co's stores, but also in Westparley Co's existing stores.

Industry norms

Westparley Co's directors may be concerned about keeping the level of gearing at or below the industry average, because of finance providers becoming worried if gearing exceeds industry levels. Keeping debt as a significant element in overall finance may act as a deterrent to acquirers becoming interested in making a bid for Westparley Co. Because of the highly competitive nature of retailing and the high fixed cost base, cash flows are likely to be volatile. This will add to concerns over taking on extra debt finance.

54 Chakula

Marking guide		Marks
(a) Shareholders	3	
Other stakeholders	3	
Other comments	2	
Maximum		5
(b) 3 marks for discussing each of the two propositions	6	
		6
(c) (i) **(Appendices 1 and 2)**		
Kawa Co, cost of capital	1	
Sales revenue years 1 to 4	1	
PBIT years 1 to 4	1	
Taxation years 1 to 4	1	
Additional asset investment years 1 to 4	1	
Corporate value	2	
Value per share	1	
		8
(ii) **(Appendix 3)**		
Lahla Co, current equity value	1	
Kawa Co, estimate of PE ratio	1	
Combined company, current equity value	1	
Estimate of additional value	1	
Cash offer: gain (both groups of shareholders)	2	
Share offer: gain (both groups of shareholders)	3	
Financing implications	3	
		12
(iii) **Report**		
Evaluation of financial and other factors *(evaluation report could include, for example, financial returns from demerger and each form of consideration, exit strategies, concerns about becoming minority shareholders, but also concerns for majority shareholders on the impact minority shareholders may have, assumptions made and whether the value created from the share-for-share exchange is realistic)*	7	
Impact on the capital structure	3	
Marks Available	10	

Maximum	$\underline{9}$

Professional skills marks

Communication

- General report format and structure (use of headings/sub-headings and an introduction)
- Style, language and clarity (appropriate layout and tone of report response, presentation of calculations, appropriate use of the tools)
- Effectiveness of communication (answer is relevant, specific rather than general and focused to the requirement)

Analysis and Evaluation

- Appropriate use of the data to determine suitable calculations
- Appropriate use of the data to support discussion and draw appropriate conclusions
- Demonstration of reasoned judgement when considering key matters for Lahla Co
- Demonstration of ability to consider relevant factors applicable to each company's situation

Scepticism

- Effective challenge of forecast information supplied and assumptions to support key facts and/or decisions

Commercial acumen

- Effective use of examples and/or calculations from the scenario information and other practical considerations related to the context to illustrate points being made
- Recognition of external constraints and opportunities as necessary

Maximum	$\underline{10}$
Total	$\underline{\underline{50}}$

(a) The key reason for a regulatory framework to exist in merger and acquisition (M&A) activity is to ensure that the interests of stakeholders are protected, and where the natural market forces may not be sufficient on their own to ensure that this happens. The regulatory framework aims to ensure a well-functioning market for corporate control.

With respect to shareholders, as a major stakeholder group, the regulatory framework aims to establish that shareholders of the target company are not affected negatively by ensuring that:

(1) minority shareholders' rights are protected;

(2) the target company's management cannot block a M&A where it is in commercial and economic interest of shareholders; and,

(3) sufficient time is made available for a proposal to be properly scrutinised. The regulatory framework also aims to ensure that sufficient information is provided about the proposed M&A for all investor groups to evaluate the proposed deal properly.

With respect to other stakeholders, the aim of the regulatory framework is to ensure that there is not a substantial lessening of competition after the M&A has taken place. This will protect the choice that consumers, suppliers and employees have in engaging with a range of organisations in that business sector, and within a properly functioning economic market.

(b) The two theoretical propositions are based on the opinion that a company's capital structure does matter to the value of the company. The first proposition posits that since debt is cheaper than equity and there is a 'tax shield' attached to debt finance, it is better for a company to be financed by as much debt as possible. This is the view presented by the Modigliani and Miller with taxes model. Since interest is paid before a company pays corporation tax, but dividends are not, a company does not have to pay taxes on profits used

to pay interest. This is referred to as a tax shield. The presence of a tax shield results in the cost of capital reducing as the proportion of debt financing increases.

The second proposition builds on this by arguing that although debt carries with it the advantage of a tax shield, at high levels of gearing this position no longer holds true. Here financial risk increases significantly and the company experiences increasing levels of financial distress, resulting in the cost of equity increasing significantly. This overrides the benefits gained from the tax shield. As a result, the cost of capital increases. At very high levels of gearing, even the cost of debt starts to increase significantly. Hence, there is a trade-off between the benefits of the tax shield and the costs related to financial distress, such that the cost of capital reduces initially but then rises, meaning that there is an optimal, minimum cost of capital where corporate value is maximised.

(c) **REPORT TO THE BOARD OF DIRECTORS (BoD), LAHLA CO**

This report evaluates and discusses the financial and other factors that both Lahla Co's and Kawa Co's shareholders would consider prior to agreeing to the acquisition. It also evaluates and discusses the impact of the acquisition on Lahla Co's capital structure under the two payment methods.

Factors to consider

Demerger (Appendix 2)	Additional value created for Kawa Co's shareholders 18.3%	
Acquisition, cash payment (Appendix 3)	Additional value created for Kawa Co's shareholders 10.0%	Additional value created for Lahla Co's shareholders 22.0%
Acquisition, share-for-share exchange (Appendix 3)	Additional value created for Kawa Co's shareholders 26.7%	Additional value created for Lahla Co's shareholders 14.0%

The initial evaluation would indicate that the demerger is the better option for Kawa Co's shareholders, compared to the acquisition, if the acquisition is paid for by cash. However, the share-for-share exchange gives a higher return compared to the demerger and therefore on purely financial grounds this is the best option for Kawa Co's shareholders. Although Lahla Co's shareholders lose some additional value derived from the acquisition if the share-for-share option is chosen, they would probably still be in favour of the acquisition because the company's value will increase and so will the value of their shares.

However, the following additional factors also need to be considered in the evaluation:

The value estimates are based on predicted variables, both for the demerger valuation and for the acquisition valuations. It is likely that there will be changes to the actual variables, and it is recommended that Lahla Co undertake sensitivity analysis and assess the results of this before making the final acquisition decision.

Kawa Co's shareholders probably have three main areas they would want considered further with respect to the acquisition with the share-for-share exchange.

Firstly, they would become part of a larger company with interests both in hotels and in coffee shops and they would own just under 36% (667m share / 1,867m shares) of the share capital of the new combined company. However, they would be minority shareholders. As such, they may feel that they do not have sufficient influence in the major decisions the company makes.

Therefore, Kawa Co's shareholders may be of the opinion that operating as a stand-alone demerged independent company may give them a better opportunity to shape the company's strategy. On the other hand, they may equally decide that they would need to be part of a large company to be able to compete effectively against Buni Co.

Secondly, Kawa Co's shareholders cannot be certain whether the 26.7% additional value is realistic or not. This may be especially pertinent because Lahla Co is an unlisted company

and therefore may keep proprietary/strategic information private, limiting the ability for external parties to undertake a full and effective evaluation.

Thirdly, because Lahla Co is an unlisted company, Kawa Co's shareholders may be concerned about how they would be able to exit the company, if they want to. For instance, if their investment portfolios become imbalanced when the companies are combined, they may need to sell some shares to rebalance it. Lahla Co should consider the possibility of undertaking a partial listing in order to make the deal more palatable for Kawa Co's shareholders.

In addition to ensuring that the acquisition is financially beneficial for them, Lahla Co's shareholders' main concern would be that Kawa Co's shareholders will own a significant portion of the combined company (just under 36%). This could mean that the new shareholders would have a significant influence on the way the company is run and its strategic direction, which may be different to what Lahla Co's current shareholders want.

Capital structure changes

Capital Structure	Equity %	Debt %
Original: Lahla Co	60.0%	40.0%
Cash payment: Combined company (Appendix 3)	46.9%	53.1%
Share-for-share exchange: Combined company (Appendix 3)	68.0%	32.0%

The cash payment option means that the proportion of market value of debt increases significantly and is higher than the market value of equity. This would probably increase the costs related to financial distress and future borrowing costs would increase as a result.

On the other hand, the share-for-share exchange, increases the proportion of equity compared to debt financing. This may reduce financial distress costs, but also reduce Lahla Co's ability to benefit from the tax shields.

On the face of it, it would appear that Lahla Co would find it difficult to raise the funds needed through just debt financing, although the BoD could explore this option further. Equity finance through a partial listing may be a necessary option which Lahla Co will need to explore as well, although this may require Lahla Co to disclose private information to the markets.

> **Tutorial note.** *Additional consideration which could be made*
>
> If the cash payment to Kawa Co's shareholders is increased to $0.71/share, to bring it in line with the value obtained from the demerger, and the funding is sought from debt financing, then the debt percentage compared to total firm value will increase to 53.8% (as shown below):
>
> $0.71 × 2,000m shares = $1,420m.
>
> Market value of equity: $2,933.7m, 46.2%
>
> Market value of debt = ($1,601.7m + $1,420m + $400m) = $3,421.7m, 53.8%]

Conclusion

The share-for-share exchange gives the highest return for Kawa Co's shareholders and also makes a good return for Lahla Co's shareholders. The impact on capital structure from this method is a higher percentage of equity and therefore scope to raise more finance through debt if required.

However, concerns that Lahla Co is unlisted and complications arising from this, might make the cash payment method the preferred one for Kawa Co shareholders. The current cash offer is less than the value generated from the demerger and therefore unlikely to be accepted. Therefore, a cash offer to match the benefit from the demerger would need to be made. The initial cash offer and a higher revised cash offer would have a significant impact on Lahla Co's capital structure in terms of increased debt. Therefore, it is recommended that

Lahla Co should consider equity finance through a partial listing. This would also enable Kawa Co's shareholders to trade their shares and thereby make the deal look better for them.

Report compiled by:

Date

Note. Credit will be given for alternative and valid discursive comments.

APPENDICES:

Appendix 1: Estimate of Kawa Co cost of capital (Part (c)(i))

Kawa Co, cost of equity = 13.51%

Kawa Co, post tax cost of debt = 3.52%

Kawa Co, cost of capital =

(13.51% × $1,200m + 3.52% × $400m) / ($1,200m + $400m) = 11.01%, say 11%

Appendix 2: Estimate of Kawa Co equity value if demerger is undertaken (Part (c)(i))

Current sales revenue attributable to Kawa Co = 20% × $4,500m = $900m

Per year, sales revenue growth rate = 6%

Profit before interest and tax (PBIT) = 21%

Tax rate = 20%

Additional asset investment = $0.25/$1

Cost of capital (Appendix 1) = 11%

Per year, free cash flow growth rate after first four years = 2.5%

Cash flows, years 1 to 4 ($m)

Year	1	2	3	4
Sales revenue	954.0	1,011.2	1,071.9	1,136.2
PBIT	200.3	212.4	225.1	238.6
Tax	40.1	42.5	45.0	47.7
Additional asset investment	13.5	14.3	15.2	16.1
Free cashflows	146.7	155.6	164.9	174.8
Present value of free cashflows (11%)	132.2	126.3	120.6	115.1

Corporate value, years 1 to 4: $494.2m

Corporate value, year 5 onwards:

($174.8m × 1.025 / (0.11 − 0.025)) × 1.11^{-4} = $1,388.5m

Total corporate value: $1,882.7m

Value attributable to equity: 75% × $1,882.8m = $1,412.0m

Per share value = $1,412.0m / 2,000 million shares = $0.71 per share

Kawa Co original value = $1,200m / 2,000 million shares = $0.60 per share

Gain = ($0.71 − $0.60) / $0.60 = 18.3%, if Kawa Co gets demerged

Appendix 3: Sale of Kawa Co to Lahla Co (Part (c)(ii)

Lahla Co PE ratio = 90% × 15.61 = 14.05

Lahla Co equity value = 14.05 × $171.0m = $2,402.6m

Kawa Co equity value = $1,200m

Kawa Co estimate of PE ratio = $1,200m / $117.1m = 10.25

Profits after tax of combined company = $171.0m + $117.1m + $62m = $350.1m

Average PE ratio of combined company = (14.05 + 10.25) / 2 = 12.15

Estimate of equity value of combined company = $350.1m × 12.15 = $4,253.7m

Additional equity value created from combining the two companies =

$4,253.7m − ($1,200m + $2,402.6m) = $651.1m

Cash offer

Chakula Co's shareholders will receive $0.66 per share from sale of Kawa Co, or

$0.66 × 2,000 million shares = $1,320m in total

Kawa Co original value per share = $0.60

Gain = $0.06 / $0.60 = 10%

Lahla Co's total shareholders' value is estimated at = $4,253.7m − $1,320m = $2,933.7m, or $2,933.7m / 1,200 million shares = $2.44 share

Lahla Co estimate of original value = $2,402.6m / 1,200 million = $2 per share

Gain = $0.44 / $2 = 22%

Share-for-share Offer

Additional shares issued by Lahla Co= 2,000 million / 3 = 667 million

Equity value of combined company = $4,253.7m

Per share value = $4,253.7m / 1,867 million shares = $2.28

Gain to Kawa Co's shareholders

$2.28 − ($0.60 × 3) = $0.48

$0.48 / $1.80 = 26.7%

Gain to Lahla Co's shareholders from combining the company

($2.28 − $2) / $2 = 14.0%

Lahla Co: Impact on capital structure from the two payment methods

Lahla Co, before acquisition

Market value of equity: $2,402.6m (see above)

Market value of debt = 40/60 × $2,402.6m = $1,601.7m

Combined company, cash payment through debt borrowing

Market value of equity: $2,933.7m or 46.9%

Market value of debt = $1,601.7m + $1,320m + $400m* = $3,321.7m or 53.1%

Note. $2,933.7m + $3,321.7m = $6,255.4m; 46.9% = ($2,933.7m / $6,255.4m) × 100% and 53.1% = ($3,321.7m / $6,255.4m) × 100%

Combined company, share-for-share exchange

Market value of equity: $4,253.7m or 68.0%

Market value of debt: $1,601.7m + $400m* = $2,001.7m or 32.0%

Note. $4,253.7m + $2,001.7m = $6,255.4m; 68.0%% = ($4,253.7m / $6,255.4m) × 100% and 32.0% = ($2,001.7m / $6,255.4m) × 100%

*In the above cases when the two companies are combined, it is assumed that Lahla Co will continue to service loan notes B or cancel them by paying them off through an equivalent borrowing.

55 Zhichi

Marking guide | **Marks**

(a) 2–3 marks per policy failure

(For example, fixed discount rate: need project specific discount rate to take account of project risk, otherwise low-risk projects can be rejected and high-risk projects might be accepted. Using equity finance. Not observed in practice. Instead pecking order of internal, then debt, then equity sources of finance. Due to information asymmetry, signalling and tax advantage of debt)

Maximum	6

(b) (i) **(Appendix 1)**

Liyu Co, asset beta	1
Sanwenyu Co, equity beta	2
Sanwenyu Co, asset beta	1
Asset beta attributable to business risk of motor scooter manufacturing	1
Cost of equity/discount rate	1
	6

(ii) **(Appendix 2)**

Sales revenue	1
Costs	2
Tax allowable depreciation	1
Tax and timing	2
Working capital invested/released: years 0 and 1	1
Working capital invested/released: years 2–4	1
Cash flows and all-equity financed NPV	1
	9

(iii) **(Appendix 3)**

Issue costs	1
Present value of tax shield	2
Present value of loan subsidy benefit and cost	3

BPP

Adjusted present value	1	
	—	
		7

(iv) **Report**

Evaluation	2	
Discussion of assumptions	4	

(For example, rival companies' asset betas represent business risk, all-equity financed project from asset beta, variable known with certainty and will not change, interest rates will not change, debt capacity is sufficient, cost of debt represents appropriate discount rate)

Discussion of appropriateness of APV

(For example, limitations of cost of capital re changes in business and financial risk, APV takes account of both risks, APV separates out areas where value is derived from, APV takes into account different levels of risk and required return, but APV does not consider financial distress, tax exhaustion or agency issues)	4	
Maximum		8

(c) Up to 2 marks per relevant point

(Maximum 1 mark if only either debt finance or asset securitisation discussed)

(For example, similarity of interest and capital repayment, conventional debt imposes restrictive covenants, security provided on assets, securitisation's security provided by pooling income, creating assets of this pool and creating different risk levels of securities, securitisation is expensive and not all income is pooled, but it gives more flexibility and does not impact debt capacity so it provides flexibility to the company)

Maximum	4

Professional skills marks

Communication

- General report format and structure (use of headings/sub-headings and an introduction)
- Style, language and clarity (appropriate layout and tone of report response, presentation of calculations, appropriate use of the tools)
- Effectiveness of communication (answer is relevant, specific rather than general and focused to the requirement)

Analysis and Evaluation

- Appropriate use of the data to determine suitable calculations
- Appropriate use of the data to support discussion and draw appropriate conclusions
- Demonstration of reasoned judgement when considering key matters
- Demonstration of ability to consider relevant factors applicable to each company's situation

Scepticism

- Effective challenge of forecast information supplied and assumptions to support key facts and/or decisions

Commercial acumen

- Effective use of examples and/or calculations from the scenario information and other practical considerations related to the context to illustrate points being made
- Recognition of external constraints and opportunities as necessary

Maximum	10
Total	50

ANSWERS

(a) **Fixed discount rate**

A fixed discount rate to appraise new investment projects, which Zhichi Co uses, can be ineffective when a decision is being made whether or not to undertake the project. This is because projects will have different risks attached to them and therefore the returns required from these projects would differ. This could result in low-risk projects being rejected which could have added to Zhichi Co's corporate value, and high-risk projects being accepted which could reduce corporate value. Zhichi Co should instead estimate an appropriate discount (or hurdle) rate which accounts for the risk of the project. In this way, the company can assess the value of projects more accurately and thereby add to its corporate value.

New project finance

Observations of how companies raise new finance for projects show that they typically prefer internal funds before accessing external markets. If new finance is raised through external markets, then companies prefer debt to equity. Debt finance may have advantages such as tax benefits and controlling the actions of managers. Investors have less information compared to managers and directors in a company, and use companies' actions on raising finance as a signal. Issuing debt finance can also be seen as a sign of confidence that the company can fulfil its interest payment commitments, and can therefore be considered to be stable and less risky by investors. Information asymmetry between investors and a company's managers sends signals that the company is only raising equity finance when share prices have peaked or shares are over-valued. This causes share prices to fall following announcements that a company is raising new equity finance. It is likely that Zhichi Co has experienced this. Therefore, Zhichi Co should finance through a long-term strategy of internal finance, followed by debt issues and then equity issues as a last resort.

(b) **Report to the board of directors (BoD), Zhichi Co**

Introduction

This report evaluates whether or not the new motor scooter project should be undertaken. It discusses the assumptions made in estimating the value of the project and whether the adjusted present value (APV) method, which is used to estimate the value of the project, is more appropriate than the conventional net present value (NPV) method.

Evaluation

Although the NPV based on an all-equity financed discount rate is negative $0.9m (Appendix 2), when the impact of the financing side effects is taken into account, the APV is positive $4.9m (Appendix 3). On that basis, the project should be accepted if the project is funded using the subsidised loan, but not necessarily without it.

However, both values are marginal and a small change in the variables (see below) could easily mean that the project is no longer viable. In addition to this, it should be noted that a large proportion of the present value of cash inflows from the project, $51.5m (Appendix 2), occur in the fourth year of the project. Projections further into the future tend to be more uncertain.

Zhichi Co may benefit from undertaking sensitivity and scenario analysis to assess the impact of changes in the input variables instead relying solely on the results of appendices 2 and 3.

Assumptions

The assumptions made in each of the three appendices are discussed in turn.

In Appendix 1, Liyu Co's and Sanwenyu Co's asset betas are calculated by degearing each company's equity beta to eliminate the company specific financial risk. The asset betas of both companies represent just the business risk element. It is assumed that Sanwenyu Co's asset beta represents the business risk of the wind farm business and Liyu Co's asset beta represents the business risks of both the wind farm and the environmentally friendly motor scooter businesses. From these it is assumed that the asset beta, representing a suitable proxy for the business risk of environmentally friendly motor scooters, can be computed and used to estimate the all-equity financed discount rate.

In Appendix 2, it is assumed that all input variables are known with certainty or reasonable accuracy. It is also assumed that these variables, and the factors which determine the variables, do not change in the future. Uncertainty increases as cash flows are predicted further into the future, and the majority of the positive cash flows for the new project occur in year 4.

In Appendix 3, it is assumed that the interest rates of the subsidised loan and the corporate tax rates remain unchanged for the period of the project. The normal borrowing rate of 6% is used to determine the present value of the financing side effects, although the risk-free rate could also be used and this will give a higher APV. The debt capacity of Zhichi Co could change as a result of undertaking the project.

In the computations, debt beta is assumed to be zero, although in practice, corporate debt is not free of default risk.

Adjusted present value or net present value

With NPV, future cash flows are discounted using Zhichi Co's average cost of capital (discount rate) since a positive NPV will ensure that the minimum return requirement of all Zhichi Co's investors is met. However, the discount rate often does not take into account (i) the changing business risk profile (since the project is a diversification) nor (ii) the changing financial risk profile (since the new project will be entirely financed by debt). With the new project, both these risks are changing and the APV method takes both changes into account.

Furthermore, the APV method will provide significantly more information about the sources of value and also about the different levels of risk applicable to different cash flows. When using the average cost of capital as the discount rate to generate the NPV, it is not possible to tell where the project's value is generated from, whether the value is from undertaking the project or from the changing capital structure. It also assumes that all cash flows have the same risk profile and should therefore be discounted at the same rate. The APV method considers the risk elements separately and considers the cash flow impact of each. It also assigns a suitable cost of capital which is relevant to each cash flow (for example, the ungeared cost of equity to base case NPV and the cost of debt to the financing side effects).

APV does not normally take into account costs of financial distress, possibility of tax exhaustion and agency costs related to financing using debt. However, in Zhichi Co's case, none of these is likely to be an issue because it has only used equity financing previously and therefore the impact of the above is likely to be minimal.

For these reasons, APV is the more appropriate method to use to evaluate Zhichi Co's new project.

Conclusion

After considering the assumptions made in the calculations and discussing why the APV is the more appropriate method, the recommendation is that the new project is undertaken because it generates a positive APV. However, sensitivity and scenario analysis should be undertaken because of the assumptions made and because the decision to accept is marginal.

Report compiled by:

Date

Appendices:

Appendix 1: (Part (b)(i)):

Liyu Co

Asset beta = 1.2 × $172m / ($172m + $48.26m × 0.8) = 0.98

This reflects the risk of motor scooters and wind farm equipment.

Sanwenyu Co

Re-arranging the CAPM equation to find the equity beta for a wind farm equipment manufacturer:

Equity beta = (15.4% − 4.8%) / 8% = 1.325

Asset beta = 1.325 × 0.8 / (0.8 + 0.2 × 0.8) = 1.1 approx.

 **BPP**

It is assumed that this asset beta of 1.1 reflects the business risk attributable to manufacturing equipment for wind farms.

Asset beta attributable to business risk of manufacturing motor scooters

0.98 Liyu asset beta = 0.6 × [asset beta, motor scooters] + 0.4 × 1.1

Asset beta = (0.98 − 0.44) / 0.6 = 0.9

It is assumed that this asset beta of 0.9 reflects the business risk attributable to manufacturing motor scooters.

Base case discount rate = 4.8% + 8% × 0.9 = 12%

Appendix 2: (Part (b)(ii)): Motor scooter project, all-equity financed

Year	0	1	2	3	4	5
	$m	$m	$m	$m	$m	$m
Sales revenue		10.0	40.0	48.0	57.6	
Costs		(12.0)	(32.0)	(19.2)	(23.0)	
TAD (W1)		(10.5)	(8.9)	(7.6)	(23.0)	
Taxable profit		(12.5)	(0.9)	21.2	11.6	
Taxation (W1)			2.5	0.2	(4.2)	(2.3)
Add back TAD		10.5	8.9	7.6	23.0	
Investment	(70.0)				42.0	
Working capital (W2)	(10.0)	4.0	(1.2)	(1.4)	8.6	
Cash flows	(80.0)	2.0	9.3	27.6	81.0	(2.3)
Discounted at 12% (Appendix 1)	1	0.893	0.797	0.712	0.636	0.567
Present value of cash flows	(80.0)	1.8	7.4	19.7	51.5	(1.3)

All-equity financed net present value is approximately $(0.9)m.

Workings

1 **Taxation**

Year	TAD (Tax allowable depreciation) ($m)	Balance ($m)
	Investment	70.0
1	TAD (15%)	(10.5)
		59.5
2	TAD (15%)	(8.9)
		50.6
3	TAD (15%)	(7.6)
		43.0
4	Balancing allowance	(23.0)
		20.0

2 Working capital

Year	0	1	2	3	4
	$m	$m	$m	$m	$m
Required		10	6.0	7.2	8.6
Invested/(released)	10	(4)	1.2	1.4	(8.6)

Appendix 3: (Part (b)(iii): Motor scooter project, adjusted present value

Issue costs

Outlay excluding issue costs = $80m.

So, outlay including issue costs = $80m / 0.97 = $82.5m

Issue costs are $82.5m − $80m = $2.5m

[Alternatively: 3/97 × $80m = $2.5m]

Tax shield

Annual tax saved on interest payable = $80m × 0.03 × 0.2 = $0.5m

This is received over 4 years from time 2–5 and is discounted at 6% (the normal cost of debt) which reflects the risk associated with these cash flows.

Present value of interest payable = $0.5m × (4.212 − 0.943) = $1.6m

Subsidised loan benefit and cost

Present value of subsidised loan benefit received from time periods 1–4

= $80m × 0.03 × 3.465 = $8.3m

Present value of tax shield lost, in time periods 2–5

= $80m × 0.03 × 0.2 × (4.212 − 0.943) = $1.6m

Note. Although 6% is used as the discount rate to calculate the present value of the tax shield and subsidised loan benefits, the risk-free rate of 4.8%, could be used as an alternative.

Adjusted present value

$(0.9)m (from Appendix 2) + $(2.5)m + $1.6m + $8.3m + $(1.6)m = $4.9m

(c) There are many similarities between debt finance and asset securitisation, and Zhichi Co would face similar obligations which it would need to fulfil. Conventional debt finance would raise an initial borrowed amount, on which Zhichi Co will pay interest and make capital repayments as required. When using asset securitisation, the borrowing aspect for Zhichi Co is similar in terms of repayments of interest and capital. The main differences are the bases on which the borrowing takes place.

In order to mitigate or take account of risk, lenders of conventional debt would probably impose restrictive covenants on Zhichi Co and require a charge to be placed on specific assets or a pool of Zhichi Co's assets. It is likely that Zhichi Co would find it easier to raise conventional debt either through approaching specific lenders or issuing debt securities like bonds. It is also likely that raising conventional debt would be cheaper. This is because markets for conventional debt are more readily available.

Asset securitisation provides a means to capitalise future income flows into an asset, in this case Zhichi Co's rental income, and then use this asset as a means of borrowing funds. Converting the future rental income into an asset would likely be undertaken through the use of a special purpose vehicle (SPV). Zhichi Co would then manage the rent collection and use the rental income stream to pay the interest and capital over a specified time period.

It is likely that obtaining funding through asset securitisation can be expensive due to search costs, management costs, legal fees and continuing administrative costs. Additionally, it is unlikely that Zhichi Co would be able to borrow funds equivalent to the full value of the rental income, and if rental incomes fall, Zhichi Co would need to fund the interest and capital from alternative sources. This could open up Zhichi Co to lower credit ratings and increased risk of financial distress.

 BPP

The advantages of asset securitisation are that Zhichi Co's debt capacity is maintained for future projects, and it provides a way for Zhichi Co of utilising income from non-core business areas.

Ultimately, the choice to Zhichi Co between debt finance and asset securitisation is that the latter probably provides greater flexibility and opportunity, but at a higher cost.

Note. Credit will be given for alternative and valid comments and approaches, where relevant, for all parts of the question.

56 Prysor Co

Course Book reference

NPV analysis, including duration and sensitivity analysis, is covered in Chapter 3. International investment appraisal is covered in Chapter 5. Ethics is covered in Chapter 1.

Top Tips

The NPV calculations were mainly done well. However, in discussing the assumptions the ACCA examining team comments noted here that 'too many candidates submitted a list of basic assumptions with nothing added and very often copied straight from the question. What was required was an identification of the **key assumptions** and a **discussion of why** they were important'.

In the section on sensitivity and duration many candidates confused duration with payback.

Nearly all candidates missed a small issue relating to tax paid in the overseas country in the sensitivity calculations. This is understandable and reinforces the key message that **you don't need to get every calculation right to get a strong pass mark at AFM.**

In the final part of the question, the ACCA examiner comments noted that 'answers that were awarded high marks included points ... such as reputation, impact on shareholders and other stakeholders, additional costs and the impact on the investment appraisal. The poorer answers repeated the facts given in the scenario without adding any further discussion or focussed too heavily on just one area like reputation'.

Marking guide — Marks

	Marks
(a) World Trade Organisation role	3
Free trade area and impact on Prysor Co's subsidiary	2
Marks Available	5
Maximum	4
(b) (i) Component costs	3
Taxation	2
Cash flows in M$	1
Additional tax on foreign profits	2
Additional contribution	2
Tax on additional contribution	1
Lost contribution	1
Tax on lost contribution	1
Net present value	1
	14

(ii) Up to 2 marks per assumption discussed

Maximum 1 mark if no discussion (points can include variable cost forecasts, tax liability, need for working capital, cost of capital, purchasing power

 BPP

parity, realisable value after four years and other scenarios)		
Maximum		4
(iii) Duration	2	
Sensitivity of sales revenue		
Post-tax sales revenue	1	
Post-tax sales revenue in M$	1	
Additional tax in Marteg	2	
Present value of after-tax sales revenue	1	
% reduction in selling price	1	
		8
(iv) Duration	3	
Sensitivity of selling price (points can include ability to increase future selling price, interaction of selling price and quantity, need to consider cost and contribution sensitivity, need for scenario analysis)	3	
Marks Available	6	
Maximum		5
(c) Up to 2 marks per relevant point		
(points can include impact on investment profitability of adopting charter, impact of boycott call, consistency with commitments made by company, employees/local community as stakeholders, overall investment framework and extent to which charter can be incorporated)		
		5

Professional skills marks

Communication

- General report format and structure (use of headings/sub-headings and an introduction)
- Style, language and clarity (appropriate layout and tone of report response, presentation of calculations, appropriate use of the tools)
- Effectiveness of communication (answer is relevant, specific rather than general and focused to the requirement)

Analysis and Evaluation

- Appropriate use of the data to determine suitable calculations
- Appropriate use of the data to support discussion and draw appropriate conclusions
- Demonstration of reasoned judgement when considering key matters
- Demonstration of ability to consider relevant factors

Scepticism

- Effective challenge of information, evidence and assumptions supplied and techniques carried out to support key facts and/or decisions
- Demonstration of the ability to probe into the reasons for issues and problems

Commercial acumen

- Effective use of examples and/or calculations from the scenario information and other practical considerations related to the context to illustrate points being made
- Recognition of external constraints and opportunities as necessary

Maximum	10
Total	**50**

(a) **Role of World Trade Organisation**

The World Trade Organisation (WTO) was established to implement the General Agreement on Tariffs and Trade. Its main aim is to reduce barriers to international trade. It does so by trying to prevent protectionist measures, such as tariffs, quotas and other import restrictions. It also offers a forum for negotiation and dispute resolution with countries.

The WTO promotes free trade by applying the most favoured nation principle between its members. This means that reduction in tariffs offered to one country by another should be offered to all countries.

Implications for Prysor Co

Prysor Co's subsidiary's position is affected by one of the exceptions to the most favoured nation principle being free trade areas, where there is no restriction on the movement of goods and services between countries. The WTO permits members to make free trade agreements and give other participating countries in an agreement favourable treatment compared with countries outside the agreement. The free trade agreement between Marteg and Elan will therefore help Prysor Co both in relation to the components imported into Elan for production and any sales to Marteg.

However, if sales are expanded to other countries outside the free trade area, Prysor Co's subsidiary's goods may be subject to tariffs and other protectionist measures.

(b)

Report to the board of directors (BoD), Prysor Co

Introduction

This report discusses the assumptions made in calculating the estimates presented below, with detailed calculations given in the appendices and workings to the appendices. It then discusses the issues connected with the calculation of duration and the sensitivity of the initial sales price.

The report finally recommends, with justification and qualifications, whether or not Prysor Co should undertake the investment.

All calculations are shown in an Appendix to this report.

(ii) Assumptions

Figures relating to variables such as revenues, costs, taxation, working capital and initial investment costs are assumed to be accurate. There may be considerable uncertainty surrounding the accuracy of some of these. A significant change in one or more figures could alter the forecast results of the investment significantly and suggest a different decision. Prysor Co will, for one, need to consider the impact on costs of adopting some or all of the standards in the Campaign For Fair Production's charter. As regards tax also, the assumption that Prysor Co will be exempt from tax in Elan for its first two years there may be doubtful.

The project appears to be a significant one, with a new subsidiary being established and a new product being sold. The assumption that Prysor Co already has sufficient working capital for the new project may therefore be doubtful.

The basis of choosing 14% as the cost of capital has not been clearly explained. If it is the 'normal' rate used to appraise investments, it may not be accurate, as investment in Elan may have different business risk characteristics.

Exchange rates have been predicted using purchasing power parity theory. This suggests that the underlying real exchange rate mainly remains stable, however, nominal exchange

rates fluctuate due to changes in inflation. Whilst this may be the case in the longer term, certainly in the short term there are other factors which could affect exchange rates. These include interest rates, market sentiment and government policy.

The realisable value figure may also be questionable if the subsidiary cannot be sold as a going concern. A zero realisable value on the investment will lower the NPV, and whilst not making it negative, sensitivity to changes in other figures will be increased. However, the figure may also be too pessimistic. Further analysis is required of the scenarios of selling the subsidiary as a going concern (and what the selling price might be), and, alternatively, the impact of Prysor Co's investment continuing beyond four years.

(iv) Duration

Duration of 2.86 years is the average time to recover the present value of the project.

If the project is discounted at the internal rate of return, it is the time taken to recover the initial investment. However, unlike simple payback, the duration calculation takes into account the time value of money and the timing of cash flows over the whole investment period.

The main problem with the duration calculation is interpreting what it actually means. The concept of average time to recover value may not be easy to understand. If a number of projects were being considered in a capital rationing situation, duration could provide a point of comparison. However, this decision appears to be a one-off. Therefore, the directors need to determine what an acceptable duration would be, which may be difficult.

The assumption implicit in duration calculations is that the shorter the duration period, the lower the risk. Basing decisions on duration may result in a bias towards short-term projects.

Sensitivity of selling price

The sensitivity analysis indicates that the initial selling price would have to be 8.1% lower for the investment to have a nil net present value, assuming that the selling price increased annually by 5% in subsequent years.

The logic behind looking at the sensitivity of the selling price is that, in theory, Prysor Co will have control over it. It is certainly worth considering whether the initial price could be set lower to increase the chances of establishing the phone.

However, if the initial selling price is set at a lower level, it may be questionable whether it will be possible to increase it by as much as 5% each year subsequently. The viability of increasing selling price will also depend on the pricing policies of competitors.

The analysis also assumes that if selling price is 8.1% lower each year, the same forecast quantities would be sold. The calculation does not consider any interaction and trade-offs between prices and quantities sold. Any change in quantities would impact on total costs and also possibly costs per unit, with lower quantities meaning the loss of bulk discounts, for example. That said, if the mobile phone's sales are not price sensitive, either because it is perceived as a must-buy or as a luxury item, then reducing its sales price will not significantly affect the quantity sold. Possibly, dropping the selling price may even lead to fewer phones being sold, as customers may perceive its lower price as indicating it is an inferior product.

Another factor in relation to costs is whether Prysor Co would reconsider the selling price of the component to the subsidiary if the selling price to the consumer was lower. All these factors would indicate a need to look at the sensitivity of contribution as well as revenue.

The sensitivity analysis of initial selling price therefore needs to be supplemented by sensitivity analysis of other elements in the NPV calculation and analysis of different scenarios, using more complex assumptions and considering, in particular, the interaction between selling price and quantity sold. Consideration of different market scenarios, and how Prysor Co might respond to them, would also be helpful. Prysor Co could consider using simulation, as it is a better method of considering more complex scenarios than sensitivity analysis.

 **BPP**

Conclusion

The financial appraisal suggests that making the investment will result in a positive NPV and the investment should therefore be undertaken. However, the financial appraisal is based on a number of assumptions. Changes in these may impact upon the commercial viability of the investment. Therefore, additional sensitivity and scenario analysis should be undertaken. The directors need to define what constitute acceptable and unacceptable outcomes in the light of the strategic reasons for undertaking the investment, before making a final decision.

Appendix 1

Project operating cash flows

	ED000	ED000	ED000	ED000	ED000
Year	0	1	2	3	4
Sales revenue		8,000	10,920	14,641	16,670
Component costs (W2)		(877)	(1,186)	(1,599)	(1,742)
Other costs		(3,508)	(4,934)	(6,230)	(6,685)
Tax allowable depreciation		(3,615)	(2,711)	(2,033)	(2,701)
Profits before tax		0	2,089	4,819	5,542
Tax (20%)				(964)	(1,108)
Tax allowable depreciation		3,615	2,711	2,033	2,701
Investment	(14,460)				3,400
Cash flows in ED000	(14,460)	3,615	4,800	5,888	10,535
Exchange rates	2.6000	2.5055	2.3906	2.2799	2.1947
	M$000	M$000	M$000	M$000	M$000
Cash flows in M$000	(5,562)	1,443	2,008	2,583	4,800
Additional tax in Marteg (10%) (W2)		(–)	(87)	(211)	(253)
Additional contribution (W3)		123	174	239	278
Tax on additional contribution (30%)		(37)	(52)	(72)	(83)
Lost contribution		(400)	(436)	(471)	(504)
Tax on lost contribution (30%)		120	131	141	151
Cash flows (M$000s)	(5,562)	1,249	1,738	2,209	4,389
Discount factor (14%)	1.000	0.877	0.769	0.675	0.592
Discounted cash flows	(5,562)	1,095	1,337	1,491	2,598
Net present value	959				

The investment has a positive net present value and on financial grounds should be accepted.

Alternative NPV presentation using spreadsheet functionality

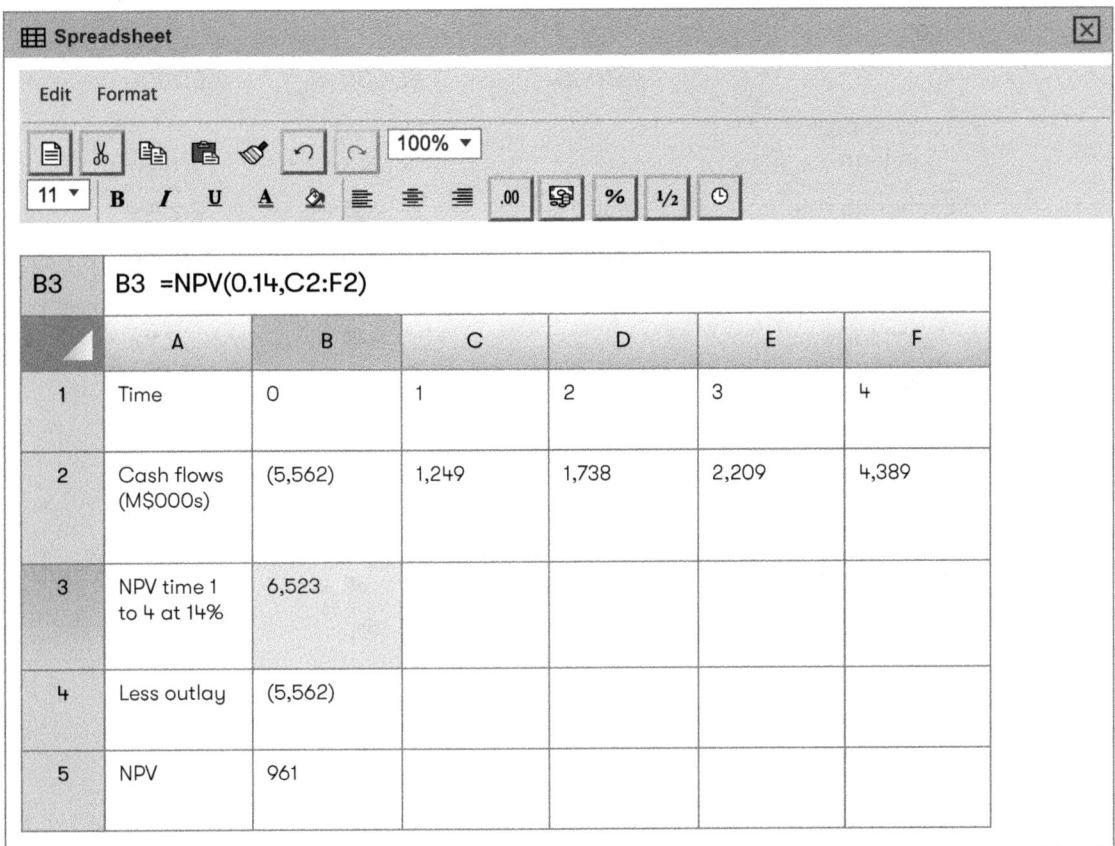

	A	B	C	D	E	F
	B3 =NPV(0.14,C2:F2)					
1	Time	0	1	2	3	4
2	Cash flows (M$000s)	(5,562)	1,249	1,738	2,209	4,389
3	NPV time 1 to 4 at 14%	6,523				
4	Less outlay	(5,562)				
5	NPV	961				

There is a slight difference in the NPV due to rounding of the discount factors in the first approach.

Workings

1 Component costs

Year	1	2	3	4
Quantity (000)	50	65	83	90
Year 1 price (M$)	7.00	7.00	7.00	7.00
Inflation		x 1.09	x 1.09 x 1.08	x 1.09 x 1.08 x 1.07
Exchange rate	2.5055	2.3906	2.2799	2.1947
Cost (ED000)	877	1,186	1,559	1,742

2 Additional tax in Marteg

Year	1	2	3	4
	ED000	ED000	ED000	ED000
Taxable profits in Elan	–	2,089	4,819	5,542
Exchange rate	2.5055	2.3906	2.2799	2.1947
	M$000	M$000	M$000	M$000
Taxable profits in Marteg	–	874	2,114	2,525
Additional tax (10%)	–	(87)	(211)	(253)

3 Additional contribution

Year	1	2	3	4
Quantity (000)	50	65	83	90
Year 1 price (M$)	7.00	7.00	7.00	7.00
Inflation		x 1.09	x 1.09 x 1.08	x 1.09 x 1.08 x 1.07
Contribution margin	0.35	0.35	0.35	0.35
Additional contribution (M$000)	123	174	239	278

Appendix 2

Sensitivity calculations

Duration

Year	1	2	3	4
Present value (M$000)	1,095	1,337	1,491	2,598
Percentage of total PV (%)	16.8	20.5	22.9	39.8

Duration = (1 x 0.168) + (2 x 0.205) + (3 x 0.229) + (4 x 0.398) = 2.86 years

2.86 years is the average time to recover the present value of the project.

 BPP

Sensitivity of revenue

Year	1	2	3	4
	ED000	ED000	ED000	ED000
Sales revenue	8,000	10,920	14,641	16,670
Tax on sales revenue in Elan (20%)	___	___	(2,928)	(3,334)
	8,000	10,920	11,713	13,336
Exchange rates	2.5055	2.3906	2.2799	2.1947
	M$000	M$000	M$000	M$000
	3,193	4,568	5,138	6,076
Additional tax in Marteg (10%) (W)	(319)	(457)	(642)	(760)
	2,874	4,111	4,496	5,316
Discount factor 14%	0.877	0.769	0.675	0.592
	2,520	3,161	3,035	3,147
Present value of revenue less tax	11,863			

Reduction in selling price = ($959,000 / $11,863,000) x 100% = 8.1%

Alternative NPV presentation using spreadsheet functionality

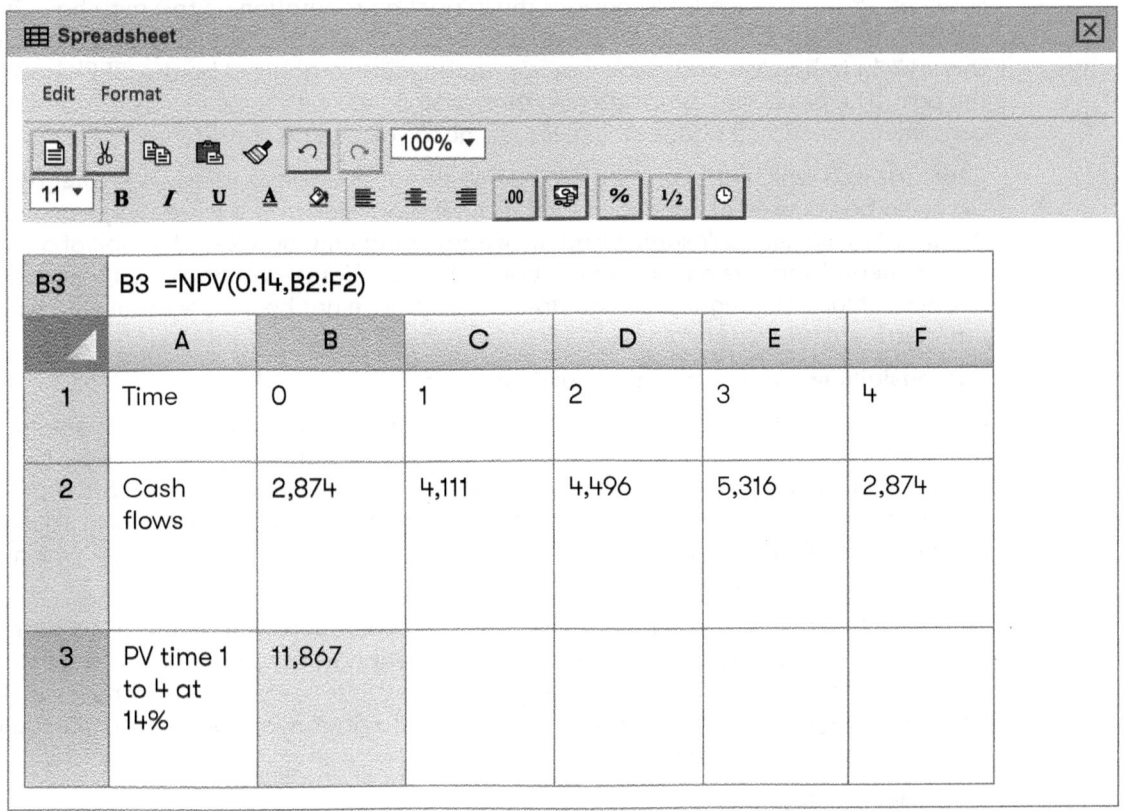

	A	B	C	D	E	F
		B3 =NPV(0.14,B2:F2)				
1	Time	0	1	2	3	4
2	Cash flows	2,874	4,111	4,496	5,316	2,874
3	PV time 1 to 4 at 14%	11,867				

There is a slight difference in the NPV due to rounding of the discount factors in the first approach.

Year	1	2	3	4
	ED000	ED000	ED000	ED000
Sales revenue in Elan	8,000	10,920	14,641	16,670
Exchange rate	2.5055	2.3906	2.2799	2.1947
	M$000	M$000	M$000	M$000
	3,193			
Taxable sales revenue in Marteg		4,568	6,422	7,596
Additional tax (10%)	(319)	(457)	(642)	(760)

Note. There is no tax on revenue in years 1 and 2 in Elan.

(c)

Responsibilities to shareholders

The commitments in the Campaign For Fair Production (CFFP)'s charter go beyond the legal responsibilities which Prysor Co has in Elan. They might therefore lead to the investment being more costly than forecast, and the responsibility to maximise value for shareholders not being fulfilled.

Reputation risk

However, Prysor Co needs to consider the impact on reputation as this may have financial implications if the CFFP calls for a boycott. Prysor Co's board needs to consider whether this is likely to happen and also what impact boycotts organised by the CFFP have had in the past. The possibility of upside risk, that compliance with the CFFP's charter will attract consumers concerned about ethical issues, needs also to be considered.

Other aspects which may prove a reputation threat are transparency and integrity. Prysor Co could be accused of concealment if it is not disclosing how it is treating workers in Elan. If Prysor Co makes disclosures about its treatment of employees and its social and environmental impacts on local communities in accordance with the charter, it could be accused of lack of integrity if its actual practices have not been consistent with what it has reported.

Responsibilities to workers and local community

If Prysor Co adopts the charter, it will have to weigh its responsibilities to its employees and the local community in Elan and see if they conflict with maximising value for shareholders. Increasing wage costs will affect profits, but may be necessary if greater foreign investment in Elan results in more competition for labour, particularly skilled labour. Paying for employee education can be seen as investment in human capital which will create future shareholder value.

The impact on the local community of production operations is difficult to evaluate, with the financial benefits of increased local employment having to be weighed against physical impacts and disturbance. If Prysor Co has to take steps to limit the impacts which its current operations in Marteg have, it may be straightforward and not too costly to adopt similar measures in Elan.

Investment policy

As regards overall investment policy, this will need to be consistent with Prysor Co's overall mission and supporting objectives, including the ethical and environmental responsibilities which it has. The CFFP's charter may provide a basis for investment policy which is consistent with Prysor Co's wider mission and objectives. However, adopting all of it may constrain Prysor Co's decision-making. Prysor Co's board may consider an approach of following the code's broad principles and adopting some specific requirements, for example, provision of education for employees.

 Videos can be viewed by accessing your ebook version on VitalSource.

57 Para Fuels

Course Book references

Investment appraisal is mainly covered in Chapter 3 of the Course Book, and the Black-Scholes model is covered in Chapter 4. Strategic and ethical issues are covered in Chapter 1.

Easy marks

About 60% of the marks are available for discussion but ensure your points are addressed to the scenario to maximise marks remember easy communication marks can be obtained by:

(1)   Providing a suitable, simple, heading to the answer (eg a simple report format)

(2)   Providing a short introduction paragraph outlining the structure of the report

(3)   Providing a clear answer (eg referencing spreadsheet calculations where appropriate).

(4)   Providing a conclusion to complete the report.

Marking guide		**Marks**
(a) 1 to 2 marks per well-discussed point (eg not just assess on a now or never basis, projects have flexibility, examples of flexibility, ability to discontinue Project B by selling to Kero Innovations Co, value of the opportunity)	<u>4</u>	
		4
(b) (i) **(Appendix 1)**		
Sales revenue	1	
Production costs	2	
Tax allowable depreciation	1	
Tax	1	
Working capital	2	
Present value of cash flows, years 5 to 25	1	
Net present value of Investment A	<u>1</u>	
		9
(ii) **(Appendix 2)**		
Cash flows: years 1 to 4	1	
Present value of cash flows, years 5 to 25	2	
Net present value of Investment B (without Kero offer)	1	
Present value of cash flows foregone (P_a)	1	
Other variables for option pricing formula	2	

ANSWERS

Put value (value of offer from Kero Innovations Co)	1
Total NPV of project with option	1
	9

(iii) **Recommendation and assumptions (in report)**

Recommendation	2
Assumptions other than real options' assumptions	4
Real options' assumptions	3
	7

(iv) **Discussion (in report)**

Benefits to company re meeting environmental goals	3
Buy-in from airlines	2
Need to improve computations	2
Cost reduction/revenue increase possibilities	3
Discussion of how Para Fuels Co might proceed	4
	11

Professional skills marks

Communication

- General report format and structure (use of headings/sub-headings and an introduction)
- Style, language and clarity (appropriate layout and tone of report response, presentation of calculations, appropriate use of the tools)
- Effectiveness of communication (answer is relevant, specific rather than general and focused to the requirement)

Analysis and evaluation

- Appropriate use of the data to determine suitable calculations
- Appropriate use of the data to support discussion and draw appropriate conclusions
- Balanced appraisal/use of information objectively to support options, determine the impact of a course of action, make a recommendation or decision

Scepticism

- Effective challenge of information and assumptions supplied and techniques carried out to support key facts and/or decisions
- Effective challenge and critical assessment of the information and assumptions provided, including identification of contradictory evidence, and ongoing questioning of the reliability of the information provided

Commercial acumen

- Recommendations are practical and plausible in the context of Para Fuels Co's situation
- Effective use of examples and/or calculations from the scenario information and other practical considerations related to the context to illustrate points being made
- Recognition of possible consequences of past and future actions and decisions, for example, relating to initial replacement of existing fuel

Maximum	10
Total	50

(a) The traditional net present value investment appraisal method assumes that an investment needs to be taken on a now or never basis and once undertaken, it cannot be reversed. Most

investments have within them certain amounts of flexibility, such as whether or not to undertake the investment immediately or to delay the decision, whether or not to pursue follow-on opportunities, and whether or not to discontinue an investment opportunity after it has started. This flexibility, known as a real option, can be valuable for companies, such as Para Fuels Co.

Kero Innovations Co is potentially offering Para Fuels Co the opportunity to discontinue with Investment B, if it felt that this opportunity is not worth pursuing, even though the project has already started. Para Fuels Co does not have to continue the investment for 25 years but can effectively abandon it after only three years. This also gives Para Fuels Co the opportunity to judge the likely commercial success of the new household waste products to paraffin conversion process. This is a real option and the Black-Scholes option pricing (BSOP) model provides a method of valuing this opportunity, which is similar to a put option. Para Fuels Co can then consider this value within its project assessment.

(b)

Report to the board of directors (BoD), Para Fuels Co

Introduction

This report provides estimates of whether the production facility which needs to be replaced should use traditional technology or new technology to produce jet fuel, in financial terms. Based on this, it makes an initial recommendation. The report discusses the assumptions made in the computations. The report then discusses the comments made at the BoD meeting and suggests how Para Fuels Co may want to proceed if the new technology is adopted.

(iii) Current estimated values

- Investment A: approximately $5,716,000 (Appendix 1)

- Investment B, prior to considering the potential offer from Kero Innovations Co: approximately $29,000 (Appendix 2)

- Investment B, including the potential offer from Kero Innovations Co using the BSOP model: approximately $4,359,000 (Appendix 2)

- Investment B, without considering the offer from Kero Innovations Co, only gives a marginal positive value and even when the potential offer from Kero Innovations Co is considered, using the BSOP model, the value of $4,359,000 is less than the value obtained from Investment A at $5,716,000. Based on this, Investment A should be undertaken.

Assumptions

Examples of assumptions which have been made are as follows, and will need further analysis, and should be supported by sensitivity analysis.

1. It is assumed that the input figures in the computations for both projects such as sales revenue, costs and working capital, and the inflation figures are correct. The accuracy of these may need to be assessed. It is also assumed that the tax rates will remain the same during the project and this is unlikely to be true.

2. Both projects are very long-term projects and the assumptions and bases of determining the figures from year 5 to year 25 need to be closely examined for reasonableness. Questions need to be asked, such as: On what basis will Investment B's cash flows remain the same from year 5 onwards? How likely is this to be the case? How has the present value of cash flows for Investment A, from year 5 onwards, been determined?

3. Para Fuels Co's cost of capital has been used as the discount rate for both projects. This assumption may not be accurate. A risk-adjusted, project specific cost of capital would give a more accurate estimate of the value of the project.

4. When calculating the value of the offer made by Kero Innovations Co, using the BSOP model, the standard deviation or volatility of the underlying asset is needed, and the BSOP model assumes that this can be estimated accurately. This may be possible for frequently traded products, but this probably is not the case for one-off projects and new projects. Such estimation is difficult to do and is open to significant errors. Therefore, the assumption of the accuracy of the volatility measure is questionable.

5. The BSOP model assumes that markets are frictionless and the project's cash flows follow a lognormal distribution, both of which are reasonable assumptions for market-traded products but not necessarily for investment projects.

6. The BSOP model assumes that, once determined, the variables will not change, but in reality, they may do.

7. In order to estimate the value of Kero Innovations Co's offer for Investment B, Para Fuels Co has assumed that the offer is binding, but currently it is only a potential offer.

The estimates of value resulting from the calculations in the appendices should therefore be treated as indicative and not definitive.

(iv) Response to the BoD meeting on the replacement of the production facility

Adherence to environmental, social and governance (ESG) aspects are becoming increasingly important criteria by which to judge a company as a good corporate citizen, from the perspective of all stakeholder groups, including investors. Whether Para Fuels Co decides to undertake the replacement of the production facility with traditional technology which uses crude oil or the new technology using household waste, this will impact on the company's expected environmental responsibilities, the perception of how it discharges these and thereby impacting its reputation as a good corporate citizen. This is probably what the chief executive officer is referring to. However, the BoD should equally be cautious about pursuing an agenda which compromises Para Fuels Co's financial strength.

As the chief marketing officer suggests, airline companies will be concerned about their responsibilities with respect to the environment and using this type of jet fuel would be of significant help in achieving a high level of environmental protection. Therefore, both Para Fuels Co and its customers, the airline companies, are in agreement. The airlines will be naturally concerned about the safety aspects of the new product. However, once the new type of jet fuel is proven to be as safe as the current type of jet fuel, these concerns should dissipate and sales revenue will probably increase rapidly.

The chief financial officer (CFO) has put forward the argument that, financially, Para Fuels Co does not benefit from moving to the new technology currently. Furthermore, whereas there should be a positive uplift once the fuel is deemed safe, the current computations do not necessarily show this. The CFO appears to be concerned that if more production facilities are replaced with the new technology, this will reduce the company's and its shareholders' value. Nonetheless, it is possible that over the coming two years, Para Fuels Co will have a much better knowledge of the new type of jet fuel and its safety. Therefore, the computations will be more reliable and might well show a substantial positive value creation impact.

The significant advantage for Para Fuels Co, if it went with the new technology, is that as an early adopter it should benefit from positive learning curve effects and ways to make the production of the jet fuel more efficient than would be the case if they continue with the traditional technology. This would result in the reduction of ongoing costs. The set-up costs in the future may also reduce if the company establishes better ways of constructing production facilities needed in two years' time. Revenues may also increase as Para Fuels Co will have more time to build better customer networks and relations, and a better marketing strategy, all built around the fuel coming from the adoption of the new technology.

How should Para Fuels Co proceed

If the new technology is adopted for the single production facility initially, Para Fuels Co may wish to proceed as follows:

1. The company should launch a public relations (PR) campaign to highlight its environmental credentials, build its reputation and thereby hopefully increase its corporate value;

2. The company should also launch a PR campaign to reassure its investors that it aims to maximise long-term corporate value and this move to new technology is very much in keeping with that;

3. Since there may be safety concerns initially, the company may want to support research investigations to assess the safety of the fuel, including financial support, especially in conjunction with airline companies involved in this research and possibly other interested companies, such as Kero Innovations Co;

4. The company should put into place effective processes to maximise learning opportunities from the investment made in the first production facility. It should then use this learning to reduce costs and to produce more accurate estimations and, where possible, reduce uncertainties of cash flow forecasts;

5. The company should ask Kero Innovations Co to make a formal, contractual offer and possibly align it to two years, when it will need to make further decisions, in case the new technology proves not to be feasible.

If Para Fuels Co decides to stick with the traditional technology instead, this technology is still environmentally friendly and the PR campaigns externally and to investors should proceed. As a result, Para Fuels Co will hopefully maintain its corporate reputation and value.

Conclusion

The report suggests that based only on financial grounds, and taking into account assumptions made, Para Fuels Co should replace the production facility with traditional technology. However, the new technology does offer significant opportunities, especially in terms of environmental benefits, and therefore suggestions are put forward of how Para Fuels Co might proceed.

Report compiled by:

Date:

Note. Credit will be given for alternative valid comments and approaches, where relevant, for all parts of the question.

Appendix 1: (Part (b)(i)): Investment A, calculation of value

(Amounts shown in $000s)

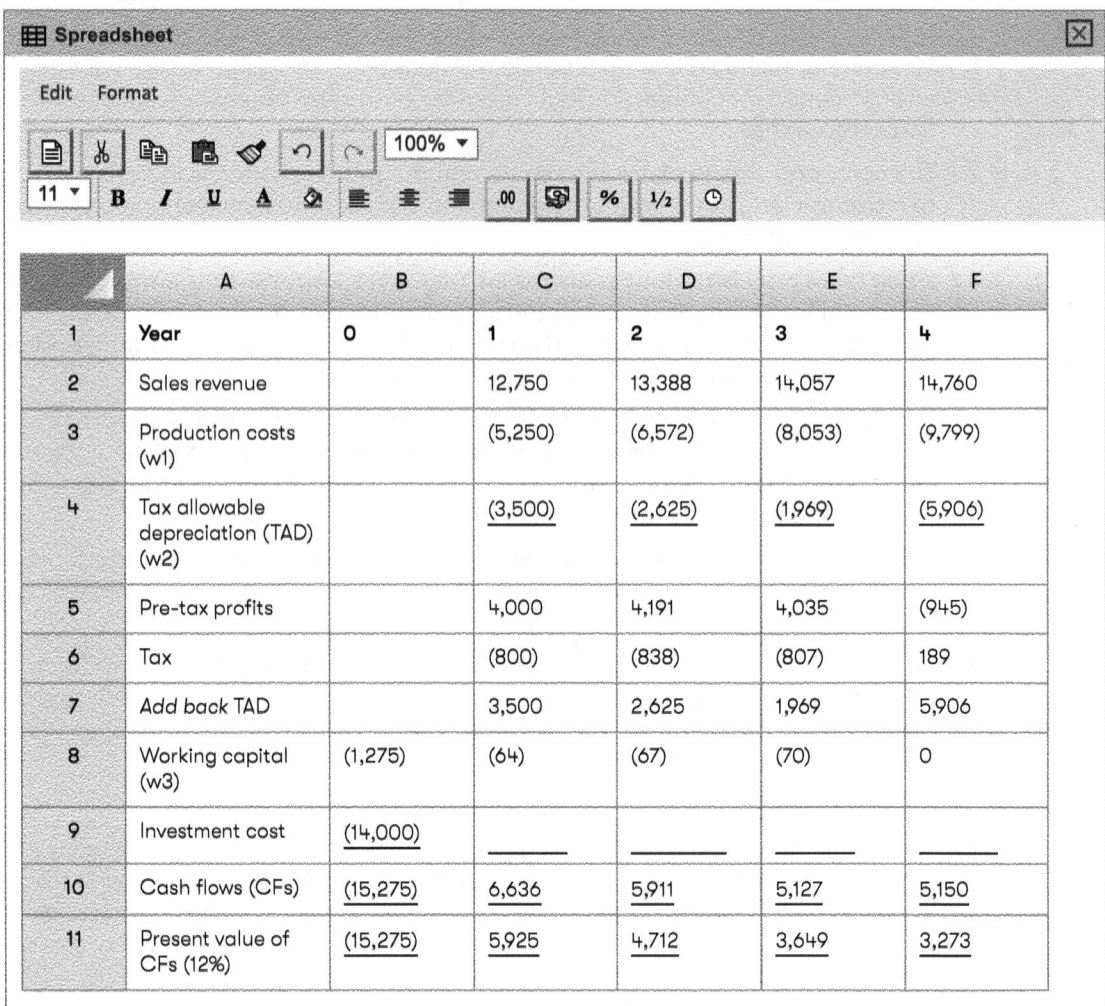

	A	B	C	D	E	F
1	**Year**	0	1	2	3	4
2	Sales revenue		12,750	13,388	14,057	14,760
3	Production costs (w1)		(5,250)	(6,572)	(8,053)	(9,799)
4	Tax allowable depreciation (TAD) (w2)		(3,500)	(2,625)	(1,969)	(5,906)
5	Pre-tax profits		4,000	4,191	4,035	(945)
6	Tax		(800)	(838)	(807)	189
7	Add back TAD		3,500	2,625	1,969	5,906
8	Working capital (w3)	(1,275)	(64)	(67)	(70)	0
9	Investment cost	(14,000)				
10	Cash flows (CFs)	(15,275)	6,636	5,911	5,127	5,150
11	Present value of CFs (12%)	(15,275)	5,925	4,712	3,649	3,273

Present value of cash flows for years 5 to 25 ($000s): $5,400 \times 1.12^{-4} = 3,432$

Net present value of Investment A: approx. $5,716,000

Workings

1 **Production costs ($000s)**

Year 2: $6,200 \times 1.06 = 6,572$

Year 3: $7,100 \times 1.06 \times 1.07 = 8,053$

Year 4: $8,000 \times 1.06 \times 1.07 \times 1.08 = 9,799$

2 **TAD ($000s)**

Year 1: $14,000 \times 25\% = 3,500$

Year 2: $(14,000 - 3,500) \times 25\% = 2,625$

Year 3: $(14,000 - (3,500 + 2,625)) \times 25\% = 1,969$

Year 4: $(14,000 - (3,500 + 2,625 + 1,969)) = 5,906$

3 Working capital (WC)

Year	WC required ($000s)	Additional WC ($000s)
0 (for year 1)	10% x 12,750 = 1,275	1,275
1 (for year 2)	10% x 13,388 = 1,339	1,339 – 1,275 = 64
2 (for year 3)	10% x 14,057 = 1,406	1,406 – 1,339 = 67
3 (for year 4)	10% x 14,760 = 1,476	1,476 – 1,406 = 70

No additional working capital needed after the start of year 4.

Appendix 2: Part (b)(ii)): Investment B, calculation of value

Without considering the offer from Kero Innovations Co

(Amounts shown in $000s)

Year	0	1	2	3	4
Cash flows (CF)	(34,600)	1,400	1,960	2,744	5,488
Present value of CFs (12%)	(34,600)	1,250	1,563	1,953	3,488

Present value of cash flows for years 5 to 25 ($000s):

$5,488 \times (7.843 - 3.037) = 26,375$

Net present value of investment B: approx. $29,000

If the potential offer from Kero Innovations Co is considered

Present value of cash flows foregone (P_a): $3.488m + $26.375m = $29.863m

Potential offer from Kero Innovations Co (P_e): $27m

Risk-free rate of return (r): 5%

Standard deviation (s): 40%

Time to expiry (t): 3 years

Using the BSOP spreadsheet:

P_a	P_e	$r_{(decimal)}$	$t^{(years)}$	$s_{(decimal)}$
29.863	27	0.05	3	0.4
d_1	0.7084			
d_2	0.0156			
$N(d_1)$	0.7606			
$N(d_2)$	0.5062			
C	10.95			
P	4.33			

According to the BSOP option pricing model, the value of the potential offer from Kero Innovations Co is approx. $4,330,000.

Net present value of investment B: $4,359,000 ($29,000 + $4,330,000)

BPP

58 Fondir

Marking guide

	Marks
(a) Explanation of exposure	3
Suggestions of how exposure could be managed	3
	6
(b) (i) (Appendix 1)	
OTC forward rate	2
$ receipt using OTC forward as hedge	1
Call option	1
Premium cost (including borrowing)	2
$ receipt using OTC option as hedge	1
	7
(ii) (Appendix 2)	
Go long/buy futures	1
Number of contracts	1
Basis remaining	1
Loss on future markets if rates increase	2
Gain on futures markets if rates decrease	2
Net return if rates increase	1
Net return if rates decrease	1
	9
(iii) Comments and addressing queries (in report)	
Comments on results	4
Alternative methods to hedge receipt	3
Margins	3

Marks Available		10	
Maximum			9

(iv) **Discussion (in report)**

Should financial risk be managed (for example, costs and benefits, impact on cost of capital, impact on cash flows, benefit to stakeholders of stable/sustainable cash flows, benefits harder to identify)   5

Communicating risk management policies (for example, communication of stability improves stakeholder engagement, reduction in agency costs, costs related to informational asymmetry, clientele effects; balanced against releasing too much proprietary information) $\underline{5}$

Marks Available   10

Maximum $\underline{9}$

Professional skills marks

Communication

- General report format and structure (use of headings/sub-headings and an introduction)
- Style, language and clarity (appropriate layout and tone of report response, presentation of calculations, appropriate use of the tools)
- Effectiveness of communication (answer is relevant, specific rather than general and focused to the requirement)

Analysis and evaluation

- Appropriate use of the data to determine suitable calculations
- Appropriate use of the data to support discussion and draw appropriate conclusions
- Balanced appraisal/use of information objectively to support options, determine the impact of a course of action, make a recommendation or decision

Scepticism

- Effective challenge of information and assumptions supplied and techniques carried out to support key facts and/or decisions
- Demonstration of the ability to probe into the reasons for issues and problems, including the identification of missing information or additional information, which would alter the decisions reached by Fondir Co

Commercial acumen

- Recommendations are practical and plausible in the context of Fondir Co's situation
- Effective use of examples and/or calculations from the scenario information and other practical considerations related to the context to illustrate points being made

Maximum $\underline{10}$

Total $\underline{\underline{50}}$

(a)

In the case of Fondir Co, falling revenues may have resulted from the strength of the dollar and the weakness of the Euro (Italian currency). Due to higher dollar production costs compared to the cheaper Euro, Fondir Co may be forced to price their goods higher compared to the European competition and therefore resulting in lower sales revenue. If this situation persists, then Fondir Co may face lower revenues over a long period of time.

Short-term exchange rate fluctuations normally occur because of trade flows or speculation, or changes in interest rates and inflation rates between countries. However, the underlying exchange rate stays largely the same. If there is a long-term, permanent shift in the underlying exchange rate, then this results in economic exposure, which appears to be what Fondir Co is facing.

Derivatives can be used to manage risks of short-term exchange rate fluctuations, and except for swaps, derivatives are not normally offered for long-term hedging purposes. Furthermore, even swaps cannot be used to manage permanent shifts in underlying exchange rates. Therefore, Fondir Co may need to take a longer-term strategic view of how to manage the economic risk it faces. It may, for example, decide that the Italian market is very important and that it should set up a subsidiary company in the Euro zone to take advantage of the cheaper costs of production. In that way, Fondir Co might face similar costs to its European competitors and be able to compete on more equal terms.

(b)

Report to the board of directors (BoD), Fondir Co

Introduction

This report shows and comments on how the income from Lothil can be hedged using currency and interest rate derivatives. The report then discusses the need for, and communication of, its risk management activity.

Comment on calculations and response to the queries raised

Results obtained in the appendices 1 and 2

Appendix 1 shows that hedging the expected receipts from Lothil in four months' time using over-the-counter (OTC) forwards, giving $4,200,000, is more beneficial than OTC options, which only give $4,043,977. This is due to the cost of the premium which is paid for options. However, options present an opportunity for Fondir Co to abandon the contract should the exchange rates move in the company's favour. With forwards, this is not possible and the amount received is fixed.

Appendix 2 shows that the futures hedge ensures that the interest earned from the invested funds is fixed at $59,500 whether interest rates increase or decrease between now and when the Lothil Lira income is received in four months' time. Fondir Co knows the interest income for certain. However, this is predicated on the assumptions that basis diminishes in a straight line and that there is no basis risk. It is by no means certain that either assumption will hold in reality. The income received may therefore vary a little due to the uncertainty of the movement in basis.

 BPP

Fondir Co could choose to use alternative methods to hedge the receipt from Lothil, instead of derivatives. It could, for example, use money markets, where it would borrow Lira today, such that the income which will be received in four months will be sufficient to pay for the amount borrowed and the interest accrued. It can then convert the Lira at the current spot rate and use the funds for other purposes from today. Alternatively, it could offer the companies based in Lothil a discount for immediate payment. Either action would reduce the exchange rate risk Fondir Co faces, but both need careful consideration. In the first case, Fondir Co is potentially using up credit facilities, although it does get use of the funds immediately. In the second case, giving discounts can be costly.

Margin requirements

Fondir Co would need to deposit margins when exchange traded derivatives are bought or sold. This is standard practice and ensures that the risk and impact of any default is minimised. If, for example, Fondir Co does not fulfil its contractual obligation, if prices move against it, the margin is used to pay for any shortfall. This deposit could tie up company funds while the futures contracts are open, although these will be returned to the company when the contracts are closed. However, dealing in futures need not be as expensive as other forms of hedging for which transaction fees may also be payable. Margins tend to be proportionally lower, especially in active futures markets, compared to the value of each contract. Therefore, large amounts of exposure can be hedged with relatively small margin deposits.

Management of financial risks

Fondir Co's marketing director is correct in his assertion that managing risks does cost money due to the operational and transactional needs of managing such risks. However, risk management activity could be beneficial as well. If costs outweigh the beneficial impact of risk management, then Fondir Co needs to think carefully about the need to engage in such activity. The potential benefits of risk management activity need to be considered in more detail to assess whether or not risk management can be beneficial.

Risk management may increase Fondir Co's value by either increasing its future cash flows or reducing its cost of capital. Risk management activity would be designed to reduce the risk or volatility of Fondir Co's cash flows. This may result in the reduction of Fondir Co's cost of capital, and the compensation it needs to provide to its capital providers. The amount of reduction depends on the risk which has not already been diversified away and whether the non-diversifiable risk can be transferred in a cost-efficient manner. Fondir Co will need to assess the extent to which its cost of capital reduces and therefore leads to the increase in the company's value.

The other consideration is whether the reduction in risk increases cash flows. A number of suggestions are put forward to suggest that this may be the case, such as reduction in tax liability, ability for companies like Fondir Co to reduce its financial distress costs, set up a beneficial capital structure for the company and allowing management to focus on the risks they can control instead of worrying about risks which are not in their control. Ultimately, Fondir Co's stakeholders will also be concerned that the company manages risks effectively in order to ensure that the benefits they derive from engaging with the company are stable and sustained.

Perhaps the view held by Fondir Co's marketing director is symptomatic of the fact that costs of managing risks are easier to quantify and their impact easier to assess, whereas benefits are less easy to identify and to quantify. Therefore, more weight is put on costs and less on the potential benefits. A fair assessment of the benefits will provide a more balanced view.

Communication of the risk management approach to stakeholders

Clear communication of Fondir Co's risk management approach should be beneficial to the company's stakeholders. Stakeholders would benefit from knowing that the company is creating value for them in a stable and sustained manner. Stakeholders such as employees and managers have to rely fully on the company's continued operation. Unlike shareholders who have diversified away specific risk, these stakeholders face the full impact of Fondir Co's risk exposure and therefore risk management. Effective risk management would help ensure that stakeholders are more engaged with the company.

Lenders would be willing to lend on favourable terms to Fondir Co, if they know that the company's cash flows are stable. Stakeholders will benefit from all these aspects and also from cash flow generation discussed above.

Effective communication of the risk management approach taken by Fondir Co will provide assurance to the company's stakeholders and corroborate their expectations. It will reduce agency-related costs and costs related to asymmetric information. Effective communication of the risk management approach will attract the appropriate shareholder clientele to invest in Fondir Co. This may result in a more stable share price and not one which is changing due to uncertainty about the company's cash flows.

Fondir Co may be concerned that divulging too much information may affect the company's competitive position and may reduce the company's cash flows as competitors react to the information provided. It is important for Fondir Co keep proprietary information confidential whilst still providing sufficient information to stakeholders. A careful balance needs to be struck between giving too much information and not providing sufficient information for stakeholders.

Conclusion

The report shows, in the appendices, how various derivative instruments can be used to hedge the risks of currency and interest rate fluctuations. The main content of the report comments on the results, which showed the highest receipt was from forward contracts and that futures contracts fix the interest return at $59,500. The report also addresses the queries raised by the BoD on alternative methods of hedging and margin requirements.

Report compiled by:

Date

Note. Credit will be given for alternative valid comments and approaches, where relevant, for all parts of the question.

(i) **Appendix 1:**

OTC forward rate

Adjusting annual interest rates to become 4-month rates by dividing the annual rates by 3 and using the IRP formula:

84.00 x (1 + (0.06 + 0.0060)/3)/(1 + (0.033 − 0.0030)/3) = 85.00 approx.

Receipt ($) = LL357m/85.00 = $4,200,000

OTC option rate

Purchase call options to hedge against falling $ income from LL sales.

Gross income if option is exercised = LL357m/84.00 = approx. $4,250,000

Premium cost

4,250,000m x LL4 = LL17,000,000

In $ = LL17,000,000/84.00 = $202,381

Add interest on borrowing for premium, $202,381 x (1 + (0.054/3)) = $206,023

Net receipt = $4,250,000 − $206,023 = $4,043,977

(ii) **Appendix 2:**

The higher receipt from the forwards contract of $4,200,000 is taken for investment.

Need to hedge against a fall in interest rates, therefore go long in the futures market.

No. of contracts needed = $4,200,000/$500,000 × 5 months/3 months = 14 contracts

Current price (on 1/1) − futures price = total basis

(100 − 3.3) − 96.10 = 0.60

Unexpired basis = 2/6 × 0.60 = 0.20

If interest rates increase by 0.50% to 3.80%

Investment return = 3.80% - 0.3% = 3.5% in annual terms so adjusting for 5 months = 3.50% × 5/12 × $4,200,000 = $61,250.

Expected futures price = 100 – 3.80 – 0.20 = 96.00

Loss on the futures market = (0.9600 – 0.9610) × $500,000 × 3/12 x 14 = $(1,750)

Net return = $59,500

If interest rates decrease by 0.50% to 2.80%

Investment return = 2.80% - 0.3% = 2.5% in annual terms so adjusting for 5 months = 2.50% × 5/12 × $4,200,000 = $43,750

Expected futures price = 100 – 2.80 – 0.20 = 97.00

Gain on the futures market = (0.9700 – 0.9610) × $500,000 × 3/12 x 14 = $15,750

Net return = $59,500

Mock Exams

ACCA

Advanced Financial Management

Mock Exam 1

Sample questions

Questions	
Time allowed	Time allowed 3 hours and 15 minutes
Section A THIS question is compulsory and MUST be attempted Section B BOTH questions to be attempted	

DO NOT OPEN THIS EXAM UNTIL YOU ARE READY TO START
UNDER EXAMINATION CONDITIONS

SECTION A

This section of the exam contains one question.

This question is worth 50 marks and is compulsory.

This exam section is worth 50 marks in total.

1 Cigno

(a) Prepare a report for the BoD of Cigno Co which:

    (i) Estimates the value attributable to Cigno Co's shareholders from the acquisition of Anatra Co before taking into account the cash benefits of potential tax savings and redundancies, and then after taking these into account **(18 marks)**

    (ii) Assesses the value created from (b)(i) above, including a discussion of the estimations made and methods used **(8 marks)**

    (iii) Advises the BoD on the key factors it should consider in relation to the redundancies and potential tax savings **(4 marks)**

(b) Discuss whether the defence strategy suggested by Anatra Co's CEO of disposing assets is feasible. **(5 marks)**

(c) Takeover regulation, where Anatra Co is based, offers the following conditions aimed at protecting shareholders: the mandatory-bid condition through sell-out rights, the principle of equal treatment, and squeeze-out rights.

Required

Explain the main purpose of each of the three conditions. **(5 marks)**

Professional marks will be awarded for the demonstration of skill in communication, analysis and evaluation, scepticism and commercial acumen in your answer. **(10 marks)**

(Total = 50 marks)

Exhibit 1: Financial information: Cigno Co and Anatra Co

Cigno Co is a large pharmaceutical company, involved in the research and development (R&D) of medicines and other healthcare products. Over the past few years, Cigno Co has been finding it increasingly difficult to develop new medical products. In response to this, it has followed a strategy of acquiring smaller pharmaceutical companies which already have successful products in the market and/or have products in development which look very promising for the future. It has mainly done this without having to resort to major cost cutting and has therefore avoided large-scale redundancies. This has meant that not only has Cigno Co performed reasonably well in the stock market, but it has also maintained a high level of corporate reputation.

Anatra Co is involved in two business areas: the first area involves the R&D of medical products, and the second area involves the manufacture of medical and dental equipment. Until recently, Anatra Co's financial performance was falling, but about three years ago a new chief executive officer (CEO) was appointed and she started to turn the company around. Recently, the company has developed and marketed a range of new medical products, and is in the process of developing a range of cancer-fighting medicines. This has resulted in a good performance in the stock market, but many analysts believe that its shares are still trading below their true value. Anatra Co's CEO is of the opinion that the turnaround in the company's fortunes makes it particularly vulnerable to a takeover threat, and she is thinking of defence strategies that the company could undertake to prevent such a threat. In particular, she was thinking of disposing of some of the company's assets and focusing on its core business.

Cigno Co is of the opinion that Anatra Co is being held back from achieving its true potential by its equipment manufacturing business and that by separating the two business areas, corporate value can be increased. As a result, it is considering the possibility of acquiring Anatra Co,

 **BPP**

unbundling the manufacturing business, and then absorbing Anatra Co's R&D of medical products business. Cigno Co estimates that it would need to pay a premium of 35% to Anatra Co's shareholders to buy the company.

Exhibit 2: Financial information: Anatra Co

Given below are extracts from Anatra Co's latest statement of profit or loss and statement of financial position for the year ended 30 November 20X5.

	20X5
	$m
Sales revenue	21,400
Profit before interest and tax (PBIT)	3,210
Interest	720
Pre-tax profit	2,490
Non-current liabilities	9,000
Share capital (50c/share)	3,500
Reserves	4,520

Anatra Co's share of revenue and profits between the two business areas are as follows:

	Medical products R&D	Equipment manufacturing
Share of revenue and profit	70%	30%

Exhibit 3: Post-acquisition benefits from acquiring Anatra Co

Cigno Co estimates that following the acquisition and unbundling of the manufacturing business, Anatra Co's future sales revenue and profitability of the medical R&D business will be boosted. The annual sales growth rate is expected to be 5% and the profit margin before interest and tax is expected to be 17.25% of sales revenue, for the next four years. It can be assumed that the current tax-allowable depreciation will remain equivalent to the amount of investment needed to maintain the current level of operations, but that the company will require an additional investment in assets of 40c for every $1 increase in sales revenue.

After the four years, the annual growth rate of the company's free cash flows is expected to be 3% for the foreseeable future.

Anatra Co's unbundled equipment manufacturing business is expected to be divested through a sell-off, although other options such as a management buy-in were also considered. The value of the sell-off will be based on the medical and dental equipment manufacturing industry. Cigno Co has estimated that Anatra Co's manufacturing business should be valued at a factor of 1.2 times higher than the industry's average price/earnings ratio. Currently the industry's average earnings per share is 30c and the average share price is $2.40.

Possible additional post-acquisition benefits

Cigno Co estimates that it could achieve further cash flow benefits following the acquisition of Anatra Co, if it undertakes a limited business reorganisation. There is some duplication of the R&D work conducted by Cigno Co and Anatra Co, and the costs related to this duplication could be saved if Cigno Co closes some of its own operations. However, it would mean that many redundancies would have to be made, including employees who have worked in Cigno Co for many years. Anatra Co's employees are considered to be better qualified and more able in these areas of duplication, and would therefore not be made redundant.

Cigno Co could also move its headquarters to the country where Anatra Co is based and thereby potentially save a significant amount of tax, other than corporation tax. However, this would mean a loss of revenue for the government where Cigno Co is based.

The company is concerned about how the government and the people of the country where it is based might react to these issues. It has had a long and beneficial relationship with the country and its people.

Cigno Co has estimated that it would save $1,600 million after-tax free cash flows to the firm at the end of the first year as a result of these post-acquisition benefits. These cash flows would increase by 4% every year for the next three years.

Exhibit 4: Estimating the combined company's weighted average cost of capital

Cigno Co is of the opinion that as a result of acquiring Anatra Co, the cost of capital will be based on the equity beta and the cost of debt of the combined company. The asset beta of the combined company is the individual companies' asset betas weighted in proportion of the individual companies' market value of equity. Cigno Co has a market debt to equity ratio of 40:60 and an equity beta of 1.10.

It can be assumed that the proportion of market value of debt to market value of equity will be maintained after the two companies combine.

Currently, Cigno Co's total firm value (market values of debt and equity combined) is $60,000 million and Anatra Co's asset beta is 0.68.

Additional information

- The estimate of the risk-free rate of return is 4.3% and of the market risk premium is 7%.

- The corporation tax rate applicable to all companies is 22%.

- Anatra Co's current share price is $3 per share, and it can be assumed that the book value and the market value of its debt are equivalent.

- The pre-tax cost of debt of the combined company is expected to be 6.0%.

Exhibit 5: Important note

Cigno Co's board of directors (BoD) does not require any discussion or computations of currency movements or exposure in this report. All calculations are to be presented in $ million. Currency movements and their management will be considered in a separate report. The BoD also does not expect any discussion or computations relating to the financing of acquisition in this report, other than the information provided above on the estimation of the cost of capital.

 **BPP**

SECTION B

This section of the exam contains two questions.

Each question is worth 25 marks and is compulsory.

This exam section is worth 50 marks in total.

2 Casasophia

(a) Advise Casasophia Co on, and recommend, an appropriate hedging strategy for the US$ income it is due to receive in four months. Include all relevant calculations and evaluate both option exercise prices. **(10 marks)**

(b) Given that Casasophia Co agrees to the local bank's offer of the swap, calculate the net present value of the project in six months' time, in €. Discuss whether the swap would be beneficial to Casasophia Co. **(10 marks)**

Professional marks will be awarded for the demonstration of skill in analysis and evaluation, scepticism and commercial acumen in your answer. **(5 marks)**

(Total = 25 marks)

Exhibit 1: Casasophia

Casasophia Co, based in a European country that uses the euro (€), constructs and maintains advanced energy efficient commercial properties around the world. It has just completed a major project in the US and is due to receive the final payment of US$20 million in four months.

Casasophia Co is planning to commence a major construction and maintenance project in Mazabia, a small African country, in six months' time. This government-owned project is expected to last for three years during which time Casasophia Co will complete the construction of state-of-the-art energy efficient properties and provide training to a local Mazabian company in maintaining the properties. The carbon-neutral status of the building project has attracted some grant funding from the European Union, and these funds will be provided to the Mazabian government in Mazabian Shillings (MShs).

Casasophia Co intends to finance the project using the US$20 million it is due to receive and borrow the rest through a € loan. It is intended that the US$ receipts will be converted into € and invested in short-dated treasury bills until they are required. These funds, plus the loan, will be converted into MShs on the date required, at the spot rate at that time.

Mazabia's government requires Casasophia Co to deposit the MShs2.64 billion it needs for the project, with Mazabia's central bank, at the commencement of the project. In return, Casasophia Co will receive a fixed sum of MShs1.5 billion after tax, at the end of each year for a period of three years. Neither of these amounts is subject to inflationary increases. The relevant risk-adjusted discount rate for the project is assumed to be 12%.

Exhibit 2: Financial information

Exchange rates available to Casasophia

	Per €1	Per €1
Spot	US$1.3585–US$1.3618	MShs116–MShs128
4-month forward	US$1.3588–US$1.3623	Not available

 BPP

Currency options (Contract size €125,000, Exercise price quotation: US$ per €1, cents per euro)

	Calls		Puts	
Exercise price	2-month expiry	5-month expiry	2-month expiry	5-month expiry
1.36	2.35	2.80	2.47	2.98
1.38	1.88	2.23	4.23	4.64

Casasophia Co local government base rate	2.20%
Mazabia government base rate	10.80%
Yield on short-dated euro treasury bills (assume 360-day year)	1.80%

Mazabia's current annual inflation rate is 9.7% and is expected to remain at this level for the next six months. However, after that, there is considerable uncertainty about the future and the annual level of inflation could be anywhere between 5% and 15% for the next few years. The country where Casasophia Co is based is expected to have a stable level of inflation at 1.2% per year for the foreseeable future. A local bank in Mazabia has offered Casasophia Co the opportunity to swap the annual income of MShs1.5 billion receivable in each of the next three years for euros, at the estimated annual MShs/€ forward rates based on the current government base rates.

3 Amberle (December 2018, amended)

(a) Calculate the adjusted present value (APV) for the project and conclude whether the project should be accepted or not. **(15 marks)**

(b) Discuss the factors which may determine the long-term finance policy which Amberle Co's board may adopt. **(5 marks)**

Professional marks will be awarded for the demonstration of skill in analysis and evaluation, and scepticism in your answer. **(5 marks)**

(Total = 25 marks)

Exhibit 1: Amberle Co

Amberle Co is a listed company with divisions that manufacture cars, motorbikes and bicycles. Over the last few years, Amberle Co has used a mixture of equity and debt finance for its investments. However, it is about to make a new investment of $150 million in facilities to produce electric cars, which it proposes to finance solely by debt finance.

Exhibit 2: Project information

Amberle Co's finance director has prepared estimates of the post-tax cash flows for the project, using a four-year time horizon, together with the realisable value at the end of four years:

Year	1	2	3	4
	$m	$m	$m	$m
Post-tax operating cash flows	28.50	36.70	44.40	50.90
Realisable value				45.00

Working capital of $6 million, not included in the estimates above and funded from retained earnings, will also be required immediately for the project, rising by the predicted rate of inflation for each year. Any remaining working capital will be released in full at the end of the project.

Predicted rates of inflation are as follows:

Year	1	2	3	4
	8%	6%	5%	4%

The finance director has proposed the following finance package for the new investment:

	$m
Bank loan, repayable in equal annual instalments over the project's life, interest payable at 8% per year	70
Subsidised loan from a government loan scheme over the project's life on which interest is payable at 3.1% per year	80
	150

Issue costs of 3% of gross proceeds will be payable on the subsidised loan. No issue costs will be payable on the bank loan. Issue costs are not allowable for tax.

Exhibit 3: Financial information

Amberle Co pays tax at an annual rate of 30% on profits in the same year in which profits arise.

Amberle Co's asset beta is currently estimated at 1.14. The current return on the market is estimated at 11%. The current risk-free rate is 4% per year.

Amberle Co's chairman has noted that all of the company's debt, including the new debt, will be repayable within three to five years. He is wondering whether Amberle Co needs to develop a longer-term financing policy in broad terms and how flexible this policy should be.

Answers

DO NOT TURN THIS PAGE UNTIL YOU HAVE
COMPLETED THE MOCK EXAM

Exam success skills

In any AFM exam it will be important to apply good general exam technique by using the six exam success skills identified at the start of the Revision Kit, in the section covering 'essential skills'. These skills are: 1. Case scenario: Managing information; 2. Correct interpretation of requirements; 3. Answer planning: Priorities, structure and logic; 4. Efficient numerical analysis; 5. Effective writing and presentation; and 6. Good time management.

Some examples of how to apply these skills in this exam are provided in the table below.

Skill	Examples
Managing information	It is crucially important to assimilate the information in the question scenario.
	In longer questions, such as the 50-mark question, it is difficult to assimilate information by simply starting at the beginning and reading to the end because there is so much information to take in.
	Instead, it is sensible to take an **active approach** to reading each question. Read enough of the question to get an idea of the basic scenario and then read the initial requirements so that you understand the first things that you are expected to do with this information.
	For example, in Question 1 the lengthy scenario makes a lot more sense if, before reading all of it, you are aware that the first requirements relate to bond valuation and the cost of capital.
Correct Interpretation of requirements	Be careful to interpret the verbs used in the question requirements carefully.
	For example, in Q3(a) the verb 'evaluate' clearly implies that calculations are expected.
	Also be careful to identify where a question requirement contains more than one instruction.
	For example, in Q1(a)(ii) where an assessment of value AND discussion of methods and estimations are requested, and in Q3(b) where there are two areas that need to be discussed.
Answer planning	This is always important in answering AFM questions.
	For example, in risk management questions (such as Q2), it is especially important that your plan correctly identifies (i) the risk being faced and (ii) the relevant timings. If you get these wrong, then there will be a cap on the number of marks that you can score (however accurate your answers are).
Efficient numerical analysis	It is essential that the marker can follow your workings and your logic.
	It is also important that you accept that under exam conditions you will not get **all** the calculations correct, and that this is not necessary in order to score a strong pass mark.
	If you make a mistake early in your calculations that affects your later calculations, then the marker will only penalise the error you have made, and not its follow-on impact on other calculations. This means that it is not normally a good use of your time to correct such errors during the exam.
	For example, in Question 2 it is important that your calculations of the options hedge clearly shows the type of contract and the number of contracts, but the exact accuracy (eg whether or not

Skill	Examples
	to use a forward contract to hedge any over or under hedge arising from the future) is not crucial.
Effective writing and presentation	In Q1 there are marks available for professional structure (eg use of sub-headings, appendices etc). Many of the techniques used here are good practice in all questions throughout the exam.
	It is also very important to relate your points to the scenario and to the requirement wherever possible. This does not mean simply repeating the details from the question but using this information to help to explain the point you are making.
	For example, in Q3(b) there is a commitment in the annual report to treat employees fairly, but why is this relevant in a discussion of ethics?
Good Time Management	The exam is 3 hours 15 minutes long, which translates to 1.95 minutes per mark.
	It is essential that you do not allow yourself to become bogged down in the harder numerical areas of the exam.
	For example, it is especially easy to get bogged down in Q1(a)(ii) in this exam
	At the beginning of a question, work out the amount of time you should be spending on:
	(a) Planning:
	(i) for a 25-mark question this will be about 1.95 × 25 marks × 20% = 10 minutes
	(ii) for a 50-mark question this should be about 20 mins.
	(b) Writing your answer to each requirement:
	(i) Take the mark allocation and multiply by 1.95 minutes per technical mark.

Diagnostic

Did you apply these skills when reading, planning, and writing up your answer? Identify the exam success skills where you think you need to improve and capture your thoughts here of what you want to achieve when attempting questions in future.

SECTION A

1 Cigno

Course Book references

This is really a question about acquisition strategy and is mainly covered in Chapters 8-11.

Top tips

The 50-mark question often mainly focusses on core syllabus areas like acquisitions.

Part (a) required a report; communication marks were available for format, structure and presentation.

Part (a)(i), for 18 marks, required an assessment of whether the proposed premium for the acquisition would result in value being created or destroyed for the predator's shareholders. This required an assessment of the value of the part of the acquired company that would be sold (using the price/earnings (P/E) method) and the value of the part of the company that remained. This latter calculation required the use of the free cash flow method discounted at a

post-acquisition weighted average cost of capital (WACC). The question also required an assessment of the post-acquisition value of synergies again using the free cash flow method.

The challenge here was mainly to conceptualise how to attack the problem – the individual calculations were not unusual and have been tested many times before. Candidates who were unsure about the approach to take could have scored easy marks for valuing the disposal, the synergies and the post-acquisition WACC – this was worth ten of the marks.

Part (a)(ii), for 8 marks, asked for assessment of the meaning of the numbers from bi and a discussion of the methods that had been used and the estimates that had been made. Candidates that had got stuck with the numbers may still have been able to gain about half of the marks for discussing the methods and the estimates.

Part (a)(iii), for 4 marks, required a brief discussion of the reputational and ethical issues associated with redundancies and tax savings.

Part (b), for 5 marks, asked for a discussion of a proposed takeover defence. This could have been satisfactorily answered by using the details of the proposal that were provided in the scenario.

Part (c), for 5 marks, asked for an explanation of the purpose of three common types of takeover regulation. Although the terminology used was a bit off-putting, with a bit of thought at least two of the three regulations were reasonably clear in their purpose and should have been easy to explain.

Easy marks

There were elements of this question (some of (a)(ii), (a)(iii), (b), (c), and the communication marks in part (a) that were available to candidates who struggled with the numerical content of this question. Targeting these easier marks is an essential element in exam technique for this exam.

Marking guide	Marks
(a) (i) Appendix 1	
Anatra Co, manufacturing business, P/E ratio	1
Estimate of the value created from sell-off	3
Appendix 2	
Cigno Co asset beta	1
Combined company asset beta	1
Combined company equity beta	1
Combined company cost of capital	1
Appendix 3	
Sales revenue, Years 1 to 4	1
Operating profit, Years 1 to 4	1
Taxation, Years 1 to 4	1
Capital investment, Years 1 to 4	1
Value from Years 1 to 4	1
Value from Year 5 onwards	1
Value for Cigno Co shareholders before impact of savings from tax and employee cost reduction	2
Appendix 4	
Value created from tax and employee cost savings	1
Value for Cigno Co shareholders after impact of savings from tax and employee cost reduction	1
Maximum	18

(ii)	Discussion of values for the equity holders, additional costs/benefits not given	4
	Methods used and assumptions made	$\frac{5}{9}$
	Marks Available	9
	Maximum	8
(iii)	Reputation factors	2
	Ethical factors	2
	Comment on value	$\frac{2}{6}$
	Marks Available	6
	Maximum	4
(b)	1 to 2 marks per point	
	Maximum	5
(c)	Up to 2 marks for explaining the purpose of each condition	
	Maximum	$\underline{5}$

Professional skills

Communication

- General report format and structure (use of headings/sub-headings and an introduction)
- Style, language and clarity (appropriate layout and tone of report response, presentation of calculations, appropriate use of the tools)
- Effectiveness of communication (answer is relevant, specific rather than general and focused to the requirement)
- Adherence to the details of the proposal in the scenario

Analysis and Evaluation

- Appropriate use of the data to determine suitable calculations to support the acquisition decision
- Appropriate use of the data to support discussion and draw appropriate conclusions
- Demonstration of reasoned judgement when considering key matters
- Demonstration of ability to consider relevant factors applicable to Cigno's situation

Scepticism

- Effective challenge and critical assessment of the information and assumptions used in the valuation of Anatra
- Demonstration of ability to consider all relevant factors applicable to the decisions made by Cigno Co

Commercial acumen

- Effective use of examples and/or calculations from the scenario information and other practical considerations related to the context to illustrate points being made
- Recognition of external constraints and opportunities as necessary

Maximum	$\underline{10}$
Total	$\underline{\underline{50}}$

(a)

Report to the BoD, Cigno Co

This report assesses the potential value of acquiring Anatra Co for the equity holders of Cigno Co, both with and without considering the benefits of the reduction in taxation and in employee costs. The possible issues raised by reduction in taxation and in employee costs are discussed in more detail below. The assessment also discusses the estimates made and the methods used.

Assessment of value created

Cigno Co estimates that the premium payable to acquire Anatra Co largely accounts for the benefits created from the acquisition and the divestment, before considering the benefits from the tax and employee costs saving. As a result, before these savings are considered, the estimated benefit to Cigno Co's shareholders of $128 million (see Appendix 3) is marginal. Given that there are numerous estimations made and the methods used make various assumptions, as discussed below, this benefit could be smaller or larger. It would appear that without considering the additional benefits of cost and tax reductions, the acquisition is probably too risky and would probably be of limited value to Cigno Co's shareholders.

If the benefits of the taxation and employee costs saved are taken into account, the value created for the shareholders is $5,609 million (see Appendix 4), and therefore significant. This would make the acquisition much more financially beneficial. It should be noted that no details are provided on the additional pre-acquisition and post-acquisition costs or on any synergy benefits that Cigno Co may derive in addition to the cost savings discussed. These should be determined and incorporated into the calculations.

Basing corporate value on the P/E method for the sell-off, and on the free cash flow valuation method for the absorbed business, is theoretically sound. The P/E method estimates the value of the company based on its earnings and on competitor performance. With the free cash flow method, the cost of capital takes account of the risk the investors want to be compensated for and the non-committed cash flows are the funds which the business can afford to return to the investors, as long as they are estimated accurately.

However, in practice, the input factors used to calculate the organisation's value may not be accurate or it may be difficult to assess their accuracy. For example, for the free cash flow method, it is assumed that the sales growth rate, operating profit margin, the taxation rate and incremental capital investment can be determined accurately and remain constant. It is assumed that the cost of capital will remain unchanged and it is assumed that the asset beta, the cost of equity and cost of debt can be determined accurately. It is also assumed that the length of the period of growth is accurate and that the company operates in perpetuity thereafter. With the P/E model, the basis for using the average competitor figures needs to be assessed; for example, have outliers been ignored; and the basis for the company's higher P/E ratio needs to be justified as well. The uncertainties surrounding these estimates would suggest that the value is indicative, rather than definitive, and it would be more prudent to undertake sensitivity analysis and obtain a range of values.

Key factors to consider in relation to the redundancies and potential tax savings

It is suggested that the BoD should consider the impact of the cost savings from redundancies and from the tax payable in relation to corporate reputation and ethical considerations.

 BPP

At present, Cigno Co enjoys a good reputation and it is suggested that this may be because it has managed to avoid large-scale redundancies. This reputation may now be under threat and its loss could affect Cigno Co negatively in terms of long-term loss in revenues, profits and value; and it may be difficult to measure the impact of this loss accurately.

Whilst minimising tax may be financially prudent, it may not be considered fair. For example, currently there is ongoing discussion and debate from a number of governments and other interested parties that companies should pay tax in the countries they operate and derive their profits, rather than where they are based. Whilst global political consensus in this area seems some way off, it is likely that the debate in this area will increase in the future. Companies that are seen to be operating unethically with regard to this may damage their reputation and therefore their profits and value.

Nonetheless, given that Cigno Co is likely to derive substantial value from the acquisition, because of these savings, it should not merely disregard the potential savings. Instead it should consider public relations exercises it could undertake to minimise the loss of reputation, and perhaps meet with the government to discuss ways forward in terms of tax payments.

Conclusion

The potential value gained from acquiring and unbundling Anatra Co can be substantial if the potential cost savings are taken into account. However, given the assumptions that are made in computing the value, it is recommended that sensitivity analysis is undertaken and a range of values obtained. It is also recommended that Cigno Co should undertake public relations exercises to minimise the loss of reputation, but it should probably proceed with the acquisition, and undertake the cost saving exercise because it is likely that this will result in substantial additional value.

Report compiled by:

Date:

Appendix 1: Estimate of value created from the sell-off of the equipment manufacturing business

Average industry P/E ratio = $2.40 / $0.30 = 8

Anatra Co's equipment manufacturing business P/E ratio = 8 × 1.2 = 9.6

Value from sell-off of equipment manufacturing business

Share of pre-tax profit = 30% × $2,490m = $747m

After-tax profit = $747m × (1 − 0.22) = $582.7m

Value from sell-off = $582.7m × 9.6 = $5,594m (approximately)

This answer would be presented as a spreadsheet in the exam (as would the other Appendices), as follows (the footnotes beneath the spreadsheet show the content of cells B1 to B5 of the spreadsheet and would not be typed out separately):

	A	B
	B6	**B6 = B5*B2**
1	Average industry P/E ratio	8 [1]
2	Anatra Co's equipment manufacturing business P/E ratio	9.6 [2]
3	**Value from sell-off of equipment manufacturing business**	
4	Share of pre-tax profit ($m)	747 [3]
5	After-tax profit ($m)	582.7 [4]
6	Value from sell-off ($m)	5,594

[1] $2.40 \div 0.3$

[2] $8 * 1.2$

[3] $0.30 * 2,490$

[4] $B4 * (1 - 0.22)$

Appendix 2: Estimate of the combined company cost of capital

Anatra Co, asset beta = 0.68

Cigno Co, asset beta:

Equity beta = 1.10

Proportion of market value of debt = 40%; Proportion of market value of equity = 60%

Asset beta = $1.10 \times 0.60 / (0.60 + 0.40 \times 0.78) = 0.72$

Combined company, asset beta

Market value of equity, Anatra Co = $3 \times 7,000m$ shares = $21,000m

Market value of equity, Cigno Co = $60\% \times \$60,000m = \$36,000m$

Asset beta = $(0.68 \times 21,000 + 0.72 \times 36,000) / (21,000 + 36,000) = 0.71$ (approximately)

Combined company equity beta = $0.71 \times (0.6 + 0.4 \times 0.78) / 0.6 = 1.08$

Combined company, cost of equity = $4.3\% + 1.08 \times 7\% = 11.86\%$

Combined company, cost of capital = $11.86\% \times 0.6 + 6.00\% \times 0.78 \times 0.4 = 8.99$, say 9%

Appendix 3: Estimate of the value created for Cigno Co's equity holders from the acquisition

Anatra Co, medical R&D value estimate:

Sales revenue growth rate = 5%

Operating profit margin = 17.25%

Tax rate = 22%

Additional capital investment = 40% of the change in sales revenue

Cost of capital = 9% (Appendix 2)

Free cash flow growth rate after 4 years = 3%

Current sales revenue = 70% × $21,400m = $14,980m

Cash flows, Years 1 to 4

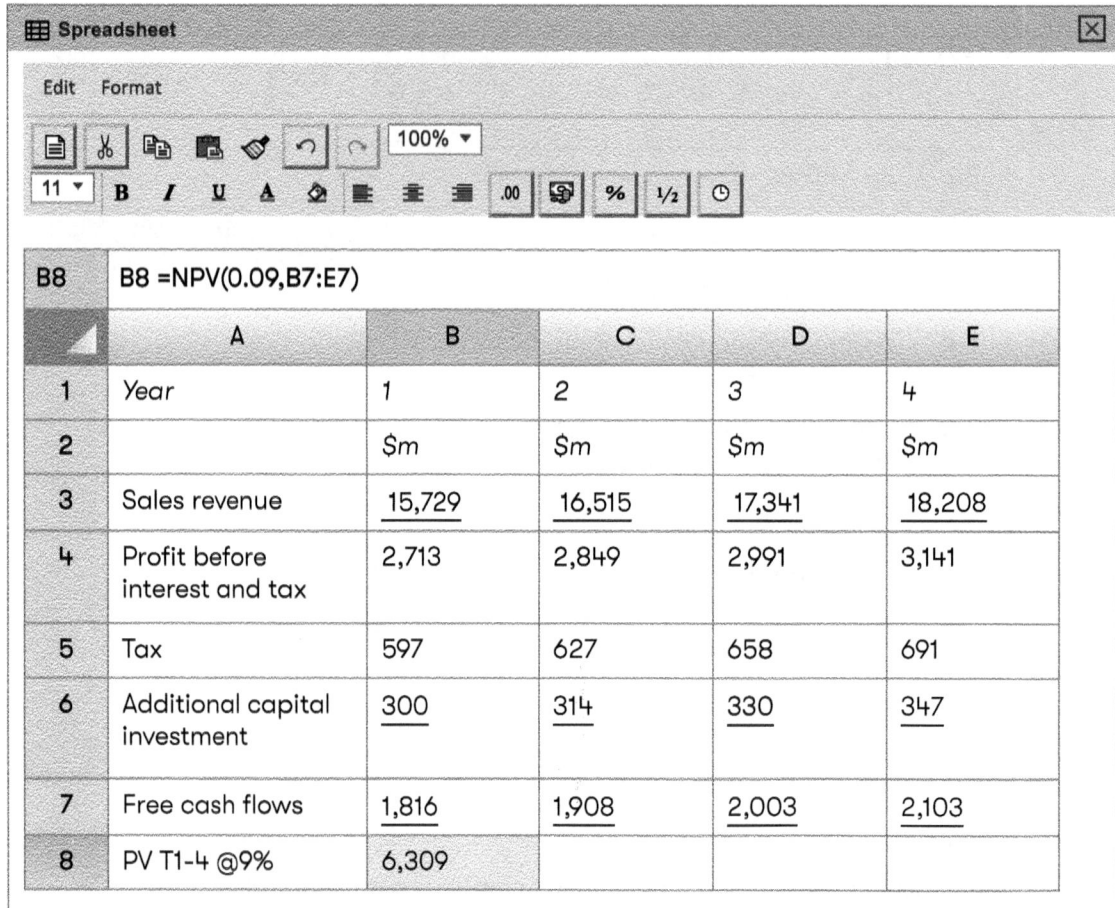

B8 =NPV(0.09,B7:E7)

	A	B	C	D	E
1	Year	1	2	3	4
2		$m	$m	$m	$m
3	Sales revenue	15,729	16,515	17,341	18,208
4	Profit before interest and tax	2,713	2,849	2,991	3,141
5	Tax	597	627	658	691
6	Additional capital investment	300	314	330	347
7	Free cash flows	1,816	1,908	2,003	2,103
8	PV T1-4 @9%	6,309			

Value, Years 1 to 4: $6,309m

Value, Year 5 onwards: $[\$2,103 \times 1.03 / (0.09 - 0.03)] \times 1.09^{-4} = \$25,575m$

Total value of Anatra Co's medical R&D business area = $31,884 million

Total value of Anatra Co following unbundling of equipment manufacturing business and absorbing medical R&D business:

$5,594m (Appendix 1) + $31,884m = $37,478m (approximately)

Anatra Co, current market value of equity = $21,000 million

Anatra Co, current market value of debt = $9,000 million

Premium payable = $21,000m × 35% = $7,350m

Total value attributable to Anatra Co's investors = $37,350 million

Value attributable to Cigno Co's shareholders from the acquisition of Anatra Co before taking into account the cash benefits of potential tax savings and redundancies = Value following unbundling ($37,478m) – Anatra's debt ($9,000m) – price paid for Anatra ($21,000m + $7,350m) = $128m

 BPP

Appendix 4: Estimate of the value created from savings in tax and employment costs following possible redundancies

Cash flows, Years 1 to 4

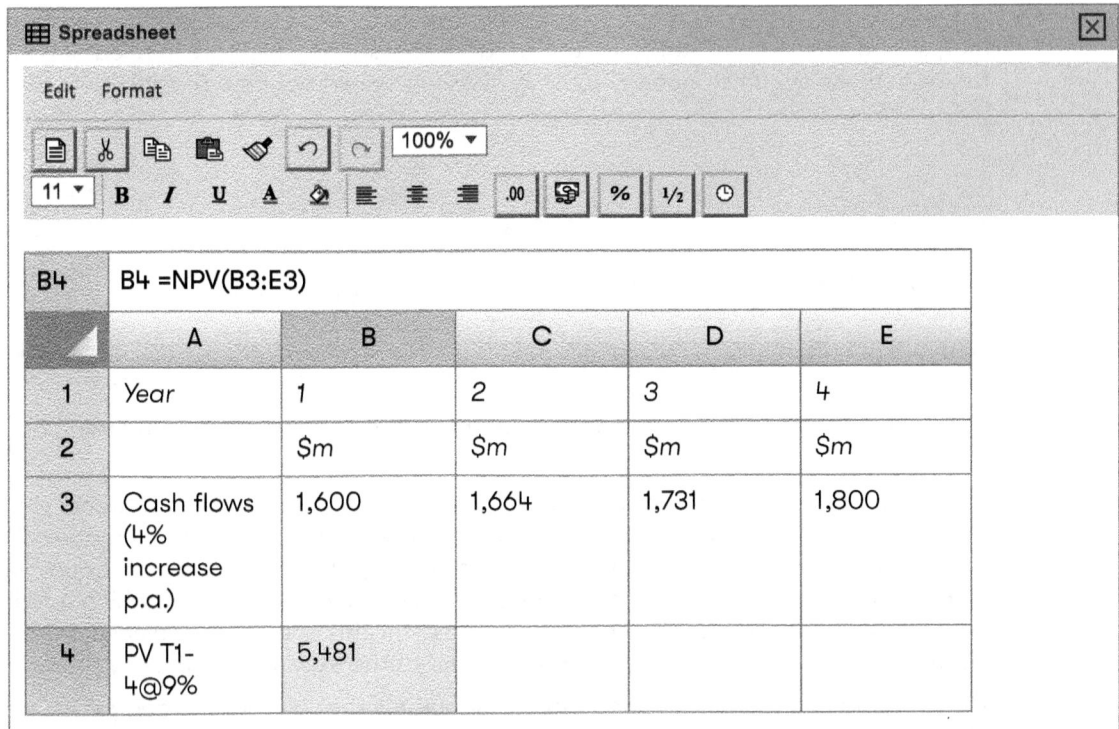

B4	B4 =NPV(B3:E3)				
	A	B	C	D	E
1	Year	1	2	3	4
2		$m	$m	$m	$m
3	Cash flows (4% increase p.a.)	1,600	1,664	1,731	1,800
4	PV T1-4@9%	5,481			

Total value = $5,481 million

Value attributable to Cigno Co's shareholders from the acquisition of Anatra Co after taking into account the cash benefits of potential tax savings and redundancies = $5,609 million. ($5,481m + $128m)

(b)

The feasibility of disposing of assets as a defence tool against a possible acquisition depends upon the type of assets sold and how the funds generated from the sale are utilised.

If the type of assets are fundamental to the continuing business then this may be viewed as disposing of the corporation's 'crown jewels'. Such action may be construed as being against protecting the rights of shareholders (similar to the conditions discussed in part (d) below). In order for key assets to be disposed of, the takeover regulatory framework may insist on the corporation obtaining permission from the shareholders first before carrying it out.

On the other hand, the assets may be viewed as not being fundamental to the core business and may be disposed of to generate extra funds through a sell-off (see part (a) above). This may make sense if the corporation is undertaking a programme of restructuring and reorganisation.

In addition to this, the company needs to consider what it intends to do with the funds raised from the sale of assets. If the funds are used to grow the core business and therefore enhancing value, then the shareholders would see this positively and the value of the corporation will probably increase. Alternatively, if there are no profitable alternatives,

the funds could be returned to the shareholders through special dividends or share buybacks. In these circumstances, disposing of assets may be a feasible defence tactic.

However, if the funds are retained but not put to value-enhancing use or returned to shareholders, then the share price may continue to be depressed. And the corporation may still be an attractive takeover target for corporations which are in need of liquid funds. In these circumstances, disposing of assets would not be a feasible defence tactic.

(c)

Each of the three conditions aims to ensure that shareholders are treated fairly and equitably.

The mandatory-bid condition through sell out rights allows remaining shareholders to exit the company at a fair price once the bidder has accumulated a certain number of shares. The amount of shares accumulated before the rule applies varies between countries. The bidder must offer the shares at the highest share price, as a minimum, which had been paid by the bidder previously. The main purpose for this condition is to ensure that the acquirer does not exploit their position of power at the expense of minority shareholders.

The principle of equal treatment condition stipulates that all shareholder groups must be offered the same terms, and that no shareholder group's terms are more or less favourable than another group's terms. The main purpose of this condition is to ensure that minority shareholders are offered the same level of benefits as the previous shareholders from whom the controlling stake in the target company was obtained.

The squeeze-out rights condition allows the bidder to force minority shareholders to sell their stake, at a fair price, once the bidder has acquired a specific percentage of the target company's equity. The percentage varies between countries but typically ranges between 80% and 95%. The main purpose of this condition is to enable the acquirer to gain a 100% stake of the target company and prevent problems arising from minority shareholders at a later date.

Note. Credit will be given for alternative, relevant approaches to the calculations, comments and suggestions/recommendations.

SECTION B

2 Casasophia

Marking guide		Marks
(a) Forward contract calculation	1	
Forward contract comment	1	
Option contracts calculations	4	
Option contracts comments	3	
Conclusion	1	
Maximum		10
(b) Estimates of forward rates	3	
Estimates of present values and net present value in euros	3	
Discussion		
Marks Available	6	
Maximum		10

Professional skills

Analysis and Evaluation

- Appropriate use of the data to determine suitable calculations to recommend an appropriate hedging strategy

- Appropriate use of the data to support discussion and draw appropriate conclusions
- Demonstration of reasoned judgement when considering key matters for Casasophia Co
- Demonstration of ability to consider relevant factors applicable to Casasophia Co's situation
- Identification of further analysis, which could be carried out to enable an appropriate recommendation to be made.
- Appraisal of information objectively

Scepticism

- Effective challenge and critical assessment of the information and assumptions provided
- Demonstration of ability to consider all relevant factors applicable to the decisions made

Commercial acumen

- Effective use of examples and/or calculations from the scenario information and other practical considerations related to the context to illustrate points being made
- Recommendations are practical and plausible

Maximum 5

Total 25

(a)

Hedging strategy

Forward contract

The company will be receiving US$ therefore we use US$1.3623 as the rate.

Receipt in € (see spreadsheet appendix) = **€14,681,054**

The hedge fixes the rate at €1 = US$1.3623. This rate is legally binding.

Options

With options the holder has the right but not the obligation to exercise the option (that is, the option will be exercised if it is beneficial to the holder). However, there is a premium to be paid for this flexibility, making options more expensive than futures and forward contracts.

To protect itself against a weakening US$, Casasophia will purchase euro call options.

Using an exercise rate of $1.36 (calculations in spreadsheet appendix)

Number of contracts = 117 (rounded down to the nearest whole contract)

Total receipts assuming option is exercised = €14,404,311

Using an exercise rate of $1.38 (calculations in spreadsheet appendix)

Number of contracts = 115 (rounded down to the nearest whole contract)

Total receipts assuming option is exercised = €14,258,316

The receipts from either of the options are considerably lower than those from the forward contract. This is primarily due to the premiums payable to secure the flexibility that options offer. The US$ would have to move significantly against the € to allow Casasophia to cover the cost of the premiums.

Conclusion

Based on the calculations above, it is recommended that Casasophia uses forward contracts to hedge against the US$ depreciating against the € in order to maximise receipts. The company should be aware that once the contract is agreed, the price is fixed and is legally binding. In addition, there is no formal exchange for forward contracts, thus giving rise to default risk.

Appendix: Forward contract (the footnotes beneath the spreadsheet show the cell content and would not be typed out separately):

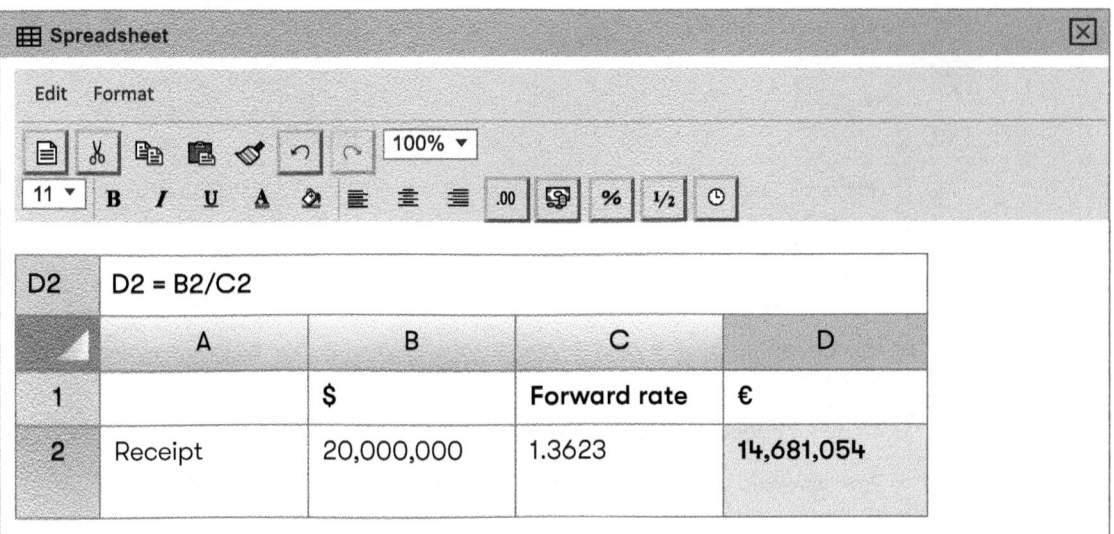

D2	D2 = B2/C2			
	A	B	C	D
1		$	Forward rate	€
2	Receipt	20,000,000	1.3623	14,681,054

Appendix: Option at 1.36

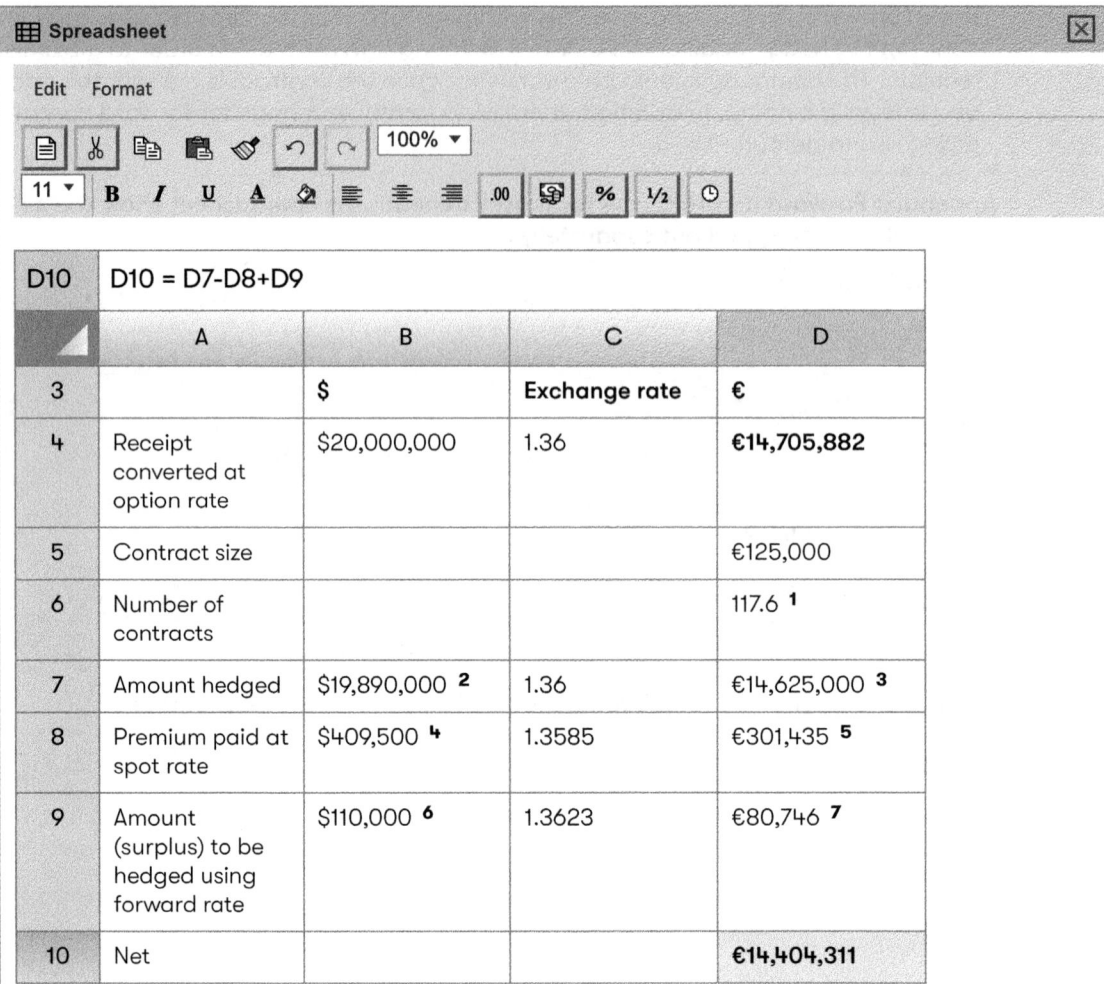

	A	B	C	D
3		$	Exchange rate	€
4	Receipt converted at option rate	$20,000,000	1.36	**€14,705,882**
5	Contract size			€125,000
6	Number of contracts			117.6 [1]
7	Amount hedged	$19,890,000 [2]	1.36	€14,625,000 [3]
8	Premium paid at spot rate	$409,500 [4]	1.3585	€301,435 [5]
9	Amount (surplus) to be hedged using forward rate	$110,000 [6]	1.3623	€80,746 [7]
10	Net			**€14,404,311**

Cell reference D10 = D7-D8+D9

[1] D4/D5

[2] C7*D7

[3] 117*D5

[4] 0.0280*B7

[5] B8/C8

[6] B4-B7

[7] B9/C9

Appendix: Option at 1.38

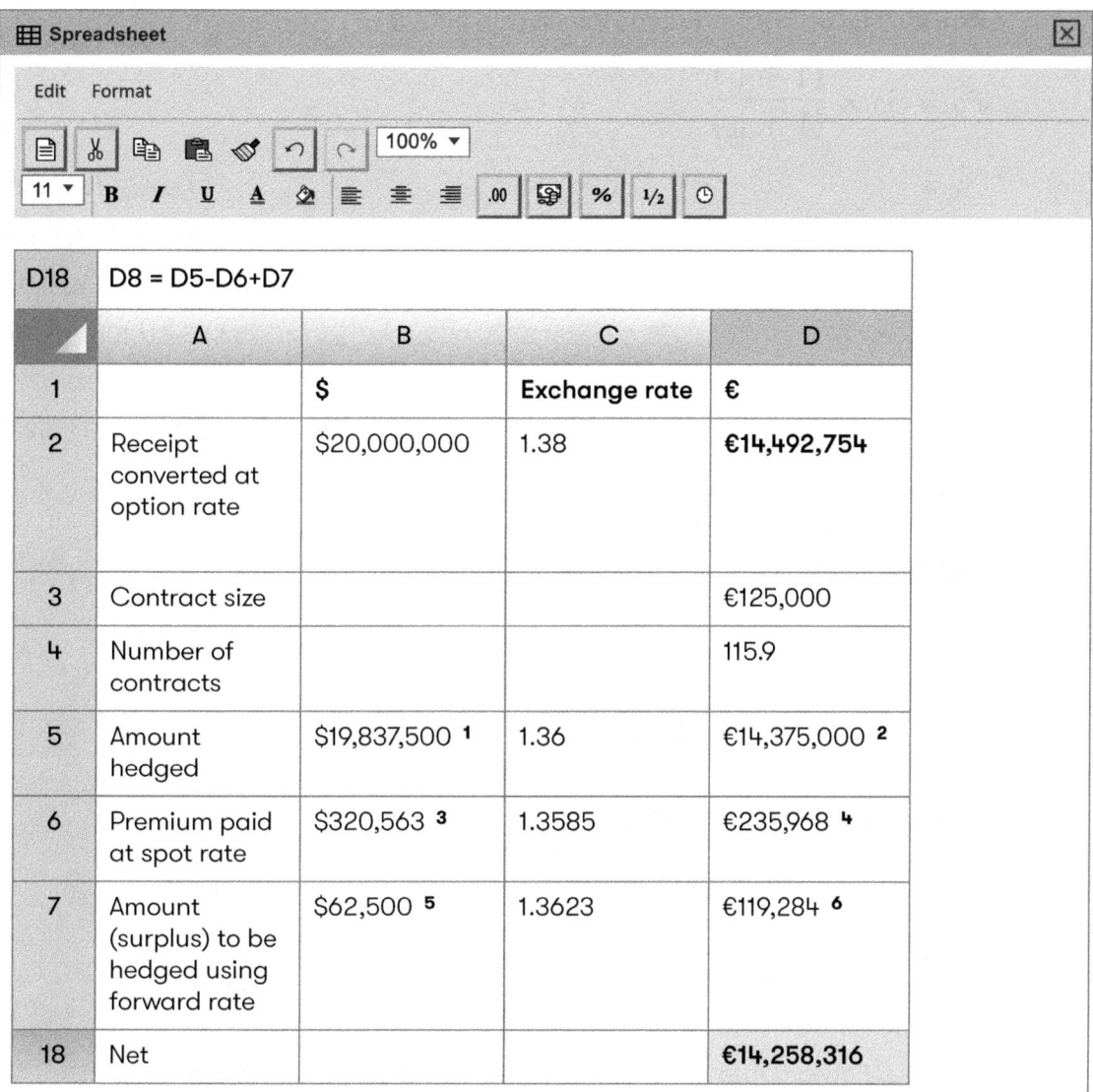

D18	D8 = D5-D6+D7			
	A	**B**	**C**	**D**
1		$	Exchange rate	€
2	Receipt converted at option rate	$20,000,000	1.38	**€14,492,754**
3	Contract size			€125,000
4	Number of contracts			115.9
5	Amount hedged	$19,837,500 [1]	1.36	€14,375,000 [2]
6	Premium paid at spot rate	$320,563 [3]	1.3585	€235,968 [4]
7	Amount (surplus) to be hedged using forward rate	$62,500 [5]	1.3623	€119,284 [6]
18	Net			**€14,258,316**

[1] C7*D7

[2] 115*D5

[3] 0.0223*B7

[4] B8/C8

[5] B4-B7

[6] B9/C9

(b) **Project NPV**

Expected forward rates (using interest rate parity)

$$F_0 = S_0 \times \frac{(1 + i_c)}{(1 + i_b)}$$

Year	Forward rate (€1 = MShs)
Half year	128 × (1.108/1.022) = 138.77
	128 + [(138.77 − 128)/2] = 133.38
1.5 years	133.38 × (1.108/1.022) = 144.60
2.5 years	144.60 × (1.108/1.022) = 156.77
3.5 years	156.77 × (1.108/1.022) = 169.96

NPV calculation (note that Year 1 actually means 1.5 years from now as project starts in six months' time)

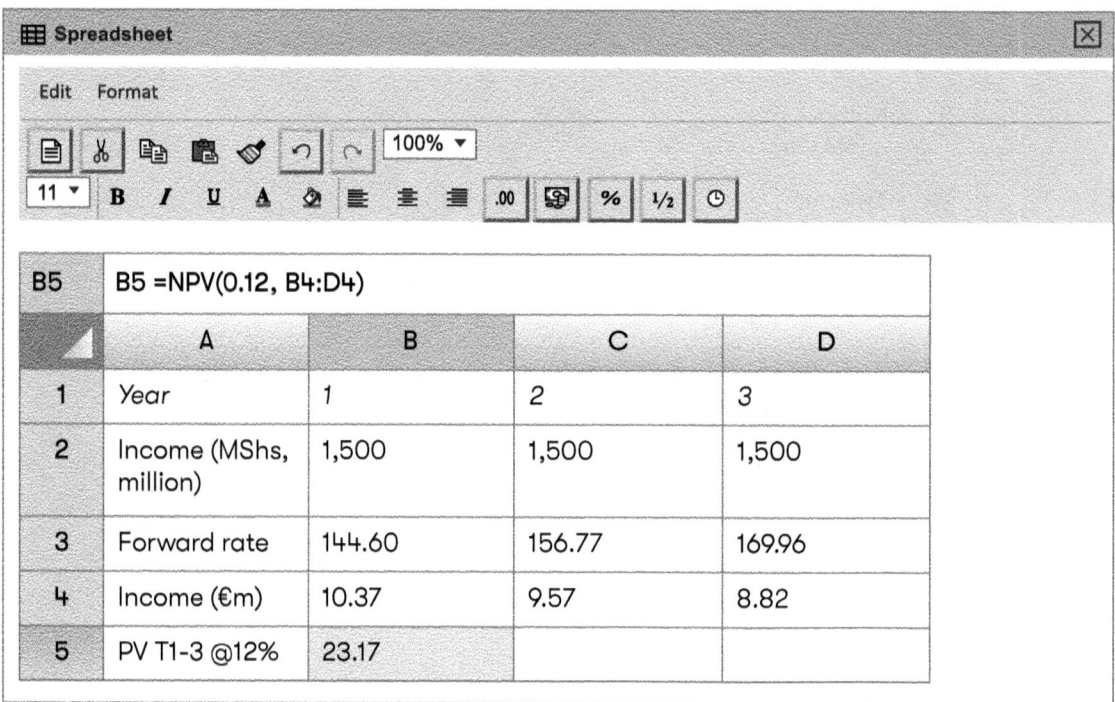

Spreadsheet

B5 = B5 =NPV(0.12, B4:D4)

	A	B	C	D
1	Year	1	2	3
2	Income (MShs, million)	1,500	1,500	1,500
3	Forward rate	144.60	156.77	169.96
4	Income (€m)	10.37	9.57	8.82
5	PV T1-3 @12%	23.17		

Total present value = €23.17 million

Expected spot rate (MShs) in 12 months' time (using purchasing power parity):

$$S_1 = S_0 \times \frac{(1 + h_c)}{(1 + h_b)}$$

S_1 = 116 × (1 + 0.097) / (1 + 0.012) = 125.74

In six months' time expected spot rate = 116 + (125.74 − 116) / 2 = 120.9

Total investment required in € = MShs2.64b / 120.9 = €21.84m

NPV = €1.33m

Will the swap be beneficial for Casasophia?

Forward rates based on interest rate parity show that MShs is depreciating against the € as interest rates are much higher in Mazabia (10.8%) than in the European country (2.2%). However, even with a depreciating MShs the project is still worthwhile (positive NPV).

 BPP

When forward rates are estimated using purchasing power parity, it is assumed that forward rates will change according to differences between the two countries' inflation rates. If Mazabia's inflation rate is greater than the European country's rate, the MShs will depreciate against the €. This may not be the case as many factors affect exchange rates.

We are told that Mazabia's inflation rate could vary between 5% and 15% over the next few years, therefore a swap would appear to be advantageous (as it would fix the future exchange rates). Without the swap there will be uncertainty over the NPV of the project.

Default risk should also be taken into consideration and Casasophia may ask the government of Mazabia to act as a guarantor in order to reduce the risk.

The grant funding will be provided directly to the Mazabian government in MShs. It may be worthwhile for Casasophia to explore the possibility of receiving the grant directly in € as this would reduce currency exposure.

3 Amberle

Course Book references

Adjusted present value is covered in Chapter 6.

Top tips

Ensure that you don't over-obsess about the tricky part of the APV calculation (the interest element of the bank loan repayments). Time would be better invested in part (b) where up to 2 marks per discussion point is available (if the point is addressed to the scenario).

Easy marks

Time invested in reading the scenario carefully should have revealed the ungeared cost of capital and post-tax project cashflows are, effectively, provided in the question. This should mean that Step 1 in APV (evaluating the project as if ungeared) should be easily accomplished.

ACCA examining team's comments

In part (a) the calculations related to the financing side effects proved more challenging. The majority of candidates were not able to deal with a loan payable in equal instalments. A minority of responses either did not discount the financing side effect cash flows at all or used the normal cost of capital used for the base case. Again, this demonstrated a misunderstanding of the purpose and relevance of the adjusted present value method of assessing capital investment projects.

Marking guide	Marks
(a) Working capital	2
Discount rate	1
Base case net present value	2
Issue costs	1
Tax shield benefit – subsidised loan	1
Tax shield benefit – bank loan	4
Subsidy benefit	1
Adjusted present value	1
Comments and conclusion	2
	15
(b) Factors determining long-term finance policy: 1–2 marks per point	5
Maximum	5

 **BPP**

Professional skills

Analysis and Evaluation

- Appropriate use of the data to determine suitable calculations to appraise the project using APV

- Appropriate use of the data to support discussion and draw appropriate conclusions

- Demonstration of reasoned judgement when considering key matters for Amberle Co

- Demonstration of ability to consider relevant factors applicable to Amberle Co's situation

- Identification of further analysis, which could be carried out to enable an appropriate recommendation to be made on whether the project should be accepted.

- Appraisal of information objectively to make a recommendation

Scepticism

- Effective challenge of information and assumptions supplied and, techniques carried out to support any investment decision

Maximum	5
Total	25

(a)

Year	0	1	2	3	4
	$m	$m	$m	$m	$m
Post-tax operating cash flows		28.50	36.70	44.40	50.90
Investment	(150.00)				
Realisable value					45.00
Working capital (W1)	(6.00)	(0.48)	(0.39)	(0.34)	7.21
Cash flows	(156.00)	28.02	36.31	44.06	103.11
Discount factor 12% (W2)	1.000	0.893	0.797	0.712	0.636
Present value	(156.00)	25.02	28.94	31.37	65.58
Base case net present value	(5.09)				

Base case net present value is approximately ($5.09 million) and on this basis, the investment should be rejected.

Alternative approach using spreadsheet functionality:

Alternatively, the present value of the cash flows from time 1–4 can be calculated using the =NPV spreadsheet function. Either method is acceptable, but the spreadsheet function gives a slightly more precise answer and, with practice, should be quicker to use in the exam.

The spreadsheet extract shown in the following section shows the =NPV formula being applied using the cost of capital of 12%.

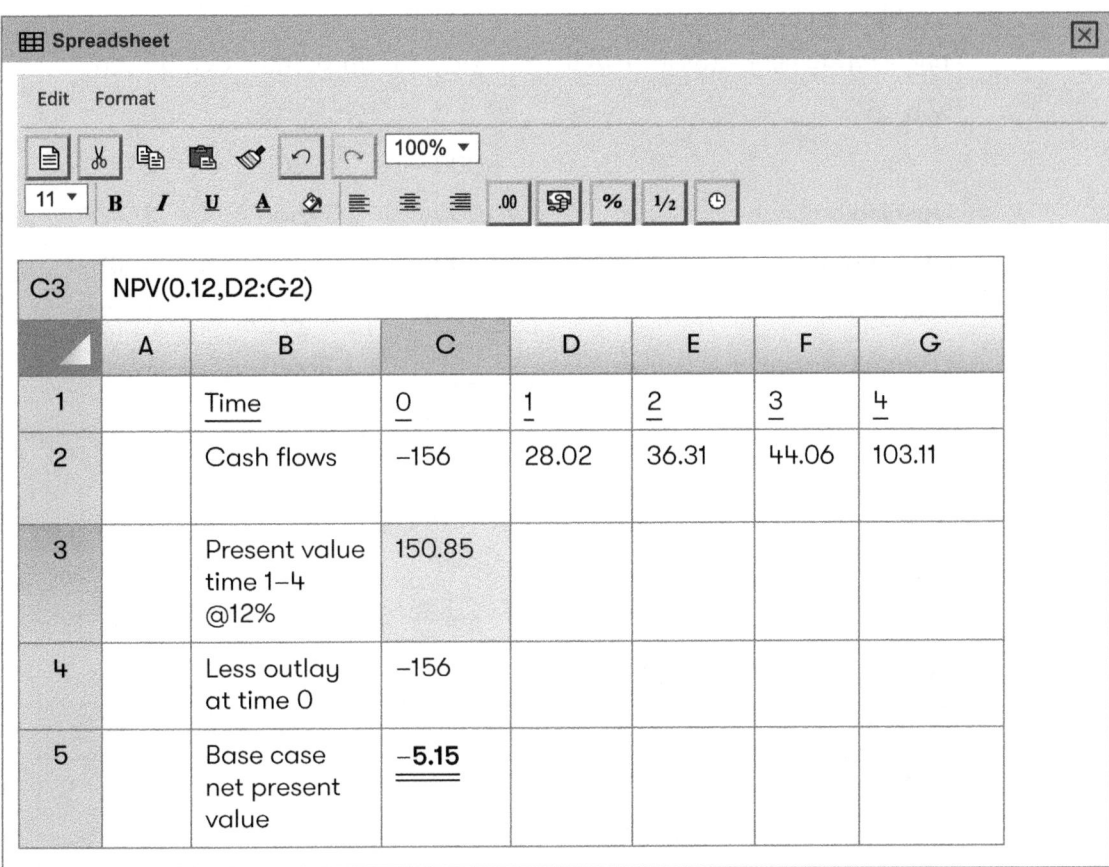

Spreadsheet

C3	NPV(0.12,D2:G2)					
	A	B	C	D	E	F	G
1		Time	0	1	2	3	4
2		Cash flows	–156	28.02	36.31	44.06	103.11
3		Present value time 1–4 @12%	150.85				
4		Less outlay at time 0	–156				
5		Base case net present value	**–5.15**				

Note that the NPV function assumes that the first cash flow is in one year's time, so you then have to subtract the time 0 cash outflows as before to give the project NPV. There is a slight difference in the answer due to rounding of the discount factors in the first approach.

Workings

1 **Working capital**

Year	0	1	2	3	4
	$m	$m	$m	$m	$m
Working capital		6.00	6.48	6.87	7.21
Required/(released)	6.00	0.48	0.39	0.34	(7.21)

2 **Discount rate**

Using asset beta

All-equity financed discount rate = 4% + (11% − 4%) 1.14 = 12%

3 **Issue costs**

$80m / 0.97 = $82,474,227

Issue costs = 3% × $82,474,227 = $2,474,227

There will be no issue costs for the bank loan.

4 **Tax shield on subsidised loan**

Use PV of an annuity (PVA) years 1 to 4 at 8% (normal borrowing rate)

$80m × 0.031 × 30% × 3.312 = $2,464,128

Note to markers

Full credit should be given if tax shield is discounted at the government interest rate of 3.1% rather than the normal borrowing rate of 8%.

5 **Tax shield on bank loan**

Annual repayment = ($70m/PVA 8% Yr 1 – 4) = ($70m/3.312) = $21,135,266

Year	1	2	3	4
	$'000	$'000	$'000	$'000
Opening balance	70,000	54,465	37,687	19,567
Interest at 8%	5,600	4,357	3,015	1,565
Repayment	(21,135)	(21,135)	(21,135)	(21,135)
Closing balance	54,465	37,687	19,567	(3)

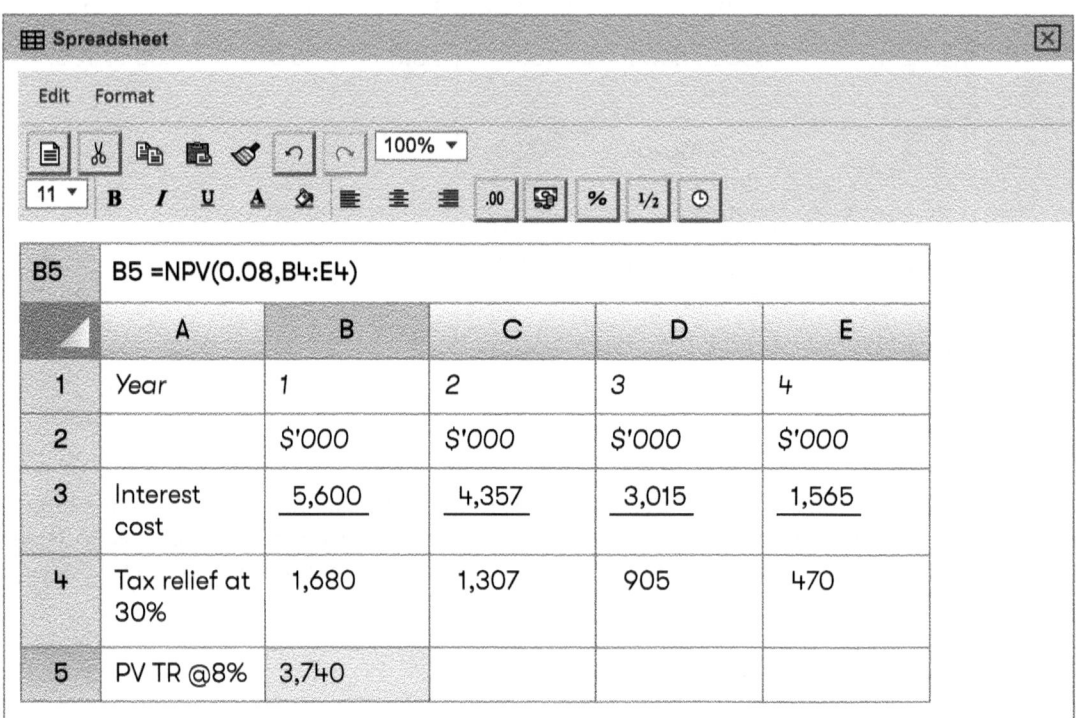

B5   B5 =NPV(0.08,B4:E4)

	A	B	C	D	E
1	Year	1	2	3	4
2		$'000	$'000	$'000	$'000
3	Interest cost	5,600	4,357	3,015	1,565
4	Tax relief at 30%	1,680	1,307	905	470
5	PV TR @8%	3,740			

6 **Subsidy benefit**

Benefit = $80m × (0.08 – 0.031) × 70% × 3.312 = $9,088,128

7 **Financing side effects**

	$'000
Issue costs (W3)	(2,474)
Tax shield on subsidised loan (W4)	2,464
Tax shield on bank loan (W5)	3,740
Subsidy benefit (W6)	9,088
Total benefit of financing side effects	12,818

 **BPP**

Financing the project in this way would add around $12.82 million to the value of the project.

The adjusted present value of the project is around $7.73 million and so the project should be accepted on the basis of this financial evaluation.

Sensitivity analysis should be undertaken on all the significant variables to identify the percentage change in the variable required for the APV to fall to zero. This will help to identify the key assumptions that have been made which can then be reviewed. Further analysis may be needed, particularly of the assumptions which lie behind the post-tax cash flows, such as sales and the tax rate. The realisable value of $45 million may be questionable.

On the other hand, the time horizon of four years seems low and analysis should be done of potential cash flows beyond that time.

Finally, it should be noted that APV is an application of Modigliani and Miller theory and, as such, assumes that there are no financial distress costs associated with using more debt finance. For Amberle this could include higher prices from suppliers if they are concerned about its ability to pay their invoices.

(b)

Amberle Co's board can use various principles to determine its long-term finance mix. The directors may aim to follow consistent long-term policies, or they may have preferences which change as circumstances change.

At present Amberle Co is using a mix of finance, raising the question of whether the directors are aiming for an optimal level of gearing, or there is a level which they do not wish gearing to exceed. If the board wishes to maintain gearing at an optimal level, this is likely to be determined by a balance of risks and advantages. The main risks are not being able to maintain the required level of payment to finance providers, interest to debt providers or required level of dividend to shareholders. Advantages may include lower costs of debt, tax relief on finance costs as shown in the APV calculation or, on the other hand, not being legally required to pay dividends in a particular year.

Another issue is whether Amberle Co's board has preferences about what source of finance should be used and in what order. One example of this is following the pecking order of retained earnings, then debt, then equity. The board may prefer this pecking order on the grounds that avoiding a new equity issue means that the composition of shareholdings is unchanged, or because retained earnings and longer-term debt are judged low risk, or because the market will assume that an equity issue is being made because directors want to take advantage of Amberle Co's shares being over-priced. Other specific sources of finance may have benefits which attract the directors or drawbacks which deter them.

This investment highlights the aspect of whether the board prefers to match sources of finance with specific investments. Matching arguably gives greater flexibility and avoids committing Amberle Co to a long-term interest burden. However, to adopt this approach, the board will need assurance either that the investment will be able to meet finance costs and ultimately repayment burdens, or these can be met from surpluses from other operations.

 **BPP**

ACCA

Advanced Financial Management

Mock Exam 2

Specimen exam

Questions	
Time allowed	Time allowed 3 hours and 15 minutes
Section A THIS question is compulsory and MUST be attempted Section B BOTH questions to be attempted	

DO NOT OPEN THIS EXAM UNTIL YOU ARE READY TO START UNDER EXAMINATION CONDITIONS

BPP

Section A

THIS QUESTION is compulsory and MUST be attempted.

1 Kingtim

The following **exhibits** provide information relevant to the question.

- Kingtim Co
- Takeover defences – to be used by Kingtim Co
- Financial details – relating to cost of capital and bond information
- Employee remuneration

This information should be used to answer the question **requirements** within your chosen **response option(s)**.

Required

(a) Discuss the feasibility and effectiveness of the defence strategies of selling off individual garden centres and enhancing directors' remuneration. **(7 marks)**

(b) Prepare a report for the board of directors of Kingtim Co which:

    (i) estimates the company's cost of capital before the new bonds are issued; **(4 marks)**

    (ii) estimates the market value and post-tax cost of debt of the new bonds; **(7 marks)**

    (iii) estimates the revised cost of equity and revised cost of capital if the new bonds are issued; **(7 marks)**

    (iv) discusses the impact of Kingtim Co's cost of capital and the reaction of equity and bond holders to the chief executive's proposal. The discussion should include an explanation of any assumptions made in the estimates in (b) (i)–(iii) above. **(9 marks)**

(c) Discuss the approach taken to employee remuneration by Kingtim Co's Northern region and the issues associated with it. **(6 marks)**

Professional marks will be awarded for the demonstration of skill in communication, analysis and evaluation, scepticism and commercial acumen in your answer. **(10 marks)**

(Total = 50 marks)

Exhibit 1: Background

Kingtim Co is a nationwide chain of garden centres, selling products such as plants, fertilisers, tools and garden furniture. It was established 20 years ago by the current team of executive directors, and achieved a listing on its local stock market four years ago. Since listing, the company has made consistent profits and has been able to increase its dividends each year. The executive directors collectively own between them 25% of issued share capital. The remaining shares are held by a number of investors, with none of them owning more than 10% of issued share capital.

Two of Kingtim Co's major competitors have been taken over in the last two years. Media coverage suggests that further takeovers are possible. Potential acquirers include other chains of garden centres, property developers and supermarket chains looking to diversify their business into the profitable garden centre sector. As yet, no potential acquirer has approached Kingtim Co to buy the whole chain, although Kingtim Co has had enquiries from other businesses wanting to purchase individual garden centres. Kingtim Co can sell a number of individual garden centres without threatening its continued existence.

Exhibit 2: New proposals

Kingtim Co's executive directors remain committed to the business. They are fearful of a takeover, believing that the new owners will want some, or all of them, to leave the company. They have therefore been considering possible defences against a takeover bid. Kingtim Co's chief executive has received two proposals from directors:

- Sell individual garden centres which would be particularly attractive to purchasers. Disposal of these centres would make Kingtim Co, overall, a less attractive purchase.

- Pay the executive directors higher remuneration and change their contracts so that they would receive much higher compensation for loss of office if their contracts were terminated early.

Kingtim Co's chief executive believes, however, that any defence Kingtim Co adopts should also strengthen the company's future. She is therefore proposing to expand the company's current limited sales of camping products in its garden centres by establishing a chain of Kingtim outdoor shops, selling camping, walking and other outdoor equipment. The outdoor retail sector is competitive, but the chief executive believes that Kingtim Co will be successful. The establishment of the chain of outdoor shops would be funded solely by debt, the idea being that changing Kingtim Co's finance structure by having significantly more debt would make it less attractive to acquirers.

Exhibit 3: Financial information

Kingtim Co currently has 25 million $1 shares in issue, with a current share price of $5.56 per share. It also has 0.45 million 6.5% bonds in issue. Each 6.5% bond has a nominal value of $100, and is currently trading at $104 per $100. The premium on redemption of the bonds in three years' time is 2%. Based on a yield to maturity approach, the after-tax cost of the bonds is 4.1%.

Kingtim Co's quoted equity beta for its existing garden centre business is 0.9.

Kingtim Co plans to issue 0.6 million, 7.5%, new bonds, each with a nominal value of $100. These bonds will be redeemable in four years' time at a premium of 8%. The coupon on these bonds will be payable on an annual basis. These bonds are anticipated to have a credit rating of BBB−. The issue of the new 7.5% bonds will not affect the market value of Kingtim Co's shares or the existing 6.5% bonds.

The market value of the new bonds will be determined by using information relating to Kingtim Co's credit rating and the four bonds which the government has issued to estimate Kingtim Co's yield curve. All the bonds are of the same risk class. Details of the bonds are as follows:

Bond	Annual yield (based on spot rate)	Redeemable in
Ga	4%	1 year
Th	4.3%	2 years
De	4.7%	3 years
Ro	5.2%	4 years

Credit spreads, shown in basis points, are as follows:

Rating	1 year	2 years	3 years	4 years
BBB−	56	78	106	135

Kingtim Co plans to invest $60m in non-current assets for the outdoor shops (working capital requirements can be ignored). Currently, Kingtim Co's non-current assets have a net book value of $150m. It is assumed that the proportion of the book value of non-current assets which will be invested in the outdoor shops and the garden centres will give a fair representation of the size of each business within Kingtim Co. The asset beta of similar companies in the outdoor retail sector is assumed to be 0.88.

Before taking into consideration the impact of this new investment, Kingtim Co's forecast pre-tax earnings for the coming year is $24m. It is estimated that the new investment will make a 10% pre-tax return and after-tax earnings will increase by $1.125m.

The corporation tax rate applicable to all companies is 25% per year. The current risk-free rate of return is estimated to be 4% and the market risk premium is estimated to be 9%.

Exhibit 4: Social issues

Kingtim Co's annual report contains a general commitment to act with social responsibility, in line with society's expectations. It also commits to paying its staff fairly in accordance with their responsibilities and states that its staff are vital to its success.

To try to improve the situation of low-paid employees, the government has recommended a basic hourly wage as the minimum level employees should be paid, although this minimum is not legally enforceable. A newspaper investigation has revealed that some staff in Kingtim Co's garden centres in the northern region of the country are paid up to 15% less per hour than the recommended minimum wage. Most of these staff are part-time staff, working limited hours each week.

The manager of Kingtim Co's northern region centres, when asked to comment, stated that Kingtim Co had obligations to its shareholders to control staff costs. Lower pay levels were necessary to differentiate between staff, ensuring that managers and staff with experience and expertise were appropriately rewarded. The manager commented that pay levels also reflected the lower commitment to Kingtim Co which part-time staff made compared with full-time staff.

Section B

THESE QUESTIONS are compulsory and MUST be attempted.

2 Colvin

The following **exhibits** provide information relevant to the question:

(1)   Colvin Co

(2)   Project information

(3)   Discount rate

This information should be used to answer the question **requirements** within your chosen **response option(s)**.

Required

(a)   Evaluate the suitability of the investment proposal in Canvia, including the impact of the country risk premium on the net present value of the project.   **(14 marks)**

(b)   Discuss the validity of the chief executive's reasons for adjusting the discount rate used in appraising the project in Canvia.   **(6 marks)**

Professional marks will be awarded for the demonstration of skill in analysis and evaluation, scepticism and commercial acumen in your answer.   **(5 marks)**

(Total = 25 marks)

Exhibit 1: Background

Colvin Co is based in the eurozone region and was established ten years ago to manufacture competition standard bicycles for professional road racers. When the company obtained a listing five years ago, the founder retained a small minority shareholding. The remaining shares are held by a number of institutional investors.

The board recently decided to expand the range of models and to look for new growth opportunities abroad. Whilst manufacturing is currently restricted to the eurozone, the board of directors has identified Canvia as a key growth market and is considering a potential investment project to manufacture and sell a new model there. This would involve establishing a subsidiary in Canvia.

Exhibit 2: Project information

The currency in Canvia is the Canvian lira (CL) and the current exchange rate is CL9.91 per euro (€). The annual rate of inflation in Canvia is expected to remain at 10% throughout the four-year duration of the project.

The finance director estimates the project's sales volumes, inflation-adjusted, pre-tax contribution and fixed costs as follows:

Year	1	2	3	4
Sales volume (units)	109,725	121,795	148,590	197,624
Pre-tax contribution (CLm)	419.4	500.2	671.3	961.2
Fixed costs (CLm)	270.0	291.6	314.9	340.1

The project will require an immediate investment of CL75m in land and buildings and CL700m in plant and machinery. Tax allowable depreciation is available on plant and machinery on a straight-line basis at an annual rate of 25% on cost. Colvin Co's finance director believes the plant and machinery will have a zero residual value at the end of the four years. The land and buildings will be disposed of at the end of the project and their tax exempt value is expected to increase at an annual rate of 30% throughout the four-year life of the investment.

The project will also require an immediate investment in working capital of CL25m. The annual incremental working capital requirements are expected to be as follows:

Year	0	1	2	3
CLm	(25.0)	(2.5)	(2.8)	(3.0)

Working capital will be released back in full at the end of the project. Colvin Co has a policy of extracting remittable cash flows as dividends at the earliest possible opportunity.

All components for the new bicycle will be produced or purchased in Canvia except for a gearing system component which will be manufactured by Colvin Co in the eurozone. The cost of acquiring this component from the eurozone is already included in the pre-tax contribution estimates, based on a transfer price of €10 per component. The finance director estimates a manufacturing cost of €2 per component. Both the transfer price and manufacturing cost are expected to increase in line with eurozone annual inflation of 4% in the first two years of the project and 2% in years three and four.

Corporation tax in Canvia is payable annually at 25% and companies are allowed to carry losses forward to be offset against future trading profits. Colvin Co pays corporation tax in its home country at an annual rate of 20%. Taxes are payable in both countries in the year the liability is incurred. A bi-lateral tax treaty exists between the two countries, which permits the offset of overseas tax against any domestic tax liability incurred on overseas earnings.

Exhibit 3: Financing information

The board proposes financing the project with a mix of equity and debt in such a way that the existing capital structure remains unchanged. For the purposes of this project, the chief executive believes Colvin Co's weighted average cost of capital of 13% should be adjusted to include a country risk premium on the basis that Canvia is a developing economy and appears to be economically less stable than the eurozone countries. She made this decision after consulting a country risk index, which compares the standard deviation of market returns in various countries.

Additional factors taken into consideration include foreign exchange risk, the fact that there have been frequent changes of government, and hence economic policies, in Canvia. You have therefore been asked to use a discount rate of 16% to appraise this investment project.

3 Boullain

The following **exhibits** provide information relevant to the question.

(1) Boullain Co and its hedging policy

(2) Hedging products

This information should be used to answer the question **requirements** within your chosen **response option(s)**.

Required

(a) Explain the rationale for the policy of hedging Boullain Co's foreign exchange risk and the potential benefits to shareholder value if that policy is effectively communicated to the company's key stakeholders. **(6 marks)**

(b) Recommend a hedging strategy for Boullain Co's foreign currency receipt in six months' time based on the hedging choices the finance director is considering. Support your recommendation with relevant calculations and appropriate discussion including the impact of the margin requirements. **(14 marks)**

Professional marks will be awarded for the demonstration of skill in analysis and evaluation, scepticism and commercial acumen in your answer. **(5 marks)**

(Total = 25 marks)

Exhibit 1: Background

Boullain Co is based in the Eurozone and manufactures components for agricultural machinery. The company is financed by a combination of debt and equity, having obtained a listing five years ago. In addition to the founder's equity stake, the shareholders consist of pension funds and other institutional investors. Until recently, sales have been generated exclusively within the Eurozone area but the directors are keen to expand and have identified North America as a key export market. The company recently completed its first sale to a customer based in the United States, although payment will not be received for another six months.

At a recent board meeting, Boullain Co's finance director argued that the expansion into foreign markets creates the need for a formal hedging policy and that shareholder value would be enhanced if this policy was communicated to the company's other stakeholders. However, Boullain Co's chief executive officer disagreed with the finance director on the following grounds. First, existing shareholders are already well diversified and would therefore not benefit from additional risk reduction hedging strategies. Second, there is no obvious benefit to shareholder value by communicating the hedging policy to other stakeholders such as debt providers, employees, customers and suppliers. You have been asked to provide a rationale for the finance director's comments in advance of the next board meeting.

Exhibit 2: Foreign currency issues

Assume today's date is 1 March 20X0. Boullain Co is due to receive $18,600,000 from the American customer on 31 August 20X0. The finance director is keen to minimise the company's exposure to foreign exchange risk and has identified forward contracts, exchange traded futures and options as a way of achieving this objective.

The following quotations have been obtained.

Exchange rates (quoted as €/US$1)

Spot	0.8707–0.8711
Six months forward	0.8729–0.8744

Currency futures (contract size €200,000; price quoted as US$ per €1)

	Price
March	1.1476
June	1.1449
September	1.1422

Currency options (contract size €200,000; exercise price quoted as US$ per €1, premium: US cents per €1)

Exercise	Calls			Puts		
price	March	June	September	March	June	September
1.1420	0.43	0.59	0.77	0.62	0.78	0.89

Assume futures and options contracts mature at the month end and that there is no basis risk. The number of contracts to be used should be rounded down to the nearest whole number in calculations. If the full amount cannot be hedged using an exact number of futures or options contracts, the balance is hedged using the forward market.

Once the position is open, the euro futures contract outlined above will be marked-to-market on a daily basis. The terms of the contract require Boullain Co to deposit an initial margin per contract with the clearing house. Assume the maintenance margin is equivalent to the initial margin.

Your manager is concerned about the impact of an open futures position on Boullain Co's cash flow and has asked you to explain the impact of the margin requirements and their significance for the hedging decision.

Advanced Financial Management

Answers

DO NOT TURN THIS PAGE UNTIL YOU HAVE
COMPLETED THE MOCK EXAM

BPP

Exam success skills

In any AFM exam it will be important to apply good general exam technique by using the six exam success skills identified at the start of the Revision Kit, in the section covering 'essential skills'. These skills are: 1. Case scenario: Managing information; 2. Correct interpretation of requirements; 3. Answer planning: Priorities, structure and logic; 4. Efficient numerical analysis; 5. Effective writing and presentation; and 6. Good time management.

Some examples of how to apply these skills in this exam are provided in the table below.

Skill	Examples
Managing information	It is crucially important to assimilate the information in the question scenario.
	In longer questions, such as the 50-mark question, it is difficult to assimilate information by simply starting at the beginning and reading to the end because there is so much information to take in.
	Instead, it is sensible to take an **active approach** to reading each question. Read enough of the question to get an idea of the basic scenario and then read the initial requirements so that you understand the first things that you are expected to do with this information.
	For example, in Question 1 the lengthy scenario makes a lot more sense if, before reading all of it, you are aware that the first requirements relate to bond valuation and the cost of capital.
Correct Interpretation of requirements	Be careful to interpret the verbs used in the question requirements carefully.
	For example, in Q1(b iv), the verb 'discuss' implies that an element of critical analysis (discussing from different viewpoints) is appropriate.
	Also be careful to identify where a question requirement contains more than one instruction.
	For example, in Q1 part b where calculation AND explanation is asked for.
Answer planning	This is always important in answering AFM questions.
	For example, in risk management questions such as Q3, it is especially important that your plan correctly identifies (i) the risk being faced (ii) the relevant timings. If you get these wrong, then there will be a cap on the number of marks that you can score (however accurate your answers are).
Efficient numerical analysis	It is essential that the marker can follow your workings and your logic.
	It is also important that you accept that under exam conditions you will not get **all** the calculations correct, and that this is not necessary in order to score a strong pass mark.
	If you make a mistake early in your calculations that affects your later calculations, then the marker will only penalise the error you have made, and not its follow-on impact on other calculations. This means that it is not normally a good use of your time to correct such errors during the exam.
	For example, in Question 2(a) an error early on in your calculations would only attract a small penalty despite its impact on the final NPV.

 **BPP**

Skill	Examples
Effective writing and presentation	In Q1 there are marks available for professional structure (eg use of sub-headings, appendices etc). Many of the techniques used here are good practice in all questions throughout the exam. It is also very important to relate your points to the scenario and to the requirement wherever possible. This does not mean simply repeating the details from the question but using this information to help to explain the point you are making. For example, in Q1(b)(iv) it is not enough to state the assumptions, you need to explain their relevance.

Good Time Management	The exam is 3 hours 15 minutes long, which translates to 1.95 minutes per mark.
	
	It is essential that you do not allow yourself to become bogged down in the harder numerical areas of the exam.
	
	For example, in Q1 it is vital to leave enough time to answer the discursive parts, especially part (c).
	
	At the beginning of a question, work out the amount of time you should be spending on:
	
	(a) Planning:
	
	    (i) for a 25-mark question this will be about 1.95 × 25 marks × 20% = 10 minutes
	
	    (ii) for a 50-mark question this should be about 20 mins.
	
	(b) Writing your answer to each requirement:
	
	    (i) Take the mark allocation and multiply by 1.95 minutes per technical mark.

Diagnostic

Did you apply these skills when reading, planning, and writing up your answer? Identify the exam success skills where you think you need to improve and capture your thoughts here of what you want to achieve when attempting questions in future.

Section A

1 Kingtim

Course Book references

Ethics is covered in Chapter 1 and cost of capital Chapters 2 and 7. Defence strategies are covered in Chapter 9.

Top tips

You will need to be very strict on your time management with this question – it is easy to overrun especially if you are attempting to produce a 100% perfect answer to part (b)(ii).

Easy marks

About 60% of the marks are available for discussion but ensure your points are addressed to the scenario to maximise marks remember easy communication marks can be obtained by:

(1) Providing a suitable, simple, heading to the answer (eg a simple report format)

(2) Providing a short introduction paragraph outlining the structure of the report

(3) Providing a clear answer (eg referencing spreadsheet calculations where appropriate).

(4) Providing a conclusion to complete the report.

 BPP

(a)	Sell-off assets (examples of points could include company less appealing, use of proceeds from sell-off, how Kingtim Co will be viewed, smaller company being more affordable)	4
	Onerous contracts (examples of points could include cost burden, acquirer may be prepared to bear it, corporate governance requirements, shareholder reaction)	$\underline{4}$
	Marks Available	8
	Maximum	7
(b) (i)	Cost of equity	1
	Value of equity	1
	Value of existing bonds	1
	WACC	$\underline{1}$
		4
(ii)	Annual spot yield curve	1
	Value of new bonds	2
	Market value of new bonds	1
	Post-tax cost of debt of proposed bonds	$\underline{2}$
		7
(iii)	Asset beta garden centre business	1
	Weighted asset beta	2
	Revised equity beta	1
	Revised cost of equity	1
	Revised WACC	$\underline{2}$
		7
(iv)	Cost of capital	2
	Assumptions	3
	Equity holders	3
	Bond holders	$\underline{3}$
	Marks Available	11
	Maximum	9
(c)	Up to 2 marks for each well-explained issue (issues could include rewarding expertise/seniority fairly, balancing shareholder and employee interests, unfair to question staff's commitment, society's expectations/law, expectations raised by Kingtim Co's statements, employee/customer reaction to poor practices)	$\underline{6}$
	Maximum	$\underline{6}$

Professional skills marks

Communication

- General report format and structure (use of headings/sub-headings and an introduction)
- Style, language and clarity (appropriate layout and tone of report response, presentation of calculations, appropriate use of the tools)
- Effectiveness of communication (answer is relevant, specific rather than general and focused to the requirement)
- Adherence to the details of the Chief Executive's proposal in the scenario

 **BPP**

Analysis and Evaluation

- Appropriate use of the data to determine suitable calculations
- Appropriate use of the data to support discussion and draw appropriate conclusions
- Demonstration of reasoned judgement when considering key matters for Kingtim Co
- Demonstration of ability to consider relevant factors applicable to increasing the level of debt finance

Scepticism

- Effective challenge of information, evidence and assumptions supplied and, techniques carried out to support key facts and/or decisions
- Demonstration of the ability to probe into the reasons for issues and problems, including the identification of missing information or additional information, which would alter the decision reached by Kingtim Co

Commercial acumen

- Recommendations are practical and plausible in the context of Kingtim Co's situation
- Effective use of examples and/or calculations from the scenario information and other practical considerations related to the context to illustrate points being made
- Recognition of external constraints and opportunities as necessary

Maximum | 10

Total | 50

(a)

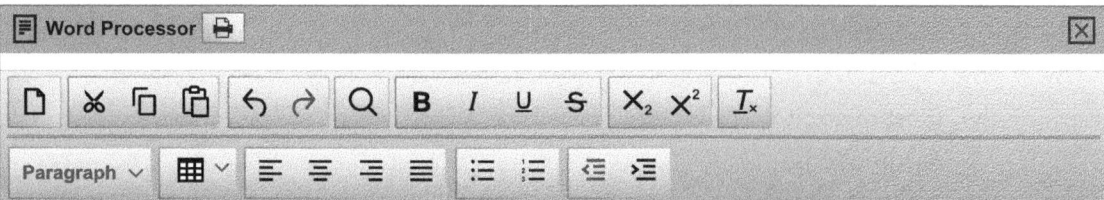

Sell-off of garden centres

Selling some of the most desirable garden centres, known as selling the crown jewels, may deter some acquirers looking to buy the whole chain if Kingtim Co sells the assets they most desire. Kingtim Co could take this option if it is able to sell off individual centres without jeopardising its overall existence.

However, if no particular use is made of the cash raised from the sales, Kingtim Co would still remain a tempting takeover target due to its cash surpluses. Returning the surplus cash to shareholders in the form of a one-off dividend might be popular with shareholders, but equally they might be concerned about their future returns given the sale of assets generating significant income. Shareholders and others interested in Kingtim Co might also question what future strategies the board had in mind if it did not use these cash surpluses for investment.

Also, if the money was distributed to shareholders, Kingtim Co would become a smaller company and perhaps more affordable to some potential acquirers.

Enhanced directors' remuneration and contracts

The enhanced commitments to the directors would represent an increased burden for acquirers, either the costs of honouring them, or the cost and the time involved in terminating the directors' employment and compensating them. This burden may deter acquirers, particularly if the decision to acquire is marginal.

However, enhancing the commitments to the directors could be ineffective. The acquirer could decide to keep the directors on and pay the increased remuneration. Alternatively, the acquirer may feel that buying out the directors' contracts and compensating them is a necessary cost that it is prepared to bear.

Corporate governance aspects are also important. As a listed company, Kingtim Co should have a remuneration committee made up of non-executive directors, who should be reviewing the executive directors' remuneration packages. Kingtim Co may have to publish a remuneration report to explain the rationale for directors' remuneration, and to allow shareholders to discuss and perhaps vote on the report.

Shareholders may believe that the directors are being given a better compensation package without having earned it, and for no other reason than to try to protect their own positions. They may doubt whether directors are acting in the best interests of the company and its shareholders.

(b)

Report to board of directors, Kingtim Co

Introduction

This report indicates the impact of the proposed investment in outdoor shops and the consequent increase in debt finance. It also discusses the possible reactions of equity and bond holders to the proposals. Financial estimates provided in the appendices are used to support the discussion and assumptions underlying the estimates are set out below.

Cost of capital

There are two impacts, in opposite directions, on the weighted average cost of capital.

Kingtim Co's cost of equity has risen significantly. This is due to increased business risk, resulting from the investment in the outdoor shops and increased financial risk from the additional debt. The increase in the cost of equity has pushed the weighted average cost of capital upwards.

However, the higher proportion of debt in the company's finance structure, with debt having a lower cost than equity and also being tax-deductible, has pushed the weighted average cost of capital downwards.

Overall, however, the weighted average cost of capital has risen, meaning the increase in the cost of equity has had the greater impact.

Assumptions

The assumptions about the returns from the new investment may depend on how much Kingtim Co can attract customers away from competitors rather than finding a new market niche itself. Competitor reaction may also impact upon returns.

The CAPM model used is assumed to be a good predictor of equity returns, although some published evidence suggests that it may not be.

The asset beta used for the outdoor shops is a representative beta for similar companies and may not be accurate for Kingtim Co. The asset beta used to calculate the revised cost of equity is a weighted average of the asset betas of the two businesses. The weighting used is the non-current assets in each business, which is assumed to approximate to the size of each business. This assumes that non-current assets currently held are valued fairly, and that their valuation represents their income-generating potential and the proportion of business risk that each business represents.

ANSWERS

The share price and price of the existing bonds are assumed to remain unchanged when the new investment is made. As discussed below, there is a strong possibility of changes in the shareholder base leading to changes in the share price and hence in the cost of capital.

Equity holders

Equity holders may consider the returns from the new investment to be insufficient. The pre-tax return of 10% is lower than the 16% pre-tax return ($24m/$150m) on the existing garden centres, and is not much above the 7.5% pre-tax finance cost of the bonds used to finance the investment.

Equity holders are likely to be concerned about the increases in both business and financial risks. The increase in business risk is due to the higher business risk for the outdoor shops, due to the competition in that sector. Equity holders will be concerned about the possible variability of returns and also of dividends, as the company is committed to an increased operating cost burden in terms of extra premises and increased finance costs. Variability of returns may also result in the share price becoming more volatile.

Other aspects concerning equity holders might be any restrictive covenants attached to the new bonds that affect payment of dividends and also the planned repayment of the bonds. Kingtim Co already has a significant commitment to repay the $45m bonds in three years' time. The new bonds would mean an additional commitment to repay $60m just a year later. The alternative is refinancing, but the terms that would be available are currently unknown.

These risks may mean that equity holders reconsider their investment in Kingtim Co, if they are risk-averse and do not feel that the additional returns compensate for the risk. They will take into account that the return on investment in the new business is lower than the current return on investment in the garden centres, although they are not required to make any additional investment themselves for the return on the outdoor shops. The share price will fall if a significant number of shareholders decide to sell their shares, although Kingtim Co may attract a new clientele of shareholders who are more risk-seeking.

Bond holders

Bond holders are likely to be most concerned about Kingtim Co's ability to meet its interest and repayment commitments. Holders of the new bonds are particularly likely to be concerned about the ability to repay their capital, given the commitment to repay existing bond holders. Bond holders may also be concerned about whether the financing of the investment allows Kingtim Co to take undue risks. They may wonder about the motivation for undertaking the new investment using debt finance, particularly if they are not convinced about its business case.

Conclusion

Assuming a strong business case can be made for the investment and the estimates are robust, Kingtim Co may be able to justify financing it solely by debt and claim that the increase in financial risk is within acceptable levels. However, before committing to further debt, Kingtim Co must provide a clear plan for repayment of both the current and new bonds, or offer sufficient assurance that it will be able to refinance its debt when it is due for repayment.

Appendix 1 Estimate of existing cost of capital (b) (i)

Cost of equity

$k_e = 4.0\% + (0.9 \times 9.0\%) = 12.1\%$

Value of equity (V_e) = $5.56 \times 25 million shares = $139m

Value of existing bonds

$V_d = \$104 \times 0.45$ million = $46.8m

Current WACC

WACC = ((12.1% × 139) + (4.1% × 46.8))/(139 + 46.8) = 10.1%

Appendix 2 Estimate of cost of new bonds (b) (ii)

Annual yield curve

Bond	Government annual yield curve	Credit spread	Kingtim Co annual yield curve
Ga	4%	56	4.56%
Th	4.3%	78	5.08%
De	4.7%	106	5.76%
Ro	5.2%	135	6.55%

Value of new bonds based on annual yield curve

$\$7.50 \times 1.0456^{-1} + \$7.50 \times 1.0508^{-2} + \$7.50 \times 1.0576^{-3} + \$115.50 \times 1.0655^{-4} = \$109.92$

Market value of new bonds

$\$109.92 \times 0.6m = \$65.952m$

Post-tax cost of debt of new bonds

Year		$	5%	$	3%	$
0	Market value	(109.92)	1.000	(109.92)	1.000	(109.92)
1–4	Interest (post-tax)	5.63	3.546	19.96	3.717	20.93
4	Redemption	108.00	0.823	88.88	0.888	95.90
				(1.08)		6.91

Post-tax cost of debt = 3% + ((6.91 / (6.91 + 1.08)) × (5% – 3%)) = 4.7%

Alternative presentation of cost of debt using spreadsheet functionality

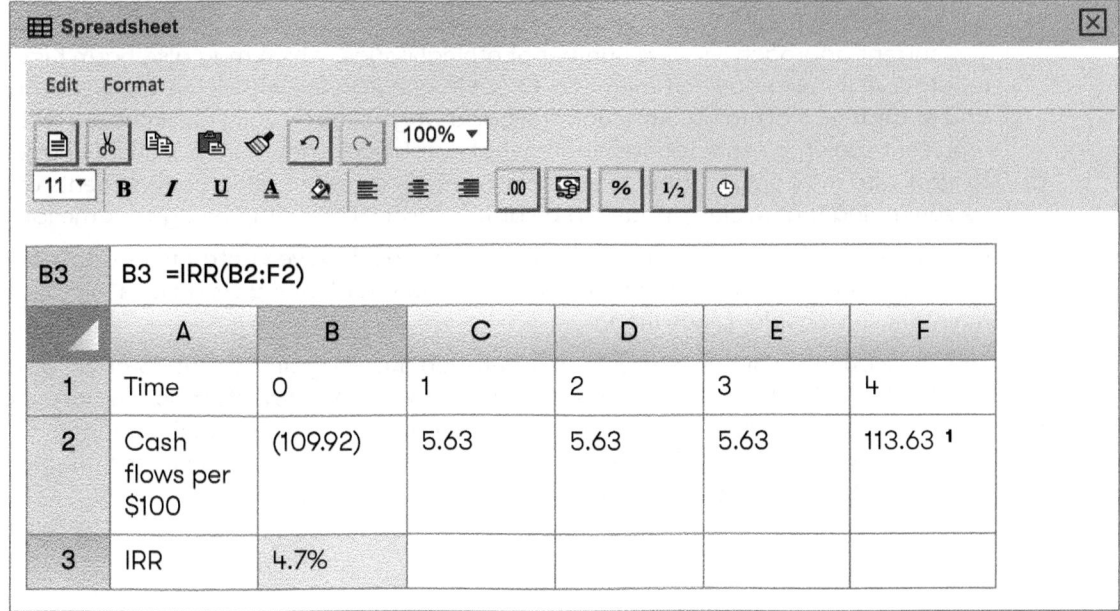

	A	B	C	D	E	F
		B3 =IRR(B2:F2)				
1	Time	0	1	2	3	4
2	Cash flows per $100	(109.92)	5.63	5.63	5.63	113.63 [1]
3	IRR	4.7%				

[1] 5.63+108

Appendix 3 Revised cost of equity and WACC (b) (iii)

βa garden centre business = 0.9 × (139 / (139 + (46.8 × 0.75))) = 0.72

Weighted average βa = (0.72 × (150 / (150 + 60))) + (0.88 × (60 / (150 + 60))) = 0.77

βe = 0.77 × ((139 + ((46.8 + 65.952) × 0.75)) / 139) = 1.24

ke = 4.0% + (1.24 × 9.0%) = 15.2%

WACC = ((15.2% × 139) + (4.1% × 46.8) + (4.7% × 65.952)) / (139 + 46.8 + 65.952) = 10.4%

(c)

Approach taken

The stated approach to employee remuneration has some business logic. Expertise, experience, seniority and commitment are all attributes that staff have that could be reflected in extra rewards for them, not only out of fairness to the staff but also because of their value to the business. If staff with these attributes believe they are not being rewarded fairly, they may leave and perhaps join a competitor.

Kingtim Co also has a duty to enhance the wealth of its shareholders and has raised expectations by recently increasing dividends. There is a stakeholder conflict, as increasing the wages of many employees would lead to lower profits and less money available for distribution to shareholders.

Issues with approach

The statement about part-time staff not having the same level of commitment may well be unjust, as they may be as committed as full-time staff during the hours they work.

The current approach raises a number of ethical issues, which may also harm Kingtim Co's reputation. It has made commitments to act in accordance with society's expectations and to treat its staff fairly. Although the basic wage is not legally enforceable, it does represent society's expectations about what employees should be paid. Limiting rewards to staff who may only be able to work part-time because of other commitments could also be something that society judges to be discriminatory and may be against the law.

In addition, if Kingtim Co's directors are given more lucrative contracts as a takeover defence mechanism, this undermines the argument for limiting staff costs in order to maintain shareholder reputation.

The consequences of these threats to reputation might again be that lower-paid staff eventually decide to leave. A high staff turnover will mean few staff develop experience and expertise over time, which may impact on customer service quality. Kingtim Co may also have problems recruiting staff for its new outdoor business. Customers may also stop shopping at Kingtim Co in protest at the poor treatment of staff.

Section B

THESE QUESTIONS are compulsory and MUST be attempted.

2 Colvin

> **Course Book references**
>
> Investment appraisal is mainly covered in Chapters 3 and 5, and managing blocks dividend remittances is covered in Chapter 16.
>
> **Top tips**
>
> **Part (a).** This required a straightforward analysis of the contribution less fixed costs, adjusting for straight line tax allowable depreciation. The only real complication is how to treat profits on internal transfers, but this was only worth 3 marks.
>
> **Part (b).** Comments need to be addressed to the rationale of the CEO for changing the cost of capital despite the fact there no change in capital structure and arguably little change in business risk. Since the logic of the CEO is based on standard deviation an awareness of the irrelevance of standard deviation (portfolio theory) is useful.

Marking guide	Marks
(a) Exchange rates	2
Tax	2
Working capital	1
Land and buildings residual value	1
Remittable cash flows in euros	1
Contribution from component	2
Tax on contribution	1
Net present values	2
Comment	3
Marks Available	15
Maximum	14
(b) Up to 2 marks per point (eg argument for WACC, total risk vs market risk, correlation across countries)	
Maximum	6

Professional skills marks

Analysis and Evaluation

- Appropriate use of the data to determine suitable calculations
- Appropriate use of the data to support discussion and draw appropriate conclusions
- Appraisal of information objectively to make a recommendation

Scepticism

- Effective challenge of information, evidence and assumptions supplied and, techniques carried out to support key facts and/or decisions
- Demonstration of ability to consider all relevant factors applicable to a given course of action

Commercial acumen

- Recommendations are practical and plausible in the context of Colvin Co's situation
- Effective use of examples and/or calculations from the scenario information and other practical considerations related to the context to illustrate points being made

(a) **Project cash flows:** All figures are in CL millions

Year	0	1	2	3	4
Contribution		419.4	500.2	671.3	961.2
Fixed costs		(270.0)	(291.6)	(314.9)	(340.1)
Tax allowable depreciation		(175.0)	(175.0)	(175.0)	(175.0)
Taxable profit / (loss)		(25.6)	33.6	181.4	446.1
Tax loss carried forward			(25.6)		
Adjusted taxable profit		(25.6)	8.0	181.4	446.1
Taxation (25%)			(2.0)	(45.4)	(111.5)
Tax loss carried forward			25.6		
Add back TAD		175.0	175.0	175.0	175.0
Cash flows after tax		149.4	206.6	311.0	509.6
Working capital	(25.0)	(2.5)	(2.8)	(3.0)	33.3
Investment cost	(775.0)				214.2
Cash flows	(800.0)	146.9	203.8	308.0	757.1

Cash flows: All figures are in € millions

Year	0	1	2	3	4
Exchange rate (w1)	9.91	10.48	11.09	11.96	12.89
Total investment cost	(80.7)				
Remittable cash flows		14.0	18.4	25.8	58.7
Component contribution (w2)		0.9	1.1	1.3	1.8
Tax on net contribution (20%)		(0.2)	(0.2)	(0.3)	(0.4)
Cash flows	(80.7)	14.7	19.3	26.8	60.1

Net present value using 16% discount rate: All figures are in € millions

Year	0	1	2	3	4
Cash flows	(80.7)	14.7	19.3	26.8	60.1
Discount rate (16%)	1.000	0.862	0.743	0.641	0.552
Present values	(80.7)	12.7	14.3	17.2	33.2

Net present value (€3.3m)

Alternative presentation of NPV at 16% using spreadsheet functionality

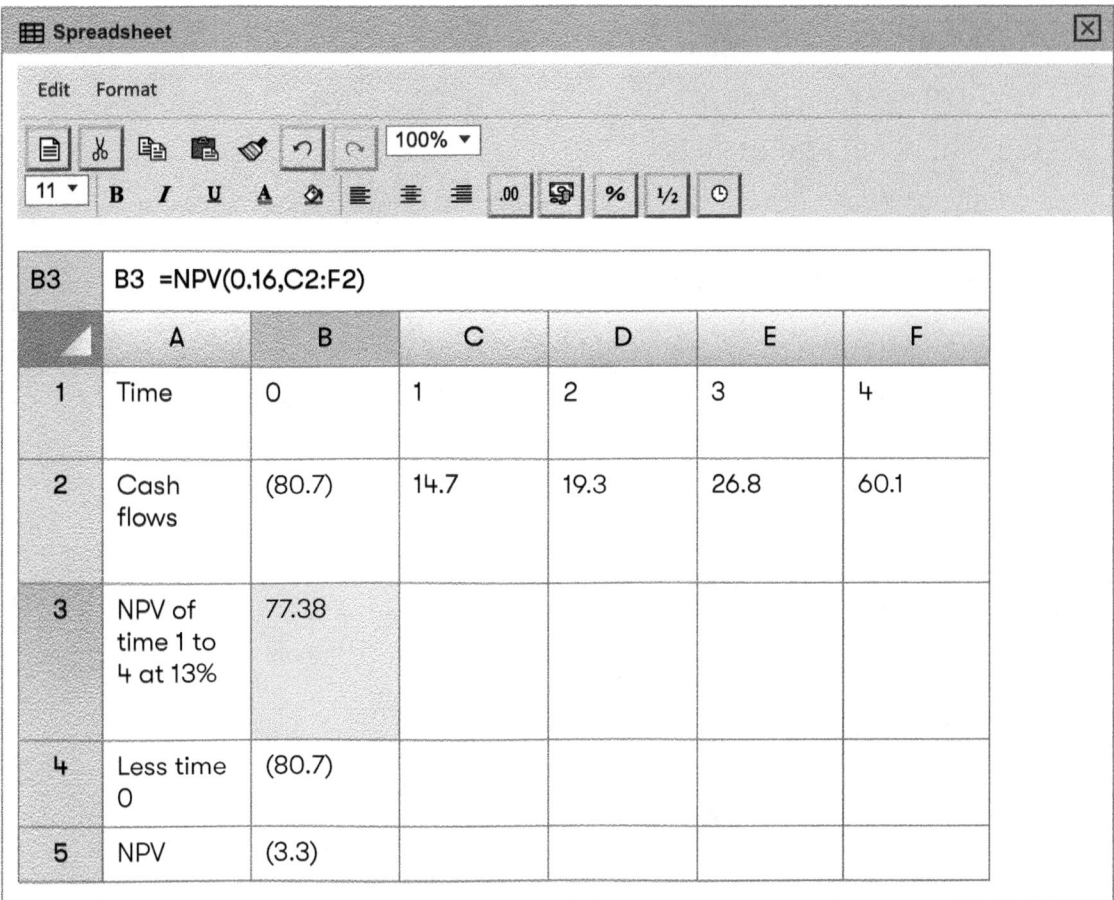

B3	B3 =NPV(0.16,C2:F2)					
	A	B	C	D	E	F
1	Time	0	1	2	3	4
2	Cash flows	(80.7)	14.7	19.3	26.8	60.1
3	NPV of time 1 to 4 at 13%	77.38				
4	Less time 0	(80.7)				
5	NPV	(3.3)				

Net present value using 13% discount rate: All figures are in € millions

Year	0	1	2	3	4
Cash flows	(80.7)	14.7	19.3	26.8	60.1
Discount rate (13%)	1.000	0.885	0.783	0.693	0.613
Present values	(80.7)	13.0	15.1	18.6	36.8

Net present value €2.8m

Alternative presentation of NPV at 13% using spreadsheet functionality

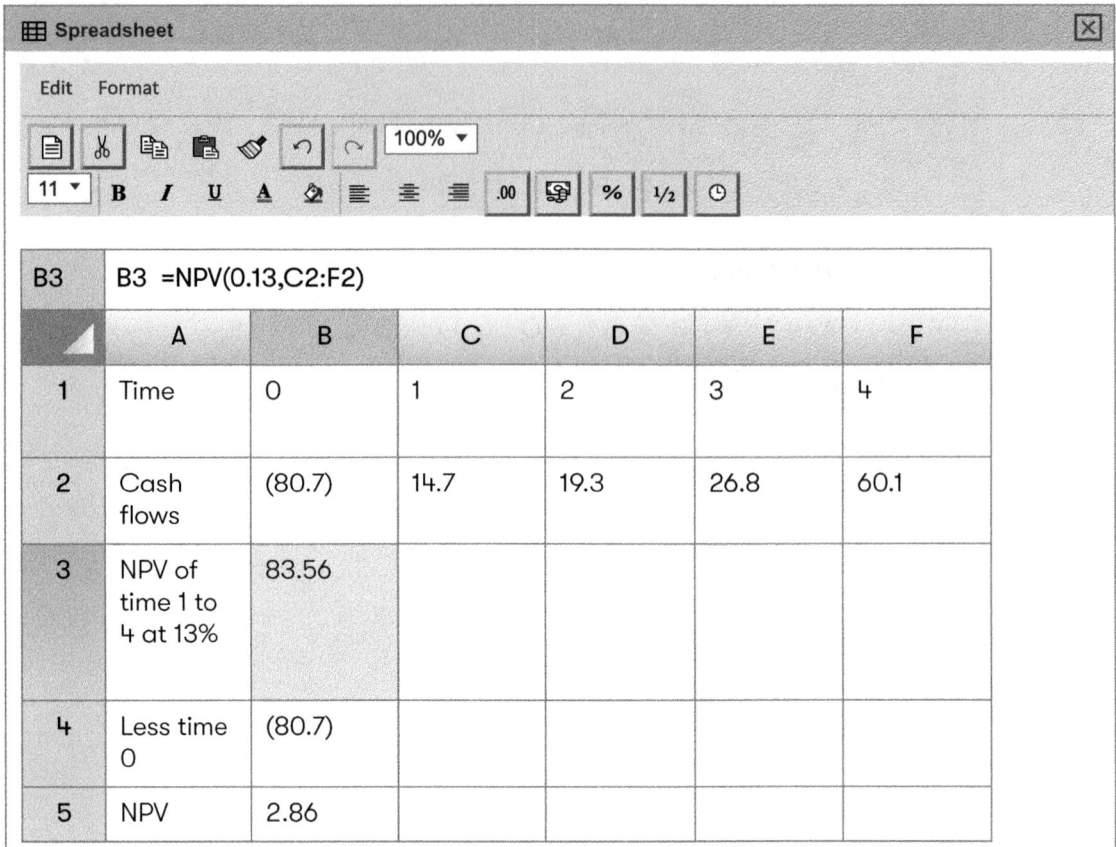

Spreadsheet ⊠

Edit   Format

B3 | B3 =NPV(0.13,C2:F2)

	A	B	C	D	E	F
1	Time	0	1	2	3	4
2	Cash flows	(80.7)	14.7	19.3	26.8	60.1
3	NPV of time 1 to 4 at 13%	83.56				
4	Less time 0	(80.7)				
5	NPV	2.86				

Workings

1   Exchange rates

Year	1	2	3	4
CL/€	9.91 × 1.10/1.04 =10.48	10.48 × 1.10/1.04 = 11.09	11.09 × 1.10/1.02 = 11.96	11.96 × 1.10/1.02 = 12.89

2   Component contribution (€)

Year	1	2	3	4
Contribution	109,725 × 8 × 1.04 = 0.9m	121,795 × 8 × 1.04^2 = 1.1m	148,590 × 8 × 1.04^2 × 1.02 = 1.3m	197,624 × 8 × 1.04^2 × 1.02^2 = 1.8m

BPP

Comment

The decision whether to accept or reject the project critically depends on the discount rate, switching from a negative net present value of €3.3m (calculations are provided in the spreadsheet appendix) when the discount rate includes a country risk premium to a positive net present value of €2.8m when there is no premium.

Given that there appears to be greater justification for the 13% discount rate it is recommended that the project should be accepted. However, the adjustment to the weighted average cost of capital requires further investigation because it is possible Colvin Co could accept a project that reduces shareholder wealth.

The outcome assumes the contribution and other cash flows are reliably estimated. Other critical inputs include the assumption that land and buildings will increase in value at an annual rate of 30% and that any disposal is tax exempt.

(b)

Colvin Co's investment in Canvia does not involve a change in business risk or capital structure. The company's weighted average cost of capital would normally be expected to provide a reasonable measure of risk for the new project. The chief executive's justification for a risk premium is based on the increased risk the company is exposed to in Canvia, a developing economy, compared to the company's existing business in the Eurozone. This perception of increased risk is based on a country risk index, which compares the standard deviation of market indices around the world. The chief executive has incorporated other factors, such as political risk and foreign exchange risk in determining this premium.

However, standard deviation is not the appropriate measure of risk for Colvin Co's investment since any portion of total risk that is uncorrelated across different markets can be diversified away at no cost to investors. For example, adverse political events in Canvia may be partially offset by more favourable events in other parts of the world. No rational investor would pay a premium for risk that can be avoided. In this sense, although Colvin Co's investment in Canvia is exposed to foreign exchange risk, this too can be mitigated by an appropriate hedging policy.

Furthermore, Colvin Co's institutional shareholders are likely to be well diversified across global markets and asset classes. The potential for further risk reduction by Colvin Co from diversifying operations globally is therefore limited when the shareholders can achieve this more efficiently on their own.

The only component of total risk that could justify a premium to Colvin Co's cost of capital is market risk or undiversifiable risk. This assumes returns across countries are significantly positively correlated. For example, there is a strong possibility that a recession in the Eurozone may lead to a downturn in Canvia too rather than offset it, transmitted through trade links and closer integration between markets. This tendency for markets across the world to move together means reduced risk reduction benefits from diversification, hence a

higher cost of capital. The key issue therefore is whether the risk of the new investment is diversifiable or not. If returns across markets are significantly positively correlated and the risk undiversifiable, the new project in Canvia may therefore command a risk premium although no justification is provided for the chief executive's premium of 3% which would require further investigation and analysis.

3 Boullain

Course Book references

The rationale for risk management is covered in Chapters 2 and 11, and foreign currency hedging is covered in Chapter 12.

Top tips

It is important to answer all parts of a requirement. For example, there are two aspects to part (a) but many candidates ignored one of these two aspects and therefore limited the number of marks that they could score to half the marks available for that requirement.

Easy marks

One twist in this question is that the question specifically says that "If the full amount cannot be hedged using an exact number of futures or options contracts, the balance is hedged using the forward market". This complicates the calculations but if this aspect to the calculations had been ignored then it was still possible to score 10 of the 11 marks, so ignoring this complication would have been understandable / sensible under exam conditions.

Examining team's comments

The examining team made the point that answers need to make clear which currency is being used to avoid basic errors such as adding together amounts that are in different currencies.

Marking guide		Marks
(a) Rationale for hedging policy	3	
Communication of policy with stakeholders		
(examples of stakeholders may include debt providers, employees, customers and suppliers, policy may include example to reduce agency and distress costs)	$\frac{4}{}$	
Marks Available	7	
Maximum		6
(b) Forward	1	
Buy futures and call option	1	
Number of futures contracts	1	
Predicted futures rate	1	
Underhedge futures	1	
Number of options contracts	1	
Option premium	1	
Underhedge options	1	
Outcome	1	
Discussion of outcome	3	
Explanation of margin requirements	$\frac{3}{}$	
Marks Available	15	
Maximum		$\underline{14}$

Professional skills marks

Analysis and Evaluation

- Appropriate use of the data to determine suitable calculations
- Appropriate use of the data to support discussion and draw appropriate conclusions
- Appraisal of information objectively to make a recommendation

Scepticism

- Effective challenge of information supplied to support key facts and/or decisions
- Demonstration of ability to consider relevant factors applicable to hedging options

Commercial acumen

- Recommendations are practical and plausible in the context of Boullain Co's situation
- Effective use of examples from the scenario information and other practical considerations related to the context to illustrate points being made

Maximum   5

Total   25

(a)

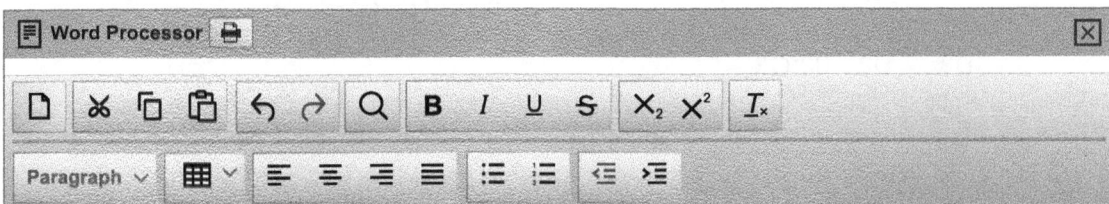

Rationale for hedging policy

Within the framework of Modigliani and Miller, Boullain Co's CEO is correct in stating that a company's hedging policy is irrelevant. In a world without transaction or agency costs, and where markets are efficient and information symmetrical, hedging creates no value if shareholders are well diversified. Shareholder value may even be destroyed if the costs associated with hedging exceed the benefits.

However, in the real world where market imperfections exist, including the transaction costs of bankruptcy and other types of financial distress, hedging protects shareholder value by avoiding the distress costs associated with potentially devastating foreign exchange fluctuations.

Active hedging may also benefit debt-holders by reducing the agency costs of debt. A clearly defined hedging policy acts as a signalling tool between shareholders and debt-holders. In this sense, hedging allows for higher leverage and a lower cost of debt and reduces the need for restrictive covenants.

Communication of policy with stakeholders

Even when foreign exchange risks are hedged, the funding of variation margin payments on exchange traded futures can create financial distress. A well communicated hedging strategy allows debt providers to make informed decisions about Boullain Co's ability to service its debt.

Agency costs and the risk of financial distress also impact the expected wealth of employees who, unlike shareholders, may not enjoy the risk reduction benefits of a diversified portfolio. A consistent hedging policy reduces the risks faced by employees which may serve to benefit Boullain Co in the form of motivational and productivity improvements.

Customers and suppliers have claims on a company which create shareholder value but are conditional upon Boullain Co's survival. Suppliers may invest in production systems which create value in the form of lower costs. For customers, these claims reflect promises of quality and after-sales service levels which enable Boullain Co to charge higher prices. In both cases, shareholder value is created as long as the customers and suppliers believe these claims will be honoured. One way of achieving this is by implementing a hedging strategy and communicating it to stakeholders.

In conclusion, management should attempt to communicate the principles underlying its hedging strategy and the benefits to shareholder value in the form of reduced agency and distress costs. In this way, stakeholders can make informed decisions about the potential risks and impact on their expected wealth.

(b) **Calculations (would be completed in spreadsheet)**

Forward contract

$18,600,000 × 0.8729 = €16,235,940

Alternative presentation using spreadsheet functionality

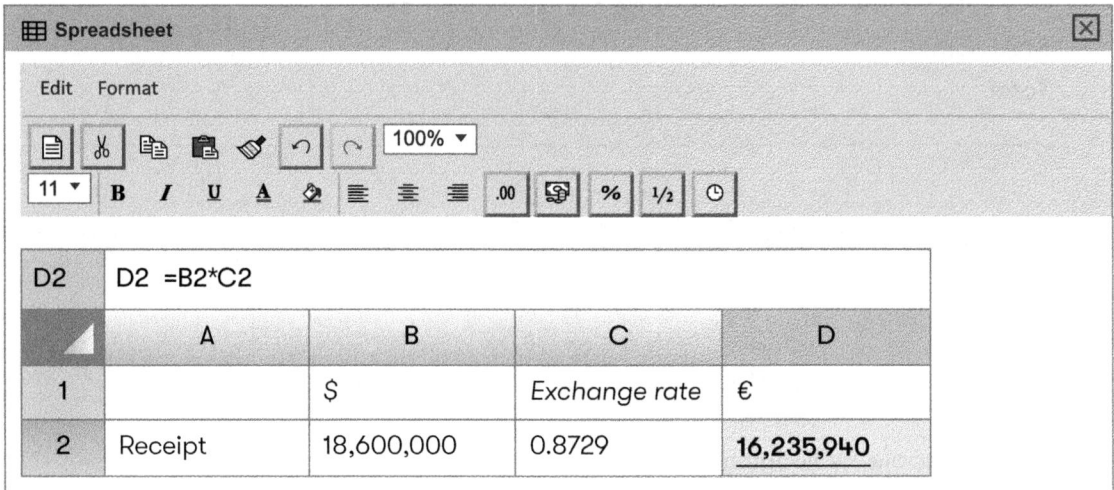

Futures

Buy September € futures

Calculation of futures price

Spot rate (US$/€1) = 1/0.8707 = 1.1485

Assume that basis reduces to zero at contract maturity in a linear fashion.

Opening basis with 7 months to end of future = 1.1422 (future) − 1.1485 (spot) = −0.0063

Closing basis on 31 August with 1 month remaining = −0.0063 × 1/7 = −0.0009

Effective futures rate = Opening future − closing basis = 1.1422 − −0.0009 = 1.1422 + 0.0009 = 1.4310

Number of contracts

Expected receipt using the effective rate = $18,600,000/1.1431 = €16,271,542

Number of contracts = €16,271,542 / €200,000 = 81.4, say 81 contracts

Amount underhedged = $18,600,000 − (81 × €200,000 × 1.1431$/€) = $81,780

Receipt at forward rate = $81,780 × 0.8729 €/$ = €71,386

Outcome

	€
Futures (81 × 200,000)	16,200,000
Forward market	71,386
	16,271,386

The outcome could also be calculated by using the expected receipt of €16,271,542 calculated earlier **using the effective rate**.

This is very slightly less accurate because it does not recognise the impact of over/under hedging. However, it avoids spending time analysing this issue, which is not likely to have a material impact on the hedging decision. This is approach is **much quicker to calculate** and would lose a maximum of 1 mark.

Options

September € call options

Number of contracts

Payment = $18,600,000/1.1420$/€ = €16,287,215

Number of contracts = €16,287,215 / €200,000 = 81.4, say 81 contracts

Premium

Premium = 81 × €200,000 × 0.0077$/€ = $124,740

Translate at spot = $124,740 × 0.8711€/$ = €108,661

Amount underhedged = $18,600,000 − (81 × €200,000 × 1.1420$/€) = $99,600

Receipt at forward rate = $99,600 × 0.8729€/$ = €86,941

Outcome

	€
Options (81 × €200,000)	16,200,000
Premium	(108,661)
Forward market	86,941
	16,178,280

Recommendation and discussion

The forward and futures contracts fix the exchange rate with the futures contract generating a slightly higher euro receipt compared to the forward. However, the futures contract is exposed to basis risk.

The futures contract is also marked-to-market daily. This means that Boullain Co deposits an initial margin with the clearing house when the futures position is opened. The notional profit or loss at each day's closing settlement price is added to or subtracted from the margin account balance. If the margin account balance falls below the level of the maintenance margin, Boullain Co is required to deposit additional funds to top-up the margin account, known as a variation margin. Boullain Co needs to consider that the initial margin and any variation margins would need to be funded and would impact cash flow in the short term.

The option outcome of €16,178,280 (see calculations in Appendix) provides a worst-case scenario based on the option being exercised. The option premium is expensive which results in a lower receipt if the option is exercised. Unlike the forward and futures contracts, however, the option allows Boullain Co to retain the upside whilst also protecting against the downside risk. Based on the forward and futures markets, the dollar is expected to strengthen and it is therefore unlikely the option would be exercised.

The final hedging choice depends on the board's attitude to risk. However, assuming there is no default risk associated with the forward contract, this may be the best choice under the circumstances. The board may also wish to consider the possibility of not hedging since the dollar is expected to strengthen.

In order to reduce counter-party risk, Boullain Co deposits an initial margin with the clearing house when the futures position is opened. The notional profit or loss at each day's closing settlement price is added to or subtracted from the margin account balance. If the margin account balance falls below the level of the maintenance margin, Boullain Co is required to deposit additional funds to top-up the margin account, known as a variation margin.

If Boullain Co makes a notional profit on any day, the amount in the margin account will be greater than the specified maintenance margin and no variation margin is required. The profit on each such a day may be withdrawn in cash.

ACCA

Advanced Financial Management

Mock Exam 3

March/June 2023 exam (amended)

Questions	
Time allowed	Time allowed 3 hours and 15 minutes
Section A THIS question is compulsory and MUST be attempted Section B BOTH questions to be attempted	

DO NOT OPEN THIS EXAM UNTIL YOU ARE READY TO START UNDER EXAMINATION CONDITIONS

Section A

This section of the exam contains one question.

This question is worth 50 marks and is compulsory.

This exam section is worth 50 marks in total.

1 Joshua

The following exhibits provide information relevant to the question:

(1)   Joshua Co

(2)   Acquisition of Fraser Co

(3)   Share buyback

This information should be used to answer the question requirements within your chosen response option(s).

Required

(a)   Discuss the agency problems created by Joshua Co's proposed takeover of Fraser Co as a defence and risk diversification strategy and explain how these could be mitigated.   **(5 marks)**

(b)   Prepare a report for the board of directors of Joshua Co that:

Professional marks will be awarded for the demonstration of skill in communication, analysis and evaluation, scepticism and commercial acumen in your answer.   **(10 marks)**

  (i)   Calculates the post-acquisition weighted average cost of capital;   **(5 marks)**

  (ii)   Estimates the additional value to shareholders from Joshua Co's proposed acquisition of Fraser Co;   **(11 marks)**

  (iii)   Compares shareholder wealth before and after the acquisition by calculating the percentage change in equity value and next year's dividend income for both companies' shareholders;   **(6 marks)**

  (iv)   Advises the board of any concerns either company's shareholders may have with the acquisition and discusses the validity of the assumptions made in evaluating the proposal in (b)(i), (ii) and (iii) above; and   **(8 marks)**

  (v)   Discusses the credibility of the CEO's alternative suggestion to use a share buyback as a takeover defence and advises whether or not this is a feasible strategy for Joshua Co.   **(5 marks)**

(Total = 50 marks)

Exhibit 1: Joshua Co

Joshua Co is a listed leading fashion retailer with stores based in flagship retail centres nationwide. For many years, Joshua Co has been highly popular but its financial performance has suffered recently due to the problems associated with its online operation. These problems are causing concern for the company's institutional shareholders.

Online rivals have emerged in recent years and are quickly reducing Joshua Co's market share. These companies have also successfully diversified into other areas such as household furnishings once they have established a well-known brand. Joshua Co recently attempted to acquire one of these online rivals, Fraser Co, but neither company's shareholders approved the deal on the grounds that it was unlikely to create value.

Following a series of profit warnings, there has been ongoing media speculation that Joshua Co is attracting takeover interest. There has been no approach made so far but Joshua Co's directors are concerned about the implications for their future in the company. Joshua Co's chairman would like to discuss defence strategies at an upcoming board meeting, particularly the

 **BPP**

suggestion that Joshua Co could defend itself against a takeover by improving its own takeover offer for Fraser Co. The rationale for this suggestion is that it would be much more difficult to acquire an enlarged Joshua Co. In addition, this would also introduce a risk diversification benefit into Joshua Co's operations.

Exhibit 2: Acquisition of Fraser Co

Joshua Co's funding options have deteriorated significantly since last year's cash offer for Fraser Co was rejected. It no longer has the cash reserves required to fund another cash offer and the shareholders are unlikely to agree to a rights issue so soon after the last attempt, which also ended in failure. In addition, Joshua Co's gearing significantly exceeds the industry average and the company is close to breaching one of its bank covenants. The CEO has therefore suggested a new offer is made for Fraser Co based on a share-for-share exchange.

The following information is available, including brief extracts from both companies' most recent annual reports:

	Joshua Co	Fraser Co
Market value of equity	$102m	$56m
Asset beta	0.85	1.18
Dividend	$2.7m	$3.2m
Ordinary shares ($1)	$40m	$10m

Cost of capital

Joshua Co's post-acquisition asset beta can be assumed to be a weighted average of both companies' pre-acquisition asset betas, weighted in proportion to their market value of equity. The board intends to maintain the company's existing debt:equity ratio of 30:70, based on market value, and expects the pre-tax credit spread on Joshua Co's debt to remain at 410 basis points above the risk-free rate if Fraser Co is acquired.

Post-acquisition cash flows

According to the finance director's forecast, Joshua Co will earn profit before interest and tax (PBIT) of $27.2m in the first year after the acquisition, growing by 5% per year in the following three years.

It is assumed that tax allowable depreciation will be equivalent to the amount of investment needed to maintain existing operations. However, an investment in assets of $2.7m will be required in year one and then $2.13 per $1 increase in PBIT from years two to four.

It is expected that the acquisition will create after-tax synergies worth $9.2m per year in each of the first four years. From year five onwards, the company's free cash flows are expected to grow annually by 3% for the foreseeable future.

Share-for-share exchange and post-acquisition dividend

The CEO's proposal for a share-for-share exchange will involve one Fraser Co share being exchanged for three Joshua Co shares. Based on last year's negotiations, the board believes it has a good understanding of Fraser Co's expectations. You have therefore been asked to incorporate a minimum acquisition premium of 35% into your analysis, which is the same premium which was requested last year.

Fraser Co's founder and majority shareholder is unlikely to approve an acquisition offer on terms which would lead to a reduction in the annual dividend. However, Joshua Co's debt includes a covenant restricting dividend payments to 25% of each year's free cash flow to the firm. The board has therefore also asked for an evaluation of the impact of the proposed terms on next year's forecast post-acquisition dividend for both companies' shareholders.

Further information

Both companies pay corporation tax at 18%. The risk-free rate of return is 3.7% and the market risk premium is 8.1%.

Exhibit 3: Share buyback

As yet, there have been no formal takeover offers for Joshua Co. However, the board wants to be fully prepared in case this changes, particularly if their own takeover of Fraser Co is not viable. The directors have been attending a series of seminars on alternative takeover defences and would like to discuss their findings at next week's board meeting. The topics to be discussed include the possibility of using a share buyback as a defence tactic. This would involve Joshua Co buying and then cancelling some of its own shares. Joshua Co's CEO has asked for advice on the credibility of such a defence and would like to discuss the effect on the company's earnings per share, cost of capital and share price amongst other issues, in the context of the company's liquidity problems and a further bank covenant which has imposed a restriction on what assets can be disposed of.

Section B

This section of the exam contains two questions.

Each question is worth 25 marks and is compulsory.

This exam section is worth 50 marks in total.

2 Oxwick

The following exhibits provide information relevant to the question:

(1)   Oxwick Co's acquisition of Ludham Co

(2)   Financial data – both companies

This information should be used to answer the question requirements within your chosen response option(s).

Required

(a)   Discuss the non-executive director's views in relation to Oxwick Co's acquisition strategy and the acquisition of Ludham Co.   **(5 marks)**

(b)   Estimate, using the data available:

- the equity value of the combination of Oxwick Co and Ludham Co; and

- the % gain in value which would be gained by Oxwick Co's shareholders from the acquisition, concluding whether it will fulfil the expected shareholder requirement of a 15% gain in value.

(10 marks)

(c)   Discuss the assumptions made in the calculations in part (b).   **(5 marks)**

Professional marks will be awarded for the demonstration of skill in analysis and evaluation, scepticism and commercial acumen in your answer.   **(5 marks)**

(Total = 25 marks)

Exhibit 1: Oxwick Co's acquisition of Ludham Co

Oxwick Co is a listed, fruit-flavoured soft drinks manufacturer which has increased its profits significantly over the last few years and is looking to expand. Oxwick Co's directors have identified Ludham Co as a potential target. Ludham Co is an unlisted, family-owned company. It produces a premium brand of soft drink, the Ludorchard brand. Oxwick Co's directors are aware that the Ludorchard brand is stocked in a number of retail outlets where Oxwick Co's drinks are not stocked.

Assuming Ludham Co is acquired, Oxwick Co's directors believe that Oxwick Co will be able to spend more on marketing the Ludorchard brand than Ludham Co has been able to spend, increasing sales significantly. It will also achieve other synergies which will increase value and justify the acquisition. However, one of Oxwick Co's non-executive directors believes that the acquisition will be of no value to Oxwick Co because it does not reduce risk. He feels that Oxwick Co's shareholders want the company to make acquisitions which reduce risk and therefore increase company value. He believes that Oxwick Co should therefore consider acquiring companies with different product streams, or one or more of its suppliers.

Exhibit 2: Financial data – both companies

Ludham Co's profits have remained static during the past three years. As it is an unlisted company, there is no information available about Ludham Co's forecast cash flows.

Oxwick Co has 200 million shares in issue and its current market price per share is $11.52. Its most recent post-tax earnings were $128m.

Ludham Co has 80 million shares in issue. Its most recent post-tax earnings were $52m.

Assume that Ludham Co's current valuation can be obtained by using Oxwick Co's P/E ratio, reduced by 40% to reflect Ludham Co's unlisted status.

The post-tax cash flows for the first year of the combined company are estimated to be $270m. These are expected to increase by the following % each year as a result of sales volume increases, synergies and inflation:

Year	2	3	4
% increase in post-tax cash flows	12%	10%	7%

Tax allowable depreciation is assumed to be equivalent to the amount of investment needed to maintain existing operations. However, an additional investment in assets (including working capital) will be required of $28m at the end of year 1. In years 2 to 4, additional investment in assets at the end of each year will be $0.80 for every $1 increase in post-tax cash flows in that year.

After four years, the annual growth rate of free cash flows is expected to be 5% for the foreseeable future. It is assumed that there will be no additional capital investment from year 5 onwards.

The combined company's cost of capital is estimated to be 12%. It is expected that the combined company's debt to equity level will be maintained at 20:80, in market value terms, after the acquisition has taken place.

The directors of Oxwick Co assume that the shareholders of Ludham Co will require a 15% premium on the fair value of their shares. To satisfy their own shareholders, Oxwick Co's directors believe that the acquisition should result in a minimum gain to their shareholders of at least 15%.

3 Blackbosca

The following exhibits provide information relevant to the question:

(1) Blackbosca Co

(2) Üskistan expansion project

(3) Business and financial risks

This information should be used to answer the question requirements within your chosen response option(s).

Required

(a) Evaluate the suitability of the investment proposal in Üskistan, including in your analysis a discussion of the chief executive officer's concerns about the consultant's cash flow estimates.

   Note. There are up to 5 marks available for discussion. **(13 marks)**

(b) Discuss the financial and business risks which Blackbosca Co will be exposed to if the project in Üskistan is approved. **(7 marks)**

Professional marks will be awarded for the demonstration of skill in analysis and evaluation, scepticism and commercial acumen in your answer. **(5 marks)**

(Total = 25 marks)

Exhibit 1: Blackbosca Co

Blackbosca Co is the market-leading online food delivery company in Turkey. The company was set up five years ago and is already highly profitable, exceeding all the founder's revenue targets by a wide margin every quarter. The founder is the company's majority shareholder and chief executive officer (CEO) and he would like to repeat this success in new territories, particularly in locations where the market has been slow to develop so far. The board is due to meet next week to review a potential expansion into the country of Üskistan.

 **BPP**

Exhibit 2: Üskistan expansion project

Üskistan's currency is the Üskistani dollar ($) and today's exchange rate is 3.82 Turkish lira (TL) per $1.

Based on Blackbosca Co's experience in its home country, the board believes that revenue growth in the early stages of a new market is likely to be non-linear. The company has therefore hired a consultant who has modelled the project's revenues based on an exponential mathematical function. The function takes into account inputs such as the potential size of the market, the rate at which new customers are likely to adopt the new technology as well as the reaction from competitors.

Blackbosca Co's consultant estimates the project will earn a pre-tax contribution margin of 40% throughout the project's four-year life and has provided the following inflation-adjusted cash flow estimates for the new project in Üskistan:

Year	1	2	3	4
	$m	$m	$m	$m
Revenue	110.0	138.0	463.0	1,160.0
Pre-tax contribution (40% of revenue)	44.0	55.2	185.2	464.0
Fixed operating costs	74	93	116	145

The directors plan to discuss the reliability of the model underpinning these cash flow estimates at the next board meeting. The CEO's main concerns are that the model is untested and that a mathematical equation is too much of a simplification to accurately model a complex scenario. He is also questioning the validity of the estimated fixed operating costs.

Blackbosca Co's finance director has provided additional information relevant to the project in Üskistan. If the project is approved, Blackbosca Co will need to make an immediate investment of $220m in plant and machinery, which is not expected to be recoverable at the end of the project's life. Tax allowable depreciation is available on a straight-line basis at an annual rate of 25% on cost.

In addition, Blackbosca Co will receive a royalty payment from the investment in Üskistan, payable annually. The first year's royalty payment is fixed at $2.5m but this will increase annually at a rate of 5% in subsequent years.

The annual rate of corporation tax in Üskistan is 20%, compared to 15% in Turkey. In both countries, taxes are payable in the year the liability arises. The tax authority in Üskistan allows companies to carry forward tax losses and offset them against future trading profits. A bi-lateral tax treaty exists between the two countries. This treaty permits Blackbosca Co to offset overseas tax against any domestic tax, which is incurred as a result of its overseas earnings.

The project will also require an investment in working capital at the start of each year, equivalent to 2% of that year's expected pre-tax contribution. It is expected that working capital will be released back in full at the end of the project. Blackbosca Co's board intends to extract positive free cash flows as dividends at the earliest possible opportunity.

Annual inflation is expected to remain constant at 3% in Üskistan and 12% in Turkey for the duration of the project.

Predicted exchange rates using purchasing power parity are as follows:

Year	0	1	2	3	4
TL/$	3.82	4.15	4.51	4.90	5.33

Blackbosca Co's cost of capital is 16%.

Exhibit 3: Business and financial risks

Although Üskistan is a developing country, it is an attractive investment opportunity because it has excellent infrastructure and important cultural links with Turkey, including a shared language.

The tax treatment of delivery riders is also favourable to Blackbosca Co since Üskistan allows delivery companies to treat their riders as self-employed workers rather than employees. This benefits Blackbosca Co since it can avoid paying employer benefit contributions for its self-employed delivery riders. This will significantly reduce the project's costs. Several years ago, the tax authority in Üskistan challenged the tax status of delivery riders as self-employed workers but recently lost its case in Üskistan's Supreme Court.

Although there have been frequent changes of government in Üskistan's recent history, the current government appears stable following a change in the country's constitution. The government also recently removed a restriction on dividend remittances, which had been in place for many years. However, the new government has inherited a high level of government debt, which is creating pressure on government expenditure.

Due to its developing country status, the online food delivery market is only just beginning to emerge in Üskistan and therefore presents excellent growth prospects. Blackbosca Co's finance director plans to pursue the same business model in Üskistan, relying on financial institutions to process customer payments online.

Answers

DO NOT TURN THIS PAGE UNTIL YOU HAVE
COMPLETED THE MOCK EXAM

Exam success skills

In any AFM exam it will be important to apply good general exam technique by using the six exam success skills identified at the start of the Revision Kit, in the section covering 'essential skills'. These skills are: 1. Case scenario: Managing information; 2. Correct interpretation of requirements; 3. Answer planning: Priorities, structure and logic; 4. Efficient numerical analysis; 5. Effective writing and presentation; and 6. Good time management.

Some examples of how to apply these skills in this exam are provided in the table below.

Skill	Examples
Managing information	It is crucially important to assimilate the information in the question scenario.
	In longer questions, such as the 50-mark question, it is difficult to assimilate information by simply starting at the beginning and reading to the end because there is so much information to take in.
	Instead, it is sensible to take an **active approach** to reading each question. Read enough of the question to get an idea of the basic scenario and then read the initial requirements so that you understand the first things that you are expected to do with this information.
	For example, in Question 1 the lengthy scenario makes a lot more sense if, before reading all of it, you are aware that the first requirements relate to the evaluation of an acquisition.
Correct Interpretation of requirements	Be careful to interpret the verbs used in the question requirements carefully.
	For example, in Q2(a), the verb 'discuss' implies that an element of critical analysis is needed.
	Also be careful to identify where a question requirement contains more than one instruction.
	For example, in Q1 part (biv) where advice AND discussion are asked for.
Answer planning	This is always important in answering AFM questions. Planning time can be used to focus on understanding the scenario. Without a good understanding of the scenario, it will not be possible to score well on the discussion parts of a question (which require application of a point to the scenario) or to score well on the professional marks.
Efficient numerical analysis	It is essential that the marker can follow your workings and your logic.
	It is also important that you accept that under exam conditions you will not get **all** the calculations correct, and that this is not necessary in order to score a strong pass mark.
	If you make a mistake early in your calculations that affects your later calculations, then the marker will only penalise the error you have made, and not its follow-on impact on other calculations. This means that it is not normally a good use of your time to correct such errors during the exam.
	For example, in Question 1 an error early on in your calculations would only attract a small penalty despite its impact on the final answer.
Effective writing and presentation	In Q1 there are marks available for professional structure (eg use of sub-headings, appendices etc). Many of the techniques used

Skill	Examples
	here are good practice in all questions throughout the exam. It is also very important to relate your points to the scenario and to the requirement wherever possible. This does not mean simply repeating the details from the question but using this information to help to explain the point you are making. For example, in Q2(c) it is not enough to state the assumptions, you need to explain their relevance.

Good Time Management	The exam is 3 hours 15 minutes long, which translates to 1.95 minutes per mark.
	
	It is essential that you do not allow yourself to become bogged down in the harder numerical areas of the exam.
	
	For example, in Q1 it is vital to leave enough time to answer the discursive parts.
	
	At the beginning of a question, work out the amount of time you should be spending on:
	
	(a) Planning:
	
	    (i) for a 25-mark question this will be about 1.95 × 25 marks × 20% = 10 minutes
	
	    (ii) for a 50-mark question this should be about 20 mins.
	
	(b) Writing your answer to each requirement:
	
	    (i) Take the mark allocation and multiply by 1.95 minutes per technical mark.

Diagnostic

Did you apply these skills when reading, planning, and writing up your answer? Identify the exam success skills where you think you need to improve and make a note of what you want to achieve when attempting questions in future.

Section A

1 Joshua

Course Book reference

Agency issues are covered in Chapter 1. Acquisitions are covered in Chapters 8, 9 and 10.

Top Tips

Part (a) caused some difficulty. A sensible approach here would have been to focus on the key point that a takeover should be in the best interest of the shareholders and not motivated by the worries of the Board about their own job prospects.

In that there is an element of risk diversification in the acquisition, this can be criticised because shareholders can diversify by creating share portfolios themselves.

Mitigation could involve identifying sources of synergy to justify the acquisition, and to ensure the company has the skills necessary to effectively manage and integrate the acquired company.

If candidates did not know how to approach this part of the question, then time would be better spent moving on to the report in part b compared to writing an answer that did not address agency issues. This is an important approach in Q1 which is normally a very time-pressured exercise.

Marking guide	Marks	
(a) Agency problems	3	
Mitigation strategies	3	
Marks Available	6	
Maximum		5
(b) (i) Appendix one		
Post-acquisition asset beta	1	
Equity beta	1	
Cost of equity	1	
Pre-tax cost of debt	1	
Weighted average cost of capital	1	
		5
(ii) Appendix two		
PBIT	1	
Tax	1	
Incremental asset investment	2	
Present value of free cash flows in years 1–4	1	
Present value of free cash flows after year 4	2	
Present value of synergies	1	
Total corporate value	1	
Post-acquisition value of equity	1	
Additional value	1	
Maximum		11
(iii) Appendix three		
Percentage change in equity values	2	
Percentage change in future dividends	2	
Discussion of results including the 35% premium	2	
		6
(iv) Shareholder concerns (eg communication, Joshua Co share of additional value, previous negotiations)	5	
Assumptions (eg accuracy, variability, perpetuity, synergy)	5	
Marks Available	10	
Maximum		8
(v) Share buyback – credibility of defence	3	
Feasibility relating to this scenario	3	
Marks Available	6	

 **BPP**

Maximum — 5

Professional skills marks

Communication

- General report format and structure (use of headings/sub-headings and an introduction)
- Style, language and clarity (appropriate layout and tone of report response, presentation of calculations, appropriate use of the tools)
- Effectiveness of communication (answer is relevant, specific rather than general and focused to the requirement)

Analysis and Evaluation

- Appropriate use of the data to determine suitable calculations
- Appropriate use of the data to support discussion and draw appropriate conclusions
- Balanced appraisal/use of information objectively to support options, determine the impact of a course of action, make a recommendation or decision

Scepticism

- Effective challenge of information, evidence and assumptions supplied and techniques carried out to support key facts and/or decisions
- Demonstration of the ability to probe into the reasons for issues and problems including the identification of missing information or additional information, which would alter the decisions reached by Joshua Co

Commercial acumen

- Advice is practical and plausible in the context of Joshua Co's situation
- Effective use of examples and/or calculations from the scenario information and other practical considerations related to the context to illustrate points being made
- Recognition of external constraints and opportunities as necessary

Maximum — 10

Total — 50

(a)

There is potential for a conflict of interest when an agent, such as Joshua Co's board, is responsible for maximising the wealth of a principal, such as Joshua Co's shareholders. When the interests of the principal and agent diverge, agency conflict is said to have arisen. The source of conflict in this case is the board members' concern for their jobs following the rumours of a potential takeover, since any action taken to address this may be at the expense of the shareholders' wealth maximisation objective. The key question for shareholders is whether Joshua Co's takeover defence strategy is value maximising.

Evidence of whether shareholder value is created through a takeover defence strategy is mixed. Research suggests that the threat of a hostile takeover is an important external mechanism for reducing agency conflict and realigning the interests of a company's board with those of its shareholders since it exposes directors to the risk of being removed from their roles. Takeover defences insulate directors from this form of market discipline to the detriment of shareholder wealth, particularly if the bidding company has the ability to

restore market confidence. Whilst there is evidence to suggest that takeover defences can benefit shareholders by encouraging long-term investment, particularly in the early years of a company's life cycle, this does not seem to apply to Joshua Co.

The risk diversification strategy is another potential source of agency conflict since shareholders can diversify their own portfolios themselves quicker and more cheaply than companies. This is particularly true if Joshua Co's investor base includes institutional shareholders since they will already hold well-diversified portfolios themselves. The risk reduction benefits of such a strategy are therefore severely limited and in the absence of a clear strategic objective, the shareholders may question whose interests are being pursued.

Mitigation

Shareholders will need to be convinced about the rationale for Joshua Co's takeover defence strategy and any plans for the company's future strategic direction. The board will also need to convince shareholders that the company can access the skills and resources required to follow through on these plans.

Any concerns the shareholders have about revisiting an acquisition proposal which had previously been rejected will also have to be addressed and effectively communicated to shareholders. The sources of synergy arising from Joshua Co's acquisition of Fraser Co will need to be identified and the board's plans for achieving synergies will need to be communicated effectively.

(b)

Report to Joshua Co's board on the acquisition of Fraser Co

This report assesses a renewed proposal to acquire Fraser Co by estimating the additional value created and the impact on both companies' shareholder wealth, including the effect on dividend income. The report considers the validity of the assumptions used in the additional value calculations and discusses the concerns which are likely to be raised by both companies' shareholders. The appendices to the report provide detailed calculations in estimating the additional value created as well as the impact on shareholder wealth.

Summary of results

Based on a free cash flow valuation, Joshua Co's equity value after the acquisition is $179.2m. The acquisition therefore creates additional value of $21.2m. The % change in equity value of Fraser Co is above the required premium of 35% and should be acceptable. However, the future dividend income is likely to reduce and may therefore cause shareholders to question the value of the offer.

The comparison of shareholder wealth is as follows:

Shareholders	Joshua Co	Fraser Co
Equity values (% change)	0.4%	37.1%
Dividend income (% change)	3.7%	(34.4%)

(iv) Shareholder concerns

Joshua Co's proposal to acquire Fraser Co was previously rejected on the grounds that it failed to create value for Joshua Co shareholders. Both companies' shareholders are likely to be concerned about the credibility of the revised calculations since very little time has passed from when that last decision was made. The board will need to communicate what

has changed between now and then to justify the sudden improvement to the shareholder wealth estimate. In addition, Joshua Co's share of the additional value is positive but only by a small margin. Joshua Co's shareholders are unlikely to approve an offer where the bulk of the additional value goes to the target's shareholders. It would have been useful to have access to any previous calculations and/or board reports leading up to that last assessment to identify any changes to the key inputs so these could be investigated further.

There is no guarantee that Fraser Co shareholders will accept an offer based on the same terms as the previous cash offer. For example, the acquisition premium may need to be increased, which would reduce the share of the additional value accruing to Joshua Co shareholders. The previous offer was to be paid in cash rather than through a share-for-share exchange, so Joshua Co's board will need to communicate the strategic benefits behind the acquisition since they are now asking Fraser Co shareholders to invest in the future of the combined company. Fraser Co's shareholders are likely to expect board representation post-acquisition and the company's current directors may themselves have concerns for their own future. It would be useful to obtain more information about the previous negotiations between the two companies to gain some insight into Fraser Co's reaction if another offer is made.

In addition, Fraser Co's founder and majority shareholder is unlikely to approve the proposed terms since it will lead to a reduction in dividend income. In addition, there does not seem to be a clear strategic objective behind the decision to make another takeover offer and this may need to be communicated more effectively if both companies' shareholders are to grant approval.

Assumptions

The following factors need to be considered before the board decides to proceed with an offer for Fraser Co. It is assumed the inputs provided for the calculations are credible estimates. For example, it is assumed that the equity values, issued shares, asset beta coefficients, credit spread, profit before interest and tax (PBIT), growth rates, incremental capital investment, tax rate and synergistic cash flows are estimated accurately. It is also assumed that inputs such as the tax and growth rates, asset betas, debt:equity ratio, credit spread, operating margin, risk free rate, market risk premium and maximum dividend restriction remain constant. Minor changes to any of the key variables may have a material impact on the final results. Therefore Joshua Co should conduct a sensitivity analysis to gain an understanding of the risks associated with the proposal and identify critical variables.

It is assumed that Joshua Co is justified in basing its post-acquisition asset beta on a weighted average of both companies' pre-acquisition asset betas and that the current equity values are the appropriate weights. There is no information provided regarding the debt:equity ratio or how Joshua Co intends to achieve this. However, Joshua Co is already experiencing liquidity issues so it may be restricted in terms of how it restructures its capital base after the acquisition. Depending on both companies' pre-acquisition debt, a capital restructuring may impact the cost of capital. It is also questionable whether the credit spread on Joshua Co's debt will be unaffected by the acquisition, particularly when the company is already highly geared.

The free cash flow valuation assumes cash flows will grow in perpetuity even though this is unlikely and will therefore overstate the additional value. The post-acquisition growth rates are highly dependent on the level of incremental capital investment, so this input will need to be assessed to ensure it is sufficient. The information provided also assumes that the acquisition will take place immediately even though in reality there are likely to be significant delays whilst both companies negotiate terms and approve the deal.

There is no basis provided for the finance director's PBIT forecast or the growth estimates, all of which will need to be substantiated. The same applies to the synergies even though these make a significant contribution to the additional value. Whilst there may be scope for achieving synergies, the estimate provided is highly material to the final outcome and will therefore need to be investigated.

(v) Credibility

In the context of a defence strategy, a buyback would reduce the number of issued shares and therefore affect the chances of an acquirer being able to obtain a controlling interest. Fewer issued shares will also result in an increase in Joshua Co's earnings per share at a time when this ratio has been in decline due to Joshua Co's deteriorating profitability.

In theory, the company's share price will increase in response to the improvement in its earnings per share although this assumes the company's price earnings ratio remains unchanged. If the buyback moves a company closer to its optimal level of gearing, the reduction in the cost of capital will lead to an increase in the share price. Ultimately, one rationale behind a buyback is that it will deter unwelcome takeover bids by increasing the overall acquisition cost.

The evidence suggests that the market normally sees through any attempt to artificially boost the share price when there is no change in the company's underlying profitability. The market may also interpret a buyback as a signal that Joshua Co lacks suitable investment opportunities, which could reduce its share price even further and enhance Joshua Co's attraction as an acquisition target rather than inhibit it.

The reduction in Joshua Co's equity will increase gearing and therefore financial risk. This effect is magnified if the buyback is financed with new debt. Since Joshua Co's gearing already exceeds the industry average by some margin, it is possible that a buyback would cause the company to move even further away from its optimal capital structure, in which case the share price would fall.

Feasibility

If the buyback successfully increases the share price, this may act as a deterrent to a potential acquirer but Joshua Co currently lacks any cash reserves. It is also close to breaching one of its covenants, which will restrict the company's ability to raise new debt and is unlikely to be able to raise additional funds from shareholders.

Alternatively, it may be possible to raise sufficient funds through an asset disposal. However, if key assets are disposed of, it will undermine future operations and damage market confidence in the company even further. In theory, it might be possible to identify non-core assets but Joshua Co's loan is also subject to an asset disposal restriction which will limit the funds which can be generated. The terms of this covenant would need to be investigated further but even if such a disposal could be made, it may take more time than the company has available to deter a takeover before the capital could be raised to fund a buyback.

Conclusion

The acquisition appears to add minimal financial value for Joshua Co's shareholders and exceeds the premium requested by Fraser Co shareholders during the last round of negotiations. However, as stated above, Fraser Co shareholders may raise their expectations about the appropriate premium this time round. In addition, Fraser Co shareholders still may not approve the offer because of a possible reduction to next year's dividend. Both companies' shareholders are likely to have concerns about the credibility of the new proposal, including the strategic rationale underlying the acquisition, and these issues will need to be addressed if the acquisition is likely to proceed. The alternative defence strategy may not be viable unless Joshua Co can identify non-core assets which could be disposed of to raise funds.

Appendix 1: Estimate of post-acquisition cost of capital

Asset beta = $((0.85 \times \$102m) + (1.18 \times \$56m))/(\$102m + \$56m) = 0.97$

Equity beta = $0.97 \times (1 + ((1 - 0.18) \times 0.30/0.70)) = 1.31$

Cost of equity = $3.7\% + (1.31 \times 8.1\%) = 14.3\%$

Pre-tax cost of debt = 3.7% plus 410 basis points = 7.8%

Cost of capital = $((14.3\% \times 0.70) + (7.8\% \times 0.82 \times 0.30)) = 11.9\%$, say 12%

ANSWERS

Appendix 2: Estimate of additional value

Cash flows, years 1 to 4 ($ million)

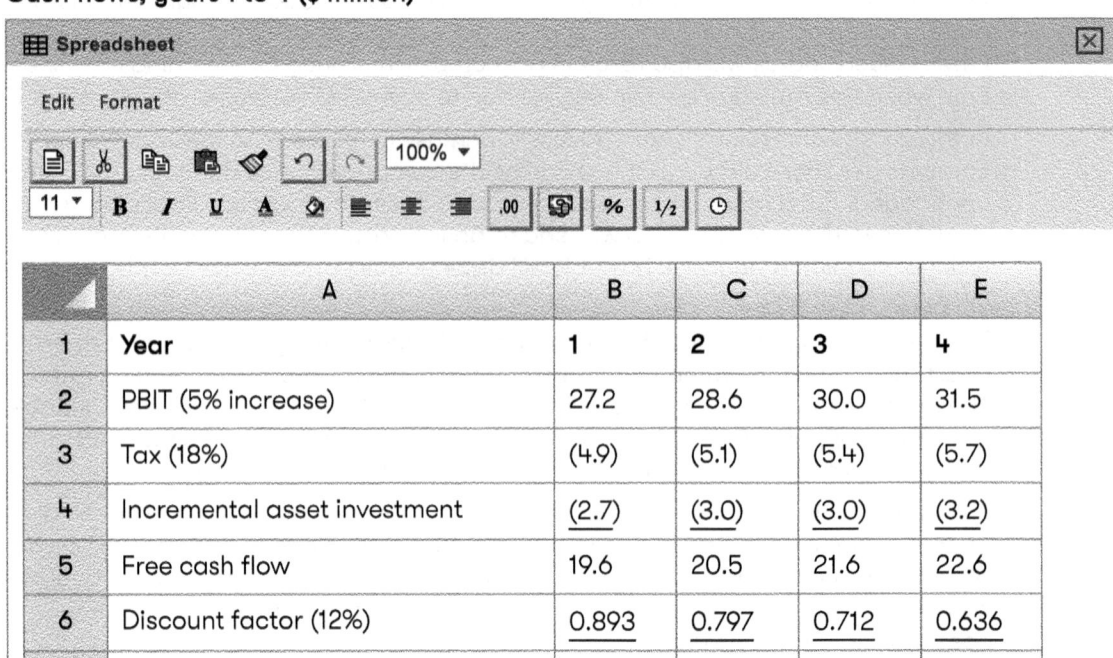

	A	B	C	D	E
1	Year	1	2	3	4
2	PBIT (5% increase)	27.2	28.6	30.0	31.5
3	Tax (18%)	(4.9)	(5.1)	(5.4)	(5.7)
4	Incremental asset investment	(2.7)	(3.0)	(3.0)	(3.2)
5	Free cash flow	19.6	20.5	21.6	22.6
6	Discount factor (12%)	0.893	0.797	0.712	0.636
7	Present value	17.5	16.3	15.4	14.4

Corporate value, years 1 to 4: $63.6m

Corporate value, year 5 onwards:

($22.6m × 1.03/(0.12 − 0.03)) × 1.12^{-4} = $164.5m

Synergy − annuity factor (12%, 4 years): 3.037 × $9.2m = $27.9m

Total corporate value = $63.6m + $164.5m + $27.9m = $256.0m

Market value of equity = 70% × $256.0m = $179.2m

Additional value = $179.2m − $102.0m − $56.0m = $21.2m

Note. The scenario was intended to explain that synergies only exist for four years. However, the question does not specify that these synergies should be excluded from the free cash flow calculation from year 5 onwards, and candidates following this alternative approach received full credit.

Appendix 3: Impact on shareholder wealth

Post-acquisition comparison

Shareholders	Joshua Co	Fraser Co
Number of shares (W1)	40 million	30 million
Pre-acquisition equity value	$102.0m	$56.0m
Post-acquisition equity value (W2)	$102.4m	$76.8m
Percentage change	0.4%	37.1%
Pre-acquisition dividend	$2.7m	$3.2m
Post-acquisition dividend (W3)	$2.8m	$2.1m
Percentage change	3.7%	(34.4%)

The acquisition premium of 37.1% exceeds Fraser Co's minimum threshold of 35%.

Workings

1 ***Share-for-share exchange***

New shares issued to Fraser Co shareholders = 10m × (3/1) = 30m

Total number of issued shares = 40m + 30m = 70m

2 ***Post-acquisition equity value***

Joshua Co: $179.2m × (40/70) = $102.4m

Fraser Co: $179.2m × (30/70) = $76.8m

3 ***Post-acquisition dividend***

Maximum dividend in year 1 = 0.25 × $19.6m = $4.9m

Maximum dividend per share = $4.9m/70m shares = $0.07

Joshua Co: $0.07 × 40m = $2.8m

Fraser Co: $0.07 × 30m = $2.1m

Note. Rounding differences may arise when producing figures to one decimal place.

 BPP

Section B

2 Oxwick

Marking guide		Marks
(a) Non-executive director's views on need for acquisition to reduce risk (points can include smoothing cash flows, reduction in cost of capital and increase in company value, clientele effect, difficulty of managing new products, shareholders' ability to diversify, supply chain benefits)	4	
Non-executive director's view of proposed acquisition	2	
Marks Available	6	
Maximum		5
(b) Current valuation – Oxwick Co	1	
Current valuation – Ludham Co	1	
Post-tax cash flows	1	
Additional investment	1	
Present value of free cash flows Years 1–4	1	
Present value of free cash flows Year 5 onwards	2	
Equity value of combined company	1	
Gain for Oxwick Co's shareholders	1	
Conclusion	1	
Maximum		10

 BPP

(c) 1 mark per point

(points can include use of Oxwick Co's P/E ratio and choice of 40% discount, possibility that Ludham Co's shareholders may make a higher valuation using free cash flows and demand higher price, assumptions about growth of cash flows (particularly after year 4), synergies and cost of capital) $\frac{5}{}$

Marks Available   5

Maximum $\underline{5}$

Professional skills marks

Analysis and Evaluation

*   Appropriate use of the data to determine suitable calculations

*   Appropriate use of the data to support discussion, draw appropriate conclusions and design appropriate responses

*   Identification of omissions from the analysis, or further analysis, which could be carried out to enable an appropriate decision/recommendation to be made

Scepticism

*   Effective challenge of information and assumptions supplied, and techniques carried out, to support key facts and/or decisions

*   Effective challenge and critical assessment of the information, evidence and assumptions provided, including identification of contradictory evidence, and ongoing questioning of the reliability of the information/evidence provided/gathered

*   Demonstration of the ability to probe into the reasons for issues and problems, including the identification of missing information or additional information, which would be required to challenge conclusions or recommendations which have already been reached

Commercial acumen

*   Effective use of examples and/or calculations from the scenario information, and other practical considerations related to the context, to illustrate points being made

Maximum $\underline{5}$

Total $\underline{\underline{25}}$

(a)

Shareholders' views

The non-executive director assumes that shareholders will welcome any acquisition which reduces risk. Diversification into new products with different income streams and possibly more certain cash flows can reduce risk in the eyes of shareholders and debt providers. The reduction in risk may reduce the cost of capital and increase the value of the company.

However, shareholders may not welcome acquisitions which reduce risk. Clientele theory suggests that companies will attract shareholders who are broadly happy with the current mix of risk and return.

Shareholders may also not welcome diversification into new products. They may doubt whether Oxwick Co's management will be able to achieve gains in value for products

which they have no experience managing. Shareholders may also be able to diversify more easily and cheaply than Oxwick Co can itself.

Acquisition of supplier

Buying a supplier would be a way of reducing risk, particularly given Oxwick Co's dependence on the supply of ingredients for its drinks. Acquisition may be the most effective method of guaranteeing a source of supply. However, Oxwick Co can currently compel its suppliers to offer the best deals in price and delivery by using competitive tendering. If it owns a supplier, the competitive element is lost and costs may increase.

Acquisition of Ludham Co

The argument that as Ludham Co produces the same products as Oxwick Co, acquiring it will have no value is very questionable. The acquisition offers market diversification into new outlets, possibly giving access to Oxwick Co's other products. Oxwick Co appears also to have greater potential resources to market and sell the Ludorchard brand. The assumption that there will be synergies appears reasonable. The acquisition could result in economies of scale, production efficiencies, wider distribution channels and greater market power, which are more likely to be exploited given Oxwick Co's success in the soft drinks industry.

(b) Oxwick Co equity market value = $11.52 × 200m = $2,304m

Oxwick Co P/E ratio = $2,304m/$128m = 18

Ludham Co P/E equity valuation = 18 × 0.6 × $52m = $561.6m

Combined company cash flows

	A	B	C	D	E
1	Year	1	2	3	4
2		$m	$m	$m	$m
3	Post-tax cash flows (W)	270.0	302.4	332.6	355.9
4	Additional investment	(28.0)	(25.9)	(24.2)	(18.6)
5	Free cash flows	242.0	276.5	308.4	337.3
6	Discount factor (12%)	0.893	0.797	0.712	0.636
7	Discounted free cash flows	216.1	220.4	219.6	214.5

Working

Post tax cash flows

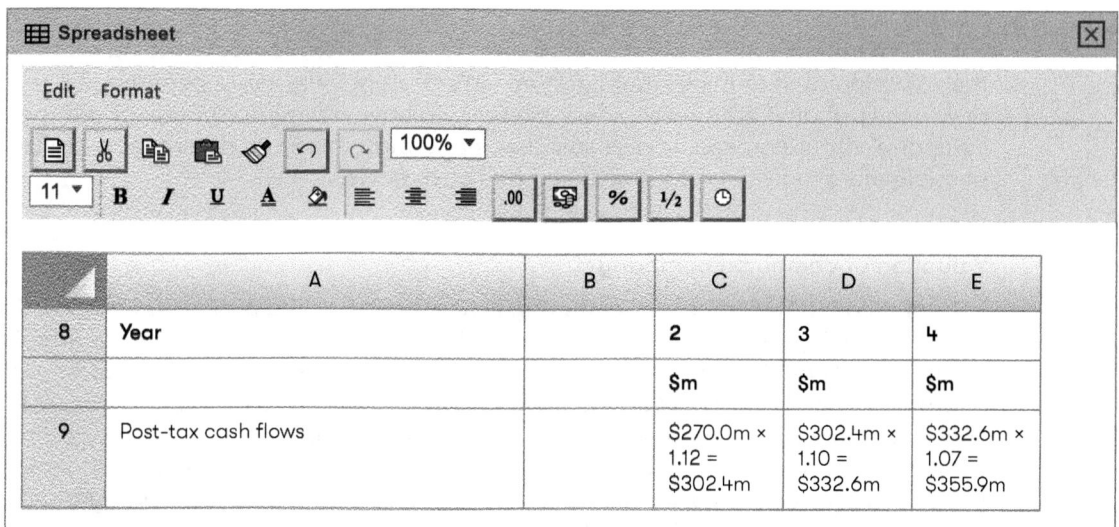

	A	B	C	D	E
8	Year		2	3	4
			$m	$m	$m
9	Post-tax cash flows		$270.0m × 1.12 = $302.4m	$302.4m × 1.10 = $332.6m	$332.6m × 1.07 = $355.9m

The spreadsheet calculations show that the discounted free cash flows years 1–4 = $870.6m

The discounted cash flows for year 5 onwards = ($355.9m × 0.636 × 1.05)/(0.12 − 0.05) = $3,395.3m

The combined company valuation is therefore $870.6m + $3,395.3m = $4,265.9m

This give a combined company equity value (80% × $4,265.9m) of $3,412.7m.

The share of gains accruing to Oxwick Co's shareholders = $3,412.7m − $2,304m − ($561.6m × 1.15) = $462.9m

Therefore the % increase in value = ($462.9m/$2,304m) × 100% = 20.1%

As the % share of gains exceeds the 15% requirement, the acquisition will be acceptable to Oxwick Co's shareholders.

(c)

Valuation of Ludham Co

Using the price-earnings ratio of Oxwick Co and reducing it by 40% may be questionable. It is normal to reduce the price-earnings ratio of a listed company to arrive at an appropriate ratio for an unlisted company, but 40% is an arbitrary %, possibly inaccurate. In addition, the only reason for the reduction is Ludham Co is unlisted, so it assumes that

Oxwick Co and Ludham Co are similar in other ways, whereas Ludham Co's recent profits have been static while Oxwick Co's profits have increased.

There is no guarantee that Ludham Co's directors and shareholders will agree with the valuation and accept the price offered by Oxwick Co. Oxwick Co's adding a premium to the valuation to determine what Ludham Co's shareholders will accept may be realistic. However, Ludham Co's shareholders are likely to have more information about the company's future prospects and cash flows and may therefore determine a higher (and possibly more realistic) valuation using free cash flows.

Valuation of combined company

The valuation of the combined company is dependent on the projected increases in free cash flows being realistic. It would be easier to assess this if information was supplied about sales quantities and prices, and operating costs. Oxwick Co does not have detailed information about Ludham Co's cash flows or forecasts, so its own forecasts in relation to Ludham Co's business may not be accurate. There has also been no specification of the value of synergies, so it is impossible to tell whether these are realistic. Management may have been over-optimistic in estimating synergies and underestimated integration costs, particularly in relation to IT and HR.

The valuation is particularly dependent on 5% growth being achievable into perpetuity. 5% is a high annual growth rate for a mature business. Oxwick Co should consider alternative scenarios which assume growth in the early years and steady cash flows thereafter.

The assumption that there will be no additional capital investment after year 4 may be unrealistic. The valuation is also dependent on the correct estimation of the cost of capital. An increase in the cost of capital will decrease it.

3 Blackbosca

Course Book references

International investment appraisal is covered in Chapter 5 and risk is covered in Chapters 2, 6 and 11.

Top Tips

Don't always look for complications in AFM questions, they may not be there and the question may be easier than you think! Here, the numerical calculations were, by AFM standards, straightforward. Unfortunately, some candidates looked for complications in the question that were not there such as inflating the cash flows when they were already given in nominal (ie inflated) terms.

More thought is required to generate good discussion points, which are especially important as they will also pick up many of the professional marks. Areas to discuss could include interpreting the final NPV (noting its reliance on cash flows in the final year and its ignoring of cash flows after time 4), and the model used to generate the forecast (which the CEO is concerned about), and potentially the use of the company's existing cost of capital (not adjusting for risk, although this also could be discussed in part b).

A discussion means not simply repeating the issues but explaining their relevance and their potential importance or lack of importance. Weaker answers failed to do this, or discussed general issues that were not relevant to this scenario.

When writing a discussion answer candidates should aim to make one point per mark available although there is quite often up to two marks if the point is developed well.

(a) Royalty fee ... 1

Tax ... 3

Working capital ... 2

Cash flow in TL ... 1

Post-tax royalty fee in TL ... 2

Net present value ... 1

Evaluation ... 2

Chief executive officer's concerns ... 3

Marks Available ... 15

Maximum ... 13

(b) Financial risk (points can include currency risk, payment risk and credit risk but credit will be given for any valid comment) ... 4

Business risk (points can include political risk, tax law change risk, health and safety legislation risk; credit will be given for any valid comment) ... 4

Marks Available ... 8

Maximum ... 7

Professional skills marks

Analysis and Evaluation

- Appropriate use of the data to determine suitable calculations
- Appropriate use of the data to support discussion and draw appropriate conclusions
- Appraisal of information objectively to make a recommendation

Scepticism

- Effective challenge of information, evidence and assumptions supplied and techniques carried out to support key facts and/or decisions
- Demonstration of ability to consider all relevant factors applicable to a given course of action

Commercial acumen

- Recommendations are practical and plausible in the context of Blackbosca Co's situation
- Effective use of examples and/or calculations from the scenario information and other practical considerations related to the context to illustrate points being made

Maximum ... 5

Total ... 25

(a)

Note. Rounding differences may arise when producing figures to one decimal place.

Project cash flows: All cash flows are in $ millions

	A	B	C	D	E	F
1	**Year**	0	1	2	3	4
2	Pre-tax contribution (40%)		44.0	55.2	185.2	464.0
3	Fixed operating costs		(74.0)	(93.0)	(116.0)	(145.0)
4	Royalty (5%)		(2.5)	(2.6)	(2.8)	(2.9)
5	Tax allowable depreciation (TAD)		(55.0)	(55.0)	(55.0)	(55.0)
6	Taxable profit/(loss)		(87.5)	(95.4)	11.4	261.1
7	Tax loss carried forward		——	——	(11.4)	(171.5)
8	Adjusted taxable profit		(87.5)	(95.4)		89.6
9	Taxation (20%)					(17.9)
10	Add loss carried forward				11.4	171.5
11	Add TAD		55.0	55.0	55.0	55.0
12	Cash flows after tax		(32.5)	(40.4)	66.4	298.2
13	Working capital (W1)	(0.9)	(0.2)	(2.6)	(5.6)	9.3
14	Investment cost	(220.0)	——	——	——	——
15	Cash flows	(220.9)	(32.7)	(43.0)	60.8	307.5

BPP

Cash flows: All cash flows are in TL millions

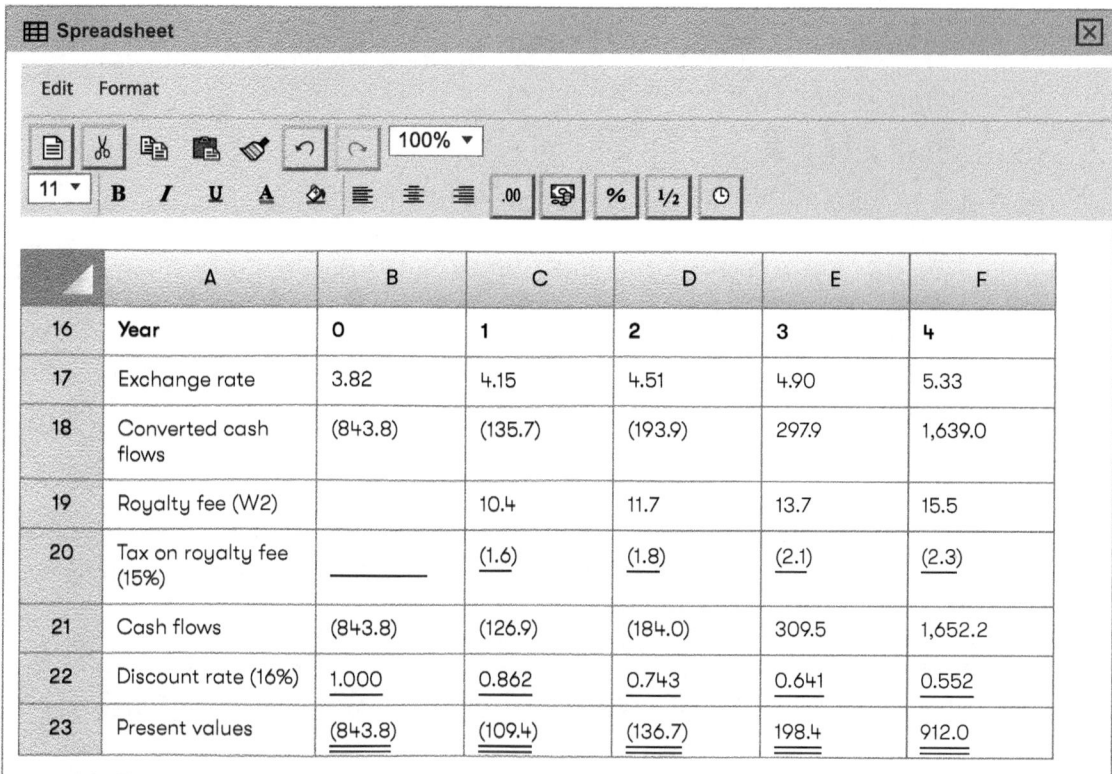

	A	B	C	D	E	F
16	Year	0	1	2	3	4
17	Exchange rate	3.82	4.15	4.51	4.90	5.33
18	Converted cash flows	(843.8)	(135.7)	(193.9)	297.9	1,639.0
19	Royalty fee (W2)		10.4	11.7	13.7	15.5
20	Tax on royalty fee (15%)		(1.6)	(1.8)	(2.1)	(2.3)
21	Cash flows	(843.8)	(126.9)	(184.0)	309.5	1,652.2
22	Discount rate (16%)	1.000	0.862	0.743	0.641	0.552
23	Present values	(843.8)	(109.4)	(136.7)	198.4	912.0

Net present value (NPV): TL20.5m

Workings

1 **Working capital**

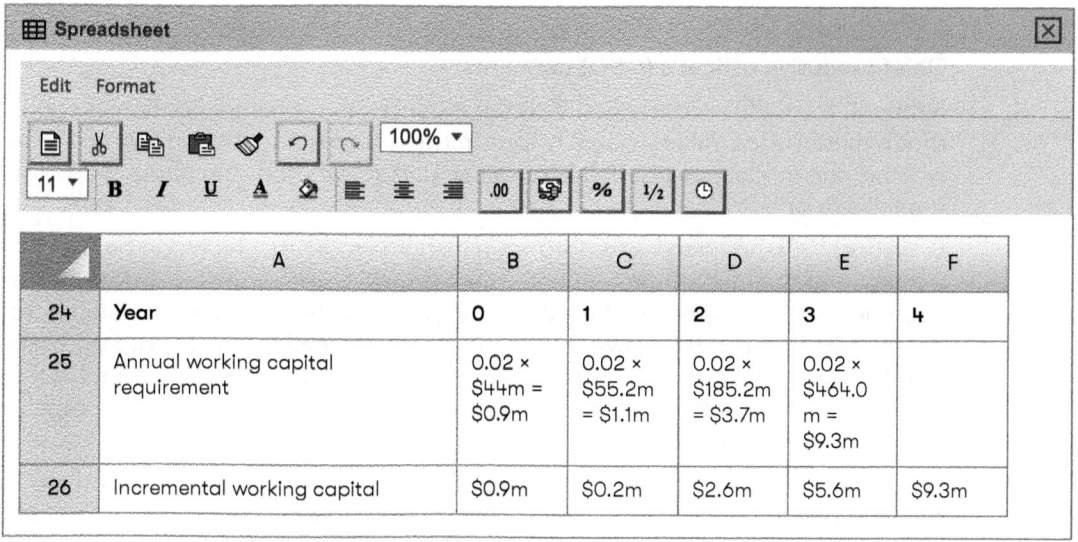

	A	B	C	D	E	F
24	Year	0	1	2	3	4
25	Annual working capital requirement	0.02 × $44m = $0.9m	0.02 × $55.2m = $1.1m	0.02 × $185.2m = $3.7m	0.02 × $464.0m = $9.3m	
26	Incremental working capital	$0.9m	$0.2m	$2.6m	$5.6m	$9.3m

2 *Royalty fee*

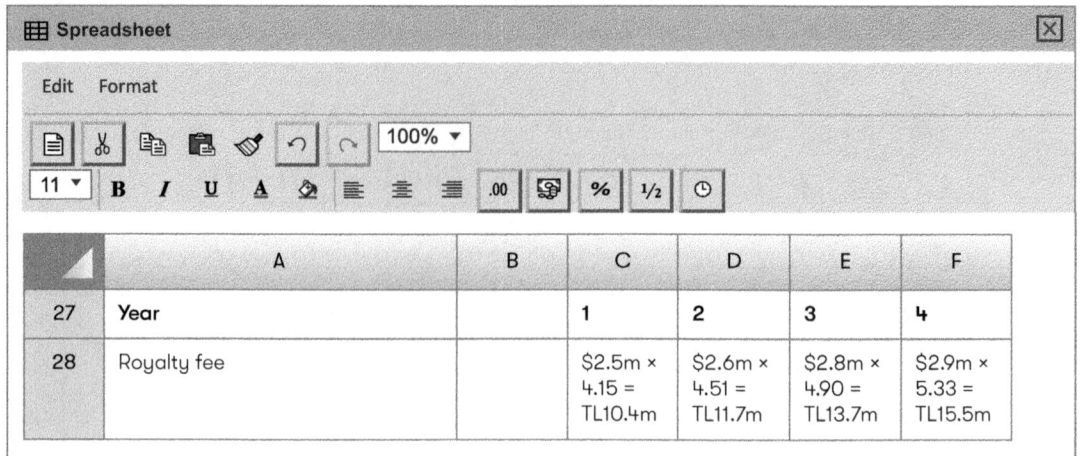

Evaluation

The net present value is positive (see calculations in the spreadsheet), implying shareholder wealth will increase if the project is accepted. However, this outcome critically depends on the accuracy of the cash flow estimates in year 4, since more than 82% of the project's positive present value is generated in that year. The board will therefore need to assess the validity of the model.

Chief executive officer's (CEO) concerns

Although the CEO is concerned that the model is an oversimplification, it could be argued that a model adds value when it approximately represents the real world. The real test is whether the model has predictive power and, if so, whether the underlying assumptions are reliable or not.

Blackbosca Co has access to data from its home market, which can be used to test the accuracy of the model's predictions. There is also publicly available data from many other countries, which can be used for the same purpose. This would allow Blackbosca Co to determine the predictive power of the model. This combination of data and experience can also be used to test the reliability of the assumptions used as coefficients in the model since the directors already have knowledge about adoption rates and competitor reactions from their home market.

Based on the cash flows provided in the scenario, it is questionable that the non-linearity assumption only applies to revenue but not the fixed operating costs. If the latter were also truly exponential, the project's NPV would be significantly lower, almost certainly negative. There is also no basis provided for the contribution margin of 40% even though competition is likely to be fierce in the early years of a new market.

(b)

Financial risk

Before deciding whether or not to accept the new project, Blackbosca Co's board needs to assess the associated financial and business risks and, if necessary, consider how these can be mitigated. The investment in Üskistan will introduce currency risk to the company for the first time and could have a negative impact on the project's cash flows if the Turkish lira weakens less than that predicted by the purchasing power parity (PPP) assumption. This is particularly relevant since there is evidence to suggest that PPP theory may be less useful in predicting short-term deviations rather than a long-run equilibrium. Any short-term deviations could adversely impact the project's net present value (NPV).

As with any business, there is a potential for credit risk if counterparties are unable to meet their obligations in accordance with the agreed terms. The financial institutions which process customer payments will be a concern and in the context of a developing country, this risk may be significant. The board will also need to consider the risk associated with transferring foreign currency across international borders, which may be less secure and involve long delays, even with electronic payments.

Business risk

It is possible that restrictions on remittances may be re-introduced if there is another change in government, limiting any positive cash flows which can be returned to Blackbosca Co. Frequent changes of government do not always imply there is a substantial political risk but in countries where there is a potential for a sudden change in political opinion, this could significantly impact the project's cash flows. This is particularly relevant since the government of Üskistan is under pressure due to an inherited public debt burden.

The board will need to consider fiscal risk since the project's NPV is based on an assumption that the tax rates in both countries are constant and that the bilateral tax treaty remains in place throughout. Blackbosca Co will also need to consider the possibility that the tax treatment of the riders may change and will need to familiarise itself with employment law in Üskistan. Even though the Supreme Court decision confirmed that the current tax treatment is correct under existing legislation, it is still possible that new legislation could be introduced, particularly if the government needs to find alternative sources of tax revenue. Since the new project involves transporting food, Blackbosca Co will also need to review existing health and safety legislation and assess the likelihood of any food regulatory changes which could impact the project's cash flows.

ACCA

Advanced Financial Management

Mock Exam 4

September/December 2023 exam

Questions	
Time allowed	Time allowed 3 hours and 15 minutes
Section A THIS question is compulsory and MUST be attempted Section B BOTH questions to be attempted	

DO NOT OPEN THIS EXAM UNTIL YOU ARE READY TO START
UNDER EXAMINATION CONDITIONS

Section A

This section of the exam contains one question.

This question is worth 50 marks and is compulsory.

This exam section is worth 50 marks in total.

1 McKeever Co

The following exhibits provide information relevant to the question:

(1) McKeever Co

(2) Project information

(3) Alternative exchange rate assumption

(4) Country risk

This information should be used to answer the question requirements within your chosen response option(s).

Required

Prepare a report for the board of directors of McKeever Co which:

(a) Estimates the project's Erat-based cash flows, in pounds;   **(8 marks)**

(b) Estimates the net present value (NPV) of the project in dollars;   **(9 marks)**

(c) Evaluates the impact of the marketing director's alternative exchange rate assumption on the project's NPV, recommending whether or not the project should be accepted;   **(6 marks)**

(d) Discusses the assumptions made in the NPV calculations and responds to the marketing director's concerns about the methodology used to estimate the expected exchange rates in (b);   **(8 marks)**

(e) Discusses the political risks the board should consider before making a final decision;
                                                                                                                      (5 marks)

(f) Discusses the validity of the chief executive officer's suggestion to adjust the project's discount rate to incorporate country risk.   **(4 marks)**

Professional marks will be awarded for the demonstration of skill in communication, analysis and evaluation, scepticism and commercial acumen in your answer.   **(10 marks)**

                                                                                                       (Total = 50 marks)

Exhibit 1: McKeever Co

McKeever Co specialises in the design and production of scientific instruments. Until now, the company has never sold or manufactured products outside its home market, the United States (US), but the chief executive officer (CEO) has identified a new growth opportunity in the country of Erat. Although Erat is an emerging market which has experienced extreme economic challenges in recent decades, the new government has introduced a series of incentives to promote inward foreign investment. These incentives were introduced after the recent election and were an important factor behind the CEO's proposal.

Exhibit 2: Project information

Erat's currency is the Eratian pound (£) and today's exchange rate is £3.31 per $. It is assumed the project will last for four years.

Operating cash flows

The number of scientific instruments expected to be sold in Erat each year is as follows:

Year	1	2	3	4
Sales (units)	55,000	67,000	82,000	90,000

McKeever Co will charge a selling price of £275 per unit in year 1, incurring estimated variable costs of £100 per unit. The selling price and variable costs are expected to increase in line with the annual rate of inflation in Erat. The variable cost estimate in year 1 already includes the cost of a component, which will be manufactured in the US. This component will be charged at a transfer price of £20 per unit, generating a pre-tax contribution of £10 per unit. Both the transfer price and pre-tax contribution are expected to increase in line with the annual rate of inflation in Erat.

The project will incur fixed costs of £750,000 in year 1, increasing at an annual rate of 5%.

Investment cost

The investment cost includes £32m for land and buildings and £18m for plant and machinery. Tax allowable depreciation is available at an annual rate of 25% on the cost of the plant and machinery on a straight-line basis with the first allowance claimed in year 1.

As an incentive to foreign investors, the government has agreed with McKeever Co to act as a buyer of last resort in the event that another buyer cannot be found for the land and buildings at the end of year 4. The cost of the land and buildings is therefore expected to be recovered in full at the end of the project but the expenditure on plant and machinery is not expected to be recoverable.

Taxation

As another incentive to foreign investors, the government has agreed to reduce the corporation tax rate, which is normally 30%. McKeever Co will therefore pay tax at an annual rate of 20% in Erat, compared to 25% in the US. In both countries, taxes are payable in the year the liability arises. A bi-lateral tax treaty exists between the two countries and under the terms of that treaty, McKeever Co will be able to offset overseas tax against any US tax liabilities incurred as a result of its overseas earnings.

Working capital

The project will also require an investment in working capital at the start of each year, equivalent to 15% of that year's contribution. Assume working capital is fully recoverable at the end of year 4.

Inflation

The expected annual inflation rates in the two countries are as follows:

Year	1	2	3	4
US	6%	6%	7%	7%
Erat	5%	5%	4%	4%

In the first instance, the board has asked you to appraise the new project using the purchasing power parity model to estimate the forecast exchange rates.

Further information

The Eratian government has removed all restrictions on dividend remittances, so the board plans to extract positive annual cash flows at the earliest opportunity.

McKeever Co normally uses its cost of capital of 14% to appraise new projects.

Exhibit 3: Alternative exchange rate assumption

The expected annual inflation rate predictions provided in the previous exhibit were made after obtaining forecasts for both countries from a number of analysts. The analysts' predictions varied widely over the period the board is planning to implement the new project although there seems to be a general consensus that inflation is likely to increase in the US and decrease in Erat. The

finance director has managed the risk associated with these forecasts by attaching probabilities to each of the analysts' predictions and then calculating the expected inflation rates provided.

McKeever Co's marketing director has concerns about the lack of consistency across the range of analysts' predictions and the methodology used by the finance director to estimate the expected inflation rates.

As an alternative approach, he has asked you to re-assess the project using alternative exchange rate assumptions for the exchange rate based on the historical trend, as follows:

Year	1	2	3	4
£/$	3.37	3.41	3.47	3.50

However, the finance director commented that a weakening of the Eratian pound was suggested by less than 5% of the analysts' predictions.

Under this alternative exchange rate assumption, an estimated present value of the post-tax component contribution has already been calculated as $485,000.

Exhibit 4: Country risk

McKeever Co's board expressed concern about the country risk associated with an emerging market economy, particularly the project's foreign exchange and political risks. For example, Erat's main opposition party is challenging the tax incentives which were introduced and has overtaken the governing party in opinion polls less than six months after the last election. In theory, the next election is more than five years away but in practice Erat has a history of more frequent changes in government. The directors' key concern is whether the company's shareholders, mainly institutional investors, will react favourably or not to the new project.

The CEO questioned whether the project's discount rate should be increased even though the project will not involve a change in the company's capital structure or its normal course of business, apart from being based in another country. According to the CEO, this adjustment to the discount rate would reflect the increase in the company's risk exposure due to both foreign exchange and political risk.

**BPP**

Section B

This section of the exam contains two questions.

Each question is worth 25 marks and is compulsory.

This exam section is worth 50 marks in total.

2 Southmed

The following exhibits provide information relevant to the question:

(1) Southmed restaurants

(2) Summarised financial statements – Southmed's summarised financial statements for years ending 31 December 20X0, 20X1, 20X2

This information should be used to answer the question requirements within your chosen response option(s).

Required

Evaluate Southmed's financial performance and business situation.

You should indicate in your discussion any omissions in the data provided, where further information would be helpful to extend your analysis.

Provide relevant calculations for ratios and trends to support your evaluation.

Note. 10 marks are available for the calculations.   **(20 marks)**

Professional marks will be awarded for the demonstration of skill in analysis and evaluation, scepticism and commercial acumen in your answer.   **(5 marks)**

(Total = 25 marks)

Exhibit 1: Southmed restaurants

Southmed Restaurants Co (Southmed) is a chain of restaurants operating in the country of Pangland, specialising in Southern Mediterranean food. Southmed aims to provide customers with a better dining experience than other chains offering similar food, with more comfortable seating and stylish surroundings. Sourcing of food and drink from suppliers is organised by a central procurement function, acting on orders from restaurants. Restaurants, however, have some discretion in the prices they charge in response to local business conditions and also in their staffing policies.

For the purposes of segmental reporting, Southmed divides its restaurants into three segments, located in:

• The six largest cities in Pangland

• Tourist centres, mostly coastal locations

• Smaller cities and towns

Southmed's board is currently reviewing its strategic positioning and financing. The directors wish to ensure, as far as possible, that Southmed will have sufficient finance to sustain investment and keep shareholders happy by maintaining dividend levels. They view as a significant competitive threat the growth of more expensive restaurants offering higher quality food and better surroundings than Southmed does, particularly in the six largest cities in Pangland.

About five years ago, Southmed expanded the number of restaurants it had in tourist centres in response to a campaign by Pangland's government aiming to increase the number of holidays taken in Pangland. The board has been pleased with the results of these restaurants, but there is considerable competition now in the tourist centres, particularly from restaurants which serve high customer numbers at cheaper prices than Southmed.

Southmed's board wishes to assess its current business situation, based on the figures in its most recent financial statements, before deciding on how it should respond to the competitive threats the company faces and how the response should be financed.

Exhibit 2: Summarised financial statements – Southmed's summarised financial statements for years ending 31 December 20X0, 20X1, 20X2

	A	B	C	D
1	Statement of profit or loss for years ending 31 December			
2		20X2	20X1	20X0
3		$'000	$'000	$'000
4	Revenue	120,900	121,500	121,900
5	Cost of sales	-101,600	-101,300	101,100
6	Gross profit	19,300	20,200	20,800
7	Administrative costs	-11,600	-11,200	-11,000
8	Operating profit	7,700	9,000	9,800
9	Finance costs	-2,400	-2,600	-2,800
10	Profit before tax	5,300	6,400	7,000
11	Tax	-1,200	-1,600	-1,800
12	Profit after tax	4,100	4,800	5,200
13	Dividends	3,000	3,000	3,000
14				
15	Statement of financial position for years ending 31 December			
16		20X2	20X1	20X0
17		$'000	$'000	$'000
18	Non-current assets (Note 1)	78,400	78,800	79,100
19	**Current assets**			
20	Bank and cash	8,000	8,000	8,200
21	Other current assets (Note 2)	3,000	2,600	2,400
22		11,000	10,600	10,600
23	**Total assets**	89,400	89,400	89,700
24	**Equity**			
25	Ordinary shares ($1)	10,000	10,000	10,000
26	Reserves	44,100	43,000	41,200
27		54,100	53,000	51,200
28	Non-current liabilities (Note 3)	23,400	26,000	28,000

 **BPP**

	A	B	C	
29	**Current liabilities**			
30	Trade payables	10,600	8,600	8,500
31	Other current liabilities	1,300	1,800	2,000
32		11,900	10,400	10,500
33	**Total equity and liabilities**	89,400	89,400	89,700
34				
35	Market price per share	4.85	5.35	5.70
36				
37	**Notes**			
38	1. Non-current assets consist of land, buildings, fixtures, equipment and vehicles.			
39	2. Other current assets consist of inventory of perishable foods and prepayments.			
40	3. Non-current liabilities consist of loan notes redeemable in seven years, market value equalling nominal value, and a bank loan repayable in instalments			
41				
42		20X2	20X1	20X0
43		$'000	$'000	$'000
44	**Revenue**			
45	Six largest cities	30,300	31,400	32,400
46	Tourist centres	29,600	29,000	28,200
47	Small cities and towns	61,000	61,100	61,300
48		120,900	121,500	121,900
49	**Gross profit**			
50	Six largest cities	4,700	5,400	5,900
51	Tourist centres	4,300	4,400	4,500
52	Small cities and towns	10,300	10,400	10,400
53		19,300	20,200	20,800
54	**Number of restaurants**			
55	Six largest cities	24	24	24
56	Tourist centres	32	32	32
57	Small cities and towns	84	84	84

	A	B	C	
58		<u>140</u>	<u>140</u>	<u>140</u>
59				
60	Industry figures (other national restaurant chains)			
61		20X2	20X1	20X0
62	Gross profit margin (%)	18.6	19.1	19.6
63	Operating profit margin (%)	8.1	8.6	9.0
64	Gearing (%)	42.0	41.6	41.4
65	(measured as (Non-current liabilities/(Non-current liabilities + Market value of equity))			
66	Change in share price (%)	-3.4	-0.8	

3 Abertafol

The following exhibits provide information relevant to the question:

(1) Abertafol Co's interest rate hedging

(2) Directors' queries about hedging

This information should be used to answer the question requirements within your chosen response option(s).

Required

(a) Advise on hedging strategies, based on the hedging choices that the finance department is considering for:

- the loan of $24m, assuming the central bank base rate rises to 5.9%;

- the investment of $18m, assuming the central bank base rate falls to 4.5%.

Support your answer with appropriate calculations and discussion.

Note. Up to 4 marks are available for discussion. **(13 marks)**

(b) Discuss the queries raised by each of the directors. **(7 marks)**

Professional marks will be awarded for the demonstration of skill in analysis and evaluation, scepticism and commercial acumen in your answer. **(5 marks)**

(Total = 25 marks)

Exhibit 1: Abertafol Co's interest rate hedging

Abertafol Co is planning a change in its arrangements for distributing its products. The company wishes to dispose of its large distribution centre in the middle of its home country and invest the proceeds of sale in two smaller distribution centres, one in the north and the other in the south of the country.

It is currently 1 February 20X8. Because of expected timing differences in the three transactions, Abertafol Co expects to take out a short-term loan of $24m from 1 May 20X8 to 1 September 20X8. It then expects to make a short-term investment of $18m from 1 September 20X8 to 1 February 20X9.

Abertafol Co intends to hedge interest rate risk using derivatives. The terms offered on derivatives are based on the central bank base rate. It can be assumed that futures or options contracts are settled at the end of each month. Basis can be assumed to diminish to zero at contract maturity

at a constant rate, based on monthly time intervals. It can also be assumed that there is no basis risk and there are no margin requirements.

$24m loan

Abertafol Co can borrow at central bank base rate plus 40 basis points. At present, the central bank base rate is 5.1%. Commentators expect the government to raise the central bank base rate by up to 0.8% to 5.9% before 1 May 20X8.

Abertafol Co's finance department intends to use forward rate agreements or futures to hedge the loan. It has already found out that using a forward rate agreement for the loan would result in a net payment of $461,600, which is an effective annual interest rate of 5.77%.

Three-month $ futures, $500,000 contract size

Prices are quoted in basis points at 100 − annual % yield.

Month	Price
June	94.55
September	94.50

$18m investment

Abertafol Co can invest at central bank base rate minus 30 basis points.

An election is due on 1 July 20X8. The main opposition party has promised that it will reduce the central bank base rate from whatever the level was before the election. Commentators expect that the central bank base rate could be a minimum of 4.5% if the main opposition party wins the election. At present, the election result cannot be predicted with confidence. It can be assumed that interest rates will not be reduced if the current government wins the election.

Abertafol Co's finance department has already found out that using a forward rate agreement for the investment would guarantee $378,750, which is an effective annual interest rate of 5.05%.

Because of the uncertainty surrounding the election result, the finance department is looking at buying call options as the alternative to using a forward rate agreement to hedge the investment.

Options on three-month September $ futures, $500,000 contract size, option premiums are in annual %

Calls	Exercise price
0.298	94.75

Exhibit 2: Directors' queries about hedging

At the last board meeting, Abertafol Co's finance director explained to the board the possible strategies for hedging the loan and the investment. She has received a number of queries from directors about the plans:

- Director A stated that Abertafol Co should not be using derivatives, as trading in derivatives was not part of the company's normal activities. Therefore, shareholders would not expect the company to be using derivatives.

- Director B understood that futures or a forward rate agreement might be the best solution if the central bank rate rose up to 5.9% or fell down to 4.5%. However, she queried what would happen if rates did not rise as high as 5.9%, nor fall as low as 4.5%. Abertafol Co could possibly lose the chance of benefiting from more favourable rates than those offered by the futures or forward rate agreement.

- Director C stated that options should not be used to hedge the $18m investment, as they would never be the best choice because of their premium. The best choice would be not to hedge at all.

 **BPP**

Answers

DO NOT TURN THIS PAGE UNTIL YOU HAVE
COMPLETED THE MOCK EXAM

Exam success skills

In any AFM exam it will be important to apply good general exam technique by using the six exam success skills identified at the start of the Revision Kit, in the section covering 'essential skills'. These skills are: 1. Case scenario: Managing information; 2. Correct interpretation of requirements; 3. Answer planning: Priorities, structure and logic; 4. Efficient numerical analysis; 5. Effective writing and presentation; and 6. Good time management.

Some examples of how to apply these skills in this exam are provided in the table below.

Skill	Examples
Managing information	It is crucially important to assimilate the information in the question scenario. In longer questions, such as the 50-mark question, it is difficult to assimilate information by simply starting at the beginning and reading to the end because there is so much information to take in. Instead, it is sensible to take an **active approach** to reading each question. Read enough of the question to get an idea of the basic scenario and then read the initial requirements so that you understand the first things that you are expected to do with this information. For example, in Question 1 the lengthy scenario makes a lot more sense if, before reading all of it, you are aware that the first requirements relate to the evaluation of an international investment.
Correct Interpretation of requirements	Be careful to interpret the verbs used in the question requirements carefully. For example, in Q1 many of the discussion requirements use the verb 'discuss,' which implies that an element of critical analysis is needed. Also be careful to identify where a question requirement contains more than one instruction. For example, the 4th requirement of Q1 asks for discussion of assumptions AND method used.
Answer planning	This is always important in answering AFM questions. Planning time can be used to focus on understanding the scenario. Without a good understanding of the scenario, it will not be possible to score well on the discussion parts of a question (which require application of a point to the scenario) or to score well on the professional marks.
Efficient numerical analysis	It is essential that the marker can follow your workings and your logic. It is also important that you accept that under exam conditions you will not get **all** the calculations correct, and that this is not necessary in order to score a strong pass mark. If you make a mistake early in your calculations that affects your later calculations, then the marker will only penalise the error you have made, and not its follow-on impact on other calculations. This means that it is not normally a good use of your time to correct such errors during the exam. For example, in Question 1 an error early on in your calculations would only attract a small penalty despite its impact on the final answer.

Skill	Examples
Effective writing and presentation	In Q1 there are marks available for professional structure (eg use of sub-headings, appendices etc). Many of the techniques used here are good practice in all questions throughout the exam. It is also very important to relate your points to the scenario and to the requirement wherever possible. This does not mean simply repeating the details from the question but using this information to help to explain the point you are making. For example, in Q1(iv) it is not enough to state the assumptions, you need to discuss their relevance.

Good Time Management	The exam is 3 hours 15 minutes long, which translates to 1.95 minutes per mark.
	
	 It is essential that you do not allow yourself to become bogged down in the harder numerical areas of the exam.
	
	 For example, in Q1 it is vital to leave enough time to answer the discursive parts.
	
	 At the beginning of a question, work out the amount of time you should be spending on:
	
	 (a) Planning:
	
	    (i) for a 25-mark question this will be about 1.95 × 25 marks × 20% = 10 minutes
	
	    (ii) for a 50-mark question this should be about 20 mins.
	
	 (b) Writing your answer to each requirement:
	
	    (i) Take the mark allocation and multiply by 1.95 minutes per technical mark.

Diagnostic

Did you apply these skills when reading, planning, and writing up your answer? Identify the exam success skills where you think you need to improve and make a note of what you want to achieve when attempting questions in future.

Section A

1 McKeever Co

Course Book references

International investment appraisal is covered in Chapter 5.

Top tips

As ever, time spent planning is time well spent. The ACCA Examiner's comments noted that 'Candidates who take the time to thoroughly understand the scenario are generally better prepared for the discussion elements of the question and are less likely to make mistakes in the cash flow calculations...In addition, candidates who take the time to understand the scenario are more likely to earn the professional skills marks with relevant comments relating to the case or the real world.'

Easy marks

Discussing assumptions should be a source of easy marks. However, this will require more a list-based approach. The key point when discussing assumptions is to comment on the implication of an assumption or why an assumed value (eg the cost of capital) may be incorrect and the impact of this.

Professional marks should also be relatively easy to achieve, especially communication marks (requiring sub-headings, reference to workings in spreadsheet, simple report format and brief conclusion) and analysis & evaluation (making suitable calculations and using numerical analysis to support discussion points).

Marking guide		Marks
(a) Contribution	3	
Fixed costs	1	
Tax allowable depreciation	1	
Taxation	1	
Working capital	$\underline{2}$	
Marks Available	8	
Maximum		8
(b) Exchange rates	2	
US$ cash flows	1	
Additional tax	2	
Component contribution	2	
Tax on component contribution	1	
Net present value	$\underline{1}$	
Marks Available	9	
Maximum		9
(c) US$ cash flows	1	
Additional tax	1	
Net present value	1	
Evaluation (eg, historical trend v purchasing power parity, impact on cash flows, impact on net present value, attitude to risk, etc)	3	
Recommendation	$\underline{1}$	
Marks Available	7	
Maximum		6
(d) Assumptions	4	
Lack of consistency	3	
Methodology	$\underline{3}$	
Marks Available	10	
Maximum		8
(e) Up to 2 marks per well explained point (eg, change of government, increased tax rate, transfer price, withdrawal of guarantee, tariffs, block on remittances)	$\underline{5}$	
Marks Available	5	
Maximum		5
(f) Up to 2 marks per well explained point (eg, diversifiability, foreign exchange risk, institutional shareholders, political risk adjustment)	$\underline{4}$	
Marks Available	4	
Maximum		$\underline{4}$

Professional skills marks

Communication

- General report format and structure (use of headings/sub-headings and an introduction)

- Style, language and clarity (appropriate layout and tone of report response, presentation of calculations, appropriate use of the tools)
- Effectiveness of communication (answer is relevant, specific rather than general and focused to the requirement)

Analysis and evaluation

- Appropriate use of the data to determine suitable calculations
- Appropriate use of the data to support discussion and draw appropriate conclusions
- Balanced appraisal/use of information objectively to support options, determine the impact of a course of action, make a recommendation or decision

Scepticism

- Effective challenge of information, evidence and assumptions supplied, and techniques carried out to support key facts and/or decisions
- Demonstration of the ability to probe into the reasons for issues and problems, including the identification of missing information or additional information, which would alter the decisions reached by McKeever Co

Commercial acumen

- Advice is practical and plausible in the context of McKeever Co's situation
- Effective use of examples and/or calculations from the scenario information and other practical considerations related to the context to illustrate points being made
- Recognition of external constraints and opportunities as necessary

Maximum	10
Total	50

Report to the board of directors on the viability of the investment in Erat

> **Word Processor** 🖨   ☒
>
> ---
> 🗋 ✂ 🗐 📋 ↶ ↷ 🔍 **B** *I* U̲ S̶ X₂ x² Iₓ
> ---
> Paragraph ∨ ⊞∨ ≡ ≡ ≡ ≡ ⦂≡ ⦂≡ ⦉≡ ≡⦊
> ---
>
> **Introduction**
>
> This report considers the suitability of a proposal to manufacture and sell scientific instruments in Erat. It takes into account the project's net present value (NPV) calculation, which is included in an appendix to the main report and discusses the assumptions on which the project's cash flows are based, including the impact of an adjustment to the exchange rate assumption, which was suggested by the marketing director. The report continues with a discussion on political risk, explaining whether or not the discount rate should be adjusted for country risk.
>
> **Results**
>
> On a purely financial basis, the NPV of $1.1m suggests the project should be approved. However, sensitivity analysis would be useful in testing the sensitivity of the project's NPV to each of the inputs in order to identify critical variables.
>
> **Evaluation**
>
> There is conflicting evidence about the future direction of the exchange rate since the inflation differentials provided in the scenario were used to predict a strengthening of the pound relative to the dollar whereas the historical trend analysis seems to be predicting a weakening pound.

If the pound does in fact weaken, the project's cash flows will be worth less in terms of dollars. A weakening currency will affect the later cash flows more than the earlier cash flows. It is therefore not unexpected that the project's NPV is significantly lower under these circumstances since the resale value of the land and buildings has a significant impact on the project's value. In fact, the NPV switches from being positive to negative (i.e. $0.5m) when the exchange rate assumption is altered.

The analysts' predictions suggest such a scenario is extremely unlikely, but the marketing director's approach would result in a project being rejected even when the overwhelming likelihood is that it would be wealth increasing, simply because there is a remote possibility that it could result in a marginally negative NPV.

Ultimately, the final decision will depend on the board's attitude to risk but based on expected values, the project will increase shareholder wealth and should, therefore, be accepted unless the board is very risk averse since the downside is only marginally negative and is considered to be an unlikely outcome.

Assumptions

It is assumed that the inputs used in the NPV calculation, such as the selling prices, market demand, variable and fixed costs, tax, working capital, investment cost, residual value, transfer price, component contribution, cost of capital and inflation differentials are estimated accurately. The project value also assumes certain inputs remain constant or adjusted for inflation for the duration of the project such as the tax rates, tax allowable depreciation, transfer price, component contribution and the working capital requirement.

The exchange rates are based on the purchasing power parity model, using analysts' predictions about future inflation differentials. However, research suggests that this model is more effective at predicting long-term fluctuations, rather than short-term movements in the exchange rate.

The calculations assume the investment will take place immediately, assuming the project is approved, although in reality there are likely to be delays. There is also an assumption that the project will only last for four years, so any change to this assumption will impact the NPV.

Marketing director's concerns

Lack of consistency between analysts' predictions

There is nothing unusual about the lack of consistency between the analysts' predictions. Predictions about the future are inherently subjective and there are a number of variables which could affect future inflation rates (eg, government spending, monetary policy and economic growth). Each analyst will rely on different methodologies and forecasting biases with different assumptions about each of the input variables.

Finance director's methodology

The theoretically correct approach to managing this type of risk is to attach probabilities to each of the possible outcomes and calculate expected inflation rates which can be incorporated into the purchasing power parity model. Therefore, the finance director's methodology is fundamentally sound. The key issue is whether the probability estimates are credible and what information was used to generate these estimates.

The marketing director's historical trend analysis predicts a weakening of the pound relative to the dollar, in contrast to the output of the purchasing power parity model. Although it is tempting to rely on historical trends, this would ignore the government's incentives for foreign investment and their likely impact on the future direction of the exchange rate. It is therefore not unexpected that the pound would strengthen when the government is actively promoting foreign investment.

However, there is some logic to the marketing director's suggestion if it is used to provide a measure of the project's risk and allows the board to attach a probability to a plausible downside scenario.

Political risk

The project in Erat may give rise to significant political risks. A recent opinion poll suggests that the governing party is already losing popular support only a few months after the last general

election. Even though the general election took place fairly recently, there is also a potential for political instability if Erat's history of more frequent changes in government repeats itself. A new government could have a significant impact on the project's cash flows, particularly if the agreement to act as a buyer of last resort for the land and buildings is withdrawn. This agreement allows McKeever Co to recoup almost all of its investment cost and forms a significant portion of the project's present value. In a stagnating property market, there is a risk that the project is not feasible without such an agreement. On the other hand, it is possible that the political reforms begin to take effect by year four and the drive to increase foreign investment has a positive impact on Erat's property market.

There is also a risk that the favourable tax regime is withdrawn. Minor increases in the tax rate would not have an impact on the project's NPV because McKeever Co profits are taxed at a higher rate in its home country anyway. However, any increase above the US corporation tax rate of 25% would have an impact on the project's cash flows. In the context of a less favourable tax regime, any reduction in the transfer price would also have an adverse impact on the expected outcome. A new regime may seek to investigate the legitimacy of the transfer price and there is a risk that this could be reduced, shifting profits from a lower to a higher tax rate. There is also a risk that Erat could impose tariffs or quotas affecting the supply of the component which is to be imported from the US and this could have an impact on the project's manufacturing capacity.

There is also a possibility that a new government could re-introduce restrictions on annual remittances. Any change in this assumption would impact the project's NPV since delayed remittances would need to be discounted at a less favourable discount rate. McKeever Co could potentially bypass such a restriction, for example, by charging a management or royalty fee, but this assumes the exchange controls are not applied to repatriations in general. Although extreme, there remains a risk that a new government might attempt to appropriate McKeever Co's assets.

McKeever Co would need to assess the likelihood of a change of government over the next four years. If the next election is more than four years away, these issues may not be a material concern as long as the government remains stable.

Discount rate

All things being equal, the cost of capital would normally be expected to provide reasonable compensation for the risk of a new project when there is no change in McKeever Co's business or financial risk. Intuitively, however, it is not difficult to understand the CEO's concern since this project carries more risk than an equivalent project in McKeever Co's home country due to the exposure to both foreign exchange and political risk. However, the key question is whether this risk is diversifiable or not.

Foreign exchange risk will affect different companies in different ways. Some companies, such as McKeever Co, will be adversely affected by a weakening of the pound whereas other companies will benefit. In addition, losses in the Eratian pound may be offset by gains in another currency assuming there is a weak correlation across different currencies. It is therefore possible to reduce most, if not all, exposure to foreign exchange risk by investing in countries whose currencies do not all move in the same direction. This is McKeever Co's first foreign investment project, which means it is not a globally diversified company. However, McKeever Co's shareholders are mainly institutional investors whose portfolios are already likely to be well diversified across global markets. It is therefore unlikely they would be willing to pay a premium in the form of a higher discount rate for a risk which is diversifiable within their own portfolios.

The evidence for political risk, on the other hand, indicates there is a significant positive correlation across countries and this relationship is becoming stronger over time as global markets become more integrated. This suggests there is an element of political risk, which cannot be diversified away, for which investors would expect to be compensated in the form of an increase to the discount rate.

Recommendation

The project generates a positive NPV of $1.1m and therefore appears acceptable. However, the project's assumptions need to be investigated, including the potential need for an adjustment

to the project's discount rate to account for country risk. Scenario and sensitivity analysis would also be useful in identifying critical variables.

Note. Rounding differences may arise when producing figures to one decimal place

(a) **Expected project cash flows:** All cash flows are in £ thousands

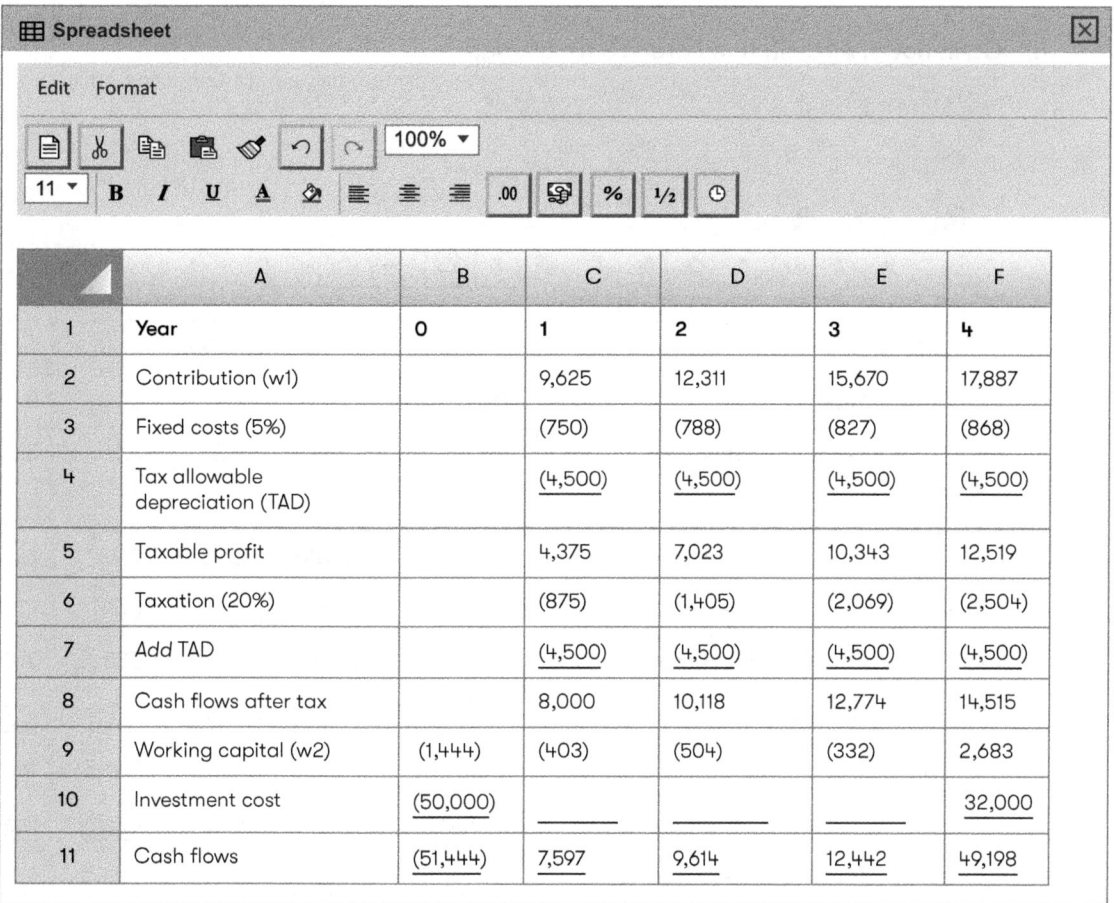

	A	B	C	D	E	F
1	Year	0	1	2	3	4
2	Contribution (w1)		9,625	12,311	15,670	17,887
3	Fixed costs (5%)		(750)	(788)	(827)	(868)
4	Tax allowable depreciation (TAD)		(4,500)	(4,500)	(4,500)	(4,500)
5	Taxable profit		4,375	7,023	10,343	12,519
6	Taxation (20%)		(875)	(1,405)	(2,069)	(2,504)
7	Add TAD		(4,500)	(4,500)	(4,500)	(4,500)
8	Cash flows after tax		8,000	10,118	12,774	14,515
9	Working capital (w2)	(1,444)	(403)	(504)	(332)	2,683
10	Investment cost	(50,000)				32,000
11	Cash flows	(51,444)	7,597	9,614	12,442	49,198

Tutorial note. The workings presented here show more detail than you would have time to write out in the exam. Under exam conditions, a good way of presenting these workings in a spreadsheet is to set up an 'input' section before the analysis of cash flows and show the key workings there, with calculations embedded in the spreadsheet cells and not written out in full as shown in the following sections.

Workings

1 *Contribution*

Year	1	2	3	4
Contribution	£175 × 55	£175 ×	£175 × 1.05	£175 × 1.05
	= 9,625	1.05 × 67	× 1.04 × 82	× 1.04^2 × 90
		= 12,311	= 15,670	= 17,887

2 *Working capital*

Year	0	1	2	3	4
Annual working capital requirement (15%)	1,444	1,847	2,351	2,683	
Incremental working capital	(1,444)	(403)	(504)	(332)	2,683

(b) **Cash flows:** All cash flows are in $ thousands

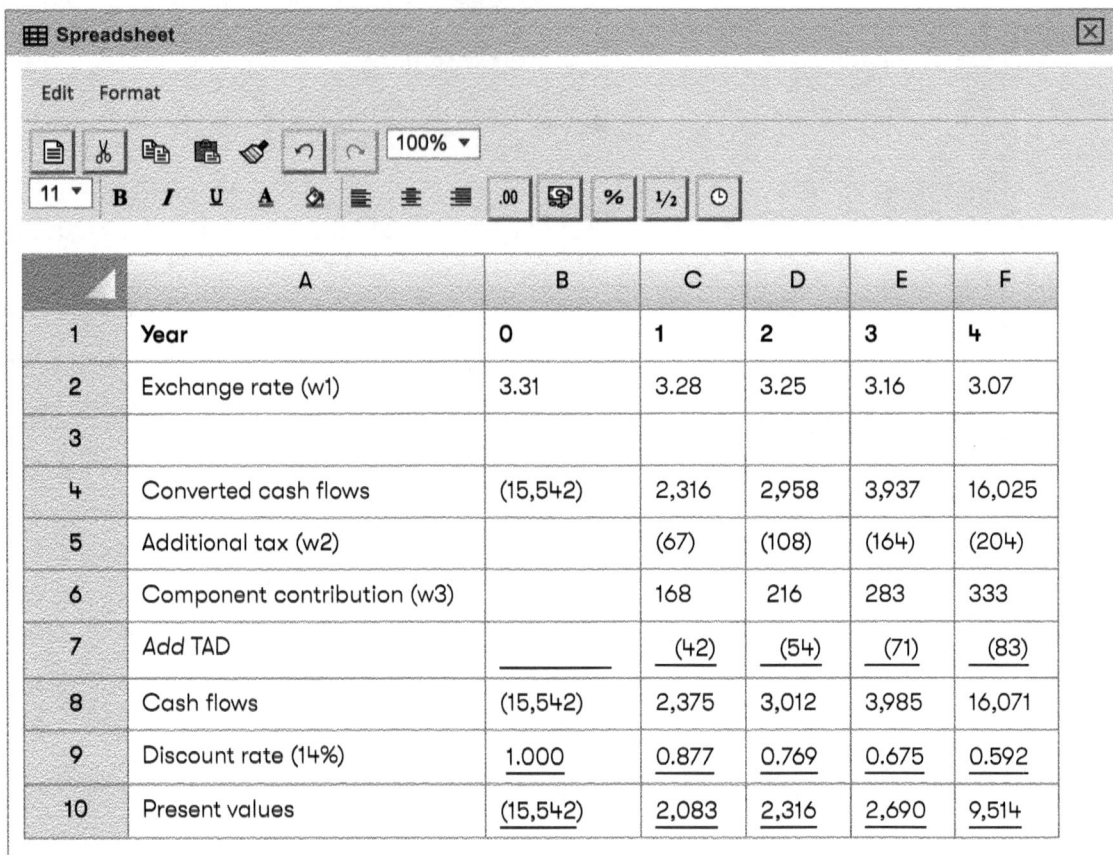

Net present value (NPV): $1,061,000

> **Tutorial note.** Two points to note:
>
> 1. Be careful converting from £s to $s, the exchange rate shows that one $ is worth over £3, so if converting from £ to $ you will need to divide by the exchange rate.
>
> 2. The =NPV function could be used. The formula to input is =NPV(0.14,C8:F8) and this would give the present value of the cash flows from time 1-4, then the outlay at time 0 would be deducted to give the project NPV. This is normally a quicker approach to use in the exam, the NPV may be slightly different as the discount tables only work to three decimal places.

Workings

1 *Exchange rates*

Year	1	2	3	4
£/$	3.31 ×	3.28 ×	3.25 ×	3.16 ×
	1.05/1.06	1.05/1.06	1.04/1.07	1.04/1.07
	= 3.28	= 3.25	= 3.16	= 3.07

2 Additional tax

Year	1	2	3	4
	(£4,375 × 0.05)/3.28	(£7,023 × 0.05)/3.25	(£10,343 × 0.05)/3.16	£12,519 × (0.05)/3.07
	= $67	= $108	= $164	= $204

3 Component contribution

Year	1	2	3	4
	(£10 × 55)/3.28	(£10 × 1.05 × 67)/3.25	(£10 × 1.05 × 1.04 × 82)/3.16	(£10 × 1.05 × 1.04^2 × 90)/3.07
	= $168	= $216	= $283	= $333

(c) **Appendix 2: NPV under alternative exchange rate assumption**

Alternative cash flows: All cash flows are in thousands

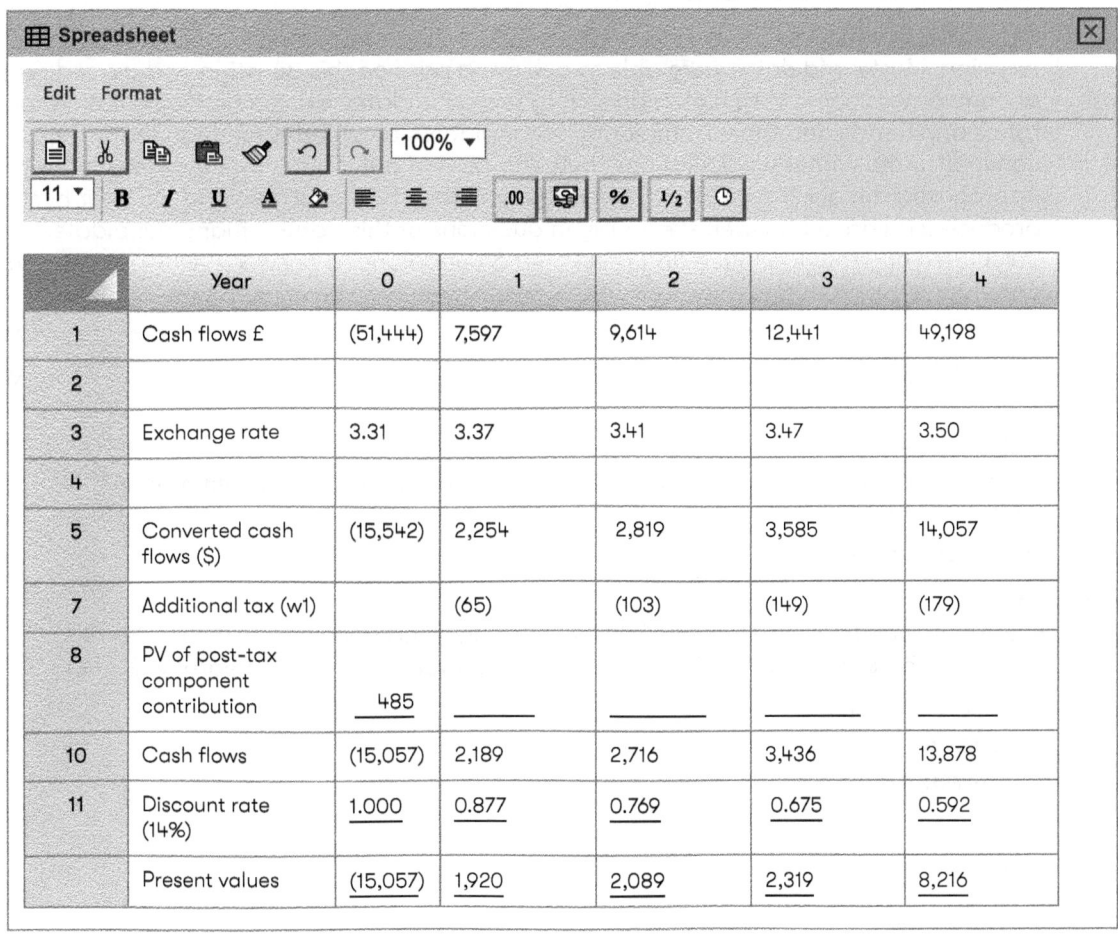

Spreadsheet

Edit   Format

	Year	0	1	2	3	4
1	Cash flows £	(51,444)	7,597	9,614	12,441	49,198
2						
3	Exchange rate	3.31	3.37	3.41	3.47	3.50
4						
5	Converted cash flows ($)	(15,542)	2,254	2,819	3,585	14,057
7	Additional tax (w1)		(65)	(103)	(149)	(179)
8	PV of post-tax component contribution	485				
10	Cash flows	(15,057)	2,189	2,716	3,436	13,878
11	Discount rate (14%)	1.000	0.877	0.769	0.675	0.592
	Present values	(15,057)	1,920	2,089	2,319	8,216

Working

Additional tax

Year	1	2	3	4
	(£4,375 × 0.05)/3.37	(£7,023 × 0.05)/3.41	(£10,343 × 0.05)/3.47	(£12,519 × 0.05)/3.50
	= $65	= $103	= $149	= $179

ANSWERS

Section B

2 Southmed

Marking guide	Marks
Calculations	
Profitability (calculations can include revenue and profit changes, profit margins, asset turnover, ROCE)	4
Capital structure	2
Liquidity	2
Investor (calculations can include earnings and dividend per share, dividend cover, change in share price, dividend yield, total shareholder return, price/earnings ratio)	4
Restaurant analysis	2
Discussion	
Profitability	3
Capital structure	3
Liquidity	2
Investor	3
Restaurant analysis	3
Conclusion	2
Marks Available	30
Maximum	20

Professional skills marks

Analysis and evaluation

- Appropriate use of the data to determine suitable calculations
- Appropriate use of the data to support discussion, draw appropriate conclusions and design appropriate responses

- Identification of omissions from the analysis, or further analysis, which could be carried out to enable an appropriate decision/recommendation to be made
- Demonstration of reasoned judgement when considering key organisational matters and impacts

Scepticism

- Effective challenge of information, evidence and assumptions supplied and techniques carried out to support key facts and/or decisions
- Demonstration of the ability to probe into the reasons for issues and problems, including the identification of missing information or additional information

Commercial acumen

- Effective use of examples and/or calculations from the scenario information and other practical considerations related to the context to illustrate points being made
- Recognition of external constraints and opportunities as necessary

Maximum $\underline{5}$

Total $\underline{\underline{25}}$

Note: Credit will be given for alternative, relevant, calculations and discussion. Candidates will not be expected to complete all the calculations shown to obtain 10 marks.

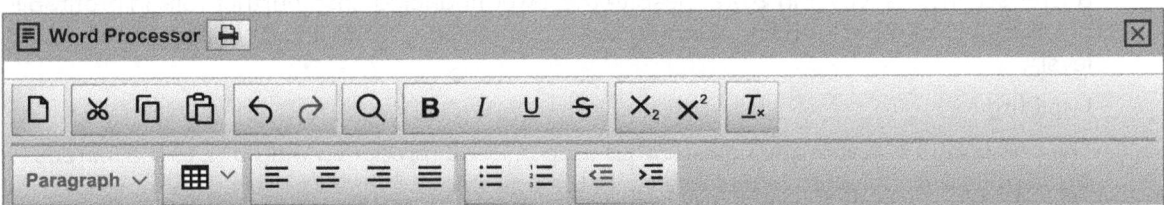

Revenue and profitability

Overall, there has been a small decrease in Southmed Co (Southmed)'s revenue over the last two years with a rather larger decrease in gross profit.

Revenue and gross profit have declined particularly in the restaurants in the biggest cities. Possibly, fewer people are dining out in city centres, but also the better dining experience offered by more expensive competitor restaurants may be appealing more to customers. The gross profit margin of these restaurants has also dropped from 18.2% to 15.5%. This may suggest a cost base which cannot easily be cut in line with falls in revenue.

The restaurants in the tourist areas have shown an increase in revenue, but their gross profits have declined slightly. This may be due to poor cost control, or it may be that restaurant managers have been charging lower prices to compete with the cheaper restaurants. This will have resulted in an increase in activity but lower gross profits if food and other costs have not fallen.

The restaurants in the small cities and towns show stable figures. This may be an indication that costs are being controlled satisfactorily, possibly because, for example, waste is being carefully controlled.

The fall in the sector's average gross profit margin over the last three years is similar to the fall Southmed has experienced, suggesting that the sector generally is having similar issues to Southmed. Although the sector's average % margins are higher than for Southmed, these may be of limited use as comparators, as these margins will be influenced by figures from chains which Southmed would not regard as competitors. Figures for Southmed's individual competitors would be better comparators, ideally broken down geographically in the same way in which Southmed's figures are.

The revenue per restaurant's figures are of limited use for comparison between the different restaurant segments, as they do not reflect the ability of the restaurants to generate revenue. Comparisons of revenue and profit per meals served or space occupied would give a better indication, whilst using revenue per employee would be a measure of efficiency. Also, each segment is an aggregation of the performance of a number of restaurants. It would be helpful to see the variation in performance in each segment.

The decrease in gross profitability has been enhanced by the rise in administration costs which has resulted in a fall in operating profit margin from 8.0% to 6.4%. More details are needed about why administration costs are rising when business at the restaurants is not increasing. Although average operating profit margin for the sector has also been falling, this appears to be mainly due to the fall in gross profit margin, with the larger fall in Southmed's operating profit margin suggesting it has greater issues with operating cost control.

The lower return on capital employed is due to the fall in profitability, as the asset base has decreased slightly over the three years. The number of restaurants has been static over the last three years, possibly due to lack of funds for investment in new sites. In addition, the decline in the value of non-current assets appears to indicate that additional investment is not being made in the asset base, when, by contrast, competitor restaurants are investing in better surroundings.

Solvency

Using market values to estimate the value of equity, gearing has remained fairly static over the three years with the fall in non-current liabilities being matched by the fall in the value of equity due to the decrease in the share price. This raises the question of why additional loan funding has not been sought, particularly as Southmed's gearing is lower than the sector average. The level of interest cover may be a factor. The fall in profitability has resulted in decreased interest cover in 20X2, despite the lower financing cost. Further falls in profitability or taking out of more loan finance may result in interest cover falling to unacceptably low levels.

Liquidity

The company's current ratio has shown a drop in 20X2, predominantly due to the increase in trade payables, reflected in an increase in the payables payment period. This may be a one-off caused by a year-end distortion in paying suppliers, but it may be an early sign of possible cash flow pressures. The main current asset is the bank and cash balance which Southmed has been able to maintain, it does not appear to require overdraft financing at present. The fact that it has not changed very much over the three years may indicate that it is a precautionary balance.

Investor

Southmed has been able to maintain the level of dividend payment, which could arguably be a sign of the directors showing confidence in the company's ability to generate cash flows. However, it does not appear to be convincing as the company's share price has fallen by 6% and 9% over the last two years. Investors may be taking the view that the decline in dividend cover from 1.7 to 1.4 is a sign that dividends are not sustainable. Any fall in dividends would lead to a further fall in total shareholder return, which has declined over the last two years despite the increase in dividends. Part of the reason for the fall may be the restaurant sector not generally being popular with investors, as shown by the sector's average fall in share price. However, Southmed's share price has declined at a faster rate, indicating shareholders have specific concerns about it.

The increase in the price/earnings ratio reflects the fact that share price has not fallen at the same rate as earnings.

Conclusion

At present, Southmed is managing to meet its loan repayments and maintain the level of dividend, but this situation may not continue if profits continue to fall. In addition, the need to invest in the non-current asset base of the company means that extra finance has to be generated. It seems doubtful whether its current operations will be able to generate the funds required. Southmed has only been able to generate increased revenue in the tourist centre segment, but the gross profits of the tourist centre restaurants have fallen. Increased debt

might send gearing up to levels which would concern shareholders and the stock market, particularly as interest commitments might threaten dividend payments. The fall in share price, despite the maintenance of dividend levels, suggests Southmed may struggle to raise sufficient funds through an equity issue.

Appendix

Edit   Format

100% ▾

11 ▾   **B** *I* U A ⬙ ≡ ≡ ≡ .00 🪙 % ½ 🕒

	A	B	C	D
1	Year	20X2	20X1	20X0
2	**Profitability**			
3	Change in revenue (%)	(0.5)	(0.3)	
4	Gross profit margin (%)	16.0	16.6	17.1
5	Change in gross profit (%)	(4.5)	(2.9)	
6	Operating profit margin (%)	6.4	7.4	8.0
7	Change in operating profit (%)	(14.4)	(8.2)	
8	Asset turnover (sales/capital employed)	1.6	1.5	1.5
9	Return on capital employed (%) (operating profit /capital employed)	9.9	11.4	12.4
10	**Solvency**			
11	Gearing (%) (non-current liabilities/(non-current liabilities + market value of equity))	32.5	32.7	32.9
12	Interest cover	3.2	3.5	3.5
13	**Liquidity**			
14	Current ratio	0.9	1.0	1.0
15	Trade payables payment period (days)	38.1	31.0	37.7
16	**Investor**			
17	Earnings per share ($)	0.41	0.48	0.52
18	Dividend cover	1.4	1.6	1.7
19	Dividend per share ($)	0.30	0.30	0.30
20	Market price per share ($) (given)	4.85	5.35	5.70
21	Change in share price (%)	(9.31)	(6.1)	
22	Dividend yield (%)	6.2	5.6	5.3
23	Total shareholder return (%)	(3.2)	(0.5)	
24	Price/earnings ratio	11.8	11.1	11.0

BPP

ANSWERS

	A	B	C	D
25	Total market value of equity ($000s)	48,500	53,500	57,000
26	**Revenue per restaurant ($000)**			
27	Six largest cities	1,263	1,308	1,350
	Tourist centres	925	906	881
29	Small cities and towns	726	727	730
30	**Change in revenue (%)**			
31	Six largest cities	(3.5)	(3.1)	
32	Tourist centres	2.1	2.8	
33	Small cities and towns	(0.2)	(0.3)	
34	**Gross profit margin (%)**			
35	Six largest cities	15.5	17.2	18.2
36	Tourist centres	14.5	15.2	16.0
37	Small cities and towns	16.9	17.0	17.0
38	**Change in gross profit (%)**			
39	Six largest cities	(13.0)	(8.5)	
40	Tourist centres	(2.3)	(2.2)	
41	Small cities and towns	(1.0)	0	

3 Abertafol

Course Book references

Interest rate risk management is covered in Chapter 13.

Top tips

To score good discussion marks in part (a) candidates need to do more than simply state which hedge would be the more financially beneficial (although this did score a mark).

In part (b), it is important to link discussion of these queries **to the context and environment in the scenario**. The ACCA examiner's report noted that often candidates failed to do this and produced general answers that did not refer to the scenario, but that 'candidates who applied their answers to the circumstances described and tried to link them to the financial information given' scored good marks'.

When setting up a derivative agreement it is important to specify the contract type and the number of contracts. The numerical calculations should be neat and can be presented in a number of ways; two alternative methods are shown in the solution, and either is acceptable.

In addition, the effective rate for the future (for the loan) could also be calculated as opening future − closing basis + 0.4% premium that the company pays above the base rate = 5.45 − 0.14 + 0.4= 5.71%

Examining team's comments

The ACCA Examiner's report noted that scepticism was not applied effectively by many candidates.

Here, this should involve challenging information and methods used, and demonstration of the ability to probe into the reasons for issues which would be required to challenge conclusions or recommendations which have already been reached eg in part (a) identifying that basis risk was likely & would affect the outcome of the futures hedge.

Marking guide		Marks
(a) Sell June futures	1	
Number of futures contracts	1	
Unexpired basis calculation	1	
Impact of interest rate increase with futures	2	
Number of contracts	1	
Unexpired basis calculation	1	
Premium calculation	1	
Exercise options?	1	
Impact of interest rate decrease with options	1	
Discussion		
(points can include loan: futures margins and basis risks, FRA counterparty risk; investment: FRA certainty of cash flow, options give upside which may be beneficial depending on government policy choices) 3–4	$\frac{4}{}$	
Marks Available	14	
Maximum		13
(b) 2–3 marks for each of three queries discussed	$\frac{7}{}$	
Marks Available	7	
Maximum		$\frac{7}{}$

Professional skills marks

Analysis and evaluation

- Appropriate use of the data to determine suitable calculations
- Appropriate use of the data to support discussion, draw appropriate conclusions and design appropriate responses

Scepticism

- Effective challenge of information and assumptions supplied, and techniques carried out, to support key facts and/or decisions
- Effective challenge and critical assessment of the information and assumptions provided
- Demonstration of the ability to probe into the reasons for issues which would be required to challenge conclusions or recommendations which have already been reached

Commercial acumen

- Recommendations are practical and plausible in the context of Abertafol Co's situation
- Effective use of examples and/or calculations from the scenario information, and other practical considerations related to the context, to illustrate points being made

Maximum	$\frac{5}{}$
Total	$\underline{\underline{25}}$

(a) **Presented as %s**

	A	B	C
1	**$24m loan**		
2	**Futures**		
3	**Basis**		
4	June futures price less base rate (1 February)	5.45 − 5.10 = 0.35%	
5	Unexpired basis on 1 May	= 2/5 × 0.35 = 0.14%	
6	**Central bank base rate increases to 5.9%**	%	%
7	Underlying borrowing cost		(6.3)
8	Expected futures price	5.9 + closing basis 0.14 = 6.04%	
9	Gain on futures market		
10	6.04 − 5.45 =		0.59
11	Net borrowing cost		(5.71)
12	Net cost in $s	0.0571 x $24m × 4/12	$456,800
13	**$18m investment**		
14	**Options on futures**		
15	**Basis**		
16	Sep futures price less base rate (1 February)	5.5 − 5.10 = 0.40%	
17	Unexpired basis on 1 Sep	= 1/8 × 0.4 = 0.05%	
18	**Central bank base rate falls to 4.5%**		
19	Futures price on 1 Sep	4.5 + 0.05 = 4.55%	
20	Exercise price (100-94.75)	5.25%	Exercise option to receive interest
21	Gain in basis points	5.25 - 4.55 =	0.70%
22	Investment return	4.5 - 0.3 =	4.2%

 BPP

	A	B	C
23	Premium		(0.298)%
24	Net	0.70 + 4.20 - 0.298 =	4.602%
25	Net receipt in $s	0.04602 x $18m x 5/12	$345,150

Alternative presentation of numbers

Spreadsheet ☒

Edit   Format

📄 ✂ 📋 🖨 🖌 ↶ ↷ | 100% ▼ |

11 ▼ **B** *I* <u>U</u> **A** 🎨 ≣ ≡ ≣ .00 💱 % ½ 🕐

	A	B	C
1	**$24m loan**		
2	**Futures**		
3	**Basis**	Current price (1 February) – futures price = basis	(100 – 5.10) – 94.55 = 0.35
4		Unexpired basis on 1 May	= 2/5 × 0.35 = 0.14
5	**Central bank base rate increases to 5.9%**		$
6	Underlying borrowing cost	6.3% × $24m × 4/12	(504,000)
7	Expected futures price	100 – 5.9 – 0.14 = 93.96	
8	Gain on the futures market	(94.55 – 93.96) × $500,000 × 3/12 × 64	47,200
9	Net borrowing cost		(456,800)
10	Effective annual interest rate	$456,800/$24m × 12/4 = 5.71%	
11	**$18m investment**		
12	**Options on futures**		
13	**Basis**	(100 – 5.10) – 94.50 = 0.4	
14	Unexpired basis on 1 September = 1/8 × 0.4 = 0.05		
15	**Central bank base rate falls to 4.5%**		
16	Exercise price	94.75	

 **BPP**

	A	B	C
17	Expected futures price	100 − 4.5 − 0.05 = 95.45	
18	Exercise?	Yes	
19	Gain in basis points	70	
20	Gain from options		$
21	0.0070 × 3/12 × $500,000 × 60		52,500
22	Investment return	4.2% × 5/12 × $18m	315,000
23	Premium	0.00298 × $500,000 × 3/12 × 6	(22,350)
24	Net receipt		345,150
25	Effective annual interest rate	$345,150/$18m × 12/5	4.60%

Loan

For FRAs, net payment is $461,600 and effective annual interest rate is 5.77%, as stated in Exhibit 1.

For futures, the required hedge is to sell June futures, as the hedge is against a rise in interest rates and the borrowing occurs in May.

Number of contracts = $24m/$500,000 × 4 months/3 months = 64 contracts

As shown in the spreadsheet calculations, for futures the net payment is $456,800 and the effective annual interest rate is 5.71%. So, the cost of the future is lower than the FRA and is preferred in terms of cost.

In each case, the worst-case scenario has been considered, ie, the higher interest rate on the loan and the lower interest rate on the investment. For the loan, the futures give a slightly better result than the FRA and Abertafol Co may choose it for that reason. The result for the futures is dependent on the assumptions that basis diminishes linearly and there is no basis risk, which may not be true in practice. The assumption that there is no margin requirement may not also be true in real-life. The FRA has a theoretical risk of default as it is an over-the-counter policy, but this should be very small if the counterparty is a reputable financial institution.

Investment

For FRAs, using a forward rate agreement for the investment would guarantee $378,750, which is an effective annual interest rate of 5.05%, as stated in Exhibit 1.

Using options would mean buying September call options as need to hedge against a fall in interest rates.

Number of contracts = $18m/$500,000 × 5 months/3 months = 60 contracts

 **BPP**

As shown in the spreadsheet calculations, if the options are exercised the net receipt is $345,150 and the effective annual interest rate is 4.60%. So, the outcome of the option is worse and the FRA is preferred.

For the investment, the FRA gives the higher guaranteed return if the interest rate falls. If Abertafol Co is primarily concerned with certainty of cash flow, it will choose the FRA. Hoowever, if Abertafol Co believes that it is unlikely that interest rates will fall (either because it believes the governing party will win the election or that the opposition party will not fulfil its promise to reduce interest rates), it should choose the options compared to the FRA.

(b)

Director A

The argument that shareholders do not expect Abertafol Co to use derivatives as it is not part of their trading purpose could apply if it was looking to make profits out of trading in derivatives for speculative purposes. Shareholders might question trading for these reasons and whether use of derivatives was increasing the risk levels they faced.

However, that is not the case here. In these circumstances, derivatives are being used for hedging purposes, to limit the risks to cash flows the company faces. It could be argued that shareholders would expect Abertafol Co to take reasonable steps to manage risks, particularly as levels and direction of interest rate movement are quite uncertain at present. If the risks are not hedged, Abertafol Co could lose out doubly, having to pay more interest and receiving less interest than if it took steps to hedge.

Abertafol Co will also generally wish to limit uncertainty when it is budgeting. Using derivatives limits how much actual payments or receipts could vary from budgeted figures, whereas the maximum possible variations from budgeted figures if derivatives are not used are uncertain and could be large.

Director B

It is true that interest rates might rise or fall, but not to the levels predicted. As regards the loan, if interest rates did not go up beyond 5.31%, Abertafol Co would end up paying more as a result of hedging. The terms for the futures and forward rate agreements reflect market expectations that rates will rise to around this level. This suggests that the risk of Abertafol Co paying significantly more on the loan as a result of hedging is small.

As regards the interest rate on the investment, the forward rate is set bearing in mind the uncertainty about the ultimate direction of interest rate change as well as its amount. If the opposition party wins the election, the forward rate agreement is likely to lead to a higher net receipt (receiving 5.05% would imply an offer rate of 5.35% on the forward rate agreement, when the opposition party is planning to reduce the central bank base rate below 5.1%). The current government would have to increase the base rate above 5.35% for the forward rate agreement to be less profitable than not hedging.

Director C

Although not evaluated here, if the central bank base rate rose to 5.9%, options would not be exercised. In this situation, options would represent a less profitable choice than not hedging because of the premium paid.

Options would be a better choice than not hedging if they were exercised and the central bank base rate fell below 4.9%, meaning interest received was below 4.6%. This would imply that the opposition party had won the election and fulfilled its promise to reduce interest rates. However, if the central bank rate fell to such an extent that options were

exercised, the forward rate agreement would give a higher effective annual interest rate than options.

Therefore, it is true from this investment's perspective that options would never be the best solution whatever the change in interest rates.

Note. Credit will be given for alternative and valid comments.

Mathematical tables and formulae

BPP

Formulae

Modigliani and Miller Proposition 2 (with tax)

$$k_e = k_e^i + (1-T)(k_e^i - k_d)\frac{V_d}{V_e}$$

Or rearranged

$$k_e + (1-T)k_d\left(\frac{V_d}{V_e}\right) = k_e^i + (1-T)k_e^i\left(\frac{V_d}{V_e}\right)$$

The Capital Asset Pricing Model

$$E(r_i) = R_f + b_i(E(r_m) - R_f)$$

The asset beta formula

$$\beta_a = \left[\frac{V_e}{(V_e + V_d(1-T))}\beta_e\right] + \left[\frac{V_d(1-T)}{(V_e + V_d(1-T))}\beta_d\right]$$

The Growth Model

$$P_0 = \frac{D_0(1 + g)}{(r_e - g)}$$

Gordon's growth approximation

$$g = br_e$$

The weighted average cost of capital

$$WACC = \left[\frac{V_e}{V_e + V_d}\right]k_e + \left[\frac{V_d}{V_e + V_d}\right]k_d(1-T)$$

The Fisher formula

$$(1 + i) = (1 + r) \times (1 + h)$$

Purchasing power parity and interest rate parity

$$S_1 = S_0 \times \frac{(1 + h_c)}{(1 + h_b)}$$

$$F_0 = S_0 \times \frac{(1 + i_c)}{(1 + i_b)}$$

Modified internal rate of return

$$MIRR = \left[\frac{PV_R}{PV_I}\right]^{\frac{1}{n}}(1 + r_e) - 1$$

The Black-Scholes option pricing model

$$c = P_a N(d_1) - P_e N(d_2)e^{-rt}$$

BPP

Present value table

Present value of 1 ie $(1+r)^{-n}$

Where r = discount rate; n = number of periods until payment

Periods (n)	Discount rate (r)									
	1%	2%	3%	4%	5%	6%	7%	8%	9%	10%
1	0.990	0.980	0.971	0.962	0.952	0.943	0.935	0.926	0.917	0.909
2	0.980	0.961	0.943	0.925	0.907	0.890	0.873	0.857	0.842	0.826
3	0.971	0.942	0.915	0.889	0.864	0.840	0.816	0.794	0.772	0.751
4	0.961	0.924	0.888	0.855	0.823	0.792	0.763	0.735	0.708	0.683
5	0.951	0.906	0.863	0.822	0.784	0.747	0.713	0.681	0.650	0.621
6	0.942	0.888	0.837	0.790	0.746	0.705	0.666	0.630	0.596	0.564
7	0.933	0.871	0.813	0.760	0.711	0.665	0.623	0.583	0.547	0.513
8	0.923	0.853	0.789	0.731	0.677	0.627	0.582	0.540	0.502	0.467
9	0.914	0.837	0.766	0.703	0.645	0.592	0.544	0.500	0.460	0.424
10	0.905	0.820	0.744	0.676	0.614	0.558	0.508	0.463	0.422	0.386
11	0.896	0.804	0.722	0.650	0.585	0.527	0.475	0.429	0.388	0.350
12	0.887	0.788	0.701	0.625	0.557	0.497	0.444	0.397	0.356	0.319
13	0.879	0.773	0.681	0.601	0.530	0.469	0.415	0.368	0.326	0.290
14	0.870	0.758	0.681	0.577	0.505	0.442	0.388	0.340	0.299	0.263
15	0.861	0.743	0.642	0.555	0.481	0.417	0.362	0.315	0.275	0.239

(n)	11%	12%	13%	14%	15%	16%	17%	18%	19%	20%
1	0.901	0.893	0.885	0.877	0.870	0.862	0.855	0.847	0.840	0.833
2	0.812	0.797	0.783	0.769	0.756	0.743	0.731	0.718	0.706	0.694
3	0.731	0.712	0.693	0.675	0.658	0.641	0.624	0.609	0.593	0.579
4	0.659	0.636	0.613	0.592	0.572	0.552	0.534	0.516	0.499	0.482
5	0.593	0.567	0.543	0.519	0.497	0.476	0.456	0.437	0.419	0.402
6	0.535	0.507	0.480	0.456	0.432	0.410	0.390	0.370	0.352	0.335
7	0.482	0.452	0.425	0.400	0.376	0.354	0.333	0.314	0.296	0.279
8	0.434	0.404	0.376	0.351	0.327	0.305	0.285	0.266	0.249	0.233
9	0.391	0.361	0.333	0.308	0.284	0.263	0.243	0.225	0.209	0.194
10	0.352	0.322	0.295	0.270	0.247	0.227	0.208	0.191	0.176	0.162
11	0.317	0.287	0.261	0.237	0.215	0.195	0.178	0.162	0.148	0.135
12	0.286	0.257	0.231	0.208	0.187	0.168	0.152	0.137	0.124	0.112
13	0.258	0.229	0.204	0.182	0.163	0.145	0.130	0.116	0.104	0.093
14	0.232	0.205	0.181	0.160	0.141	0.125	0.111	0.099	0.088	0.078
15	0.209	0.183	0.160	0.140	0.123	0.108	0.095	0.084	0.079	0.065

Annuity table

Present value of an annuity of 1 ie $\frac{1-(1+r)^{-n}}{r}$

Where r = discount rate; n = number of periods

Periods (n)	Discount rate (r)									
	1%	2%	3%	4%	5%	6%	7%	8%	9%	10%
1	0.990	0.980	0.971	0.962	0.952	0.943	0.935	0.926	0.917	0.909
2	1.970	1.942	1.913	1.886	1.859	1.833	1.808	1.783	1.759	1.736
3	2.941	2.884	2.829	2.775	2.723	2.673	2.624	2.577	2.531	2.487
4	3.902	3.808	3.717	3.630	3.546	3.465	3.387	3.312	3.240	3.170
5	4.853	4.713	4.580	4.452	4.329	4.212	4.100	3.993	3.890	3.791
6	5.795	5.601	5.417	5.242	5.076	4.917	4.767	4.623	4.486	4.355
7	6.728	6.472	6.230	6.002	5.786	5.582	5.389	5.206	5.033	4.868
8	7.652	7.325	7.020	6.733	6.463	6.210	5.971	5.747	5.535	5.335
9	8.566	8.162	7.786	7.435	7.108	6.802	6.515	6.247	5.995	5.759
10	9.471	8.983	8.530	8.111	7.722	7.360	7.024	6.710	6.418	6.145
11	10.368	9.787	9.253	8.760	8.306	7.887	7.499	7.139	6.805	6.495
12	11.255	10.575	9.954	9.385	8.863	8.384	7.943	7.536	7.161	6.814
13	12.134	11.348	10.635	9.986	9.394	8.853	8.358	7.904	7.487	7.103
14	13.004	12.106	11.296	10.563	9.899	9.295	8.745	8.244	7.786	7.367
15	13.865	12.849	11.938	11.118	10.380	9.712	9.108	8.559	8.061	7.606

(n)	11%	12%	13%	14%	15%	16%	17%	18%	19%	20%
1	0.901	0.893	0.885	0.877	0.870	0.862	0.855	0.847	0.840	0.833
2	1.713	1.690	1.668	1.647	1.626	1.605	1.585	1.566	1.547	1.528
3	2.444	2.402	2.361	2.322	2.283	2.246	2.210	2.174	2.140	2.106
4	3.102	3.037	2.974	2.914	2.855	2.798	2.743	2.690	2.639	2.589
5	3.696	3.605	3.517	3.433	3.352	3.274	3.199	3.127	3.058	2.991
6	4.231	4.111	3.998	3.889	3.784	3.685	3.589	3.498	3.410	3.326
7	4.712	4.564	4.423	4.288	4.160	4.039	3.922	3.812	3.706	3.605
8	5.146	4.968	4.799	4.639	4.487	4.344	4.207	4.078	3.954	3.837
9	5.537	5.328	5.132	4.946	4.772	4.607	4.451	4.303	4.163	4.031
10	5.889	5.650	5.426	5.216	5.019	4.833	4.659	4.494	4.339	4.192
11	6.207	5.938	5.687	5.453	5.234	5.029	4.836	4.656	4.486	4.327
12	6.492	6.194	5.918	5.660	5.421	5.197	4.988	4.793	4.611	4.439
13	6.750	6.424	6.122	5.842	5.583	5.342	5.118	4.910	4.715	4.533
14	6.982	6.628	6.302	6.002	5.724	5.468	5.229	5.008	4.802	4.611
15	7.191	6.811	6.462	6.142	5.847	5.575	5.324	5.092	4.876	4.675

Additional CBE Mock Exam

Please find below information and a link relating to an additional CBE Mock Exam. This Mock Exam has been written by the BPP team and built in the ACCA exam software. Please sit this exam at home at a time convenient to you and self-review using the model answers available at the end of the assessment.

It is extremely important to follow the below guidelines when attempting this Mock Exam:

- Please make sure that you launch the exams using **Google Chrome** in order to enjoy the full functionality of the Software.
- Only launch the exam once you are ready to fully complete it.
- Remember to retain a copy of the pdf output of your script as this will be useful for you to self-review and self-mark the script.
- The Mock Exam is set to time out after 4 hours. There will be a timer on the top right of the screen. You will be warned if the 4 hours is about to expire.
- We recommend that you use a wired internet connection wherever possible to reduce the likelihood of any internet outage during the Mock Exam.
- In the same way as the real exam environment, this Mock Exam must be sat in one attempt. Once you close out of the exam it will save your output to pdf. You will not be able to re-enter the exam or pick it up where you left off.

Link here:

https://ondemand.questionmark.eu/delivery/open.php?session=0434309000434309&customerid=612294&NAME=x&GROUP=x

Tell us what you think

Got comments or feedback on this book? Let us know.
Use your QR code reader:

Or, visit:
https://www.smartsurvey.co.uk/s/BFO4OC/

Need to get in touch with customer service?

www.bpp.com/request-support

Spotted an error?

https://learningmedia.bpp.com/pages/errata